DICKENS STUDIES ANNUAL
Essays on Victorian Fiction

DICKENS STUDIES ANNUAL
Essays on Victorian Fiction

DICKENS
STUDIES
ANNUAL

Essays on Victorian Fiction

VOLUME
39

Edited by
Stanley Friedman, Edward Guiliano,
Anne Humpherys, Talia Schaffer, and Michael Timko

AMS PRESS, INC.
New York

Dickens Studies Annual
ISSN 0084–9812

COPYRIGHT © 2008 by AMS Press, Inc.
Dickens Studies Annual: Essays on Victorian Fiction is published in cooperation with Queens College and The Graduate Center, CUNY.

International Standard Book Number
Series: 978–0–404–18520–6 / Series ISBN-10: 0–404–18520–7
Vol. 39: 978–0–404–18939–6 / Vol. 39 ISBN-10: 0–404–18939–3

Dickens Studies Annual: Essays on Victorian Fiction welcomes essay- and monograph-length contributions on Dickens and other Victorian novelists and on the history of aesthetics of Victorian fiction. All manuscripts should be double-spaced and should follow the documentation format described in the most recent *MLA Style Manual*. The author's name should appear only on a cover-page, not elsewhere in the essay. An editorial decision can usually be reached more quickly if two copies of the article are submitted, since outside readers are asked to evaluate each submission. If a manuscript is accepted for publication, the author will be asked to provide a 100- to 200-word abstract and also a CD-ROM containing the final version of the essay. The preferred editions for citations from Dickens's works are the Clarendon and the Norton Critical when available, otherwise the Oxford Illustrated or the Penguin.

Please send submissions to The Editors, *Dickens Studies Annual*, Ph.D. Program in English, The Graduate Center, CUNY, 365 Fifth Avenue, New York, NY 10016-4309. Please send inquiries concerning subscriptions and/or availability of earlier volumes to AMS Press, Inc., Brooklyn Navy Yard, 63 Flushing Ave., Unit #221, Brooklyn, NY 11205-1005, USA.

Manufactured in the United States of America

All AMS books are printed on acid-free paper that meets the guidelines for performance and durability of the Committee on Production Guidelines for Book Longevity of the Council on Library Resources.

Contents

Preface

These two quotations, referring to two Londons over eight decades apart, may help to explain the continued interest of scholars of different critical persuasions in the fiction of Dickens and his contemporaries: so much is offered that there is something for everyone.

A preface to one of our volumes is always a statement of gratitude for different kinds of support. We depend, of course, on the scholars who submit their work to us, and we also rely heavily on our outside readers for recommendations that guide our editorial decisions and include useful suggestions that we forward to our contributors.

We are very grateful to Natalie Cole for her extensive survey of studies of Dickens and gender appearing from 1992 to 2007 and to Timothy Spurgin for his lively review essay examining Dickens scholarship published in 2006.

For important practical assistance, we are indebted to the following administrators: President William P. Kelly; Acting Provost Linda N. Edwards; and Ph.D. Program in English Executive Officer Steven F. Kruger, all of The Graduate Center, CUNY; and President James L. Muyskens; Dean of Arts and Humanities Tamara S. Evans; and Department of English Chair Nancy R. Comley, all of Queens College, CUNY.

We are grateful to John O. Jordan, Director of The Dickens Project at the University of California, Santa Cruz; JoAnna Rottke, Project Coordinator for The Dickens Project; and Jon Michael Varese, the Project's Research Assistant and Web Administrator, for placing on the Project's website the tables of contents for volumes 1–27 of *DSA*, as well as abstracts for subsequent volumes. (These items are included in a link to *Dickens Studies Annual* on the Project's website, which can be reached at <http://dickens.ucsc.edu>.)

We offer thanks to Gabriel Hornstein, President of AMS Press, who generously acts as an enabler for this enterprise; to Jack Hopper, retired Editor-in-Chief at AMS Press, who still helps *DSA* in many important ways; and to David Ramm, Editor-in-Chief at AMS Press, who has very skillfully responded to (and at times anticipated) our requests for assistance. In addition, we express appreciation to our editorial assistant, Matt Lau, a Ph.D. candidate at the Graduate Center, for his conscientious, valuable help with this volume.

—The Editors

Notes on Contributors

KIMBERLE L. BROWN recently began her doctoral studies at the University of New Hampshire Department of English, where she teaches writing. Her current research includes gender and sexuality in Wharton and her contemporaries and in Anglophone postcolonial texts. At present she is at work on an essay exploring Gothic doubling and ambiguous identity in British and European Romantic poetry.

JAMES BUZARD has written two books, *Disorienting Fiction: The Autoethnographic Work of Nineteenth-Century British Novels* (Princeton UP, 2005) and *The Beaten Track: European Tourism, Literature, and the Ways to "Culture," 1800–1918* (Oxford UP, 1993), as well as numerous essays on nineteenth- and twentieth-century British literature and culture, the history of travel, and cultural theory. He is co-editor of a special *Victorian Studies* issue on "Victorian Ethnographies" and of *Victorian Prism: Refractions of the Crystal Palace* (U of Virginia P, 2007). He is currently working on a second volume of the *Disorienting Fiction* study, covering United Kingdom fiction from George Eliot to Joyce. Buzard is Professor and Head of the Literature Faculty at MIT.

NATALIE B. COLE is Associate Professor of English at Oakland University in Rochester, Michigan. She has published work on Hawthorne, Meredith, Dickens, and Collins. Her most recent work, "*Private Snuggeries*: The Spaces of Masculine Identity in *Armadale*," will appear in *Armadale: Wilkie Collins and the Dark Thread*, ed. Mariaconcetta Costantini (Arachne, 2008). Her current research is on masculinity and spaces of leisure and travel in work by Dickens and Collins.

CAROLYN DEVER is Professor of English and Executive Dean of the College of Arts and Science at Vanderbilt University. Her research interests include Victorian fiction, psychoanalysis, and gender theory. She is writing a book about art, marriage, and the journals of Michael Field, as well as co-editing the forthcoming *Cambridge Companion to Anthony Trollope*. Dever's books include *Death and the Mother from Dickens to Freud* (Cambridge, 1998), *Skeptical Feminisms* (Minnesota, 2004), and the co-edited volume *The Literary Channel,* (Princeton, 2002).

KEITH EASLEY, an associate professor at Aichi Shukutoku University in Japan, is very slowly writing a book on Dickens and Bakhtin. The first part appeared in volume 34 of *Dickens Studies Annual*. Current work is on Bakhtin's move from authoring to dialogism, with particular reference to *Little Dorrit*. A separate project focuses on the role of character in Victorian detective fiction.

JOHN GLENDENING is an English professor at The University of Montana, where he specializes in nineteenth-century British literature and culture and serves as Director of Literature for his department. He is author of two books: *The High Road: Romantic Tourism, Scotland, and Literature, 1720–1820* (St. Martin's, 1997) and *The Evolutionary Imagination in Late-Victorian Novels: An Entangled Bank* (Ashgate, 2007).

MARK M. HENNELLY, JR. is Professor of English and former Department Chair at California State University, Sacramento. He is also a trustee of the International Dickens Society and has published widely in Victorian fiction. His most recent work appears or is forthcoming in *Victorian Literature and Culture* (essays on *Adam Bede* and the *Alices*), *Journal of Dracula Studies* (on *Dracula*), *Hitchcock Annual* (on Alfred Hitchcock's *The Ring*, *Strangers on a Train*, and *Frenzy*), and *Contemporary Literature* (on A. S. Byatt's *Possession*).

BERT HORNBACK has been writing about Dickens for 40 years, publishing three books and some 30 essays about Dickens's novels. He has also published books on Thomas Hardy, George Eliot, and Richard Nixon, and essays on Homer, Sophocles, Dante, Shakespeare, Keats, Tennyson, Joyce, and other writers. He is the editor of the Norton Critical Edition of *Middlemarch* and a volume of essays on Jane Kenyon. His most recent book is *The Wisdom in Words: How Language Carries Our Earliest Cultural Values*. He taught Dickens at the University of Michigan for 28 years and is a past president of the Dickens Society. He lives now in Amsterdam and New Orleans.

LISA HARTSELL JACKSON is a lecturer in both British literature and technical writing for the English Department at the University of North Texas. Her research interests are Dickens, Hardy, and film adaptations of Victorian novels. She is an active member of the Dickens Fellowship and a contributor to the *Oxford New Dictionary of National Biography*.

BRITTA MARTENS is Senior Lecturer in English at the University of the West of England in Bristol, UK. She is review editor for the *Browning Society Notes* and reviewer of the Year's Work on Robert Browning for *Victorian Poetry*. Her research interests lie in Victorian poetics and cross-cultural aspects of Victorian writing on Europe, especially Italy and France.

NATALIE KAPETANIOS MEIR is a Language Lecturer in the Department of Expository Writing at New York University, where she received her Ph.D. in English. This article is part of a larger project in which she considers the construction of dining norms in Victorian fiction and social instruction manuals. Her recent publications in *Victorian Literature and Culture* and *Studies in the Novel* discuss how dining practices are codified through narrative in a range of nineteenth-century works, including novels, etiquette books, household manuals, and restaurant guides.

DANIEL POLLACK-PELZNER is a Ph.D. candidate in English at Harvard University. His dissertation explores the relationship between Shakespearean reception and the nineteenth-century British novel. His articles have appeared in the *Dickens Quarterly*, the *Keats-Shelley Journal*, and the *Journal of the P. G. Wodehouse Society*.

TIMOTHY SPURGIN is Associate Professor of English and the Bonnie Glidden Buchanan Professor of English Literature at Lawrence University. His writing has appeared in *The Chronicle of Higher Education* and the *minnesota review*. He has also recorded a series of lectures on the history of English fiction, including two talks on Dickens, for the Teaching Company.

IGOR WEBB, Professor of English at Adelphi University, is author of *From Custom to Capital: The English Novel and the Industrial Revolution* (Cornell UP, 1981) and *Ideas Across Time: Classic and Contemporary Readings for Composition* (McGraw-Hill, 2007). He is at work on a study of the nineteenth-century novel in the light of the revolutions in criticism over the past three decades.

The Gamut of Emotions from A to B: *Nickleby*'s "Histrionic Expedition"

Carolyn Dever

In Nicholas Nickleby, *Charles Dickens develops a new technique for his representation of complex, conflicted, deeply interior human emotions. By means of the novel's hyperbolic, melodramatic approach to emotions, Dickens constructs a universe of affective polarization that enables him to explore the complexities and subtleties of feelings that are not polarized but mixed. Melodrama is the means by which Dickens signifies ambivalence, the simultaneous experience of powerful, oppositional emotions, and the normative emotional state of family life for the Nicklebys and other characters. For Dickens as for Freud in the theory of ambivalence he articulates later in* Totem and Taboo, *fathers and father-figures catalyze uniquely charged, uniquely ambivalent emotions for their sons and daughters, and children reflect heavily ambivalent feelings for their parents.*

In *Nicholas Nickleby*, Dickens invests blatantly in a state of nearly constant hysteria. The novel is replete with dastardly villains and damsels in distress; with bewigged Crummleses, fainting Kenwigses, and suicidal Mantalinis; with leering, pimping, dueling, vegetable-hurling old men and young men of stout heart and hair-trigger temper. For its first half at least, the plot jackknifes from one emotional extreme to the next. Indeed, the advertisement trumpeting Vincent Crummles's "histrionic expedition" across the Atlantic seems but a shadow of the pilgrim's progress undertaken by Nicholas and his fellow traffickers in affective extremity.

Dickens Studies Annual, Volume 39, Copyright © 2008 by AMS Press, Inc. All rights reserved.

1

Nickleby is a novel of high emotional highs and low emotional lows. Though the novel's "Cheeryble period" is nominally less fractious than its first half, it bears witness nonetheless to multiple deaths and a suicide, the dramatic revelation of paternity, the martyrdom of true love (twice, followed by martyrdom's failure, twice), and the perpetuation of the family fetish as the next generation dedicates itself to tending the grave of its "poor dead cousin," strategically located at the spot of Kate Nickleby's infantile debut in a plot of loss and redemption. The novel is so very melodramatic, in other words, that it begs the question of melodrama's functions and, indeed, limitations in Dickens's emerging repertoire of novelistic techniques.

In *Nickleby*, I argue, Dickens deploys melodrama not as an end in itself but as the means to an end. Melodramatic emotions offer Dickens access to such extremes that they enable him, perhaps paradoxically, to signify emotional subtleties. By focusing almost hyperbolically on emotional polarization—love! hatred!—Dickens makes visible the spaces between polar extremes. Dickens highlights family relations as the foremost site of contradictory passions. And, through the vehicle of the family, he posits ambivalence—the simultaneous and unresolvable experience of conflicting emotions—as the engine of affective synthesis, and the prime signifier of psychological complexity.

Though *Nicholas Nickleby* makes great use of the theatricality of melodramatic emotional display, the novel undermines the presumption that all feelings are created equal, that emotions are worn perforce on the sleeve, and that affect can be turned on and off with whipsaw abruptness. Melodrama serves an important function here, to be sure: its extremes are the delivery vehicles for powerful emotions. Helena Michie points out that "Melodramatic gesture . . . embodies the possibility of an emotion,"[1] indexing for Victorian theatergoers and readers alike not artifice but authenticity (95). "Melodrama proves the catalyst for growth and change" in *Nickleby*, suggests Carol MacKay, insofar as it offers both "the tools of self-expression and a critical, dramatic stance on . . . life" (152, 155). But, as Robert Patten argues, "Exactly how to write through theatrical claptrap to the spiritual and moral principles underlying melodrama's stock figures and black-white contrasts was a vexing issue for Dickens" (27).

To get at that "vexing issue," I suggest that *Nickleby*'s high emotional tone betrays an investment in the power of emotional understatement, and indeed in emotional *un*-statement: that is, in feelings that are felt before they are known or understood, if ever they are known or understood. *Nickleby* is a novel about emotions, but not about their clarity or comprehensibility. Instead, this is a novel about emotion's conflicted underside, about the guilt-riddled inextricability of love and hatred. The very fever pitch of the novel's affective demonstrations suggests the ferocity of the conflicts raging below its surface. The tropes of melodramatic passion offer Dickens a vehicle for affective expression and lead him toward the deconstruction of emotional extremes. The production in turn of "grey areas" of guilty conflict, ambiguity, and ambivalence situates the family as the source of and the signifier for psychological conflict.

I. Why Nicholas and Ralph Hate Each Other so Much, Right Away

The novel's very first chapter attributes the origin of human personality to a complex process of identification and repression. The young Nickleby boys, Ralph and Nicholas (uncle and father of our Nicholas and Kate), were shaped for life by their dramatically different responses to conflicting models of masculinity: a father who is weak and poor and an uncle who is rich, powerful, and cruel. Young Ralph Nickleby over-identifies with his uncle's power by repressing his identification with his father's weakness, and his brother Nicholas does exactly the reverse. Thus, by page 2, in two generations of Nickleby men, we have already encountered two among the novel's many significant pairs—let's call them twins—who stand in sharp opposition to one another: strong and rich; weak and poor. Linked by blood and history, each of these Nickleby pairs presents a study in contrasts. But Dickens immediately dismantles this impression by suggesting that the brothers' differences are a self-fulfilling prophecy, that the extremity of their differences creates itself: they are mirror images of one another, and thus they set the stage for the circumstances that will propel Nicholas and Kate into the malign hands of *their* Uncle Ralph.

Dickens offers up antagonists such as Squeers, Gride, and Sir Mulberry Hawk as melodramatic villains through and through, and such protagonists as Smike and the Cheerybles as correspondingly virtuous. This leaves plenty of room in between for characters such as Nicholas himself, split between violent rages on one hand and dedication to truth, justice, Kate, Madeline, and the Cheerybles on the other. In the case of Verisopht, Dickens dangles the possibility of redemption only to cut it tragically short, and in Newman Noggs he gives us a secret agent who knows how to work both sides of the fence on the younger Nicholas Nickleby's behalf.

Central to its catalogue of moral agents, however, is the novel's most persistently powerful villain, Ralph Nickleby. Ralph may be a violent, amoral reptile, but he is one of the few characters to whom the novel's narrator attributes flashes of introspection. Just after Ralph learns that his son was his son, and shortly before his suicide in the very room of the boy's early terror, the narrator reports one of these moments:

If [Ralph] had known his child to be alive, if no deceit had ever been practiced and he had grown up beneath his eye, he might have been a careless, indifferent, rough, harsh father—like enough—he felt that; but the thought would come that he might have been otherwise, and that his son might have been a comfort to him and the two happy together. He began to think now, that his [son's] supposed death and his wife's flight had had some share in making him the morose, hard man he was. He seemed to remember a time when he was not quite so rough and obdurate, and almost thought that he had first hated Nicholas because he was young and gallant . . .   (751)

In light of the bond his dead son had forged with Nicholas, Ralph has the impulse to reexamine his role as a father: "his son might have been a comfort to him and the two happy together." Yet, in fantasizing that the boy would have been "a comfort to him," Ralph reveals that he has something in common with other parents in the novel, asking not what he could have done for his son, but what his son could have done for him. Traveling further on this train of thought, Ralph begins to imagine that the boy's "supposed death and his wife's flight had had some share in making him the morose, hard man he was." Just before his suicide, Ralph conjures his softer, gentler, youthful counterpart—indeed, a young man much like Nicholas, to whom Ralph's own son had pledged eternal fealty.

Ralph reaches back into the past to explain not only his actions but his very personality. He attributes his character to the primal loss of his wife and son, and submits that his behavior has been governed by forces beyond both his understanding and his control. The novel demonstrates a great deal of sympathy for this explanation, to the point that it reflects Ralph's psychologizing impulse in its very structure. The first chapter, after all, opens with an account of the Nicklebys' past: Mr. Godfrey Nickleby, father of Ralph and his dead brother Nicholas, tried to marry for money but failed—and found for himself a love match that predicts, if a bit anemically, the possibility of the "comfortable coupledom" later enjoyed by Tim Linkinwater and Miss La Creevy (761). The Nicklebys' life was one of poverty and obscurity until the death of Mr. Nickleby's uncle, the first villainous Ralph, who left the family his fortune of five thousand pounds. Young Ralph and his brother, Nicholas, "had often heard, from their mother's lips, long accounts of their father's sufferings in his days of poverty, and of their deceased uncle's importance in his days of affluence, which recitals produced a very different impression on the two" (18). The story launches the younger brother into a quiet country life, while Ralph, in contrast, concludes "that there was nothing like money" (19).

Regarding Ralph, the novel remains, to say the least, ambivalent: by psychologizing his behavior, Dickens intermittently introduces the question of whether to let Ralph off the hook. In citing the formative effects of the

Nickleby family story—the suffering, poor father and the powerful, rich uncle—the narrator offers us a glimpse of Ralph as a child still, split between
paternal castration and avuncular potency, and threatened by Nicholas's
youthful virility. Ralph, too, construes himself as a victim when he recurs to
the formative implications of his son's death and his wife's flight. In this he
reveals, unwittingly, his persistent identification with the castrated father,
stripped of son and wife, behind the mask of the powerful uncle. In her
analysis of *Nickleby*'s uncles, mothers-in-law, aunts, and siblings, Michie
points out that Dickens constructs family bonds in highly attenuated terms,
and thus mines legal, economic, and erotic ambiguities. *Nickleby*'s weak
fathers leave a power vacuum, and into the breach step powerful uncles like
the Ralph that Ralph models himself after, and the Ralph he himself becomes.
In Michie's account, uncles and nephews stand in for fathers and sons. With
roles more fluid and less codified than those governing the "natural" relations
of parent and child, the family rules are up for grabs.

Ralph's emotional vulnerability to his niece Kate reveals his ambivalence
still further, showing other aspects of what his robber-baron persona re-
presses. Kate is Nicholas's unthreatening counterpart, the one who makes
her uncle tremble with guilt and desire even as he engineers her sexual
exploitation: "The lock of hair that had escaped and curled loosely over her
brow, the traces of tears yet scarcely dry, the flushed cheek, the look of
sorrow, all fired some dormant train of recollection in the old man's breast;
and the face of his dead brother seemed present before him, with the very look
it wore on some occasion of boyish grief, of which every minute circumstance
flashed upon his mind, with the distinctness of a scene of yesterday" (240).
In his young niece Ralph sees his dead brother and that brother's very weakness; the domestic promise lost with his child and his wife; and his own
naked, feminized vulnerability. As Michie points out, the relationship of uncle
and niece is ambiguous, like that of uncle and nephew, both legally and
"naturally" (86–88). In the space of that ambiguity emerges erotic desire,
which Ralph, being Ralph, instantly converts to his only available currency
for the expression of desire: money. Ralph sublimates—barely—his own
desire for Kate's innocent femininity by constructing a sexual marketplace
for her: he dangles Kate as the bait to catch any one of a series of men with
whom alliances suit Ralph's purpose. Ralph's ambivalence toward Kate is
constituted not only by her contrast to Nicholas, but by the rich mix of desire,
loss, guilt, and anxiety she alone inspires in her uncle:

> To say that Ralph loved or cared for—in the most ordinary acceptation of those
> terms—any one of God's creatures, would be the wildest fiction. Still, there
> had somehow stolen upon him from time to time a thought of his niece which
> was tinged with compassion and pity; breaking through the dull cloud of dislike
> or indifference which darkened men and women in his eyes, there was, in her

case, the faintest gleam of light—a most feeble and sickly ray at the best of times—but there it was, and it showed the poor girl in a better and purer aspect than any in which he had looked on human nature yet.   (329)

Ralph's love for Kate is a tiny ray of light in the darkness, a light which glows modestly but steadily brighter as the novel continues. At the same time, however, like the father of Madeline Bray—and, Ralph would argue, the mothers of most marriageable daughters—parental love in this novel is inextricable from commerce: Kate is displayed for the highest bidder by the uncle for whom "there was nothing but money" (7).

When taken as a pair—a gesture both Ralph and the narrator make continually—Kate and Nicholas together represent the full spectrum of emotions for Ralph. His violent hatred of Nicholas and his flawed affection for Kate represent the distribution into melodramatic extremes of strong, oppositional emotions. Only when those distributed emotions are consolidated—when the Kate desire is laid over the Nicholas hatred—does the full complexity of Ralph's ambivalence emerge. In this novel, Dickens explores conflicting emotions that mirror one another through recourse to characters that double one another. Dickens splits ambivalent emotions into their component parts, and only rarely ventures their dangerous reintegration.

Godfrey and Ralph, Nicholas and Ralph, Ralph and Nicholas, Nicholas and Kate, Nicholas and a lost boy known as Smike, who perhaps began the world as Ralph—the Nickleby family heritage is one of emotional disintegration, and it finds its reflection in the text's wider world. This serves a purpose for Dickens. The novel's investment in emotional extremes represents a way of sorting out—and thus managing and containing—those complex oppositional emotions that originate from the same source. Contradictory though they may seem, in the Nickleby family drama, opposites attract: family members become who they are relative to their relatives.

II. Mixed Feelings

In 1910, the Swiss psychiatrist Eugen Bleuler coined the term "ambivalence" to describe the phenomenon in which polarized feelings toward another person, or an object or situation, coexist simultaneously: "The very same concept can be accompanied simultaneously by pleasant and unpleasant feelings (*affective ambivalence*): the husband both loves and hates his wife. The patient's hallucinations reveal to the mother the 'longed-for' death of the child by the unloved husband. She breaks out in endless sobbing and moaning . . . " (53, emphasis original). In his *Dementia Praecox*, Bleuler identified ambivalence or uncertainty as well as affective and thought disorders as the hallmarks of schizophrenia, ubiquitous components of the illness signified consistently, in terms both grand and subtle, in a patient's affect, will, and intellect (53–55).[2] Almost immediately, however, psychoanalysts extrapolated from Bleuler's conclusions, suggesting not that ambivalence is pathological but that it is normative. The term offers a means of understanding the complexity of all strong emotions, and in English the word itself underscores the simultaneous, oppositional, and passionate feeling it describes: the prefix "ambi" means "both," and the suffix "valent," strong or vigorous. The *Oxford English Dictionary* defines the term this way: "The coexistence in one person of contradictory emotions or attitudes (as love and hatred) towards a person or thing."

Sigmund Freud makes three major claims on behalf of ambivalence in *Totem and Taboo*, first published in 1912:

1. Love and hostility are inextricable from one another. They originate together, define each other mutually, and stand as the prototype for all other ambivalent emotions. On this point, Freud writes: "In almost every case where there is an intense emotional attachment to a particular person we find that behind the tender love there is a concealed hostility in the unconscious. This is the classical example . . . of the ambivalence of human emotions" (13:60).
2. The passionate expression of love masks the equally passionate repression of hostility when hostility is the more dangerous and less acceptable emotion. Conversely, under circumstances in which love is the more dangerous emotion, hostility will instead govern conscious expression.
3. Fathers embody ambivalence, especially for their sons. The father is the icon of all that is good and bad, beloved and loathed, powerful and weak; the son's first object of masculine identification, he is also a son's competitor for status and recognition. Just as the father represents *eros*, or the life drive, he embodies *thanatos*, or the death drive.

Psychoanalysts Otto Rank and Melanie Klein respectively suggest that the imagery of twinning and doubling indicates the splitting-in-two, and thus the management, of ambivalent emotions that originate in the psychic crucible of a child's relations with its parents (Klein 83).[3] For Freud, too, all powerful emotions originate in families and in relation to fathers and mothers; thus, for Freud as for Klein after him, powerful emotions are by definition ambivalent. A person is capable of expressing a strong emotion—hostility, for example—only insofar as that emotion is bound by its opposite. Hostility finds its means of expression only insofar as its dangerous counterpart, love or desire, remains safely repressed in the unconscious, emerging only as "the faintest gleam of light—a most feeble and sickly ray at the best of times." In the hall of mirrors that is human emotion, then, hostility is the governing motive of repressed love, and love of hostility. Thus, a son's emulation of a strong and powerful father-figure—let's call him an uncle—is simply an overdetermined response to the fear provoked by paternal weakness, a fear which flourishes unacknowledged in the younger man's unconscious. For Freud and for Dickens, fathers and their surrogates crystallize precisely those strong, contradictory emotions that require the repression of one in favor of the other.[4]

III. Scary Parents, Frightened Children

Throughout *Nicholas Nickleby* Dickens twins love and hostility, strength and weakness, sex and death, the erotic and the economic. Yet the fluctuations of ambivalent passions emerge with the most damaging ferocity in the novel's parent-figures. Adult love for children is riddled with guilt because children invariably mean something financial, for good or for ill, to the adults in their lives. Reflecting his own ambivalence about his actions toward Kate, Ralph Nickleby rationalizes to Mr. Bray the exchange of young Madeline for financial solvency and security: "Why, how often do men of family and fortune [who] have all the means and superfluities of life within their reach—how often do they marry their daughters to old men, or (worse still) to young men without heads or hearts, to tickle some idle vanity, strengthen some family interest, or secure some seat in Parliament!" (588). Mr. Bray, reflecting Ralph's ambivalence back, is torn between avarice and natural affection for his girl:

> "Hush! hush! cried Mr. Bray, suddenly starting up, and covering Ralph's mouth with his trembling hand. "I hear her at the door!" . . . There was a gleam of conscience in the shame and terror of this hasty action, which, in one short moment, tore the thin covering of sophistry from the cruel design, and laid it bare in all its meanness and heartless deformity. The father fell into his chair pale and trembling; Arthur Gride plucked and fumbled at his hat, and durst not raise his eyes from the floor; even Ralph crouched for the moment like a beaten hound, cowed by the presence of one young innocent girl!   (588–89)

The novel couldn't be clearer about its ambivalence toward the ambivalence even its most loving parents feel toward its children. Like *Oliver Twist*, *Nickleby* is preoccupied with the commodification of and trade in innocent childish flesh by parents or parent-figures who should know better. John Bowen contends that "the peculiarly ambivalent transformational energies of Dickens's writing undercut the domestic ideology of early Victorian capitalism through the frankness of its recognition of the economic forces beneath it . . . ; through its recognition or half-recognition of incestuous and murderous desires within families . . . ; and through the hysterical and carnivalesque laughter and inversion that permeate [*Nickleby*], mischievously and promiscuously intermixing and confusing distinctions, identities, places, families" (109). In the dark, unbounded, and, indeed, ambivalent world of this novel, children mean something mercantile to those entrusted not to exploit them but to protect them.

Thus, though Bray, Gride, and Ralph remain undaunted in their quest for virgins, they are sufficiently human to know their desire is wrong. The same cannot be said for Squeers: he has identified a market in extraneous children that stepfathers and mother-aunts want to offload. The rhetoric of plain education clads only thinly the claims of conscience. The Infant Phenom serves a market function, too: "[T]he infant phenomenon, though of short stature, had a comparatively aged countenance, and had moreover been precisely the same age—not perhaps to the full extent of the memory of the oldest inhabitant, but certainly for five good years. But she had been kept up late every night, and put upon an unlimited allowance of gin-and-water from infancy, to prevent her growing tall, and perhaps this system of training had produced in the infant phenomenon these additional phenomena" (283). Like the Phenom, Miss Morleena Kenwigs will insist on having a body that changes—she incites her mother's ire for the sinful possession of growing hair. And even before the traumatic haircut episode, Morleena and her sisters are understandably terrified by their female parent's rather menacing observation of her daughters: "[O]h! they're too beautiful to live, much too beautiful" (169). The Kenwiggian father, too, shares his wife's unnerving rhetorical tendency to recur to his children's mortality. Upon learning that baby and siblings were disenfranchised by Mr. Lillyvick's marriage: " 'Let [that baby] die,' cried Mr. Kenwigs, in the torrent of his wrath. 'Let him die. He has no expectations, no property to come into. We want no babies here,' said Mr. Kenwigs recklessly. 'Take 'em away, take 'em away to the Fondling!' " (444). Reflecting the "we want no babies here" mentality, Mrs. Nickleby recalls her late husband. Careening through one of her patented monologues, she gets hung up on the details of a long-ago menu: "Roast pig! I hardly think we ever could have had one, now I come to remember, for your papa could never bear the sight of them in the shops, and used to say that they always put him in mind of very little babies, only the pigs had much fairer complexions; and he had a horror of little babies, too, because he couldn't very well afford any increase to his family, and had a natural dislike of the subject" (502).

Ranging from the sadistic extreme of Squeers to the declamatory expostulations of the Kenwigses, *Nickleby* represents parents as menacing, violent, and exploitative, all in the interest of capital; like the patient in Bleuler's first description of ambivalence, it would seem that the death of a child is at once a parent's dearest wish and worst nightmare. Parents have the power of life and death over their offspring, and the novel's children register a range of responses to malign parental influence. Madeline Bray is stolid in the face of her father's exploitation of her youth and good looks, and Kate Nickleby is noteworthy for her patience in the face of her mother's idiosyncrasies. Like Ralph, Mrs. Nickleby is not without a gleam of insight into what her eccentricities cost her daughter: witnessing Kate's rare expression of her grief for her dead father, "Mrs. Nickleby began to have a glimmering that she had been rather thoughtless now and then, and was conscious of something like self-reproach as she embraced her daughter, and yielded to the emotions which such a conversation naturally awakened" (533). As this suggests, Kate's relationship with her mother requires the careful management of emotional self-display. Yet Kate's repressed rage at Mrs. Nickleby's role in her sexual exploitation gives way before Mrs. Wititterly. Kate appeals to her decidedly unmaternal employer based on the protection and sympathy an older woman owes a younger:

> "Is it possible! . . . that any one of my own sex can have sat by, and not have seen the misery these men have caused me! Is it possible that you, ma'am, can have been present, and failed to mark the insulting freedom that their every look bespoke? Is it possible that you can have avoided seeing, that these libertines, in their utter disrespect for you, and utter disregard of all gentlemanly behaviour and almost of decency, have had but one object in introducing themselves here, and that the furtherance of their designs upon a friendless, helpless girl, who, without this humiliating confession, might have hoped to receive from one so much her senior something like womanly aid and sympathy?"   (352–53)

Like her brother, too, Kate has no compunction at voicing her rage at her disgrace to Ralph Nickleby. Ralph's response speaks right to the heart of his ambivalence: "although Ralph felt no remorse at that moment for his conduct towards the innocent, true-hearted girl; although his libertine clients had done precisely what he had expected, precisely what he most wished, and precisely what would tend most to his advantage, still he hated them for doing it, from the very bottom of his soul" (357).

If Ralph leaves his son Smike a paternal legacy at all, it is the ambivalence of desire and loss for which Kate is the catalyst. Like father, like son, the two are bound by a love for Kate that they will live neither to express nor to realize. For this reason Miss La Creevy recognizes that the possession of a secure home and family unnerves young Smike as much as it comforts him. Smike's personal history includes no mother, no father, not even a wire monkey—just a room. Nicholas tries to prompt the boy's hurt memory: " 'Do you remember no woman, no kind gentle woman, who hung over you once, and kissed your lips, and called you her child?' . . . 'No,' said the poor creature, shaking his head, 'no, never.' . . . 'Nor any house but that house in

Yorkshire?' . . . 'No,' rejoined the youth, with a melancholy look: 'a room—I remember I slept in a room, a large lonesome room at the top of a house, where there was a trap-door in the ceiling. I have covered my head with the clothes often, not to see it, for it frightened me, a young child with no one near at night, and I used to wonder what was on the other side' '' (268). From that very trap door, Smike's father and double, Ralph, later hangs himself.

Charles Cheeryble dismisses the presumption that "natural" love can flourish in an emotional starvation economy, even between a parent and a child:

> "Parents who never showed their love, complain of want of natural affection in their children—children who never showed their duty, complain of want of natural feeling in their parents—law-makers who find both so miserable that their affections have never had enough of life's sun to develop them, are loud in their moralisings over parents and children too, and cry that the very ties of nature are disregarded. Natural affections and instincts, . . . are the most beautiful of the Almighty's works, but like other beautiful works of His, they must be reared and fostered, or it is as natural that they should be wholly obscured, and that new feelings should usurp their place, as it is that the sweetest productions of the earth, left untended, should be choked with weeds and briars."
>
> (564)

Brother Charles allocates responsibility for the maintenance of love and "natural affection" to parents and children alike. Consequences have actions, he suggests: love may be the natural first state of the parent-child relationship but it is easily obscured by the "weeds and briars" that choke out its "sweetest productions." Notice, however, that Charles describes love *obscured* by neglect—not love lost. Is it conceivable that deep beneath the violent hatred Nicholas feels for Ralph and Ralph for Nicholas, beneath Ralph's vicious exploitation of Kate and Bray's of Madeline, thrive powerful feelings of love and desire obscured by other motives?

Again and again, the novel supports this suggestion. Recall the glimmers of conscience Ralph feels relative to Kate and Bray relative to Madeline. Recall, too, Ralph's fantasy that he would have been a good father to Smike, or more precisely, that Smike would have been a good son to him, had Ralph only had the chance to know him. Ambivalence offers us a framework for understanding the extreme depth and violent passion of Nicholas's hatred for Ralph, and vice versa. The novel reflects Charles Cheeryble's theory of parent-child relations, consistently underscoring the tenacity of children's "natural" love for their parents. There are consequences to its abuse, however. That natural love is fragile—it can be choked into the dark obscurity of the unconscious when the "weeds and briars" are left to flourish. This underscores the narrative function of doubling, which shows simultaneous, conflicted emotions safely distributed between two different characters rather than conflated in one. Ralph is clearly a double for his brother, Nicholas's father, a man whom we know to be quiet, retiring, affectionate, impecunious, afraid of babies, and dead. As an uncle, Ralph is a safe repository for all the negative emotions Nicholas cannot admit he holds for his father. In the real time of the text, Ralph's malevolent paternity is offset by the doubly overdetermined Cheeryble duo. Bad father, Ralph; good father, Cheerybles. In turn, Ralph, who is the son of an ineffectual father and the father of a lost son, demonizes Nicholas to defend against the feelings of guilt, loss, and anger called to semi-consciousness by Nicholas's virile youth. Though Ralph struggles with his would-be love for Kate and for his lost son, he displaces those emotions into a safer channel: his disproportionately violent hatred for Nicholas, the person who is at once his niece's sibling, his dead brother's son, his son's surrogate father, and his own surrogate son.

To apply the concept of ambivalence to the Nickleby family drama is in some sense to shoot fish in a barrel. I want to suggest, however, that this representational strategy marks a new turn for Dickens in his development as a novelist. Putting the conventions of melodrama to new use for the first time in his career, Dickens finds new machinery for his representation of complex emotional conflict. Because such conflict is by definition deeply interior and often unacknowledged to his characters' conscious minds, Dickens relies for its expression on its projection outward and its spatial distribution. Thus, in his rendering of the Nicklebys' emotional life, Dickens deconstructs ambivalent feelings of love and hatred and assigns the component parts to pairs of characters. Remember that ambivalence requires the simultaneous experience of powerful, conflicting emotions about a person, a concept, or an event. The stronger, more complex, and less acceptable of the two emotions in question—say, hostility toward the father or hatred toward one's own child—is repressed into the subject's unconscious. The act of repression leaves its other half—love for the father or for the child—in florid display, its overdetermination verging on the grotesque, the extreme, even the melodramatic. His characters feel extreme emotions, but Dickens signifies the conflicted quality of ambivalence by assigning the polarized extremes of "good" and "bad" to figures that function as doubles for one another. This affords Dickens a narrative technique for the representation of complex emotions—emotions that refuse, by and large, to be integrated and whose polarization resists resolution. The proliferation of doubles throughout *Nicholas Nickleby*, and the florid overdetermination of melodramatic emotion, signifies the unspoken complexity of emotions that are too disturbing to express, too hot to handle in the light of day.

IV. Why Are There Two Cheerybles?

Ralph Nickleby may be very, very bad, but Ralph's nephew Nicholas is *not* very, very good. In the novel's 1848 preface, Dickens underscores the fact that Nicholas is no easy foil for the novel's figures of melodramatic vice: ''If Nicholas be not always found to be blameless or disagreeable, he is not always intended to appear so. He is a young man of an impetuous temper and of little or no experience'' (9). Nicholas is indeed too violent and impetuous to conform easily to an ideal of sentimental virtue, and in his infatuation with Madeline Bray, conceived anonymously in a public place, he bears a passing resemblance to those in the novel who traffic in women for seamier motives. (In fact, to my mind Nicholas is redeemed as an interesting protagonist by the persistent gap between his virtuous ideals and his impetuous actions.) The Cheeryble brothers, in contrast, are indeed very, very good—*too* good in fact, their goodness so overdetermined that it threatens to stop the plot's momentum in its tracks. That goodness is multiplied exponentially by the Cheerybles' doubleness, identical twins and loving surrogate fathers beaming approvingly at one another as they dispense wisdom along with cash and property. Plainly they are the anti-Ralph and the anti-Squeers, the diametric opposite of every careless, neglectful, hostile, abandoning, abusive, exploit-ative, or dead parent in this book and also in Dickens's fiction more gener-ally—and there are many of them. Anchoring the regime of virtue against the prevailing darkness, Cheerybles proliferate: their very twinnedness is an overdetermined expression of the threat that must be forestalled.

Dickens gives us plenty of room to perceive the Cheerybles as the flip side of the Ralph Nickleby coin. They represent a certain mode of virtue that the novel idealizes: an even balance of dedication to family, business, and social good which Joe Childers describes as ''the last hurrah for a naïve representa-tion of an unsullied, middle-class goodness that was never without its darker side'' (63). What interests me most, though, about the abundant Cheerybles is their very awkwardness as a deus ex machina. In they swoop, not just one good father but two; not just wise but good; not just good but rich.

It is almost as if the novel itself needs a benevolent patriarch, wants a good father, as earnestly as Nicholas Nickleby himself. Fairly early on, Dickens visits Nicholas and Smike on the road to Portsmouth that will eventually take them to the Crummles players. The narrator finds them at a very low moment: ''The whole capital which Nicholas found himself entitled to, either in posses-sion, reversion, remainder, or expectancy, after paying his rent and settling with the broker for whom he had hired his poor furniture, did not exceed by more than a few halfpence the sum of twenty shillings. And yet he hailed the morning on which he had resolved to quit London with a light heart, and sprang from his bed with an elasticity of spirit which is happily the lot of young persons, or the world would never be stocked with old ones'' (264). Given the fate of children in this novel, the narrator's association of youth with ''elasticity of spirit'' seems almost ludicrously optimistic. But indeed, in the end, things turn out well for Nicholas, if less so for Smike and other refugees of the Squeers academy. To be young is not yet to understand the competing claims death holds over life, *thanatos* over its counterpart, *eros*.

This novel is on the side of life and of *eros*; its concluding glow of domestic bliss includes not just the marriages of the young lovers but that of a pair of much older characters, the novel's "comfortable couple," Tim Linkinwater and Miss LaCreevy (761). The novel's expression of hope extends to its social advocacy on behalf of innocent and abused children, and even more subtly, to its emotional embrace of the "elasticity of spirit" that propels Nicholas out of bed each morning. *Nicholas Nickleby* is a novel written by a man of just twenty-six, a very early novel of a writer whom it is hard to extricate from the weight of the long and distinguished career that followed. And, as Steven Marcus reminds us, "While *Nicholas Nickleby* was being written, John Dickens was again arrested for debt and rescued by his son" (122). This young novel believes in Cheerybles even as it fears the real malign power of the Ralph Nicklebys of this world. The Cheerybles and Ralph are the novel's two most intimately rendered figures for paternal potency. Symbols of good father and bad father respectively, they remain polarized and unintegrated. Dickens associates such painful complexity of emotions with fathers in *Nicholas Nickleby* that even in the end, good father and bad are unintegratable within a single figure. In this young novel, for this young novelist, the ambivalence goes unresolved but not unmarked.

Dickens undertakes a noteworthy formal experiment in *Nicholas Nickleby*. Perhaps ironically but quite effectively, the novel's melodramatic extremism lends Dickens a new novelistic technique for the investigation of complex and seemingly irreconcilable emotions: the novel attributes oppositional emotional qualities to characters who serve as doubles or mirror images for one another. Embracing a certain "elasticity of spirit," the novel ends on an optimistic note—both young Nicklebys married for love and money, the elderly "comfortable couple" established at the hearthside—but leaves unintegrated its powerful ambivalence toward fathers and their symbolic surrogates. The very overdetermined quality of the novel's domestic conclusion, its resolute exchange of tranquility for high drama, comfortable coupledom for passion, suggests in the end a new phase in the ambivalent development of Nicklebys and *Nickleby*.

NOTES

1. Elaine Hadley provides a materialist account of the melodramatic mode in nineteenth-century British culture. On melodrama and affect, see Brooks, and on literature, politics, and affect in Victorian Britain, see Ann Cvetkovich.

2. See also Brody.

3. For Freud's discussion of Rank's theory of the *Doppelgänger*, see pp. 252–53 of his essay "The 'Uncanny.' "

4. In the psychoanalytic tradition ambivalence replicates infantile attitudes toward powerful parental figures. While for Freud this drama is embodied in the father, for Melanie Klein and the object-relations tradition that followed her, the mother is the anchor of ambivalence. On the "maternal" challenge to psychoanalytic phallocentrism posed to Freud by object-relations theorists, see my *Death and the Mother from Dickens to Freud*, 51–57.

WORKS CITED

Bleuler, Eugen. *Dementia Praecox or the Group of Schizophrenias*. Trans. J. Zinkin. New York: International Universities P, 1950.

Bowen, John. *Other Dickens: Pickwick to Chuzzlewit*. Oxford: Oxford UP, 2000.

Brody, Morris W. "Clinical Manifestations of Ambivalence." *Psychoanalytic Quarterly* 25 (1956): 505–14.

Brooks, Peter. *The Melodramatic Imagination: Balzac, Henry James, Melodrama, and the Mode of Excess*. New Haven: Yale UP, 1976.

Childers, Joseph W. "*Nicholas Nickleby*'s Problem of *Doux Commerce*." *Dickens Studies Annual* 25 (1996): 49–65.

Cvetkovich, Ann. *Mixed Feelings: Feminism, Mass Culture, and Victorian Sensationalism*. New Brunswick, NJ: Rutgers UP, 1992.

Dever, Carolyn. *Death and the Mother from Dickens to Freud: Victorian Fiction and the Anxiety of Origins*. Cambridge: Cambridge UP, 1998.

Dickens, Charles. *Nicholas Nickleby*. Ed. Mark Ford. New York: Penguin, 2003.

Freud, Sigmund. *Totem and Taboo. The Standard Edition of the Complete Psychological Works of Sigmund Freud*. Trans. and ed. James Strachey. Vol. 13. London: Hogarth, 1986. 1–162.

———. "The 'Uncanny.' " *The Standard Edition*. Vol. 17. 217–56.

Hadley, Elaine. *Melodramatic Tactics: Theatricalized Dissent in the English Marketplace, 1800–1885*. Stanford: Stanford UP, 1995.

Klein, Melanie, and Joan Riviere. *Love, Hate and Reparation*. New York: Norton, 1964.

MacKay, Carol Hanbery. "The Melodramatic Impulse in *Nicholas Nickleby*." *Dickens Quarterly* 5:3 (1988): 153–63.

Marcus, Steven. *Dickens: From Pickwick to Dombey*. New York: Basic Books, 1965.

Michie, Helena. "The Avuncular and Beyond: Family (melo)drama in *Nicholas Nickleby*." *Dickens Refigured: Bodies, Desires, and Other Histories*. Ed. John Schad. Manchester: Manchester UP, 1996. 80–97.

Patten, Robert. "From *Sketches* to *Nickleby*." *The Cambridge Companion to Charles Dickens*. Ed. John O. Jordan. Cambridge: Cambridge UP, 2001. 16–33.

Rank, Otto. *The Double: A Psychoanalytic Study*. Trans. and ed. Harry Tucker, Jr. Charlotte: U of North Carolina P, 1971.

Enumeration and Exhaustion: Taking Inventory in *The Old Curiosity Shop*

James Buzard

The Old Curiosity Shop *marks a crisis in Dickens's early career. Over-committed to projects, a victim of his own success, Dickens soon found his episodic model of fiction, first practiced in* Pickwick *and devoted to furnishing "a constant succession of characters and incidents," pushed to its limit. Of his new periodical* Master Humphrey's Clock *he complained, "wind, wind, wind, always winding I am." His fourth novel became a metafictional reflection on the conditions of his own creativity, a work seemingly intent on thwarting the very delineating power—the power of invention, and of inventory—that multiplies fresh characters and incidents in the Dickensian episodic narrative.*

> He excels in inventories of poor furniture, and is learned in pawnbrokers' tickets.
>
> —Walter Bagehot

> Mr. Shandy's clock was nothing to mine [i.e., *Master Humphrey's Clock*], wind, wind, wind, always winding I am; and day and night the alarum is ringing in my ears, warning me that it must not run down.
>
> —Charles Dickens

> Of the making of many books there is no end.
>
> —Ecclesiastes

Dickens Studies Annual, Volume 39, Copyright © 2008 by AMS Press, Inc. All rights reserved.

Inventory—traceable to Late Latin *inventarium*, "a finding out," or "enumeration," from the Latin *invenire*, "to come upon, find, invent." The word preserves the archaic meaning of *invention*, whose modern sense (to quote the *OED*) of "devising, contriving, or making up" rests upon this buried, contrary idea of "coming upon or finding . . . of finding out; discovery (whether accidental, or the result of search and effort)."

Item

Coming upon, or making up?

Charles Dickens's novel *The Old Curiosity Shop*, serialized between April 1840 and February 1841, begins with Master Humphrey's account of meeting by chance a lost little girl in the London street, of escorting her back to her grandfather's shop, of conversing with the grandfather and mingling with the dissolute Fred Trent and Dick Swiveller, the loyal Kit, the fiendish Quilp. Yet if we are to believe what he says upon concluding his narration, none of that ever happened. I refer here to Master Humphrey's notorious announcement (in the remarks following *The Old Curiosity Shop* in Dickens's periodical *Master Humphrey's Clock*) that his "share . . . in the pages we have read" was not, after all, that of the chance discoverer of Nell and her old grandparent, that his initial appearance was "fictitious," and that he is in fact the "single gentleman" who entered the narrative in its thirty-fourth chapter, that old grandparent's long-expatriated younger brother who searches England—too late—in hopes of being reunited with his kin (680).

It has been easy for critics and editors to discount this "confession" as an afterthought irreconcilable with the tale it follows, but then, a standard of narrative consistency would seem ludicrously misapplied to such a wayward and improvised text as *The Old Curiosity Shop*. And to engage in the thought-experiment of taking the confession seriously for even one minute is to realize that its being "true" would mean that the narrator of this work never saw Nell Trent alive—for the "single gentleman" arrives with his search party at Nell's final resting-place (in chapter 71) two days after her death, to find her lying in state and his brother insensible to anything but Nell. Between his entrance into the story and this tardy arrival, he personally interacts with most of the other characters, but a *living* Nell has no place on any inventory of those he has dealt with. He made her up. And knowing her only as a corpse, he has retrospectively invented an illusion of a walking and talking and weeping and laughing Nell that seems permanently out of place in the world of the living. Inventing her, he has made a "oner," something wonderful and one-of-a-kind. Nell is a "wax-work child" of "classical" repose, placed in the domain of mutability and history, "surrounded and beset by everything that was foreign to its nature'' and endowed with a spiritual prestige befitting her incipient angelhood, an allure by contrast with which all the contents of that historical domain fade into undifferentiated ''heaps of fantastic things,'' all its actors into ''a crowd of wild grotesque companions,'' all its events into so much ''useless strife'' (308, 271, 56, 187). ''It would be a curious speculation,'' Master Humphrey says to himself at the end of the opening chapter, ''to imagine her in her future life, holding her solitary way among a crowd of wild grotesque companions; the only pure, fresh youthful object in the throng. It would be curious to find'' (56)—but he interrupts himself there. If Master Humphrey is the single gentleman, then the speculation is a sham: he already knows that Nell has no future life, no way to make. However many pages are heaped up, however much narrative invention is expended to distract us from the fact, there is nothing to find: Dickens seems to have abidingly felt as much in the writing of this most curious of books, a tale that makes a mockery of the curiosity on which narrative feeds. Or rather, there's only *one* thing: but whether that one thing is the black hole of Nell's always inevitable absence or the surviving ''single gentleman'' who creates and destroys her—who else but Dickens, terribly alone at his desk?—neither of these ''oners'' can make up a narrative, or an inventory, all by itself.

Item

''The author's object in this work, was to place before the reader a constant succession of characters and incidents; to paint them in as vivid colours as he could command; and to render them, at the same time, life-like and amusing'' (41). So wrote Dickens in the preface to the 1837 volume edition of *Pickwick Papers*, a work of episodic serial fiction whose miraculous comic inventiveness may be described by the trope of the inventory—a list of separate items (''characters and incidents'') placed one after another, preserved in their plurality. All the items in an inventory contribute to a total value, but, arrayed in succession, they are amenable to line-item evaluation, and the value of the whole is nothing more than the sum of their separate worths. ''The publication of this book in monthly numbers,'' Dickens noted, ''rendered it an object of paramount importance that, while the different incidents were linked together by a chain of interest strong enough to prevent their appearing unconnected . . . the general design should be so simple as to sustain no injury from this detached and desultory form of publication . . . '' (41). A collection of installments essentially ''complete in [themselves]'' might strive for only the modest aim of a ''tolerably harmonious whole'' (41); literary creativity simply meant, in this instance, the capacity for continual production of new material, the capacity to keep extending a list by adding to it fresh items not identical with or subsumable under what has come before. ''And if it be objected to the Pickwick Papers, that they are merely a series of adventures, in which the scenes are ever changing, and the characters come and go like the men and women we encounter in the real world,'' Dickens added, ''they claim to be nothing else'' (41).

Inventory *proliferates*: it implies a point of view alert to differences, interested and indeed invested in the difference it makes to move from one item to another and to tally each judiciously. If one pays close enough attention and is sufficiently discriminating, missing no chance to exploit a distinction and so add a new line, there is no intrinsic reason why an inventory, like a picaresque novel, cannot be prolonged almost indefinitely. This was a consideration that arose during the serial run of *Pickwick*, once the work's phenomenal success was assured—for, surely, there was no internal logic in the text, no constraining plot, requiring the rounding off and closure of its narrative at any particular point: why should it not be extended as long as the market would bear? (''Which nothing but death will terminate'' are in fact the last words of *Pickwick Papers*.) Certainly the book's self-appointed continuators, in such works as *Pickwick Abroad* and others, recognized the open-endedness of the tale Dickens had commenced. Yet in an announcement accompanying the tenth installment (in December 1836), the author made clear ''his intention to adhere to his original pledge of confining his work to twenty numbers,'' in spite of his having received, as he no doubt took pleasure in recounting, ''every temptation to exceed the limits he first assigned to himself, that brilliant success, an enormous and increasing sale, the kindest notice, and the most extensive popularity, can hold out'' (902). (We might say that Dickens here indulges in a little inventory of ''reasons for self-satisfaction.'') Having to make this decision probably heightened Dickens's awareness that, short of death, and as long as the work enjoyed its success, nothing but his authorial fiat would put a stop to the story and bring its wayfaring characters to rest. His situation was like that of Mr. Codlin in *The Old Curiosity Shop*, the Punch-and-Judy patterer on whom alone rests ''the responsibility of deciding on [the puppet show's] length and of protracting or expediting the time for the hero's final triumph over the enemy of mankind, according as he judged that the after-crop of halfpence would be plentiful or scant'' (191). In the event, a death did halt the forward progress of the *Pickwick* juggernaut for awhile—Dickens's sister-in-law Mary Hogarth's death, in the spring of 1837, which caused Dickens to miss his deadline for the only time in his career, and, of course, supplied the germ of Nell, the always-already-an-angel heroine of *The Old Curiosity Shop*—a lavishly idealizing piece of work that is also prone to Codlin-esque cynicism about its creator's inventive genius.

Item

"He was for some days restrained by business from performing any particular pranks, as his time was pretty well occupied [in] taking . . . a minute inventory of all the goods in the place" (141). This is the villain Quilp, in chapter 11 of *The Old Curiosity Shop*, newly in possession of Nell's grandfather's property and for once, it seems, doing something *rational*: for even he, with his demonic energies and abiding "taste for [always] doing something fantastic and monkey-like" (124), appears to defer, at least for a time, to another exigency, subordinating his usual malign acrobatics to the business of sorting and counting and record-keeping. Still at this point believing the old man he has ousted to be a miser with a cache of treasure hidden amongst the miscellaneous oddities of the shop, Quilp settles down to determine, item by item, exactly what it is he now owns.

So what *is* there in the old curiosity shop—or in *The Old Curiosity Shop*? Master Humphrey says—and remember, he may be making this up, since he may never have been there—that "There were suits of mail standing like ghosts in armour here and there, fantastic carvings brought from monkish cloisters, rusty weapons of various kinds, distorted figures in china and wood and iron and ivory: tapestry and strange furniture that might have been designed in dreams" (47). But this is *inefficient* inventory, exhibiting only the most minimal discriminating energy: a half-hearted gesture at enumeration employing a few rough-and-ready distinctions to form fuzzy, unhelpful classes (such as "tapestry and strange furniture"). The point of view expressed here is one almost entirely lacking in the commitment, the *curiosity*, to delineate more and yet more items, to extend the catalogue and avoid lumping possibly distinguishable items together, so as to miss no opportunity of extracting value. As Henry James would say, we have been given "the circumstances of the interest," "but where is the interest itself?" (James 319). Indeed, one gets the feeling that, even if Master Humphrey were to tell us in greater detail what the shop contained, the effect of his doing so would be comparable to the one that arises from John Bunyan's description, in *Pilgrim's Progress*, of the Vanity Fair of this fallen world, where (says Bunyan) "all such merchandise [is] sold, as houses, lands, trades, places, honours, preferments, titles, countries, kingdoms, lusts, pleasures, and delights of all sorts, as whores, bawds, wives, husbands, children, masters, servants, lives, blood, bodies, souls, silver, gold, pearls, precious stones, and what not" (125). To the Nell-fixated gaze—and how many of this novel's *characters* have it, as well as readers?—spin the list out as one may, it all reduces in the end, and even before that, to a mass of "what not," or to what the single gentleman sums up as "the wreck of life," the assorted, heaped-together, unworthy-to-be-delineated contents of history's old curiosity shop (652). Bunyan says that one might see in Vanity Fair "jugglings, cheats, games, plays, fools, apes, knaves, and rogues, and that of all sorts" (125): a pretty fair description, one might be disposed to think, of the narrative business, the narrative *busy-ness*, set serially before us between our first view of Nell, as she lies sleeping in the shop, and our last, as she lies dead upon her bier (figs. 1 and 2). The uncanny sameness-and-difference of these two well-known illustrations, the seemingly typological relationship in which the former appears inevitably to forecast the latter, threatens to reduce "reading" this novel to the act of flipping back and forth between the two framing, static images, and to evacuate all significance from the in-between.

In *The Old Curiosity Shop*, Dickens hurls against his own narrative-propagating powers, so gloriously deployed in *The Pickwick Papers*, the story-negating inertia of Nell. With our eyes fixed on her in her passage from one picture to another, we will be inclined to regard all the energetic comings and goings of *The Old Curiosity Shop* and, for that matter, of mortal existence as such, in the manner Master Humphrey attributes to a bedridden man listening to the foot-traffic outside his window: as just so much maddeningly pointless "pacing to and fro," as an "incessant tread of feet," a "stream of life that will not stop [but] pour[s] [senselessly] on, on, on" (43) in the delusion that there is anywhere to get to in life other than where we always knew we were always headed.

Tennyson, in the fifty-sixth section of *In Memoriam*, fills out an inventory that is just as pointlessly, tragically prolonged as the narrative of *The Old Curiosity Shop* might seem to us, when he responds to the evidence of a suspectedly indifferent Nature by asking:

And he, shall he,

Man, Her [Nature's] last work, who seem'd so fair,
Such splendid purpose in his eyes,
Who roll'd the psalm to wintry skies,
Who built him fanes of fruitless prayer,

Who trusted God was love indeed
And love Creation's final law—
Tho' Nature, red in tooth and claw
With ravine, shriek'd against his creed—

Who loved, who suffer'd countless ills,
Who battled for the True, the Just,
Be blown about the desert dust,
Or seal'd within the iron hills? (399)

As this single sentence grows and grows, the poet unwinds and unwinds the whole long scroll of human history, its prayers, loves, sufferings, battles,

ideals, theories, purposes—*what not*—as if to defer his arrival at the terminus
he has seen lying before him all along.

In *The Old Curiosity Shop*, if we are really to pay attention to what fills
up the middle, to *inventorize*, delineating and involving ourselves in the affairs
of Quilp and Dick Swiveller and the Punch performers and Mrs. Jarley's
waxworks and the factory fire-watcher and the impoverished unemployed
and the bereft old schoolmaster—and what not—we must distract ourselves
from the static spectacle of Nell, must practice what James Kincaid calls "the
massive . . . evasion" of the dying or already dead child: our challenge as
readers of this unreadable novel, Kincaid says, is to "show Nell and her
corpse that they can't claim all the attention" (36, 37). Because to look at
Nell is to miss everything else. Witness Nell's grandfather, a man blasted
loose from all attachment to the world by the experience of living with an
angel. By the end of the book, he has come to inhabit a condition in which
"[w]hatever power of thought or memory he retained, was all bound up in
her," such that he can feel "no love or care for anything in life" (660, 661).
His plight may remind us of the opening lines of Rilke's *Duino Elegies*,
where the poet writes,

> Who, if I cried, would hear me among the angelic
> orders? And even if one of them suddenly
> pressed me against his heart, I should fade in the strength of his
> stronger existence. For Beauty's nothing
> but the beginning of a Terror we're still just able to bear,
> and why we adore it so is because it serenely
> disdains to destroy us. Each single angel is terrible. (21)

Nell's is the image, as her grandfather puts it, that "sanctifies the game"
(306), but to look upon that image is to forget the point of playing. By the
end, this curiosity shop keeper has been rendered "quite incapable of interest
or curiosity" (649).

Item

"Inventory," Roland Barthes once wrote, "is never a neutral idea; to catalogue is not merely to ascertain, . . . but also to appropriate" (222). Quilp's
attention to the business of reckoning the value of his new property restrains
him from fully indulging in his usual menacing monkey-business. To be sure,
even while conducting his inventory Quilp manages to make a thorough
nuisance of himself to both Nell (whose bed he commandeers with salacious
glee) and his own lawyer, Mr. Brass (whom he compels to smoke as inces-
santly as himself). But, whereas most of the time he functions in this novel

Fig. 1. Nell asleep in the Curiosity Shop

Fig. 2. Nell on her death-bed

as a superlatively busy and finally self-defeating devil incarnate who merely moonlights as a businessman, here the calculative protocols of the latter assume temporary priority, making this maliciously mobile enemy of peace and rest accept temporary confinement in the shop, for as long as the process of counting and assessing lasts. And confinement is something "foreign to [his] nature." Like the book in which he appears, and like all the other houses and buildings in that book, and indeed like Quilp's small body itself, the shop and its rooms and furniture seem scarcely able to hold his errant energy. When he goes to sleep in the very coziest of the book's enclosures, Nell's little bed, Quilp "hang[s] so far out of [it] that he almost seem[s] to be standing on his head" (150).

A parodic reflection of Quilp's inventory-taking can be found a few chapters earlier, when a character who is destined to counterbalance Quilp in the novel—Dick Swiveller—takes "a greasy memorandum-book from his pocket and [makes] an entry therein" (109). Having just consumed another delivered dinner and incurred another debt he cannot defray, Dick explains,

> I enter in this little book the names of the streets I can't go down while the shops are open. This dinner to-day closes Long Acre. I bought a pair of boots in Great Queen Street last week, and made that no thoroughfare too. There's only one avenue to the Strand left open now, and I shall have to stop up that to-night with a pair of gloves. The roads are closing so fast in every direction, that in about a month's time, unless my aunt sends me a remittance, I shall have to go three or four miles out of town to get over the way.   (109)

Where Quilp finds it necessary to take stock of what he owns, his comic counterpart defers to calculative rationality so far as to keep careful track of what, and where, he *owes*. In both cases, on the credit side of the ledger and on the debit, concession to the necessity of accounting requires that a character defined by his capacity for movement—the restless troublemaker and the constantly "swiveling" evader of debt—accept or acknowledge a measure of limitation, checking or at least redirecting his steps.

Like other villains in early Dickens, Quilp achieves his primary effect through his apparently incessant and unpredictable motion: not only does his body jerk and caper its way through every scene, as if unable to control the force it harbors; more than this, whenever Quilp is compelled to remain indoors, he tends to smoke so volcanically as to suggest he is liable to erupt. He also exhibits the alarming tendency (visible as well in the behavior of *Oliver Twist*'s Monks and Fagin) suddenly to materialize from out of nowhere. When Kit is arrested on the trumped-up charge of stealing from the lawyer Brass, the innocent dupe looks out of the window of the carriage bearing him away and sees, "all at once, as though it had been conjured up by magic, . . . the face of Quilp" (548). Here again—and strikingly captured in the accompanying illustration (fig. 3)—the baleful power in Quilp shows itself straining against enclosure: "It was from the open window of a tavern that [Quilp] looked out," we read; "and the dwarf had so spread himself over it, with his elbows on the window-sill and his head resting on both his hands, that what between this attitude and his being swoln with suppressed laughter, he looked puffed and bloated into twice his usual breadth" (548). In another passage, Nell has a close call when Quilp turns up unexpectedly, seeming "to have risen out of the earth," in the town she has just arrived in with Mrs. Jarley's traveling waxworks show, and the fright makes her feel "as if she were hemmed in by a legion of Quilps, and the very air were filled with them" (276, 278). It appears as if the driving force in Quilp is something, to borrow language Dickens will later apply to the Inspector Bucket of *Bleak House*, that "[t]ime and space cannot not bind" (769).

As for Dick Swiveller, he is reminiscent of figures like Jingle and Bob Sawyer in *Pickwick Papers*, men of boundless appetite and verbal self-invention who love the wide world for its ample provision of more and more places in which to contract new obligations and escape having to repay them. For such locomotive appetites, as for Tennyson's Ulysses in the dramatic monologue of that name, "all experience is an arch wherethro'/Gleams that untravell'd world, whose margin fades/For ever and forever as [they] move" ("Ulysses" 142, lines 19–21). From the mouths of such men comes an outflow of chatter proportionate to the amount of free food and drink that goes in. Other people exist, for such characters, for the almost exclusive purpose of affording them what Swiveller is looking for from Nell's grandfather when he first appears in the novel: "The watch-word to the old min," Dick says, "is—fork" (68)—as in *fork over*, or provide the means of feeding me. Embodied in Swiveller is the comic potential so rapturously exploited in Dickens's inaugural novel, that of the man self-invented on the move, unfettered by relationships, by institutions, and most of all by the women who control them: the man who makes it up as he goes along, his creative powers seeming equal to the variety of the world. When Jingle, in *Pickwick Papers*, announces that his place of residence is "No Hall, Nowhere" (584), he defines himself and his ilk as the instruments of a boundless, *unhouse-able* desire, the radical extension of that cornerstone of English liberty, the principle of habeus corpus. As Sam Weller memorably puts it, "The have-his-carcase, next to the perpetual motion, is vun of the blessedest things as wos ever made" (701).

Yet in *The Old Curiosity Shop*, as Dick perceives, the roads are closing fast in every direction. By the middle of the novel he finds himself installed in a kind of curiosity shop, that lawyer's trap for ensnaring the innocent, the House of Brass. Here he takes up his station alongside other oddities such as (in a kind of inventory) "She-dragons in the business, conducting themselves like professional gentlemen [Sally Brass]; plain cooks of three feet high appearing mysteriously from under ground [the Marchioness]; strangers walking

Fig. 3. Quilp in the window

in and going to bed without leave or license in the middle of the day [the single gentleman]'' (334). No better able to bear confinement than Quilp is, Swiveller is liable to burst into ''the performance of a maniac hornpipe'' (329) when left alone, and to play at attacking his jailer (Sally Brass) when her back is turned. For this comic law-unto-himself, being compelled to serve as clerk to a lawyer is tantamount to being what he imagines his destiny making him next, ''a convict . . . trotting about a dockyard with [his] number neatly embroidered on [his] uniform, and the order of the garter on [his] leg'' (330).

When these restless characters stay inside and pay attention to their lists, they acknowledge the power that places *them* on a list—the power that constructs and manages the dramatis personae. They defer, that is, to the narrator, who enumerates, apportions, and delimits the domains of his characters.

Item

''Everything in our lives, whether of good or evil, affects us most by contrast'' (*OCS* 493). As Audrey Jaffe observes in her excellent study *Vanishing Points: Dickens, Narrative, and the Subject of Omniscience*, the roving Dickensian narrator possesses his authorizing mobility and freedom ''in relation to and at the expense of'' its characters, producing the effect of omniscience and omnipresence by opposition to characters who are, finally, made to remain in their places, however much they may long to roam free (12). Narrative omniscience, Jaffe maintains, is not just a phenomenon of Dickens's fiction but a, or perhaps *the*, project of that fiction, and *The Old Curiosity Shop* in particular shows us that project in faltering and self-conscious operation, revealing ''not the unproblematic achievement of distance and detachment, but rather a blurring of the boundaries that define and separate narrator and narration'' (49–50). As readers cannot help noticing, the Master Humphrey who participates in the narrative of the book's opening chapters removes himself from the story's action at the end of chapter 3 in what seems the most ham-fisted of manners, announcing his intention of ''detach[ing] [him]-self from its further course'' (72). Subsequently he will make full and ironically knowing use of the omniscient narrator's unique ability to leap from setting to setting and storyline to storyline, demonstrating and indeed flaunting the narrator's privilege in such passages as the following:

> As the course of this tale requires that we should become acquainted, some-where hereabouts, with a few particulars connected with the domestic economy of Mr Sampson Brass, and as a more convenient place than the present is not likely to occur for that purpose, the historian takes the friendly reader by the hand, and springing with him into the air, and cleaving the same at a greater

rate than ever Don Cleophas Leandro Perez Zambullo and his familiar travelled
through that pleasant region in company [in Le Sage's romance *The Devil on
Two Sticks*], alights with him upon the pavement of Bevis Marks.   (319)

And yet, as we have seen, he will make a "return" to the domain of the
story's participants that feels just as clumsy as his exit from it, as if he is
unsatisfied with having to choose only one side of the opposition between
narrator and narrated. As Jaffe puts it, "the status of the narrator—whether
he is 'in' or 'out'—is not fully settled by his departure" at the end of chapter
3 (49). It remains an open question whether the narrator should be listed on
or omitted from an inventory of *The Old Curiosity Shop*, whether he intends
to accept the self-erasure that is the price of omniscience or whether he
considers that price too high. Not content with being the peripatetic student
of human affairs, he ambivalently occupies a position we might label *peripa-
thetic*, at once free to move about the fictional landscape he surveys and
affectively involved in it. He can't *just* stay "out."

At the same time, the characters whose limitation and *inventoriability* defines the narrator's mobility and invisibility by contrast, can appear to chafe,
as we have already begun to see, against the restriction they are obliged to
accept under the terms of their fictional contract. When, at the end of chapter
21, Quilp encounters and then taunts to fury a chained dog (fig. 4), the
interaction travesties the Dickensian differential relationship of narrator and
characters: from a position of "perfect safety," Quilp "triumph[s] over [the
dog] in his inability to advance another inch" (228). "The dog tore and
strained at his chain with starting eyes and furious bark," we read, "but there
the dwarf lay, snapping his fingers with gestures of defiance and contempt.
When he had sufficiently recovered from his delight, he rose, and with his
arms a-kimbo, achieved a kind of demon-dance round the kennel, just without
the limits of the chain, driving the dog quite wild" (228). In a later passage
(fig. 5), we need hardly ask the true identity of the "figure-head of some
old ship," "much too large for the apartment which it was . . . employed to
decorate," which is propped in a corner of Quilp's room "like a goblin or
hideous idol whom the dwarf worshipped" (564). Quilp says it looks like
Kit, but to say so is to screen himself from what stares him in the face: who
else but his creator and confiner could provoke such a torrent of aggression
as he rains down upon the colossal effigy? The churl "batter[s] the great
image until the perspiration stream[s] down his face with the violence of the
exercise"; he boasts of "screwing gimlets into him, and sticking forks in his
eyes, and cutting [his] name on him," intending "to burn him at last" (566).

A comparable effect arises from the fact that our attention is repeatedly
directed, both by Dickens's text and by its accompanying pictures, to the
permeability of the spaces characters occupy. If we recall that illustration of

Fig. 4. Quilp and the dog

Fig. 5. Quilp and the effigy

Quilp emerging from the tavern window to crow at the captured Kit (fig. 3), we confront just one of this novel's images of a barely successful restraint or an endangered threshold, with the frame of an insufficiently large window coming to suggest the frame of the illustration itself and the frame of the book that contains it. If you see a window in this book, chances are that Quilp will be thrusting himself through it. Similarly, there appears to be no half-opened doorway in this novel without its eavesdropper or unexpected entrant. And doors that are closed are often being pounded upon, a situation that more than once stirs up a threshold anxiety about what might happen if they are suddenly opened.

For example, the morning after Nell and her grandfather abscond from the shop they have forfeited to Quilp, the antagonist and the lawyer Brass are awakened by "a knocking at the street-door, often repeated and gradually mounting up from a modest single rap into a perfect battery of knocks, fired in long discharges with a very short interval between" (152). It's Dick Swiveller, laying siege to the shop—in answer to whom Quilp, "opening the door all at once, pounce[s] out upon the person on the other side" (154), whom he mistakenly believes to be his wife, a sort of substitute Nell he delights in terrorizing (fig. 6). This sequence involves the replacement of Quilp's opposite and victim (Mrs. Quilp; Nell) by a figure who at this point in the narrative is his rival pursuer of Nell (for Swiveller is acting here on Fred Trent's plan that he woo Nell to get hold of the grandfather's supposed fortune). A line of demarcation between opposed characters' spaces is crossed with an explosive sense of release, and a distinction temporarily collapses, as two men with similar aims engage in the one activity this novel provides in plenty: pointless violence, "useless strife" (187).

Later on, once Swiveller has become something of a victim himself, entrapped in the House of Brass, he hears "a loud double knock" at the street door that is "repeated with increased impatience" up to the point at which "the door [is] opened, and somebody with a very heavy tread [goes] up the stairs and into the room above" (332). This is followed by a further "rapping of knuckles at the office door" (332), which Dick, who ignored the first summons, is compelled to answer. In walks the small servant—her very existence a surprise—whom Dick will eventually rechristen the Marchioness (and later, Sophronia Sphynx), to announce the arrival of the "single gentle-man" who has come to take the room for rent upstairs. A complex transaction is taking place here. Though he does not yet recognize the fact, just as he does not admit the knocker into the house, Dick is *himself* a "single gentleman" in search of a loved one; and insofar as we are willing to entertain the idea that the brusquely intrusive single gentleman is Master Humphrey, we might also observe that Dick Swiveller is, for his part, the poet, the story-maker, the word-spinner, in this novel. Had he opened the street door, he would have

Fig. 6. Quilp and Swiveller at the door

looked into a mirror, he would have *been* a mirror to the single gentleman who looked at him, and the narrative would have foundered on the spectacle of a Dick(ens) "[a]ll alone," a "Swiveller solus" (514). But the Marchioness mediates, helping to keep apart the teller and the told, to keep narrative going and to ensure a different, happier destiny for Dick Swiveller than the one that awaits his fellow bachelor.

Nor is this the last of the door-business. A few pages later, the new lodger's preternatural powers of sleeping have so disturbed the other inhabitants of the house that they gather outside his chamber determined to roust him out, even though they fear "[i]t would be an extremely unpleasant circumstance if he was to bounce out suddenly" (341). "Hallo there! Hallo, hallo!" shouts Mr. Brass (fig. 7),

> as a means of attracting the lodger's attention, and while Miss Brass plied the hand-bell, Mr Swiveller put his stool close against the wall by the side of the door, and mounting on the top and standing bolt upright, so that if the lodger did make a rush, he would most probably pass him in its onward fury, began a violent battery with the ruler upon the upper panels of the door. . . . [He] rained down such a shower of blows that the noise of the bell was drowned . . . Suddenly the door was unlocked on the inside and flung violently open. (341)

One can imagine a passage like this in an acutely self-reflexive modern text such as Flann O'Brien's *At Swim-Two-Birds*, in which we would not be surprised to find a group of characters laboring to awaken their slumbering storyteller so that he might invent something for them severally to *do*, might divide and distribute and mobilize them by means of an efficacious fictional plot. Perhaps they just want him to tell them whether he intends to stay in or go out.

But perhaps the uncanniest instance of this threshold anxiety in *The Old Curiosity Shop* occurs when Mrs. Jarley's carriage is put in motion at the end of chapter 26. Nell is on board, the recipient of the waxwork proprietress's hospitality, and as the vehicle takes to the road we read that "away they went, with a great noise of flapping and creaking and straining, and the bright brass knocker, which nobody ever knocked at, knocking one perpetual double-knock of its own accord as they jolted heavily along" (269). Ask not for whom the invisible knocker knocks. The north-by-northwest journey Nell is on makes a gloomy rejoinder to the sunny picaresque of *Pickwick*, in which the road and the book always promise something new, something more around the next bend. In *The Old Curiosity Shop*, as Hilary Schor has put it, "the central activity of any reader . . . is watching Little Nell walk herself to death" (32). Even when she gets to ride for a time, her foreordained fate is out there, importunately knocking.

Fig. 7. Knocking at the single gentleman's door

The *inventoriable* world of Dickens's early fiction, like the whole universe
as John Milton imagined it in his *Doctrine and Discipline of Divorce*, requires
what Milton called the "divorcing command" of its creator if it is to rise,
and remain, "out of Chaos": it requires the exertions of a power capable of
drawing a line between and "separating . . . unmeet consorts" like Light and
Dark, dry land and water, Nell and Quilp (Milton 420). But in *The Old
Curiosity Shop*, as Robert Frost puts it, "something there is that doesn't love
a wall" (33). And so we face a catalogue of items exhibiting what seems a
compulsive failure to stay distinct from one another. There's Abel Garland—Abel without a Cain, a clone of his father, down to the club-foot. There
are the brother and sister Brass, of whom it is said that "so exact . . . was the
likeness between them, that had it consorted with Miss Brass's maiden modesty and gentle womanhood to have assumed her brother's clothes in a frolic
and sat down beside him, it would have been difficult for the oldest friend
of the family to determine which was Sampson and which Sally" (320).
There are Mrs. Jarley's waxwork figures, so malleable to their mistress's
hand that "Mr Grimaldi as clown" can be transformed into "Mr Lindley
Murray as he appeared when engaged in the composition of his English
Grammar," that "a murderess of great renown" can undergo wholesale
moral revision and turn into "Mrs Hannah More," that "Mr Pitt in nightcap
and bedgown, and without his boots" can represent "the poet Cowper with
perfect exactness," and "Mary Queen of Scots in a dark wig, white shirt-
collar, and male attire" can become "a complete image of Lord Byron"
(288). There is the "I and five hundred other men" of the desperate unemployed, the pitiful aggregate never permitted to diversify into individuals
(427). There is Nell, and Mrs. Quilp, and Miss Edwards, and her sister, and
perhaps the Marchioness, all versions of each other. There are Quilp and
Swiveller, two masks for "the uncontainable." There is Kit, who surrenders
his separate consciousness entirely to his image of Nell, determining his
conduct by the principle of "always try[ing] to please her," of "always
be[ing]," as he puts it, "what I should like to seem to her if I was still her
servant" (632). There is Nell's grandfather, who convinced himself that his
gambling addiction was a selfless service to Nell, and who winds up so
thoroughly lost to himself that, as we have seen, "whatever power of thought
or memory he retained, was all bound up in her" (660). There are Nell and
Quilp—but then, as Steven Marcus noted, the one exists not just as the antithesis but as the other half of the other (151). The exaggerated carnality that
must shadow Nell's exaggerated purity, Quilp without Nell is a rebel without
a cause. There is Nell's family tree, which generates generations without
differences, and which features "the same sweet girl through a long line of
portraits—never growing old or changing—the Good Angel of the race"
(*OCS* 637). And then, of course, there are the bachelors.

Item

"When Death strikes down the innocent and young, for every fragile form from which he lets the panting spirit free, a hundred virtues rise, in shapes of mercy, charity, and love, to walk the world, and bless it. . . . In the Destroyer's steps there spring up bright creations that defy his power, and his dark path becomes a way of light to Heaven" (659). The narrator of *The Old Curiosity Shop* here imagines a vibrant growth economy of goodness rooted in the fertile soil of buried Nell. Yet by the end of this novel, Dickens's own capacity for bringing hundreds of new shapes and bright creations into the world is straining to its utmost. In the last scene in which we see Nell alive, the old sexton tells her that the deep, dry well into which he compels her to gaze is "to be closed up, and built over" (511). In a later work, such as *Bleak House*, what is meant to get constructed over the gaping hole left by a child's passing is a revitalized national culture determined to prevent the neglect that condemned the child to penury, ignorance, and disease. In dying, Jo the street-sweeper assumes a nation-energizing power comparable to that of the "Unknown Soldier": he becomes a site of commemoration and rededication for an entire people, belonging to all of them equally, since he is both *theirs* and none of theirs *in particular.*

One can discern a tentative gesture in this direction in *The Old Curiosity Shop*, in the nation-implying center-to-periphery radius Nell's itinerary draws from London to a Shropshire hamlet "within sight of the primeval heart of Britain, 'the blue Welch mountains far away' " (Marcus 141). *Bleak House* describes a similar circuit in reckoning the Chancery Court's baleful effect upon Mr. Gridley, "the man from Shropshire," and so suggesting that the evil it concerns itself with is fully national, infecting not just the metropolis but "every shire" (*Bleak House* 54, 51). But in the earlier novel, any progress we might want to make toward this expansive vision is checked by the vision of the little community, if we can call it that, constituted around Nell's grave. In seeming mockery of his celebrated fecundity and variety as a storyteller, Dickens turns and turns his crank and gives us a series of insufficiently distinguishable deformed or wounded aged bachelors: Master Humphrey, the single gentleman, the old schoolmaster, the "little old gentleman" called "the bachelor," the old sexton, another old man who talks with him, and while we are at it why not include Nell's grandfather (so long ago married it hardly counts), and the village clergyman (ditto), and Mr. Garland (surely a bachelor, even though married), and Quilp (who in the course of the story leaves his wife and declares himself a bachelor), and, of course, the other members of Master Humphrey's club, that "bizarre distortion of the Pickwickians" (Marcus 131). Thinking about this self-negating inventory of spent men gathered around the figure of Nell can call to mind the obscure mechanical and fruitless ritual taking place in Marcel Duchamp's so-called *Large Glass* (fig. 8), that masterpiece of twentieth-century conceptual art whose full title, in English, is *The Bride Stripped Bare by Her Bachelors, Even.*

Bottom Line

What saves us, and Kit, and Dick Swiveller—insofar as Dickens considers any of us worthy of salvation—is the little servant Dick names, the woman for whom he harrows the hell of Brass's kitchen-dungeon. Without her, his only possible future is that of the single gentleman, condemned to join the queue. As Dick learns through his near-fatal illness and recuperation under her care, he must have someone else to play off, and play *with*. Until he has the Marchioness, all he can do is give a self-pleasuring solo performance, like his performance of the tune ''Away with Melancholy,'' which he plays—one blushes to recall—''very slowly on [a] flute in bed'' for ''half the night, or more'' (535). Whatever gratification he gets from this, his neighbors may prefer not to know about it. G. K. Chesterton called the union of Swiveller and Sophronia Sphynx ''the one true romance in the whole of Dickens'' (156), and John Bowen has more recently contended that in this couple the cold ''spiritual heaven'' of Nell ''is answered and outplayed'' by the more mundane, material satisfactions, such as they are, ''of having enough to eat and drink, and some fun'' (156). Both of these critics take a more sanguine view of the matter than I am able to adopt. For me, the fascination of this breathtaking Dickensian anti-novel, or anti-Dickensian Dickens novel, can be summed up by saying that the whole gaudy apparatus it parades before us can be, exactly, summed up—in a slogan. Innumerable writers undergo crises of creativity; Dickens turned his into a substantial work of fictional narrative that questions in the most radical and remorseless fashion the very principles he understood his art of fictional narrative to follow. It is a work that, by repeatedly threatening to negate that divorcing power with which Dickens's imagination multiplied characters and incidents, brought the novelist again and again to the brink of his terrible singleness. The slogan? I imagine Dickens muttering it to himself as he wound and wound and wound his Clock and churned out page after page: *stop sniveling; keep swiveling.*

Fig. 8. Marcel Duchamp, *The Large Glass*, or *The Bride Stripped Bare by Her Bachelors, Even*. Philadelphia Museum of Art: Bequest of Katherine S. Dreier, 1952.

WORKS CITED

Barthes, Roland. "The Plates of the *Encyclopedia*." *A Barthes Reader*. Ed. Susan Sontag. New York: Hill & Wang, 1982. 218–35.

Bowen, John. *Other Dickens: Pickwick to Chuzzlewit*. Oxford: Oxford UP, 2003.

Bunyan, John. *The Pilgrim's Progress*. 1678; Harmondsworth: Penguin, 1980.

Chesterton, G. K. *Chesterton on Dickens*. London: Everyman, 1992.

Dickens, Charles. *Pickwick Papers*. 1837; Harmondsworth: Penguin, 1986.

———. *The Old Curiosity Shop*. 1841; Harmondsworth: Penguin, 1985.

———. *Bleak House*. 1853; Harmondsworth: Penguin, 1971.

Frost, Robert. "Mending Wall." *The Poetry of Robert Frost*. New York: Holt, 1974. 33–4.

Jaffe, Audrey. *Vanishing Points: Dickens, Narrative, and the Subject of Omniscience*. Berkeley: U of California P, 1991.

James, Henry. "The New Novel." *Henry James: Selected Literary Criticism*. Ed. Morris Shapira. Cambridge: Cambridge UP, 1981. 311–42.

Kincaid, James. *Annoying the Victorians*. New York: Routledge, 1995.

Marcus, Steven. *Dickens from Pickwick to Dombey*. New York: Simon and Schuster, 1965.

Milton, John. *The Works of John Milton*. Vol. 3, Part 2: *The Doctrine and Discipline of Divorce*. New York: Columbia UP, 1931.

Rilke, Rainer Maria. *Duino Elegies*. Trans. J. B. Leishman and Stephen Spender. New York: Norton, 1963.

Schor, Hilary. *Dickens and the Daughter of the House*. Cambridge: Cambridge UP, 1999.

Tennyson, Alfred. *In Memoriam*. *Tennyson: A Selected Edition*. Ed. Christopher Ricks. Berkeley: U of California P, 1989. 321–484.

———. "Ulysses." *Tennyson: A Selected Edition*. Ed. Christopher Ricks. Berkeley: U of California P, 1989. 138–45.

Little Nell's Nightmare: Sexual Awakening and Insomnia in Dickens's *The Old Curiosity Shop*

Lisa Hartsell Jackson

Although The Old Curiosity Shop *often seems to be a gentle pastoral picaresque, there is something far more sinister going on—Little Nell is driven to wander, in part, by her budding sexuality. Nell's immaturity and inexperience lead to a repetition of erotically-charged scenarios that is part of the cycle of "compulsive recurrence" that happens when someone is trying to achieve mastery over behavioral patterns. While Nell sees herself as a little girl, others obviously see her as a nubile young woman. Her situation is aggravated by the cycle of insomnia, which lends itself to weakening her already delicate system. Nell's sense of self-consciousness is heightened by puberty, and her increased self-awareness lends itself to a decrease in self-worth since she senses that she attracts unwanted attention wherever she goes. The cyclical nature of insomnia plays directly into Nell's need to repeat experience. Her "dreams are endeavouring to master the stimulus retrospectively, by developing the anxiety whose omission was the cause of the traumatic neurosis" (Freud 37). Nell's nightmares and sleeplessness are exacerbated by her feelings of depression and helplessness in a vicious cycle that ultimately forms the gestalt of the novel.*

Almost more than any of Dickens's other characters, Little Nell has suffered at the hands of literary critics. Mark Spilka, among others, has called her

Dickens Studies Annual, Volume 39, Copyright © 2008 by AMS Press, Inc. All rights reserved.

43

nothing more than "a sentimental textual blur" (Cox 174). Oscar Wilde
claimed, "One must have a heart of stone to read the death of Nell without
laughing" (Schlicke 426). The relative dearth of scholarly attention paid to
Nell over the last decade is a testament to the derision in which she is frequently held. Why then was she so popular, reportedly inducing crowds on
the shores of America to shout, "Does Little Nell die?" to the ships bringing
the next installment of her chronicle? In short, *The Old Curiosity Shop*, Dickens's fourth novel, is more than simple sentimental hogwash. Although the
novel is often a gentle pastoral picaresque, there is something far more sinister
going on—Little Nell is driven to wander, in part, by her budding sexuality.
Three of the themes of the novel—wandering, insomnia, and fatigue—make
her death a given from the opening pages. And Little Nell emerges not as a
timid, sickly little girl, but as a uniquely assertive, brave heroine.

    In discussing "texts of compulsive recurrence," Peter Brooks states that
"If repetition is mastery, movement from the passive to the active, and if
mastery is an assertion of control over what man must in fact submit to . . . [-
then] repetition, taking us back again over the same ground, could have to
do with the choice of ends" (98). Nell's journey definitely qualifies as a text
of "compulsive recurrence" since virtually every episode sees her working
through some aspect of the "nightmare" her life has become. She is unable
to rest until all of the information and symbolic imagery of her dreams are
untangled, and every destination is a repetition of some aspect of her initial
bad dream that leads her to the ultimate conclusion that there is no escape.
If she lives, she will get older and will have to face her sexuality by choosing
to marry (which she must do for financial reasons). Not marrying could imply
a failure in her role as a dutiful daughter. What I am suggesting is that while
Nell is not truly suicidal, she is driven by what Brooks calls "nightmare
energy" (138), which leads to her incessant wandering and eventual death.
If we consider Brooks's assertion that "The most effective, or at the least,
the most challenging texts may be those that are most delayed, most highly
bound, most painful" (102), we may have a fresh appreciation of why so
many readers and scholars have found Nell's story simply too sickly sweet
to gobble whole. Nell's journey and subsequent death are more than just a
maudlin manipulation to sell more copies of the serial, but are, instead, the
whole reason for the text itself.

    Little Nell (who is thirteen) is introduced as a wanderer who is lost, late
at night, roaming through the wilderness of London's streets. Because it takes
place at night, this episode has a dream-like quality that sets the tone for the
rest of the novel. Nell has a trusting, child-like nature, and it does not occur
to her to question the trustworthiness of a "solitary gentleman" she encounters on her rambles. Although her grandfather kindly shows his gratitude to
the old man for bringing Nell home safely, he shows his lack of consideration

for her by becoming defensive when the old man admonishes him to ''[take] more care of [his] grandchild'' (5). Her grandfather acknowledges that ''in many respects, I am the child, and she the grown person'' (10). His failure to perform as the adult in their relationship, along with his mysterious nocturnal ventures, forces Nell to take on adult responsibilities without the benefit of an adult's experience or perception.

The old man Nell has brought home seems benign, but he takes an inordinate interest in her physical appearance, her sleeping arrangements, and the lack of protection she is given during her grandfather's evenings out. The old man, who has noticed Nell's hair ''hanging loose about her neck'' and her ''flushed'' face (6), tells her grandfather that ''it always grieves me to contemplate the initiation of children into the ways of life, when they are scarcely more than infants. It checks their confidence and simplicity—two of the best qualities that Heaven gives them—and demands that they share our sorrows before they are capable of entering into our enjoyments'' (6). On the surface, this statement sounds harmless enough, but it has sinister, pedophilic undertones. Nell's fallen, loose hair and flushed face are evocative of sexual arousal, and although she is clearly unaware of this, the old man intuitively perceives her artless sensuality. Nell is a very young adolescent, who is barely more than an ''infant.'' Her purity and ''simplicity'' make her incapable of believing that anyone would try to harm her, which is precisely why she is a perfect target for pedophilia, and why the old man contemplates Nell's ''initiation'' in the first place. He is perfectly aware that Nell is too young to engage in sexual ''enjoyments,'' yet he feels compelled to think about that possibility. Even after he leaves the Trent household, the old man continues to think about ''a region on which [he] was little disposed to enter'' (13). The old man senses that Nell really has no dependable source of protection, and that the wicked forces that surround her will inevitably destroy her innocent defenselessness.

As the old man contemplates what he has seen at the old curiosity shop, he ponders how odd it would be ''to imagine [Nell] in her future life, holding her solitary way among a crowd of wild grotesque companions; the only pure, fresh youthful object in the throng'' (13). If this old, infirm man can see Nell's budding sexuality and the lack of concern her grandfather exhibits in protecting it, other more capable predators will sense it too. In this scenario, and indeed throughout the rest of the novel, Nell is the real curiosity. The old and musty medieval weapons that fill her grandfather's shop are reminiscent of the bygone custom of chaste, chivalric love, and suggest that the idealization of chastity is in danger of becoming an anachronism. Like the rusty, broken-down weapons themselves, Nell's grandfather is a quixotic, rapidly decaying shield that offers inadequate protection, and renders Nell defenseless. The antiquated arsenal in the shop is as insufficient to protect

Nell as is her limited knowledge of the outside world. Thomas Hood observed that Nell's bedchamber was "like an Allegory of the peace and innocence of Childhood in the midst of Violence, Superstition, and all the hateful or hurtful Passions of the world" (McCarthy 20). The Old Curiosity Shop could, then, represent "a need to restore an earlier state of things" (Brooks 106), making Nell's journey more of a regression than a progress. This makes her story an "effort to reach an assertion of origin through ending, to find the same in the different, the time before in the time after" (110). Nell, instead of moving toward the eventual mature return of the typical bildungsroman, repeatedly longs for a return to her past, when life was less threatening, when it still held the promise of dreams yet to be fulfilled rather than nightmares to be avoided. This may explain part of the Victorians' obsession with this novel, since it chronicles a way of life that was rapidly vanishing in the wake of progress and urbanization.

Nell's relationship with her dissipated brother Fred shows how vulnerable she is to attack. Fred is an utter failure as a sibling because he fails to conform to the idealized Victorian paradigm of the brother-sister relationship, wherein brothers were expected to act as intellectual, practical guides for their sisters, particularly if the sister were the younger sibling (Gorham 45). Gorham states that "more than any other relationship, the sister-brother dyad was perceived as free of conflict" and that because of this, sibling rivalry "could simply be discounted" (45). Fred is convinced that his grandfather has spurned him in favor of Nell, and that she will be the beneficiary of what Fred assumes is a large inheritance. Like the nameless old man who brought her home, Fred has noticed that "Nell will be a woman soon" (20). His observation carries none of the tender, protective anticipation of a devoted brother for his beloved sister, but is, instead, an ominous foreshadowing of a more self-serving interest. Fred is planning to "sell" his sister in marriage to his ne'er-do-well friend, Dick Swiveller, so that they can share in her "inheritance." He is patently unconcerned with Nell's safety or happiness, and concentrates only on the enjoyment he and Dick will get from spending her money. He takes sibling rivalry to a new extreme and violates the sanctity of his role as Nell's protector by planning his future around sexually, emotionally, and financially exploiting her. Peter Brooks states that "the image of incest (of the fraternal-sororal variety) . . . is a sign of a passion interdicted because its fulfillment would be too perfect, a discharge indistinguishable from death, the very cessation of narrative movement" (109). He continues, "Incest is the only exemplary version of a temptation of short-circuit from which the protagonist and the text must be led away, into detour, into the cure that prolongs narrative" (109). Fred and Nell's relationship has too much potential for explosion, too many elements that Dickens's audience would have found unpalatable. Therefore, we must turn our narrative gaze away from the Fred-Nell complication, and toward her journey. As threatening as this scenario is for the unsuspecting Nell, a more ominous predator is pursuing her.

Daniel Quilp is a bestial antithesis to Nell's angelic sweetness, and his deformed, dwarfed body is an outward manifestation of his misshapen psyche. Quilp's manipulative powers belie his small stature and extend to his business dealings. He eventually moves into the curiosity shop after Nell's grandfather forfeits the business, and in a terrifying scene, uses smoking to frighten, humiliate, and intimidate Nell. This scene has rightfully received a great deal of scholarly attention. While most scholars agree that the cigar itself is a blazing phallic symbol that underscores Quilp's smoldering desire for Nell, it may also be regarded as the spark that ignites her funeral pyre and fuels her quest for death.

Part of the moral outrage that we as readers sense in Dickens's narrative is a result of this sexualization of an innocent like Nell. Elsie Leach states that "At first, one may shrink from regarding Little Nell as a nymphet"; however, Dickens does not allow her "to remain an ordinary girl or to become an ordinary woman" (72). By equating Nell with Lolita, one of literature's most famous "nymphets," Leach demonstrates how potently sexual Nell's character truly is, and our desire to have her front and center in the narrative makes us as readers slightly voyeuristic as well. Quilp's lust for Nell is obvious, and his name, which is reminiscent of the word "quilt," takes on sinister implications when we consider Nell sleeping under such a covering. Because his passion for Nell is so intense, Quilp cannot conjure up enough smoke to satisfy his longing, and he invites two of his friends to join him in smoking and lounging in the shop, thus increasing the threat to Nell's unprotected innocence threefold. He is menacingly patronizing to Nell as he asks her whether she is going to "sit upon [his] knee" or go "to bed in her own little room" (86). Both suggestions are clearly sexual and patently inappropriate. In his determination to occupy her bed in some capacity, no matter how trivial, he takes it as "a sleeping place by night and as a kind of Divan by day" (86). This makes it difficult for Nell, who has moved to another room, to fall asleep, and marks the first of many instances in which her sleep will be disturbed by anxiety and fear. She is intuitive enough to understand that Quilp's small stature disguises the enormity of his lascivious intentions, and that his frighteningly distorted appearance is a reflection of the nightmarish existence involvement with him entails. Michael Steig contends that "Nell's response to the sexuality of Quilp grows into a pattern of flight, obsession, and death" (168). When her grandfather reminds Nell of her earlier entreaty that they "walk through country places" (71), she overcomes her fear of Quilp long enough to devise a plan of escape in order to save her chastity, as well as what little remains of her grandfather's sanity. As she plans, she has "no thought of hunger or cold, or thirst, or suffering" (94). She can no longer sleep peacefully inside her home, and the risks awaiting her in the outside world seem small in comparison.

There is no distance that will put Nell out of danger, because her naïveté makes it difficult for her to know whom she can and cannot trust. This becomes particularly apparent when she and her grandfather meet Codlin and Short, two performers who operate a Punch and Judy show. In fact, once Nell and her grandfather join Codlin and Short, they are surrounded by traveling carnival performers, and Nell's life takes on a surrealistic, nightmarish quality that makes it difficult to distinguish appearance from reality. Once again, Nell is the real curiosity among all these other curiosities because her physical appearance matches the reality of who she is—a sweet, naïve young girl. The Punch and Judy puppets thus become an eerie reminder of Nell's vulnerability to potentially abusive relationships, and her anxiety is manifested in her inability to sleep soundly. Codlin in particular is mesmerized by her—he looks at her "with an interest which did not appear to be diminished when he glanced at her helpless companion" (124). Nell is startled the next morning to discover that "she had been moved from the familiar chamber in which she seemed to have fallen asleep last night," and she does not know "whither she had been conveyed" (128). This indicates that she is unsafe both waking and sleeping, and her inability to rest soundly escalates as the novel progresses. Her apprehension increases when Codlin cryptically admonishes her that "it's me that's your friend—not him" (145), just as she is planning to retire for the night. Although she is exhausted by walking all day, Nell is unable to fall asleep right away. Her fears are realized the next day when "Codlin testified his jealousy and distrust by following close at her heels, and occasionally admonishing her ankles with the legs of the theatre in a very abrupt and painful manner" (147). Although "a change in style of dress was the most obvious physical sign of a girl's transition from childhood to young womanhood" (Gorham 93), Nell has not yet lowered her skirts to a length that is suitable to her burgeoning sexuality, and, thus, her exposed legs are highly erotic. Codlin's insistence on poking and thrusting the legs of the theater into Nell's legs is emblematic of the hostility and viciousness of rape, and he keeps "his eye steadily upon [Nell]" (147). In fact, his name itself suggests a type of erotic, passive-aggressive coddling aimed at lulling Nell into a compromising situation. Nell fears Codlin's uninvited attentions, and since her grandfather is incapable of protecting her, she knows that they must flee before it is too late.

At this point, we as readers may wonder why Nell seems to find herself in these types of situations over and over. The repetition of erotically-charged scenarios is part of the cycle of "compulsive recurrence" that happens when someone is trying to achieve mastery over behavioral patterns. Because Nell is so vulnerable, predators sense that she is a prime target for a variety of abuses—but Nell herself is part of the problem, unconsciously helping to perpetuate her young and vulnerable appearance because she longs for someone else to take control. While Nell sees herself as a little girl, others obviously see her as a nubile young woman. Flight, the only solution she sees available, actually causes more difficulty for her because it does not allow her sufficient time or opportunity to examine what is happening. On some level, Nell has comfort in her own discomfort because flight allows her to temporarily feel as though she is asserting herself and taking control of her situation. Freud states, "the compulsion to repeat also recalls from the past experiences which include no possibility of pleasure, and which can never, even long ago, have brought satisfaction" (21). Familiarity with the boundaries of her discomfort enables Nell to repeat her experience over and over in the text since "there really does exist in [her] mind a compulsion to repeat which overrides the pleasure principle" (24). In Freudian terms, Nell's paranoia can be viewed as proof of her "compulsion to repeat" since her conviction that she is being followed "is for the most part arranged by [herself]" (23). This "arrangement" is somewhat functional, however, since it is an unconscious attempt to resolve her problems.

Nell's situation is aggravated by the cycle of insomnia, which lends itself to weakening her already delicate system. In fact, Victorians treated female adolescence as a time when girls were particularly delicate, since "physicians generally held that the physical events of puberty triggered the psychical manifestations of femininity" (Gorham 86). Nell's sense of self-consciousness may be heightened by puberty, and her increased self-awareness lends itself to a decrease in self-worth since she senses that she attracts unwanted attention wherever she goes. Most medical experts agree with this idea because the "normative increase in self-consciousness and the tendency to rely heavily on external feedback for self worth" often results in a "sharp rise in depressive symptoms and depressive disorders during early to mid-adolescence" (Burwell and Shirk 480). Interestingly, there is a "strong association between the report of nightmares in women and the presence of either a depressive disorder, an anxiety disorder, or both disorders together" (Ağargün et al. 200). Nell's dreams include "depressive themes, such as hopelessness and helplessness, and an excessive focus on the past" (200), and feed on her depression and fatigue. The cyclical nature of insomnia plays directly into Nell's need to repeat experience, since her "dreams are endeavouring to master the stimulus retrospectively, by developing the anxiety whose omission was the cause of the traumatic neurosis" (Freud 37). Because "sleep is a primary aspect of adolescent development," the way Nell sleeps (or does not sleep) has a significant impact on her "ability to think, behave, and feel during daytime hours" (Wolfson and Carskadon 875). Indeed, research suggests that adolescents who suffer from sleep problems have "higher levels of depression" and "lower social competence" than teenagers who get enough sleep (884). Therefore, insomnia could have a detrimental impact on Nell's ability to make good, sound decisions that is separate from her chronological immaturity. Furthermore, medical research indicates that "it is not the incidence of nightmares which is the critical variable in predicting greater psychological disturbance but the reported distress associated with the nightmare experience which is of paramount importance, particularly for anxiety and depression" (Levin and Fireman 209). Nell's nightmares and sleeplessness are exacerbated by her feelings of depression and helplessness in a vicious cycle that ultimately forms the gestalt of the novel.

In the next leg of their journey, Nell and her grandfather encounter a kindly schoolmaster in a village where she has a brief respite. The schoolmaster is a sympathetic, selfless man who has projected his paternal longings onto one of his students who is ill and has been "wandering in his head" (Dickens 184). This schoolmaster's compassion for and devotion to this child indicate to Nell that he is someone she can trust, since he has no interest in using her for any personal gain. The security she feels in this man's presence is most evident in the fact that Nell is able to sleep soundly while she is under his roof. Once she is secure in her own room, Nell grieves deeply over the little boy, giving "free vent to the sorrow with which her breast was overcharged" (194). Her grief, however sincere, is really for the life she herself has lost; Nell has had to give up her own childhood and her own innocence in order to protect herself and her beloved grandfather. As she ruminates on "How many of the mounds in that old churchyard where she had lately strayed, grew above the graves of children" (194), it is obvious that she too will die while still really a child.

But Nell and her grandfather then set out once again on their journey, this time "at a much slower pace [because they were] very weary and fatigued" (195). Clearly, Nell's strength is being diminished by her wanderings, and as her physical health declines, so do her spirits. When she and her grandfather meet Mrs. Jarley, the proprietress of a "famous" wax-work, Nell learns that her reputation has suffered because of her involvement with Codlin and Short. Mrs. Jarley admonishes her by saying that she was "very sorry . . . to see you in company with a Punch; a low, practical, wulgar wretch, that people should scorn to look at" (196). Mrs. Jarley overlooks Nell's poor judgment because she is "young and inexperienced" (197), while she scolds the grandfather because "[she] should have thought [he was] old enough to take care of [himself]" (205). Mrs. Jarley extends an offer for Nell to sleep in her caravan "as a signal mark of [her] favour and confidence" (207). Although this should alleviate Nell's anxieties about her safety and her financial situation, she is immediately thrust back into the nightmarish scenario that forced her initial flight from London. Just as she is taking a pre-slumber stroll, Nell sees Quilp. She is successful in keeping herself hidden from him, but when she tries to go to sleep, "she could get none but broken sleep by fits and starts all night, for fear of Quilp" (209). Clearly, her life has become like a living nightmare in which it is difficult to distinguish between waking and sleeping terrors. Joan D. Winslow comments, "These imagings of Quilp that recur again and again throughout the journey [are] always associated with fear and danger, [and] greatly augment our awareness of intended pursuit and keep this threat alive, even though he never again sees Nell and her grandfather after they leave London" (164).

In spite of her fear, Nell knows that she must earn some type of living to support herself and her debilitated grandfather, and so she sets out to learn all about each wax figure in order to perform as a kind of tour guide for the waxworks. Mrs. Jarley pays particular attention to her instruction about Jasper Packlemerton, one of the wax figures "who courted and married fourteen wives, and destroyed them all, by tickling the soles of their feet when they were sleeping in the consciousness of innocence and virtue" (214). While the idea of tickling someone's feet sounds like something one would do to a child, the fact that Packlemerton reputedly did this while his victims were sleeping sexualizes this seemingly innocuous activity. Packlemerton's figure is particularly menacing since he represents the type of man who is capable of destroying virginal women like Nell, while it simultaneously underscores the idea that "repetition always takes place in the realm of the symbolic . . . where the affects and figures of the past are confronted in symbolic form" (Brooks 124). It is also a sinister reminder of the nightmarish existence that awaits Nell if any of the men who pursue her, including Quilp, Codlin, Dick Swiveller, or her brother Fred is able to locate her. In fact, each of these men has the power to be either protector or destroyer of Nell's innocence. It is this dichotomy that "works to produce [an] erotic seam between trust and violation and to create in our conception of Nell a constant, vivid, erotically desired awareness of violation and loss" (Kucich 64).

As readers, our outrage over the idea of Nell's "violation" creates a need in us to "protect" her by prolonging her narrative. Additionally, it demonstrates Nell's need for repetition to master "the moment of the buried yet living past which insists on repeating itself in the present" (Brooks 134). The reality of what the wax figures represent makes Mrs. Jarley's waxworks take on the ghoulish, dreamlike quality that renders this type of exhibition both fascinatingly compelling and horrifyingly repulsive. Once she begins her job as Jarley's tour guide, Nell's presence has an immediate impact: "The beauty of the child, coupled with her gentle and timid bearing, produced quite a sensation in the little country place" (216). The narrator continues, "Grown-up folks began to be interested in the bright-eyed girl, and some score of little boys fell desperately in love'' (216). This suggests, once again, that Nell's nubile attractiveness renders her vulnerable, and, in spite of her success, Nell is still plagued by dreams of Quilp. He "was a perpetual nightmare to the child, who was constantly haunted by a vision of his ugly face and stunted figure'' (217). However, she has much more to fear from an unexpected source that is terrifyingly close to her.

One evening, after a long walk, Nell and her grandfather are forced to take refuge from a sudden rainstorm by spending the night at a pub. While they are there, her grandfather finally reveals the secret he has been keeping from Nell for so long—he is a compulsive gambler. His sudden interest in a game of cards fills Nell "with astonishment and alarm [because] his whole appearance had undergone a complete change. His face was flushed and eager, his eyes were strained, his teeth set, his breath became short and thick, and the hand he laid upon her arm trembled so violently that she shook beneath its grasp'' (221). The grandfather's reaction is so strongly evocative of sexual arousal that Gareth Cordery says there is a distinct possibility that "gambling is a symbolic substitute for sexual activity'' (48), which makes the subsequent theft of Nell's money a "symbolic rape'' (43). While it may stretch credulity to imply that Nell's grandfather is sexually attracted to his own grandchild, it is indisputable that his gambling does put Nell at risk and is a great violation of her innocence and trust. Nell's dismay over this situation causes her intense anguish because she thinks that she herself is the "cause of all this torture'' (224), a reaction that is consistent with the behavior of incest victims; in fact, much of her subsequent behavior is in keeping with the stereotypical responses to this type of abuse. While their relationship may not be literally incestuous, it is certainly emotionally incestuous since Nell has been forced to take on an adult role. Rest, which has been difficult for her prior to this incident, becomes virtually impossible now. The narrator's declaration that as a result of the grandfather's gambling spree "Nell's little purse was exhausted'' (225) takes on erotic implications in light of Cordery's argument. Nell's "purse'' is inadequate for any type of activity, whether the activity is sexual, financial, or emotional.

When Nell tries to sleep, she falls into "a broken, fitful sleep, troubled by dreams of falling from high towers, and waking with a start and in great terror'' (228). Symbolically, Nell's sexual awakening promises to be a terrifying experience if it involves the feeling that she is falling out of control and into an uncomfortable, startling arousal where she is surrounded by the large, phallic images the towers imply. It is therefore understandable that termination of her sexual "sleep'' looms like a horrific dream she cannot escape. Her imaginary fears are realized when a shadowy specter enters her room and begins "groping its way with noiseless hand, and stealing around the bed'' (228). Like the stereotypical rape victim, Nell is too frightened to speak or cry out, and instead falls back onto her pillow "lest those wandering hands should light upon her face" (228). Nell is traumatized by the creeping, animalistic stealth of the intruder, and as soon as she can, she takes flight to the only safety she has ever known—her grandfather. Her grandfather, who is "counting the money of which his hands had robbed her" (229), is finally revealed as a reprehensible character. He has put his own selfish needs above the safety and comfort of his innocent, defenseless granddaughter, and from this point on, Nell will be unable to awake from the nightmare of her existence. Nell has essentially been "sleeping" with an enemy whose own selfish desires will constantly compel her to continue her interminable journey.

Like many victims of incest, Nell falls into a deep depression and seeks to absolve her abuser. She is terrified that her grandfather will repeat his nocturnal visit because "in [her] imagination it was always coming" (230). As is also typical of incest victims, Nell fears that others will be able to sense the stigma of her private life. This fear is realized in her encounter with the inflexibly stern schoolmistress Miss Monflathers, who scolds her by saying, "it's very naughty and unfeminine, and a perversion of the properties wisely and benignantly transmitted to us, with expansive powers to be roused from their dormant state through the medium of cultivation" (235). Nell fears that Miss Monflathers has somehow sensed that her innocence has been shattered by her grandfather's perversion, and that she has somehow been naughty and unfeminine by enabling the "cultivation" of his gambling habit. After all, her grandfather has told her that "it's all for thee, my darling" (223), a statement that reminds us of the pedophile's injunction to keep molestation a secret.

The grandfather's gambling persists, and becomes a "constant drain upon [Nell's] scanty purse" (312); not only is it a financial drain—it is a physical, emotional, and psychological drain that saps Nell's already delicate health. Even in her solitary "rambles which had now become her only pleasure or relief from care" (311), she remains depressed because gambling has wedged "a gradual separation" (312) between her grandfather and herself. This separation is partially a result of Nell's realization that "her own beloved grandfather embodies corruption, and, while she can flee from the malicious villains whose corruption she has conceptualized but has experienced only briefly in her dealings with Quilp, she cannot flee from her own grandfather" (Schiefelbein 28). The separation seems deeper and more sinister when her grandfather becomes involved with a group of Gypsies. As John Reed observes, Gypsies were believed to be "outcasts, of an idle and thieving nature, and untrustworthy to any but their own kind" (364). Nell watches in horror as the Gypsies plot against her grandfather, and then runs "homeward as quickly as she could, torn and bleeding from the thorns and briars, but more lacerated in mind, and threw herself upon her bed" (317). The tearing and bleeding are emblematic of her grandfather's figurative rape of his granddaughter, while the lacerations to Nell's mind illustrate just how deeply she has been psychologically and emotionally scarred. The grandfather is gambling with her virtue and her innocence; losing money is a mere side effect of his addiction. Once again, Nell's sleep is disturbed, and she runs to her grandfather's side "Half undressed, and with her hair in wild disorder" (318). This description is frighteningly sexual, but it is clear that Nell does not intentionally make herself appear to be erotically aroused. Her disheveled outer appearance reflects the disarray her grandfather's gambling has wrought upon both her countenance and her psyche. Although she feels tainted and bruised, she is not at fault because she is patently unaware of her sexual attractiveness—no one has explained it to her. The narrator constantly refers to Nell as a "child," even though almost everyone around her sees her nubile sensuality. She feels she has no recourse other than retrieving her grandfather and fleeing again, and she tells him they must leave because, "I cannot sleep, I cannot stay here . . . Nothing but flight can save us" (318). Nell's determination to flee is a "search for safety" and "an attempt above all to elude the nightmare enemies" (Kincaid 87) whom she is certain are following her. Her daydreams of leading a better life with her grandfather by traveling through the countryside are shattered, and Nell must resume her journey.

As they leave, Nell is tempted to look back. Not only is she looking back to make certain they are undetected, she is also looking back on her innocence and on her childhood. She realizes that "There was no divided responsibility now; the whole burden of their two lives had fallen upon her" (320). It becomes increasingly apparent that Nell will not be able to survive the trauma of her burgeoning sexuality; the narrator says she is like "childhood fading in its bloom," ready to rest "in the sleep that knows no waking" (320). As they walk on, fatigue eventually overtakes Nell, and she falls asleep. Once again, she awakes to find a strange man watching her slumber. This nameless man and his partner offer to take Nell and her grandfather down the river to an unnamed location. When they ask where she and her grandfather are going, Nell gives her destination no other distinction than saying it is somewhere in the West—the symbolic direction of death. Her journey now becomes reminiscent of archetypal journeys over the river Styx to Hades, and indeed, her life has taken on some of the same hellish, incessant qualities as the wanderings of Odysseus. However, unlike that ancient hero, Nell will not have a glorious homecoming on earth. She is already "tired and exhausted" (324) when one of the men on the boat insists that she sing to him as entertainment. For him, as well as for the other men on the boat, Nell's singing is as sweet and enticing as the Sirens' song, and it is just as likely to arouse their interest in her in other ways. Joan D. Winslow remarks that this incident "with [its] sense of forced reluctance, unrestrained indulgence, and physical exertion, suggest[s] a sexual assault'' (164). Miraculously, Nell and her grandfather are able to leave the barge unharmed, but what awaits them in the next town holds little comfort. They cannot find anyone to help them, and are eventually forced to sleep outside in the rain. This exposure to the harsh elements of nature parallels Nell's physical and emotional exposure, and indicates that as the journey continues, it becomes less and less likely that she will ever find adequate protection.

Just as they are about to take refuge in a doorway, a mysterious stranger appears out of the darkness and offers to give them a meager sleeping place. The stranger, like both Mrs. Jarley and the old gentleman at the beginning of the novel, scolds the grandfather for not making more of an effort to protect his grandchild: ''Do you know . . . how wet she is, and that the damp streets are not a place for her?'' (329). However, the grandfather is more incapable than ever of protecting Nell, and makes little, if any, effort to do so. Although the stranger is tender and kind to Nell, the place he takes her and her grandfather is a fiery furnace that looks eerily like a living hell. Nell sleeps comfortably, but awakes to find the stranger staring intently into the fire. He tells her, ''It's my memory, that fire, and shows me all my life'' (331). It is apparent that if Nell cannot find safety and rest, her life too will continue to be the burning hell of memory and regret that is already consuming her. Because she is so weary both physically and emotionally, it is no surprise that Nell ''soon yielded to the drowsiness that came upon her'' (332). People who feel hopeless and are chronically depressed often sleep deeply for long periods of time as an escape from their troubles, and Nell is no different. Her sleep, which has been disturbed so frequently, now offers protection she cannot find anywhere else. If she cannot stand to be sexually awakened, she can find refuge in the eternal sleep of death.

As they head toward their new destination, Nell's deepening depression becomes more and more obvious. Her journey has taken an enormous physical toll on her, and she ''walked with more difficulty than she had led her companion to expect, for the pains that racked her joints were of no common severity, and every exertion increased them'' (335). Her slumber becomes less troubled, partly because there is ''nothing between her and the sky'' (336). This, along with her decreasing appetite and ''a dull conviction that she was very ill, perhaps dying'' (335), indicates that Nell will soon succumb to her depression and ascend into the heavens. The trauma of her adolescence has been too deep, and the narrator makes it more emphatically obvious than ever that Nell will not recover. Gabriel Pearson contends that ''Dickens protects Nell from sexuality by early sounding the mortuary note that is to keep her for ever a child'' (Gross and Pearson 84–85). Just as she is about to collapse from fatigue, Nell and her grandfather again encounter the kindly schoolmaster. Nell immediately faints, and the schoolmaster admonishes her grandfather, "You have taxed her powers too far, friend" (340). Under the schoolmaster's tender, fatherly care, Nell is able to rest soundly. At last she has found someone whom she can trust as both a parent and a friend, and Nell lays down the burden she has solitarily had to carry.

Nell is deemed too ill to travel on foot, and is put into a carriage that will carry her to her new home. As she drowses in safety and comfort, the carriage becomes a living hearse that is carrying a breathing corpse to its final resting-place. Once they arrive in the village, Nell asks the schoolmaster to leave her on the steps of the church while he goes to make the final arrangements for his new job. Her utter fascination with the graveyard indicates that she is already prepared to give up the will to live. Nell soon befriends the sexton of the church, and spends an inordinate amount of time visiting both the graveyard and the tombs, where she feels "now she was happy, and at rest" (398). Reading the tombstones offers "no authority for the plot of life" because Nell's story is a "plot that can never find satisfactory resolution, that unresolved must play over its insistent repetitions, until silenced by death" (Brooks 136). We as readers have reached what Brooks calls "the non-narratable" (134), since the only plot left for Nell is the funeral plot. There is no happy ending, no return, no absorption into a "happily ever after." Her determination to give up the will to live is apparent since she thinks, "It would be no pain to sleep amidst" the other dead souls in the graveyard (398).

Nell now transfers her need to be a good daughter to her grandfather into her devoted attention to caring for the graves of the dead. The only thing that keeps her alive is the overriding fear that she will be forgotten. Once the schoolmaster tells her that "There is nothing . . . no, nothing innocent or good, that dies, and is forgotten" (406), Nell is able to begin her descent into death. Her grandfather's claim that she "would be a woman, soon" (408) is a reminder to her of the fear involved in taking the final steps into maturity and helps in her determination to put an end to her struggles, to let her sexuality "sleep." Ironically, the grandfather finally realizes his complicity in Nell's declining health, and, as he does, he understands that she will never be able to embrace womanhood and all it holds because she has become a living angel. During her decline, she takes on a spiritual quality because of "her warmth and the promise of redemption and new hope" (Polhemus and Henkle 83) that her sweetness and purity bring to the old church.

For Nell, the secrets of sexuality will have to remain secrets. She has been too frightened for too long to be able to embrace the sexual awakening that is a necessary step in undertaking the role of the idealized Victorian wife and mother. Sexuality is not a terminus for Nell, not a place where she can achieve the ideal of femininity made ripe and gloriously whole. It is, instead, a place where she will lose herself entirely by sublimating herself and disappearing both from her own identity, and from the text itself. Laurie Langbauer contends that "Dickens's emphatic denial of Nell's sexuality suggests how powerful that sexuality is, [and] how much it [has kept] her character moving" (420). Nell's obsession with death grows daily, and as she looks into the well in the crypt beneath the church, she tells the sexton that "It looks like a grave itself" (413). The church, which "had once had a convent or monastery attached" (348) is a perfect cloister for this virginal child. Clearly, Nell desires the eternal sleep that comes with death because it will enable her to maintain her child-like innocence, as well as her sexual purity. Robert Polhemus and Roger Henkle assert that "It seems crucial that Nell [dies] a virgin, unpolluted by sexuality" since "Her virginity [has been] ripe for exploitation" (81) throughout the novel. When she does die, the narrator says she is borne to her grave "pure as the newly-fallen snow" (542). Nell's death gives her a saintly aura because she is, like the snow, frozen in time, and she will forever retain the sanctity of her virginity, which will never be tarnished. In dying, Nell's tombstone becomes her life's story, her own autobiographical text that serves as a warning or moral fable of what her life's journey was. The secrets of sexuality and her continuous pursuit by a multitude of roguish characters have killed both Nell and her potential to grow into the stereotypical ideal of mature Victorian femininity. Ultimately, Nell dies, not because Dickens "kills" her off, but because she is tired of struggling, tired of secrets, and tired of the subsequent sorrow the truth has brought her.

WORKS CITED

Ağargün, Mehmed Y., et al. "Repetitive and Frightening Dreams and Suicidal Behavior In Patients with Major Depression" *Comprehensive Psychiatry* 39:4 (1998): 198–202.

Brooks, Peter. *Reading for the Plot: Design and Intention in Narrative*. Cambridge: Harvard UP, 1984.

Burwell, Rebecca A., and Stephen R. Shirk. "Self Processes in Adolescent Depression: The Role of Self-Worth Contingencies." *Journal of Research on Adolescence* 16:3 (2006): 479–490.

Cordery, Gareth. "The Gambling Grandfather in *The Old Curiosity Shop*." *Literature and Psychology* 33:1 (1987): 43–61.

Cox, Don Richard, ed. *Sexuality in Victorian Literature*. Knoxville: U of Tennessee P, 1984.

Dickens, Charles. *The Old Curiosity Shop*. Oxford: Oxford UP, 1984.

Freud, Sigmund. *Beyond the Pleasure Principle*. New York: Norton, 1961.

Gorham, Deborah. *The Victorian Girl and the Feminine Ideal*. Bloomington: Indiana UP, 1982.

Gross, John, and Gabriel Pearson, ed. *Dickens and the Twentieth Century*. London: Routledge and Kegan Paul, 1962.

Kincaid, James R. *Dickens and the Rhetoric of Laughter*. Oxford: Clarendon, 1971.

Kucich, John. "Death Worship Among the Victorians: *The Old Curiosity Shop*." *Publications of the Modern Language Association* 95 (1980): 58–72.

Langbauer, Laurie. "Dickens's Streetwalkers: Women and the Form of Romance." *ELH* 53:2 (Summer 1986): 411–31.

Leach, Elsie. "Lolita and Little Nell." *San Jose Studies* 3:1 (1977): 70–78.

Levin, Ross, and Gary Fireman. "Nightmare Prevalence, Nightmare Distress, and Self-Reported Psychological Disturbance." *Sleep* 25:2 (2002): 205–12.

McCarthy, Patrick J. "The Curious Road to Death's Nell." *Dickens Studies Annual* 20 (1991): 17–34.

Polhemus, Robert M., and Roger B. Henkle, ed. *Critical Reconstructions: The Relationship of Fiction and Life*. Stanford: Stanford UP, 1994.

Reed, John R. *Victorian Conventions*. Athens: Ohio UP, 1975.

Schiefelbein, Michael. "Bringing to Earth the 'Good Angel of the Race.' " *Victorian Newsletter* 84 (Fall 1993): 25–28.

Schlicke, Paul, ed. *The Oxford Reader's Companion to Dickens*. Oxford: Oxford UP, 1999.

Steig, Michael. "The Central Action of *The Old Curiosity Shop* or Little Nell Revisited Again." *Literature and Psychology* 15 (1965): 163–70.

Winslow, Joan D. "*The Old Curiosity Shop*: The Meaning of Little Nell's Fate." *The Dickensian* 77:3 (Autumn 1981): 162–67.

Wolfson, Amy R., and Mary A. Carskadon. "Sleep Schedules and Daytime Functioning in Adolescents." *Child Development*. 69:4 (1998): 875–87.

Charles Dickens in America:
The Writer and Reality

Igor Webb

Dickens's disenchanted first visit to the United States in 1842 occasioned a new departure in his writing. The visit cast in a garish light the role of the writer in the new mass market for fiction, a role Dickens seemed to have mastered back home, as well as highlighting the problem of form in relation to the unprecedented social realities of nineteenth-century life. Addressing the latter, Dickens now sought methodically for a form of narration that might successfully depict the "naked and aggressive existence," to use Dorothy Van Ghent's words about the view from Todgers's, that his American visit brought to the fore. After reassessing his campaign for international copyright and his role in the U.S. as celebrity, this study rereads American Notes *and* Martin Chuzzlewit. *In the latter, a novel with multiple centers of authority and as many narrative modes, Dickens seems especially to identify with Nadgett's form of narrative as surveillance, an amoral but comprehensively informed method that makes sense of dizzying realities without losing either control or spontaneity, a literature that, Dickens suggests hopefully, can counteract the malign energies of Pecksniff, Jason, and Tigg.*

In the preface to the third volume (1842–1843) of the Pilgrim Edition of Dickens's *Letters* (1974), the editors remark that his "American visit [of 1842] has never been thoroughly examined" (vii). This is certainly not true any longer, for, after a hiatus following the remarkable contextualization of

Dickens's visit provided by the Pilgrim Edition, a number of studies of Dickens's journey have appeared.[1] Moreover, groundbreaking work on *Martin Chuzzlewit*, arguably the main outcome of Dickens's trip, had already been published prior to the 1974 volume of letters.[2] I propose to bring the earlier criticism into dialogue with the more recent body of scholarship and on that basis to attempt a reassessment of Dickens's journey and a rereading of *American Notes* and *Martin Chuzzlewit.*

I. Wider Views

Charles Dickens and his young wife Catherine first set foot on American soil at Boston, on January 22, 1842, but already by the time the couple arrived in New York on February 12, five days after Dickens's thirtieth birthday, he was unsettled and disillusioned; and soon he wanted nothing better than to be back home. A journey that began with high hopes ended just this side of disaster. A number of critics have advanced the view that Dickens's months in America ought to be understood as a period of determining transition in his career, a series of mainly disturbing experiences that were the making of the mature Dickens, who first shows himself in *Martin Chuzzlewit* (1843–44).[3] Indeed John Foster says in his biography that Dickens "returned from America with wider views . . . and with more maturity of mind" (I, 291).

What were these wider views? And what happened? Dickens's experiences during his American journey can be divided into two broad categories, each, I believe, offering a window not only onto the development of Dickens as a man and a writer—but also onto the whole landscape of the nineteenth-century novel. The first category of experiences has to do with the new role of the writer in the new mass market for fiction. The second has to do with the problem of form in relation to the unprecedented social realities of nineteenth century life. Under the first, I would include Dickens's obstinate campaign in the United States for international copyright, his distaste for but collusion in his role as celebrity (he was literally mobbed everywhere he went), and his revulsion with American social democracy. These topics reveal the central motif governing Dickens's visit, which might be called the disenchantment of unexamined premises. Dickens came to the United States expecting, like other English travelers, that he would glimpse the future but, of course, he assumed confidently that the future would conform nicely to expectations.[4] The obdurate, offensive, unexpected, unsettling reality he encountered in America, the future as America seemed to foreshadow it, disenchanted him.

The second aspect of his travels has to do with Dickens's effort to translate this disenchantment into writing. The vexing problem of how to convey the subjective nature of ostensibly objective experience, especially when that experience is literally unprecedented, may not have been new to Dickens but was given new force and even a suggestion of danger in his encounter with America. In this respect his American trip included most importantly an element of aesthetic revaluation. Dickens failed in his first effort to put his disenchantment into words, the half-hearted *American Notes*. But *Martin Chuzzlewit* opens a new phase in Dickens's career and can be seen as a kind of laboratory in which the paramount formal and thematic dilemmas confronting the major nineteenth-century novelists are defined and an initial effort to ''solve'' them is made. Alexander Welsh argues persuasively that Dickens's time in the United States is best understood as a ''moratorium,'' a term he borrows from Erik Erikson that is intended to define a kind pause for breath, usually early in the life of an active individual, a pause in which to reflect and gather one's resources, consider one's options, and rediscover with new fervor one's life mission (10–12). Dickens's American visit clearly offered him a fresh perspective from which to reconsider the direction of his writing career or indeed whether he ought to abandon that career altogether and try something else. In this light, *Martin Chuzzlewit*, as the main literary outcome of Dickens's visit, is a book that is as much about the efficacy of literature as it is a study of selfishness.

The questions that loom over the book are fundamental questions about writing given a special edge by the perspective of travel. When reality seems to evade all preconceptions, how should or can a writer proceed? Can the writer hope to capture the reality that is ''out there'' or is the reality of fiction necessarily a matter of form and invention? Is fiction necessarily a study in how to finesse the limitations of epistemology? Dickens seems to have entertained any number of answers to these questions. In *Martin Chuzzlewit* we find a curious mixture of assured, authoritative narration by a storyteller apparently standing on the absolutely solid ground of certainty and conviction—Dickens the satirist; a storyteller devoted to unity and coherence of composition; a storyteller persuaded that narrative is the surest route through the labyrinth of history; a storyteller committed above all to the orderliness and efficacy of literature, indeed of literature as a collective value in the form of a library (Joseph passim). And we find a radically different storyteller, one who is apparently at a loss about where to stand; a storyteller able to mimic a vivid cast of theatrical voices, personas, and viewpoints but uncertain that any one vantage point can or should be controlling; an improviser extraordinaire; a storyteller for whom the observing or all-seeing eye of the narrator seems complicit in the unsavory and monolithic qualities of surveillance; a storyteller in the grip of a multifaceted crisis about authority. Thus, the novel seems less to resolve the questions it poses than to display a vivacious tableau of possible answers. Before proceeding to explore how these arise in a reading of *Martin Chuzzlewit*, I want first to go back to look in more detail at Dickens's American journey.

II. Dickens, William Cullen Bryant, and International Copyright

The most important and representative person Dickens met during his first visit to the United States was, I believe, William Cullen Bryant, who provides a perspective on Dickens's experience from an American point of view. Bryant's reputation has plummeted in the last half-century, and he now requires something of an introduction.[5] Perhaps his earlier stature can best be suggested by saying that he is the George Washington of American letters. He was the nation's first great poet and the greatest public intellectual of his day. For half a century or more American schoolchildren memorized "Thanatopsis," the main stanzas of which Bryant wrote when he was seventeen. But Bryant's stature derived as much from his editorship of the New York *Evening Post* as from his poetry. Founded by Alexander Hamilton, the *Post*, in Bryant's hands, became the nation's leading serious newspaper. Bryant began working on the *Post* in 1827 and ran it until his death in 1878. No person other than Franklin had so dominated the press. He was the supreme artist of the newspaper editorial (Nevins 134), and the first to use the editorial pages for various campaigns—the campaign for abolition of slavery (in the early years of the century New York was an anti-abolitionist town), for the preservation of the Union, for Central Park (it was Bryant who first proposed the creation of such a park in the city) and, along with many other civic improvements, for a cause that Dickens imprudently espoused while in the U.S., international copyright. Many of these ideas can be traced to another of Bryant's important contributions to the culture, his travel writing. His letters from abroad were one of the most popular sections of the *Post.*

When Dickens arrived in New York, he told Bryant that, aside from Washington Irving, he was the person in the United States he most wanted to see (*Letters* 58). The two men, and their wives too, saw a good deal of each other while Dickens was in New York, and they seem to have to hit it off (Sargent 190). Still, despite Dickens's professed interest in meeting Bryant, he doesn't seem to have read Bryant's poems[6] and it is safe to assume that what he most wanted was the support of the *Evening Post* for U.S. approval of an International Copyright Agreement with Great Britain.

The first time that Dickens mentioned international copyright, his reference was made almost casually (see *Letters* 59n4), and the subject was not entirely new. The Federal Act of 1790, establishing copyright in the United States, explicitly excluded foreign books from copyright protection. The immediate consequence for the young republic was rapid growth of reading, although also intellectual domination by writers from the mother country. In the nineteenth century, the U.S. far more than Britain was the land of the general reader and the print runs for British books in the United States were often larger than the print runs for the same books in Britain (St. Clair 386). Ironically, copyright protection in Great Britain steadily restricted access to literature among the general population, and for a time sharply restricted readership as a consequence of the passage of the 1842 Copyright Act (St. Clair 355–56). The results of copyright policy in the two nations were therefore diametrically opposed, and came out of conflicting needs, traditions, and cultures. In the U.S., copyright laws served the democratic end of expanding the reading public and the economic end of expanding the printing and publishing industries; in Britain, they tended to create monopoly and raise prices.

At the same time, however, the underlying movement toward a mass market forced British writers and publishers to reconsider the relation between literature and readers well before the same dilemmas faced American writers. The British literary culture was, obviously, far more developed in every way than the American. Whatever the impact of copyright laws on the size and nature of the reading public in Britain, there was no shortage of writers or, even more, of notable journals. British writers, moreover, were fully aware of a world audience for their work. In the U.S. the situation was altogether different. When Bryant first came to New York in the 1820s, he looked for work on a literary journal but was forced to shift to a newspaper because of the difficulty of sustaining a literary journal at that time in New York. There were neither enough readers nor enough writers to keep a journal going. In the early years of the century, consequently, there simply weren't any American publications to compare with the British periodicals of the time (Brown 128–30). Far from being the economic hub of the world, or the center of an empire, the United States was a young nation building every aspect of its society.

The impact of the economic depression from 1837 to 1843 on American publishing made the case for international copyright a lost cause in 1837 and even more so when Dickens raised the subject five years later. The depression spawned the ''mammoth'' papers, newspapers of enormous physical size that specialized in literary piracy, led by *Brother Jonathan*, which Park Benjamin launched in 1839, and the *New World*, which Benjamin later came to edit. The *New World* was four feet long and divided its pages into eleven columns! These cheap papers circulated across the nation and—unlike the established book publishers—thrived despite very narrow profit margins on the volume of their sales, fueled by complete runs of mainly British works of fiction and nonfiction. These ran both in the pages of the papers proper and in what they boasted of as ''extras,'' often complete books in themselves. The mammoths forced the book trade, wounded like most industries by the dreadful economic climate, to cut costs and otherwise to scramble to survive. In this respect international copyright would have been a direct threat to an industry struggling to keep afloat while rethinking its way of doing business. All of this is not to say that Dickens and other British writers had no grounds for complaint. *Brother Jonathan* carried *Nicholas Nickleby* in its early numbers, without any recompense to Dickens. In 1842 alone the *New World* printed 21 complete works as extras; in 1843 it produced 36. To add insult to injury, the *New World* ran Dickens's *American Notes* almost immediately after it appeared in England, attracting 50,000 readers to the paper—and affording Dickens not a penny (Barnes 11; Houtchens 22–23).

Dickens first raised the question of international copyright in a speech in Boston on February 1 and then in Hartford on February 8. After the latter, the papers began to attack him for barging in where he did not belong, for venal motives, for violating the courtesies a guest owes his host, and so on. Dickens responded more or less in kind, albeit largely in private. "I'll tell you what the two obstacles to the passing of an international copyright law with England, are," he wrote to John Forster at the beginning of May; "firstly, the national love of 'doing' a man in any bargain or matter of business; secondly, national vanity" (*Letters* 231). He secretly organized an open letter from eminent British writers, many his friends, in support of a copyright agreement,[7] which he presented to the American newspapers as unsolicited; and he also, through the good offices of Irving, secretly organized a complementary petition to Congress signed by 24 leading American writers, including, in addition to Irving, Bryant, W. A. Duer (the president of Columbia), a number of prominent editors, and Fitz-Greene Halleck (Houtchens 19–20). Dickens personally took the petition to Henry Clay, then at the very end of his years in the Senate.

The United States did not sign a copyright agreement with Britain until 1891, for a variety of reasons well articulated in 1842 but that Dickens refused to heed. The first, and at the time of Dickens's visit the most powerful, was, as I have outlined above, economic. In addition to the paper-makers, the printers and publishers fought an agreement, persuasively marshalling charts and statistics to show how many people would be thrown out of work and how much capital lost if a copyright agreement were signed. Quite simply, the printers, publishers, and paper-makers asked Congress to protect home industry at a time of poor trade. No argument on the side of copyright could outweigh this obvious practical counter-argument. But the trade had other points to make, too. The American publishers saw themselves as at a distinct disadvantage with respect to the British. Although Bryant and others argued that America was well on the way to producing sufficient talent to compete in the international market, the publishers worried that they would be thrown out of business by the burden of paying for what they now could have for free. There was an emphasis too on what was perceived as necessary cultural protectionism. Once international copyright made the U.S. profitable to writers, the publishers anticipated entry into the U.S. of a foreign literature that they could no longer control or adapt "to our wants, our institutions, and our state of society" (Houtchens 22). In the most detailed study of the failure of the campaign for international copyright at midcentury, James J. Barnes concludes that as "a young nation, the United States wanted the freedom to borrow literature as well as technology from any quarter of the globe" (ix).

There was another argument advanced, one that particularly angered Dickens. "Has Mr Dickens yet to learn," the *New World* wrote on February 12, "that to the very absence of such a law as he advocates, he is mainly indebted for his widespread popularity? To that class of his readers—dwellers in log cabins, in our back settlements—whose good opinion, he says, is dearer to him than gold, his name would hardly have been known had an international copy-right law been in existence." The *New World* may have been advancing a cynically self-serving argument but on its face the argument is not only true but exposes one of the most confusing circumstances governing the production of literature in the age of a mass audience, which is that the interests of writer and reader are sometimes at odds.

Bryant, for example, would have liked best to have pursued a career as a poet—but at the time there was no such career. No one could earn a living in the United States of his day, not to say raise a family, as a poet. He became a newspaper proprietor and editor. Bryant's actual circumstances confirm (if confirmation were necessary) that the essential condition that makes it possible for a person in a market economy to become a professional writer is, naturally enough, pay for work. Ignoring for the moment the nature of publishing and distribution and the market, the obvious interest of the writer is to be paid as much as possible, whereas the obvious desire of the reader is to pay as little as possible. If this sounds ridiculously simple, think of the situation of a pop singer today and the confusion and acrimony caused by the ability of listeners simply to pirate songs onto their computers. So the argument of the *New World*, outrageous as it seemed to Dickens, was nonetheless fair enough: by printing huge runs of his work and selling them at extremely cheap prices the paper was indeed providing him with a mass audience he could not possibly have had otherwise. The interest of the reader is to have access to the greatest number of books or their equivalent at the lowest price, or if possible for no price at all. The more this situation obtains, the larger the reading public and the stronger the literary culture. Again, the situation of music today persuasively illustrates the general point. Looked at strictly from the point of view of the reading public, the pirating of Dickens's writing spread literature widely, encouraged literacy, and diffused not only knowledge but a whole world of values, including appreciation of reading and of the book, across American society. For a young nation, all of these results were good.

It is also obviously the case that if Dickens had been paid nothing at all by his publishers in Great Britain he, like Bryant, would have had to seek another trade. American pirates evaded the truth that they were stealing Dickens's labor by taking comfort in his considerable income at home; besides, their activities were not only legal but were in truth encouraged by American law. And American law protected and encouraged their literary piracy because American lawmakers judged the growth of reading (and the industries associated with it) to be a more urgent national interest than pay for Dickens. Having said that, it's important to add that although Dickens did not, like Bryant, seek another trade, he did reinvent his trade: he sought as much control as he could gain over the publication of his own works. He became, insofar as possible, his own publisher, and aimed for a relation to his readers just like that of the *New World*. He aimed for huge print runs and for communication with a mass audience. He achieved huge sales by writing serially, so that people of modest means who could not afford the very high cost of a three-volume novel could afford the cost of a weekly or monthly serial. The cheap price of installments of his fiction earned him a very handsome return because of the volume of sales.

In this respect as in so many others, the absence of international copyright forced upon Dickens a different, often unpleasant or alarming, perspective on practices and beliefs that, in the British context, he not only considered proper but that he took pride in vigorously promoting. Dickens thrived on the system of serial production, materially, of course, but even more as a writer. He seemed to derive enormous creative energy from the pressure of writing for a deadline. The very mass audience that international copyright would have denied him in the U.S., and that publication strictly in three-volume format would have denied him at home, Dickens avidly pursued through serial publication. He clearly relished his intimacy-at-a-distance with a mass readership. His reading tours later in his career show, I think, that from the start Dickens understood—and also craved—the absolutely essential requirement of the mass reading public: that the writer as personality be as vivid, and present to the reader, as the writer's work. Dickens courted the mass reading public as no writer had before him. But when he arrived in the U.S., Dickens suffered a kind of Frankenstein moment. As he was mobbed, touched, forced to shake hands for hours, as intrusive fans invaded his hotel rooms, he experienced the fame he created and courted, this figure he had concocted called ''Boz,'' as a monster; and more than once he must have asked, What have I done?

III. Dickens and Celebrity

I can do nothing that I want to do, go nowhere where I want to go, and see nothing that I want to see. If I turn into the street, I am followed by a multitude. If I stay at home, the house becomes, with callers, like a fair. . . . I go to a party in the evening, and am so inclosed and hemmed about by people, stand where I will, that I am exhausted for want of air. I dine out, and have to talk about everything, to everybody. I go to church for quiet, and there is a violent rush to the neighbourhood of the pew I sit in . . . I take my seat in a railroad car, and the very conductor won't leave me alone. I get out at a station, and can't drink a glass of water, without having a hundred people looking down my throat when I open my mouth to swallow. . . . I have no rest or peace, and am in a perpetual worry. (Dickens to John Forster, 24 Feb. 1842, *Letters* 87)

Dickens's visit to the U.S. was the most important visit by any foreigner in the first half of the nineteenth century. He was welcomed triumphantly to the New World as the champion of American values within the corrupt old heart of Great Britain. The mammoths had circulated his novels to a huge audience and made him greater than any king. The man himself, however, was horrified. He was horrified in the main because living as a celebrity was an unbearable, exhausting nuisance. Perhaps he felt something alarming, too, about the disappearance of his actual identity into that mobbed public figure. Indeed he became only a public figure—his privacy was severely curtailed, invaded, and all but obliterated (he was identified everywhere as "Boz"; the extravagant evening mounted for thousands in his honor in New York was called the "Boz Ball"). But no matter how one might sympathize with Dickens the man under these circumstances, Dickens the writer and Dickens the man of business vigorously, ingeniously, and successfully exploited the new conditions of literary production and in this way helped significantly to create the celebrity culture he found, when writ large in America, to be repulsive. Dickens was the greatest literary entertainer and the best literary man of business of his age.[8] Everything in his career led logically to celebrity status for the writer. In this respect too his American experience reflects a new reality, one from which there was to be no turning away. In *Martin Chuzzlewit* Dickens satirized the impudence and presumptuousness, the vulgarity of American celebrity culture. But as the master literary marketer, the supreme literary promoter and entertainer of the nineteenth century, he could not avoid the hard truth that the very methods essential to his enterprise—artistic and financial—were not only the same as but led directly to the very celebrity culture that horrified him in the United States.

The emergence of celebrity culture in the nineteenth century—already in the early nineteenth century[9]—announced the triumph of urban, democratic society and of the public domain well before politics was fully transformed from its exclusively aristocratic basis, its male system of privilege, into a

voting system based on all the people—rich and poor, male and female, free
and ex-slave. The cultural revolution established new sources of authority
and revealed a new relation to time, both of determining importance to literature. By the date Dickens visited the U.S., however, the end of aristocratic
society was in sight. "The divine right of the masses," wrote Gustav Le Bon
in his seminal study of the crowd, "[was] about to replace the divine right of
kings" (16).[10] The mass society produced by industrial capitalism, urbanism,
technology and commodities rendered hierarchies irrelevant and archaic. The
market in ideas that came into existence to bond civil society around acceptable, democratically arrived-at policies—that is, the public domain—at once
elevated culture and degraded it. The cultural system based on the landed
estate consciously fashioned a complete, coherent, purposeful way of life,
well represented by Augustan verse. But prose made to sell in the market
necessarily raised entertainment as the paramount value and relegated literary
tradition to a very dusty corner, to be lit up or left dark as the writer chose.
Although then as now it seemed impossible to conceive of art as incoherent
and purposeless, nonetheless the novel from the outset incorporated conflict
and gave play to many competing voices within its two covers. At the very
least just what total social vision should replace, in society and in art, the
vision represented by the estate was not at all obvious. In all these respects
Dickens as celebrity reflected the rise of a mass society he both championed
and dreaded, dreaded especially once he saw where things were going in
America.[11]

   The movie star Esther Williams, having absorbed a century of experience,
memorably captured the wisdom of her kind. "Walk fast," she said. "You
touch them, they don't touch you" (Schickel 5). If celebrity announces the
boundless possibilities of a free society (of democracy and the free market),
and is therefore at least arguably "touchable by the multitude" (Marshall 6),
it simultaneously signals the impossibility of grand attainment and indeed
insists on celebrity as fantasy rather than reality. The celebrity has to fulfill
every conscious and unconscious expectation of the millions of non-celebri-
ties. Celebrity culture is therefore full of danger, as Dickens discovered. He
constantly found himself betraying expectations he could not have known he
had aroused. "This man is offended because I won't live in his house; and
that man is thoroughly disgusted because I won't go out more than four times
in one evening" (*Letters* 87). Not only does celebrity, to quote Le Bon once
more, "represent the disintegration of the distinction between the private and
the public" (247), so that Dickens's admirers thought nothing of barging into
his hotel room uninvited, since after all Dickens was not a real but rather a
symbolic person and hence could not possibly have about him anything private; but celebrity culture literally endangers the celebrity and can quickly
turn adulation (touching what you want to be and may become) to violence

and violence to murder, "the most intimate of acts" (Schickel 8). As Richard Schickel argues, the fan wants intimacy from the celebrity, wants the celebrity to be at one and the same time a glorious "star" and a regular gal or guy, just like the man or woman in the street. It is very easy to be disappointed. "The worst fears of rejection surface," he writes. "And [these] are expressed as democratic resentment: 'Who does she think she is, anyway?' " (5). It is a short step from resentment to murderous rage, for all the obvious reasons. So, as Esther Williams says, it is necessary to walk fast, because the touch of adulation can turn into something dangerous in a flash. In *Martin Chuzzlewit* Dickens explores celebrity culture in a number of ways, including a murder that is illuminated, I think, when seen as the vengeance of a resentful fan against a celebrity who has disappointed him and exposed his miserable pettiness. Isn't what Jonas thinks of Tigg precisely: "Who does he think he is, anyway?"

Being forced to see America from the vantage point of a celebrity, Dickens was repulsed by what he saw. His revulsion took the form of "This is not what I meant at all." By March 22 he was writing in distress to his friend the actor W. C. Macready:

> I *am* disappointed. This is not the Republic I came to see. This is not the Republic of my imagination. I infinitely prefer a liberal Monarchy . . . to such a Government as this. In every respect but that of National Education, the Country disappoints me . . . In everything of which it has made a boast . . . it sinks immeasurably below the level I had placed it upon. And England, even England, bad and faulty as the old land is, and miserable as millions of her people are, rises in comparison [. . . .] The man who comes to this Country a Radical and goes home again with his old opinions unchanged, must be a Radical on reason, sympathy, and reflection, and one who has so well considered the subject that he has no chance of wavering.   (*Letters* 156)

Presumably Dickens is the man who came to the U.S. a Radical and went home with his opinions changed. He came to the U.S. in the same way that later many Americans would go to the Soviet Union—to see the next stage of human progress in its concrete development, to find progressive, Radical ideals given shape and form in everyday life. But American realities were not what he expected. Worse, he hated the place. The full impact of America on Dickens is hard to gauge and may have taken some years to work itself through.[12] But Dickens had little time to reflect. He had engaged to write a travel book about the country and had to set to work more or less immediately after he arrived back home.

IV. Dickens the Traveler

The literature of travel confronts us immediately with the unpleasant truth that preconceptions are almost always impermeable to reality. It seems there are two recurring possibilities: the writer finds what he or she seeks, and is pleased; the writer does not find what he or she seeks, and is disappointed. But then, what about what's *there*? How can the travel writer recognize and then convey the truth of what he or she sees? And isn't this very close to the dilemma of the novelist trying to convey the experience, the unprecedented experience, of life in the nineteenth century? Dickens came at the problem of conveying the American reality twice, first in *American Notes* and second in *Martin Chuzzlewit*. In the former, Dickens, in haste and often inattention, takes his role as travel writer not too seriously. But in *Martin Chuzzlewit* he comes at the problem again, this time if not with complete success then certainly with greater seriousness, both interestingly anticipated by an earlier visitor to the United States, the formidable Harriet Martineau.

Hundreds of Britons traveled to the U.S. in the early nineteenth century but of this number, only Martineau, to my knowledge, felt the need to go beyond recording her impressions and went ahead to publish a quasi-academic guide to how one's visit should be properly, even scientifically, conducted. About a year after completing her influential *Society in America* (1838), Martineau brought out *How to Study Manners and Morals* (1839), a book actually penned several years earlier while Martineau was at sea on her way to the U.S. in 1834. The book opens with these words of caution, words that Dickens may have read (we know he read *Society in America* [*Letters* 91]) but that in any event seem aimed directly at him:

> There is no department of inquiry in which it is not full as easy to miss the truth as to find it, even when the materials from which truth is to be drawn are actually present to our senses. A child does not catch a goldfish in water at the first trial . . . knowledge and method are necessary to enable him to take what is actually before his eyes and under his hand. . . . [But] every man seems to imagine that he can understand men at a glance; he supposes that it is enough to be among them to know what they are doing; he thinks that eyes, ears, and memory are enough for morals, though they would not qualify him for botanical or statistical observation.   (2–3)

Martineau proposes what we would now call a social science, or sociological, approach to travel writing.[13] The dilemma she brings into focus is epistemological. The goldfish "truth" is right there in front of our eyes, but can we catch it? We can only catch it, she maintains, by study and intellectual discipline. In seeking to overcome the disabilities of prior assumptions, Martineau relies on method to achieve objectivity. The traveler Charles Dickens was not a particularly methodical writer when he first came to the United States, but one consequence of his American journey was his intention to compose *Martin Chuzzlewit* far more carefully than his earlier novels.

At the time of his arrival in the States Dickens's writing could be better described by Martineau's advice later in *How to Study*. "The observer must

have sympathy; and his sympathy must be untrammeled and unreserved . . . .
Unless a traveler interprets by his sympathies what he sees, he cannot but
misunderstand the greater part of that which comes under his observation''
(52). She uses this example to clarify what she means: ''A stranger who has
never felt any strong political interest, and cannot sympathize with American
sentiment about the majesty of social equality, and the beauty of mutual
government, can never understand the political religion of the United States''
(55). Martineau, then, proposes two not unrelated but certainly distinct ways
of getting at the truth of what the travel writer is observing: rigorous scientific
method and unreserved sympathy. These alternatives clearly have their parallels in the outlook of nineteenth—century writers—in the dispassionate intensity of Flaubert's search for le mot juste, for example, and its apparent
contrary in Keats's negative capability. And both approaches appear, sometimes in harmony and sometimes in tension, in *Martin Chuzzlewit.*

    American Notes, however, seems much less thoughtfully or methodically
put together than either *Society in America* or *Martin Chuzzlewit.* The editors
of the Pilgrim Edition of the *Letters* remark dryly that Dickens's itinerary in
the U.S. simply retraced the routes that everyone who visited from England
followed: ''he saw nothing new, nor . . . did he think very profoundly about
what he saw; yet all his descriptions bore 'Boz's peculiar colours,' characteristic of his novels'' (ix). Dickens may not have thought very profoundly about
what he saw; but it does seem he was deeply moved, albeit not in ways he
expected. And his emotions—of distress, of disgust, of dismay—contributed
to the ultimate rethinking of and indeed the formal abandonment of Boz.
Boz's peculiar colors turned out not to be quite right, quite enough to capture
the emotional truth of Dickens's American experience.

    American Notes gets off to a good start, which is with an entertaining
account of Dickens's first glimpse of his quarters aboard the Brittania. But
all too soon, when Dickens has to get down to the business of conveying
what's *there* in the New World, his usual inventiveness deserts him. Neither
the cities of the U.S. nor the vast unsettled country towards the West seem
truly to have interested him. He is detached, cavalier, whimsical. The most
obvious qualities of American cities, such as their newness, qualities that can
hardly have come as a surprise to Dickens, these very qualities, when he
actually comes upon them, seem to have been precisely those that either
bored or offended him. Compare, for example, Bryant's and Dickens's descriptions of burgeoning cities in Massachusetts. Here is Bryant writing, in
1847, of Lawrence:

> A year ago last February, the building of the city was begun; it has now five
> or six thousand inhabitants, and new colonists are daily thronging in. . . . The
> place, I was told, astonishes visitors with its bustle and confusion. The streets

are encumbered with heaps of fresh earth, and piles of stone, brick, beams, and boards, and people can with difficulty hear each other speak, for the constant thundering of hammers, and the shouts of cartmen and wagoners urging their oxen and horses with their loads through the deep sand of the ways. "Before the last shower," said a passenger, "you could hardly see the city from this spot, on account of the cloud of dust that hung perpetually over it." "Rome," says the old adage, "was not built in a day," but here is a city which, in respect of its growth, puts Rome to shame.   (Godwin II, 32)

And this is Dickens on Lowell:

It was a very dirty winter's day, and nothing in the whole town looked old to me, except the mud, which in some parts was almost knee-deep, and might have been deposited there, on the subsiding of the waters after the Deluge. In one place, there was a new wooden church, which, having no steeple, and being yet unpainted, looked like an enormous packing–case without any direction upon it. In another there was a large hotel, whose walls and colonnades were so crisp, and thin, and slight, that it had exactly the appearance of being built with cards. I was careful not to draw my breath as we passed, and trembled when I saw a workman come out upon the roof, lest with one thoughtless stamp of his foot he should crush the structure beneath him. . . . One would swear that every "Bakery," "Grocery," and "Bookbindery," and other kind of store, took its shutters down for the first time, and started business yesterday. The golden pestles and mortars fixed as signs upon the sun-blind frames outside the Druggists', appear to have been just turned out of the United States' Mint; and when I saw a baby of some week or ten days old in a woman's arms at a street corner, I found myself unconsciously wondering where it came from: never supposing for an instant that it could have been born in such a young town as that.   (65)

Bryant assumes that the reader of his matter-of-fact report will admire the hectic, dusty chaos of a city being built at an unprecedented pace. It would be possible to use the details of Bryant's description to suggest any number of unpleasantnesses, but obviously that's not the point. The cartmen driving their oxen through the "deep sand of the ways" reflect rather the unparalleled energy and drive of the young republic. They put Rome to shame.

For Dickens the deep sand of the ways brings to mind the mud deposited after the Deluge. The ancient earth recalls to his startled perception that there is (thank goodness!) such a thing as historical time and contingency, because otherwise the place is all new, all too new. Does Dickens find the mud comforting and the newness of everything else in Lowell a sorry contrast? If it *were* the case that every bakery and other store *had* opened for business yesterday, what should we think? Is there a problem? Dickens's implicit judgment is that *such* newness is somehow vulgar or, because it is new, evanescent, revealing so thin a veneer of civilization that, like the walls of the hotel, it all might vanish again as easily as it has arisen. Dickens seems to feel he need not go any farther in spelling out his reaction: obviously, anything *this* new has to be insubstantial. And when we come to New York, his account is so brief, episodic, and hasty that often it reads as though he could barely be bothered to write about the city at all. How can his apparently superficial responses to the American city, his disengagement with American urban life, be explained?

One answer is that New York turned out not to be London. Here is Dickens in 1841 inviting Washington Irving to tour London with him:

> I wish I could find in your welcome letter some hint of an intention to visit England. I should love to go with you, as I have gone, God knows how often, into Little Britain, and East Cheap, and Green Arbour Court, and Westminster Abbey.... It would gladden my heart to compare notes with you about all those delightful places and people that I used to walk about and dream of in daytime when a very small and not-over-particularly-taken-care-of-boy.
>
> (Forster I, 171)

Nineteenth-century London appears in discussions of Dickens and the city as a place of epochal darkness, the city as disrupter of human community, the city as baffling, the city as a cacophony without discernible meaning, the city as a chaos threatening to reduce the individual, and individual identity, to nullity. But in this letter, with its loving list of evocative names, its protective desire to take a friend to see "all those delightful places and people," Dickens evokes an altogether different London, London seen through his childhood's eye. It's worth recalling that this long-established perception of Dickens's sense of London includes threat, yes, but also dreams; anxiety but also delight. The London he invites Irving to tour is a city of delightful fantasy and cherished memories. It is a city the creative force of which lies in the past, depends on the past, emerges from the past. The London Dickens wants to show Irving is the commercial London of the eighteenth century, partly the London of Johnson (and Hazlitt) in the sense of London as a vivacious place that contains all of humanity, but mainly the London of Defoe. I don't mean London as it *was* in the eighteenth century or in *Moll Flanders*, but rather that eighteenth-century city sentimentalized, or, if you prefer, transformed by the passage of time, by history, tradition, childhood, and memory into the Dickensian city of the nineteenth century.

The Dickensian city of the novels is the city of Defoe and Johnson that Dickens daydreamed through as a boy and recalled as a man, confronting the other London, the hard-nosed capital of the industrial revolution. The centers of the industrial revolution—Manchester, Leeds—rarely appear in Dickens's fiction: but industrial capitalism does, in the powerful but indirect ways it affects London. Defoe's actual London is much more like Lowell or New York than like Dickens's recollected London. When Moll comes to the New

World she is not, like Dickens, horrified by its lack of history: rather, for
Moll, Virginia no less than London is a place to make money, a place whose
focus is always on its prospects and where, as in London, everyone has his
and her eye on Number One. This way of seeing the world seems either
infantile or threatening to Dickens when he encounters it in the nineteenth-
century cities of the United States. Lowell and New York were rambunctious
cities where the future was all. When in the nineteenth-century a fire destroyed
a New York building, as fires often did, it was simply replaced fast in a new
form. Whatever history the young city of New York may have had was
constantly being erased and then, just as constantly, reinvented. This turmoil
seemed to offer Dickens nothing he could draw on for his creative purposes.

It is true that Dickens set a good deal of *Martin Chuzzlewit* in the United
States. But if the U.S. appears in the novel as a setting, as a subject for satire,
even as a warning, it remains just material to be used rather than, as I think
Dickens expected on setting out, as a source of new creative energy, an
impetus for creative growth. The U.S. did not feed Dickens's creative imagination in the ways he had expected. But the U.S. does seem both to have
overturned some of Dickens's fundamental convictions and to have shown
him a face of reality he found, at least on initial encounter, deeply upsetting.
The struggle to transform the more disturbing realities of his American encounter into fiction absorbed the rest of his writing career, both as a matter
of form and content.

For *Martin Chuzzlewit* these were most obviously the realities of Cairo,
Illinois and of the Mississippi, recorded by Dickens in well-known passages
of *American Notes* (171–72). He states that Cairo was "more desolate"
than any place he had seen, a "dismal swamp" half-flooded by that "slimy
monster," that "enormous ditch," that "hotbed of disease" the Mississippi.
Dickens's account suggests he has penetrated to the heart of darkness. Many
European visitors saw nature in America in the same way. The very openness
of open country, the absence of hedged cultivation, of country seats, neat
villages, ancient towns, the essential non-humanity of American nature seems
to have stirred some unconscious phobias in the Europeans.[14] Dickens's picture has the quality of a horrified encounter with primeval slime. From the
point of view of the evolution of his fiction, Dickens's disgust with nature in
America goes hand-in-hand with his revulsion with American democratic
(read: boorish) manners and democratic (read: vulgar and demagogic) values,
with his disdain for the ideology of Make It New, and with his boredom with
evanescent New York. He came to the U.S. after several years of mounting
success, a confident, willful, headstrong, but not-yet-thirty young man. Angry
about injustice at home, he expected to find a more democratic and hence, as
he perhaps rashly assumed, more just society in the U.S.; he expected to be
able to appreciate America as had no English traveler before him; he expected

that his gifts as entertainer would receive new impetus from the confirmation America would give to his worldview. He expected that he would have no trouble translating his experiences into memorable prose. In sum, Dickens came to the U.S. a young man confident in his essentially comic view of life, comic in the sense of belief in the ameliorative power of democratic government, belief that the essential goodness of human beings could be nurtured and made to flourish in the commerce and culture of a nation through progressive institutions and policies. Similarly, Dickens came to the U.S. if not altogether complacent about his ability to improvise out of his enormous verbal facility and imaginative inventiveness an endless number of fictional entertainments, then anyway confident that fresh sights would sufficiently invigorate his powers, and nothing more was required.[15]

All his expectations were dashed. Maybe the thing that Dickens came away with most from his American journey was that his expectations *could* be dashed, that he could profoundly misunderstand. As I have already observed, much of his experience in the U.S. took the form of "That is not what I meant at all." He never meant his democratic inclinations to extend to the braggadocio of leveling he encountered in the U.S. or the ridiculousness of American political and cultural pretensions. Egalitarianism in the U.S. seemed to embrace presumption in a way he had not anticipated. Everyone took too many liberties. But the hardest thing, what I believe especially jolted him, was that the New World, able to start afresh, able to reinvent and recreate nonetheless revealed the same old worn human face. His comic worldview could not withstand the evidence to the contrary in America—in the cities, in nature, in institutions, in the quality of human relations. He discovered not only that in the American Eden men are not better than in their fallen state back on the other side of the Atlantic; but, worse, that he was deeply attached to humanity as he had known it in the corrupt Old World. America revealed to Dickens a tragic dimension to human life he seems not to have fully registered before, that he had not fully acknowledged. Many of his initial responses to the U.S., in his letters and in *American Notes*, seem to be protective of his comic worldview and of how he had given that worldview expression in his art. He seemed to recoil in order to sustain his creative powers. But now he had to make room in his art, to recreate his fiction so as to give full expression to the tragic realities revealed by his American journey. His first attempt to incorporate his American experience—literally but also in its implications—into his fiction is *Martin Chuzzlewit*.

V. Martin Chuzzlewit

The essential challenge posed to Dickens by his American journey was to his art. A famous occasion in Tolstoy's *Anna Karenina* clarifies the nature of that challenge. Unable to live together in Russia, Vronsky and Anna Karenina travel abroad, and in Italy Vronsky takes up painting, for which he fancies he has a gift. The resident Russian painter, Mikhailov, baffles and irritates the Count, but when Mikhailov finishes his portrait of Anna, Vronsky is astonished: " 'One needs to know her and love her as I have loved her to discover the very sweetest expression of her soul,' Vronsky thought, though it was only from this portrait that he had himself learned this sweetest expression of her soul" (543).

By this account, even the truth about those we love most is hidden from us, and can only be discovered through art. The role of the artist is to capture the truth and show it to us. But the passage leaves unexplored a number of vexing epistemological questions: Is this truth that we cannot see in life only present in the work of art? Is there a truth "out there" or does the artist simply persuade us through the elusive tricks of art (method? sympathy?) that what we see on the canvas is truth; and do we only then, looking away from the canvas and back to Anna, find this truth in her too? Is the point of the work of art to have us turn back to "reality" with fresh eyes?

We first meet Pecksniff in the second chapter of *Martin Chuzzlewit*, at the end of a series of paragraphs tracking the night wind:

> Out upon the angry wind! how from sighing, it began to bluster round the merry forge, banging at the wicket, and grumbling in the chimney. . . . The scared leaves only flew faster for all this, and a giddy chase it was: for they got into unfrequented places, where there was no outlet, and where their pursuer kept them eddying round and round at his pleasure . . . But the oddest feat they achieved was, to take advantage of the sudden opening of Mr Pecksniff's front-door, to dash wildly into his passage; whither the wind following close upon them, and finding the back-door open, incontinently blew out the lighted candle held by Miss Pecksniff, and slammed the front door against Mr Pecksniff who was at that moment entering, with such violence, that in the twinkling of an eye he lay on his back at the bottom of the steps. Being by this time weary of such trifling performances, the boisterous rover hurried away rejoicing, roaring over moor and meadow, hill and flat, until it got out to sea, where it met with other winds similarly disposed, and made a night of it.   (58–61)

Vronsky discovers a core truth about Anna through Mikhailov's painting but fails to realize it: he believes, rather, that the marvel of Mikhailov's painting is that the artist was somehow able to capture a quality in Anna that only someone who loved her deeply, in fact, only Vronsky, could possibly have glimpsed. The artist's secret then, at least as Tolstoy reveals it here, is that he makes us believe that he has uncovered a truth we had previously thought no one could have discovered except ourselves; when in fact we only come into possession of that truth when we encounter it in the work of art. But, ironically, the reader only knows that Vronsky has been deceived, and has deceived himself, because Tolstoy as narrator tells us. This is the narrator both as deity and as inextricable from, or invisible within, the narration itself. Tolstoy's voice, his "telling," in the novel is so absolute, his authority so total, that paradoxically we are unaware of any narrator doing the narration: we experience the narration as the truth.

Where is Dickens in the passage above? We know that Mikhailov has revealed to Vronksy the very sweetest expression of Anna's soul. What is Dickens showing us? Vronksy is unmistakably led to apprehension of the goldfish truth: Mikahilov reveals Anna's inner being, and Tolstoy tells us explicitly that that's what he's doing, too. Is Dickens's purpose analogous? One way to read the passage is to see Dickens as the wind. The wind here is petulant, impulsive, mischievous, vengeful, tyrannical but recognizable in its classical guise as inspired creator or maker. All of this is suggested in Dickens's word "incontinently," meaning at once without restraint, morally loose, and acting without hesitation, acting immediately and decisively. That's how Dickens whacks Pecksniff, foreshadowing our final glimpse of him in our first. Both at the beginning and at the end Pecksniff suffers a literary comeuppance. It is important to note that the appearance of Pecksniff in these paragraphs seems incidental: the main story is the wind's fraternity house romp. The introduction of Pecksniff, one of the great malicious energies of the book, as a slapstick victim of the elements assures us at the very outset that the real power lies with the wind. The wind not only can, when it wishes, knock the man flat on his back just like that, but to the wind the man is of no consequence: the "boisterous rover" rushes on to make a night of it with his mates. Dickens the narrator is in control, can and will have his fun, and not to worry. The narrator of this scene combines two qualities that, it seems, represent, in combination, Dickens's ideal form of narration—that is, a union of spontaneity and control, of planned composition and improvisation.

Another way to read the passage, however, is suggested by Dorothy Van Ghent in her brilliant essay "The Dickens World: A View from Todgers's." "The course of things demonically possessed," Van Ghent begins, in something of a startling opening, "is to imitate the human, while the course of human possession is to imitate the inhuman. This transposition of attributes . . . is the principle of relationship between things and people in the novels of Dickens." Dickens's world, she goes on to say, is "a world undergoing gruesome spiritual transformation" (3–5). Dickens's anthropomorphizing of the wind and leaves, in this reading, is an instance of a world in the throes, unending, of "gruesome" reversal and metamorphosis. All of the inanimate objects in the passage have a curious life of their own. To follow Van Ghent, they are possessed and have, as it were, been puffed up with human purposes, which they sometimes comically and sometimes horrifically and tragically enact in their helter-skelter mimicry.

Van Ghent reads Dickens as working with meanings through figurations rather than through character or plot. His meanings are his world. Sylvère Monod, drawing on Dickens's account of his method of composing *Dombey and Son* as he reports it to John Forster, says that Dickens distinguished "two elements" in his writing: "the elements he has determined on, and the rest. His materials, he knows, will proliferate spontaneously, not perhaps uncontrollably, but without needing much guidance from him" (109). In *Martin Chuzzlewit* and the great novels that follow, these elements might be described as comprising theme and plot, on the one hand, and most of what it takes to flesh those out, one the other. The former involve conscious composition and intentional control; the latter are best left to the inspired process of improvisation. As I have said about the scene that introduces Pecksniff, Dickens seems to be aiming for a union of spontaneity and control.

But it's necessary to say that this union is difficult to achieve and even more difficult to sustain. For one thing, the relation between fiction and the reality "out there" tends to emphasize control over improvisation and Dickens—like most nineteenth-century novelists—saw fiction as "a self-conscious effort," in the words of George Levine, "usually in the name of some moral enterprise of truth telling and extending the limits of human sympathy to make literature appear to be describing directly not some other language but reality itself" (8). This claim is the essence of realism. And the claim seems as it were natural and to arise from every page of every writing, intentionally realistic or not, because of our lifelong and inescapable acculturation to words as referents. Even as we delight in Dickens's spontaneous flights in *Martin Chuzzlewit,* we too are unable to quash questions such as: shouldn't there be a strong connection between the two elements of Dickens's composition, the one conscious and plotted and the other spontaneous? Shouldn't Dickens's spontaneous effects express his themes and coherently develop his plots? *Martin Chuzzlewit* has not lacked for critics exasperated by what they see as the novel's incoherence, disorganization, and lack of unity, among them such shrewd readers of Dickens as George Gissing and Barbara Hardy.[16] The coherence and unity of *Martin Chuzzlewit*—or the lack of these qualities—go to the heart not only of how we should read Dickens but also the nineteenth-century novel as a whole. Is a work of fiction true to reality on account of its consciously constructed composition, its plotted coherence and unity, or on account of its inspired improvisation?

These questions are not made easier, in any discussion of *Martin Chuzzlewit,* by the fact that the novel provides plenty of evidence for contradictory answers. The relation between small, easily overlooked details and theme, for instance, is often remarkable. I will offer one example, which has to do with the way books and reading are used in the novel. Often in Dickens a character or an object or an idea matters less for itself and more as a test for others: if the person or thing is good, then we know good characters will value it and bad will despise it. That's one way to look at the role of books in *Martin Chuzzlewit*. Moreover, in a novel that wants to identify literature as a primary source of value, the place of books in the novel might be said to stand for Dickens's recommitment to his vocation as writer.

Early in the novel Mary Graham is tending to Old Martin at the Dragon, a chore Mrs. Lupin offers to share with her. Mary returns her "many thanks for her solicitude and company, [but tells her] that she would remain there some time longer; and she begged her not to share her watch, as she was well used to being alone, and would pass the time in reading" (85). Mary's reading seems inconsequential, in no way a detail bearing thematic weight, until Pecksniff draws attention to it when he appears on the scene. He and Mrs. Lupin enter Old Martin's room unannounced and find him asleep and Mary reading. "I am afraid that this looks artful," Pecksniff says. "I am afraid, Mrs Lupin, do you know, that this looks very artful!":

> As he finished this whisper, he advanced before the hostess; and at the same time the young lady, hearing footsteps, rose. Mr Pecksniff glanced at the volume she held, and whispered Mrs Lupin again: if possible, with increased despondency.
> "Yes, ma'am," he said, "it is a good book. I was fearful of that beforehand. I am apprehensive that this is a very deep thing indeed!'' (87)

At this point we know nothing about Mary, except that she's reading a book. Pecksniff's characteristic effort to twist this innocent activity into something ominous—artful!— alerts us immediately to her goodness and is yet another foreshadowing of Pecksniff's end.

Just as our first associations with Mary are in this way directed toward reading, so too our early acquaintance with Tom Pinch involves books. Tom has been sent to Salisbury to meet Pecksniff's new pupil, Young Martin. He wanders happily among the shops.

> But what were even gold and silver, precious stones and clockwork, to the bookshops, whence a pleasant smell of paper freshly pressed came issuing forth. . . . That whiff of Russia leather too, and all those rows on rows of volumes . . . what happiness did they suggest! And in the window were the spick-and-span new works from London, with the title-pages, and sometimes even the first page of the first chapter, laid wide open. . . . Here too were the dainty frontispiece and trim vignette . . . and store of books, with many a grave portrait and time-honoured name, whose matter he knew well, and would have given mines to have, in any form, upon the narrow shelf beside his bed at Mr Pecksniff's. What a heart-breaking shop it was! (125)

At the tavern, waiting for Martin, Tom, like Mary, reads to pass the time.

All this—Tom's unalloyed delight in all the sensuous qualities of books, the echo in his reading of Mary's reading, the contrast between Tom's and Mary's direct and as it were selfless immersion in the imaginative, lusciously described world of books and Pecksniff's hypocritical, stinting relation to the same (Pecksniff allows Tom only a narrow shelf for this by implication useless activity)—all this establishes a web of associations that the novel densely elaborates. Young Martin, shortly after his arrival at Pecksniff's, asks Tom to read to him. Tom readily complies.

> "What will you like? Shakespeare?"
> "Aye!" replied his friend, yawning and stretching himself. "He'll do. I am tired with the bustle of to-day, and the novelty of everything about me; and in such a case, there's no greater luxury in the world, I think, than being read to sleep."   (155)

And having hogged the fire, go to sleep he does. But Tom "went on reading . . . He gradually became so much interested, that he quite forgot to replenish the fire" (156). The contrast between Tom's virtue and Martin's exasperating, voluminous self-regard is emphasized by their contrary responses to books.

Soon after Tom reads Martin to sleep, they encounter Mr. Chevy Slyme:

> "I swear," cried Mr. Slyme . . . "that I am the wretchedest creature on record. Society is in a conspiracy against me. I'm the most literary man alive. I'm full of scholarship; I'm full of genius; I'm full of information; I'm full of novel views on every subject; yet look at my condition! I'm at this moment obliged to two strangers for a tavern bill!"   (164)

Well, in fact, Tom pays for the lot, and is shown to be the exploited (but worthy) subscriber even to this debased literary man. Just as Tom is always ready to enter sympathetically into another point of view, to lose himself in books, so Slyme is the bragging self-promoter for whom literature is the agency of narcissism, sly grandiloquence, cynicism, and emotional dishonesty. When the novel takes Martin to the U.S., Slyme's self-promotion and self-invention are writ large in the grotesqueries of American culture. General Choke condescends to lecture Martin on the Queen's residences, insisting she resides mainly in the Tower of London. When in disbelief Martin asks "Have you been in England?" the General, unabashed, replies: "In print I have, sir . . . not otherwise. We air a reading people here, sir. You will meet with much information among us that will surprise you, sir." Martin, by this time on the way to his conversion—among the Americans Martin suddenly sounds sensible and mature—has the good humor to reply, "I have not the least doubt of it" (412).

Books are the currency of kindness, virtue, and finally justice in the novel. When Martin is forced peremptorily to quit Pecksniff's, he receives a book from Tom, a book containing as a gift all the money Tom has. The morning after he has eaten of Ruth Pinch's first-ever beef pudding, John Westlock gives her a cookbook "with the beef-steak-pudding-leaf turned down and blotted out" (692). The full dimensions of this motif are unveiled in Tom's mysterious windfall, his London job as a "kind of secretary and librarian" (681) and, finally, in the climactic scene in which the tables are turned and Old Martin beats Pecksniff.

Tom's place of work is four dusty and apparently long-disused rooms in a dark courtyard deep in the Temple. The place is a shambles, "a tomb" with a "haunted air":

> Movables of every kind lay strewn about, without the least attempt at order, and were intermixed with boxes, hampers, and all sorts of lumber. On all the floors were piles of books, to the amount, perhaps, of some thousands of volumes: these, still in bales: those, wrapped in paper, as they had been purchased: others scattered singly or in heaps: not one upon the shelves which lined the walls.
> (687)

Tom is charged with putting all these books in order, "an occupation full of interest for me" (687), he confesses. In dutifully performing his assigned tasks, Tom redeems the place from death to life, building a kind of animated shrine to literary values, a neat, clean, handsome library, which, upon Old Martin's arrival, becomes a place of reckoning with the books themselves coming into service as agents of the administration of justice. In Phiz's illustration Pecksniff is felled not only by Old Martin but by the books themselves, in particular by *Paradise Lost* and *Tartuffe*, pictured as tumbling on Pecksniff's head. In this chapter of revelations, a not unimportant revelation is the representative power of literature to combat the wrongs of Self, of which, in Old Martin's eyes, Pecksniff "had become the incarnation" (875). Books are shown in the novel to perform just the function that, in immediate response to his American experience, Dickens the novelist wants all the more effectively to perform.

The novel's use of books as a moral touchstone is one example, then, of a sustained coherence in *Martin Chuzzlewit*, albeit in a minor key. Having said that, I hasten to add that nonetheless the book's most powerful passages are those where Dickens, rather like a jazz saxophonist, a Victorian Charlie Parker, spontaneously elaborates his theme, in particular in his improvisations on place. Among these the most characteristic, and important, and the most often discussed, is his long description of Todgers's, both as a neighborhood and, as he says, "as a house in that neighbourhood" independent of "its merits as a commercial boarding establishment" (187). Dickens's narration

takes us from the baffling labyrinth of alleyways around Todgers's to its
cellarage and finally to the rooftop. For a moment the view from the rooftop
seems benign—"Then there were steeples, towers, belfries, shining vanes,
and masts of ships: a very forest" (188)—and echoes Wordsworth's "West-
minster Bridge" (1802):

> The city now doth, like a garment, wear
> The beauty of the morning; silent, bare,
> Ships, towers, domes, theatres, and temples lie
> Open to the fields, and to the sky.

But where the spondaic listing of figures in Wordsworth reflects the vivacity
of the city clothed in the peaceful beauty of morning, in the view from
Todgers's this prospect quickly darkens: "Gables, housetops, garret-windows,
wilderness upon wilderness." Abruptly the "crowd of objects" turns on the
viewer and possesses him. There is no way to improve on Dorothy Van
Ghent's reading of the passage that follows, but I would like to borrow her
insights and adapt them to purposes not altogether her own. After noting the
animate, dizzying activity of the objects in view, Dickens's passage concludes:

> . . . the tumult swelled into a roar; the hosts of objects seemed to thicken and
> expand a hundredfold; and after gazing round him quite scared, [the onlooker]
> turned into Todgers's again, much more rapidly than he came out; and ten to
> one he told M. Todgers afterwards that if he hadn't done so he would certainly
> have come into the street by the shortest cut: that is to say, head-foremost.
>
> (188–89)

Van Ghent comments: "The prospect from Todgers's is one in which categor-
ical determinations of the relative significance of objects . . . have broken
down, and the observer on Todgers's roof is seized with suicidal nausea at
the momentary vision of a world in which significance has been replaced by
naked and aggressive existence." She adds: "The grotesque transpositions
are a coherent imagination of a reality that has lost coherence" (29). These
incoherent transpositions, Van Ghent goes on to say, create a ubiquitous but
somehow unmoored anxiety. If Dickens's meanings are his world, the view
from Todgers's shows us a world cut loose from meaning, not liable to
coherent summation, scary, a world whose dislocations are so dizzying that
one might at any moment leap for succor to one's death.

The approach to Todgers's, through the labyrinth of streets, reveals the
London that Dickens wanted to show Washington Irving, the city whose
history and associations delight and fascinate Dickens, the labyrinth city to
which Dickens the writer has privileged access. But the view from Todgers's

is another thing altogether. Where the approach to Todgers's might be under-stood as representing conscious composition and control, the view from Todg-ers's radically undermines control and suggests that what a controlled vision can reveal for us is not just incomplete but maybe untrue. But if the view from Todgers's reveals the essential reality of the new London of the industrial age, it also opens for us a dangerous prospect. Is the vantage point on the roof of Todgers's the place where the narrator should perch himself? How can the dangerous, unsettling reality visible from Todgers's rooftop, in its impact on the viewer not unlike the reality, in life and in fiction, of Cairo and the Mississippi, best be observed? What is the narrative form appropriate to, or analogous to, this reality?

The ultimate observer, in this novel, is the professional spy Nadgett. Al-though Dickens tries on a variety of narrative voices and perspectives in the novel, from the wind to Old Martin, his identification with Nadgett is the most revealing.[17] When we first meet Nadgett, Dickens stresses a paradoxical quality of his, which is that "he was born to be a secret." This seems to have several meanings: "How he lived was a secret; where he lived was a secret; and even what he was, was a secret. . . . And yet he belonged to a class; a race peculiar to the City; who are secrets as profound to one another, as they are to the rest of mankind" (517). Nadgett is the epitome of—to use the contemporary word— surveillance. On the one hand, then, everything he does, everything he values, is secret. No one knows what he does, who he is, where he lives. He exemplifies the city as a congregation of the anonymous, every person unknown to every other person. On the other hand, because of the class of Nadgetts, London is a city where no one can have a secret, where all secrets will out, where everyone is under surveillance. Nadgett's spying on Jonas is total, and as the moment of murder approaches is transposed into nature itself, becomes, as it were, metaphysical. As Jonas, riding into the country to trap Tigg, sleeps in his coach,

> in their stalls and pastures beasts were quiet; and human creatures slept. But what of that, when the solemn night was watching, when it never winked, when its darkness watched no less than its light! The stately trees, the moon and shining stars, the softly-stirring wind, the over-shadowed lane, the broad, bright countryside, they all kept watch. There was not a blade of growing grass or corn, but watched; and the quieter it was, the more intent and fixed its watch upon him seemed to be. (798)

At the same time, Nadgett's surveillance creates a web of connections among people in the city who appear to have nothing to do with one another, who pass each other on the thronged streets unaware:

> In walking from the City . . . Tom Pinch had looked into the face, and brushed against the threadbare sleeve, of Mr Nadgett. . . . As there are a vast number

of people in the huge metropolis of England who rise up every morning not knowing where their heads will rest at night, so there are a multitude who shooting arrows over houses as their daily business, never know on whom they fall. Mr Nadgett might have passed Tom Pinch ten thousand times . . . yet never once have dreamed that Tom had any interest in any act or mystery of his. Tom might have done the like by him, of course. But the same private man out of all the men alive, was in the mind of each at the same moment; was prominently connected, though in a different manner, with the day's adventures of both; and formed, when they passed each other in the street, the one absorbing topic of their thoughts. (661–62)

This topic, of course, is Jonas. As in so many aspects of urban life, the web of connections is curiously ambiguous, binding each actor in the huge melodrama to each other actor but not necessarily for the purposes of community. In fact, no one of this trio—Tom, Nadgett, Jonas—would have been anything but dismayed to discover how they are bound, one to another. The point seems to be that the *life* of the city, where each person pursues his or her cares—an individualism that can be seen as naked and aggressive existence—is at once the dynamic product of these aggregated individuals and, as a general mode of being, as experience and ideology, also feeds back into the individual life, so that each person participates in and draws on each other individual, not for the purposes of community but for good or for bad. As a narrative form surveillance is hugely informed and informative—but lacks a moral.

The book's intensely observed locations reinforce this point. While Todgers's is the outstanding instance of Dickens's depiction of the city, of the heart of the labyrinth of London, which is to say the heart of Dickens's world,[18] it has nonetheless received undue attention. There are other significant locales in the book, especially Eden and Fountain Court. In the following passage the emigrants Young Martin and Mark Tapley, after a pause on the outskirts of Western American civilization, finally are approaching Eden, the place where Martin expects to make his fortune:

As they . . . came more and more towards their journey's end, the monotonous desolation of the scene increased. . . . A flat morass, bestrewn with fallen timber; a marsh on which the good growth of the earth seemed to have been wrecked and cast away, that from its decomposing ashes vile and ugly things might rise; where the very trees took the aspect of huge weeds, begotten of the slime from which they sprung, by the hot sun that burnt them up; where fatal maladies, seeking whom they might infect, came forth at night in misty shapes. . . .

At last they stopped. At Eden too. The waters of the Deluge might have left it but a week before: so choked with slime and matted growth was the hideous swamp which bore that name. (442)

The view from Todgers's seems, at first glance, an unnecessary "element" in the novel, extraneous to the aims announced in the novel's opening chapter. Unlike most of Dickens's openings, which pull us immediately, dramatically, into the action, the opening of *Martin Chuzzlewit* is a long, ironic genealogy of the Chuzzlewits, who by dint of "their ancient birth [have had] a pretty large share in the foundation and increase of the human family [and indeed] have still many counterparts and prototypes in the Great World about us" (56). The novel's title plays with this conceit: does the title refer to Old or Young Martin? If we read the novel following the lead of its title and its opening, the purpose of the story is to catch the human family at a moment of portentous transition, the genetic inheritance of horrible Chuzzlewitian self-centeredness about to be dispersed throughout the continents, or anyway from Europe to America, unless the new generation, in the person of Young Martin, can find within itself a way to save the race. It is, throughout, a very close thing, not least because Young Martin is a papier maché hero. What Dickens shows us of the Chuzzlewits is a diverse family unified, up to if not beyond the last moment, by all varieties of voracious self-interest. Can anything save this bunch?

The novel's way of answering this question is one part of Dickens's attempt to grapple with the impact of his American journey. He anticipated finding in the U.S. a new departure, a kind of refutation of the premises that, in his eyes, were the foundation for practices, attitudes, valuations he detested in England. He found instead the very things he hated taken to extremes that horrified him.[19] Hoping to find in the U.S. new sources of vitality for his fiction, he found instead of narrative possibilities only endless verbiage. Consequently Dickens wants his readers to see where England might find itself—in the dystopia he, not very subtly, calls Eden—if the system of each against all is not countered. The description of Eden, following closely the description of Cairo in *American Notes*, emphasizes the heart-of-darkness quality of the place. This is as far from civilization as you're likely to get: but the real distance here is not between the new world and the old but rather between the world before time and history.

Here again is the primordial slime that revolted Dickens when he actually traveled the Mississippi; but in this passage he once more associates the slime of Eden with the Deluge, using almost verbatim the words he used to describe not the Mississippi or Cairo but the mud of the newly-minted Lowell, Massachusetts. The real contrast is between Lowell or its representations in the novel and Todgers's, that is, between the brand new American city, built, as it were, in a flash on the slime left by the Deluge, and hence a city without history; and the vital center of a labyrinth of human purposes accumulated over such a great stretch of time as to be impenetrable, immured by its long chain of associations between past and present, and available for discovery only to the sympathetic observing eye of the novelist. Steven Marcus has superbly captured *this* Todgers's:

> Congested, shabby, haphazard, impenetrable, irrational, and withal utterly hu-
> manized, the visible and palpable presence of a complex civilization and its
> history, eccentric, elaborate, thick, various, outlandish, absurd, Todgers's . . . -
> very chaos is human, inundated by the past, and reeking of mortality.   (257)

But if *this* Todgers's is a fitting antithesis to Eden, what about the other one,
the one Dorothy Van Ghent so persuasively explicates?

Before answering this question, let me bring in Fountain Court, which
stands in the same relation to the Temple as Todgers's does to the Monument.
After each day's work Tom has arranged with his sister that he

> should always come out of the Temple . . . past the fountain. Coming through
> Fountain Court, he was just to glance down the steps leading into Garden Court,
> and to look once all round him; and if Ruth had come to meet him, there he
> would see her. . . .
>
> Whether there was life enough left in the slow vegetation of Fountain Court
> for the smoky shrubs to have any consciousness of the brightest and purest-
> hearted little woman in the world, is a question for gardeners. . . . But, that it
> was a good thing for that same paved yard to have such a delicate little figure
> flitting through it; that it passed like a smile from the grimy old houses . . . there
> is no sort of doubt. The Temple fountain might have leaped up twenty feet to
> greet the spring of hopeful maidenhood . . . the chirping sparrows . . . might
> have held their peace . . . as so fresh a little creature passed . . . old love letters,
> shut up in iron boxes in the neighbouring offices . . . might have stirred and
> fluttered with a moment's recollection of their ancient tenderness, as she went
> lightly by. Anything might have happened that did not happen, and never will,
> for the love of Ruth.
>
> Something happened, too. . . . Why, the fact is, that Mr Westlock was passing
> at that moment.   (762–63)

Todgers's lies at the center of a labyrinth that no stranger can penetrate; at
Todgers's the houses and their objects lord it over the people; at Todgers's
urbanity is so begrimed with time that it seems nothing could grow there;
that no light could penetrate there; and no human action make any impact
there. But Fountain Court has at its center a fountain; its vegetation may be
"slow" and "smoky" but it lives; and most important Ruth is not only more
potent than the "grimy old houses, and the worn flagstones" but it seems
possible that her power of love will brighten up even the "dry and dusty
channels of the Law." And, as if to force the point home, whom should she,
accidentally, run into just there at Fountain Court but John Westlock, the
book's only altogether sane, competent, and effective person, and so naturally
the perfect mate for such a delicate, pure-hearted little woman? Whatever we
may think about the gross sentimentality of this passage, it clearly serves to
advance both plot and theme. But insofar as it does so, it depicts a city
significantly different from, and significantly more hopeful than, Todgers's.

These contrasts—between the two kinds of elements in Dickens's narration, between different views both of Todgers's and of the city—are, I think, ultimately about authority, authority in the moral and political sense, and authority in the guise of the authority of the writer.[20] The failures of authority in the novel, for Steven Marcus, mimic the failures of the social and political world. For Marcus what Barbara Hardy calls "the hypocritical and aggressive selfishness of America" ("*MC*" 115) is only the most extreme evidence of a profound modern error, well encapsulated in the slogan laissez-faire. Martin, thinking of what is due to him rather than what he owes others, appropriately, therefore, seeks his fortune in the United States, where a whole nation is being "built," to borrow Dickens's architectural metaphor, on the false foundation of belief in the possibility that human beings can be made anew if only left to their natural self-development. There is no hope that way, in Marcus's view: rather "we must turn back toward society, and somehow undertake to live in it" (255). This sounds right, and may even be right as a general truth, but society in *Martin Chuzzlewit* is grimly unattractive, and no persuasive way of living in it is narrated by Dickens.

The book's opening chapter shows us history as the long unfolding and accumulation over time of human actions and purposes. But the opening also shows that far from being creatures of nineteenth-century laissez-faire, of a modern error, the Chuzzlewits were vile and venal right from the start, aeons ago. In this respect, Dickens as historian resembles Sir Walter Ralegh more than Marx. In the unfinished *The History of the World* (1614), the first such work in English, Ralegh saw the record of human affairs as a revelation of God's will, as providential. From the moment of Creation to the development of English history, Ralegh draws attention to what he views as the underlying divine order unfolding below the chaos and disorder of so much misguided human activity.[21]

This kind of historical authority is what Marcus attributes to Dickens as a writer. "The transaction between Dickens and his reader," Marcus writes, "in respect of what is being experienced, or 'observed,' is an epitome of the relation between author and audience which characterizes the first major phase of the modern novel" (216). He means that the "presence of the novelist—of his disciplined, magisterial sensibility, acting as a kind of deity, freely creating and controlling the experience he imposes on his readers—is as natural and appropriate here [in *Martin Chuzzlewit*] as is his absence in the later James and in Joyce" (217).

The essence of the natural is that we are oblivious to its having been created: it just *is*. Something that is natural *must be* the way it is; the very question whether it could take any other form, or of how it came to be, does not arise. No one was more aware of this than Marx, who spent prodigious energy in his writing trying to unmask the apparently natural features of man-made society. Insofar as the writer mimics God-the-historian, he functions, I believe, like Tolstoy in *Anna Karenina*. Tolstoy's narration is natural, he narrates as "a kind of deity," precisely in that we are *unaware* of him; in *Anna Karenina* we experience the narration as truth. We are lost in the narration, unaware of ourselves as reading and simply immersed in experience.

Gerhard Joseph indicates how different Dickens as narrator is from Tolstoy. Joseph remarks that in reading "the mature Dickens, we seem to experience the thrust toward omniscience . . . [Dickens] would become a kind of god, freely creating and controlling experience . . . [Nevertheless] the later Dickens serves to explode the progressivist myth that totalized vision is either feasible or that its mimicry in the novelist's 'omniscience' would supply the redemptive vantage point above a corrupt society" (20). Joseph concludes that *Martin Chuzzlewit* "prepares for one of the major emphases of the mature Dickens, his disillusioned sense of man's (and the artist's) cognitive limits" (21). To put this slightly differently, I would say that whereas we are unaware of Tolstoy as narrator, deceived into experiencing the narration as truth, we are, in *Martin Chuzzlewit*, supremely aware of Dickens as narrator precisely because of his dispersal among kinds of narration in the novel. From what vantage point should the unsettling reality of the novel be narrated? Where should Dickens stand, in the middle of the labyrinth leading to Todgers's or on the roof? Should he be like the wind or like Nadgett?

To paraphrase Alexander Welsh, Boz as narrator is everyplace in *Martin Chuzzlewit*. Consequently, even Dickens's main effects in the novel can either be contradictory or can appear to be incompletely realized, or both. Chapter 9, "Town and Todgers's," where Todgers's first appears, is a good example. The chapter opens with an account of the neighborhood as a "labyrinth, whereof the mystery was known but to a chosen few" (185). The essence of Todgers's as labyrinth is its historical density—that is, its having been built not on purpose or with a plan but rather haphazardly over time. Everything about Todgers's is very old. "Among the narrow thoroughfares at hand, there lingered, here and there, an ancient doorway of carved oak, from which, of old, the sounds of revelry and feasting often came, but now these mansions, only used for storehouses, were dark and dull . . . " (186). But paradoxically this ancient, apparently abandoned quarter is actually full of life—that is, full of narrative possibilities of the kind Dickens delights in: the "wine-merchants and wholesale dealers in grocery-ware had perfect little towns of their own"; tales of "the queer old taverns . . . would fill a goodly book." The "ancient inhabitants" who frequented these establishments "were much opposed to steam and all new-fangled ways . . . the major part of the company inclined to the belief that virtue went out with hairpowder, and that Old England's greatness had decayed amain with barbers" (187).

Only now do we arrive at Todgers's itself. The neighborhood, insofar as it represents London as a whole, is affectionately portrayed, a locale full of color and colorful old codgers; its essential qualities are all associated with age; the place flourished when England—Old England—was great, and although things sound as if they've gone very badly to seed, the quarter continues to flourish. Up to this point in Dickens's description, this neighborhood, in the heart of the City, betrays no evidence of the City as the business and financial center of the modern world. What we first see of Todgers's itself is also quaint if not archaic, as if the house were no more than a relic of a livelier time and livelier circumstances: "the grand mystery of Todgers's was the cellarage, approachable only by a little back door and a rusty grating: which cellarage within the memory of man had had no connexion with the house . . . and was reported to be full of wealth: though in what shape—whether in silver, brass, or gold, or butts of wine or casks of gunpowder—was a matter of profound uncertainty and supreme indifference to Todgers's, and all its inmates" (187–88). We would not have been surprised to find this cellarage as playing a part in the novel, revealing a hidden stream of the plot. But that's not how the novel develops. Instead, the description of the top of the house begins with the next sentence: if Dickens had moved us inside without ever having inserted the next two paragraphs, Van Ghent's explication of the view from Todgers's could never have been written, and we would have a very different sense of the place altogether.

Dickens's effects in this respect depend on our awareness of ourselves as readers and our awareness of Dickens as writer. We are far from Tolstoy. The dizzying encounter between ancient and contemporary London, between what we can experience in the labyrinth on the ground and what we can see from the housetop, like the contrast between Dickens's realistic characters and his amazing types (say between Westlock and Sairey Gamp), draws us up sharply into the realization that we are reading something made-up; the illusion of actually entering another world ends with a jolt. Far from displaying the narrator-as-deity, *Martin Chuzzlewit*, as I read it, repeatedly undermines or displaces the totalistic authority of the narrator. In all ways, *Martin Chuzzlewit* is a novel in search of or perhaps simply uncertain about authority. And this search, I believe, is at once a reaction to, and best understood in the light of, Dickens's American journey, with its simultaneous impact on Dickens's outlook and on his art.

The world as seen from Todgers's, which shows us not significance but "naked and aggressive existence," is the world as Dickens saw it before ever going to America. His letters from America, *American Notes*, and *Martin Chuzzlewit* show that what he hoped to find in the United States was a different world, a confirmation that people could not only start anew but could get somewhere else. He discovered quickly, already in Lowell, how foolish he had been. What he saw in Lowell was that human society, from its primitive life in the slime following the Deluge right up to the present in

London, the heart of the civilized world, had never taken any other form than naked and aggressive existence. The Chuzzlewits are not made into modern monsters of Self by laissez-faire; laissez-faire is simply the form which naked and aggressive existence, the life of Self, has taken in the modern world Dickens inhabits. The "quaint old guests" of "the queer old taverns" around Todgers's represent what Dickens seems to see as a supplanted standard of authority rooted in "Old England's greatness." Obviously such a view is self-consciously sentimental and anyway doubtful. (What were the Chuzzlewit ancestors up to in Old England?) But still it is the only social standard of authority in a novel otherwise demonstrably anxious about the efficacy of all the sources of authority it can imagine.

The examples in the novel of ways of being that portend death are many, potent, and make for gripping reading. What can contain, never mind overcome Pecksniff, Jonas, and Tigg? Not Tom Pinch or Young Martin, who survive strictly and solely on the provender charitably awarded them by the deus ex machina Old Martin. Moreover, social existence in the novel shows us two faces: a public face masking a whole universe of secrets. Deception is the real currency of the world of *Martin Chuzzlewit*. Over and over, things are not what they seem; worse, almost everyone seems involved in secret machinations. These observations apply obviously to Pecksniff—whose distinctive acts are acts of spying—but even more dramatically to Jonas, Tigg, Sairey Gamp, and, lest we forget, to Old Martin. The world of the novel is a world of schemes, secrets, spying, deception. The characters neatly divide between those who are gullible and guileless and those who are schemers. Old Martin is an uncomfortable exception, because it's essential, if we are to be offered any ray of hope, that the story show us on what, in such a world, we might rely for safety. Old Martin's magical intervention, however, is no solution. Tom, Young Martin, Mary, and Ruth cannot take care of themselves. The one character whom we might credibly count on is John Westlock, and perhaps this explains his otherwise puzzling presence in the novel. Westlock appears at the opening of the novel as the sole figure to see through Pecksniff. His sanity is displayed in the fact that he can assess and judge Pecksniff without bitterness. Then he vanishes from the novel only to reappear after several hundred pages when there's need of someone to take care of business. The plot could easily have been managed without him. But when Westlock is absent the novel drifts ominously: Dickens needs him for ballast. Nevertheless Westlock, without occupation, family, social place, is way too thin a reed to pit against the fully-developed, engrossing malice of Pecksniff, Jonas, and Tigg.

Where does Dickens stand in this world without authority? Nadgett comes once more to mind. More than any other narrative persona he tries on in the novel, Dickens seems best represented as the Nadgett-like ubiquitous observer of the novel, master of surveillance, writing notes to himself, connecting the apparently unrelated personages of his world, uncovering the secret truth, the unseen web of meanings. It's true that Nadgett has, or appears to have, a master; but famously the great spies are in the game for the sake of the game, and are as likely to control their handlers as the other way around. Like Nadgett, then, Dickens is a rapt, amoral observer. His curiosity, and his negative capability, are attracted to every nook and cranny both of the labyrinth leading to and the dizzying world visible from Todgers's. What is exposed in this way can be, as is the case with Nadgett's discoveries, neither altogether moral nor without danger. Characters like Mrs. Gamp foreshadow Bertolt Brecht's "alienated" personages, who never let us forget that we are watching a play even as they rouse us to anger or tears. Similarly, Dorothy Van Ghent's slap at lazy readings of Dickens—"In the *art* [sic] of Dickens . . . there is a great deal of 'inner life' transposed to other forms than that of character'' (27)—also points beyond the nineteenth century to Kafka. The sentimental rendition of the good and guileless in the novel reflects not so much a moral laziness on Dickens's part, then, as that he comes most fully to life, he is most vividly creative, as an observer. From the point of view of the observer, Todgers's incoherent vista necessarily eludes any effort to reduce it by plot or frame into a single or uniform meaning. It would be pointless to draw a single theme from the aggressive vitality of the city.

The authority of the novel in this way resides not in its plot or in its characters but as it were in itself, in its act of narration. As Gerhard Joseph suggests, this is a narration tending to or apparently pulled toward omniscience but in the end, in its multiplicity of views, in its exuberant surveillance, negating the very possibility of omniscience. Dickens tells us that he tried to compose *Martin Chuzzlewit* more carefully than his earlier work. In response to his unsettling American experience he aimed for a new gravity, and a recommitment to literature, through greater control. But in the end the matter of the novel eludes careful composition, and a different kind of literature emerges. This is what Phiz captures in his illustration of the novel's climax, all the characters artfully distributed around the central event, Old Martin with his stick raised, and the volumes of Moliere and Milton literally felling the momentarily cowed Pecksniff. What can overcome Pecksniff, Jonas, Tigg; what can salve the naked and aggressive existence of Dickens's world? Why, Dickens seems to say hopefully, the improvisations of literature can.

NOTES

1. See for example, in chronological order, the introduction by Michael Slater and articles by Gerhard Joseph, John Hildebidle, David Parker, Patricia M. Ard, David

Stevens, and books by Alexander Welsh, Jerome Meckier, Jeremy Tambling, and Efraim Sicher. More generally on Anglo-American travel literature, see Jane Louise Mesick, Max Berger, Christopher Mulvey, James Buzard, and Rupert Christiansen. Full citations in Works Cited.

2. E.g., Barbara Hardy, "The Change of Heart in Dickens," Dorothy Van Ghent, and Steven Marcus.

3. "*Chuzzlewit*," writes Sylvère Monod, as the last book Dickens signed as Boz, "is thus either the last novel of the first period or the earliest of the later novels" (8).

4. Christopher Mulvey offers a number of illuminating remarks about the differences between English and American travelers (9–14) including the comment that the Englishman "often gave the impression that he had crossed the Atlantic to confront his fears; the American often gave the impression that he had crossed the Atlantic to take possession of things long dreamt about" (14). He observes that Dickens's "instinct to compare districts of New York with those of London in 1842 . . . reflected the habit of the English traveler to refer all back to the country that he had left behind him" (161).

5. Little has been published about Bryant in the last twenty years. The most recent biography, by Charles H. Brown, is from 1971, and the best source of information about Bryant as editor is still Allen Nevins's 1922 study of the *Evening Post*. The introductions and apparatus to Bryant's *Letters*, edited by William Cullen Bryant II and Thomas G. Voss, are immensely informative about his life.

6. Dickens's editors note that only the copy of Bryant's poems given Dickens in Boston by Bryant's close friend the elder Richard H. Dana was found in his library at his death (*Letters* 59n2).

7. The letter was signed by, among others, Bulwer, Thomas Campbell, Tennyson, Hood, Leigh Hunt, Sydney Smith, Rogers, Forster (of course), and Carlyle (*Letters* 213n1; Godwin II, 397).

8. Dickens, according to J. A. Sutherland, "had the keenest business mind of all his colleagues" (47).

9. Cf. Bulwer on Byron in the still illuminating and entertaining *England and the English* (266–67).

10. See also the useful etymology of "celebrity" in Marshall (6–7).

11. Steven Marcus believes Dickens's American experience led him to see "through to the deeper social implications of what it meant to be a quasi-heroic figure, a 'celebrity' " (243).

12. Cf. Jeremy Tambling's observation that "*Bleak House* comes ten years after Dickens's visit to the United States, as if not until *Bleak House* can the city which before he thought could be read, be looked at in the decentring terms which align it with the language generated by the sense of America" (19).

13. Seymour Martin Lipset, in his introduction to Martineau's *Society in America*, states that *How To . . .* is "the first book on the methodology of social research in the then still unborn disciplines of sociology and anthropology (*Society in America* 7).

14. Cf. Mulvey: "The American wilderness filled most [English] travelers with a sense of threat and oppression. It contrasted so absolutely with the garden-like appearance of England that so impressed American travelers" (11).

15. "As a young man of radical tendencies," writes Steven Marcus, "Dickens had the most pious preconceptions about America. . . . America seemed the promise of humanity's oldest dream, the world made new again" (241).

16. David Cecil maintains that it was "very rare for a Victorian novelist before George Eliot to conceive the story as an organic whole of which every incident and character forms a contributory and integral part" (5). Gissing, in any event, says that "a novel more shapeless, a story less coherent than *Martin Chuzzlewit*, will not easily be found in any literature" (54), a judgment with which Barbara Hardy, in "The Change of Heart," agrees.

17. Alexander Welsh, who sees a "radical dispersal of Dickens" in *Martin Chuzzlewit* (12), says that "Boz can be discovered almost anywhere in *Martin Chuzzlewit*" (73). He means that Dickens identifies himself with almost all of the novel's characters. I am more interested in his various identities in the novel as narrator.

18. Cf. J. Hillis Miller's observation that, for Dickens, "the concrete embodiment of this totality ['the world'] is the great modern commercial city, made up of millions of people all connected to one another without knowing it, and yet separated from one another and living in isolation and secrecy" (1).

19. David Parker contends that "America excited Dickens' rage because it repeatedly placed before him behavior and attitudes calling up unresolved conflicts in his mind, testing habits of response laden with anxiety . . . For Dickens America was an unflattering glass" (58).

20. Cf. Marcus: "The problem of self in *Martin Chuzzlewit* is synonymous with the problem of authority" (225–26).

21. "Now we have told the success of the trumperies and cruelties of our own kings," Ralegh writes for example, " . . . so we find that God is everywhere the same God. And as it pleased him to punish the usurpation and unnatural cruelty of Henry the First and our third Edward in their children for many generations; so dealt he with the sons of Louis Debonaire, the son of Charles the Great, or Charlemagne" (II, xx). But the see Ralegh's "Preface" and the *History* passim.

WORKS CITED

Ard, Patricia M. "Charles Dickens' Stormy Crossing: The Rhetorical Voyage from Letters to *American Notes*." *Nineteenth Century Prose* 23 (1996): 34–42.

Barnes, James J. *Authors, Publishers, and Politicians: The Quest for an Anglo-American Copyright Agreement 1815–1854*. Columbus: Ohio State UP, 1974.

Berger, Max. *The British Traveller in America, 1836–1860*. 1943. Gloucester, MA: Peter Smith, 1964.

Brown, Charles H. *William Cullen Bryant*. New York: Scribner's, 1971.

Bryant, William Cullen. *Letters of a Traveller. Second Series*. New York, 1859.

————. *The Letters of William Cullen Bryant*. 6 vols. Ed. William Cullen Bryant II and Thomas G. Voss. New York: Fordham UP, 1977.

Bulwer, Edward Lytton. *England and the English*. 1833. Ed. Standish Meacham. Chicago: U of Chicago P, 1970.

Buzard, James. *The Beaten Track: European Tourism, Literature, and the Ways to Culture 1800–1918*. Oxford: Clarendon, 1993.

Cecil, David. Victorian Novelists: Essays in Revaluation. 1935. Chicago: U of Chicago P, 1958.

Christiansen, Rupert. *Victorian Visitors: Culture Shock in Nineteenth-Century Britain*. New York: Atlantic Monthly, 2000.

Dickens, Charles. *American Notes* and *Pictures From Italy*. Oxford: Oxford UP, 1989 [1957].

————. *The Letters of Charles Dickens*, Vol. 3: 1842–1843. Pilgrim Edition. Eds. Madeline House, Graham Sorey, and Kathleen Tillotson. Oxford: Clarendon, 1974.

————. *Martin Chuzzlewit*. Ed. P. N. Furbank. Harmondsworth: Penguin, 1968.

Forster, John. *The Life of Charles Dickens*. 2 vols. London: J. M. Dent, 1966 [1927].

Gissing, George. *Charles Dickens: A Critical Study*. London: Gresham, 1903.

Godwin, Parke. *A Biography of William Cullen Bryant with Extracts from His Private Correspondence*. 2 vols. New York, 1883.

Gross, John, and Gabriel Pearson, eds. *Dickens and the Twentieth Century*. Toronto: U of Toronto P, 1962.

Hardy, Barbara. "The Change of Heart in Dickens' Novels." Price 39–57.

————. *"Martin Chuzzlewit."* Gross and Pearson 107–20.

Hildebidle, John. "Hail Columbia: Martin Chuzzlewit in America." *Dickens Studies Annual* 15 (1986): 41–54.

Houtchens, Lawrence H. "Charles Dickens and International Copyright." *American Literature* 13 (1941): 18–28.

Joseph, Gerhard. "The Labyrinth and the Library: A View from the Temple in *Martin Chuzzlewit. Dickens Studies Annual* 15 (1986): 1–22.

Le Bon, Gustave. *The Crowd: A Study of the Popular Mind*. 1896. New York: Viking, 1960.

Levine, George. *The Realistic Imagination; English Fiction from Frankenstein to Lady Chatterley*. Chicago: U of Chicago P, 1981.

Marcus, Steven. *Dickens from Pickwick to Dombey.* New York: Simon and Schuster, 1965.

Marshall, David. *Celebrity and Power: Fame in Contemporary Culture.* Minneapolis: U of Minnesota P, 1997.

Martineau, Harriet. *How To Observe Morals and Manners.* 1838. Ed. Michael R. Hill New Brunswick, NJ: Transaction, 1989.

————. *Society in America.* 1837. Ed. Seymour Martin Lipset. Garden City, NY: Anchor-Doubleday, 1962.

Meckier, Jerome. *Innocent Abroad: Charles Dickens's American Engagements.* Lexington: UP of Kentucky, 1990.

Mesick, Jane Louise. *The English Traveller in America, 1785–1835.* 1922. Westport, CT: Greenwood, 1950.

Miller, J. Hillis. *Charles Dickens, The World of His Novels.* Cambridge: Harvard UP, 1958.

Monod, Sylvère. *Martin Chuzzlewit.* London: George Allen & Unwin, 1985.

Mulvey, Christopher. *Anglo-American Landscapes; A Study of Nineteenth Century Anglo-American Travel Literature.* London: Cambridge UP, 1983.

Nevins, Allen. *The Evening Post: A Century of Journalism.* 1922. New York: Russell and Russell, 1968.

Parker, David. "Dickens and America: The Unflattering Glass." *Dickens Studies Annual* 15 (1986): 55–64.

Price, Martin, ed. *Dickens: A Collection of Critical Essays.* Englewood Cliffs, NJ: Prentice-Hall, 1967.

Ralegh, Sir Walter. *The History of the World*, Vol. 2 in *The Works of Sir Walter Ralegh, Knight.* 8 vols. Oxford, 1829.

Sargent, Robert B. "Anglo-American Encounter: William Cullen Bryant, Dickens, and Others." *William Cullen Bryant and His America. Centennial Conference Proceedings 1878–1978.* Hoftra University Cultural and Intercultural Studies No. 4. New York: AMS, 1983. 179–94.

Schickel, Richard. *Intimate Strangers: The Culture of Celebrity.* Garden City, NY: Doubleday, 1985.

Sicher, Efraim. *Rereading the City Rereading Dickens: Representation, the Novel, and Urban Realism.* New York: AMS, 2003.

Slater, Michael, ed. *Dickens on America and the Americans.* Austin: U of Texas P, 1978.

St. Clair, William. *The Reading Nation in the Romantic Period.* Cambridge: Cambridge UP, 2004.

Stevens, David. "Dickens in Eden: The Framing of America in *American Notes.*" *Nineteenth Century Prose* 23 (1996): 43–52.

Sutherland, J. A. *Victorian Novelists and Publishers.* Chicago: U of Chicago P, 1976.

Tambling, Jeremy. *Lost in the American City: Dickens, James and Kafka.* New York: Palgrave, 2001.

Tolstoy, Leo. *Anna Karenina.* Intr. Mona Simpson. Eds. Leonard J. Kent and Nina Berberova. Trans. Constance Garnett. New York: Modern Library, 2000.

Van Ghent, Dorothy. "The Dickens World: A View From Todgers's." Price 24–38.

Welsh, Alexander. *From Copyright to Copperfield: The Identity of Dickens.* Cambridge: Harvard UP, 1987.

Dickens's Daniel-Plato Complex:
Dombey and *Bleak House*

Mark M. Hennelly, Jr.

Throughout his canon, Dickens significantly adapts the writing on the wall from Daniel 5, often haunted by Plato's "Allegory of the Cave" wall in The Republic, *to illustrate spectral "truths" requiring the reader's comparable intertextual interpretation. The shared components of what we might call Dickens's Daniel-Plato complex include ghostly script, shadowy walls, delusive lighting, critical interpretations, rewards and punishments, judgments, prophecies, and apocalyptic cataclysms. From* Sartor Resartus *to* Dracula, *Victorian fiction is riddled with hybrid Danielic-Platonic metaphors, but Dickens's novels most consistently appropriate the trope to figure cryptic foreshadowings, enigmatic hermeneutics, and often blurred and ironic interfacings between illusions and realities. The comparative character clusters and plots in* Dombey and Son *and* Bleak House *invoke Dickens's Daniel-Plato complex more creatively than those in any of his other novels. Dickens employs the complex in* Dombey *chiefly to help dramatize and evaluate major characters from Captain Cuttle to Carker, Florence, and Dombey himself, while in* Bleak House *the complex more subtly suggests transpersonal (and overlapping) religious, sociological, political, psychological, and aesthetic possibilities. Ultimately, then, Dickens's Daniel-Plato complex challenges his readers to discover the mysteriously hidden "interpretation thereof" in his fiction.*

Dickens Studies Annual, Volume 39, Copyright © 2008 by AMS Press, Inc. All rights reserved.

[Sissy Jupe is] trying hard to know her humbler
fellow-creatures, and to beautify their lives of
machinery and reality with those imaginative
graces and delights, without which the heart of
infancy will wither up, the sturdiest physical
manhood will be morally stark death, and [as]
the plainest national prosperity figures can show,
will be the Writing on the Wall....
—Charles Dickens, *Hard Times* (313)

I saw in [Miss Havisham's raising Estella to
wreak revenge on men], the distinct shadow of
the darkened and unhealthy house in which her
life was hidden from the sun.... As I looked
round at them, and at the pale gloom they made,
and at the stopped clock, and at the withered
articles of bridal dress upon the table and the
ground, and at her own awful figure with its
ghostly reflection thrown large by the fire upon
the ceiling and the wall, I saw in everything the
construction that my mind had come to, repeated
and thrown back to me.
—Dickens, *Great Expectations* (321)

The gaming/bookkeeping metaphor masking, if not carnivalizing, the last
sentence of fiction Charles Dickens ever wrote carries a hidden agenda: "Before sitting down to [breakfast, Datchery] opens his corner-cupboard door,
takes his bit of chalk from its shelf; adds one thick line to the score, extending
from the top of the cupboard-door to the bottom; and then falls to with an
appetite." The inscrutable Datchery identifies such curious marking, a repeated trope in Dickens, as "the old tavern way of keeping scores. Illegible
except to the scorer. The scorer not committed, the scored debited with what
is against him," namely, the customer's mounting bar bill owed to the tavern
(score) keeper (*The Mystery of Edwin Drood* 272, 270).[1]

Princess Puffer has just fingered John Jasper as both an addicted opium
dreamer, to whom the "real ... seems unreal" (261), and probably the last
person to see Drood alive. Consequently, the interpreting Datchery finds the
sacrilegious choirmaster wanting when he tallies the "score" of the evidence—which remains "illegible" to everyone else—branding Jasper as the
murderer of Edwin. Less apparently, Dickens's final words become an en-
crypted death sentence which caps his lifelong habit of adapting the wall
writing from Daniel 5, often haunted by Plato's "Allegory of the Cave"
wall in *The Republic*, to illustrate spectral "truths" requiring comparable
intertextual interpretation. In *Drood*, the shady truth of what we might call
Dickens's Daniel-Plato complex (an allusive cluster of motifs and a more
personally elusive constellation of spectral/psychological affects) forecasts

that the days of Jasper's kingdom are numbered and his darkly deluded crime will soon see the true light of solar day and be divinely, or at least authorially, punished.

To be sure, past scholarship has recognized the general heuristic value of "writing" in Dickens's fiction. Murray Baumgarten, for example, stresses Dickens's "self-conscious concern to map the social and psychological consequences of writing" (69), while Monique Morgan emphasizes that "writing and crime overlap" in Dickens, and "Forgery creates the closest possible link between writing and crime; it is a case when writing itself *is* a crime" (92). More generally, Daniel Hack has recently indicated that "Dickens's novels are filled with references to the presence, creation, appearance, physical features, and sheer tangibility of marked, written, printed and inscribed surfaces and objects" (*Material Interests* 37). Various readers have even noted the separate significance of Danielic and Platonic tropes in particular novels.[2] For instance, Michael Ragussis mentions Krook's scriptural "writing on the wall" (264) in *Bleak House* (see fig. 1); and Elaine Showalter argues that "Mrs. Clennam's house" in *Little Dorrit* "is modeled more on Plato's Cave than any London Terrace: its reality is only the exaggerated projection of her own darkness" (28). But past studies have not linked these two traditions, which creatively inform virtually every Dickens novel. After reviewing Daniel's and Plato's related scenes of wall writing and their impact on Victorian literature, my purpose here is consequently to discuss, in much greater detail, their critical and often ironic reinscriptions in Dickens's novels, particularly *Dombey and Son* and *Bleak House*.

I

The plot of Daniel 5 seems relatively straightforward. Belshazzar, King of Babylon, orders a great feast for the local aristocracy, their wives, and "concubines." Emboldened by wine, he demands that the sacred vessels, which his father Nebuchadnezzar removed from the Jerusalem temple, be utilized at the banquet. The revelers subsequently praise the gods of the different minerals adorning these precious goblets. Suddenly, against the candlelight, appear the shadowy fingers of a hand which writes a mysterious text on the wall: "MENE, MENE, TEKEL, UPHARSIN." Terrified, Belshazzar offers a king's ransom to "the astrologers, the Chaldeans, and the soothsayers" if one can "read this writing, and show me the interpretation thereof," but none meets this hermeneutic challenge. Finally, the queen suggests that Belshazzar ask Daniel, whom Nebuchadnezzar revered as a riddle-solver and dream-interpreter (renaming him Belteshazzar), to decipher the writing on the wall. After condemning Nebuchadnezzar's prideful downfall (humility

Fig. 1. "The Lord Chancellor Copies from Memory," illustrated for *Bleak House*, chapter 5, by Hablot K. Browne.

later restored him) and Belshazzar's sacrilegious arrogance, Daniel interprets the text to signify that the King's reign is over, his conduct has been weighed, measured, and found wanting, and his kingdom will be divided between the Medes and Persians. Belshazzar perishes that very evening, and Daniel is exalted.

Daniel's narrative unfolds like an extended dark conceit, and Dickens's revisions suggest more subtlety and complexity than John Gammie's representative reading: "so deeply has this chapter entered into Western consciousness [that] the expression 'handwriting on the wall' is widely understood to mean 'clear indications that a calamity is about to strike' " (60) or than Robert Anderson's more particular postcolonial interpretation "that arrogance leads to a fall. In this case it is the fall not merely of the man but of the empire" (51).[3] Before exploring Dickens's specific revisions of Daniel, we should note here its (meta-)representation of a spectral synecdoche, or transcendental signifier (the hand *is* God's), which, nevertheless, signifies a crisis in representation and referentiality, a crisis that assumes apocalyptic proportions since, ironically, Belshazzar's feast was a New Year's festival intended to renew, not destroy, Babylon (Collins 243).[4] And so Jacques Derrida's deconstruction of the so-called "transcendental signified" seems telling: "from the moment that one questions the possibility of such a transcendental signified, and that one recognizes that every signified is also in the position of a signifier, the distinction between signified and signifier becomes problematical at its root" (*Positions* 20).

Daniel's allegorical romance typically doubles critical issues and characters: Belshazzar's test of character, the wisemen's test of exegesis; King Belshazaar, Daniel Belteshazzar; polytheism, monotheism; fathers and sons; queens and "concubines"; spectral script, artificial light. And it also features related motifs appropriated by Dickens: profanation of sacred objects ("golden and silver vessels"); the originary spectral hand and finger; enigmatic text; the candlestick and illuminated "plaster of the wall"; critical interpretations and arcane readings; creative word play (*Peres/peres*: *Persians/half-piece*); measuring and weighing; judgments, rewards and punishments; apocalyptic cataclysms; and the nation-(re)building of Babylon.

Plato's "Allegory of the Cave" seems less problematic than Daniel since Socrates' monologue (masquerading as a dialogue) clearly proposes to educate future rulers "to ensure the welfare of the commonwealth as a whole," as a unified, virtuous Republic (234). Dickens suggests as much when he cites Plato's "Republic of the Virtues" in *Great Expectations* (294); and yet his appropriation of Plato's allegory often ironically transforms its "puppet-show" (Plato 228) features into a puzzling shadow-play, "the oldest form of Puppet Theatre" (Blackham xi).[5] Plato describes a "cavernous chamber underground" where prisoners, chained since childhood, watch the spectral shadows of screened figures performing with artificial objects, projected "by the fire-light on the wall of the Cave facing them" (228). As Socrates interprets this shadow-play of apparently floating signifiers and mock metonymies, "such prisoners would recognize as reality nothing but the shadows of those artificial objects" (229). If a prisoner (predictably male) were freed and ascended to the truthful sunlight, his "meaningless illusion" would disappear, and he would "see things in that upper world" (229) as they really are. If "our released prisoner" (230) returned to the darkness, however, to enlighten the remaining blind captives, they would indict his solar claims as sheer madness. Rather, the prisoners, Socrates prophesies, must all be educated empirically about the Sun's a priori, physical and metaphysical truth: "They must be made to climb the ascent to the vision of Goodness, which we called the highest object of knowledge" (233).

In spite of their contrasting representations of "truth," Dickens seems to have realized that many of Plato's motifs almost chiastically double Daniel's (including the motif of doubling itself): blinded analysts, liberated seers; artificial fire, (super)natural sun; infectious darkness, illuminating light; a posteriori, shadowy walls, a priori sunlight; artifacts, realities; interpretations, judgments, and prophecies; punishments, rewards; apocalyptic transformations. And his Daniel-Plato complex characteristically and creatively, if often problematically, integrates their allegories into hybrid parables that sometimes preview Derrida's unmasking of divinely solar signifiers in "White Mythology." Addressing *The Republic* directly, Derrida ironizes the Sun's empowering "truth," noting that "[o]ne looks at it directly on pain of blindness and death," and "every metaphor which implies the sun [and the Son] . . . does not bring clear and certain knowledge" (242, 250). But even Benjamin Jowett's Victorian commentary (1870) emphasized that Plato's solar brilliance may become "a sort of luminous mist or blindness" to "enthusiastic half-educated person[s]" (360). Dickens goes much further in deifying "THE SHADOW" itself as a "Power[ful,]" free-floating signifier prefiguring some imaginative dreamscape. In fact, he considered creating a periodical by that name which would function as a kind of Victorian shadow-show: "the Thing at everybody's elbow, and in everybody's footsteps," "an odd, unsubstantial, whimsical, new thing: a sort of previously un-thought of Power" (Forster 2:78–79). In Dickens, as we will see, walls themselves function like shady characters, often recalling the debate between Theseus and Hippolyta about the Wall character in the play-within-the-play in *A Midsummer Night's Dream*:

> Theseus: The wall, methinks, being sensible, should curse again. . . .
> Hippolyta: This is the silliest stuff that I have ever heard.
> Theseus: The best in this kind are but shadows; and the worst are no worse, if
> imagination amend them.   (V:1,181–2,209–11)

II

Again, my aim here is to explore Dickens's Danielic and Platonic metaphors of "writing" on the wall, but in order to appreciate their often vexing diversity and subtlety, we should first briefly survey other Victorian examples. For instance, while Thomas Carlyle's Editor confides that Teufelsdrökh "doubt[s] God's existence" in *Sartor Resartus*, the "bewildered Wanderer" himself insists on the spiritual promise of his own agnosticism: if some " 'miraculous Handwriting on the wall, convincingly proclaimed to me *This thou shalt do*, with what passionate readiness, . . . would I have done it, had it been leaping into the infernal Fire' " (161–62). In *Daniel Deronda*, George Eliot's Zionist Mordecai prophetically compares Biblical and Victorian Daniels as equally lost children of Israel, diagnosing Deronda's unremembered "remnant of national consciousness" and "heritage of Israel" much as Freud analyzes the mystic writing pad of the unconscious—but with also a problematic nod to Plato: "it is the inborn half of memory, moving as in a dream among writings on the walls, which it sees dimly but cannot divide into speech" (595–96).

When Jekyll awakens as Hyde without benefit of his elixir, Daniel 5 relevantly contextualizes the collapse of his psychic "city of refuge": "this . . . seemed, like the Babylonian finger on the wall, to be spelling out the letters of my judgment" and climax of "my double existence" (Stevenson 92, 88). Bram Stoker pushes the figure to more international, if not apocalyptic, proportions in *Dracula* when Van Helsing ominously prophesies that "our enemy" has escaped back "to his Castle in Transylvania. I know it so well, as if a great hand of fire wrote it on the wall" (405). In *The Return of the Native*, Thomas Hardy characteristically diminishes the divine metaphor when little Johnny Nunsuch invisibly tends Eustacia Vye's November 5th "beacon fire" (though hints of Plato's tragically blind prisoners and Guy Fawkes's scapegoated rebellion simultaneously raise the stakes here): "Close watching would have shown [the spectral movement] to be a small human hand, in the act of lifting pieces of fuel into the fire; but for all that could be seen the hand, like that which troubled Belshazzar, was there alone" (59). In "The Palace of Art," Alfred Lord Tennyson invokes Daniel to indict the artistic soul embowered among Platonic representations regressing from the Real (thus, like Dickens, blurring the distinctions between Daniel and Plato): "When she would think, where'er she turn'd her sigh/The airy hand confusion wrought,/Wrote, 'Mene, mene,' and divided quite/The kingdom of her thought" (lines 225–28). Against these spiritual, politico-racial, psychological, metaphysical, and aesthetic contexts, stands the period's most memorable example, Charlotte Brontë's "Biographical Notice" of her sister Emily, which stresses critical reading while mocking contemporary interpretations of *Wuthering Heights* and anticipating a more visionary Victorian Daniel: "reviewers remind us of the mob of Astrologers, Chaldeans, and Soothsayers gathered before the 'writing on the wall,' and unable to read the characters or make known the interpretation. We have a right to rejoice when a true seer comes at last . . . who can accurately read the 'Mene, Mene, Tekel, Upharsin' of an original mind'' (xxiii).

III

We might now ask why Dickens uses Daniel and Plato more frequently, more variously, and more creatively than any of these writers? Like Daniel, Plato, and any Victorian author, Dickens is a writer whose scripted pages often offer enigmatic texts for reader interpretation. Unlike the other writers (with the exception of Eliot with *Daniel Deronda*), though, Dickens sometimes employs characters named *Daniel* to connote the scriptural double. I have elsewhere suggested that Daniel Doyce, the imaginative inventor in *Little Dorrit*, "resembles his Biblical namesake in abjuring the value of wealth 'like an amused spectator at cards' and thereby imitating 'the Divine artificer' '' (Hennelly 204), while Dan Peggotty's Noah's-ark boathouse in *David Copperfield* even features a fantastically "coloured picture" of "Daniel in yellow cast into a den of green lions" (79), which implies a redemptive rather than revengeful Danielic context.[6] Furthermore, David's own struggles with "the noble art and mystery of stenography," particularly that "procession of . . . horrors, called arbitrary characters; the most despotic characters [David has] ever known" (608–09), recall Dickens's struggles as a young Parliamentary reporter (before reputedly becoming the most accomplished stenographer in England). Dickens's word play with "arbitrary characters" also recalls Daniel's autobiographical and punning account of the cryptic writing on the wall (with his own self-division into narrator and character, scorer and scored) and its arguably "arbitrary" and "despotic characters." Dickens's traumatic sojourn at Warren's Blacking Factory (while his family resided at Marshalsea debtor's prison) likewise suggests Daniel because of its literal context of inky or shady staining and its projected context of stigmatizing crime and punishment. Sun-dialing, Platonic wall shadows invariably recur in Dickens's prison novels like *Little Dorrit*, where prisoners mark (profane) time, while Warren's often reappears in Danielic contexts in Dickens's fiction. In *Bleak House*, for instance, "blacking bottles" accompany various "inscriptions" lining Krook's window—notably Esther's mysterious father Nemo's advertisement for legal copying, which juridically contextualizes her own "crime" of illegitimacy and its punishment (67–68), besides suggesting the problematics of absolutely tracing any "copy" to some alleged and mysteriously affiliated original, whether Nemo, Daniel, or Plato.

Dickens's recurring nightmare, "when I am in a strange country and want to read important notices on the walls and buildings, but they are all in an unknown character" (Ackroyd 676), also reprises the "unknown character[s]" in Daniel. It further adds autobiographical significance to illiterate Jo's existential alienation in *Bleak House*—more projected crime and punishment—as the marginalized crossing sweeper "shuffle[s] through the streets, unfamiliar with the shapes, and in utter darkness as to the meaning, of those mysterious symbols, so abundant over the shops, . . . and in the windows" (257). A nightmare from Dickens's childhood (reappearing in *The Pickwick Papers* and *Nicholas Nickleby*) conjures "a figure that [Dickens] once saw, just after dark, chalked upon a door in a little black lane," an "oppressive" form with a monstrous "Amouth" and "goggle eyes," which haunts his dreams as it nightly chases him home ("Lying Awake" 433–34). Arguably self-parodic (note the possible pun on *Lying*), this diabolic image is still in keeping with both uncanny, return-of-the-repressed implications in Daniel and the shadowy borders between truth and delusion in Plato and so again autobiographically broadens and deepens Dickens's imaginative integrations of the two texts.

Moving to Dickens's novels, we see that even when Daniel explicitly appears in the "Final" chapter of *Hard Times* (cited above), Dickens ironizes the "national prosperity figures" tabulated in Victorian blue books and links Britain's possible downfall with Babylon's since without "imaginative graces and delights," the "heart of infancy will wither up, the sturdiest manhood will be morally dark, and the plainest national prosperity figures . . . will be the Writing on the Wall" (313). "Morally dark" may well imply Platonic delusions; on the other hand, the cherished "heart of infancy," punningly rooted in fancy, suggests that the fanciful heart has darkly imaginative "reasons," which enlightened reason knows not of. Sometimes Dickens clearly and critically displaces wall writing to somatic script (or some other marked facade), for instance, in representing Rosa Dartle's fury against Steerforth in *David Copperfield* when her scar, from his childhood blow, blazons "forth like the old writing on the wall" (353), thus illustrating Derrida's query, "is not a mark, wherever it is produced, the possibility of writing?" (*Of Grammatology* 302). This prophetic script prefigures both Rosa's judgmental, if not apocalyptic, tirade against little Emily and even Esther's later smallpox scars as alleged judgment against her illegitimacy. In fact, it not only authorizes Rosa's Danielic judgment of Steerforth's imperious class arrogance (like Belshazzar's) and her own hegemonic hostility against his "concubine" Emily's sexual impropriety, but mixing the sacred and profane in a bitterly carnivalesque reversal, it may even suggestively displace Steerforth's assault on his scorned lover's "upper" lip to its lower-body equivalent. In any case, it generally illustrates Derrida's contention that "What writing itself, in its non phonetic moment, betrays, is life" (*Of Grammatology* 25). But more specifically, it suggests textual criteria for treating different kinds of "mural" marking as part of Dickens's Daniel-Plato complex—that is, as long as their thematic context and resonance include several of the shared motifs listed earlier: especially crime, punishment, and imprisonment; catastrophic fore-shadowing or finger-pointing; critical hermeneutics; and (often blurred, ironic, or parodic) interfacing between shadowy delusions and bright realities. Some examples are clearly more obvious than others, which only merit inclusion by their metonymic associations. Nevertheless, tangentially related instances of mural writing, like the "shape of the letters" and "turn of the inscription" (35) on Pip's parents' tombstones, must be disqualified *not*, as we will see, because they could possibly be horizontal rather than vertical (though surely they are vertical), but because the motifs shared by Daniel and Plato are simply not present beyond the general context of criminality.

Other examples of Dickens's Daniel-Plato complex include the fallen wall brick's "strange and curious inscription of unquestionable antiquity" which sunny Pickwick "scientifically" glorifies and the interpretation of which provokes the "Pickwick controversy" (*The Pickwick Papers* 217, 229). This rum rune is later debunked, which might suggest that Pickwick is no Daniel and that Platonic "truth" must always be deconstructed. Still, after Pick-wick's deluded descent into Fleet Prison, recalling Plato's Cave, Dickens ultimately proclaims that "There are dark shadows on the earth, but its lights are stronger in the contrast." Consequently, "the brief sunshine of the world should be treasured" (896)—*not* because it is Platonically truthful but be-cause it nurtures mutual friends like the Pickwickians. The initially fallen, if not disgraced wall writing thus becomes "an illegible monument of Mr Pick-wick's greatness" (229). The uncanny "kind of allegory" of old curiosities or Awild grotesque companions" (56) haunting the wall behind sleeping beauty Nell in *The Old Curiosity Shop*, on the other hand, foreshadows Nell's tormenting mentor Quilp as well as her fairy tale's transformation into a (per)version of "Beauty and the Beast." Revolving Dick Swiveller finally reverses this transformation when he awakens the Marchioness, his sleeping beauty, from her cellar cavern and leads her to the light of true love. The walls stained with Nancy's blood after Sikes bludgeons her and "stains" himself in *Oliver Twist* advertise his crime and foretell his punishment, espe-cially when the "radiant glory" of "the bright sun" reveals the "reflection of the pool of gore that quivered and danced in the sunlight on the ceiling" (426, 423). Similarly, the sacrilegious "tall joker" apocalyptically prophesies revolution as revelation in *A Tale of Two Cities* when he "scrawl[s] upon a wall with his finger dipped in muddy wine-lees—BLOOD'' (61), which also prefigures the revelation of Dr. Manette's blood-written note in the Bastille chimney wall, incriminating Darnay and ultimately implicating Carton as vicarious redeemer. In *Little Dorrit*, Clennam's birth mother "haunts [his former] house'' and "marks the walls with long crooked touches'' (854), which suggest both his benighted, false mother's Platonic deceptions as well as Danielic retribution against those deceptions. Finally, when John Harmon reads a darkened wall poster "describ[ing] myself, John Harmon, as found dead and mutilated in the river under circumstances of strong suspicion'' (365) in *Our Mutual Friend*, the reader knows the writing on the wall is apocryphal. At the same time, though, Harmon is actually leading a delusive life, and he must be reborn and bring his true identity to light so that he can more genuinely love, and be loved by, the enlightened Bella.

Since most of these examples begin, at least, with Danielic implications, an extended Platonic instance from *Great Expectations*, cited partially above, may serve to balance them. Again, we should note that Dickens explicitly cites Plato's "Republic of the Virtues'' (294) in this novel. When Pip and Estella visit Miss Havisham, self-imprisoned at Satis House, they discover "the intensity of a mind morally hurt and diseased'' evident in the Platonic "shadow of the darkened and unhealthy house in which her life was hidden from the sun.'' And this solar truth could enlighten the delusive, "withered articles of [her] bridal dress'' and other artificial objects. Although Miss Havisham projects "an awful figure with its ghostly reflection thrown large by the fire upon the ceiling and wall,'' the Cave-wall implications here deepen Pip's insight that his great expectations share her delusions since he "saw'' the false "construction that [his own] mind had come to, repeated and thrown back to [him].'' It only remains for Estella's application of Plato (and echo of Socrates' argument about the difficult transition from shadow to light) to drive home the uncanny solar truth behind Miss Havisham's eclipsing self-deceptions: "If you had brought up your adopted daughter wholly in the dark confinement of these rooms, and had never let her know that there was such a thing as the daylight. . . , and then, for a purpose had wanted her to understand the daylight and know all about it, you would have been disappointed and angry'' (320–21, 324). Still, like Dickens's Roman "Allegory'' in *Bleak House*, his adaptation of Plato's Cave "Allegory'' here does not produce absolute clarity (any more than do his often ironic adaptations of Daniel 5), but it does create an intriguing spectrum of possible and problematic interpretations.

It is *Dombey and Son* and *Bleak House*, however, that most creatively capture the nuances of Dickens's Daniel-Plato complex. And this may have something to do with the ways *Dombey*'s dreamy fabulist plot of retribution and redemption seems compulsively repeated but rendered more "symbolically real'' in *Bleak House*.[7] Dickens uncannily matches the ingenues Florence and Esther, masked ''mothers'' Edith and Lady Dedlock (with their memorably matched, multiple-mirrored boudoirs), their self-divided, lower-class shadows Alice Marwood and Hortense, repatriated lovers Walter and Woodcourt, benevolently avuncular Captain Cuttle and John Jarndyce, arrogantly patriarchal but finally redeemed Dombey and Sir Leicester, and villainous Carker and Tulkinghorn as jealous foils. Even Edith's mother Mrs. Skewton with her ''peach-velvet bonnet'' and ''charming manner'' of ''leering and mincing at Death'' (612, 614) appears reincarnated in the antique, aristocratic matrons surrounding Lady Dedlock: ''peachy-cheeked charmers with the skeleton throats . . . reduced to flirting with grim Death, after losing all their other beaux'' (928). Further, *Dombey*'s chapters alternating between the personable Florence and her impersonal father seem doubled by *Bleak House*'s alternating personal and impersonal narrators. Most importantly, though, these two texts present more significant overlappings and more subtle explorations of the Daniel-Plato complex than any other of Dickens's novels.

Although *Dombey* may appear more Platonic and *Bleak House* more Danielic, two crucially common motifs link both novels and further extend the boundaries of the Daniel-Plato complex to horizontal (besides vertical) facades. First, Dickens often implies the haunting power of Daniel 5 by creating a kind of New Testament/Old Testament palimpsest with Daniel lurking beneath John 8:1–11's account of Jesus' finger writing in the dust, signifying that only ''He that is without sin'' may cast the first stone at an adulteress. Dombey likewise ''trac[es] figures in the dust with his stick,'' while mentally staging a theomachia between the self-projected, enlightening ''angel'' Florence and the delusively demonic ''spirit crouching in his bosom'' (356) personified by Carker. Ironically, Jehovah's Old Testament avenging finger would prove more judgmental against female sexuality than Jesus' New Testament merciful finger in measuring Dombey, destroying his Counting House, and ultimately converting him through redemptive love. In much the same way, Miss Rachel's cautionary verses in *Bleak House* prove more judgmental against illegitimate Esther than Esther's own merciful ''reading, from St. John, how our Saviour stooped down, writing with his finger in the dust, when they brought the sinful woman to him'' (32), though Dickensian irony brands the judging Rachel as the actual ''sinful woman.'' And Dickens's *The Life of Our Lord*, written for his children at the same time he was writing *Dombey*, documents his commitment to ''the teachings of our great Master. . . . All my strongest illustrations are derived from the New Testament'' (Ackroyd 504).

Secondly, both novels make significant use of writing under erasure (*sous rature*). The ''creeping track of [Rob's] hand upon the table'' momentously chalks ''D.I.J.O.N.'' and then quickly ''obliterate[s] the word. . . , rubbing and planing all trace of it away with his coat-sleeve'' (832) in *Dombey*, while

Krook similarly rubs out letters as he chalks ''the word JARNDYCE, without once leaving two letters on the wall together'' and then, repeating the process, ''rubbed out singly, the letters forming the words BLEAK HOUSE'' (76). Rob's literal motive is his fear of ''criminal'' punishment if Carker discovers that the pathetic Grinder has revealed the location of his tryst with Edith, while Krook's motives are twofold: pride in posturing to imitate, scripturally, his delusions of becoming the Lord Chancellor; and avarice in serially destroying evidence that could dispossess him of any rewards from such delusions of grandeur. Rob's Platonic pretense of absence may prevent the discovery of his original act, but it predestines Carker's Danielic fate at the hands of the railway's avenging angel. Krook tries to have it both ways: present pride of achievement, absent any evidence that might rob him of future benefits. In other words, he resembles Plato's prisoners in confusing signifiers with signifieds, while he also approximates Daniel's Belshazzar in sacrilegiously imitating the Lord (Chancellor) and coveting his possessions. Finally, Rob's erased script is still accessibly recorded in the conscious memory of Dombey, who (melo)dramatically eavesdrops and acts upon the first scene of writing; Krook's erased lettering, prefiguratively, is also memorialized somewhere in the mystic writing pad of narrating Esther's psyche (not to mention her readers'). And, whether remembered or not, the critical evidence which settles the ''JARNDYCE'' case—less with an apocalyptic bang than with Richard's whimper—*is* ultimately found buried in Krook's papers.

IV

In pursuing Dickens's Daniel-Plato complex in *Dombey*, one needs to imitate neither Rob's ''Grinders' School'' approach to ''the tribes of Judah'' and proceed ''by the monotonous repetition of hard [scripture] verses,'' nor Captain Cuttle's analysis of the ''Divine Sermon'' on ''a Mount'' and ''write any number of fierce theological disquisitions on its every phrase'' (629). Rather, one should specify more precisely the ''process of marking and wiping of marks'' that Michal Peled Ginsburg notes in the novel (62). In fact, the clearest way to appreciate the Daniel-Plato complex in *Dombey* is to see how it evaluates major characters like those complementary nautical companions Solomon Gills and Captain Cuttle, who sometimes seem the serious and comic faces of the same avuncular figure presiding over the Midshipman. ''Sol'' graces his instrument shop with ''[o]ld prints of ships with alphabetical references to their various mysteries, hung in frames upon the walls'' (89); and his enacted solar truth and nominal scriptural wisdom preview his nephew Walter's mysterious and monumental disappearance at sea. When Captain Cuttle identifies with the instruments waiting to be ''weighed, measured''

(98), he plays a more comic Belshazzar—and his wavering faith in Walter's return supports this interpretation. Nonetheless, the good Captain prophetically deciphers the ballad of "lovely Peg," which had "a profound metaphysical bearing on the case of Walter and Florence" and "had long fluttered among many others . . . on a dead wall" (172). Later, Cuttle's correct interpretation of this mural writing and renewed faith in Walter are appropriately rewarded (with Florence as astonished witness and H. K. Browne's Platonic plate "The Shadow in the Little Parlour" [fig. 2] as ironic proof of the actual link between delusive shadows and documented realities and the fact that some dreams do come true):

> "Yes," roared the Captain. "Steady, darling! courage! Don't look round yet. See there! upon the wall!"
> There was the shadow of a man upon the wall close to her. She started up, looked round, and with a piercing cry, saw Walter Gay behind her! (784–85).[8]

In a darker, nightmarish sense, Dickens's Daniel-Plato complex further contextualizes the comparable characters of those decidedly not-good-enough-mothers Mrs. Brown and Mrs. Skewton. In the chapter titled "Another Mother and Daughter," the "figure of Good Mrs Brown," Alice's mother, appears as a shadowy "gigantic and distorted image of herself thrown half upon the wall behind her." And the narrator playfully wonders whether, if Florence observed "the original of the shadow thrown upon the wall," her memory of her childhood abductor would realize that this "terrible old woman was as grotesque and exaggerated a presentment of the truth, perhaps, as the shadow on the wall" (566–67). Dickens's "perhaps" again deconstructs Plato's "truth" since Mrs. Brown's actual terror seems no less "exaggerated" than her authentically ominous shadow on the wall.[9] Similarly, the "black hatchments of pictures blotching the walls" (509) of Mrs. Skewton's house in Grosvenor Square, borrowed from wealthy Cousin Feenix "for nuptial purposes" (504), foreshadow the criminal and punitive results of her daughter Edith's marriage to Dombey—which mercenary Mrs. Skewton has contrived. Nicknamed Cleopatra, match-making Mrs. Skewton, like Mrs. Brown, plays more procuring courtesan than queen. And the somatic writing of her glaring cosmetic artifice, her inside scripted outside her outside, prophecies her own deluded death as truly as the sun's Platonic judgment: "Such is the figure, painted and patched for the sun to mock" as she awaits the imagined "stone arm—part of a figure of some tomb, [which] she says—is raised to strike her" dead (673).

Short-lived little Paul most memorably establishes Dickens's Daniel-Plato complex as he grows "intimate with all the paperhanging" at Doctor Blimber's and "saw things that no one else saw in the patterns" on the wall. Paul's

Fig. 2. ''The Shadow in the Little Parlour,'' illustrated for *Dombey and Son*, chapter 49, by Hablot K. Browne.

visions of "miniature lions and tigers" (234) appear innocently illusory but, in fact, become companionable forms after Paul adapts to the scholastic realities at Blimber's academy: "the lions and tigers climbing up the bedroom walls became quite tame and frolicsome" (251). When Paul falls ill, however, the wall writing grows more poignant, and the increasing shadows more profoundly prophetic: "When the sunbeams struck into his room through the rustling blinds, and quivered on the opposite wall like golden water, he knew that evening was coming on, and that the sky was red and beautiful. As the reflection died away, and a gloom went creeping up the wall, he watched it deepen, deepen, deepen, into night" (292).

Again, it would create a false binary to typecast Dickens's wall writing here as essentially either Danielic or Platonic, since the context creatively dovetails the two traditions and thereby de-authorizes both a strict Christian and a strictly Platonic reading. The "sunbeams" create clear "reflection[s]," not shadows, of their celestial source, though these transform into an eclipsing "gloom" which "deepen[s] into night." As in Daniel, the spectral writing prefigures death; as in Plato, it foreshadows solar virtues and verities; as in neither, it may even illuminate the eternal cycle between sun and shade, if not little Paul's redemptive return from terrestrial shadow lands to his heavenly origin. In this sense, and refuting Plato's disparagement of poetry as delusion (and Dombey's delusion that "gold," one of Plato's "artificial objects," is the only real truth), Dickens's "golden water" simile becomes a kind of Keatsian truth when beautifully mysterious, mural seascapes replace solar script: "How many times the golden water danced upon the wall; how many nights the dark, dark river rolled towards the sea . . . Paul never counted, never sought to know" (295). During this spectral process, Paul even significantly wonders "whether that had been his father in the room, or only a tall shadow on the wall" (275), which itself adumbrates Dombey's own growing "spectralization" and suicidal night thoughts as he stands in the bright shadow of his son.

Dombey, however, is ultimately humanized; his shady double Carker is not. Carker's only truth is falsity; his "affectation of humility" appears "as false as the face of the too truly painted portrait hanging" on his wall, "or its original at breakfast in his easy chair below it" (554). Consequently, "the shadow of their guilty brother" Carker haunts Harriet and John's house like a "wraith" as it "flitted about in frightful shapes" and conjured "shadowy terrors" in their living room (845). It is only poetic, or better, Platonic justice that a "shadowy postillion" carries delusive Carker to his predestined doom as enlightening "[s]hadows of familiar people, . . . strange apparitions of [Dombey,] the man he was flying from, or of Edith" (865) haunt his last ride.

Edith often seems self-stigmatized by a false face like the painted one that graces Carker's wall. Whether Juno, Potiphar's adulterous wife (Genesis 29),

Judith about to slay Holofernes (Apocrypha), or "some scornful Nymph" (554), this wall-hanging figuratively suggests Edith's dark double, her fallen cousin Alice Marwood, whom Carker has ruined as he attempts to ruin her. When shamed, though, Edith genuinely "flushe[s] indignant scarlet" (467). The night before her wedding, she even self-consciously brands her body with scarlet script as "her broad white bosom [blazes] red with the cruel grasp of the relentless hand with which she spurned it from her[self]" (515), and later her "white limb [also] showed a bar of red" (653) from her violently rubbing it with Dombey's bracelet gift. Both brands herald the bar sinister of her legalized prostitution and conjugal bondage. When the "sun is shining down, upon the golden letters of the ten commandments" on Edith's wedding day, the narrator queries, "which is it that appears to leave the wall, and print itself, in glowing letters, on her [prayer] book"—"False Gods; murder; theft: the honour that she owes her mother"? (523–24). Edith may yet be guilty of all these trespasses, but the scarlet letter of adultery (which she never actually commits) seems to be the missing "interpretation thereof" here.

When their marriage finally dissipates into looking-glass distortions, Dickens's Daniel-Plato allusions turn even more spectral as both partners grow increasingly "reflective" and apart: Dombey appears more abstract and Edith more absent as she takes no more "heed of him, in the mirror, than if he had been an unseen spider or the wall" (657). When Carker kisses her hand, Edith, "with a flush upon her cheek," again obsessively indulges in self-punishing somatic writing, striking it on the "chimney-shelf" so that "it was bruised, and bled." Then, like Plato's prisoners, she sits alone by a "sinking" fire and watches "the murky shadows looming on the wall. . . . Whatever shapes of outrage and affront, and black foreshadowings of things that might happen, flickered, indistinct and giant-like, before her, one resented figure marshalled them against her. And that figure was her husband" (692–93). Here the "sinking" fire reflects Edith's dwindling delusions of possible happiness, while the "black foreshadowings" conversely forecast apocalyptic retribution, perhaps even the "giant-like" train which crushes Carker. Another "giant-like" or ironically "god-like" apparition is "her husband" Dombey, who again seems more spectral "figure" than fact, and whose crime of self-idolatry, like Belshazzar's, will soon also be punished.

Dombey is himself haunted by undeciphered, often mural figures—"those two figures clasped in each other's arms" and the "imperfect shapes of meaning with which [his represented wife and daughter] were fraught" (83). The obstacle to his interpreting these figures and his own "imperfect" feelings about them is his pride, which again rivals Belshazzar's. Ordering Paul's memorial mural, he also plays Danielic deity: "Mr Dombey intimates where he would have it placed; and shows [the designer], with his hand upon the wall, the shape and size. . . . Then, with his pencil, he writes out the inscription, . . . adding, 'I wish to have it done at once' " (312). When he abandons

Florence in the Dombey mansion while traveling, the mansion (resembling the inner man) also appears like Plato's Cave with "wronged innocence imprisoned": "a monstrous fantasy of rusty iron"; a "Gorgon-like" visage; graffiti chalked on the exterior walls; "[d]amp started on the [interior] walls"; and all "seemed to say, 'Who enter here, leave light behind!' " (393–94). After he loses his son and his marriage (not to mention Florence), Dombey, the empire-builder, is haunted by that very world he commercially attempted to colonize, if not create: "there are eyes in [the world] map, hanging on the wall" as he tries to "hide the world within him from the world without" (809, 808).[10] Finally, "the staring announcement that the lease of [Paul Dombey's] desirable Family Mansion was to be disposed of" is posted outside the house; and the days of his kingdom seem surely numbered unless this Saul, on his own figurative road to Damascus, can be miraculously converted to Paul.[11] Inside, Dombey again sits self-reflectively before a mural mirror and sees himself literally and figuratively disfigured: "in the glass, from time to time, this picture: A spectral, haggard, wasted likeness of himself, brooded and brooded over the empty fireplace" (938). Whether this miserific vision be a grim delusion or grim reality, "it" (dehumanized from "he") contemplates self-destruction by its own "guilty hand": "how wicked and murderous that hand looked"; and it even imagines "many prints of [the bloody] feet" whose owners will dispose of its corpse. Ultimately, though, and recalling Nebuchadnezzar's reformation, the wall mirror reveals a more beatific vision to the refigured and rehumanized Dombey, another shadowy dream-come-true—"his own reflection in the glass, and at his knees, his daughter!" (938–39).

Lastly, then, Florence's appearance in a wall print at Dr. Blimber's "where, in the centre of a wondering group, one figure that [her father] knew, a figure with a light about its head—benignant, mild, and merciful—stood pointing upward" (264) becomes the "figure" that Dombey seeks but cannot find nor adequately interpret. Her prefiguration of Agnes Wickfield's allegorical posture in Dickens's next novel *David Copperfield* is clearly problematic, and yet her finger-pointing, like Allegory's, if not Bucket's in *Bleak House*, also seems appropriately Danielic. More humanizing is the fact that Florence appreciates the beatified "golden water, dancing on the wall" which her brother Paul had so admired. For Florence, whose name suggests both flowing water and flowering buds, this mural figure incarnates her own compassion, "the pouring out of her full heart—to let one angel love her and remember her" (318). Later, she interprets "[t]he golden water she remembered on the wall" compassionately "as a current flowing on to rest, and to a region where the dear ones, gone before, were waiting, hand in hand" (427). Nevertheless, "on her breast there was [still] the darkening mark of [her father's] angry hand" (772); much later, this "cruel mark was on her bosom yet. It rose against her father with the breath she drew, it lay between her and her lover when he pressed her to his heart.'' Unlike Edith and Rosa Dartle, and more like Esther Summerson, however, Florence finally ''forg[ets]'' her stigmatizing somatic script (884) and its vengeful letter of the law, which killeth. And this spiritual act of self-negation prepares her to become the real writing on the wall in Dombey's mirror, the flowing, flowering figure of redemption which he can finally and feelingly interpret.

The days of Dombey's Counting House are numbered, but his golden years have truly just begun when he, too, can finally see the golden water on the wall and hear ''the voices in the waves speak low to him of Florence, . . . his blooming daughter'' and his own ''altered heart'' (975–76). As Cousin Feenix, that kinsman with the magically renewing name, concludes, ''all I can say is, with my friend Shakespeare,'' that life is ''like the shadow of a dream'' (969).

V

Developing beyond the character traits in *Dombey*, Dickens's Daniel-Plato complex in *Bleak House* significantly suggests transpersonal (and overlapping) religious, sociological, political, psychological, and aesthetic problems and possibilities. Even ''the great Cross on the summit of St. Paul's Cathedral,'' like Allegory's finger on Tulkinghorn's ceiling, seems a Danielic figure until Jo ironically interprets this ''sacred emblem'' as a floating signifier of ''the crowning confusion of the great, confused city'' (315).[12] On his deathbed, Richard projects himself spectrally as a ''stray shadow'' ultimately ''irradiated'' by angelic Ada's kiss—a ''dreamer'' forsaking ''this world'' of ''many faults and blindnesses'' for the heavenly ''world that sets this right.'' Nevertheless, Richard's Christian ''Allegory'' also appears too Platonically ideal, especially when John Jarndyce queries, ''What am I but another dreamer, Rick?'' (979). Of course, Ada, too, is ''another dreamer''; and Jarndyce's (a)gnostic qualification here recalls Dickens's earlier disturbing image of Ada and Richard's ''shadows blended together'' on ''the wall . . . surrounded by strange forms, not without a ghostly motion caught from the unsteady fire'' (93). This enigmatic chiaroscuro may simply adumbrate their shared Platonic delusions, but it also foreshadows their very different dreams: Rick's of a successful Chancery verdict; Ada's of a disillusioned and enlightened Rick.

Sociological references to Daniel and Plato are fewer and seem clearer as they cry out for sanitary reform and social justice, but they are equally disorienting. For instance, a prophetic ''thick humidity broke out like a disease'' on ''the walls'' of Tom-All-Alone's ''filthy houses'' before Esther discovers her dead mother. Consequently, and again subverting Plato, "the unreal things were more substantial than the real" (913) in London's latter-day version of Babylon's class-divided wasteland (and Dickens often referred to London as a modern Babylon). As the diseased outcast Jo becomes the lower-class scapegoat in England's perverse process of purgation, so too the dis-eased, saturnine Lady Dedlock becomes the upper-class target of social injustice since her "story" may soon be "chalked upon the walls and cried in the streets" (653) when she falls from the social status of queen to that of disgraced concubine. Indeed, *Bleak House* represents Dickens's most identifiably Victorian version of Daniel 5 because the social and cultural condition of "England has been in a dreadful state" for some time. And "the smoke from [this] vaporous Babylon" (638, 953) clearly signals its specific Danielic symptomology (with a nod to Revelation 19:3). Put differently, the entire novel appears as arbitrary writing on the wall like the ironically fashionable "view from my Lady Dedlock's own windows"—"alternately a lead-coloured view, and a view in Indian ink" (21).

England's two nations further reveal political overtones that merge Danielic and Platonic representations, especially pictorial representations recalling Plato's "artificial objects," in the ancestor worship of aristocratic "pictured forms [of deceased Dedlocks] upon the walls" (639) at Chesney Wold (reinforced by Browne's spectral illustration). This vision of Götterdammerung apocalyptically involves what Gillian Beer calls the Victorian fear of the "death of the sun" (169) or *Sonnenuntergang*, which Dickens' features in the first paragraph of *Bleak House*, that is, the waning twilight of Plato's solar godhead's mythology of white lies: "the fire of the sun is dying. . . . Higher and darker rises [the] shadow on the wall—now a red gloom on the ceiling—now the fire is out" (641). Such passages again anticipate Derrida's questioning of solar origins and Apollonian truth since "one of the terms directly or indirectly implied in the substitution (the sensory sun) cannot be known in what is proper to it" ("White Mythology" 250). England's middle class ironically brands itself with the same kind of Platonic/Danielic idolatry and national death wish as Weevle's delusive heroine worship of the Galaxy Gallery of British Beauty gracing his walls suggests. In a parody of Plato's shadow-play between originals and artificial copies, Weevle even boastfully "seems to know the originals" (331), including Lady Dedlock, who is now but a fading imitation of Esther's lost maternal (re)source.

Back at Chesney Wold's portrait gallery, the declining sun "throws a broad bend-sinister of light that strikes down crookedly" across "the picture of my lady" (182), prophetically branding her false self-representation and her offspring with the bar sinister of heraldic bastardy like that with which Edith Dombey brands herself. This solar metaphor foreshadows Browne's later detailed Platonic illustration of it, "Sunset in the long Drawing-room at

Chesney Wold'' (640; fig. 3), which further portends the political waning and, indeed, illegitimate entitlement of the British (like the Babylonian) aristocracy. A rising shade suggestively penetrates the lower midsection of Lady Dedlock's light-colored gown after it has already eclipsed the idealized central statuary of a mother and angel embracing on a pedestal like the figures which haunted Dombey. Also recalling the raised arm haunting Mrs. Skewton, it is as if, Dickens's Danielic metaphor suggests, ''a great arm held a veil or hood watching an opportunity to draw it over her'' (641) and remove any hope of the fallen woman's reunion with her cherubic child. In fact, several other plates reflect Dickens's Daniel-Plato complex (see 77 [fig. 1], 585, 751, 815 [fig. 4], and 914), especially those ''dark plates'' Jane R. Cohen relevantly views as ''complement[ing] the action of the novel, which seems always under the shadow of impending or accomplished tragedy'' (108). These illustrations often feature geometric figures (rectangular picture frames and serial arches)-within-figures, further suggesting endlessly abyssal regression from their origin. Dickens's wordplay implies that such sinister semiotics are also signatures of the mock Lord Chancellor Krook, who self-definitively makes ''a crooked mark on the panelling of the wall'' (75), while scripting déclassé ''walls of words'' which regressively double and politically deconstruct ''the High Court of Chancery.'' In this context, its ''members'' seem ''mistily engaged in one of the ten thousand stages of an endless cause, tripping one another up on slippery precedents, groping knee-deep in technicalities, running their goat-hair and horse-hair warded heads against walls of words, and making a pretense of equity'' (14). Chancery consequently becomes an ''endless'' serial killer in *Bleak House*.

The philosophical implications of the Daniel-Plato complex suggest a deconstructive and frequently existential interrogation of transcendental signifiers, a priori presence, and absolute origins. It's not just that the painted lyres on Turveydrop's wall indict this immodest Model of Deportment as a *liar* deserving deportation because his self-representations are too distant or ''degenerated'' from the Real when he postures, like Krook as the Lord Chancellor, in self-mocking ''imitation of the print of his illustrious model,'' his ''Royal Highness or the Prince Regent'' (228). It's also that Krook again ''make[s] all the [crooked] letters separately, and he knows most of them separately . . . but he can't put them together'' (512).[13] In other words, he can't serially trace the letters, *sous rature*, back to some original Word. Later, Pantagruelian Krook's ''dark greasy coating on the walls'' (517) mock-heraldically reaffirms that writing's arbitrary characters combust spontaneously and so signify nothing but absence in this grotesque example of a carnivalesque inside-out implosion. No wonder Krook's secretarial heir Charlie's trials ''with her copy-book'' testify generally that ''[w]riting was a trying business.'' In her deconstructing ''hand every pen appeared to become

Fig. 3. ''Sunset in the long Drawing-room at Chesney Wold,'' illustrated for *Bleak House*, chapter 40, by Hablot K. Browne.

Fig. 4. ''Shadow,'' illustration for *Bleak House*, chapter 53, by Hablot K. Browne.

perversely animated, and to go wrong and crooked,'' so that Charlie's ''copy of the letter O,'' for instance, is supplementarily ''represented as square, triangular, pear-shaped, and collapsed in all kinds of ways'' (486).[14]

Conversely, *Bleak House* also presents ontologically present and permanent wall writing. For example, prison walls ironically afford George a firm ''point of view'' (795), and ''with his head against the wall,'' Mr. Jellyby also seems to discover perspectival ''consolation in walls'' (484), which lack Daniel's divine authority. Paranoid Mrs. Snagsby, on the other hand, obsessively ''runs her delicate-formed head against a wall'' (908), trying to incriminate and punish her innocently enlightened husband. Crippled Phil Squod finds simple support ''with his shoulder against the wall''; and his endearing endurance leaves a dark ''smear all round the four walls, conventionally called 'Phil's mark' '' (351), which permanently represents his self-authorizing signature on the real world. Such graphic empiricism, the materiality of writing, further suggests existential ''realities'' which eclipse the sun's glare. Less enduring than Phil, scapegoat Jo suffers stigmatic anomie and alienation—more projected crime and punishment—as, again, he spectrally replays Dickens's recurring Danielic nightmare like any common Chaldean ''unfamiliar with the shapes, and in utter darkness as to the meaning, of those mysterious symbols, so abundant'' on shop walls (257).

Psychological motifs in *Bleak House* usually appear in either the Platonic context of shadowy delusions or the Danielic context of the pathology of guilt, whether projected or introjected. For instance, Ada's and Rick's ''shadows blended together'' on the wall seem a Platonic indictment of the deluded inbreeding of these two kissing cousins. Rick's faith in Chancery and Ada's fidelity to Rick may also seem figuratively incestuous or, at least, narcissistic. And the pastoral ''papering on the walls'' at the second Bleak House, copying the original Bleak House, likewise creates regressive ''doll's rooms'' (962–63), thereby branding Esther's marriage to Woodcourt as a family-romance equivalent of her near marriage to paternalistic Jarndyce. On the other hand, the Danielic suggestiveness of ''Richard's name in great white letters on [his office door's] hearse-like panel'' (783) betrays guilt-ridden Rick's self-retributive death wish. The somatic script of Esther's smallpox scars, like Florence's and Edith's violent somatic markings, similarly suggests the ''writing on the wall.'' Unlike Rosa Dartle's scars (which Dickens explicitly identified as wall writing), Esther's imply less the divine retribution that Miss Rachel projectively predicts, or the maternal guilt Esther may introject, than Dickens's own projection of guilt upon anyone, like Guppy, who reads this writing as a telltale bar sinister scored against Esther. Related examples of somatic script include ''the inky condition'' (79) of Caddy Jellyby's body, the ''curious little dark marks . . . faint remembrances of poor Caddy's inky days'' (768) stigmatizing her baby Esther, which recall attempts to stigmatize her baby's namesake, and the "notched memoranda of [Caddy's siblings'] accidents in their legs, which were perfect little calendars of distress" (78). Ironizing Daniel, such script indicts its own author, Mrs. Jellyby, whose malign, maternal neglect seems far more guilty and more genealogically far-reaching than Lady Dedlock's unwitting abandonment of Esther, who she thought was dead. Unlike the working-class, naturally "tanned" Mrs. Bagnet, "freckled by the sun" (439) of Platonic authenticity, Volumnia Dedlock's "indiscrete profusion . . . of rouge" (447), like Mrs. Skewton's cosmetic glare, temporarily brands her aristocratic artifice until her authentic affection for the stricken Sir Leicester ultimately absolves Volumnia's class guilt. It may even seem, vicariously, to atone for Lady's Dedlock's self-serving affectations toward her husband.

"Artifice" introduces our last motif, aesthetic reproductions of the Daniel-Plato complex "formed" ideally, as Turveydrop boasts of Esther, "to be graceful both by Art and Nature" (228), but actually suggesting a real crisis of representation and referentiality. In this context, Danielic finger-pointing comparisons between Roman Allegory and its figurative incarnation in Mr. Bucket—both the British detective and the affiliated "Roman . . . [often appear] together, comparing forefingers" (803)—prove especially telling. As an alleged transcendental signifier (if not signified), Allegory graces Tulkinghorn's "painted ceilings," where its typically pointless pointing "makes the head ache—as would seem to be Allegory's object always," like the logocentric lawyer's "boxes labelled with transcendent names" (158) and like the Babylonian finger's absolutist (but still arbitrary) characters.[15] Nevertheless, the monologic contention "[o]nce pointing, always pointing—like any Roman, or even Briton, with a single idea"—is gradually replaced with some undecidable "new meaning" involving heartfelt "mystery and awe." This, in turn, becomes the pointed "deadly meaning" that not only is heartless Tulkinghorn appropriately "shot through the heart," but also the equally heartless "body and soul of Allegory" have turned "stark mad" (750–52) through their monomaniacal representations. Suggesting again that the Platonic copy may outshine the original, Bucket's similarly represented, "fat forefinger seems to rise to the dignity of a familiar demon"; and, like the famed Babylonian finger, it appears "invariably [to] predict" that "a terrible avenger will be heard of before long." Yet, unlike the representations of Daniel's ghost writer, Bucket "on the whole [becomes] a benignant philosopher not disposed to be severe upon the follies of mankind" (803). Even as his "cruel finger . . . prob[es] the life-blood of [Sir Leicester's loving] heart" (821), Bucket appears more Danielic than divine, more compassionately charitable than critically Chaldean, since his "interpretation" of Sir Leicester's "writ[ing] upon the slate"—"Full forgiveness. Find—" (859–60) does, in fact, discover both his missing word and his missing wife. In this sense, the

Daniel-Plato complex in *Bleak House* ultimately replaces Old Testament law with New Testament love (and solar truth with a more compassionate, if shadowy, beauty) even as, like *Dombey and Son*, it questions any such absolute interpretation of Dickens's own writing on the wall.

Since we began with the scene of wall writing secreted in the final sentence Dickens wrote, one which analogized "the old tavern way of keeping scores" in *Drood*, we might conclude with a similar scene from Dickens's first novel. Here, the "names" of his two blasphemous clowns, Ben Allen and Bob Sawyer, "very often [appear on tavern walls and doors], at the head of long and complex calculations worked in white chalk" (825). In *Pickwick*, especially early in the novel, such writing on the wall simply measures Ben and Bob's Pantagruelian excesses. If, like Belshazzar, they profane sacred vessels, it is only in a mock-heroic sense; if, like Plato's prisoners, they inhabit a cave (or wine cellar) of shadowy delusions, these delusions are surely benign and even liberating: the days of their eternally comic kingdom seem, indeed, endless. In between Dickens's first and last scenes of wall writing, however, his Daniel-Plato complex performs a variety of significant roles, particularly prefiguring the unforseen destinies of characters and foreshadowing subtly interrelated tropes and themes. Ultimately, then, it challenges Dickens's own readers to discover the mysteriously hidden "interpretation thereof" in his fiction.

NOTES

1. See Pip's innocent but parodic "account" of the "alarmingly long chalk scores . . . on the wall" of the Three Jolly Bargemen tavern, "which seemed . . . never paid off." Since "there was a quantity of chalk about our country," however, this wall writing provides economic "opportunity of turning it to account" (*Great Expectations* 103) as writing, drinking, and producing chalk all contribute to consumer culture.
2. Still, Janet Larson's book-length analysis of Dickens's Biblical motifs devotes only an endnote to "the writing on the wall at Belshazzar's feast" (339n54).
3. Norman Porteus suggests that Daniel "is writing what we may call a romance" (77); John Collins discusses Danielic examples of folklore, riddles, and allegories (246, 252–53), and Louis Hartman and Alexander Di Lella note Daniel's various puns (185nn25–28; 189).
4. As Anderson puts it, "The task set the wise men was twofold. It was necessary to read the writing, and then to interpret it . . . . Despite their collective talents they were unable to meet the demands even of the first test. We can only conjecture the reason for this failure. Either the words were written in an unknown script, or they were presented in such a way that it was not possible to make sense of them" (54).

5. See Blackham (95–112) for a general account of the Victorian shadow-show.
6. See Dennis Walder, 151.
7. Many have noted Dickens's symbolic realism in *Bleak House*. Robert Newsom, for example, emphasizes "Dickens's interest in the 'canny' and the 'uncanny' (or the homey and the unhomey)" (59).
8. See Ella Westland's discussion of this plate's relation to "Victorian shadow theater" (101–03) and Gillian Gane's analysis of Captain Cuttle's reading abilities and general literacy (*passim*).
9. Michelle Mancini links Mrs. Brown's walls to Gaston Bachelard's "claim" that "walls are optional" (138n18).
10. See Malvern van Wyk Smith's post-colonial reading of the waves' eternal whisper (especially 130–36).
11. See Larson (75–121) and Walder (124–39) for different Biblical accounts of *Dombey*'s conversion theme.
12. See Paul Kran's Lacanian account of signifiers in *Bleak House*.
13. Claudette Kemper Columbus also notes Krook's "handwriting on the wall," but without suggesting any scriptural context (612).
14. The examples in this paragraph support J. Hillis Miller's famous statement that *Bleak House* "is a document about the interpretation of documents" (179) as well as, perhaps, Hack's amendment that the novel is "a document about the materiality of documents and the interpretation of that materiality.... *Bleak House*'s engagement with the physical materiality of writing may well be the most intensive of any Victorian novel" (*Material Interests* 38).
15. See Hack's discussion of allegory in *Bleak House* (" 'Sublimation Strange,' " *passim*).

WORKS CITED

Ackroyd, Peter. *Dickens*. New York: HarperCollins, 1990.

Anderson, Robert A. *Daniel: Signs and Wonders*. Grand Rapids: Eerdmans, 1984.

Baumgarten, Murray. "Calligraphy and Code: Writing in *Great Expectations*." *Dickens Studies Annual* 11 (1983): 61–72.

Beer, Gillian. " 'The Death of the Sun': Victorian Solar Physics and Solar Myth." *The Sun is God: Painting, Literature, and Mythology in the Nineteenth-Century*. Ed. J. B. Bullen. Oxford: Clarendon, 1989. 159–80.

Blackam, Olive. *Shadow Puppets*. Drawings by S. K. S. New York: Harper, 1960.

Brontë, Charlotte. "Biographical Notice of Ellis and Acton Bell." *Wuthering Heights*. Emily Brontë. Intro. Royal A. Gettmann. New York: Modern Library, 1978. xix–xxvi.

Carlyle, Thomas. *Sartor Resartus: The Life and Opinions of Herr Teufelsdröckh*. Ed. Charles Frederick Harrold. New York: Odyssey, 1937.

Cohen, Jane R. *Charles Dickens and His Original Illustrators*. Columbus: Ohio State UP, 1980.

Collins, John C. *Daniel*. Minneapolis: Fortress, 1993.

Columbus, Claudette Kemper. "The (Un)Lettered Ensemble: What Charlie Does Not Learn about Writing in Bleak House [*sic*]." *Studies in English Literature* 28 (1988): 609–23.

Derrida, Jacques. *Of Grammatology*. Trans. Gayatri Chakravorty Spivak. Baltimore: Johns Hopkins UP, 1976.

———. *Positions*. Trans. and annotat. Alan Bass. Chicago: U of Chicago P, 1982.

———. "White Mythology: Metaphor in the Text of Philosophy." *Margins of Philosophy*. Trans. Allan Bass. Chicago: U of Chicago P, 1982. 207–71.

Dickens, Charles. *Bleak House*. Ed. Nicola Bradbury. London: Penguin, 1996.

———. *David Copperfield*. Ed. Trevor Blount. London: Penguin, 1988.

———. *Dombey and Son*. Ed. Peter Fairclough. Intro. Raymond Williams. Harmondsworth, Middlesex: Penguin, 1985.

———. *Great Expectations*. Ed. Angus Calder. London: Penguin, 1985.

———. *Hard Times*. Ed. Kate Flint. London: Penguin, 1995.

———. *Little Dorrit*. Ed. John Holloway. Middlesex: Penguin, 1967.

———. "Lying Awake." *Reprinted Pieces*. [No vol. no.] *The Oxford Illustrated Dickens*. 21 vols. London: Oxford UP, 1951–59.

———. *The Mystery of Edwin Drood*. Ed. David Paroissien. London: Penguin, 2002.

———. *Nicholas Nickleby*. Ed. Michael Slater. Harmondsworth: Penguin, 1986.

———. *The Old Curiosity Shop*. Ed. Angus Easson. Intro. Malcolm Andrews. Harmondsworth: Penguin, 1986.

———. *Oliver Twist*. Ed. Peter Fairclough. Intro. Angus Wilson. Harmondsworth: Penguin, 1985.

———. *Our Mutual Friend*. Ed. Adrian Poole. London: Penguin, 1997.

———. *The Pickwick Papers*. Ed. Robert L. Patten. London: Penguin, 1986.

———. *A Tale of Two Cities*. Ed. George Woodcock. London: Penguin, 1988.

Eliot, George. *Daniel Deronda*. Ed. Barbara Hardy. London: Penguin, 1986.

Forster, John. *The Life of Charles Dickens.* 2 vols. London: Chapman & Hall, n.d.

Gammie, John G. *Daniel.* Atlanta: John Knox P, 1983.

Gane, Gillian. "The Hat, the Hook, the Eyes, the Teeth: Captain Cuttle, Mr. Carker, and Literacy." *Dickens Studies Annual* 25 (1997): 91–126.

Ginsburg, Michal Peled. "House and Home in *Dombey and Son.*" *Dickens Studies Annual* 36 (2005): 57–73.

Hack, Daniel. *The Material Interests of the Victorian Novel.* Charlottesville: UP of Virginia, 2005.

———. " 'Sublimation Strange': Allegory and Authority in *Bleak House.*" *English Literary History* 66 (1999): 129–56.

Hardy, Thomas. *The Return of the Native.* Ed.Tony Slade. Intro. Penny Boumelha. London: Penguin, 1999.

Hartman, Louis F., and Alexander A. Di Lella. *The Book of Daniel: A New Translation The Anchor Bible.* Vol. 23. Garden City, NY: Doubleday, 1978. 181–91.

Hennelly, Mark M., Jr. " 'The Games of the Prison Children' in Dickens's *Little Dorrit.*" *Nineteenth-Century Contexts* 20 (1997): 187–213.

The Holy Bible. King James Version. New York: Simon & Schuster, 1948.

Jowett, Benjamin. "Analysis of Book VII." *Plato: The Republic.* Trans., intro., analyses, and summary Benjamin Jowett. Norwalk, CT: Heritage, 1972. 344–62.

Kran, Paul A. "Signification and Rhetoric in *Bleak House.*" *Dickens Studies Annual* 26 (1998): 147–67.

Larson, Janet L. *Dickens and the Broken Scripture.* Athens: U of Georgia P, 1985.

Mancini, Michelle. "Demons on the Rooftops, Gypsies in the Street: The 'Secret Intelligence' of *Dombey and Son.*" *Dickens Studies Annual* 30 (2001): 113–40.

Miller, J. Hillis. "Interpretation in Dickens' *Bleak House.*" *Victorian Subjects.* Durham, NC: Duke UP, 1991. 179–99.

Morgan, Monique R. "Conviction in Writing: Crime, Confession, and the Written Word in *Great Expectations.*" *Dickens Studies Annual* 33 (2003): 87–108.

Newsom, Robert. *Dickens on the Romantic Side of Familiar Things:* Bleak House *and the Novel Tradition.* New York: Columbia UP, 1977.

Plato. *The Republic of Plato.* Trans., intro., annotat. Francis MacDonald Cornford. New York: Oxford UP, 1945.

Porteous, Norman W. *Daniel: A Commentary.* Philadelphia: Westminister, 1965.

Ragussis, Michael. "The Ghostly Signs of *Bleak House.*" *Nineteenth-Century Fiction* 34 (1979): 253–80.

Shakespeare, William. *A Midsummer Night's Dream. The Complete Pelican Shakespeare.* Ed. Stephen Orgel and A. R. Braunmuller. New York: Pelican, 2002. 258–84.

Showalter, Elaine. "Guilt, Authority, and the Shadows of *Little Dorrit.*" *Nineteenth-Century Literature* 34 (1979): 20–40.

Stevenson, Robert Louis. *The Strange Case of Dr Jekyll and Mr Hyde. Dr Jekyll and Mr Hyde and Other Stories.* Ed. Jenni Calder. London: Penguin, 1979. 27–97.

Stoker, Bram. *Dracula.* Ed. Maurice Hindle. London: Penguin, 1993.

Tennyson, Alfred. "The Palace of Art." *Poems of Tennyson.* Ed. Jerome H. Buckley. Boston: Riverside, 1958. 39–47.

van Wyk Smith, Malvern. " 'What the waves were always saying': *Dombey and Son* and Textual Ripples on an African Shore." *Dickens and the Children of Empire.* Ed. Wendy S. Jacobson. Houndmills: Palgrave, 2000. 128–52.

Walder, Dennis. *Dickens and Religion.* London: George Allen & Unwin, 1981.

Westland, Ella. "Dickens's *Dombey* and the Storied Sea." *Dickens Studies Annual* 35 (2005): 87–108.

Williams, Katherine. "Glass Windows: The View from *Bleak House.*" *Dickens Studies Annual* 33 (2003): 55–85.

"What would you like for dinner?":
Dining and Narration in *David Copperfield*

Natalie Kapetanios Meir

By focusing upon the many moments when David confronts the conventions of ritualized dining in David Copperfield, *this article argues that the novel raises questions regarding the adoption and implementation of shared paradigms for social behavior. As it repeatedly draws attention to a conflict between two different ways of learning proper dining etiquette—a process that is associated with book learning and a method that is represented as either intuitive or beyond the narrative—the novel provides a commentary on the very concept of learning social norms. Even as the novel progresses, certain conventions remain outside of David's comprehension, and the kind of knowledge associated with domestic handbooks fails David. Dickens thus calls into question the assumption that social conventions can be learned and that routines can be formed through mimicry and repetition. Since David does not learn the proper routines but instead ends up relying on another person's intuition, the novel idealizes a kind of social knowledge that is not, and perhaps cannot, be narrated.*

1.

" 'You said I wasn't comfortable!' said Dora.
'I said the housekeeping was not comfortable.'
'It's exactly the same thing!' cried Dora.
And she evidently thought so, for she wept
most grievously."

—David Copperfield (ch. 44)

Dickens Studies Annual, Volume 39, Copyright © 2008 by AMS Press, Inc. All
rights reserved.

David Copperfield, serialized in parts from 1849 to 1850, is punctuated by a series of dining scenes in which David confronts the conventions of ritualized social practices. These moments consistently replicate the premise that Dora expresses when she weeps that David will find both her and the housekeeping uncomfortable: the person becomes subsumed by the practice. This idea can be seen both in the novel's narrative devices and in David's emotional responses to his problems with following social conventions. David can go through the motions of hosting meals by following others' cues—in other words, he can attempt to adhere to the conventions—yet in doing so he invariably experiences an internal conflict. From his drunken feast with Steerforth and friends to his raw mutton with the Micawbers to his tea with his Aunt Betsey, David is plagued by a feeling that he is not "master" of his social experiences (580). This feeling is only intensified when he marries Dora and moves into their new home. The servants take advantage of him, the purveyors cheat him, and Dora makes mistakes that he cannot rectify. In short, as the disorder in the illustration "Our Housekeeping" demonstrates, nothing works out according to the type of instructions that household manuals offer (fig. 1). As Brenda Ayres rightly explains, "the Copperfield domestic sphere conspicuously contrasts with what was expected of the middle-class home, as outlined in Sarah Ellis's *The Wives of England*" (14).

Most critics have focused on Dora's memorable domestic mishaps as Dickens's way of asserting the importance—and the difficulty—of learning domestic economy.[1] For instance, Joel Chaston writes, "Murdstone's speller, Dora's cookery book, and David's stenography handbook all present a practical system of knowledge, which causes problems for its users" (148). The problem with these types of books, according to Chaston, is that they "do not include any representation of human feelings and are therefore extremely artificial" (148). I believe this point is important, and I want to add to this body of work on the novel by using a narratological approach. In doing so, I suggest that Dickens calls into question the assumption that social conventions can be learned and that routines can be formed through mimicry and repetition. The novel's dramatization of the problems that arise from a poorly regulated home thus becomes important not for what it suggests about the conventions of domesticity in general, but for what it suggests about how such conventions become commonplace.

Moreover, it is important to consider that the private rituals in the home, such as hosting dinner parties and keeping house, have an analogue in the numerous occasions when David dines at public houses. In this essay, I broaden my focus to include the many moments when David learns public eating conventions, particularly in the dining-out scene, for in these urban moments David must present and position himself in relation to the standard practices of the city.[2] Through a focus upon both public and private meals, I

Fig. 1. ''Our Housekeeping''

argue that the dining experiences in *David Copperfield* raise questions regarding the adoption and implementation of shared paradigms for social behavior.[3]

Throughout the novel there is often a disconnection between what David knows and what he is supposed to know about dining rituals. Dickens delineates a conflict between two different ways of learning proper etiquette: a process that is associated with book learning and a method that is represented as either intuitive or beyond the narrative. While David has successfully embraced the conventions of the domestic sphere by the end of the novel when he marries Agnes, his narrative introduces the child Agnes as already familiar with the routines of household management and the conventions of proper social behavior.[4] To the extent that Agnes is represented as possessing intuitive knowledge about proper domesticity, David's imaginative returns to the moment when he first saw his "little housekeeper" as a child with her basket of keys call into question the concept of formation. After all, the ending of the novel can be seen to suggest that what has been wanting in David is intuition: the ability to intuit what he wants to eat, how to rectify a cookery accident, and how to regulate a household. Since David does not learn the proper routines but instead ends up relying on another person's intuitive knowledge, the novel ends by validating a non-narrative knowledge of conventions—a term I use to invoke a kind of knowledge that is felt rather than learned by studying a formal narrative, or a kind of script for proper behavior. Indeed, one of the problems with David and Dora's attempt to acquire knowledge by reading a cookery book is the notion that a narrative of conventions, with its step-by-step instructions and unwavering procedures, can determine behavior.

It is thus striking that *David Copperfield* was published during a time when the social instruction handbook was at its peak. By 1850, cookery books, household manuals, and restaurant guides codifying dining behavior were being mass-produced and circulating widely.[5] These works convey a spirit of optimism about what could be achieved by reading, including self-improvement, respectability, and order. Even the "Copperfield Advertiser" (a tear-out pamphlet surrounding each monthly installment of the novel) regularly contained advertisements for a multitude of how-to books. In a sense, these works can be seen to offer connections to the knowledge that David is missing. Here is a partial list of titles:

Lessons on Housewifery

A Word to Parents, Nurses, and Teachers on the Rearing and Management of Children

Botanical Garden and Fruitist: How to Make a Small Garden Pleasant and Profitable

The Good Boy Henry; or The Young Child's Book of Manners

Walker's Manly Exercises; Instructions in Riding, Hunting, Shooting, Walking, Running, Leaping, Vaulting, Swimming, Rowing, Sailing, and Driving

Handbooks for the People
Social Distinction; or, Hearts and Homes
The Universal Pronouncing Dictionary
Handbook for the Continent
Court Etiquette
The Young Sportsman's Manual
Manners and Customs in Ye England in 1849

Although *Household Words*, Dickens's own periodical, is given prominence by means of tear-out advertising cards (similar to what we find in magazines today), the "Copperfield Advertiser" also includes a number of periodicals devoted to domestic harmony. Examples include *The Magazine of Domestic Economy*, *The Ladies' Companion*, *The Domestic Economist*, and *Eliza Cook's Journal*. The "Advertiser" conveys the notion that correct social comportment can be learned by all who purchase the latest books and periodicals; in other words, it suggests that proper social behavior is a social product rather than a natural, or innate, state of being. Books such as *The Good Boy Henry; or The Young Child's Book of Manners* or advertisements for "Dodney's Tailors for Gentlemen" suggest that through these products and services one can become—or at least appear to be—a proper young gentleman, as David strives to be. Ironically, then, the novel helps to generate revenue by means of a premise that it consistently reveals to be problematic, yet desirable and necessary in the absence of an Agnes figure that is an innate housekeeper.

The fact remains, however, that, even as the novel progresses, certain conventions remain outside of David's comprehension, and the kind of knowledge associated with domestic handbooks fails David. Given that regardless of David's repeated practice with dining conventions he nevertheless struggles, the novel calls into question the very concept of transformation that is at the heart of the bildungsroman and that traditionally informs quests to learn proper etiquette. Instead, in problematizing the possibility of a smooth trajectory toward increased understanding and mastery of dining conventions, Dickens provides a commentary on the very concept of learning social norms.[6] As it repeatedly draws attention to what is missing—that is, to the inadequacy of David's dining skills—the novel idealizes a kind of social knowledge that is not, and perhaps cannot, be narrated.[7]

2.

" 'Young gentlemen is generally tired of beef and mutton, have a weal-cutlet!'
I assented to this proposal, in default of being able to suggest anything else.''
—A Waiter and David, *David Copperfield* (ch. 19)

In contrast to social instruction handbooks' elaboration of the minutiae of proper dining—from how to arrange a meal to how to hold one's fork—Dickens often sidesteps such details, even though he devotes significant attention to dining itself. He does so through a technique that narratologists have called paralipsis, "an alteration that consists in giving less information . . . than should presumably be given" about a narrative event; paralipsis occurs when the narrative fails to mention "one or more components in the situation that is being recounted" (Prince 69).[8] In the dining scenes in *David Copperfield* the "information" that "should presumably be given" but that is often left out relates to the conventions of the dining scenarios that David encounters. By leaving out particulars surrounding dining rituals, Dickens implies that certain routines exist prior to the narrative and are so commonplace that they need not be narrated.[9] On the other hand, this technique creates the impression that these ideals are unattainable, beyond the scope of David's ability and experience.

Yet, even though the novel recognizes the difficulty of achieving faultless dining knowledge, it does chart what has the potential to be a gradual process of increased insight into questions of etiquette that parallels David's maturity. As such, a traditional reading of the novel might emphasize the extent to which the repeated social rituals contribute to Dickens's characterization of David. It could be argued that in repeatedly using dining scenes to narrate the development of David's identity, Dickens suggests that participation in such rituals is fundamental to one's development as a social subject. For, in a sense, David is, quite literally, constructed by social practices related to eating, and *David Copperfield* can be seen as a bildungsroman as narrated through eating scenes. Indeed, the many critics who have noted the novel's sustained focus on domestic issues have linked these themes to questions about the development of self. For instance, in "Cookery, not Rookery: Family and Class in *David Copperfield*," Chris Vanden Bossche argues that David embraces the middle-class values of midcentury cookery books in his search for a "legitimate social position" (87). I share Vanden Bossche's belief that David's struggle with the moral economy associated with cookery books bears an important relationship to his development of a class identity. In fact, I regard the novel's dining scenes as depicting David's struggle to master the conventions of a social type, the young gentleman.[10] However, rather than focus upon issues of narrating the self, my reading shifts the emphasis to what such repeated scenes suggest about narrating the dining conventions themselves.

By repeating similar dining scenes that contain less information than would be expected about a particular dining ritual, Dickens uses each consecutive dining scene to narrate a subtlety of what was not narrated in the prior scene. For the most part, David, the retrospective first-person narrator, only narrates what he knew at the time and withholds a complete explanation of what he now knows about the social rituals he discusses.[11] While this technique of paralipsis is common to the retrospective mode of narration, Dickens does something more than gesture toward David's limited point of view at particular points in his life. Instead, he draws attention to the very limits of David's experiences in furthering his dining knowledge.

One example of this method is David's description of his first visit to a coffee-room. In the following description, even though the adult David is familiar with coffee-rooms, he captures the strangeness of the experience from the child David's perspective:

> It was a large long room with some large maps in it. I doubt if I could have felt much stranger if the maps had been real foreign countries, and I cast away in the middle of them. I felt it was taking a liberty to sit down with my cap in my hand, on the corner of the chair nearest the door, and when the waiter laid a cloth on purpose for me, and put a set of castors on it, I think I must have turned red all over with modesty.
>
> He brought me some chops, and vegetables, and took the covers off in such a bouncing manner that I was afraid I must have given him some offence.
>
> (70)

Dickens describes the many instances when David dines out in narratives of such great detail that they constitute dramatic plot events in themselves. Here, David is a humble young boy who cannot imagine that he would deserve attention from the waiter. When the waiter proceeds to divest him of each course of his meal—including ale, chops, potatoes, and pudding—David cannot see that he has been taken advantage of. Instead, he concludes that he has never met such a "friendly and companionable" fellow.

Because ordering at a public house is a social ritual, Dickens does not necessarily have to spell out each and every detail. For example, he does not specify that this moment is not exemplary of a routine occurrence, and that the waiter has told a series of lies and preyed upon the boy's naïvete to fulfill his gluttonous appetite. Instead, this narrative is marked by a gap in information. The fact that Dickens does not articulate this lesson verbally, as part of the narration of the scene, suggests that the novel assumes a certain level of familiarity with the social routines it represents. In other words, Dickens implies that the conventions of proper dining are readily recognizable in the popular imagination and do not necessarily require spelling out. However, as Mieke Bal explains in her discussion of the spatial aspects of narrative, not all readers will have a similar response to the details a narrative provides—or, as in this case, does not provide: "Those who are already familiar with the atmosphere will immediately be able to visualize much more, and for them the notations 'in the kitchen' and 'in the parlour' will evoke much more precise images'' (136). I share Bal's idea that not all readers will fill paralipses with the same information; in this coffee-room example, not all readers will be familiar with the conventions that Dickens does not explain.

My point, rather, is that the very fact that Dickens does not narrate the conventions of such a scene is significant. For it implies the assumption that there is an ordinary procedure for such a scenario, even though David's particular experience does not conform to standard practice. Furthermore, the fact that this scene is atypical and, more specifically, that there is a distinction between David's presentation of events and the waiter's behavior, serves to emphasize the routine itself. That is, the aberrant nature of this scene highlights the extent to which David's knowledge of standard dining practices departs from the social norm.[12]

In case the reader should fail to notice this discordance, the illustration accompanying this dining moment can be seen to provide additional commentary.[13] In making this point, I am following Gerard Genette's argument in *Paratexts* that the elements surrounding a text—such as tables of contents, chapter titles, or illustrations—can be regarded as functioning as part of the text and thus contribute to its effects (1–2). In the illustration associated with this dining scene, entitled ''The friendly Waiter and I'' (fig. 2), the innocent look in David's upturned eyes is in marked contrast to the devious smirk on the waiter's face. This image depicts the gap that is at the heart of this dining experience and others: one between the standard social practice and the individual's awareness (or lack thereof) of the routine at hand. In ''Reading Illustrations: Pictures in *David Copperfield*,'' Stephen Lutman also argues that through its illustrations the novel poses discrepancies between David's self-presentation and an ''objective'' point of view. He suggests that an important function of the novel's illustrations is to present information about David that supplements or contradicts his conception of himself.[14] Both in its illustrated and narrative forms, then, a dining event such as this one can provide a gloss on the conventions of the ritual being represented. In this case, David's experience with the waiter can be read as a lesson in how not to dine in a restaurant: do not allow yourself to be taken advantage of by duplicitous waiters.

For David himself, though, this lesson is not spelled out. While later in life he may realize that the waiter's behavior was inappropriate, he does not describe himself as having arrived at this level of awareness at this particular point in time. In contrast to *Great Expectations*, in which, upon his arrival in London, Pip receives ''friendly suggestions'' from Herbert Pocket regarding the proper handling of his silverware, wine glass, and dinner napkin (141–42), David lacks either a friend or a restaurant guide elaborating standard dining practices. His experiences with waiters are therefore consistently

Fig. 2. ''The friendly Waiter and I''

unpredictable. This unpredictability, in turn, allows the dining-out scene to function as a point of reference for his development in learning the proper way to comport himself in society. For example, David's retrospective narrative invokes his experience years later in the coffee-room of the Golden Cross, an inn: "I was still painfully conscious of my youth, for nobody stood in any awe of me at all: the chambermaid being utterly indifferent to my opinions on any subject, and the waiter being familiar with me, and offering advice to my inexperience" (269). Unlike David's first experience with waiters, he is now "conscious" of his youth. Yet, as the word "still" suggests, he has not progressed socially: waiters continue to fail to respect him, and he "still" experiences conflict when dining out, much as he had in his first visit to a public-house. David regards the fact that the chambermaid ignores his preferences and that the waiter offers "advice" as an affront to the impression that he would like to convey.

Once again, Dickens figures David's conduct in deciding what to order as a power struggle between David and the waiter, only this time David seems slightly more aware that there is indeed a conflict at work:

> "Well now," said the waiter, in a tone of confidence, "what would you like for dinner? Young gentlemen likes poultry in general, have a fowl!"
>
> I told him, as majestically as I could, that I wasn't in the humour for a fowl.
>
> "Ain't you!" said the waiter. "Young gentlemen is generally tired of beef and mutton, have a weal-cutlet!"
>
> I assented to this proposal, in default of being able to suggest anything else.
>
> "Do you care for taters?" said the waiter, with an insinuating smile, and his head on one side. "Young gentlemen generally has been overdosed with taters."
>
> I commanded him, in my deepest voice, to order a veal-cutlet and potatoes, and all things fitting; and to enquire at the bar if there were any letters for Trotwood Copperfield, Esquire—which I knew there were not and couldn't be, but thought it manly to appear to expect.   (270)

As is the case here, Dickens's narratives of David's individual dining experiences persistently invoke the paradigm of the perfectly mannered "young gentleman" who is well-versed in the codes for proper dining. Ever-present yet elusive, this ideal of civility not only serves as a benchmark for David's development as a social subject but also, and, more interestingly, sheds light on the complexities of mastering the conventions of dining through repetition and mimicry. In narrating David's indoctrination into the ritualized dining behavior of the young gentleman, this passage illuminates how such norms undergo a transformation from being alien to what may appear to be second nature.

Dickens depicts this process as involving a repetition of what is expected in such a scenario (what young gentlemen "generally" do) until David no longer resists. At first, in his refusal of fowl, David opposes being regarded as the generic young gentleman. Yet eventually he finds it easier to give in to the expectations associated with this paradigm than to try to voice his own preferences. In fact, as he admits, he does not even know what he wants to eat—or what he should want to eat. As Rebecca Spang points out in *The Invention of the Restaurant*, coffee-rooms in the nineteenth century did not regularly offer menus from which patrons could choose available meals. Spang thus views the "creation of a list," one of the distinctive features of the restaurant, as allowing the individual to make "personal choices" (76). In light of Spang's argument that ordering a meal is linked to questions of individual expression, the very question "what would you like for dinner?" becomes an issue that tests one's dining preferences as well as one's knowledge of the conventions for dining out. In contrast to the "highly individual statement" that Spang believes the restaurant menu enables a diner to make, David's acquiescence to the waiter's proposed meal implies that he conforms to a set of conventions that are predetermined and "fitting" for a young gentleman. Once David "commands" the "veal-cutlet and potatoes," he accepts the role of a young gentleman named Trotwood Copperfield, Esquire, and thus becomes what the waiter expects him to be. Of course, as both David and the waiter seem to know, the young gentleman is a prescribed social role, a socially constructed appearance of manliness rather than a natural expression of personality.

Thus, although David may begin to become acclimated to the social rituals of the young gentleman, he does not necessarily understand how to assert himself as such. Through the technique of repetition, however, Dickens gradually narrates David's exposure to experiences that contain the possibility of informing his comprehension of how best to comport himself in formal dining experiences. The following breakfast scene can be read as a repetition of the previous narrative in which David learns what he should want to order, much as that narrative can be read as a repetition of his first experience in a public house. The repetition that links these narratives together is highlighted by the fact that the events unfold in the novel in the chronological order in which they presumably occurred in the story of David's life. To the extent that the repeated narratives share basic similarities, each one can be read as providing information that the previous one left out; taken together, they have the potential to contribute to a greater body of knowledge about the customs of dining out.

For instance, unlike David's awkward dialogue with the waiter, in which the waiter must inform David how he should dine, the following narrative explains how a seasoned young gentleman would typically arrange a meal. Dickens uses David's friend Steerforth as a foil to David's dining inexperience. For, in contrast to David, who awkwardly plays the role of gentleman in the absence of his own tastes and desires, Steerforth appears to be a true gentleman, one who seems to possess an innate conception of appropriate social behavior. When David runs into Steerforth at a play after his "young gentleman" dining experience, Steerforth arranges a breakfast the next morning. David explains:

> It was not in the coffee-room that I found Steerforth expecting me, but in a snug private apartment, red-curtained and Turkey-carpeted, where the fire burnt bright, and a fine hot breakfast was set forth on a table covered with a clean cloth; and a cheerful miniature of the room, the fire, the breakfast, Steerforth, and all, was shining in the little round mirror over the sideboard. I was rather bashful at first, Steerforth being so self-possessed, and elegant, and superior to me in all respects (age included); but his easy patronage soon put that to rights, and made me quite at home. I could not enough admire the change he had wrought in the Golden Cross; or compare the dull forlorn state I had held yesterday, with this morning's comfort and this morning's entertainment. As to the waiter's familiarity, it was quenched as if it had never been. He attended on us, as I may say, in sackcloth and ashes.   (273–74)

David and Steerforth share their own private, domestic scenario, with David as guest and Steerforth as host. It is telling that David attributes the "change" that has been "wrought in the Golden Cross" to Steerforth rather than to his own state of mind. For, although at this meal the waiter treats David like a gentleman, as he treats Steerforth, David still feels young and inferior. David's social awkwardness is apparent in the fact that he is absent from his own description of the mirror reflection of this scene of domestic bliss. The phrase, "the breakfast, Steerforth, and all, was shining in the little round mirror over the sideboard," leaves David out, and only the ambiguous word "all" stands in for his presence. Quite simply, David does not notice himself. He perceives a difference in his emotions, material comfort, and treatment by the waiter, but does not necessarily believe himself to be any different.

After all, the air of "self-possession" that Steerforth exhibits remains elusive to David. David's lack of social ease is not only heightened by his being surrounded by Steerforth but also other figures who have achieved a kind of mastery over ritualized dining, including Micawber. Although Micawber functions as a parody of a man who has achieved success with the conventions of cookery, the fanfare, pride, and enjoyment that characterize his making of punch nevertheless shed light on David: Micawber's confidence in matters of dining emphasizes David's inability to figure out how he might comport himself so that he might convey a similar impression of familiarity and effortlessness with formal dining practices (383). When David's dinner with the Micawbers goes awry and Steerforth's servant intervenes and takes over the serving, while Micawber is "humming a tune, to show that he was quite at ease," David describes himself as "a mere infant at the head of my own table" (386).

David's failure to achieve the composure of Steerforth, Micawber, and others can be attributed in part to his lack of confidence in his social position. As Vanden Bossche writes, "David Copperfield, though born and raised in a gentleman's home, never feels certain that he belongs among gentlemen as we are constantly reminded by his fears that servants and other social inferiors can see through his pretenses to that estate" (88). Building on Vanden Bossche's reading, I would emphasize that his words "never" and "constantly" gesture toward the repetitive nature of certain aspects of the novel. What is particularly significant is that these terms suggest that repetition can be synonymous with stasis rather than with development. Ultimately, David's process of learning the "pretenses" to the "estate" of gentleman is rather static, for his attempts at learning how to master the conventions are consistently fraught with complications. By repeating the dining-out scene, and by placing the event in a time frame from David's childhood to adulthood, Dickens problematizes repetition as a tool for both narrating and learning conventions. The notion that repetition is not a guarantor of progress applies to Dickens's narrative techniques as well as to the portrait of David that emerges from these narrative techniques. For even though the repetitive nature of David's dining experiences may seem to suggest that repetition, over time, is fundamental to attaining proper social behavior, something is invariably missing—typically David's ease with himself.

3.

> "It occurred to me that I really ought to have a little housewarming"
> —David, *David Copperfield* (ch. 24)

Just as David experiences a kind of absence, something is wanting in the very narrative methods Dickens uses to convey David's tribulations in proper dining. As I have shown, there is often something that is not being articulated, that is being withheld from David. This technique implies that there is not simply a problem with the individual trying to master the social conventions of dining but rather a problem with the narratives of conventions themselves, including how they are taught and perpetuated. Specifically, Dickens draws our attention to the perils of mimicry and to the loss of self that invariably ensues. This notion can be seen in the fact that, much as he fails to recognize himself in the mirror reflection of his breakfast with Steerforth, David often loses himself in eating scenes. I read these gaps in David's self-narrative as signs that, in the process of attempting to become a social type, David experiences a crisis in identity.

David's dinner with Steerforth and friends, a ritual for the establishment of the social identity of a middle-class man, is the most striking example of this conflict. When David writes, "it occurred to me that I really ought to have a little housewarming" (334), he recognizes this social ritual; the word "ought" signifies his familiarity with the convention of hosting a housewarming in a bachelor's chambers. It is significant, however, that David does not specify how he knows that he should do so. His representation of this social knowledge as simply entering his consciousness ("it occurred to me") suggests that the social "ought" penetrates the individual much as the waiter's repetition of the norms of dining overpowers David. In both cases, however, although David may embrace the ritual he nevertheless has trouble mastering it.[15] The novel thus continually reminds us of the often conflicting relationship between narratives of social conventions and the experience of ritual.

In its step-by-step fashion, the following narrative of the conventions for a bachelor dinner emphasizes David's lack of familiarity with the way in which one follows the routine of hosting a dinner. David plans his first dinner party in consultation with his landlady, Mrs. Crupp, and narrates the series of steps that he undergoes in preparation for it. First they choose the proper servants, both for serving and for washing dishes. Next, they discuss the meal:

> Mrs. Crupp then said what she would recommend would be this. A pair of hot roast fowls—from the pastry-cook's; a dish of stewed beef, with vegetables—from the pastry-cook's; two little corner things, as a raised pie and a dish of kidneys—from the pastry-cook's; a tart, and (if I liked) a shape of jelly—from the pastry-cook's. This, Mrs. Crupp said, would leave her at full liberty to concentrate her mind on the potatoes, and to serve up the cheese and celery as she could wish to see it done.
>
> I acted on Mrs. Crupp's opinion, and gave the order at the pastry-cook's myself.
>
> (335)

Dickens specifies each detail necessary for the bachelor dinner—except how the host should behave.

The dinner party becomes a time for self-questioning and self-doubt, in part because, as Dickens's phrasing emphasizes, David is dependent upon the advice and services of others: both Mrs. Crupp's recommendations and the pastry-cook's creations.[16] In contrast to the repeated phrase "Mrs. Crupp said," which is representative of received dining wisdom, the parenthetical phrase "if I liked" highlights that David's preferences in hosting this dining ritual are an afterthought. Along with this phrase, David's emphasis of the fact that he "gave the order at the pastry-cook's" himself suggests that he wants to be a part of the preparations and hence provide his own stamp on the ritual. He therefore takes the liberty of buying a slab of "Mock Turtle" on his own, but when Mrs. Crupp cooks it it shrinks into "a liquid state"

(335). Similarly, although he tries to maintain a semblance of autonomy, when the guests arrive David feels "much too young to preside" and makes Steerforth "take the head of the table" (336).

When the dinner turns into a drunken feast, owing to the "rather extensive order" David placed at the retail wine merchant's (335), David loses awareness of who he is. He explains:

> Somebody was leaning out of my bedroom-window. . . . It was myself. I was addressing myself as 'Copperfield' . . . . Now, somebody was unsteadily contemplating his features in the looking-glass. That was I too. I was very pale in the looking-glass; my eyes had a vacant appearance; and my hair—only my hair, nothing else—looked drunk.   (337)

Dickens represents David's attempt to establish himself as equal to Steerforth and the other young gentlemen by hosting a dinner party as causing distance from the self. As David's reference to himself in the third person as "somebody" and "Copperfield" suggests, he regards himself from an outsider's perspective, the perspective of the social world. At the same time, he experiences a vertiginous confusion of perception and reality, which the "looking-glass" eventually sets straight. With the help of the mirror, David is able visually to identify each body part that makes up the entity called "David Copperfield," as the repetition of "my" and "I" demonstrates.

In this nightmarish scene, Dickens implies that self-abnegation is a consequence of ritualized behavior that can occur if one relies excessively on convention as a substitute for one's own preference. This feeling only intensifies when, as David begins to sober up, the void of self becomes replaced by the accoutrements of his dinner party:

> How, as that somebody slowly settled down into myself, did I begin to parch, and feel as if my outer covering of skin were a hard board; my tongue the bottom of an empty kettle, furred with long service, and burning up over a slow fire; the palms of my hands, hot plates of metal which no ice could cool!
> (339)

Contrasted to the moment above when David recognizes himself as "I" by naming each body part ("my eyes," "my hair"), this moment suggests the full complexity of his situation. The fact that David experiences himself as composed of kitchen utensils—"a hard board," "an empty kettle," "hot plates of metal"—captures the way in which one can be empty of meaningful substance if one relies exclusively on social ideals at the expense of one's own preferences.[17] Given that this novel's narrative devices, particularly its repetitive structure and the use of David's experiences as exemplary of the routines of the young gentleman, also contribute to this effect of lack of individuation, Dickens provides a warning regarding blind adherence to social norms.

In marked contrast, one of David's most self-assured dining-out experiences is his "magnificent order at the public-house" as a small child, for in this moment he is uninhibited by the knowledge of what he should do in this social situation. David describes himself as a small child asking the landlord of a public-house, "What is your best—your *very* best—ale a glass?" After the landlord acquaints him with the house's best ale, he continues, " 'Then,' says I, producing the money, 'just draw me a glass of the Genuine Stunning, if you please, with a good head to it' " (156–57, emphasis in original). Here, David does not wait for others' instructions as to how he should place his order or consume his ale. Instead, he simply asserts his own desire with what Gareth Cordery describes as "an air of insouciance and superiority in keeping with his assumed gentlemanly status" (63).

Cordery emphasizes David's class aspirations in this scene, explaining that "David pretends to be something that he is not but wants to be, and pretends to be able to afford the very best ale, which he can't" and pointing out that the landlord and his wife are certainly not fooled by David's performance (63). I would observe that it is significant that David tries at all, for the "air of insouciance" he exudes while ordering conveys a confidence in his ability to embrace the conventions of dining out that is not found elsewhere in the novel. As in the illustration of David's dinner with "the friendly waiter," the illustration accompanying David's public-house experience once again implies a gap between David's behavior and social expectations (fig. 3).[18] Only here the contrast is between David's proud posture and the owners' sympathetic glances. Considered in relation to David's subsequent dining episodes, this moment crystallizes the notion that when one learns proper social behavior by simply following others' cues rather than asserting one's own sense of propriety, one is at risk of losing self-assurance.

Throughout the novel, the kind of knowledge that David relies upon in this public-house scene—an instinctive conception of proper social behavior—has been depicted as external to the narrative. It becomes manifest at times, but it is not narrated in detail. In the end, the novel's emphasis through Agnes on an awareness of proper social conventions that does not necessarily emerge from step-by-step, verbal paradigms may seem to contradict the logic of the many dining handbooks being published at the time, such as those very manuals contained in the "Copperfield Advertiser." However, Dickens's concentration on intuitive knowledge can also express an ideal that such handbooks perpetuate: a scenario in which one places an order at a restaurant or hosts a dinner party without worrying about each consecutive step.

Fig. 3. ''My magnificent order at the public-house''

NOTES

1. In "The Women of *David Copperfield*," Brenda Ayres offers a different perspective on this issue by arguing that Dora's resistance to learning proper domesticity can be read as a form of dissent (16). A number of other articles have focused to some extent on domesticity in *David Copperfield*. See Poovey, Chaston, Darby, Grill, McCarthy, and Andrade.

2. For a consideration of urban moments in *David Copperfield*, see Craig 25–31.

3. See Watt for a discussion of the symbolic implications of eating in Dickens's work, particularly as it relates to character traits, power relations, and psychoanalytic issues. For a discussion of *David Copperfield* in particular, see 169–70.

4. Critics have focused on the two different models of domesticity that the novel explores, as symbolized by Dora and Agnes, and the ways in which David's relationship to each woman contributes to his growing sense of self. For example, in "The Man-of-Letters Hero: *David Copperfield* and the Professional Writer," Mary Poovey is attuned to the complexity of the novel's attempts to figure a domestic model provided by the image of woman as a guarantor of middle-class male identity (115).

5. For further discussion of the ideals of nineteenth-century dining handbooks, see Meir, " 'A fashionable dinner is arranged as follows.' "

6. Patrick McCarthy also places David's journey toward middle-class domesticity within the context of the logic of social instruction manuals. However, he has a different perspective. He argues that David's "*modus operandi* [is] straight out of Samuel Smiles's *Thrift* and other handbooks of middle-class ethics" (24). Although McCarthy acknowledges the "sufferings" implicit in Dickens's domestic models, he suggests that "his was the optimistic scenario for the young, capable male for whom success was possible" (25).

7. My focus upon what Dickens does and does not narrate about eating suggests that what novels do not narrate can be rich sites for critical inquiry. My reading is indebted to D. A. Miller's concept of the nonnarratable, which he explains in *Narrative and Its Discontents*.

8. For more on paralipsis, see Genette, *Narrative Discourse* 52.

9. In *The Victorian Parlour*, Thad Logan also considers Victorian novelists' tendency to offer "surprisingly scarce" descriptions, though she does so in the context of domestic interiors. She suggests that perhaps novelists have difficulty describing that which is so familiar to them, their immediate surroundings (206).

10. My reading is informed by Mary Poovey's discussion of *David Copperfield*, in which she describes the "paradox of individualism" in class society (118). Poovey explains: "What we have in *David Copperfield* . . . is a novel in which the identity of the 'hero' is never completely stabilized or fully individuated because the main character is split and distributed among so many other characters and parts" (119–20). In problematizing the notion of "fully individuated" characters, Poovey raises the issue that individual characters can be suggestive of larger concepts or traits.

11. In his discussion of the way in which the illustrations in the novel function, Robert Patten makes a similar point. He suggests that "each plate may add to

implications of preceding ones, may foreground what was previously a minor feature'' and notes that this process is also the way ''the text makes its sense'' (120).

12. For further discussion of the way very similar narrative techniques also gesture toward how social conventions become norms in nineteenth-century novels, see Meir, '' 'Household forms and ceremonies.' ''

13. In his perceptive analysis of the complexities of illustrating a retrospective narrative, Patten describes this technique as follows: ''Browne must provide illustrations of David that incorporate the child as he feels himself to be and the adult reflecting back on the child he was. Browne must also depict the child as he is seen by the author, in places where neither David the Younger as child nor David the Younger as older narrator sees all that is going on; consequently, only the 'author' Charles Dickens, 'parent' of this 'favourite child,' and the reader through the mediation of the illustration that enlightens and elucidates the text, can see some things'' (97). In addition to Patten, for a consideration of the way in which the novel's illustrations function, see Lutman and Cordery.

14. Lutman also focuses on dining to some extent; he examines patterns in the novel's illustrations and notices a repetition of images of David sitting in chairs at tables as a poignant sign of his uneasiness (208).

15. Gareth Cordery explains David's difficulties in hosting this dinner: ''David wishes to be like Steerforth but can only act out these desires when the moral values drummed into him by Aunt Betsey and Dr. Strong are suspended'' (71). While this scene certainly underscores a moral conflict, I am suggesting that this conflict also has to do with the very nature of following the conventions associated with Steerforth's social station.

16. Nonfiction works circulating around the same time as the novel offer similar instructions. For example, the restaurant guide *London at Dinner* recommends that a bachelor procure his food for dinner parties from local shops rather than trying to cook using a Dutch oven in his chambers (27).

17. A similar moment occurs when David becomes part of a cookery book. David describes how Dora literally inscribes him in her book: ''But the Cookery Book made Dora's head ache, and the figures made her cry. They wouldn't add up, she said. So she rubbed them out, and drew little nosegays, and likenesses of me and Jip, all over the tablets'' (558).

18. See Cordery 63–69 for more on this illustration, including its historical context and its relationship to previous illustrations by George Cruikshank contained in Dickens's works. See also Patten, who points out that this illustration represents David handling the responsibilities of being a ''city boy'' better than the text itself does (105, 118).

WORKS CITED

Andrade, Mary Anne. ''Pollution of an Honest Home.'' *Dickens Quarterly* 5 (1988): 65–74.

Ayres, Brenda. "The Women of *David Copperfield.*" *Dissenting Women in Dickens's Novels: The Subversion of Domestic Ideology.* Westport, CT: Greenwood, 1998. 13–32.

Bal, Mieke. *Narratology: Introduction to the Theory of Narrative.* 2nd ed. Toronto: U of Toronto P, 1997.

Chaston, Joel. "Crusoe, Crocodiles, and Cookery Books: *David Copperfield* and the Affective Power of Reading Fiction." *University of Mississippi Studies in English* 9 (1991): 141–53.

Cordery, Gareth. "Drink in *David Copperfield.*" *Redefining the Modern: Essays on Literature and Society in Honor of Joseph Wiesenfarth.* Ed. William Baker. Madison, NJ: Fairleigh Dickinson UP, 2004. 59–74.

Craig, David. "The Interplay of City and Self in *Oliver Twist, David Copperfield,* and *Great Expectations.*" *Dickens Studies Annual* 16 (1987): 17–38.

Darby, Margaret Flanders. "Dora and Doady." *Dickens Studies Annual* 22 (1993): 155–69.

Dickens, Charles. *David Copperfield.* Ed. Jeremy Tambling. New York: Penguin, 1996.

———. *Great Expectations.* Ed. Edgar Rosenberg. New York: Norton, 1999.

Genette, Gerard. *Narrative Discourse: An Essay in Method.* Trans. Jane Lewin. Ithaca, NY: Cornell UP, 1980.

———. *Paratexts: Thresholds of Interpretation.* Trans. Jane Lewin. New York: Cambridge UP, 1997.

Grill, Neil. "Homes and Homeless in *David Copperfield.*" *Dickens Studies Newsletter* 11 (1980): 108–11.

Logan, Thad. *The Victorian Parlour: A Cultural Study.* New York: Cambridge UP, 2001.

London at Dinner; or, Where to Dine. London: Robert Hardwicke, 1858.

Lutman, Stephen. "Reading Illustrations: Pictures in *David Copperfield.*" *Reading the Victorian Novel: Detail into Form.* Ed. Ian Gregor. London: Vision Press, 1980. 196–225.

McCarthy, Patrick. "Making for Home: David Copperfield and His Fellow Travelers." *Homes and Homelessness in the Victorian Imagination.* Ed. Murray Baumgarten and H. M. Daleski. New York: AMS, 1998. 21–33.

Meir, Natalie Kapetanios. " 'A fashionable dinner is arranged as follows': Victorian Dining Taxonomies." *Victorian Literature and Culture* 33 (2005): 133–48.

———. " 'Household forms and ceremonies': Narrating Routines in Elizabeth Gaskell's *Cranford.*" *Studies in the Novel* 38 (2006): 1–14.

Miller, D. A. *Narrative and Its Discontents: Problems of Closure in the Traditional Novel*. Princeton, NJ: Princeton UP, 1981.

Patten, Robert. "Serial Illustration and Storytelling in *David Copperfield*." *The Victorian Illustrated Book*. Ed. Richard Maxwell. Charlottesville: UP of Virginia, 2002. 91–128.

Poovey, Mary. "The Man-of-Letters Hero: *David Copperfield* and the Professional Writer." *Uneven Developments: The Ideological Work of Gender in Mid-Victorian England*. Chicago: U of Chicago P, 1988. 89–125.

Prince, Gerald. *A Dictionary of Narratology*. Lincoln: U of Nebraska P, 1987.

Spang, Rebecca. *The Invention of the Restaurant: Paris and Modern Gastronomic Culture*. Cambridge, MA: Harvard UP, 2000.

Vanden Bossche, Chris. "Cookery, not Rookery: Family and Class in *David Copperfield*." *Dickens Studies Annual* 15 (1986): 87–109.

Watt, Ian. "Oral Dickens." *Dickens Studies Annual* 3 (1980): 165–81.

"When I Kissed Her Cheek": Theatrics of Sexuality and the Framed Gaze in Esther's Narration of *Bleak House*

Kimberle L. Brown

In Bleak House, *Charles Dickens's theatrical ventriloquism of Esther Summerson's voice, shaped by conventions of the theater and combined with a special framed gaze technique, expresses the simultaneous possibilities of innocent intense friendship and lesbian encounter. The blushing, crying, kissing, and hyperbolic use of pet names in Esther's dramatic vignettes, combined with rhythmic delays, repetitions, and exclamatory punctuation, embody and articulate a sensibility that channels characters to act toward social good. Concurrently, as synesthesia blends the visual and aural, Dickens invites a gendered role-reversal for female and male characters and readers to assume power and envision empathetic action.*

Bleak House swings like a pendulum in the fog between two very different narrators, an omniscient observer and the novel's protagonist, Esther Summerson. Esther, separated from her mother and raised by a woman she later learns is her aunt, becomes a companion to Ada Clare, who, with her cousin Richard Carstone, joins the household of their guardian, John Jarndyce. Ada and Richard await judgment in the Chancery case of Jarndyce and Jarndyce—an inheritance morass that crushes everyone in its path except for the vampiric lawyers that feed for generations on its claimants. Along the way, the novel reveals a sex scandal whose secret threatens to taint our heroine

---

Esther and succeeds in killing her parents. We encounter abused and grossly neglected children, love triangles, childish adults, feuding neighbors, ambitious law clerks, money-grubbing families, and mysterious deaths. Through it all, it is Esther's voice, whose pulse of life and action combats the surrounding bleakness. Esther's point of view is one of keen observation, dramatic sensibility, and veiled sexuality.

In the pages that follow, I will define and examine how Esther's gaze—her voice and acts—amplifies Dickens's message of sexuality and compassion in *Bleak House*.[1] Building upon the foundation of the gaze as defined by Sigmund Freud, Jacques Lacan, Laura Mulvey, and others, I invite readers to envision the framed gaze as a technique that allows Dickens to control the narrative flow, both in tone and pace, to enact a variety of synesthesic effects that blend the visual and the aural.[2] Dickens's fusion of framed gazing and theatrical devices such as direct address and exaggeration in Esther's narration evidences his intent to use sexuality in the novel to elicit action from the readers. This exploration will raise the curtain on Esther's narrative performance by examining how the connection between voice and gaze affects narration, gender, and sexuality in *Bleak House*.

Dickens, through the gaze, emphasizes theatrical aspects and apparent heightened sexuality. Numerous provocative scenes in the novel beg questions: does Dickens lose control of his experimental appropriation of the female voice through Esther's narration or does he seek a purposeful titillation with a dash of lesbian eroticism to bolster Victorian sales?[3] Is it possible that we fixate on sexuality and thus lesbianism stemming from a contemporary hypersensitivity to sexuality? Yet, as Dickens flirts with us through an exploration of transgender boundary crossing in *Bleak House* and his depictions of what contemporary readers may construe as unconventional female friendships, he just as radically plays on conventional narrative techniques of voice and gaze; *Bleak House* is transgressive in more ways than one.

The irony of Esther's point of view helps us to see that Dickens commandeers the female voice and invites the female reader to gaze upon the world as a man, while still retaining her femininity—''she may find herself secretly, unconsciously almost, enjoying the freedom of action and control over the diegetic world that identification with a hero provides'' (Mulvey, ''Afterthoughts'' 24). The novel, in turn, requires male readers to don the role of woman by empathizing with Esther. Dickens successfully effects this role-reversal by deploying synesthesia, blending voice and gaze; this revolutionary narrative technique emphasizes our own bodies and our ability to act.

My discussion will illuminate Dickens's technique of framing the gaze and how this visual position (apparently paradoxically) heralds his reliance on a theatrical voice for Esther's narration, which offers an alternative perspective to the cinematic voice of the omniscient narrator.[4] Esther's narration includes theatrical soliloquies, direct address, and exaggeration of action and speech, but the cinematic voice merely observes, employing aerial shots and montage, especially evident in the opening sequence of the novel. Comparing two distinct visual voices exposes variations in tone, energy, and tempo that go farther to elucidate Dickens's sexual intent in *Bleak House* than subtle charges of pornography or justifications of intense friendliness. The sensory narrative strategies of framed gaze and theatrical voice signal Dickens's controlled message that audiences should poise themselves for a virtuoso literary performance.

Dickens's art manifests itself in the twofold ability to permit audiences both to lose themselves in the stimulating sensation of emotional sensibility through identification with characters' feelings and simultaneously to distance themselves in analytic pleasure. Dickens accomplishes this by juxtaposing an overflow of emotion, brought about by his transmission of theatrical conventions and energy, to a delight in analysis that allows us to view the scaffolding he has erected for our perusal. I argue against the notion that *Bleak House* completely follows the nineteenth-century realistic novel convention of encouraging readers to lose themselves in the story as though it were transparent. By framing the gaze, Dickens presents a device similar to the *verfremdungseffekt*,[5] proclaiming the coming theatrics as theatrics and allowing for the conscious apprehension of his rhetoric, as critics like Frederick Karl promote the idea that Dickens was "writing with a sense of high moral purpose" (141). Thus, through the staging of theatrical scenes, spotlighted by a framed gaze, Dickens both showcases and shrouds sexuality in the novel.

Given his own passionate involvement in the theater, an art form most closely related to the expression of the energy of human interactions, it is not surprising that Dickens should deploy theatrical conventions in his novels. According to Edgar and Eleanor Johnson, Dickens's "imagination and personality were steeped in the stage; the world in which his spirit dwelt was a world brilliant in theatrical hue and violent in theatrical movement, crammed with a huge cast of fantastic actors" (3). As I will illustrate, Dickens's use of theatrical conventions attempts to convey through his writing the energy and pleasure of the sexual experience without being overtly sexual. As Ronald Pearsall notes, "Of all the writers that could have explored the sexual nexus between man and woman, none was better equipped than Dickens, but like his contemporaries he fought shy of the explicit . . . using analogies to indicate . . . sexuality" (68). Dickens's ability to both amplify and mute sexual, perhaps lesbian, scenes in *Bleak House* has led to scholarly contemplation.[6] In particular, when we examine the framed gaze and theatrical voice of Esther's narration, we witness the directed rhythms and patterns of sexuality. Certainly, patterns of rising action and rhythmic delays are not unique to Dickens's writing; however, in Dickens, we find an emphasis and showmanship that directs us to these scenes and their artful mimicry of sexuality. Dickens encourages his audience to become voyeurs—but then the writer goes a step beyond voyeurism by also eliciting social action.

The framed gaze demands our notice, and once Dickens has our attention, he presents a theatrical, cathartic session that dispels the gloomy problems that afflict the residents of the world of *Bleak House*. Dickens doesn't want us to melt into the novel, entertained, and spent—he has pedagogical concerns. Throughout the novel he sets up intense scenes of gazing and drama; characters meet other characters and are instantly delighted and courteous—so full of emotion that it overflows in them, enacting an interaction that makes the importance and humanity of others foremost. Characters see how loved, appreciated, and respected they are—this in turn causes them to experience emotion and this generation of energy is meant to cycle powerfully in the reader. The energy, in turn, is released outward in the form of social action—it is this energy that may inspire characters and readers to act compassionately. Esther's sensibility empowers her attempt to save the orphaned boy Jo by nursing him back to health despite some characters' fears of his contagion. The overflow of emotions that Esther and Ada bring forth mimics conventions of the human sexual experience. Dickens manipulates sexuality for social good. This is one way Dickens suggests to stamp out the cruelty of the world he envisions—the exchange of energy at the level of excitement that live theater and the sexual experience reach to transform the reader. This transformation through the devices of the framed gaze and theatrical voice encourage characters like Esther to work for social good and to ease suffering and illness, exemplified in her surrogate mothering of Caddy Jellyby, her attentions to the pitiful Peepy Jellyby, and her attempt to provide Jo with nursing care.

Theatrical Voice

Following a long tradition of *Bleak House* critics viewing the omniscient and first-person narrations as dichotomous, I propose that the omniscient narration resembles the cinematic in scope and tone, while Esther's first-person narration presents a theatrical model. By theatrical voice, I posit that the writing that follows theatrical conventions (direct address and exaggeration) is intended as spoken performance rather than solely silent reading. It exists as composition so filled with the energy of performance that the subjective reader yearns for its aural fulfillment. Theater performance holds forth the prospect of more potential interaction and engagement between the spectator and the players than cinematic performance. The cinematic voice is a flatter reproduction of a live performance, and its perfection through editing separates itself from the delightful "mistakes," second thoughts, and improvisation that make live art wonderful and energetic; these possibilities, even in a perfectly performed, scripted, theatrical performance, loom in the air of the playhouse, but less in the editing cuts of the cinematic work. In *Bleak House*, theatrical audiences may exist as partners to the conventions of the theater, poised to act out, especially when *verfremdungseffekt* and fourth wall conventions are broken, while cinematic audiences serve as receivers of consciousness-raising, setting up but not necessarily partaking in the action. Viewed this way, the cinematic and theatrical voices work together to inspire characters to act toward social good, but it is only in Esther's narration that this inspiration translates itself into deed.

The best example of cinematic omniscient narration occurs at the opening of the novel, in a sequence which critic Robert Alan Donovan likens to an image of a "roving eye, which, like the movie camera mounted on an overhead crane, can follow the action at will" (103):

London. Michaelmas Term lately over, and the Lord Chancellor sitting in Lincoln's Inn Hall. Implacable November weather. As much mud in the streets, as if the waters had but newly retired from the face of the earth, and it would not be wonderful to meet a Megalosaurus, forty feet long or so, waddling like an elephantine lizard up Holborn Hill. Smoke lowering down from chimney-pots, making a soft black drizzle, with flakes of soot in it as big as full-grown snowflakes—gone into mourning, one might imagine, for the death of the sun. Dogs, undistinguishable in mire. Horses, scarcely better; splashed to their very blinkers. Foot passengers, jostling one another's umbrellas, in a general infection of ill-temper, and losing their foot-hold at street-corners, where tens of thousands of other foot passengers have been slipping and sliding since the day broke (if this day ever broke), adding new deposits to the crust upon crust of mud, sticking at those points tenaciously to the pavement, and accumulating at compound interest.

(1)

This establishing shot sets the voice of the omniscient narrator as an uninvolved spectator—he or she notices the mud, the smoke, and the frustrations of the beings it views, but takes no action to alleviate the bleak scene. The cinematic voice and eye surveying the scene raise consciousness but do not act. The most pronounced evidence of this lack of action reveals itself through the absence of verbs throughout the passage. The sufferings "accumulate" and "compound," yet the emotional concern, sympathy, or sentiment remains one of disinterest. Just as in the narration, there is no sense in the description of meaningful interaction by characters, only "jostling" and "ill-temper." The narrator's move from "London" to "Smoke," "Dogs," "Horses," and "Foot passengers" acts as a cinematic montage of associative editing—a series of contiguous shots materializing a metaphorical and symbolic relationship. The "smoke" of "London" settles on all beings, where "foot passengers" are as "undistinguishable in mire" and as "splashed to their very blinkers" as their pitiful beastly counterparts.

In contrast to this cinematic voice, Esther's narration blossoms as theatrical. In her introduction, three chapters into *Bleak House*, her vibrant voice rings out as if from the stage: "I have a great deal of difficulty in beginning to write my portion of these pages for I know I am not clever" (15). This direct address to the reader announces Esther's subjectivity, her characterization; she has the floor even as she pretends not to. Her self-effacing comments so abhorred by some critics read like a direct address to a live audience with the effect of dividing and compartmentalizing them from the rest of her narration.[7] Set off parenthetically, Esther's direct address reveals a desire to speak to her audience and clarify possible misunderstandings. In the midst of the introductory soliloquy quoted above, Esther states, "I have mentioned that, unless my vanity should deceive me (as I know it may, for I may be very vain, without suspecting it—though indeed I don't) my comprehension is quickened when my affection is" (16). Esther's awareness that she requires emotional attachment to enact understanding contrasts sharply to Dickens's depiction of other characters like Lady Dedlock, who "by suppressing [her] true feelings follow[s] the path to self-destruction" (Karl 133).

We see many instances of this theatrical soliloquizing and direct address throughout Esther's narration. Later in the novel, Esther comments on Richard's well-being and the unfortunate effects of the Chancery on his character. At the conclusion of her matter-of-fact oratory she perorates: "I write these opinions, not because I believe that this or any other thing was so, because I thought so; but only because I did think so, and I want to be quite candid about all I thought and did" (227). Although some readers may view Esther's comments as awkward or paranoid, I believe her language points to her theatrical perspective and how this perspective indicates a sophisticated awareness of the world and her role in it—an awareness that other characters in the novel seem to lack. Her direct address to readers confirms that she recognizes her audience and wishes to ensure that they grasp her motivations. The impact of Esther's interactive theatrical voice lends her narration not only more humanity, but also an energy and excitement less present in the plodding, divorced, omniscient narration that in its cinematic model is once removed from the energy of live human interaction with which Dickens imbues Esther's voice.

Dickens's use of theatrics through Esther's narration emerges strikingly in a private scene between Esther and Ada in which the latter confesses what Esther has already surmised—that Ada and Richard are secretly in love. This passage remains one of the best examples of Dickens's dual ability to mesmerize his audience in excited sensibility and concurrently to distance the audience to allow for scrutinized analysis and interpretation. Dickens sets his frame through Esther's gaze:

Now I observed that evening, as I had observed for some days past, that Ada
and Richard were more than ever attached to each other's society; which was
but natural, seeing that they were going to be separated so soon. I was therefore
not very much surprised, when we got home, and Ada and I retired up-stairs,
to find Ada more silent than usual; though I was not quite prepared for her
coming into my arms, and beginning to speak to me, with her face hidden.

(176)

Starting the scene sedately, Esther's calm can be seen in her report that she
is "not very much surprised." Esther and Ada "retire" and, their interaction
is described as "silent." In the continuing passage, Dickens quickly moves
to histrionics sparked by the close intimate proximity of Esther and Ada.
Once Ada's face is "hidden" in Esther's breast as Esther hugs Ada, we enter
the realm of the body. The narrative pace increases rapidly with short rhythmic bursts copying sexual intensity as masterfully as live theatrical performance. The vacillation between exclamations and questions quickens and
excites as the repeated "O"s mimic a clichéd lover's surprise of desire.

If Dickens flaunts sexuality between these two women for sensational reasons, we might ask whether his writing becomes pornographic. Or could
Dickens be using sexuality as a theatrical tool to increase energy that leads
to ideation and action, as Esther hints in her opening soliloquy, "my comprehension is quickened when my affection is" (16)? The scene's intense titillation begs attention:

> "My darling Esther!" murmured Ada. "I have a great secret to tell you!"
> A mighty secret, my pretty one, no doubt!
> "What is it, Ada?"
> "O Esther, you would never guess!"
> "Shall I try to guess?" said I.
> "O no! Don't! Pray don't" cried Ada, very much startled by the idea of my
> doing so.
> "Now, I wonder who it can be about?" said I, pretending to consider.
> "It's about," said Ada, in a whisper. "It's about—my cousin Richard!"
> "Well, my own!" said I, kissing her bright hair, which was all I could see.
> "And what about him?"
> "O Esther, you would never guess!"
> It was so pretty to have her clinging to me in that way, hiding her face; and
> to know that she was not crying in sorrow, but in a little glow of joy, and pride,
> and hope; that I would not help her just yet.   (176–77)

Ada murmurs exclamations while burrowed in Esther's arms, discussing a
secret about which it seems impossible for audiences not to venture guesses,
and mumbling murmurs that turn to whispers, kisses, and clinging. In my
view, reading the exchange as an attempt by Dickens to use theatrics as a
spectacle for the simultaneous expression, sublimation, and manipulation of

sexuality assists in untangling positions of unexamined voyeurism. Yet this teasing volley is itself a self-conscious performance on Esther's part complete with all the necessary vigor of live action. Esther occupies a decidedly poly-morphic gendered position, inviting audience members to try out the role as the strong protector of Ada's secret and physicality, acting as a brace for Ada to lean upon as she confesses the secret that Esther, through her mastery of observation and assessment, has already gleaned.

We learn of Esther's delight in her privileged position through her direct address to the audience, starting with "It was so pretty to have her clinging to me in that way." This position is one she desires to sustain, as Dickens milks the scene in repetitions and delays that enhance sentimental pleasure. Dickens allows Esther the complete freedom to express her desire for Ada, and she does so with oral professions of love, visual delight, and physical en-thusiasm:

> "He says—I know it's very foolish, we are both so young—but he says," with a burst of tears, "that he loves me dearly, Esther."
> "Does he indeed?" said I. "I never heard of such a thing! Why, my pet of pets, I could have told you that weeks and weeks ago!"
> To see Ada lift up her flushed face in joyful surprise, and hold me round the neck, and laugh, and cry, and blush, and laugh, was so pleasant!   (176–77)

Dickens's mastery of what may be regarded as sublimated sexuality, in a scene that has nothing literally to do with sex, seems most pronounced here, as Ada's speech, broken by dashes and description poises breathy before her orgasmic "burst of tears" followed by "joyful surprise" with the requisite physical manifestation of the blush. The evidence of theatrics exists in Es-ther's direct address to the audience "To see Ada lift up her flushed face." Esther's theatrical voice lends some credence to the argument that the scene contains lesbian overtones, yet at the same time, if we view dramatic art as an attempted mimicking of sexual rhythmic motifs to enact a recognition of human interactions, we find Dickens to be not simply a tantalizer but an enactor of social good. This dual purpose promotes emotional love and the passion often inextricably connected to love as a vehicle for social good, allowing characters and urging readers to act in both a performative and real sense.

The speed with which the continued scene moves with its ubiquitous ex-clamatory punctuation, marks a sexual pattern, evidenced by the women's clipped dialogue, which crescendos, not to diminish until after several bursts of tears and cries when "Ada was soon quiet and happy":

> "O, that's not quite the worst of it, Esther dear!" cried Ada, holding me tighter, and laying down her face again upon my breast.

"No?" said I. "Not even that?"

"No, not even that!" said Ada, shaking her head.

"Why, you never mean to say—!" I was beginning in joke.

But Ada, looking up, and smiling through her tears, cried, "Yes, I do! You know I do!" and then sobbed out, "With all my heart I do! With all my whole heart, Esther!"

I told her, laughing, why I had known that, too, just as well as I had known the other! And we sat before the fire, and I had all the talking to myself for a little while (though there was not much of it); and Ada was soon quiet and happy.   (177)

The scene winds down with a tearful confession masked in ambiguity, as the women remain entwined. In my examination of the language of Ada's actual confession, the object of her affection, though easily assumed to be Richard, remains unclear. Ada clearly states to Esther that Richard has made his love for her apparent. She relates to Esther: " 'he says,' with a burst of tears, 'that he loves me dearly, Esther' " (177). However, the language moves from clear to ambiguous when Ada pleads her own feelings. Esther, without naming Richard, questions Ada: " 'Why you never mean to say—!' And Ada replies, 'Yes, I do! You know, you know I do!' and then sobbed out, 'With all my heart I do! With all my whole heart, Esther!' " (177).

Some may argue that the subsequent plot movements confirm that the object of Ada's affection is indeed Richard; however, why in the midst of the scene in question, as Esther "kisses [Ada's] bright hair, which was all [she] could see," does Dickens choose to cloak the love object in ambiguity? Esther and Ada's interactions play out through their bodies—touching, voicing, and crying. Note how Ada, described by Esther, in the above scene "look[s] up," orienting her body, in this case her head, to Esther's position. Ada looks "through her tears" focusing attention to her gaze and to how her tears may veil the view and the way of seeing as she voices with her cry, "Yes, I do!" Esther's theatrical voice and performance announce the synaesthesic link of the visual and aural to the "acting" body, clarifying for her audience her ability to act to relieve Ada's ambiguous anxiety and confusion. Social action on this personal, micro-level buffers larger social catastrophes like Chancery and exists as first movements in meaningful social change.

The Framed Gaze[8]

As Esther performs, she also witnesses and her gaze frames the action of *Bleak House*. The first frame of the novel invites the reader to gaze at Esther's narrative performance articulated in her direct address, qualifications, and the quirks that have angered some critics, not recognizing Dickens's theatrical modes.[9] The second frame highlights Esther's gazing at another character, and at times a third layer materializes where we gaze at Esther gazing at another character who is gazing at yet another character. These layers call special attention to the gaze and how its specific frames inform the coming theatrical scene.[10] Esther and other characters in these framed scenes exhibit the elements necessary for a staged performance that emphasize increased energy, histrionics, and melodrama.

In *Bleak House* we witness an example of the triple-layered framed gaze described sequentially above, when Esther, Ada, Mr. Skimpole, and Mr. Jarndyce attend a small church service while visiting Mr. Boythorn. In this exchange, Esther first encounters the "pretty girl" Rosa, the Frenchwoman Mademoiselle Hortense, and Lady Dedlock. Esther narrates:

> The pretty girl, of whom Mr. Boythorn had told us, was close by her. She was so very pretty, that I might have known her by her beauty, even if I had not seen how blushingly conscious she was of the eyes of the young fisherman, whom I discovered not far off. One face, and not an agreeable one, though it was handsome, seemed maliciously watchful of this pretty girl, and indeed of every one and everything there. It was a Frenchwoman's.   (249)

Already gazing at Esther, we follow her to the church and in the second frame of the gaze we stare impressively at the beauty of Rosa through Esther's narrative direction. Dickens has our complete attention as Esther's exaggerated enamored attention to Rosa and her beauty present evidence of erotic scopophilia—blushing by Rosa and staring by the young fisherman, as well as Esther. The second frame intensifies the energy and the voyeuristic "pleasure in looking" in the scene significantly, as Esther watches the fisherman admire both Rosa's prettiness and Rosa's uncomfortable consciousness that she is being surveyed. The third frame presents an element of danger as Esther notices Mademoiselle Hortense gazing not only at Rosa, but also at "everyone and everything." Why does Esther describe the Frenchwoman's gaze as malicious when she, too, has been ogling the entire congregation?

Dickens excites our gaze and frames our attention in this memorable scene by using theatrical conventions that increase energy and mimic conventions of seduction and sexual tension. The above scene, set in a church audience, uses the gaze in place of dialogue to convey dramatic action. Emphasis remains on the erotic look that slips between characters amidst "close" bodily proximity and blushing. The gaze transmits a link of desire or strong interest from Esther and Rosa, Rosa and the fisherman, and Mlle. Hortense and "everyone" through the repeated description that Rosa is "pretty." Rosa's "beauty" contrasts sharply with Mlle. Hortense's "handsome" controlling male gaze that to Esther seems "malicious." Esther's gaze upon Mlle. Hortense and her identification of Hortense's face as "not an agreeable one," along with Esther's power to pronounce the French maid's watching ''malicious,'' combine to condemn ''the Frenchwoman'' in Esther's narration. At the same time, the gaze and theatrics call attention to class and xenophobia—the menacing French maid dares to transcend class barriers that would normally prohibit the lower-class, especially service-class members, from eyeballing those of the upper class. The scene's energy multiplies through forbidden notions of sexuality and hints of its transmission between distinct classes.

Dickens, unwilling to describe any overtly sexual events, yet desiring to capture the whole of the truth of human experience,[11] must, in the Victorian sense, sublimate sex to the unspoken level of the pre-symbolic. William A. Cohen argues that in Dickens's work ''literary language functions simultaneously to connote and to obscure sexual meanings,'' and that ''by locating the collection of rhetorical techniques . . . a sexual pulse can be felt beating subcutaneously in a novel that does not overtly represent sex'' (23). Dickens mimics nature by framing a stage of sexual rhythms, and the reading (or hearing, when we consider how often Dickens's novels were read aloud) of cadenced language allows sensual enjoyment and titillation in scenes of apparent innocence.

The following passage increases the sexual tension, not only by its histrionic description of Esther's autonomic nervous system, but also by interruption of the tension with a paragraph devoted to description of the church. This lull relaxes the energy yet sustains it enough for the next round of theatrical excitement—a masterful mimicking of the sexual experience. My analysis inserted between these two passages should have a similar effect in delaying the excitement from this excerpt of the scene until the next as Esther's narration erupts suddenly:

> Shall I ever forget the rapid beating at my heart, occasioned by the look I met, as I stood up! Shall I ever forget the manner in which those handsome proud eyes seemed to spring up out of their languor, and to hold mine! It was only a moment before I cast mine down—released again, if I may say so—on my book; but I knew the beautiful face quite well, in that short space of time . . . the lady was Lady Dedlock. But why her face should be, in a confused way, like a broken glass to me, in which I saw scraps of old remembrances; and why I should be so fluttered and troubled (for I was still), by having casually met her eyes; I could not think.   (250)

Despite the scene's delicate foreshadowing of Esther's eventual discovery that Lady Dedlock is in fact her mother, Dickens presents us with an exchange drenched in sexual excitement. Lady Dedlock's eyes ''spring up'' and ''hold'' Esther causing her to ''flutter'' and lose her ability to project her gaze outward, suggesting the power to move and control and the power of self-conscious reflection, which we find in the sexual experience and in its transmission to the realm of dramatic art. Lady Dedlock's "broken glass" face acts as a mirror in which Esther views herself with excited fascination. *Bleak House*'s subjective reader, Esther, and Lady Dedlock form a framed gaze tripod signaling the theatrical excitement gleaned from the energy of human interaction that Dickens captures so vividly—the rapid heartbeats and locked gazes known so well in a live theatrical performance.

The last passage of this framed scene occurs, again after an interlude, allowing us to recover; and, before Esther brings us back to the overt staring, Dickens circles our attention back to our heroine with a pronounced "I—I, little Esther Summerson" (250). Through the exaggeration of Esther's physical state and hence the body in the upcoming passage, the statement focuses our attention on the framed gaze:

> It made me tremble so, to be thrown into this unaccountable agitation, that I was conscious of being distressed even by the observation of the French maid, though I knew she had been looking watchfully here, and there, and everywhere, from the moment of her coming into the church. By degrees, though very slowly, I at last overcame my strange emotion. After a long time, I looked towards Lady Dedlock again. It was while they were preparing to sing, before the sermon. She took no heed of me, and the beating at my heart was gone. Neither did it revive for more than a few moments, when she once or twice afterwards glanced at Ada or at me through her glass.   (250–51)

Now it is Esther who is occupying Rosa's original position in the church scene, distressed by the scopophilic gaze, trembling in a histrionic fit of "unaccountable agitation." Gazing highlights Esther's sexual sensibility as she is again examined by the French maid and by Lady Dedlock. Left without the explanation of Dickens's theatrical aim, readers may wonder why Esther seems so concerned by the gazing for which she is equally responsible. Dickens strives to emphasize key scenes dramatically through sexual subtext and to lend a more emotional, interactive quality to Esther's voice. Dickens wants his readers to feel—as much as they can—*with* Esther because her subjective human communication is one key to compassionate acting.

The framed gazes and theatrical voice of Esther's narration draw readers to the realization that Dickens offers sentimentality and emotion as barometers for social action. Dickens allows Esther to interact with other characters in a more emotional and thus more realistically human way than the cinematic omniscient narrator who, at times, coldly records events and interactions from an aerial view seemingly above the range of human existence. It is the cinematic narrator who reports Jo's death and all of the events that lead up to the tragedy, but it is Esther who feels Jo's predicament and *acts* to save him. The cinematic and theatrical narratives work together—the cinematic voice allowing the distancing necessary for analytical pleasure and Esther's voice allowing a sentimentality that urges action.

To view this dynamic let us examine the novel's first meeting of principal players: Esther, Ada, and Richard. In this convergence of characters at the law office of Mr. Kenge, Dickens frames his theatrics through the gaze of Esther. Mr. Kenge leads Esther "along a passage, into a comfortable sort of room, where a young lady and a young gentleman were standing near a great, loud-roaring fire. A screen was interposed between them and it, and they were leaning on the screen, talking" (29). Esther focuses immediately on the young lady, Ada, and by depicting Esther as the watcher of another female, Dickens imbues her with traits commonly associated with masculinity, allowing female readers to imagine themselves dramatically possessing the power and privilege of men. The gaze signals this role-play as Esther, upon first meeting Ada, a ward of the court, exhibits the penetrating gaze normally employed by men watching women. According to Mulvey, "the determining male gaze projects its fantasy onto the female figure, which is styled accordingly" ("Visual Pleasure" 1448). Through the gaze, Esther punctuates her description of Ada with exclamations: "I saw in the young lady, with the fire shining upon her, such a beautiful girl! With such rich golden hair, such soft blue eyes, and such a bright, innocent, trusting face" (29). It is difficult to ignore such a burst of enflamed desire coming from Esther, and as the meeting progresses she quickly takes possession of Ada with her first pet name—"my darling" (30).

Recognizing the historically testosterone-soaked literary canon that Gilbert and Gubar expose in *Madwoman in the Attic*, female critics and readers alike are no strangers of the necessity to identify with a male narrator, despite its incongruence, at times, to their own feminine sensibilities. How novel that Dickens empowers readers with the ability to cross gender lines, at least polymorphically, and imagine the other's sphere. To interpret this as lesbian overture or attempt to explain it away as intense friendship, misses the profound invitation to act in the role Dickens intends—for his female audience, retaining their femininity through identification with a *female* narrator to see the world through the eyes of a man with the transfer of power and possession the role bequeaths.[12] By writing through an ambiguous narrator, he transfers feelings of power and privilege enjoyed by men to his female audience. Ellen Moers's accentuation of Esther's freedom of motion "far from the confines of *Bleak House*" and Esther's outspokenness throughout the novel evidence this narrative dynamic (20).

The catharsis Dickens offers women readers through role-play, the identification with maleness through a woman's eyes that allows them to behold power, and the requirement that men play the role of women could explain the difficulty some male critics have had with Esther's narration.[13] As the group grows with the addition of the Lord Chancellor, we witness another male trait in Esther—sizing up the competition for her newly claimed possession. As Ada is presented to the Lord Chancellor, Esther narrates: "That he admired her, and was interested in her, even *I* could see in a moment" (31). Esther is keenly aware of the position in the room of "her" Ada at all times, noticing both when Mr. Kenge and Richard exit and when her "pet" is finally "released" by the Lord Chancellor (31–32). As the group of three—Esther, Ada, and Richard—are left alone, Esther stamps her possession of Ada more powerfully with a diminutive name, calling her "my love." Any threat to Esther's possession of Ada by Richard is dismissed, for he is simply a "youth" and a "light-hearted boy" in Esther's calculation (30).

Along with a gendered role reversal, crucial to our understanding of the gaze and the framed gaze in *Bleak House*, is the required presence of an audience. The significance of the framed gaze becomes manifest only when an audience forces an alienation of the gazing, causing a self-reflexive consciousness ripe for "acting" toward social good. This is why the connection between the framed gaze and Esther's theatrical voice, with its awareness of being watched, is so important; it highlights Esther's position in the novel as both spectacle and spectator.

Voice and Gaze

Dickens does not limit the theatrical voice and framed gaze to scenes involving only women. The following passage occurs a few pages before the preceding example of Ada's confession to Esther. In this scene at a theater in London, Esther narrates that she is hounded by Mr. Guppy, who several chapters before proposed marriage to her at only their second meeting and was promptly but politely rejected:

> I was sitting in front of the box one night with Ada; and Richard was in the place he liked best, behind Ada's chair; when, happening to look down into the pit, I saw Mr. Guppy, with his hair flattened down upon his head, and woe depicted in his face, looking up at me. I felt, all through the performance, that he never looked at the actors, but constantly looked at me, and always with a carefully prepared expression of the deepest misery and the profoundest dejection. (171)

Again, we see the framed gaze present, focusing our attention on the upcoming dramatic scene; it is no coincidence that the exchange unravels at a theatrical performance, adding another layer to the complexity of the interaction. Dickens winks at readers here, providing a scene implementing theatrical conventions set at an actual theater performance attended by Esther, Ada, and Richard, a scene in which more drama unfolds between Esther and Mr. Guppy in the theater's audience than on the actual proscenium. The scene follows the framed gaze formula: we gaze at Esther gazing at both the actors in the play and at Mr. Guppy. He, in turn, directs his male gaze, complete with all the oppression inherent in its visage, upon Esther. Here the theatrics are transferred from Esther to Mr. Guppy with his "carefully prepared expression." The contrast between this heterosexual gazing and theatrics and the homosocial exchange between Esther and Ada that follows reveals a frozen Esther, unable to act, unable to emote:

> I really cannot express how uneasy this made me. If he would only have brushed up his hair, or turned up his collar, it would have been bad enough; but to know that that absurd figure was always gazing at me, and always in that demonstrative state of despondency, put such a constraint upon me that I did not like to laugh at the play, or to cry at it, or to move or to speak. I seemed able to do nothing naturally. . . . So there I sat, not knowing where to look—for wherever I looked, I knew Mr. Guppy's eyes were following me—   (172)

On this occasion, to contrast with the previous scene between Esther and Ada, Esther suffers from a form of blindness ("not knowing where to look") that drains her sensibility and her reason and leaves her unable to "laugh," to "cry," "or to speak." Here we see the oppressive nature of the gaze, for the control and power of Guppy's gaze render Esther unable to act "naturally." Yet this oppression of the gaze also renders Esther self-conscious; the gaze she normally directs outward toward others now beams back upon herself, bestowing upon her important powers of self-reflection that she learns from and uses in her future intercourse with Ada. Esther's blindness and muteness in the face of Mr. Guppy draw attention to the free gazing and the voiced narration that launches desire and social action in her interaction with Ada.

As the play ends, Esther continues describing her voluntary blindness in relation to Guppy: "After we got home, he haunted a post opposite our house. The upholsterer's where we lodged, being at the corner of two streets, and my bedroom window being opposite the post, I was afraid to go near the window when I went up-stairs, lest I should see him (as I did one moonlight night) leaning against the post" (172). Throughout the scene, Esther remains oppressed, avoiding her normal behavior in the fear of additional gazing and action by Mr. Guppy, who leans against the phallic post, stalking her from the street. Yet the emotions and theatrics of the passage, with all of the hints of sexuality expressed through energy, allow Esther to act with her true convictions when she next encounters Mr. Guppy later in the novel. For, when she next interacts with him, she seeks him out, and she remains composed enough to accept Mr. Guppy's withdrawn proposal of marriage. Guppy's action reinforces Esther's fears that the facial scarring she received during a life-threatening illness, contracted during her care of the orphan boy Jo, affects the way others view her. However, Esther learns through the course of the novel that while some people may see the scars on her face as evidence of a taint to be avoided, other characters, like Allan Woodcourt, equally invested in acting for social good, regard Esther's scars as a badge of honor representing her performance of good works.

At the novel's end, Dickens recalls Mr. Guppy's proposal scene when he describes another proposal, this one from Allan Woodcourt to Esther. The scene where Allan first confesses his love to Esther contrasts sharply with the earlier excerpts of framed gazing, theatrics, and sexual subtext. Esther narrates:

> We were standing by the opened window, looking down into the street, when Mr. Woodcourt spoke to me. I learned in a moment that he loved me. I learned in a moment that my scarred face was all unchanged to him. I learned in a moment that what I had thought was pity and compassion, was devoted, generous, faithful love. O, too late to know it now, too late, too late. That was the first ungrateful thought I had. Too late.   (832–33)

Gone are the intense gazing sessions prominent in the church scene with Esther, Mlle. Hortense, and Lady Dedlock. Here Esther and Mr. Woodcourt look away from each other as the emphasis leans toward reason rather than emotion with the repetition of "I learned" and "thought." The emotional and profuse touching and weeping we witness between Esther and Ada is replaced with a controlled calm with no tactile action.

As Esther and Mr. Woodcourt discuss the matter of love, the only similarity to earlier examples of Esther's interactions with women is her duplication of exclamatory statements. Mr. Woodcourt, as she refers to him formally throughout the entire exchange despite the revelation of their mutual love and her penchant for nicknames, disjointedly speaks of Esther in the third person, creating an emotional distance not present even with Mlle. Hortense or Mr. Guppy. Again, Mr. Woodcourt's dialogue shuns love and emotion, privileging "the truth" over "lover's praise":

> "When I returned," he told me, "when I came back, no richer than when I went away, and found you newly risen from a sick bed, yet so inspired by sweet consideration for others, and so free from a selfish thought—
> "O, Mr. Woodcourt, forbear, forbear!" I entreated him. "I do not deserve your high praise. I had many selfish thoughts at that time, many!"
> "Heaven knows, beloved of my life," said he, "that my praise is not a lover's praise, but the truth. You do not know what all around you see in Esther Summerson, how many hearts she touches and awakens, what sacred admiration and what love she wins."
> "O, Mr. Woodcourt," cried I, "it is a great thing to win love, it is a great thing to win love! I am proud of it, and honoured by it; and the hearing of it

causes me to shed these tears of mingled joy and sorrow—joy that I have won it, sorrow that I have not deserved it better; but I am not free to think of yours.''

(833)

Their interaction unfolds so formally that when Esther reports she is crying, readers must wonder whether the couple has taken their eyes from the street throughout the entire conversation. The conspicuous visual fixation of previous scenes is replaced with an emphasis on audition. As if the pair were indeed still peering out the open window, Esther states she ''heard his voice thrill'' before he ''broke the silence'':

> I said it with a stronger heart; for when he praised me thus, and when I heard his voice thrill with his belief that what he said was true, I aspired to be more worthy of it. It was not too late for that. Although I closed this unforeseen page in my life to-night, I could be worthier of it all through my life. And it was a comfort to me, and an impulse to me, and I felt a dignity rise up within me that was derived from him, when I thought so.
> He broke the silence.
> (833)

The speech that breaks the silence reads more like a letter than a heartfelt admission of love in the direct presence of the lover. ''Truth'' and ''dignity'' replace crying, blushing, and burying faces in breasts. Gone are the physical expressions of desire we see in Esther's relations with Ada:

> ''Dear Mr. Woodcourt'', said I, ''before we part to-night, something is left for me to say. I never could say it as I wish—I never shall—but—''
> I had to think again of being more deserving of his love, and his affliction, before I could go on.
> ''—I am deeply sensible of your generosity, and I shall treasure its remembrance to my dying hour. I know full well how changed I am, I know you are not unacquainted with my history, and I know what a noble love that is which is so faithful. What you have said to me, could have affected me so much from no other lips; for there are none that could give it such a value to me. It shall not be lost. It shall make me better.''
> He covered his eyes with his hand, and turned away his head. How could I ever be worthy of those tears?
> (834)

Just as Esther finally begins to work up more intense sentiment, evidenced by her faltering dashes, she stops herself ''to think,'' and the polite composure in her subsequent speech reads more like a declining of an invitation. Why are the theatrics and the honest communication of desire present in so much of Esther's narrative so hollowly absent here? What could account for Dickens's sudden, striking lack of energy between two characters enamored of each other from early in the novel? The answer dwells within the lovers' near-miss fate. As a result of this controlled scene between Esther and Allan, they almost tragically end up apart. Esther, already obligatorily engaged to John Jarndyce, fails to mention the specifics of her promise while speaking with Allan, simply stating that she is "not free to think of" Allan's proposal (833).

Dickens uses a layer of sexual energy as the quintessence of sentimental, extemporaneous relations between human beings to teach us, through the characters in the novel, how this kind of interaction, along with ethical and responsible dutifulness, leads to action that will make us and those around us happy. Absence of the framed gaze, which can express desire, exert power, and reflect upon ourselves and others honestly, saps Esther's and Allan's energy to perform both as spectacle and spectator. The coded, scripted interactions of Esther and Allan cause a reticence that subjugates emotion and causes an inhibition of action that potentially impairs characters' ability to act on a social level for the good of others.

Sexuality

No discussion of the sublimation of sexuality in *Bleak House* could be complete without the recognition that Esther herself teems with an unspoken sexuality. The dramatizations of touching, crying, blushing, and professions of love, the nicknames she acquires, the constant jiggling of her household keys, and the frequent communications of her observations all connote desire.

Esther generates energy in the novel, while many of the other characters like Mr. Skimpole, Mr. Vholes, and Mr. Tulkinghorn, as well as the Chancery and other institutions, drain energy. As the representation of a source of energy, Esther's narration fittingly includes scenes embedded with sexual innuendo. A particularly apt example of a scene charged with sexual subtext occurs after Esther recovers from the life-threatening illness that leaves her face scarred. The contagious nature of Esther's illness has prevented Ada from coming close to her. The scene that follows reunites them for the first time since Esther's recovery. Esther narrates:

> There were more than two full hours yet to elapse, before she could come; and in that interval, which seemed a long one, I must confess I was nervously anxious about my altered looks. I loved my darling so well that I was more concerned for their effect on her than on any one. . . . When she first saw me, might she not be a little shocked and disappointed?   (516)

The framed gaze signals the drama to come, as it teases out sexuality in what seems like a purposed titillation. Esther spends the time anticipating the reunion with Ada, worrying that when Esther gazes upon Ada gazing back upon Esther, Ada will find fault in Esther's altered visage. Note the emphasis on delay, "more than two full hours to elapse" in an "interval, which seemed a long one,'' as the dramatic voicing of Esther's confession harkens back to the sexually charged and ambiguous scene of Ada's confession to Esther that Ada and Richard are in love. Here, Esther's confession focuses on her nervous anxiety, a tell-tale awareness of her own excited state that builds in intensity to mimic conventions of human sexuality. Esther's nervousness pivots on her body—her ''altered looks''—that threaten to compromise her performance as a spectacle for Ada's pleasure. We see this evidenced by her worried question that Ada may be ''shocked'' or ''disappointed'' as opposed to pleased. Esther's mention of love, ''my darling'' and Ada's prominence in Esther's esteem more than ''any one'' further suggests a romantic reunion.

Esther, in exaggerated anticipation of Ada's arrival, contemplates the ''various expressions of my sweet girl's face,'' walks along the road looking for her coach, and runs back to the house in an awkward display that sounds more like romance than friendship. Finally, the scene produces Ada's arrival:

> At last, when I believed there was at least a quarter of an hour more yet, Charley all at once cried out to me as I was trembling in the garden, ''Here she comes, miss! Here she is!''
> I did not mean to do it, but I ran up-stairs into my room, and hid myself behind the door. There I stood trembling, even when I heard my darling calling as she came up-stairs, ''Esther, my dear, my love, where are you? Little woman, dear Dame Durden!''   (517)

The suspense of the scene has worked Esther up to a ''trembling'' in her garden—the most fertile and sexually powerful setting on the grounds of *Bleak House*. The delay is finally satisfied with the announcement of the coming climax, ''at last'' and its erupting cry ''all at once.'' At her maid Charley's excited announcement punctuated by exclamation points, Esther bursts into a running dash to her room, where she tries to hide, trembling behind the door in what resembles sexual sensibility. In the confines of her room, Esther reverts to the pre-symbolic and pre-spectacle as she silently and secretly watches Ada searching and calling for her, echoing Esther's pet name for her ''my love.''

Ada also reintroduces the persistent nicknames that Ada and her lover/ husband Richard have assigned to Esther: ''little woman,'' ''Dame Durden,'' and ''little old woman.'' According to Cohen, ''the homology between proper names and sexual discourses is one of the crucial junctures of indeterminacy that enable the erotic and the literary mutually to generate each other. The names of characters, . . . are loaded with provocative suggestion, and in some cases they overlap with sexual meanings'' (22). Esther's nicknames may reveal an un-virginal quality—the older, experienced (perhaps sexually experienced) woman. This connection with sexuality links itself to Esther's taint from her mother's sexual indiscretion and may influence her dealings with men and the possibility of marriage. Esther's facial scarring could represent a physical manifestation of this taint—marking her as potentially unmarriageable. Only characters who view Esther's scarring as emblematic of her work toward social good continue their relations with Esther undaunted.

As the flight/chase scenario continues, further evidencing conventions of human sexual experience, Esther and Ada freely express their sensibility, in a manner unlike the later stilted interaction between Esther and Allan Woodcourt that reduces their ability to act. Esther persists:

> She ran in, and was running out again when she saw me. Ah, my angel girl! the old dear look, all love, all fondness, all affection. Nothing else in it—no, nothing, nothing!
> O how happy I was, down upon the floor, with my sweet beautiful girl down upon the floor too, holding my scarred face to her lovely cheek, bathing it with tears and kisses, rocking me to and fro like a child, calling me by every tender name that she could think of, and pressing me to her faithful heart.   (517)

The scene epitomizes the body, voice, gaze compendium that frames a stage of sexual rhythms through cadenced language patterns. Ada presses Esther to her body as she holds, bathes with tears, rocks, and voices her calls to Esther of ''every tender name.'' This is made possible by ''the old look''—the gaze that enables self-reflexive consciousness. Ada's gaze mirrors Esther's acceptance of her own ''altered looks.'' The cadenced language beginning with ''Ah, my angel girl!'' produces a rhythmic pattern marked by regular punctuated stress most commonly achieved through comma placement.

The culmination of the scene seems at its most climactic with lesbian overtures, frustrating a critic like Geoffrey Carter, who worries that ''what upsets us here, perhaps, is that in the guise of portraying an innocent girl's sisterly altruism, Dickens is, in fact titillating us with a scene of sexual hysteria, set up by weeks of subtly sadistic postponement of gratification'' (144). Yet, when understood through Esther's unspoken sexuality with its framed gazes and theatrical devices, a sensibility is revealed that allows Ada to accept Esther despite any possible taint in the eyes of society. This acceptance evokes such overflowing relief in Esther that a circuit of energy pulses, imitating sexual rhythms and carrying with it Dickens's message of sensibility and social action. Esther and Ada's extemporaneous interaction breaks codes and scripts allowing a dress rehearsal for kind action—a practicing of behavior that will allow them to act to help others dutifully and responsibly when called upon.

Another aspect of Esther's unspoken sexuality is alluded to in Cohen's suggestion of a correlation between women's sexuality and objects of material value (175). Following Freud, he discusses jewels specifically and their representation of genitalia, positing that jewels manifest male genitalia and jewel boxes, female genitalia.[14] Jewelry is conspicuously absent in *Bleak House*; however, there exist abundant references to keys. Near the beginning of Esther's narrative, during her first moment alone, after her arrival with Ada and Richard to John Jarndyce's home, Esther is approached by an unknown maid and given two sets of keys.

> Our luggage having arrived, and being all at hand, I was dressed in a few minutes, and engaged in putting my worldly goods away, when a maid (not the one in attendance upon Ada, but another whom I had not seen) brought a basket into my room, with two bunches of keys in it, all labeled.
> "For you, miss, if you please," said she.
> "For me?" said I.
> "The housekeeping keys, miss."
> I showed my surprise; for she added with some little surprise on her own part: "I was told to bring them as soon as you was alone, miss." (68)

If we view houses as representations of their owners, then the bestowing of all the keys of Bleak House to Esther to unlock every room is significant. As Esther begins the scene, alone in her room dressing and thus undressing, suggesting a subtle connection to sexuality, it is her surprise that seizes our attention. The connection of these household keys to male Freudian symbolic sexuality and power culminates when Esther, after reading her guardian's letter of proposal and deciding obligatorily to accept, relinquishes her keys and "gave them a kiss" (612). Esther's resignation of the keys that unlock her power provide a symbolic representation of her temporary folly. As she touches the keys to her lips and denies her body's desires, she denies the gazing that would warn her not to silence her voice but instead to decline Jarndyce's offer of engagement.

How do we account for Esther's lack of power in relinquishing her keys and accepting the proposal of marriage from her "guardian," thereby blocking the expression of her desire for Allan? As a father-figure to whom Esther believes she is deeply in debt, John Jarndyce complicates her agency temporarily. Here we see a glimpse of the limits of Dickens's experiment. Where a man may follow his desire whether or not its reciprocation is confirmed, Esther, not knowing yet that Woodcourt wishes to marry her, must seriously consider the consequences of declining Jarndyce's offer of marriage. Esther enjoys her blended view of the world through the eyes of a man, but her female status trumps polymorphism as a subordinate in Victorian society where marriage reigns as a survival mechanism.

Now her desire must work indirectly as another direct address hints at her revised agency. The morning after Esther receives the proposal letter from Mr. Jarndyce, after crying for most of the night, she describes her guardian's demeanor, "there being not the least constraint in his manner, there was none (or so I thought there was none) in mine" (613). Still partially blinded to her situation with her eyes "red and swollen," her direct address suggests the return of her agency despite societal limits (611). Her deep connection to her emotions prevents her from being without constraint, signaling to Jarndyce her alternate feelings through the performance of her body. Even as she accepts his proposal verbally with a kiss, Jarndyce has already guessed her true answer as the acceptance "made no difference presently" (613). Regaining her power (though this time through her own feminine lens), she is next heard "jiggling about with [her] keys" (614).

Perhaps it is Esther's bold comments of opinion and judgment often expressed in the form of theatrical direct address throughout the novel that reveal most pointedly her sexual position. If we accept the argument that sexuality is indeed closely tied to power, then the outward expression of distinct opinion and judgment connotes desire. The ability to express desire promotes a calculable power and signals sexuality. Esther's ability to communicate her desire with characters like Ada and work through her temporary blindness with Mr. Guppy, John Jarndyce, and Allan Woodcourt, allows her to assert her thoughts to troubling characters like Mr. Skimpole and transform herself from a passive observer to an actor.

Bleak House represents one of Charles Dickens's virtuoso literary performances. Through his use of a unique synesthesic narrative technique combining visual and aural devices through framed gazing and theatrical voicing in Esther's narration, voice, and gaze combine to deploy an emotional sensibility of self-conscious reflection, revealing erotic desire through the body that builds a foundation for acting with empathy in interpersonal circles. This agency, buttressed by a gendered role-reversal that allows Esther and female readers, through identification with her, to enjoy some aspects of a male perspective, encourages a first wave of movement toward social action and the alleviation of institutional brutality and indifference.

When the symmetry and harmony between cold reason and flaming emotion is broken, favoring reason devoid of sensibility, Dickens suggests that it is sensuality which leads us to action and on the path back to balance. Sexuality expressed artfully empowers characters and potentially readers. Dickens's synesthesic blending of the visual and aural senses, through the framed gaze and the theatrical voice, manifests a subtext of sexuality that seduces characters and readers toward action on personal levels that ripple toward social reform.

Esther's framed gazing creates a mirror through which she excitedly peers at herself through others' eyes. In her scenes with Ada, this consciousness of self (an inherently intellectual endeavor) constructs Esther as both a spectator and a spectacle in a performance that casts her in the role of a compassionate actor. Esther is instrumental in improving the lives of many of the characters she meets, including Caddy Jellyby, Charley, and Miss Flite.

The realization that the ability to express sensual aspects of one's being gives individual characters the agency to act constitutes one of Dickens's crowning designs. Characters' and readers' evolution of consciousness through the expression of sensual sensibilities frees them to enhance their communities and work toward overturning crippling institutions like Chancery and constraining gender ideologies. Dickens's appropriation of the female voice through Esther effects a role-reversal pivotal to the success of his design, empowering female readers through Esther's narration and inviting male readers to discover feminine consciousness.

Dickens expresses this dynamic in Esther's reaction to the death of the brickmaker's infant, an event that prefigures Esther's action toward Jo:

> How little I thought, when I raised my handkerchief to look upon the tiny sleeper underneath, and seemed to see a halo shine around the child through Ada's drooping hair as her pity bent her head—how little I thought in whose unquiet bosom that handkerchief would come to lie, after covering the motionless and peaceful breast! I only thought that perhaps the Angel of the child might not be all unconscious of the woman who replaced it with so compassionate a hand.
>
> (111)

NOTES

1. Scores of literary and rhetorical effects have been noted in Dickens scholarship. Sensuality represents one of these many layers. To suggest the primacy of sensuality in such a complex artistic novel borders on the prurient, since readers will no doubt notice good acts not arising from sexual motivations; however, I invite a rendition that notes sensuality as an underlying interest that does play a sublimated yet pivotal role in the motivation of specific social action.
2. Synesthesia is a condition where the senses are disordered, as we see in Arthur Rimbaud's visualization of vowels as colors in his poem "Vowels," or in the writings of Vladimir Nabokov.
3. Tess Cosslett warns that "we must beware of trying to read Victorian representations of female friendship . . . [as] anticipatory images of modern feminist solidarity or lesbian consciousness" (3). Geoffrey Carter, however, argues specifically that Dickens's writing suggests "the scandalous subject of lesbianism" (146), while Sara Putzell-Korab states to "recogni[ze] that the Victorians were aware that women can feel passion for each other may help . . . to clarify such ambiguous scenes in Victorian novels." She cites evidence that "French novels, schoolgirls' experiences, observation—all are means by which Victorians learned that women can love women sexually" (Putzell-Korab 184). James Eli Adams points out that sexual desires outside the norm are difficult to apprehend and assess:

"this has proved a special challenge with regard to lesbian relationships . . . confined within traditionally feminine privacies . . . under the guise of 'romantic friendship' or spinsterhood" (134).

4. In *Aspects of the Novel*, E. M. Forster contends that Dickens bounces readers from the omniscient narrator to Esther, at times snatching the pen from Esther's hands (79). Leonard W. Deen splits the two narrations into "the sentimental and the ironic-satiric" (216). Albert J. Guerard calls the two narrators Esther and the "roving conductor" (333). Joan D. Winslow describes the difference between the novel's main voices as largely imaginative, declaring that "Esther is straightforward, responsible, involved, while the third-person narrator is an extravagantly fantastical yet aloof spectator" (2).

5. The German term for alienation effect attributable to specific devices used to limit audiences' ability to involve themselves emotionally during a performance, with the assumption that emotional identification blocks didactic aims.

6. See n. 3 for the discussion of representative critical views of sexuality and lesbianism in the Victorian era.

7. In "The Trouble with Esther," William Axton raises scathing criticism of Esther's character, calling her "ambiguous, if not repugnant" and stating that "Esther's portion of the narrative has . . . a disingenuous ring" (545). Axton also notes Esther's "ironic commentary; she damns with faint praise, employs paraphrase with devastating effect," and to this he argues that "many readers find in Esther a dreadful parody of the ideal Victorian woman" (545). Robert Garis positively seethes concerning Esther's performance, calling it "actively detested and quietly ignored" and " a clumsy mistake which does not damage the book as a whole" despite how "disastrously unsuccessful, irritating, and repelling its heroine actually is" (141).

8. My discussion of the gaze is informed by the insights of critics like Mary Devereaux and Laura Mulvey. Devereaux asserts that "the gaze has both a literal and a figurative component. Narrowly construed, it refers to actual looking. Broadly, or more metaphorically, it refers to a way of thinking about, and acting in, the world" (337). This adds to the foundation set by Lacan, who states that "in our relation to things, in so far as this relation is constituted by the way of vision, and ordered in the figures of representation, something slips, passes, is transmitted, from stage to stage, and is always to some degree eluded in it—that is what we call the gaze" (73). Dickens uses the gaze (in some scenes in the place of dialogue) to transmit drama and power. This slippage creates ambiguous gaps that demand interpretation. Building upon Lacan's and Devereaux's definitions, Mulvey's theory of the gaze assumes a masculine observer and is informed by Freud's theory of scopophilia, the voyeuristic "pleasure in looking" that he describes as "taking other people as objects, subjecting them to a controlling and curious gaze" (qtd. in Mulvey, "Visual Pleasure" 1446). Freud's gaze suggests that part of the transmission of the gaze involves pleasure and power; we will see this presence of sexuality, further developed through Mulvey's theory, emerge through the gaze. Exploring cinematic representation of the gaze, Mulvey argues that "by structuring the film around a main controlling figure with whom the spectator can identify. . . . the power of the male protagonist as he controls events

coincides with the active power of the erotic look . . . giving a satisfying sense of omnipotence'' while ''the man controls the film fantasy and also emerges as the representative of power . . . as the bearer of the look of the spectator'' (''Visual Pleasure'' 1449). Mulvey connects the slippage and sexual pleasure to gender, situating the gaze as male and allowing contemporary readers to set up Dickens's construct of a male gaze through female eyes as an agency of rebellion. And, as members of the audience are situated by the film Mulvey discusses, so also are they constructed by Dickens.

9. John Forster, in an 1853 review of the novel, doubts Dickens's control over Esther's voice when he states: ''Mr. Dickens undertook more than man could accomplish when he resolved to make her the naïve reader of her own good qualities. We cannot help detecting in some passages an artificial tone, which, if not self-consciousness, is at any rate not such a tone as would be used in her narrative by a person of the character depicted'' (644). James H. Broderick and John E. Grant perceive that ''Dickens frequently allows the surface of his narrative, especially in connection with Esther, to become openly sentimental'' and that ''such sentimentality must finally be judged a stylistic flaw'' (252).

10. While admittedly ironic, the use of film to discuss stage conventions may help contemporary readers come to a more nuanced understanding of how Dickens employs these techniques.

11. I build here upon Edgar Johnson's ''anatomy of society'' argument, the belief that Dickens reflects experience and serves as a ''penetrating vision of modern life'' (79). Commenting upon Johnson's ideas, J. Hillis Miller states that ''the network of relations among the various characters [in *Bleak House*] is a miniature version of the interconnectedness of people in all levels of society'' (11–12). In Q. D. Leavis's estimation of Dickens's aims, she posits that ''it is not therefore the Law as such, but the laws of human nature and the society that man's nature has produced as the expression of our impulses'' (131).

12. In this way, Dickens allows for an ideation of power that arguably must precede actual power in an entrenched, gendered hegemony.

13. See n. 7.

14. See Cohen for a more detailed discussion of unspoken sexuality and an application to several Victorian novels, including Dickens's *Great Expectations*.

WORKS CITED

Adams, James Eli. ''Victorian Sexualities.'' *A Companion to Victorian Literature and Culture*. Ed. Herbert F. Tucker. Oxford: Blackwell, 1999. 125–38.

Axton, William. ''The Trouble with Esther.'' *Modern Language Quarterly* 26 (1965): 545–47.

Broderick, James H., and John E. Grant. ''The Identity of Esther Summerson.'' *Modern Philology* 55 (1958): 252–58.

Carter, Geoffrey. "Sexuality and the Victorian Artist: Dickens and Swinburne." *Sexuality and Victorian Literature*. Ed. Don Richard Cox. Knoxville: U of Tennessee P, 1984. 141–60.

Cohen, William A. *Sex Scandal: The Private Parts of Victorian Fiction*. Durham, NC: Duke UP, 1966.

Cosslett, Tess. *Woman to Woman: Female Friendships in Victorian Fiction*. Atlantic Highlands, NJ: Humanities, 1988.

Deen, Leonard W. "Style and Unity in *Bleak House*." *Criticism* 3:3 (1961): 206–18.

Devereaux, Mary. "Oppressive Texts, Resisting Readers and the Gendered Spectator: The New Aesthetics." *Journal of Aesthetics and Art Criticism* 48:4 (1990): 337–47.

Dickens, Charles. *Bleak House*. New York: Oxford UP, 1948.

Donovan, Robert Alan. "Structure and Idea in *Bleak House*." *The Victorian Novel*. Ed. Ian Watt. New York: Oxford UP, 1971. 83–109.

Forster, E. M. *Aspects of the Novel*. New York: Harcourt Brace, 1927.

Forster, John. Rev. of *Bleak House*, by Charles Dickens. *The Examiner*. 8 Oct. 1853: 643–45.

Garis, Robert. *The Dickens Theater: A Reassessment of the Novels*. Oxford: Clarendon, 1965.

Guerard, Albert J. "*Bleak House*: Structure and Style." *Southern Review* 50:2 (1969): 332–49.

Johnson, Edgar. "*Bleak House*: The Anatomy of Society." *Nineteenth-Century Fiction* 7.2 (1952): 73–89.

———. *Charles Dickens: His Tragedy and Triumph*. 2 vols. New York: Penguin, 1986.

Johnson, Edgar, and Eleanor Johnson. *The Dickens Theatrical Reader*. Boston: Little, 1964.

Karl, Frederick R. *An Age of Fiction: The Nineteenth Century British Novel*. New York: Farrar, 1964.

Lacan, Jacques. *Four Fundamental Concepts of Psychoanalysis*. Trans. Alan Sheridan. New York: Norton, 1977.

Leavis, Q. D. "*Bleak House*: A Chancery World." *Dickens the Novelist*. F. R. Leavis and Q. D. Leavis. New Brunswick, NJ: Rutgers UP, 1979. 118–83.

Miller, J. Hillis. Introduction. *Bleak House*. By Charles Dickens. New York: Penguin, 1971.

Moers, Ellen. "*Bleak House*: The Agitating Women." *The Dickensian* 69:369 (1973): 13–24.

Mulvey, Laura. "Afterthoughts on 'Visual Pleasure and Narrative Cinema' Inspired by *Duel in the Sun*." *Psychoanalysis & Cinema*. Ed. E. Ann Kaplan. New York: Routledge, 1990. 24–35.

———. "Visual Pleasure and Narrative Cinema." *The Critical Tradition: Classic Texts and Contemporary Trends*. Ed. David H. Richter. 2nd ed. Boston: Bedford, 1998. 1445–53.

Pearsall, Ronald. *The Worm in the Bud: The World of Victorian Sexuality*. New York: Penguin, 1983.

Putzell-Korab, Sara M. "Passion Between Women in the Victorian Novel." *Sexuality and Victorian Literature*. Ed. Don Richard Cox. Knoxville: U of Tennessee P, 1984. 180–95.

Winslow, Joan D. "Esther Summerson: The Betrayal of the Imagination." *Journal of Narrative Technique* 6:1 (1976): 1–13.

Self-Possession in *Great Expectations*

Keith Easley

*Mikhail Bakhtin's work on the authoring of heroes offers ways of read-
ing* Great Expectations *(1860–61) that do justice to Dickens's sense of
the dynamic relationship between author/reader and characters. Readers, like authors, would give characters aesthetic form and make those
they care for into heroes. However, the wish to lovingly consummate
another as another is contested in the nineteenth-century novel by the
growing social power of the Romantic will to consummate oneself.
Pervading our own culture, that power inflects our very critiques of
Victorian individualism. In the society of* Great Expectations, *Pip's
knowledge of himself is blocked by others' performances of self and by
his own complicity in self-consummation. Those who would love their
hero therefore have the task of providing that knowledge and of giving
him "self-possession." Instead of trying to make himself into a hero,
Pip will then be freed to take responsibility for his authoring of others.
Pip as authorial narrator helps his younger self to become a true hero
through a process of objectification that allows him to see his shaping
relationships with those around him. Realizing his authorial power, he
will offer Estella both hope for herself and an understanding of her
own authorial role. She may have a future because he has given her his
past in the form of the novel she is reading. Self-possession, bestowed on
Pip by others and passed in turn to another, defines the individual as
social at a particular moment in history.*

> " 'For whose sake would you reveal the
> secret?' "
> —*Great Expectations*, 426; ch. 51

Dickens Studies Annual, Volume 39, Copyright © 2008 by AMS Press, Inc. All
rights reserved.

Introduction

This essay, the third in a series applying Mikhail Bakhtin's thinking to Dickens's novels, considers *Great Expectations* in the light of "Author and Hero in Aesthetic Activity" (c. 1924–27). In my first article, "Dickens and Bakhtin: Authoring in *Bleak House*," I proposed that

> readers participate with the writer in the "authoring" of heroes. The giving of form through aesthetic love—in its fullest sense, "consummation"—attempts to create and find a value in the hero distinct from but interlocking with his or her[1] cognitive/ethical search for values based on knowledge. Historically, the development of the novel brings authoring into Western cultural consciousness while extending the franchise for the reader's exercise of aesthetic power. As "character" becomes ever more important, and as characters' own authoring activities are foregrounded, one main area of conflict in Victorian novels is between pluralistic consummation of another person and individualistic *self-consummation*. (185)

Dickens shares Bakhtin's sense that self-consummation, the attempted fulfillment of the Romantic belief that one can author oneself, represents the major cultural crisis of his time, and Graham Pechey's comment that the Russian thinker's "Author and Hero" stands as "a reproach to modernity's hubristic claim to self-grounding, its exciting though perverse fiction of the hero as self-authoring" (58), could be applied with equal felicity to the Victorian novelist.

In a second, unpublished essay, which focuses on *David Copperfield*, I initially consider Bakhtin's pluralistic view of human consciousness, divided internally yet capable of unity with another while insisting on individual difference. Each person is split between a cognitive-ethical "I-for-myself" and an aesthetic "the-other-for-me," the latter a baffling but accurate way of referring to our giving of ourself to another.[2] Rarely singular, we tend to do more than one thing at the same time: our cognitive and aesthetic selves act simultaneously but unseen to each other within the individual. "Author and Hero" is dedicated to proving that human beings cannot coincide in the value-producing activities that define their humanity. And this is right and proper, contends Bakhtin, because the I-for-myself depends on being unfinished: "In order to live and act, . . . I need to be open for myself—at least in all the essential moments constituting my life" (13). The aesthetic concern, on the other hand, is with encompassing the whole of its object, "and all values that are ethical and cognitive must be subordinated to that whole" (13) in the act of lovingly shaping another.

Bakhtin's argument for non-coincidence allows the reader to treat fictional characters as though they are real. As I explain in the second piece:

> Believing in another consciousness (the hero), the reader relives and re-creates
> the authorial experience, putting aside his or her consciousness of self in the
> giving of form to another. Neither writer nor reader can be self-aware in the
> creative act: they "experience themselves *in* their object, but they do not experi-
> ence the process of their own experiencing" (6–7).[3] . . . The finite nature of
> self-consciousness, the fact that in the aesthetic activity of belief we cannot
> regard our cognitive selves, makes it impossible for us to judge whether the
> hero is the product of our own cognitive self or whether we have actually
> encountered another.   (2007, 7–8)

In short, we cannot know whether the hero is another consciousness or our own *sense* of one. This necessary ignorance in the act of reading frees us to entertain the apparently impossible while appreciating that it could be exactly that. It frees us to believe.

That said, belief in David Copperfield exposes the reader to the lure of the authorial hero's attempted self-consummation. The novel is marked by David's failure to establish the vital non-coincidence between past and present selves. Given the supposed reality of David's story to himself as authorial narrator, we can expect him to follow the defining rule of (auto)biography: he should leave his younger self with a loophole out of artistic consummation into life. However, David's portrayal of his younger self is compromised by present entanglements with figures of passion in his past, and he is determined to consummate himself. If we would love our hero, we would therefore have to *de*consummate him in order to save him from himself. We identify with the hero while pulling back from him. In a self-perpetuating movement between the making and unmaking of the protagonist, we are drawn into confirming his view of his own goodness while working to uncover his failings. As a result, *David Copperfield* is the most emphatically decent and the most perverse of the great Victorian novels of growing up, a pattern-book for middle-class respectability and a manual for sexual transgression, the one reading itself into the other.

The stifling author-hero mutuality of *David Copperfield*, unable to find a way past or through desire, compromises the authorial narrator, who both embraces and makes a weapon of his extreme subjectivity. I will argue in the present essay that *Great Expectations* sets out more objectively to depict a self-consummating society that deforms passion. Unlike David, Pip does establish the grounds for the expression of desire. He can do this because, through a process of objectification whereby he sees others in himself and himself in others, he achieves the non-coincidence between his older and younger selves that is so lacking in the earlier novel. He will be helped in the objectification by the reader's own participation in the non-coincidence between ourselves and the older Pip, the authorial narrator. We make him our hero as he makes a hero of his younger self.

In the self-consummating societies of *Bleak House* and *Great Expectations*, knowledge of oneself is blocked by those who would impose their performances of self on others. Faced with such power, those who would lovingly offer aesthetic consummation have instead the task of freeing the hero or heroine cognitively, of bringing them knowledge of themselves. Only then might they be able eventually to give or receive love. I have called this giving of knowledge about oneself "self-possession," as opposed to self-consummation.

I wrote before that at the end of *Bleak House* a "collision of narrators [Esther Summerson and the Dickensian narrator with whom we have identified] makes the issue of self-possession vertiginously our own" (227), daring us to go back in our reading to the beginning to reconsider our relationship with a heroine who may in fact have been authoring *us*. I now argue that in *Great Expectations* Pip, like Esther Summerson, comes into his authoring power during the novel. Unlike her, he would give self-possession, not to the reader, but to another character, Estella. He offers her the written text of the novel itself, in which she can find knowledge of herself and of the ways in which she has been authored, and through which she may take responsibility for her own authoring of Pip. His life has been dominated by the hopeless hopefulness of passion for Estella, winding him up and wearing him down. Pip's achievement is to act on the realization that love actually consists of giving hope to Estella, not of pursuing it for himself. And passion (*hers*, not his—therein lies Pip's true generosity) can only develop properly from hope. Reading is to be Estella's task, if she chooses. In this, she will participate in and shape the act of love that is the continuing life of the novel.

Part 1

The young Pip's first meeting with Estella opens into a labyrinth of passion. Pip gives himself utterly to her. As he says later of his adult self:

> I loved her simply because I found her irresistible. Once for all; I knew to my sorrow, often and often, if not always, that I loved her against reason, against promise, against peace, against hope, against happiness, against all discouragement that could be. Once for all; I loved her none the less because I knew it, and it had no more influence in restraining me, than if I had devoutly believed her to be human perfection.   (253–54; ch. 29)

Latent desire, provoked and denied by Estella and Miss Havisham, cannot develop naturally. Passion twists into snobbery since the only way open for Pip to follow the initially overwhelming impulse of romantic love to be at one with the object of his desire is to take on her class attitudes. Pip is pushed into both aggrandizing and belittling himself as well as denigrating those who love him. " 'I want to be a gentleman on her account,' " he says to Biddy, aware that he is making a "lunatic confession" (156; ch. 17). The madness lies in the simultaneous commitment to self-authoring *and* to love of another. Knowing the wrongness of the snobbery cannot dam the only channel for the child's feeling. This portrayal of love warped into an unnaturally intense and self-punishing obsession with bettering oneself in the other person's eyes is the basis of Dickens's representation of a society distorted by and distorting passion. The language of romance and potentially of sex becomes the language of class, so that passion is everywhere, permeating society, and yet is nowhere because it cannot be admitted. Not quite nowhere: rather, passion is displaced into plot.

Seeking for that plot, the older Pip traces the forward movement from the past that has made him what he is. As his narrative builds towards his present self, the narrator becomes increasingly aware of another time-scale prefiguring the meeting with Estella. With Magwitch's revelation of himself as the source of his gentility, Pip begins to find his way back to an earlier time in his own life, but, as he links Magwitch with Estella, so he goes back even further to the events that produced Estella and made *her* as she is. The closer the main narrative comes to the narrator's present, the further he is taken back to the moment that set in motion a train of events leading to his meeting and falling in love: the sexually-motivated murder by Estella's mother of her rival for Magwitch.

The most important moment should be the opening meeting between Pip and Magwitch in the graveyard, but we find with the older narrator that the returned convict's gratitude towards and love for him have their deepest roots in the love for the daughter long lost to him through the violence of Estella's mother. Magwitch's life has anticipated Pip's own in being twisted by passion, one in relation to the mother and the other to the daughter. The resulting loss of family and the need for secrecy in order to protect mother and child put Magwitch at the mercy of Compeyson, who "held the knowledge over his head" (419; ch. 50), and whose exploitation bred Magwitch's enduring hatred for his tormentor, expressed in the defining violence at both ends of the novel.

As Jaggers notes, Estella lived in a context of disfiguring passion before being passed into Miss Havisham's deforming hands (424–26; ch. 51). And Miss Havisham's attempt to stop time at the precise moment of thwarted desire is directly caused by the hidden Compeyson's deliberate abuse of her feelings for him. Such knowledge, going back as Pip goes forward after the collapse of his genteel world when he learns the source of his expectations, informs Pip's authoring of Magwitch. Flight together, pure and simple, is his loving intention. In practice, however, the past reaches into the present with the revelation of Magwitch's erstwhile author. Compeyson would confirm his mastery and ensure his safety through the arrest of Magwitch. In the event, Pip's plan exposes and destroys the powerful and hidden figure who has throughout dedicated himself to wasting others.

Magwitch has long known and hated Compeyson as his author, resenting his helplessness in the face of the other's shaping manipulation. For him, the original disparity in the sentencing enacts the injustice of a world in which the educated gentleman, Compeyson, can shuffle responsibility off onto his pressed servant, publicly presenting him at the earlier trial as the organizing spirit of evil.[4] In revenge, Magwitch creates own gentleman, Pip, who is to rise above his oppressors. It will all come true, although not in the way originally envisaged by Magwitch, whose fantasy is partly shaped by the loving impulses ingrained in his personality. In a terrible way Pip helps to free him from lifelong imprisonment by Compeyson. Hence, Magwitch can face his subsequent imprisonment and death with dignity. He has gained freedom from the man who exploited the womans passion for her lover and the fathers love for their daughter. Taking hold of Compeyson, he makes him *his* prisoner in death. This anticipates Bradley Headstone's deathlock on Rogue Riderhood in *Our Mutual Friend*, with the difference that Magwitch can finally release Compeyson and find his own freedom.

Magwitch dies with dignity because Pip has made a hero of him. It has been a long, if circular, journey from Pip's churchyard fear of having his heart and liver torn out by the convict's ghostly companion, through the lifelong terror of being made into a criminal himself by association with Magwitch, coupled with his own intense desire to save himself by becoming a respectable romantic hero. The journey is made possible and takes the course it does because in the first place Pip does not invite identification between author and hero in the manner of David Copperfield. The authorial narrator's distance from his younger self is vital. Rather than subordinating that younger self to his own adult self-interest, this authorial narrator is more concerned with self-condemnation. And, since the child is far more practiced upon than practicing, the very excessiveness of the older Pip's judgment serves in turn to emphasize our outsideness in relation to *him*.

Kathleen Sell insists on the importance of shame (''uneasiness over one's self'') in addition to guilt (''uneasiness over one's actions'') as a central motivation for Pip's narrative. It marks his relations with others all his life. From his childhood he is ashamed of possible association with the criminal world and of those who love him, even though he knows at the time that he is being unfair and is then ashamed of himself for being ashamed of them. Sell thinks that Pip desires above all to ''to turn the shaming gaze away from himself and onto others'' (203). I would say that, moved by the later awareness that he has conflated the shame of being criminal with the shame of being loved, he insists too much on his own culpability. Indeed, Pip's ability both to see and suffer for his denial of Joe and Biddy makes him dear to us. As a result, the authorial narrator is viewed by the reader as morally admirable in a way that undermines his strictures on himself and gives a measure of freedom to his younger self that evades moral finalization. Also, the young Pip is capable of an active aesthetic love to which the older Pip, the narrator, seems blind in his censure of his younger self, but which the mature character, in fact, allows to inform his dealings with others.

There is a continuity in Pip of the capacity for and practice of authoring, another fundamental constituent of his character. The young man brings out the unexpected humanity of those whose trade is inhumanity, particularly Wemmick and Jaggers. They should be and are to some extent made mechanical by their subjugation of self to the machinery of the law, and by their calculating exploitation of human weakness. Wemmick's Castle and its appurtenances, both human and non-human, might be seen as the eccentric excrescences of a repressive society that divides public life from private, encouraging the fantastic freedom of the latter in order to subordinate the individual to the public dehumanization of the law. Yet Pip's appreciative presence makes it possible to surmount the division, or perhaps to make it irrelevant. His observant and imaginative participation helps him to realize the animating power of the Castle and its company:

> We ate the whole of the toast, and drank tea in proportion, and it was delightful to see how warm and greasy we all got after it. The Aged especially, might have passed for some clean old chief of a savage tribe, just oiled.
>
> (315; ch. 37)

In the privacy of his home, the Aged is presented as a domestic version of the Noble Savage. The comic abuse of a Romantic icon conveys, not the splendid or tragic isolation from conventional society associated with the image, but *sharing* in all its absurdity. With the Aged still in mind, we picture the Noble Savage, not in the jungle but at home "just oiled" as though he has had his bath and is ready for bed. It's the domesticity of "clean old chief" that does it. Private becomes public, and then rebounds so that an exotic character haunting the Western imagination is now peacefully lodging in the Englishman's castle. Whatever else this is, it is not alienation. Pip's jokes, like his author's, have a dynamically reciprocal power when granted the freedom to do their work.

More straightforwardly, Pip's unashamed humanity in offering his hand to Wemmick at Barnard's Inn evokes first astonishment and then self-realization:

> I put out my hand, and Mr. Wemmick at first looked at it as if he thought I wanted something. Then he looked at me, and said, correcting himself,

"To be sure! Yes. You're in the habit of shaking   hands? . . . I have got so
out of it!" said Mr. Wemmick—"except at last. Very glad, I'm sure, to make
your acquaintance. Good day!"   (197; ch. 21)

Wemmick's further responses will be all his own, but Pip makes them possible
in the first place.

Outside the deep but narrow seam of his snobbery, Pip has the authorial
gift of making others valuable to themselves and to us. Jaggers's constant
washing can be seen as an obsessive effort to preserve the purity of his private
self from the dirt of his public life. Again, though, Pip's active presence helps
to make a bridge. He makes a person of a character so constrained that his
creaking boots have to do his laughing for him (221; ch. 24), partly of course
by noticing the boots in the first place. After bringing out the brutality in
Drummle at dinner, Jaggers finds himself forced into humanity by Pip's
apology for Drummle's behavior. Warning Pip to keep clear of the upper-
class lout, he starts to muse on Drummle's likely future as he towels himself
dry after washing off the violence of the evening: "Looking out of the towel,
he caught my eye. 'But I am not a fortune-teller,' he said, . . . 'You know
what I am, don't you? Good-night, Pip' " (239; ch. 26). It seems paradoxical.
Jaggers treats Pip with the honesty due to innocence, and yet, if Pip were so
innocent, he could not understand him. It is probably a compliment. He does
not expect Pip to know exactly what he is. Rather, during the evening he has
witnessed the young man's capacity for observation and understanding even
while maintaining the innocence secretly valued by the lawyer. Pip's own
humanity has been demonstrated by his weakness in allowing himself to be
baited by Drummle, along with his strength in taking responsibility for the
weakness and apologizing to his guardian.

Jaggers lives by secrecy, and the greatest compliment he can pay is to
admit that someone knows him. Furthermore, he has actually offered knowledge during the evening by forcing Molly, his housekeeper, to show her
wrists. This certainly demonstrates his power over her, but, if Pip wanted to
know the truth, it could also show something else: Jaggers's one proven act
of kindness in preserving Molly and Estella. Without that demonstration, Pip
could not link mother and daughter. Pip's authoring presence impresses itself
enough upon Jaggers for him to hint in his bullying fashion at the proof of
his own humanity, which in turn will help Pip in his authoring and knowledge
of others.

Later, in desperation at losing all hope of Estella, Pip successfully orches-
trates the scene in which Wemmick and Jaggers accuse each other of compassion:

I have never seen two men look more oddly at one another than Mr Jaggers
and Wemmick did . . .

"What's all this?" said Mr Jaggers. "You with an old father, and you with pleasant and playful ways?"

"Well!" returned Wemmick. "If I don't bring 'em here, what does it matter?"

"Pip," said Mr Jaggers, laying his hand upon my arm, and smiling openly, "this man must be the most cunning imposter in all London."

"Not a bit of it," returned Wemmick, growing bolder and bolder. "I think you're another."

Again they exchanged their former odd looks, each apparently still distrustful that the other was taking him in.   (423–24; ch. 51)

Against the odds, Pip can bring out the best in others, and, for all his moral emphasis, the older self consistently respects and leaves room for the authoring activity of his younger self. How else could the one develop into the other? Magwitch first recognized this capacity in Pip at the beginning of the book. The end of his life is illumined by Pip's present authoring of that memory: "A smile crossed his face then, and he turned his eyes on me with a trustful look, as if he were confident that I had seen some small redeeming touch in him, even so long ago as when I was a little child" (466; ch. 56). The clicks in the convict's throat register the child's kindness, expressed as the basic giving of food to a starving wretch, and as a willingness to speak, to acknowledge the man as a fellow human being. More than this: Pip would steal, *does* steal for another, making a near fatal link between love and crime. On his deathbed, the same noise in Magwitch's throat expresses his grateful response to Pip's unselfish lies about himself and Estella being happy together. Pip's "poor dreams" are at last put to good use in convincing the dying man that his striving on Pip's behalf has redeemed the abandonment of his daughter, and his life has been proven worthwhile. Pip turns the material of his failed self-consummation into loving consummation of the other person.

The differences between Bakhtinian thinking and Peter Brooks's seminal deconstructive/psychological approach in *Reading for the Plot*, to which the present essay is much indebted, are shown very clearly by Brooks's interpretation of the discovery of Estella's origins. In proving himself a "successful detective," Pip only proves "there is no gain to be had from knowledge," since he must repress it (135). "We are in the heart of darkness," says Brooks, for this detective work "produces no authority for the plot of life."

It depends, however, on whose life we think is being plotted, and whether we see characters as only singular to themselves. From a Bakhtinian perspective, Pip's gaining of knowledge helps him to achieve true authority, responsibility for authoring, through being employed *for another*. We are not in the heart of darkness, and the articulation of meaning is not simply repressed; it is *e*xpressed in a new way, first for Magwitch's and later for Estella's sake. Brooks thinks that key scenes transmit

a "wisdom" that is in the deconstructive mode, a warning against plot.
        We confront the paradox that in this most highly plotted of novels, where
    Dickens performs all his thematic demonstrations through the manipulation of
    plot, we witness an evident subversion and futilization of the very concept of
    plot.   (136)

Illuminating though this is, it provokes the response that the plots rebound
upon each other, creating the lived events expressive of characters' authoring
relationships. Events are, in Bakhtin's terminology, "transgredient" to plots.
The concern with integrating plotting into a singular psychology makes it
difficult for Brooks to see that Pip at different times in his life can't and
shouldn't coincide with himself.

    The openness of the relationship between Pip as author and Pip as hero is
also achieved through the adult narrator's use of fairy tale to counter fairy
tale. The young Pip would let himself be a hero consummated through the
agency of a fairy godmother who is magically to reward him for his unique
but unspecified worth:

> She had adopted Estella, she had as good as adopted me, and it could not fail
> to be her intention to bring us together. She reserved it for me to restore the
> desolate house, admit the sunshine into the dark rooms, set the clocks a going
> and the cold hearths a blazing, tear down the cobwebs, destroy the vermin—in
> short, do all the shining deeds of the young Knight of romance, and marry the
> Princess.   (253; ch. 29)

Time will indeed reassert itself, fire will return, and the vermin will be
destroyed. The magic, though, exerts a price. Pip will play a heroic role, but
in the process he will also be the unwitting agent for the fairy godmother's
destruction. Long before that, he gives himself to Estella. As he does this, he
is made to experience repeatedly the certainty that his self-sacrifice has no
effect on her. Living constantly with the knowledge that his authoring power,
the shaping activity of love, is nothing, Pip has to deny his capacity for love
in the very giving of himself in its name. And this is done in the hope that
love will be given to him and will make him into a hero! Miss Havisham and
Estella really do have much to answer for.

    The young Pip's fairy tale, conjured with Miss Havisham's connivance,
takes its shape from his helpless longing, the shame awoken in him by Estella,
his imaginative response to Miss Havisham's fantasy world, and from finding
that his imagination has power over others. He gets as far as thinking "that
perhaps Miss Havisham was going to make my fortune when my time was
out" (160; ch. 17). Thus, he has the seed of his story, like the seeds he thinks
of as having intention at Pumblechook's (and which will later be stuffed in
Pumblechook's mouth by Orlick). Seeds need to be propagated, and it takes

a *second* fairy tale, known to the adult Pip but not to the child, to do this. This other story of magic and witchcraft (hence "Mag"-"witch") tells of a child, himself treated as a wretch, whose kindness to a "hunted dunghill dog" makes him human. The price, and eventual reward, is the transformation of the giver's own life. In authoring humanity in the place of death, the child opens himself to being made into a hero who will have to prove himself in the underworld. Dickens is fond of such stories: Oliver Twist, Little Nell, Florence Dombey, Esther Summerson, and Eugene Wrayburn, among many others, all author humanity and pay a price in the underworld that may be realized as a reward.

Pip, however, attempts to use his expectations to develop his own magic story, shaped to his own desires. Magic is to serve him. Daydream is to become the reality of a self-consummation guaranteeing him wealth, status, and love. In the process, Miss Havisham changes from the spectral old lady of their first meeting, and now encourages Pip from her own selfish and sadistic motives to see her as "the fairy godmother who had changed me, . . . bestowing the final gift" (183; ch. 19) with a wave of her stick like a wand. In accepting this transformation, Pip helps the pattern of his gentlemanly future to take shape. He cedes control of his life and his responsibility for authoring to others because he thinks it will give him what he wants. He should have been warned by his first impression of Miss Havisham as a living ghoul.

Magic, at least in its Dickensian forms, is not to be constrained by those who would conjure it. Pip's wishes may come true, but not in any sense foreseen or willed by him. The adult's tale of Magwitch and the criminal world at every point counters the youthful effort romantically to idealize Estella. No sooner does Pip tell Miss Havisham of his expectations (183–84; ch. 19) and move his dreams up a gear than he finds himself in the criminal society of Little Britain (188–94; ch. 20). Returning to the marshes to see Miss Havisham and Estella, he sits behind the convicts on the coach talking about Magwitch and the events of his own past (250–51; ch. 28). Estella's request to Pip to meet her in London (279; ch. 32) has him arriving so early that Wemmick, in passing, takes him on a brusquely deathlike tour of Newgate (280–83; ch. 32). Pip's railing against Estella's treatment of him (328–30; ch. 38) is followed immediately by the reappearance of Magwitch and the collapse of his genteel world. This is more complex than the oppositional binarism of *David Copperfield*. If one story simply answered another, the falling of the ceiling on Pip's dreams would end everything. He might dig himself out of the rubble, but at best he would be older, sadder, and wiser. The action of the second story on the first, however, unlocks the door to knowledge, and Magwitch's self-revelation tests Pip's love. He gains the knowledge of Magwitch that allows him to understand his own and his benefactor's past, and through this to offer Estella knowledge of herself.

The gaining of knowledge is no small matter, for *Great Expectations* is bound in secrecy. Compeyson's shadow obscures the lives of others. So does Magwitch's for much of the narrative. Central characters lack parents, important keys to their past. When parents like the Pockets do appear, they are disconnected from their children. Others besides Compeyson and Magwitch are notable for their influence in their absence. Clara's father, Bill Barley, expires noisily but unseen above the loving couple on the floor below, their courtship shaped by him. Clara herself remains hidden from Pip until he has to find help for Magwitch. Secret, shifting relationships are continually hinted at. Orlick dogs Pip all his life without his quite knowing until nearly too late. Not telling Joe about the convicts works its way into his life and character: "The secrecy had so grown into me and become part of myself, that I could not tear it away" (149; ch. 16). In Dickens's animistic world secrets assume their own life, feeding on the maiming of Mrs. Joe and on Pip's expectations.

Magwitch's self-revelation does not simply clear the way for the truth. Indeed, Pip becomes deliberately oblique even as he becomes less ignorant. His generosity is authenticated by the confidentiality of his plan to help Herbert. He determines never to tell Magwitch about Estella, and when he changes his mind he lies about her instead. Pip and Jaggers keep the fact of the inheritance being lost from Magwitch. Secrecy seems to turn back upon itself in order to find its truth. For all their intimacy since childhood, Biddy won't inform Pip directly of his sister's death. Neither will she and Joe tell him about their wedding. At the close, in leaving the reader uncertain about Pip and Estella, in keeping final knowledge from us, the published ending of the book strikes truer than the original, clear-cut version.

Secrecy encourages Pip to confound Magwitch's fundamental goodness with Miss Havisham's selfish wish to break hearts and punish her family. The manager of confidentiality and ignorance is Jaggers, who makes a covenant of silence with Pip. The lawyer's success is his skillful linking of secrecy with guilt, a universal police principle. If you don't know something, you could have done wrong. Can you deny that? Can you? Jaggers's entire masterful performance is based on making people feel he knows more about them than they do themselves. He wins by convincing others, including the innocent and those administering justice, that he knows of their guilt. As Pip realizes on his first visit to the aptly named Little Britain, everyone has private business with Jaggers. His charisma depends on the continuing preservation of secrecy, to the point where he refuses to let his own clients know what he is doing. Hence, his virtuoso performance in court leaves Pip dumbfounded: "Which side he was on, I couldn't make out" (225; ch. 24). He wins, however, not despite this ambiguity but because of it.

The secrets are about desire. Knowledge of the workings of passion (or the lack of it) is crucial to the exercise of power. Mrs. Joe's tyranny depends upon her use of Joe's guilty secret, namely, that he didn't marry her for love. He never desired her. Instead, as he hints to Pip after allowing for a '' 'little redness or a little matter of Bone' '' in this '' 'fine figure of a woman,' '' he married her for the child's sake:

> "When I got acquainted with your sister, it were the talk how she were bringing you up by hand. . . . When I offered to your sister to keep company, and to be asked in church at such times as she was willing and ready to come to the forge, I said to her, 'And bring the poor little child. God bless the poor little child,' I said to your sister, 'there's room for *him* at the forge!' ''   (78; ch. 7)

The emphasis falls on Pip, not Joe's wife, never addressed or referred to by her own name, not even or especially by Joe.

His wife doesn't have to know explicitly about Joe's reasons for marrying her. A glimpse of the other's guilt will suffice. With the best of intentions, the gentle Christian man has done his wife wrong. His very goodness makes love guilty. We learn from those we love, and Pip learns his lesson all too well. However, the extent of Joe's goodness is only appreciated later by Pip, through his experience with Magwitch. Joe marries a woman he doesn't love and submits himself to a lifetime of bondage. Nasty to begin with, if she once senses the insult in judging her to be undesirable, she can justifiably crank up the viciousness. Pip notes that she "consciously and deliberately" (142; ch. 15) works herself up into hysteria. Her eroticized reaction to Orlick's insults is to make Joe guilty for accepting them and for not accepting her. He has given her the right to do this, a self-sacrifice for which he expects no reward from the child. His secret, though, in its linking of love with guilt, has prepared for Pip's secrecy, to be amplified, complicated, and confused by the repercussions of the boy's churchyard experience. Even Joe's goodness can be turned into murder by Orlick, who certainly does understand that Pip is loved at the expense of others, namely himself, and acts accordingly in his own mad way.

Part 2

Like many oppressors in Dickens's novels, Mrs. Joe operates through a performance of knowingness. Her cognitive self turned outwards, she projects herself upon her little stage at the forge. In her self-consummating drama, her perfection and knowledge are defined by the imperfection and ignorance of those around her. Hence her unceasing activity directed at impressing their stupidity upon Pip and Joe. Such theatricality acts to block rather than express knowledge: '' 'Ask no questions, and you'll be told no lies' '' (45; ch. 2). Fools who do ask will feel the consequences.

Other social actors understand Mrs. Joe very well. Pumblechook's own performance plays shamelessly to her sense that dramatically she has much to learn, since she knows little beyond the use of angry self-dramatization. Pumblechook does know something: how to gain social authority and its perquisites through emphasizing his performance as performance. Drama commands respect. More artful predators can manipulate him by pretending to play lesser, deferential roles in his production: "You're a man that knows what's what" (63; ch. 5), says the sergeant, flatteringly encouraging him to make free with the wine originally brought for others. That fact, though, goes by the board. In the first few chapters, the self-consummating theatricality of the society of the marshes indicates the operation of social power as a whole, confidently projecting knowingness while suppressing knowledge and manipulating others in the service of self-interest.

Theatrical self-projection, however, does not by itself constitute "Dickensian" characterization. I have argued elsewhere that in *Bleak House* Dickens typically compounds theatricality, pushing it over the edge:

> In a *doubling* of aesthetic activity, impossible self-consummation is enjoyed, mocked, matched, and answered by a further consummation that memorably fixes the personality, crystallizing it in a typical action or form of words. The consciousness vivified in Guppy is that of a foolish young city clerk, a type well-known and beloved by Dickens on account of a capacity for silly self-dramatization. [Suddenly, Guppy inexplicably thrusts his head into the office safe. The search for meaning is on.] We try empathy, projecting ourselves forward with the clerk until our heads are also in the darkness of the safe. Not much meaning is to be found in there. We can then look with the author from the outside and consummate Guppy in the beautiful realization that in his mind he must try to cool his head down because, despite all appearances to the contrary, his thoughts run on so feverishly. For he is a man with a plan. Guppy sticks his head into the law's secrets, and from this action by himself and others the meanings of the book will be produced. The memorable crystallization into a typical action, sticking his head into the safe, simultaneously unlocks the cognition imprisoned within the character's own self-consummation, opening the world of meaning for the reader who, with Dickens, makes and finds Guppy to be greater than he knows in his foolishness.   (2004, 202)

Doubling typicality makes it possible for Dickens to conjure artful life in a few words. Witness Guppy's protégé, Young Smallweed, a mini-monster of knowingness. Holding "up the *Times* to run his eye over the columns, he seems to have retired for the night, and to have disappeared under the bedclothes" (259; ch. 20). The childishness within the boy's studied performance of adulthood is beautifully exposed. The action meant to convey his maturity demonstrates the opposite, and in opening up the paper Small opens up himself.[5]

Great Dickensian characters go one step further and seem to provide the means for their own double aestheticization, transforming their singular performances and conveying a striking effect of autonomy. They "walk off the page." Mrs. Gamp exemplifies such autonomy. Towards the close of *Martin Chuzzlewit*, Dickens as author distances himself critically from his creation: "Mrs. Gamp had observed, not without jealousy and scorn, that a favourable impression appeared to exist in behalf of Mr Sweedlepipe and his young friend [Bailey]; and that she had fallen rather into the background in consequence" (866; ch. 52). The authorial doubling is performed instead by Mrs. Gamp's own creation, Mrs. Harris, whom she here invokes in an attempt to sideline possible rivals. With an eye on work as nurse/midwife should the newly widowed Merry Pecksniff happen to need her, she claims the nonexistent Mrs. Harris will vouch for her. Mrs. Harris should be listened to in this instance, according to Mrs. Gamp's chop-logic, because she unexpectedly saw her sister's pickled baby on display at Greenwich Fair (866; ch. 52).

Mrs. Gamp is self-interestedly claiming that she has a right to the company's attention because she knows people who have seen more extreme natural curiosities than the concussed Bailey presently staggering around the room. Mrs. Harris is said to have been so surprised to see the dead baby because it was still-born and yet was pictured outside " 'quite contrairy in a livin' state, . . . many sizes larger, and performing beautiful upon the Arp.' " In other words, Mrs. Harris, used here by Mrs. Gamp to advertise her services, complains of the deceptiveness of advertising. Her character's performance thus undermines Mrs. Gamp's own act. Further, the talk of a baby, dead in its mother's womb—" 'since breathe it never did, to speak on, in this wale' "—is hardly likely to appeal to Merry Pecksniff if she did need a midwife. On the other hand, if she were pregnant by her dead husband and abuser, the murderer Jonas, Merry might indeed wonder whether such a child would be better stillborn. And who better than this particular midwife to ensure just such an unhappy event? Even as Mrs. Gamp meekly submits to Mr. Chuzzlewit's closing dismissal, Mrs. Harris shows her as a dark rock, over and against which the happy endings break.

There are not many such characters in *Great Expectations*. Pumblechook reprises Pecksniff's parasitic hypocrisy from *Martin Chuzzlewit*, although he narrows and intensifies the focus of his self-creation. Pecksniff magnificently makes the resisting world his foil, enlisting everyone and everything as props for the construction of his own reality, inevitably failing and just as inevitably continuing in the attempt to re-create the world as Pecksniff. Pumblechook concentrates on Pip himself, for he would use him as the foil for his self-dramatizing autonomy. That is, Pumblechook would make the narrator his own creation. Flowering annuals may be stuffed in his mouth to shut him up (475; ch. 57), but he still pops up to upbraid Pip one more time for his supposed ingratitude (485; ch. 58), his vitality drawing its persistence from Pip's indignation. Because of Pip's resistance, Pumblechook does not exactly walk off the page. Neither do we do what Pip would prefer: turn the page and forget about the Imposter. The doubling principle animating Pumblechook won't let him stay down, however dismissive Pip may be. Trabb's boy has the same india-rubber quality.

Wopsle is the negative, imploded image of a great Dickensian character. He would make himself great through acting a part, but in the event his acting only succeeds in making nothing of him as a man. The meanings conveyed by his drama, important though they are, are never guided by his intention or shaped by his direction. Nor do they change him. It is a withering view of the acting profession. Wemmick, however, does achieve true Dickensian greatness. His singular performance is to present himself as a wooden human being, projecting both the lack of humanity of the legal world and its corresponding creation of a private sphere in which freedom reigns. As we have already suggested, the doubling effect is achieved through the mimic life of that private world, made possible by Pip's appreciative presence, and by Wemmick's disciplined dedication to fantasy. Discontented with separation from the public sphere, it insists instead on a crazy unity. Gifts received from murderers as tokens of humanity are valued by Wemmick in the first place for their material worth as portable property, and he dismisses their former owners as liars. Yet his private life turns the materialism upon itself. When given to Miss Skiffins, the deathly adornments live out their originally intended feeling and prove their romantic worth. The degradation in which Wemmick daily participates turns back on itself to express the feeling normally (or abnormally) hidden by its routine inhumanity.

The post-office mouth is the most concentrated expression of this double-aestheticization. At first sight, it seems a sure sign of inhumanity in its freezing of the face into a mask. From behind the mask Wemmick projects his performance of knowing indifference upon the criminal world. Yet, as a postbox, it also works even more obviously. Wemmick is a human postbox, a channel of communication between worlds: between the criminal and the respectable, the public and the private, and even the author and the hero. The note left by Wemmick warning Pip not to go home will bring the latter into the criminal world, while Wemmick's stage-management of his own wedding (462–65; ch. 55), with the emphasis on Pip playing a central but necessarily supporting role, would suggest to Pip shortly before Biddy and Joe's wedding (486–89; ch. 58) that he must allow others the authorial stage if he is to realize his own authorial powers.

Dickens's more naturalistic writing involves a different relationship between author and hero. Instead of the external author doubling the would-be hero's self-consummating performance (or the character appearing to do this for him—or herself), a character within the narrative acts to some extent as the author of the other's singular or natural theatricality, using doubling to offer knowledge the other would rather suppress. In *Dombey and Son*, the young Paul's preternatural performance as an adult authors Mrs. Pipchin. He unnervingly refuses to play the juvenile role in her drama of respectable adult obfuscation. Rather, he is unashamedly fascinated by the ego within: "Once she asked him when they were alone, what he was thinking about. 'You,' said Paul, without the least reserve" (117; ch. 8). This authoring activity also reflects back on Paul, bringing his part in the relationship into focus. We wonder about this old-fashioned child who can author adults. Paul is too young to take such power upon himself, but love for his father pushes him to compensate for Mr. Dombey's willful ineptitude, and the attempt to be father to the man will kill the child.

In *Great Expectations*, the natural or singular theatricality of Mrs. Joe is mediated through the consciousness of Pip. His authoring makes her unforgettable as he wonders "whether it was possible she washed herself with a nutmeg-grater instead of soap" (40; ch. 2), and describes her "trenchant way of cutting our bread-and–butter" (42; ch. 2), forcing the pins and needles in her bib into the food and from there occasionally into their mouths. Superbly evocative of her angry self-righteousness, Pip's descriptive powers are, however, limited, and do not quite penetrate the secret of the anger, namely that "her near-hysteria of self-assertion springs from a fear of her own impotence" (Barickman, MacDonald, and Stark, 71). The singular performances tend to prevail, which is appropriate given that the author is a child and to him the sister's actions remain arbitrary. The older Pip, finding the words and making the selection, shows the capacity of his younger self for authorial doubling while also conveying its incompleteness and limitations in the face of overbearing adults' self-consummating performances.

Authoring is therefore more likely in naturalistic writing to be partial, qualified, and expressive of the relationships between characters. At the same time, prominence is often given to the doubling of *narratives*. Stories rebound upon each other, undoing the knowledge locked up within the characters' singular performances of self and the stories they promote to serve those performances. Pip's singular narrative is the fairy tale of his expectations, his version of what they mean for him, including the central link between his good fortune and Estella. Young Pip's story, partly encouraged by the need to escape from his convict memories, is a locking up of knowledge. In accepting Jaggers's terms, Pip agrees to defer his right to know where the wealth comes from that is to make him a gentleman. As Peter Garrett observes, "Circumstances contribute to his error of fact, but the willingness to be directed by an outside force is his own" (86). Pip's gentility is based on a commitment to ignorance. The second story, Magwitch's fairy tale and its accompanying criminal mimicry of the genteel world, consistently questions the ignorance imposed by respectability, teasingly insisting instead on hidden meanings.

With Magwitch's self-revelation, the returned convict's active role as author of the second fairy tale and of Pip would seem to be done, but the story has its own impetus, opening the doors locked for Pip by the first story and changing him as an author. The older narrator and the younger Pip begin to come together. The authorial narrator is still telling the story of his younger self, but he no longer does so from such an overtly outside position. Rather, he enters further into his own narrative, absorbing himself formally in the provision of knowledge that enables his younger self to absorb *him*self in shaping Magwitch into a true hero. Seeing and participating with him in this activity, we in turn make Pip the author *our* hero.

Like Esther Summerson in *Bleak House*, Pip has to know the past. Unlike her, he shut it out in the first place. For he has seen what a child is not supposed to see in the society of *Great Expectations*. Goodness and fear involve him in magical events that bring him a dangerous understanding of love's power and the importance of secrecy. The most intense experience of his childhood demonstrates that his goodness must be kept secret. Precisely because love of others is forbidden (since it threatens self-consummation), and because the society around him reinforces that ban at every turn, the child comes to fear that his very goodness may be bad. No wonder he falls easy prey to Miss Havisham and seeks refuge in a magic romance that would keep him safe from knowledge. To his credit, the self-stupefaction does not work. Instead, the true love within the romance awakens when the ceiling falls. Perversity undoes perversity.

The knowledge that gives Pip the power to act decisively for the first time is intimately associated with a growing sense of himself as the object of others' perception, rather than solely as a subject living outwards from within himself. Seeing how he appears to others, that is, as someone else, he can place his subjective self. In a highly influential essay, "The Hero's Guilt: The Case of *Great Expectations*," Julian Moynahan notes the possible moral insight offered by objectification when Pip, seeing himself as Magwitch, "defines his neglectful behaviour towards Joe as criminal" (74). Moynahan, however, prefers a psychological approach in which Orlick, a "distorted and darkened mirror-image" (78) of Pip, embodies and enacts the hero's repressed malevolence, sharing in the creation of a "complex unity" called "Pip-Orlick." I would argue that objectification is more important than Moynahan gives it credit for. Unlike the psychological approach, it entails both identification *and* separation, similarity *and* difference. Also, it is both a vehicle for moral insight and a structural principle made necessary and shaped in response to a self-consummating society intensely hostile to traditional methods of consummation by another.

   Objectification is important in all Dickens's fiction, but rarely is it used to
such effect as in *Great Expectations*. It engages all the mysteries in Pip's life,
however dark or comical or both: on the night coach to Rochester, for instance, listening to the convict talking about the secrets of his, Pip's, life; or
finding himself the object of a street performance by Trabb's boy that bur-
lesques his own treatment of Joe. Pip begins to feel this more fully soon after
Magwitch's self-revelation, when he goes back to the marshes and Satis
House to tell Miss Havisham about the real nature of his expectations. Meeting by chance at the Blue Boar, he and Drummle ape each other. Shoulder
to shoulder in front of the fire, each refusing to give way, they half-wittingly
mimic each other's stance and actions: ''Mr. Drummle looked at his boots,
and I looked at mine, and then Mr. Drummle looked at my boots, and I
looked at his.'' They do the same with conversation:

> ''Have you been here long?'' I asked, determined not to yield an inch of the fire.
>   ''Long enough to be tired of it,'' returned Drummle, pretending to yawn,
> but equally determined.
>   ''Do you stay here long?''
>   ''Can't say,'' answered Mr Drummle. ''Do you?''
>   ''Can't say,'' said I.   (369; ch. 43)

Such doltish provocation belongs to youth: you throw the other back at himself
or herself through mimicry while being so locked by anger in the drama that
you are not really sure who is mocking whom. The younger Pip thinks he
feels only the pain at losing Estella to the brute next to him. Supplanted in
love, as he sees it, he won't be supplanted in front of the fire. The older
narrator conveys the absurdity in the pain, a point not completely lost, perhaps, on his younger self.
   Part of Pip's chagrin may be the reluctant awareness that Drummle's idiotic
complacency at thinking himself meant for Estella distortedly mirrors his
own previous assumptions. Of course, he rages: ''I felt inclined to take him
in my arms (as the robber in the story-book is said to have taken the old
lady), and seat him on the fire'' (370; ch. 43). The violence of David Copperfield's hatred of Uriah Heep—''I had a delirious idea of seizing the red-
hot poker out of the fire, and running him through with it'' (355; ch. 25)—is
repeated with a difference. Wanting to put the enemy on the fire is made
ridiculous by the anti-climactic ''seat'' and ''old lady,'' and by the distancing
effect of the story-book reference. The ambiguity (our not knowing whether
the older or younger Pip is making the comparison) leaves it open for the
younger Pip to be the one who creates that distance, even in his anger. While
hating Drummle, he may also see something of himself in the other person,
and through that objectification he may begin to admit his own absurdity.
This seeing himself in another is the starting point for understanding his past
and himself from a different perspective.

It is also possible to see a second person *in* a third. One example is both simple and common: the awareness of family resemblance. Pip sees Estella in Jaggers's servant Molly (403–04; ch. 48), and thus finds a key to the mysteries of his love. The resemblance has been heavily trailed, which helps to convey the shock of knowing what he has already sensed but could not quite grasp, something both obvious and strange. More enigmatic is the association between Estella and Newgate, through which Pip senses without quite realizing her resemblance to Magwitch:

> [Coming out of Newgate] I beat the prison dust off my feet as I sauntered to and fro, and I shook it out of my dress, and I exhaled its air from my lungs . . . and I was not yet free of the soiling consciousness of Mr Wemmick's conservatory, when I saw her face at the coach window and her hand waving to me.
> What *was* the nameless shadow which again in that one instant had passed?
> (284; ch. 32)

Seeing one person in another changes both of them in our eyes. It may also affect our own relationship with each of them by bringing us new knowledge. Realizing that Magwitch is Estella's father, Pip knows more than Jaggers and can make more informed decisions than anyone around him. Gaining in knowledge, and working with increasing self-possession, Pip exerts a more deliberate authority when he reveals the identity of Estella's father to Jaggers (422–23; ch. 51). He refuses to accept the lawyer's crabbed performance that would congratulate itself on eliciting information without giving anything in return, insisting instead on his right to know the truth because of his lost love for Estella (423; ch. 51). When his direct expression of feeling fails, Pip appeals to Wemmick, and by exposing that man's secret humanity he allows Jaggers to momentarily reveal his own:

> Mr Jaggers nodded his head retrospectively two or three times, and actually drew a sigh. "Pip," said he, "we won't talk about 'poor dreams;' you know more about such things than I, having much fresher experience of that kind."
> (424; ch. 51)

The lawyer who would deny feeling is moved by seeing himself in and against Wemmick, and by seeing his youthful self in Pip. Jaggers's performance has been calculated to protect his heart by hiding it. Pip reminds him that he has one and proves to him that he is alive.

Pip's learning of the truth about himself and others is a story of reflection and response. Reflection, not as contemplation, but as a seeing of himself in and through others, and others in and through himself. This method of perception allows incident and action to convey the complexities and ambiguities of consciousness while avoiding the self-consummating tendency of narrative centered on interior thought processes. Seeing himself in another, Pip gains energy and clarity.

The scene with Drummle may help him to find his voice when he visits Miss Havisham and Estella immediately afterwards. In the most painfully loving speech of the novel, Pip reverses the romantic convention of identifying with the object of his love, of directly merging his subjectivity into hers. Instead of Cathy's "I am Heathcliff" in *Wuthering Heights*, Estella is "part of myself" (378; ch. 44), which emphasizes *her* influence on him and also her separateness in the very act of identification. For Pip, she is both actually "in every prospect I have ever seen," and ideally "the embodiment of every graceful fancy that my mind has ever become acquainted with." So she is in his life while remaining an object of perception, another person who can be loved for her difference as well as for being part of him. Pip then accounts for his love morally: Estella is "part of my character, part of the little good in me, part of the evil." Her identification with him—their sharing of good and evil—is again both stressed and kept incomplete by the double meaning of the much repeated "part," which denotes both merging and separateness. If you are a part of something, you are joining with it, but at the same time you are only a part, not the whole. That difference allows Pip to see value in Estella: "In the separation I associate you only with the good." On her side, Estella has always stressed her lack of responsibility, claiming to be the product of Miss Havisham's desire for revenge. Pip's closing words "O God bless you, God forgive you!" get their charge from the opposing insistence on *choice*. He cannot help loving her, but in deciding to think only of her good influence on himself, he can turn love into moral choice and back into renewed love.

As he expresses and masters his pain, Pip offers Estella a template for love. If she cared to see it, she might trace the coexistence of both identification and separateness, and of both compelling passion and choice. But his words apparently have no effect on her. Instead, they change Miss Havisham. Suffering forces Pip to present his past to Estella, and as he does this he unwittingly shows the older woman an image of her own passionate grief. She sees herself in him. Through him she understands what she has done to herself and then to those around her, including Pip. This takes some time to work into her consciousness, and at their next meeting (just before her death) she is able to confess: "Until you spoke the other day, and until I saw in you a looking-glass that showed me what I once felt myself, I did not know what I had done" (411; ch. 49). Miss Havisham is not broken solely by Estella's choice of Drummle, or by Estella's refusal to return her love. The manner of her breaking that leads directly to the manner of her death (her burning) is decided by Pip. He brings her the *knowledge* that forces her to go back over her life and leaves her with no excuse in her own eyes. He does this by presenting her with the objectified image of herself that she sees in him and then has to live and die with. Objectification has the power of life and death.

At this point, however, Pip still lacks control of his authority, for in addressing Estella he has authored Miss Havisham. It only comes when he himself is authored through objectification by the adult narrator. Returning to London, he finds the note from Wemmick—"DON'T GO HOME" (379; ch. 44)—and is expelled from his own life. Alone at night in the Hummums (the name indicative of estrangement), he finds the sense steal upon him that he has become the criminal he always feared to be, on the run like Magwitch. Inspecting the sheets on his bed for the blood of a man said to have committed suicide in this place, he loses himself and he loses us. The authorial self is dislocated. We don't know whether Pip fears his own suicide, or the ghost of the dead man, or committing violence on another, or being overwhelmed by bloodshed. Perspectival moorings have been cut.

Pip's lifelong fear of how he appears to others now coalesces into the objectified image of everything bad in society. It turns into Magwitch, and Pip has to live with himself as the returned convict. He finds himself observed all night long in the Hummums by "the wide-awake pattern on the walls" (389; ch. 46) cast by the perforated tower of the rush-light, pictured as "a foolish Argus" with a hundred eyes: "And thus, in the gloom and death of the night, we stared at each other." The awareness, *becoming aware* of oneself as the object of others' attention, makes one think again about oneself: "Once received, it is a haunting idea" (393; ch. 46). Later, the lamplighters are said to open "more red eyes in the gathering fog than my rushlight tower at the Hummums had opened white eyes in the ghostly wall" (401; ch. 48), while the death masks in Jaggers's office looked "as though they were playing a diabolical game at bo-peep with me" (401; ch. 48). They teasingly dare him to find the meaning in their game. Is he perceiver, or perceived? An onlooker or a participant in the world of criminal violence, or both?

The need to know about Magwitch and the self-forgetting activities of looking after him push Pip's sense of himself as an object to the fore. Trying to keep the other out of danger, he finds his own world changing. Home is no longer home since he cannot return, and he has to see his world from the outside. The understanding is forced upon him that he, as well as Magwitch, has become the object of the hidden Compeyson's plotting.

The reversal of the usual sense of self is made graphic by being acted out in the theater. For Tore Rem, the emphasis falls on Pip's awareness of the relationship between Wopsle's bad acting and his own life:

> Wopsle and his parodic playacting are in effect made into a model of inauthenticity for Pip and the reader. Pip must examine his own life, his own theatrical illusions, and find a new language in the light of his glaringly inept performances. Within the plot, Wopsle's performance as Hamlet acts as a catalyst for Pip's realization of his own status as imitator.   (120)

We might add that for Pip, involved in the plot through action and through mirrored rather than contemplative reflection, imitation is not something to be shunned. Rather, it is to be lived in all its present danger.[6]

Wopsle's ludicrous acting is the object of Pip's attention as he watches him pretending to be an enchanter. But Wopsle is watching *him*, transfixed by the sight of Compeyson secretly behind Pip. The enchanter enchanted! The real object of attention, Pip, is the one who thought he was naturally protected by the privilege of his subjective position. In conversation after the performance, Wopsle presents him with the secrets of his, Pip's, subjective self, objectifying the hero's experience by giving the Wopsle version of the events long ago on the marshes that have marked Pip for life. Past merges into present with the news that Compeyson was behind Pip in the theater. In watching Pip, Wopsle has been watching Compeyson. He says that he had a sense of Compeyson "belonging to me [Pip] in the old village time" (399; ch. 47), and he unwittingly puts Pip in Magwitch's position, since from Pip's perspective it has always been Compeyson and Magwitch who belong together. This sense of being Magwitch translates directly into Pip's life, because he must deliberately lead a fugitive existence for Magwitch's sake. Instead of continuing to deny the haunting childhood associations with the criminal, he becomes what he always feared, the object of dread.

Part 3

"Being Magwitch" is not a willed identification with the other person, and it touches upon important issues of individual identity. The nineteenth-century concern with individuality is seen in a very broad sense by Charles Taylor as the partial usurpation of the sacred by the secular (401). If a belief in God does not fill the mental horizon of the individual, and the possibility of other beliefs is entertained, then the individual consciousness organizing and evaluating those beliefs becomes of crucial importance. The very admission of choice of belief necessarily puts it center stage. But what constitutes such a consciousness? What validates it? One culturally important answer is that the self simply constitutes and validates itself through its own activity. We make of ourselves what we are.

Somehow, though, if solipsism is to be avoided, the relation between self and others must be accounted for. For Romantics from Rousseau onwards, this can be provided by the apparent paradox of sympathy. To put it crudely, in sympathizing with others I can realize the humanity in myself and become a stronger individual. For the Wordsworth of "Intimations of Immortality," this prospectus can be achieved with great profundity, but as Romanticism enters the Victorian cultural marketplace it becomes ever more subject to willful manipulation. In response, an awareness of the dangers of sympathy when subordinated to self-consummation gradually enters into the art of many working within the Romantic tradition. In their very different ways, the greatest novelists of mid century—Melville, Thackeray, Emily and Charlotte Brontë, and Dickens—develop forms of writing that resist both self-consummation and the merging of author and hero.

Romantic sympathy (segueing into modern empathy) depends upon an identification between author and hero in which one party may absorb the other. In Bakhtin's view, the loss of one's self in another is likely to prove worthless for both parties, particularly if the issue is human suffering. In making a hero's pain my own through identification, I may simply join him or her without doing either of us any good. Complete identification brings an "infection with another's suffering" ("Author and Hero," 26). If I merge myself, for example, with Oedipus through coexperience, I cannot enrich the event of his life as an author/contemplator. Merging with another through sympathy, says Bakhtin, would leave Oedipus alone with himself, unable to become a tragic hero. For this he needs an outside author able to give a shape whose progenitor is hidden to his consciousness. And yet, as Bakhtin well knows, sympathy is necessary to authoring activity.

How does one steer between willful self-consummation and a useless loss of self? One strategy is for the author to present the hero to himself, as it were, as the object of others' attention. And yet, although "seeing yourself as others see you" is easy enough to comprehend rationally, it cannot simply be produced from within the hero's consciousness. As Bakhtin notes:

> I am incapable of feeling *myself* in my own exterior, of feeling myself encompassed and expressed by it, since my emotional and volitional reactions attach to objects and do not contract into an outwardly finished image of myself. My exterior is incapable of becoming *for me* a constituent in a characterization of myself. In the category of *I*, my exterior is incapable of being experienced as a value that encompasses and consummates me.   (35)

It takes a second consciousness to see one's self from the outside, since for each consciousness all others are objects: "The other human being exists for me entirely in the object and his *I* is only an object for me" (38). Successfully seeing ourselves as an object is impossible from within ourselves, but it can be presented to us through another's art:

> Our portrait, when painted by an artist who is authoritative for us, is an entirely different matter. In this case, what I have is indeed a window into a world in which I never live; this is truly a seeing of oneself in the other's world through the eyes of a pure and whole other human being—the artist; a seeing as divination that has an inherent tendency to predetermine me.   (34)

By letting the hero see how he appears to others, the author may enable him to measure his cognitive knowledge of himself, his sense of himself from within his own subjectivity, against the external view. Such a perspective formatively influences the hero's view of himself. Pip provides it for his younger self, in the first place by bringing one fairy tale to bear on another, and, growing out of this, by facing his younger self with the image of himself as a criminal. Provided with the means to measure his subjective sense of self against the view from outside, Pip can begin to understand both his failings and his strengths. It no longer remains possible for him to hide his selfishness, and yet at the same time he can be sure that he is neither wicked like Compeyson, nor sadistic like Miss Havisham. Pip can stop being a secret criminal to himself as he comes to understand something of his fundamental, terrifying conflation of love and evil.

We said that Bakhtin sees the individual as comprised of an ''I-for-myself'' and ''the-other-for-me.'' However, in the early *Toward a Philosophy of the Act*, he adds a third term, ''I-for-the-other'' (54), or how one's self appears to the other.[7] Objectification is really a special application of this term. I would suggest that what we call character is created by the lived interrelationship between these aspects of the self, which varies according to historical circumstances. In *Great Expectations*, the dominating I-for-myself in a self-consummating society would use any available means to deny and destroy another's shaping power over oneself. In such a situation, with straightforward aesthetic love of another rendered impossible, there may be intense pressure to bring the I-for-the-other into play on the same axiological plane as the I-for-myself. In other words, objectification becomes of crucial importance in mid-century English society, drawing on the moral strength of the tradition of Biblical exegesis from which it partly derives, and on the emotive intensity of the Gothic romance, its other main source.

Objectification necessarily affects the operation of sympathy. Pip's brilliantly conveyed initial horror at Magwitch's reappearance—''the scene is the highest proof of the fineness of Dickens's imagination,'' according to Q.D. Leavis (407)—is changed into love by learning that the returned convict is Estella's father, and by a self-possessed sympathy that develops from the experience of objectification. In seeing oneself as someone else's object of perception, the hero has to live with a sense of being another. Art imposes the experience upon him. Others would place him within the same frame as Magwitch, that is, as a criminal. Only in living with that perception can Pip realize his own honesty and innocence. In consciously countermining the law, and in feeling himself the object of another's plotting, he finally knows what it means to be Magwitch. Repulsion changes to respect and the love necessary to Pip's later authoring of the returned convict, his mentor.

In this way, the pitfalls of Romantic identification may be avoided. One does not become the other person through an unmediated act of sympathy from within oneself. Rather, a similar experience to that of another person is imposed upon oneself from the outside (by life, as it would appear to the younger Pip; by art, as it would appear to us), and an understanding of another is made possible through living with the similarity. At the same time, you see and have to live with a previously unknown image of yourself. The sympathy is certainly vital in the first place. It prepares for and gives way to outsideness. Wondering what to do about the returned convict, Pip feels that he himself would be a murderer if he allowed Magwitch to surrender to the law and execution (358; ch. 41). If this remained internalized, singular to Pip's consciousness, it would merely provide more grist for the mill of his guilt, but it is cut short and made objectively real by the note from Wemmick that evicts Pip from his interiority.

Objectification's modern roots lie in the Gothic, perhaps because the horror genres necessarily lay such stress on the reader *not* identifying with the hero or heroine, despite appearances to the contrary. Noël Carroll argues in *The Philosophy of Horror* that the terror felt by a character is not the same as that felt by the reader: "Speaking loosely, the character's emotions in such cases [as facing a monster and a grisly death] will always be self-regarding or egoistic, whereas the audience's emotions are other-regarding and altruistic [in our sympathy for the threatened character]." He adds that, "construed this way, there can be no character-identification because the audience has emotions (suspense, concern, pity, etc.) that the characters do not, while protagonists have emotions and fears that the audience lacks (e.g., fear of extinction)" (91–92). This applies to all fiction to some extent, as Carroll recognizes, but it is particularly important in the Gothic, I would argue, because straightforward identification with the protagonist would quickly overwhelm the reader with the supposed reality of the experience. And the more violent that experience, the more the emphasis on formally separating reader and character in order to make enjoyment possible.

Coming very close to Bakhtin's thinking,[8] Carroll insists on the importance of outsideness:

> I would like to stipulate that what we do is not identify with the characters but, rather, we assimilate their situation. . . . Part of this involves having a sense of the character's internal understanding of the situation, that is, having a sense of how the character assesses the situation. . . . [And yet] we can assimilate her internal evaluation of the situation without becoming, so to speak, possessed by her.
>
> But in assimilating the situation, I also take an external view of it. . . . I see the situation not only from the viewpoint of the protagonist, though I know that viewpoint, but rather, I see it as one who sees the situation from the outside as well.   (95)

The next step, taken by some Gothic writers, but not by Carroll himself, is to integrate the author-hero relationship outlined here into the text itself, presenting the awareness of the other's situation as some form of objectification.

By the mid-nineteenth century, major fiction, drawing on common Gothic sources and methods, uses objectification to question Romantic identification and redefine individual personality. Emily Brontë's *Wuthering Heights*, often taken as a key text in the establishment of Western interiority, actually insists on presenting characters' inner lives through others' objectifications, playing one off against the other, the private against the social.[9] Jane Eyre's self-definition takes shape initially in reaction against the images of her self envisaged by others. Rochester affords her the freedom to see those objectifications (including his own) for what they are, rather than struggling blindly from within herself against others' authoring. Of course, he offers freedom while simultaneously trying to imprison her. For this, he will pay the price of literally losing his power to see and shape the world. It passes to Jane, who can in turn confer freedom on Rochester's blind, solitary self by presenting the world to him.

Perhaps uneasy with an equality won through mutilation of her hero, Charlotte Brontë follows a different path in *Villette*. Lucy Snowe's power of objectification extends to unremitting self-surveillance: she is engaged full-time in examining how she appears to herself and others. By judiciously policing the urge towards a calculating self-consummation, she guards the freedom to act with imaginative spontaneity. Tim Dolin writes of "her strong capacity to imagine and create new ways of being in response to immediate and always shifting needs. Lucy is able to move herself—led not by ambition or by any rational plan—from one identity to another" (xxv). Paul Emmanuel, by contrast, assumes that freedom for others follows from his authoritatively facing them with images of themselves. The novel offers no synthesis of these different uses of objectification. Rather, they express irreducible defining differences between individuals, between a man and a woman of the time. Whether and how Lucy and Paul Emmanuel might or might not adapt to each other's authority is left open by the famously ambiguous ending.

A reconcilement of a kind will be effected in *Great Expectations*, but first Pip's self-possession, made possible by the lived act of sympathy, gains more substance through the testing encounters that follow. Running into the main narrative of the attempted escape and its apparent failure are the two sub-narratives of Orlick and Pumblechook, both of whom forcefully face Pip with images of himself as he appears to others: as a "Wolf" intent upon destroying Orlick, and as a wretch in his ingratitude to his benefactor Pumblechook. In both cases, the sympathy involved earlier in seeing himself as Magwitch is cut away. The attention is now focused on others' unsympathetic, unredeeming views of Pip. They force him back upon himself. Significantly, the

Pumblechookian account of Pip is presented at one remove by an inn landlord "in a little octagonal common-room, like a font" (431; ch. 52). In this baptism, the version of his identity bestowed on him concentrates his attention on his behavior to Joe. The concentration is made all the more effective by the objectified presentation through the landlord, which avoids the competing presence of Pumblechook himself. The baptism turns into a brief catechism, with the landlord's assumption of Pumblechook's righteousness making Pip taste his own folly in the gullibility of the other man.

Monsters of egotism, Pumblechook and Orlick foist their misconceptions on the object of their attention, and from their ignorant versions of authoring that hold him responsible for their own blindness they gain vitality. Their power, though, draws upon truths felt by Pip. Pumblechook is gallingly right in his wrongheadedness since Pip has indeed been ungrateful to his true patron, Joe, guiltily patronizing the blacksmith instead. Orlick is right on two counts. Pip *was* a favorite at the forge. Persecuted, yes, but always favored with Joe's love, and perhaps more intensely persecuted because of that. And Pip was loved by Biddy.

The mixture of lies and truth in Orlick's and Pumblechook's versions of Pip reveals him to himself in his helplessness. One after the other, the comic and melodramatic elements of the narrative convey to Pip a sense of himself as an object of others' attention. He has much to face with Orlick. Not fear of the other man's violence, for it is made clear that he is not frightened of dying at his hands. Rather, Orlick's rapturously hateful version of him holds his past burningly in front of his eyes, illuminating both himself and the man who has shadowed his life. Yet the waking nightmare of Orlick, like Esther's sickness in *Bleak House*, frees the hero. Seen in Orlick's eyes, the falsity in Pip is demonstrated violently and cauterized by the other man. His treatment of Orlick has contained malevolence, and he has never been honest with Biddy, but he is still not the Wolf Orlick wants him to be.[10]

The prospect of imminent death, whether by violence at Orlick's hands, or through illness in Esther's case, forces different perspectives impossibly together. Pip's ordinary thinking is supplanted by a concentrated sequence of objectified images of himself in the past, present, and future. This pre-cinematic series, intercut with and given urgency by Orlick's accusatory monologue, condenses Pip's life, showing him how he will be seen (and not seen) after death by those he loves (436–39; ch. 53). He must live in order to stop those images becoming reality. Objectification here spurs him to life. At the same time, he perceives Orlick subjectively, from within himself, concentrating on the other's every movement, almost holding himself back, which is strange since he is supposedly helpless. Subjectively in the scene, and objectively everywhere else in his life, Pip finds freedom when "I had no grain of hope left" (440; ch. 53).[11] Orlick's mad authoring and the impossible state it engenders in the hero unwittingly confer a vital authorial gift on Pip: *timing*. At the crucial moment he shouts for help that would otherwise have arrived too late or not at all: Herbert, listening outside "while my mind was so busy," "began to doubt whether I [Pip] was there" (442; ch. 53), and was on the point of turning away.

Alex Woloch comments on Orlick and the scene at the limekiln:

> If Orlick is the lightning rod for all the other minor characters (the servants, Bill Barley, Mike, and the Jack) who surge forward in Volume 3, the narrative enfolds Pip's conflict with Orlick as a penultimate climax that leads up to the final clash between Magwitch and Compeyson. In their struggle at the limekiln, Orlick confronts the protagonist not primarily as an externalization (and return) of Pip's psychological tendencies but rather through his insistence on Pip's own exteriority. This is an important, but underrecognized, narrative dimension of the doppelgänger in nineteenth-century fiction, whose purely *exterior* configuration (are the thoughts of a double ever narratively articulated?) forces the protagonist to confront or conceptualize himself as an object rather than a subject, as a *social* rather than a merely psychological being (and thus as a minor rather than central character). This play between exteriority and interiority seems intrinsic to the very structure of the doppelgänger plot. (238)

Woloch is right to qualify Moynahan's view that Orlick functions thematically to dramatize elements of Pip's unconscious, and also to argue that by insisting on Pip's exteriority Orlick forces him to see himself as an object. But Pip's awareness is of simultaneous objectification and subjectivity, and Woloch is wrong, I think, to conclude that, after the (double-)awareness of objectification and subjectivity, Pip's interiority is reconstituted as a "psychological retreat."[12] Orlick intentionally shows Pip to himself while unintentionally making him aware that he is more than the mirror image of his enemy. Objectivity and subjectivity come together in the event, Bakhtin's term for the key moment of action that changes one's life. It is not interiority that is reconstituted, but the power of authoring that is reaffirmed. Woloch comes closest when he writes that "this revision posits consciousness through the connection to others" (242). Orlick's ability to call the protagonist's centrality into question through his similarity to Pip does not undermine Pip's identity. It strengthens him.[13]

Objectification works both ways, affecting and defining minor characters as well as the hero upon whom they reflect. For Robert Caserio, in his magisterial *Plot, Story, and the Novel*, characters are related through coincidence:

> Dickens's sense of plot relies upon a notion that small groups of characters or persons are somehow all the same person. Dickens sees character as an agent of literal coincidence; and his characters themselves, in shock and wonder, recognize the ways in which they are practically each other.   (113–14)

Caserio presciently allows the characters self-awareness of their inter-identity. In my view, they are also capable of (and are defined by) *not* recognizing or *mis*recognizing their sameness, as well as by responding or not responding to the differences within that inter-identity. A character such as Wemmick differs from the Jack at the Ship Inn in not only providing Pip with objectified images of himself (as someone who can find new ways of communication) but also in responding to the objectified image (of his own affection) that Pip reflects back upon him. The Jack certainly reflects the deathliness of his life upon Pip, but his confined self is incapable of reacting to any image of himself that he might see in Pip or Magwitch.

Wondering whether "the thoughts of the double [are] ever narratively articulated," Woloch simultaneously makes and misses the central point about Dolge Orlick. For his interiority is in plain sight, acted out as melodramatic performance: every movement and every word conveys his thoughts. His performance centers obsessively on Pip because he is everything Orlick is not. For all his selfish limitations and his ignorance of Biddy, Pip is Orlick's twisted ideal, a man capable of awakening love, and therefore the one who must be demonized. Although Pip can see his own suppressed bad faith magnified in Orlick, the other man sees nothing in the Pip who is necessarily different from his idea of himself. Of course, Dickens as external author makes the decisions, but within the novel characters decide their own position as major or minor according to their openness to objectification. Orlick marginalizes himself by surrendering to his obsession, crystallizing his inner life as performance.

In traditional terms, Orlick has sacrificed his soul in order to possess Pip's. From a Bakhtinian perspective, he would consummate himself through murder. Orlick does not have an interior life as understood by normative psychology, and is perhaps best approached through the Gothic romances from which his characterization is derived and which are often nudging into Pip's narrative consciousness. In creating new life, for instance, Mary Shelley's Frankenstein tries to invest another consciousness with his own suprahuman desires: he would re-create himself in perfect form as another. The ugliness he is then faced with is something more than an externalization of the horrors hidden within himself. Rather, the very externalization expresses, in the same way as Orlick, the nullifying of interiority per se. In seeking to remake Nature, he has given himself to the ultimate performance of self-consummation. Conversely, the unnamed creature's tragedy lies in his desire for the individuality of an interiority denied by his author in the very manner of his creation.[14]

Part 4

Out of the turmoil of the meetings with death at Satis House and the limekiln, Pip returns to the escape attempt with purpose and clarity. He greets the next day—the most important of his life—with a renewed sense of self: ''a veil seemed to be drawn from the river, and millions of sparkles burst out upon its waters. From me too, a veil seemed to be drawn, and I felt strong and well'' (444; ch. 53).

Trying to save Magwitch, the younger Pip makes him his hero. Through the telling of that story, the older Pip authors *his* hero, his younger self, providing the means for him to see himself from the outside, thereby further developing the movement towards self-possession. The narrator has shown his younger self how he is seen by other *people*. It remains for us, Dickens and his readers, to relate him to *place*. For character can be shown in relief against the physical world in which all experience takes place.

Naturally (sic), the physical world has been there all along, observed with that keen eye characteristic of Pip (at any age), and of Dickens himself. The constant action of imagination upon observation has been equally characteristic. Indeed, it is a major reason for Dickens's enduring popularity. Getting up early to take the stolen food and drink to the escaped convict at the beginning of the book, the young Pip notes that the frost on the window-pane looked ''as if some goblin had been crying there all night, and using the window for a pocket-handkerchief'' (48; ch. 3). The cows on the marshes startle the child in the early morning mist, ''staring out of their eyes, and steaming out of their nostrils, 'Holloa, young thief!' '' (48; ch. 3) ''One black ox, with a white cravat—who even had to my awakened conscience something of a clerical air,'' forces the little boy into blubbering out a confession.

The action of animistic imagination on closely observed detail is splendid in its surprising aptness. It is also dangerous, for it can bend the world to itself. The danger comes home to Pip in an extraordinary vision just before the ceiling falls. At Miss Havisham's, he notes every detail in the room, celebrating his power to bring the world to life. At the same time, he wonders whether that life only reflects his own consciousness:

> The candles that lighted that room of hers were placed in sconces on the wall. They were high from the ground, and they burnt with the steady dulness of artificial light in air that is seldom renewed. As I looked round at them, and at the pale gloom they made, and at the stopped clock, and at the withered articles of bridal dress upon the table and the ground, and at her own awful figure with its ghostly reflection thrown large by the fire upon the ceiling and the wall, *I saw in everything the construction that my mind had come to, repeated and thrown back to me.* My thoughts passed into the great room across the landing where the table was spread, and I saw it written, as it were, in the falls of the cobwebs from the centre-piece, in the crawlings of the spiders on the cloth, in the tracks of the mice as they betook their little quickened hearts behind the panels, and in the gropings and pausings of the beetles on the floor.
>
> (321; ch. 38; emphasis added)

Even after the realization that everything in the room may only repeat and reflect ''the construction that my mind had come to,'' his imaginative observation continues apace. We are there with the authorial narrator, quickening the hearts of the mice, informing ''the gropings and pausings of the beetles,'' compulsively entering into animation.

Pip's self-possession comes, almost finally, from *us. We* free him for a time from the burden of the imaginative gift so that he can concentrate on Magwitch. If there is more to the world—and there always is—it doesn't have to be his business right now, although it does have to be observed and its possible significance kept in mind. The physical world is presented to Pip as what he sees in his absorbed contemplation of his younger self, itself absorbed in Magwitch. In this intensified state, his consciousness is left free for us to define in outline against what he sees—the real world, as far as he is concerned.

In some of his finest writing, Dickens (carrying us with him) devotes himself and his art to depicting a narrator who is open to the world because he has no interest in trying to make an effect or to strive for art. With his eyes open, and through our art, we, Pip's authors, can show him what he sees preparing to go down the Thames and past the end of the world, Gravesend: ''It was one of those March days when the sun shines hot and the wind blows cold: when it is summer in the light, and winter in the shade'' (444; ch. 54). The poised simplicity of the rhythm and the complex image of wholeness through division are set against and give reality to Pip's own absorption in the consciousness of loving activity, itself made acute by his removal from actual physical exertion due to his injuries: ''Where I might go, what I might do, or when I might return, were questions utterly unknown to me; nor did I vex my mind with them, for it was wholly set on Provis's safety'' (444–45; ch. 54). The completeness of that concern is unwittingly indicated by his reluctance to say Magwitch's name, even now when there is no reason for continued pretense. The picking up of the rhythm that conveys the movement of the river resonates within Pip himself, giving him hope: ''The crisp air, the sunlight, the movement on the river, and the moving river itself—the road that ran with us, seeming to sympathize with us, animate us, and encourage us on—freshened me with new hope'' (445; ch. 54). Yet there is a desperate note in the determined anthropomorphism and in the slowing repetition of ''us.'' The significance is kept latent, to be noted, but no more. Pip's imagination is restrained from within by his need to remain alert for Magwitch's sake, and from without by us, while we, as the world, simultaneously keep in mind the imaginative potential of his vision:

> Old London Bridge was soon passed, and old Billingsgate market with its oyster-boats and Dutchmen, and the White Tower and Traitor's Gate, and we were in among the tiers of shipping. Here, were the Leith, Aberdeen, and

Glasgow steamers, loading and unloading goods, and looking immensely high out of the water as we passed alongside; here, were colliers by the score and score, with the coal-whippers plunging off stages on deck, as counterweights to measures of coal swinging up, which were then rattled over the side into barges; here, at her moorings was tomorrow's steamer for Rotterdam, of which we took good notice; and here tomorrow's for Hamburg, under whose bowsprit we crossed. And now I, sitting in the stern, could see with a faster beating heart, Mill Pond Bank and Mill Pond stairs.   (446; ch. 54)

Pip can notice and respond to his own heart rather than having to animate the hearts of mice. Maybe we try to warn him through what he sees, suggesting intimations of death in the "coal-whippers plunging off stages on deck." Here is Pip, almost on his way with Magwitch back to the marshes of his childhood and the gibbet to which even at that earlier time the escaped convict seemed to be returning, "going back to hook himself up again" (39; ch. 1). And here are the coal-whippers so realistically mimicking execution. And here, also, is the future: the Hamburg steamer, "under whose bowsprit we crossed." Yet we cannot linger. With us affirming Pip's imagination while holding it in abeyance, the narrative rhythm in which he is absorbed moves us calmly and firmly towards Mill Pond stairs and the escape attempt.

Pip's attention is given to Magwitch, himself made equable by Pip, and aware, perhaps, of what we also sense: that the present softness of the current carrying them downriver masks other movements in the depths beneath. They have as little control of events, he says, as they do of the tide (448; ch. 54). It is the tides that have to be taken carefully into account—as indeed they are by Pip—and yet cannot be fully understood. The Jack in the Ship Inn where they lodge lives on the dead washed ashore by the tide. Yet waiting for it to turn at the same inn after Compeyson's death and Magwitch's recapture gives Pip the time and place to give himself in loving consummation to Magwitch:

For now, my repugnance to him had all melted away, and in the hunted wounded shackled creature who held my hand in his, I only saw a man who had meant to be my benefactor, and who had felt affectionately, gratefully, and generously, towards me with great constancy through a series of years. I only saw in him a much better man than I had been to Joe.   (456–57; ch. 54)

Seeing the loving man in "the hunted wounded shackled creature" brings home Pip's failure to love Joe. Realizing humanity in another, he recognizes his own inhumanity. At this point, and for this reason, he would earn our true respect, and we would confer humanity upon him. Yet once more we cannot stop, for the rhythm of the narrative moves readers and characters back again from the marshes to London.

Pip's life has all along moved to a basic rhythm of flight and return that is brought more fully into consciousness and insisted upon by the tidal currents against and with which he and his friends try to effect an escape for Magwitch. The returned convict's freedom changes into an imprisonment that in turn makes an escape from degradation possible, for a final escape is provided by mortality, or rather, by the manner of dying. Something similar moves Pip himself, returning to the marshes from which he has escaped, only to find another kind of freedom in the return. As for Compeyson, who would direct the currents of others' lives, the man is "tumbling on the tides, dead" (458; ch. 55). A fundamental movement of the world, the tide, is felt to shape and relate place, events, and character. The attempted escape, interception, arrest, and death depend on the tide. Timing, learned by Pip from Orlick, is everything, and the tides are the movement of the world in time, the most abstract and the most physical of movements, deciding the moment when the Hamburg steamer will run them down, and when Pip and the reader will feel the full worth of another person.

The primal shaping movement of the sea parallels the primal shaping movement of art: repetition with difference. Pip has been here before, watching Magwitch and Compeyson locked in hate. That time, they were at the bottom of a ditch, in the arresting sergeant's words, like "two wild beasts" (67; ch. 5). Now, though, they are in the water proper, and this time Pip goes in with them as the boat sinks under him, a part of the experience instead of apart from it. The degradation, a sense of being infected by having given comfort to the animals fighting in the ditch, has stayed with Pip from his childhood onwards, to be washed away by his involvement in the repeated act.

After that baptism, with Magwitch a prisoner again and all his possessions forfeit, the convict's confidence in him brings home to Pip his responsibility for the other man. When Magwitch bestows authority on him with "I've seen my boy, and he can be a gentleman without me" (457; ch. 54), Pip's only thought is that "he need never know how his hopes of enriching me had perished." Authoring truly passes to him with that thought and those words, and he is capable of the fine depiction of Magwitch's courtroom dignity.

Yet Pip can still stumble, and he needs the help of those he once denied, although not in the way he thinks. Christopher Morris, among others, points to his self-serving use of the parable of "The Pharisee and the Publican." The Biblical quotation used as an epitaph for Magwitch—"O Lord, be merciful to him, a sinner!" (470; ch. 56), rather than "to *me*, a sinner!"—does indeed twist the parable into "a prayer for Magwitch rather than a confession of his own unworthiness [and this] disingenuously allows him to preserve an altruistic sense of his own selfhood" (83; see also Moynahan 74, and Welsh 108). Yet we may not accept this as just another example of Pip's "seemingly irreducible egotism'' (Morris 77). Rather than acting throughout in bad faith disguised as virtue, Pip has had to try and fail and try again for a good faith that can only be won through authoring relationships. The twisting of the parable is especially painful, given the strength of Pip's love for the dying Magwitch, and it prepares the way for the sickness immediately following this act of bad faith.

The tangle of self-love and love for others can catch critics, as well as characters. In his study of Dickens, J. Hillis Miller says with great acuity that ''In place of the self-assertive love which requires the other to make himself the basis of one's selfhood, there is substituted by Magwitch and Pip the mutual sacrifice of their dearest claims to selfhood'' (276). And yet a page later, he concludes that

> At the center of Dickens' novels is a recognition of the bankruptcy of the relation of the individual to society as it now exists, the objective structure of given institutions and values. Only what an individual makes of himself, in charitable relations to others, counts. And this self-creation tends to require open revolt against the pressures of society. Human beings are themselves the source of the transcendence of their isolation.   (277)

Under the auspices of rejecting the relationship between the individual and the social structure, ''self-creation'' now enters and assumes a leading role. This is not self-assertive, since it takes place ''in charitable relations with others,'' but that last phrase damagingly modifies the previous ''mutual sacrifice of their dearest claims to selfhood.'' What will happen when, inevitably, self-creation is at odds with or would nullify the charitable relations? Miller does not tell us, and if Pip stumbles, so may we. The renunciation of self-creation is a formidable task for both Victorians and ourselves.

During his fever, Pip's objectification goes beyond its human limit. Earlier, from seeing himself *in* another, he moved to seeing himself *as* another. Since that other person, Magwitch, was himself practiced upon, and since Pip became the object of plotting against Magwitch, the identification conferred upon him also allowed Pip to see how others make an object of him. Pumblechook's surrogate and Orlick have then shown him objectified, hateful images of himself. Now, fever pushes the objectification into complete inhumanity.

Pip envisages himself from the outside, objectifying his own subjectivity as ''a brick in the house wall . . . entreating to be released from the giddy place where the builders had set me'' (471; ch. 57). He sees himself as ''a steel beam of a vast engine,'' imploring to have ''my part in it hammered off'' (471–72; ch. 57), impossibly experiencing himself as someone and something, again echoing Esther Summerson's recollection of her illness. For Esther, the frightening realization of her own plurality marks a beginning, an entry effected into her own life by seeing herself through others' eyes. Knowing herself as an object frees her subjectivity (Easley 2004, 213–17). For Pip, it seems too horrible to accept. It blasts his egotism. At least there was feral life in Orlick's version of him, and there is beauty of a kind in Esther's vision of herself as part of a flaming necklace or starry circle. But the helplessness of being reduced to the most insensate object of physical existence while knowing that this is happening to him is a nightmare tailored for and by Pip himself. It takes to the logical extreme his lifelong ability to animate the world. He is made the prisoner of that which he animates: this is what the world would make of him.

Pip wakes with relief to the gradual recognition of being tended by Joe, who serves as a consummating point of reference to keep the nightmare of objectification in check. As he convalesces with Joe's help, Pip reprises his childhood through an adult lens and comes to the conclusion that he must relive his former life by marrying Biddy. It seems that he cannot bring himself to accept his recent experiences that have culminated in the visions during his illness. However painful it may be, experiencing oneself as an object can focus the subjectivity of a hero and position him better to author others. Pip, though, in wishing to return to and rework his childhood, would cling to his practice of making the world in his own image in order to consummate himself. The need to be forgiven for such weakness also belongs to his past. Resurfacing, that need has to be lived and surmounted again, and as this happens it will give even greater value to Pip's own forgiveness of Estella.

If he married Biddy, Pip thinks, he could make up for previous mistakes. This admirable rejection of his former selfishness would, however, renege on his recent understanding. In an attempt to recover the past on his own terms from within his own cognitive self, he would make himself the penitent hero. The warning note is sounded by the description of the countryside on his return and of the ways in which he expects life on the marshes to shape itself around his morally reborn self:

> The June weather was delicious. The sky was blue, the larks were soaring high over the green corn, I thought all that countryside more beautiful and peaceful by far than I had ever known it to be yet. Many pleasant pictures of the life that I would lead there, and of the change for the better that would come over my character when I had a guiding spirit at my side whose simple faith and clear home-wisdom I had proved, beguiled my way.   (486; ch. 58)

The idealization of his hopes founders and is revealed for what it is by unbeguiling Biddy. Martin Price sees this as "the sharpest moment of confrontation" (120) between two kinds of romanticism: Pip's perverse, self-imposed fantasy set against

> the dignity of the natural rural life. It is a dignity that . . . accepts the narrowness or stupidity of such a life as the cost of its depth and directness of feeling. This kind of romanticism uncovers reality that others overlook or despise.   (120)

Biddy's marriage to Joe, and more particularly their not informing Pip of it, denies once and for all his ruling them through his subjectivity. They do not depend upon the wishes of a would-be hero, and Biddy does not allow Pip to absorb her into his own story.[15] She never did, which is why so often in the past he had to turn away, evading the uncomfortable awareness by criticizing her attitude. At the wedding, however, when he finds himself loved but not at the center of others' happiness, Pip stifles the criticism. He could justifiably have reacted against a cruelty made all the more hurtful by his accidentally arriving on their wedding day and finding them already married. Joe's excuse is that he thought Pip wasn't strong enough to take the news. Biddy says, "I ought to have thought of it, dear Joe, but I was too happy" (487; ch. 58). So there it is. And by explicitly addressing Joe, she insists in Pip's presence on giving her attention to her husband. However, the narrator gives no hint of criticism. Instead, he participates in the love of Biddy and Joe rather than expecting them to love him: "They were both so overjoyed to see me, so touched by my coming to them, so delighted that I should have come by accident to make their day complete!" (487; ch. 58) He thus acknowledges himself as the agent for others' consummation and finally becomes responsible for his own authoring of others rather than directing them to make him a hero. Biddy said earlier, "I was your first teacher, though, wasn't I?" (153; ch. 17) She is also his last. By putting humanity into the nightmare of being "something" as well as "someone," Biddy has helped Pip to understand that the experience of such a perspective is necessary for him as an author.[16]

From a Foucauldian viewpoint, Pip is only confirming power relations that he has learned to internalize throughout the book. Far from learning from Biddy, when he suggests towards the close that she should lend him her baby, Pip is, according to Jeremy Tambling, "offering to play Magwitch to Biddy's child. He has learned nothing: is indeed a recidivist, unaware of how much he has been made himself a subject of other people's power and knowledge" (127). In short, "the production, and reproduction, of oppression is what the book charts" (128), and "if the hero learns at all, it is only within his terms of reference, so there is no breaking out from the obsession with the self" (133). The Bakhtinian approach of the present essay differs in its argument that the individual self can be constituted in a number of ways at any given time, depending on varying author-hero relationships. The Foucauldian view assumes both that there is only one kind of nineteenth-century individuality, and that writers such as Dickens necessarily subscribe to it.

For all the pertinence of the Foucauldian reading—its analysis of the ways in which human beings make instruments of others and of themselves in their very expression of freedom—it remains limited by its singular conception of the self. Bakhtinian plurality, however, makes for a measure of choice. In asking for Joe and Biddy's forgiveness, and in giving his blessing to their marriage, Pip can be free of the marshes and their legacy. If he returns, it will be at his own choosing. He has been freed from the need to impose his vision of himself upon others, and he receives a wedding gift from those who have loved him since childhood that ensures his awareness of himself as an author of others. For he sees that he makes *their* happiness complete.

That is why Pip can meet with Estella one more time, and offer her a future by giving her his past. It doesn't really matter whether they walk away together, or whether she drives away alone in a carriage. Despite the suffering she has caused, he offers her creative love in the form of the book that we are reading and that she can read for herself. That is his gift of loving forgiveness to her. It is in the reading of the novel that Estella would find herself *re*-presented, for it provides the knowledge of her self shaped by others' love, passion, hatred, and ignorance.

Jaggers characteristically advocates silence: "For whose sake would you reveal the secret?" (426; ch. 51). For once, though, his emotion revealingly outruns his theme. At the climax of a powerful harangue, he advises Pip to cut off his left hand and then get Wemmick to chop off the other rather than reveal the names of Estella's parents. His rhetorical intensity seems out of place, given that Pip has not even mentioned the possibility of making the secret known. Rather, he has told Jaggers with a view to the other man responding in kind and relating his own part in events. Yet Jaggers immediately assumes that Pip wants to tell the people involved, especially Estella, while the advice about chopping off hands suggests with visceral force that the revelation would be in writing. Pip only wanted to "come at the bare truth" (420; ch. 51), but the lawyer's reaction points instead to its actual use.

The lawyer's clerk apparently agrees with his employer: "I looked at Wemmick, whose face was very grave. He gravely touched his lips with his forefinger. I did the same. Mr Jaggers did the same" (426; ch. 51). That most duplicitous and yet most obvious of postmen would seem to commit them to yet another pact of secrecy. Yet the very gesture advocating silence in fact insists only on spoken noncommunication, leaving open the possibility of writing, the very means of communication that filled Jaggers's thoughts so powerfully. That writing will be the book we are reading, an open secret hidden from us by our own assumptions that it is all fictional. Which it is, of course, but not to the characters themselves. "Tell her" is hidden in plain sight in the very name "Es*tell*a." The book is dedicated to her. Or, more accurately, Pip silently dedicates himself to her through the book, disappearing as a true author should, according to Bakhtin,[17] quite different from David Copperfield, a narrator intent on putting himself before us as an author. In his most intense moment of love in disillusionment, Pip says that Estella is everywhere and in everything: "You are part of my existence, part of myself. You have been in every line I have ever read'' (378; ch. 44). We might add that for Pip Estella is in every line he is writing here.

Part 5

Pip's life has been haunted by the need to be forgiven. His achievement is to turn that need for himself into an offer of forgiveness to a woman who has authored his enduring shame, and who herself has every reason to be haunted by the same need. Whether baiting Pip at their first meeting, or throwing herself away on Bentley Drummle, Estella has always shown a pride which is intended to make her invulnerable but which could just as well achieve the opposite. Pride has to defend itself against shame, which may make Estella human by making her conscious of her need for others. To the extent that in the reading she makes a hero of and experiences herself *as* Pip, seeing how she has used him and has been used by him, perhaps Estella could recognize and surmount her own shame.

We saw that the last two syllables of Estella's name form the admonition to "Tell her." The pun also indicates both the similarity with and difference from Esther Summerson, her near-namesake. At the end of *Bleak House*, Esther pushes the reader into returning to the beginning and into reconsidering his or her own relationship with the heroine. Esther herself disappears into the silence of authorship: her part as heroine is finished and there is no more to be told. Dickens forms Estella's name by putting "tell" into the middle of "Esther." In *Great Expectations*, there is more to be told about the heroine. And there is more to tell her: the truth.

Pip's ending of the book would go forward by taking *Estella* back, reprising *her* life, not his. It would draw her into a reconsideration of her relationship with the author, and through him with a society that makes individuals secret to others and to themselves. No one seems more hidden than she, presented to the world and to herself as an object of beauty.[18] She acts as though she can only think of herself as that object, although in taking alienation to an extreme she also fashions a very particular revenge on Miss Havisham, which suggests feeling even as she denies it. The determination to be nothing more than a self-avowed puppet in Miss Havisham's hands, and to deny her own personality, indicates a thorough-going resistance within the apparent acquiescence.

Estella sets herself against the heightened individualism of her author, the woman who boasts of making her what she is, a breaker of men's hearts. By emphasizing her subordination to Miss Havisham's determining influence, she focusses with devastating reasonableness on the responsibility of the older woman. Estella's insistence on herself as an object is her weapon against her deforming author, as well as the expression of her deformation. Miss Havisham has built a life, or a living death, around her own passion. However, her reclusive eccentricity does not separate her from society. Rather, it publicly affirms her dominant social position. The social acceptance and support of her eccentricity express her power. She alone can behave exactly as she wishes, unconstrained by any thought for others and guided solely by her desires. Society respects the isolation and power of passion backed by wealth and position, and nearly all accede to Miss Havisham's importance. She is the ultimate expression of passionate, privileged individualism in a self-consummating society.

Miss Havisham twists Compeyson's denial of desire into hope that her creation will take revenge for her. She parallels Magwitch (just as Estella parallels Pip), but her vengeance is shaped by her wish for romance to consummate herself. Everything at Satis House is about *her*, nothing about the man, Compeyson, in whose menacing anonymity she is complicit. Despite the similarities, Magwitch's revenge takes its shape from the love for others that persists in his character and actions, and that pushes him towards life. The older woman would preserve herself at the expense of the younger, with Estella fulfilling Miss Havisham's hopes of making men suffer. It would be a self-consummation effected by one woman acting through another, her automaton.

Estella's answer to Miss Havisham is to discard herself, to throw herself away upon a man whose only recommendation is the social superiority he shares with her author and on which Miss Havisham's power has depended. Her action makes nothing of Miss Havisham's life, and as such is a condemnation of society as well as of her adoptive mother.

Earlier, Pip could only see the hopelessness of his love in terms of his own desire (288; ch. 33). The dedication of himself as an author to Estella reaccentuates everything previously taken for granted by formally responding to what she has actually been telling him all along, namely that she cannot love him or anyone else because *she* has no hope for herself. In her reading of the novel, Estella will be set a real task, as opposed to the virtual tasks of her previous virtual life: to act in the sense of doing, rather than solely playing a role. In gaining knowledge of herself through Pip's authorship, she may achieve self-possession. Estella may also consciously participate in her own authoring of Pip, and through him she may learn to take responsibility for her authoring of others. She may find subjectivity through the objectified experience of herself *as* another. Pip offers Estella the consummating power of an author, and the hope that belongs to a heroine, without which passion makes everything nothing.

Quite different from that retreat into "a society of two" voiced most influentially by Matthew Arnold's "Ah, love, let us be true/To one another"

(*Dover Beach*, c.1851), and brought to a grim conclusion a century later and an ocean away by Kurt Vonnegut in *Mother Night* (1961), Pip's gift would make no pact of love. Rather, in an act that is itself social, he freely offers Estella the opportunity to realize the social nature of individuality, and to act for herself upon that awareness. This giving of self-possession draws upon traditional Christian concepts of Love but articulates and takes its shape from the historical circumstances of a society in the toils of self-consummation. As such, it marks a moment in British culture that is democratic in the deepest sense, and that satisfies Bakhtin's criteria for the greatest kinds of bildungsroman, those novels in which the development of the hero "is no longer man's private affair. He emerges along with the world and he reflects the historical emergence of the world itself" (1986, 23).

NOTES

1. Authors are masculine for Bakhtin, a male Russian academic of his time. Heroes can be masculine or feminine. He is not much bothered about the distinction between the reader and the writer. In reading, we necessarily relive and recreate the authorial experience, with the writer acting as our unseen guide. Vital to the authoring is the *outsideness* that links reader and writer. See Morson and Emerson:

   > Artistic creators and their audiences are alike in that they must remain outside the heroes' event in both space and time, or, more accurately, in a kind of space and time. So important to Bakhtin is this shared status of outsideness that he often combines the functions of author and reader into one composite term, *author-contemplator*. (189)

2. In my essay on *Bleak House* I relabelled this aesthetic giving of oneself as "I-for-the-other," which seemed clearer than Bakhtin's "the-other-for-me." I now realize that Bakhtin is more accurate in his jettisoning of the subject "I," and I revert to his terminology with due apologies. This allows us to follow Bakhtin when he applies "I-for-the-other" (or "I-for-others") to a *third* category of self, how my self appears to those outside me. See Morson and Emerson 180.

3. The author cannot and must not assume for us the determinateness of a person, for we are *in* him, we enter into and adapt to his active seeing. It is only upon finishing artistic contemplation, i.e., only when the author no longer actively guides our seeing—it is only then that we objectify our author-guided self-activity (our self-activity is his self-activity) in the form of a certain person, in the form of an individualized countenance of the author. (Bakhtin 1995, 207)

4. Like Orlick, Magwitch takes a magically literal approach to authoring. A gentleman is characterized by his ability to read, to master words, while the Word of

the Bible is something to swear by since it is a testament to truth (349; ch. 39). Orlick gloats over Compeyson's counterfeiting ability: there's " 'them that writes fifty hands, and that's not like sneaking you as writes but one' " (439; ch. 53).

5. Double-aestheticization can be a wonderful thing. In *Martin Chuzzlewit*, Mr. Moddle, the youngest of Mrs. Todgers's lodgers, aims to show his superiority by separating himself from society, standing out as a non-performer in a lodging-house crammed with exhibitionists. Authorial doubling exaggerates the youth's romantic intensity: he is "pale, but collected, and still sits apart; for his spirit loves to hold communion with itself, and his soul recoils from noisy revellers" (187; ch. 9). The well-thumbed Romanticism points to Moddle's abuse of the idea of his own uniqueness, here degraded into a social style. The comic intensification of his infatuation with Death as he gets closer to marriage with Charity Pecksniff pushes him into common sense flight, and then revels in the young man's confirmation of his soul's investment in loss: " 'I love another. She is Another's. Everything appears to be Somebody else's. Nothing in the world is mine' " (889; ch. 54). And now he is off to Van Diemen's Land on the clipper schooner *Cupid*, languishing over his farewell letter " 'amid the howlings of the—sailors' " (889; ch. 54). The momentary hesitation of that last dash does for Moddle. It should surely be the howling of the wind or suchlike, but the authorial mimicry insists instead that, far from exposing himself to the elements and solitude, Moddle is condemned to being perpetually immersed in and generally ignored by society. Wherever he goes, he will never get away from others—from the howlings of the sailors—despite a performance dedicated to romantic isolation.

6. Rem thinks that *Great Expectations*, "in many ways one of the great ironic novels of the Western canon," achieves "some of its peculiar dynamism and vitality through the use of a melodrama problematized by its own parody" (121). For all this, we should not underplay the unexpected reciprocity between characters, from which the events (as opposed to calculated plotting) take shape. See also Brooks 49–51.

7. Attempting to explicate Bakhtin's view of the self, Morson and Emerson refer to a triad of "related categories" (180), although in the later *The First Hundred Years of Mikhail Bakhtin* Caryl Emerson combines the two terms of otherness, and many critics are simply content with "self" and "other." Those concerned with ideology, however, tend to emphasize "I-for-the-other" as the social self.

8. See Bakhtin's comment in "Author and Hero":

> I must empathize or project myself into this other human being [the hero], see his world axiologically from within him as *he* sees this world; I must put myself in his place and then, after returning to my own place, "fill in" his horizon through that excess of seeing which opens out from this, my own, place outside him. (25)

9. Self-possession has little traction in *Wuthering Heights* since Catherine would not let any author bestow it upon her. As Michael Macovski says, her priority is to know the critical faculty of her listeners in order to distinguish her own. She

must "become the other" (143) in order to interpret herself, which throws self-possession into reverse. Macovski argues that "characters engaged in this projective type of self-analysis assume the stance of the other, a position that actually enables them to inhabit another's critical faculty and apply it to themselves" (143). I suspect that in attempting this objectification through another they necessarily experience resistance and the possibility of a genuine objectification that goes beyond their original self-projection. The result is not self-possession, but neither is it quite the protagonists' recreation of "the externality of the other" that Macovski envisages. Rather, they become subject to the others' views of them through which they would see themselves.

10. As Moynahan says, Orlick and Drummle "enact an aggressive potential that the novel defines, through patterns of analogy and linked resemblances, as belonging in the end to Pip and to his unconscionably ambitious hopes" (84). But only up to a point, rather than "in the end," for their performances also reveal equally important differences. The same applies to Moynahan's previously mentioned illuminating comment that Pip engages in objectification and changes places with the criminal when he sees Magwitch as " 'a much better man than I had been to Joe.' " (74). The truth in the mirror is so sharply before us that it is difficult to see the difference: Pip never had the active power over Joe's life that Magwitch had over his. Once again the older narrator goes too far in condemning his younger self. It remains for Biddy to show Pip that truth of difference.

11. For Bakhtin, consummation finds its form as hope reaches its limits (128–29).

12. John Mullan says that for Woloch "the sense of a protagonist's complexity requires the effacement of the inner being of others" (3–4), with the corollary that the minor characters resonate memorably for us, resisting their marginalization and leaving us with a sense of alternatives not contained by the official hero and plot. This is really deconstruction applied to character rather than discourse, although Woloch does think that writers retain the ability to use marginalization creatively.

13. According to Woloch,

> the narrative ends with a realistic representation of psychological retreat— retreat from both ambition and social knowledge— while embedding this retreat in a larger representation of the complex social structure that has both catalyzed and extinguished Pip's expectations. Dickens himself follows Joe's wise adage: like life itself . . . this narrative is nothing so much as these "partings welded together." (243)

The closure of the character is thus set against the openness of the text-cum-life, with the proviso that the latter may cause the former.

For Peter Garrett, there is "a dialogue of perspectives":

> Dickens' most compressed single-focus novel condenses without synthesising divergent meanings. . . . "Pip, dear old chap," Joe explains, "life is made of ever so many partings welded together" (27). The

double force of divisions that also bind together, splitting the self and identifying opposites, disperses the single center of *Great Expectations* into undecidable alternatives. (88–89)

14. Pip initially views Magwitch's reappearance and revelation of his expectations as catching him in a horrific Frankenstein situation:

The imaginary student pursued by the misshapen creature he had impiously made, was not more wretched than I, pursued by the creature who had made me, and recoiling from him with a stronger repulsion, the more he admired me and the fonder he was of me. (354; ch. 40)

Unlike Frankenstein, Pip realizes that the creature is as much a creator of himself as he is of the other. He uses the Gothic to convey his own unnaturalness in finding love repulsive. Unlike Orlick, he does not belong to the Gothic.

15. My analysis reaccentuates Price's comment that "the place of return is now a self-contained world where Biddy is for once too preoccupied to imagine Pip's feelings except as part of her own" (120). She may, may be more astute than this comment suggests.

16. Another way of putting this is to say that Biddy naturalizes the uncanny for Pip, resolving the paradox of his visions of himself as a brick in the wall and as part of an engine, some*thing* as well as some*one*. That sense of himself as ultimately other is punishingly contradictory because it comes from within himself. Unbeguiling Biddy, always a quietly awkward outside person, makes Pip's sense of being other real and not just a product of his own imagination. She makes him human to himself.

17. See "Author and Hero":

The author is authoritative and indispensable for the reader, whose relationship to the author is not a relationship to him as an individual, as another human being, as a hero, as a determinate entity in being, but rather a relationship to him as a *principle* that needs to be followed. . . . The author's individuality as a creator is a creative individuality of a special, nonaesthetic order; it is the active individuality of seeing and forming, and not the individuality that is seen and formed. The author becomes an individuality proper only where we assign to him the individual world of the heroes that he created and shaped or where he is partially objectified as a narrator. (207)

See also nn. 1 and 3.

18. See Price on Estella's depersonalization (121–23).

WORKS CITED

Bakhtin, Mikhail. ''Author and Hero in Aesthetic Activity.'' *Art and Answerability: Early Philosophical Essays.* Trans. V. Liapunov. Ed. M. Holquist and V. Liapunov. 1990. Austin: U of Texas P, 1995. 4–256.

———. ''The *Bildungsroman* and Its Significance in the History of Realism (Toward a Historical Typology of the Novel).'' *Speech Genres and Other Late Essays.* Trans. Vern W. McGee. Ed. Caryl Emerson and Michael Holquist. Austin: U of Texas P, 1986. 10–59.

———. *Toward a Philosophy of the Act.* Trans. V. Liapunov. Ed. M. Holquist and V. Liapunov. Austin: U of Texas P, 1993.

Barickman, Richard, Susan MacDonald, and Myra Stark. *Corrupt Relations: Dickens, Thackeray, Trollope, Collins, and the Victorian Sexual System.* New York: Columbia UP, 1982.

Brooks, Peter. *Reading for the Plot: Design and Intention in Narrative.* Oxford: Clarendon, 1984.

Carroll, Noël. *The Philosophy of Horror.* New York: Routledge, 1990.

Caserio, Robert. *Plot, Story, and the Novel: From Dickens and Poe to the Modern Period.* Princeton: Princeton UP, 1979.

Dickens, Charles. *Bleak House.* Ed. Andrew Sanders. London: Everyman, 1994.

———. *David Copperfield.* Introduction and Notes by Jeremy Tambling. London: Penguin, 1996.

———. *Dombey and Son.* Afterword by Alan Pryce-Jones. New York: Signet, 1964.

———. *Great Expectations.* Ed. Angus Calder. 1965. Harmondsworth: Penguin, 1968.

———. *Martin Chuzzlewit.* Ed. Edgar Johnson. New York: Dell, 1965.

Dolin, Tim. Introduction and Notes. *Villette.* By Charlotte Brontë. Oxford: Oxford UP, 2000.

Easley, Keith. ''Dickens and Bakhtin: Authoring in *Bleak House.*'' *Dickens Studies Annual* 34 (2004): 185–232.

———. ''David Copperfield's Self-Consummation.'' Unpublished essay, 2007.

Emerson, Caryl. *The First Hundred Years of Mikhail Bakhtin.* Princeton: Princeton UP, 1997.

Garrett, Peter K. *The Victorian Multiplot Novel: Studies in Dialogical Form.* New Haven: Yale UP, 1980.

Leavis, F. R., and Q. D. Leavis. *Dickens the Novelist.* 1970. Harmondsworth: Penguin, 1972.

Macovski, Michael. *Dialogue and Literature: Apostrophe, Auditors, and the Collapse of Romantic Discourse.* Oxford: Oxford UP, 1994.

Miller, J. Hillis. *Charles Dickens: The World of His Novels.* Cambridge: Harvard UP, 1958.

Morris, Christopher D. "The Bad Faith of Pip's Bad Faith: Deconstructing *Great Expectations.*" *Charles Dickens.* Ed. and Introduced by Steven Connor. London: Longman, 1996. 76–90.

Morson, Gary Saul, and Caryl Emerson. *Mikhail Bakhtin:*

   Creation of a Prosaics. 1990. Stanford: Stanford UP, 1992.

Moynahan, Julian. "The Hero's Guilt: The Case of *Great Expectations.*" *Critical Essays on Charles Dickens's "Great Expectations."* Ed. Michael Cotsell. Miami: U of Miami P, 1990. 73–87.

Mullan, John. "Why always Dorothea?" *London Review of Books* (5 May 2005): 30–31.

Pechey, Graham. "Philosophy and Theology in 'Aesthetic Activity.' " *Dialogism: An International Journal of Bakhtin Studies* 1 (1998): 57–73.

Price, Martin. *Forms of Life: Character and Moral Imagination in the Novel.* New Haven: Yale UP, 1983.

Rem, Tore. *Dickens, Melodrama, and the Parodic Imagination.* New York: AMS, 2002.

Sell, Kathleen. "The Narrator's Shame: Masculine Identity in *Great Expectations.*" *Dickens Studies Annual* 26 (1998): 203–26.

Tambling, Jeremy. "Prison-Bound: Dickens and Foucault (*Great Expectations*)." *Charles Dickens.* Ed. and Introduced by Steven Connor. London: Longman, 1996. 117–34.

Taylor, Charles. *Sources of the Self: The Making of the Modern Identity.* 1989. Cambridge: Cambridge UP, 2002.

Welsh, Alexander. *The City of Dickens.* Oxford: Clarendon, 1971.

Woloch, Alexander. *The One vs. the Many: Minor Characters and the Space of the Protagonist in the Novel.* Princeton: Princeton UP, 2003.

Death as Spectacle: The Paris Morgue in Dickens and Browning

Britta Martens

As an object of macabre fascination, the Paris morgue is without paral-
lel in the Victorian imagination. This article explores the representation
of visits to the morgue in Dickens's Uncommercial Traveller *and in*
Browning's dramatic monologue "Apparent Failure." In both cases,
this gruesome display of French sensational culture is used to explore
a very British middle-class dilemma in the 1860s: how to reconcile the
attraction to new forms of sensational entertainment (notably through
journalism and fiction) with the fear of succumbing to a "vulgar"
sensationalism that had hitherto been the preserve of the working class.
Dickens's traveler experiences the voyeuristic crowd as an extreme
version of the mass readership, echoing the idiom of reviewers of sensa-
tion novels; yet despite distancing himself from these working-class
foreigners, he inescapably shares their fascination with the sensational.
Similarly, Browning's poem exposes the tourist's (ultimately vain) effort
to deny his fascination with the sensational and to claim the moral high
ground over French mores. This article thus combines instructive cross-
national comparisons with reflections on a specifically British middle-
class anxiety over the growth of sensational culture.

In the second half of the nineteenth century, Paris was at the forefront of an emerging culture of spectacle, visual display, voyeurism, and sensationalism. While the *flâneur* is the aspect of this new culture which has received the greatest critical attention, the fame of the city's morgue, which attracted up

---

Dickens Studies Annual, Volume 39, Copyright © 2008 by AMS Press, Inc. All rights reserved.

to 20,000 visitors per day, is certainly its most gruesome illustration.[1] Visitors
to the morgue included tourists, most conspicuously those drawn from the
growing number of Britons traveling to the French capital. As a result, accounts of visits to the morgue appeared in letters, private journals, travel
literature, and the British press; it even featured in some British novels, most
famously in George Du Maurier's *Trilby*, where it is a perfectly normal stop
on the afternoon strolls of the British artists (26).[2] The morgue therefore
gives not only an insight into French sensational culture; it also offers an
opportunity for examining British responses to a manifestation of the sensational from which the observer was culturally distanced.

British texts on the morgue have attracted some critical attention. In these
analyses the emphasis tends to be on the writers' personal responses when
confronted with the anonymous dead and on their perception of the difference
between the morbid French who flock to look at hideous corpses and the
more refined British culture (Veyriras; Vita). This applies particularly to
Charles Dickens, a frequent visitor to the morgue who wrote about it in five
of his journalistic pieces and let one of his characters, Fred Trent in *The
Old Curiosity Shop*, turn up as a corpse there (553).[3] Dickens scholars have
considered this fascination with the morgue to be something specific to him.
Harry Stone sees it as a reflection of his interest in cannibalism (86–102);
John Carey and others read it as motivated by his fascination with corpses
(81–84); and Andrew Sanders argues that Dickens saw the morgue as a
reminder of the cruelties of the French Revolution, which also allowed him
to articulate his concern for social outcasts (*Resurrectionist* 46–48; *Spirit*
104–05).

These readings do not take into account two significant points. Firstly, it is
important to note that Dickens's two longest texts on the morgue, "Travelling
Abroad" (1860) and "Some Recollections of Mortality" (1863), are not
directly autobiographical. They are written in the persona of the Uncommercial Traveller, who shares characteristics and experiences with his author but
appears in these articles also as a type of the British tourist. These texts, with
their fictional narrator from whom the author distances himself to some extent,
articulate not only a cultural critique of the French but, more interestingly,
also a personal critique of the Victorian tourist's attitude towards the foreign
culture. Secondly, with the exception of two fleeting references (Drew 129;
Vita 243), none of the analyses of British writings on the morgue comment
on the similarities between French sensationalism and British culture in a
period which saw the development of the sensation novel and sensational
journalism. As an author and magazine editor, Dickens found himself at the
center of this new culture. It is the contention of this article that his texts
about the morgue reflect a problem raised by the fashion for the sensational

among the Victorian middle class: they were attracted to new forms of sensational entertainment but afraid of succumbing to a "vulgar" sensationalism that has hitherto been the preserve of the working class.

Of course there is a difference between the direct confrontation with the sensational through the gaze at a real corpse and the textualized, mediated experience of the sensational through fiction or journalism. However, as far as the attitude of the "consumer" of the sensational is concerned, this is arguably a difference of degree rather than kind, as the same fundamental attraction to the sensational both draws visitors to the morgue and motivates readers to read sensational narratives. Dickens's texts on the Paris morgue present a graphic picture of the sensationalism that also lies at the heart of British middle-class culture, making the alert reader aware how close the taste for the sensational among members of Dickens's audience comes to what they would condemn as the repulsive, degenerate French attraction to spectacular corpses.

The analysis of Dickens's essays will be complemented by that of a contemporary text, Robert Browning's "Apparent Failure" (1864), which has so far also been read only as a record of the author's personal response to the morgue (Elliot 211; Lucas). This poem is in fact a dramatic monologue by a British tourist, and, as in all of Browning's dramatic monologues, the poem's interest lies in discovering how the speaker perceives the world around him and how he conceptualizes himself in relation to it. Although Browning seems at first sight to approach the subject of the morgue in a very different manner from Dickens, his poem likewise exposes the difficulties of the British middle class when confronted with this extreme expression of the sensational.

* * *

The morgue's official function was the identification of corpses that had been found in the public domain, since establishing the identity of the dead was considered by the authorities crucial to the preservation of social order (Maillard 42–43). The morgue had originally been visited only by members of the public in search of missing relatives. For sanitary reasons and in order to encourage more citizens to enter it and help identify the dead, it was in 1804 transferred from a dark, humid basement in the Grand Châtelet prison to its own building on the Quai du Marché Neuf on the southern side of the Ile de la Cité, not far from Notre-Dame (Gozlan 301–2; Maillard 15).[4] This functional building with a showy Doric façade contained a dissection chamber, a washing room, a room for identified corpses and those that were too decomposed to be exhibited, a storage chamber for the clothes of unidentified, buried corpses, an office where the morgue's registers were kept, the living quarters of the clerk and the guard, and, most importantly, the *salle d'exposition*, where up to ten corpses at a time were displayed to the public on two rows of inclined, brass-covered, marble slabs behind a large glass window (Gozlan 305–32; Maillard 23–32; "The Morgue" 715–16).

The corpses were naked except for a leather apron covering the groin, while their clothes were hung above them to help with identification (see fig. 1). Water taps were installed above the corpses' heads from which water trickled over the dead bodies to slow down decomposition, so that they could be exhibited for a few days. Members of the public could stroll into a spacious room and comfortably view—but not smell—the dead behind the sanitizing screen. This morgue was demolished in the course of Baron Haussmanns redesign of central Paris, the event which motivates the utterance of Brownings speaker, and in 1864 a new building, almost four times as big, was constructed at the eastern tip of the Ile de la Cité, where it remained until 1923, though closed to the general public from 1907 (Elliott 212; Schwartz 53–65, 83–88). An illustration of 1886 bears witness to the growing number and excitement of visitors to the morgue, which necessitated on busy days a queuing system and the intervention of several guards (see fig. 2). The crowd consists here not only of middle-class adults, as in the 1845 engraving, but also of children and members of the working class like the female domestic trying to jump the queue.

There are obvious parallels between the layout of the morgue and the department store, which developed in the 1850s and where the wares were also exhibited to the gaze of the passer-by behind a glass screen. In "Railway Dreaming" (1856), Dickens observes: "[A]ll the world knows that the bodies lie on inclined planes within a great glass window, as though Holbein should represent Death, in his grim Dance, keeping a shop, and displaying his goods like a Regent Street or Boulevard linen-draper" (*Journalism* 3: 375). Similarly, an article entitled "The Morgue" in *Once a Week* of 1864 refers to the screen as "a sort of shop window" (715). And already in 1831, Léon Gozlan comments: "On va là pour voir les noyés, comme ailleurs on va pour voir la mode nouvelle . . . " ("You go there to see the drowned as elsewhere you go to see the latest fashion" 303).[5]

The morgue also imitated the theater, a resemblance emphasized in the 1864 morgue, where the glass screen was fitted with curtains which would be drawn while a new corpse was being put on display (Schwartz 57–58). Given this heightened theatrical quality of the morgue, it is not surprising that the many references to it in the French press abounded with comparisons to the theater and other types of spectacular display such as waxworks and fair attractions. Maxime Du Camp, for instance, reports: "[L]es gamins, qui y viennent comme à un spectacle, appellent les corps exposés, *les artistes*; lorsque par hasard la salle d'exposition est vide, ils disent: Il y a relâche" ("the kids, who go there as they would to a theatrical representation, call the

Fig. 1. *Vue intérieure de la morgue*, engraving (c. 1845) after a painting by Carrie (reproduced with the author's permission from Harry Stone, *The Night Side of Dickens: Cannibalism, Passion, Necessity* [Columbus: Ohio State UP, 1994], 94).

Fig. 2. Paul Destez, ''Le Mystère de la Rue di Vertbois: Exposition du Petit Cadavre à la morgue,'' *Le Monde illustré*, 15 August 1886.

exhibited corpses *the artists*; if the exhibition room happens to be empty, they say: *The theater is temporarily closed today*" 431).[6] With its crowd-pulling power, the morgue even attracted other spectacles. The open space in front of it was, as Dickens noted, "a reasonably good spot for mountebanks" ("Railway Dreaming" in *Journalism* 3: 375).[7] In sum, a visit to the morgue was commonly perceived as a free-of-charge public spectacle. In the words of Emile Zola, "La Morgue est un spectacle à la portée de toutes les bourses, que se payent gratuitement les passants pauvres ou riches. La porte est ouverte, entre qui veut" ("The morgue is a spectacle within the reach of every purse and which poor and rich passersby alike can get for free. The door is open, whoever wants to can come in" 131).

The article in *Once a Week* also compares the morgue with the theater and makes the connection with sensational narrative when it comments on the morgue's "regular frequenters": "The Morgue is their theatre and their literature. Hither they come for their 'sensation' dramas and novels, and assuredly they get them" (715).[8] As Vanessa Schwartz has shown, the morgue served as a complement to the *faits divers*, the brief, curious and often sensational newspaper articles which would alert readers that the corpse on which they were reporting was displayed in the morgue. It was not uncommon for sensational novels which were serialized in newspapers to be based on *faits divers*, and some French commentators blamed the craze for the morgue among working-class women in particular on these novels (Schwartz 82). Zola's *Thérèse Raquin* (1867), a serialized novel inspired by a *fait divers* and in which the murderer pays daily visits to the morgue until he discovers his victim there, would certainly have helped to awaken curiosity in its readers. The popularity of the morgue can thus be considered a symptom of the taste for sensationalized realities in the *faits divers* and for realistically presented sensational fiction which exploited *faits divers* for their plots. Textual versions of the sensational were an important feature of Parisian culture during this era when newspapers became much more widely available, but so was the act of looking at the sensational corpse. As Firmin Maillard, the first historian of the morgue, points out, the morgue still had the advantage over sensational journalism and fiction of showing its visitor "the real thing" instead of mere representation: "Que voulez-vous, s'il préfère à vos récits les plus dramatiques, à vos peintures les plus effrayantes, la réalité, et quelle réalité!" ("What can you do if he prefers to your dramatic stories, to your most horrifying paintings, reality, and what reality!" 95).

By contrast, in Britain, where visual culture was also rapidly developing, unidentified corpses were not publicly exhibited. Until 1872, when a mortuary without access to the general public was opened in London, factual descriptions of the anonymous dead were posted outside police stations (Veyriras 52). This encounter with death was thus only available through official, textual

representations or through newspapers and broadsides with their rather crude
woodcut illustrations (Gates 46–48). Leaving aside domestic deathbed scenes,
where corpses were viewed in a decidedly unsensational context and the
observers' thoughts revolved around their personal relationship with the deceased, the only staged opportunity to see real corpses would have been
offered by executions. The public humiliation of the executed criminal
through the exhibition of his corpse to the crowd was integral to the punishment and purported to deter potential criminals among the spectators. Although executions continued to be public until 1868, their number decreased
significantly after the 1832 Reform Bill (Gatrell 9–10). They were mainly
attended by the lower classes, who were also the primary audience for textual
and pictorial representations. However, some members of the middle class
(including Dickens and Thackeray) also attended them, and many were eager
consumers of representations of executed criminals in various media, especially narrative. In a letter of 28 July 1845 to Macvey Napier which argues
for the abolition of the death penalty, Dickens comments on the unsettling
fascination with death which he observes within British society:

> I observe the strange fascination which everything connected with [capital]
> Punishment or the object of it, possesses for tens of thousands of decent, virtu-
> ous, well-conducted people, who are quite unable to resist the published por-
> traits, letters, anecdotes, smilings, snuff-takings, &c &c &c of the bloodiest and
> most unnatural scoundrel with the Gallows before him. I observe that this
> strange interest does not prevail to anything like the same degree, where Death
> is not the penalty.   (*Letters* 340)

This bears some resemblance to the Parisians' attraction to the morgue,
though in that case it is not the perpetrators but often the victims of crime
who are on display.

Throughout the century, an industry developed to cater for the interest in
sensational deaths among the British middle class. They had been the appreciative target group of the expensively produced and illustrated *Newgate
Calendars* of the 1820s and of the Newgate novels of the 1830s and 1840s;
and from 1835 onwards, they flocked to see the waxwork effigies of executed
criminals in Madame Tussaud's permanent exhibitions in London (Gatrell
112–17; Pilbeam 100–02,108–09). Although the midcentury middle class had
this access to ''lifelike'' visual representations of criminals' corpses, the
newspapers and increasingly sensation fiction were the prime media in which
they encountered sensational death and its attendant narratives. From the
mid-1850s onwards, daily newspapers like the *Daily Telegraph* and the *Times*
began to devote considerable column space to crime reporting, and in the
1860s, the blurring of distinctions between middle-class and working-class
literature which had started with the Newgate novel was taken further by

the sensation novels which were serialized in the new middle-class family magazines and which transferred the sensational plots of working-class fiction to middle-class settings (Brantlinger 148; Debenham 213). The fear that middle-class readers who consumed this "literature of the Kitchen" in their drawing-rooms would be contaminated by the craving of the lower orders for strong excitement without much consideration of moral values shines through the metaphors of corruption, disease, and addiction in reviews of works in this new genre (Mansel 482–83, 512; Rae 204). Middle-class readers found themselves in a dilemma in this period: they were attracted to sensation novels and other sensational phenomena, but if they indulged in the same taste as the lower orders, they put at stake part of their identity, namely their view of themselves as upholders of high culture (Pykett 9; Debenham 213).

Writers who wanted to exploit potential interest in the extreme sensationalism of the Paris morgue among the British middle class therefore had to present their subject in a way that allowed their readers to enjoy the thrill of the sensational without feeling the guilt of engaging in reprehensible, lower-class voyeurism. The solution to this challenge was to surround a brief passage on the viewing of the corpse by a larger framework and to present the account of the morgue as driven by moral and sociological considerations. Frances Trollope adopts this strategy in her *Paris and the Parisians in 1835* (251–60). After an anecdote about the recognition of a murdered woman in the morgue—a favorite plot device in texts about the morgue—she gives a short personal account of her visit, which does not mention the reaction of other visitors at all. This mild sensationalism is followed by information about the causes of death among the exhibited corpses, especially that of suicide, which she attributes to a depravity in the Parisians that has no equivalent in London.

Similarly, Dudley Costello in an article for *Household Words* includes a pathetic, restrained scene of a mother recognizing the corpse of her son who has committed suicide out of disappointed love (112–16). This brief scene is framed by a factual account of the morgue's history, a tour of the building, and an interview with the clerk who explicates his statistics, dilating on the causes of suicide. Costello's article was published in 1853, after Dickens's two very short references to the morgue in "A Monument to French Folly" (1851) and "Lying Awake" (1852). Dickens's longer pieces of 1856, 1860, and 1863 on the morgue, with their greater emphasis on its spectacular aspect, and the article in *Once a Week* of 1864, which recounts the stories of three spectacular corpses, reflect the growing acceptance of more overtly sensational subjects in magazines over this period.

Unlike Trollope and Costello with their (purported) interest in elucidating the causes and circumstances of a social phenomenon, and unlike the Parisians, who had the tenuous justification that their visits to the morgue might lead to the identification of a corpse and that they were thereby fulfilling a civic duty, ordinary foreign tourists had no morally sound pretext for going there. They went out of a voyeuristic desire to see the corpses and to observe the effect of the sensational on the French. Fortunately, English guidebooks to Paris made it easy for the tourist to justify his visit to the morgue, since it was presented as an integral part of a tour of other social institutions and workplaces which combined to give the visitor an understanding of the mechanisms of French society.[9] In *Galignani's New Paris Guide for 1851*, for instance, the morgue featured along with the sewers, the catacombs, and the abattoir as a way of experiencing real Parisian life (and death) (84, 325). Listings in guidebooks were usually brief, explaining the function of the morgue and devoid of sensational descriptions of corpses. Yet as Paul Vita points out, guides which did pass judgments on the morgue sent out mixed messages to their readers: they condemned both the morbid enjoyment and the indifference to the horrible sights of the morgue among the Parisian lower orders, but by listing the morgue, they were, of course, promoting it (248–49).

The curiosity of British tourists clearly outweighed any disgust or moral reservations. The morgue boasted such illustrious visitors as Thomas Carlyle, who "never felt more shocked in [his] life" (Carlyle 282), John Ruskin (*Works* 19: 115; 34: 278–80), Walter Pater (190), George Gissing (Korg 98), Oscar Wilde (201), Edith Cooper (the younger "half" of "Michael Field," Veyriras 56–58), George Moore ("Ode to a Dead Body" and "The Corpse"), and Arthur Symons (36), who both wrote poems on corpses in the morgue, and Dante Gabriel Rossetti, who in a private verse letter draws a graphic picture of a drowned man and imagines his murderer among the viewers, "watching, as/An artist, the effect of his last work" (Doughty and Wahl 76). Thomas Hardy even dragged his wife there on their honeymoon. She found the morgue "*not offensive* but repulsive" (Gittings 199).

Although written by an American, Mark Twain's paragraph on the morgue in *The Innocents Abroad* (1869) is quite representative. He introduces the subject with a sentence that echoes the guidebooks' denunciation of the morgue as repellent: "Next we went to visit the Morgue, that horrible receptacle for the dead who die mysteriously and leave the manner of their taking off a dismal secret." After a description of the hanging clothes and a corpse, and of his own response of revulsion to it, he turns his attention to the other visitors:

> Men and women came, and some looked eagerly in, and pressed their faces against the bars; others glanced carelessly at the body, and turned away with a disappointed look—people, I thought, who lived upon strong excitements, and who attend the exhibitions of the Morgue regularly, just as other people go to see theatrical spectacles every night. When one of these looked in and passed on, I could not help thinking—
> Now this dont afford you any satisfaction—a party with his head shot off is what *you* need.   (132–33)

Twain points out the macabre resemblance to the theater and denigrates the sensationalism and callousness of the Parisian crowd. Like other Anglo-American writers, he suggests that the French visitors to the morgue do not consider their attitude towards the exhibited corpses as problematic. Two possible explanations for this representation of the French suggest themselves. Firstly, Twain may be implicitly subscribing to a theory still widespread in the nineteenth century—and endorsed, for instance, by Ruskin (*Stones* 174–75) which posits a causal relationship between climate and national temperament. According to this theory, the French could be stereotyped as passionate Mediterranean people who needed strong sensual stimuli and were less well equipped with the rational and moral faculties that predominated among North European cultures. The French could thus be seen as insensitive to the monstrosity of their behavior and unable to reflect critically on it. Secondly, the alleged French insensitivity to unnatural death and the unreflecting acceptance of it as a conspicuous aspect of public life could be interpreted as a result of the French Revolution, which had accustomed the people to sights of brutality, especially to the public exhibition of guillotined corpses. Twain, like other foreign observers, implies that his attitude towards the corpses is morally superior to theirs. Ironically, though, he is guilty of the same lack of self-consciousness which he criticizes in the French, as he does not reflect on his own motivation for going to the morgue.

Nor is there any overt probing in Dickens's and Browning's texts into the tourist's reasons for being attracted to the morgue. Both authors, who distance themselves from their characters, expose instead to the attentive reader the tourist's efforts to suppress his fascination with the sensational. Their texts draw attention to the paradoxes inherent in the relatively new phenomenon of middle-class tourism abroad. The tourist's first-hand experience of the foreign culture should eliminate prejudices, but in fact prejudices—in this case the image of the French as indulging unreflectively in strong sensual stimuli and as morally inferior to the British—are often confirmed because he is on the lookout for evidence that confirms them. The analysis will show that the experiences of these two characters are interpreted in the light of post-revolutionary, post-Napoleonic national prejudice. Dickens's texts reveal the tensions between, on the one hand, the tourist's inclination to see the popular spectacle of the morgue as inferior to British middle-class culture and, on the other hand, the similarities with the less visual British sensational culture, while Browning offers a psychological insight into a middle-class Briton trying to disavow his attraction to the sensational.

The reading of these texts as explorations of the spread of sensationalism from the lower classes to the middle class, and of the vital role played in this by sensational journalism and fiction, is suggested by the prominence of the hypothetical narratives which Browning's and Dickens's tourists attribute to the corpses they see. It is not surprising that faced with unknown corpses which bear perhaps an indication of the immediate cause of death but reveal none of the motivations or events leading up to it, the observer should feel an impetus to construct stories explaining their unnatural deaths. In both Dickens's and Browning's texts, these embedded narratives are clearly informed by sensational narratives. While these narratives exploit the fascination that arises from them, they also invite critical scrutiny of the protagonist's attraction to the sensational.

"Some Recollections of Mortality" offers a catalogue of possible causes of death for the latest inmate of the morgue which is contained in a passage that also displays how torn the middle-class Briton is between enjoyment and rejection of the sensational. As the Uncommercial Traveller strolls around Notre-Dame, he notices a procession of people in their characteristic working-class blouses bringing a body to the morgue. He joins them as they wait impatiently outside the building while the body is being prepared for display. His decision "to constitute [him]self a Blouse likewise" (Dickens, *Journalism* 4: 220) at first seems a mere device to get a better insight into the crowd's experience, but in the course of the passage he becomes genuinely absorbed in the communal "we," and the first-person singular, which is so distinctive in most essays in this series, disappears completely:

> We had been excited in the highest degree by seeing the Custodians pull off their coats and tuck up their shirt-sleeves as the procession came along. It looked so interestingly like business. Shut out in the muddy street, we now became quite ravenous to know all about it. Was it river, pistol, knife, love, gambling, robbery, hatred, how many stabs, how many bullets, fresh or decomposed, suicide or murder? All wedged together, and all staring at one another with our heads thrust forward, we propounded these inquiries and a hundred more such. Imperceptibly, it came to be known that Monsieur the tall and sallow mason yonder, was acquainted with the facts. Would Monsieur the tall and sallow mason, surged at by a new wave of us, have the goodness to impart? It was but a poor old man, passing along the street under one of the new buildings, on whom a stone had fallen, and who had tumbled dead. His age? Another wave surged up against the tall and sallow mason, and our wave swept on and broke, and he was any age from sixty-five to ninety.
>
> An old man was not much: moreover, we could have wished he had been killed by human agency—his own, or somebody elses: the latter, preferable—but our comfort was, that he had nothing about him to lead to his identification, and that his people must seek him here. Perhaps they were waiting dinner for him even now? We liked that.   (*Journalism* 4: 221)

The breathless list of potential causes of death rehearsed here suggests that the crowd's expectations may be shaped by the crimes reported in sensational journalism. They are not just interested in the immediate cause of death ("river, pistol, knife"), but also want to know the plot and motivations that have led to this death ("love, gambling, robbery, hatred"). The crowd is here hoping for the kind of narrative of which Dickens's readers would have found the most exciting instances in sensation novels, inspired as they sometimes were by newspaper reports on such crimes.[10] As in the sensation novel, in which mystery is so crucial, and in the detective story, the genre whose birth is closely linked to sensation fiction, the crowd's excitement is heightened by the lack of information regarding the corpse. Later during the long wait their craving for a narrative of the old man's death goes so far that they eagerly listen to even unreliable "witnesses": "Rivals of the tall and sallow mason sprang up into being, and here again was public inconstancy. These rivals attracted audiences, and were greedily listened to; and whereas they had derived their information solely from the tall and sallow one, officious members of the crowd now sought to enlighten *him* on their authority" (*Journalism* 4: 223).

There is an implied hierarchy of more or less spectacular corpses, with homicide at the top and accidental death at the bottom of the scale, especially if the victim is already quite old—as Twain so pointedly remarks, a party with his head shot off is what *you* need. When the cause of the old mans death turns out to be insufficiently spectacular, the crowd spins a new exciting plot about his unsuspecting family, which bears further witness to their need for sensational fare. The diction in this second paragraph of the above quotation highlights the gulf between the insensitive crowd, apparent in the incongruous "our comfort was," and the relatives of the old man who are those in need of comfort but are referred to with the distancing "his people." The paragraph culminates in the blunt admission that the crowd derives perverse enjoyment from the anticipation of the sentimental scene which will be acted out by the family when they discover their relative in the morgue: "We liked that." Through such irony, the Uncommercial Traveller tries to signal his aloofness from the brutalized crowd which he cannot at this point assert by becoming a detached first-person singular narrator.

The crowd's desire to see the corpse is portrayed in terms of the natural force of a surging ocean wave, and, more significantly, aggressive consumption ("ravenous to know all"). The Uncommercial Traveller singles out from the crowd a "homicidal worker in white lead" biting his collar "with an appetite" and "a pretty young mother, [who] pretending to bite the forefinger of her baby-boy, kept it between her rosy lips that it might be handy for guiding to point at the show," and just before the doors of the morgue are opened, the crowd appears "as if they were of the cannibal species and hungry" (*Journalism* 4: 221, 223). The same metaphor of ravenous consumption is commonly found in contemporary reviews of sensation fiction. In a review of Wilkie Collins's *The Moonstone*, for instance, Geraldine Jewsbury compares the act of reading this serialized novel in the "tantalizing portions" of weekly installments to the torment of hunger: "When persons are in a state of ravenous hunger they are eager only for food, and utterly ignore all delicate distinctions of cookery; it is only when this savage state has been somewhat allayed that they are capable of discerning and appreciating the genius of the *chef*" (106). Similarly, Henry L. Mansel in his famous attack on "Sensation Novels" writes: "There is something unspeakably disgusting in this ravenous appetite for carrion, this vulture-like instinct which smells out the newest mass of social corruption, and hurries to devour the loathsome dainty before the scent has evaporated" (502).[11] Dickens draws no explicit comparison with sensation fiction here, but through the use of this pervasive metaphor and the inclusion of his tourist figure in the crowd, he seems to hold a mirror up to the British middle-class reader, whose taste for sensational narrative can be seen as a milder form of the French hunger for spectacular corpses.

After much ungracious shuffling, the crowd is finally let into the building. As soon as he has seen the corpse, the Uncommercial Traveller can distance himself again from the crowd and analyze them critically, using the food metaphor for the last time: "The uncommercial interest, sated at a glance, directed itself upon the striving crowd on either side and behind: wondering whether one might have guessed, from the expression of those faces merely, what kind of sight they were looking at" (*Journalism* 4: 223). His seamless transition from identification with the crowd to objective distance evokes again the internal conflict of a member of the middle class torn between the desire for the sensational *frisson* and the belief that this is contemptible and worthy only of the lower orders. Dickens's text draws attention to this dilemma at the moment when the sensation novel resolves it by creating sensational plots in middle-class contexts and when the increasing number of middle-class periodicals make these novels and sensational journalism more acceptable to their audience. Among these, Dickens's own *All The Year Round*, in which this article first appeared, played a prominent role, not only because it serialized the first sensation novel, Collins's *The Woman in White* (1859–60), but also because for a middle-class magazine an unusually high proportion of its content was devoted to sensational topics (Wynne 39). This focus on sensational content may have reflected the magazine's aspiration to attract a mass audience. While Dickens the editor thus tried to bridge the distance between middle—and lower-class readers, his character in "Some Recollections of Mortality" expresses discomfort at this blurring of boundaries through the shared attraction to the sensational. The distinction between the middle and lower classes has been effaced by the participation of the middle-class tourist in the supposedly lower-class activity of gazing at the corpse. In the subsequent section the Uncommercial Traveller therefore seeks to reestablish this difference by stressing his distance from the working-class crowd.

He arrives at a predictable judgment of them: they show "little pity" and are "selfish" (*Journalism* 4: 223). "There was a wolfish stare at the object, in which the homicidal worker in white-lead shone conspicuously" (*ibid.*). This sentence echoes a passage in "Railway Dreaming," which states more explicitly the opinion voiced by the critics of the morgue that its sights have a demoralizing effect and reduce the inhibition to commit crimes.[12] Dickens here finds himself standing next to "an evil-looking fellow of two or three and twenty," to whom he attributes the following thoughts: " 'Now, if I were to give that pretty young fellow, my rival, a stroke with a hatchet on the back of the head, or were to tumble him over into the river by night, he would look pretty much like that, I am thinking!' He could not have said it more plainly;—I have always had an idea that he went away and did it (*Journalism* 3: 375). There is no indication of the mans class here, and we are not told what makes him evil-looking, whereas in "Some Recollections of Mortality," the homicidal character is clearly working-class and we are made to observe how the Uncommercial Traveller comes to suspect him. At his first appearance he is identified by a "gloomy malformation of brow" (*Journalism* 4: 221), and the Uncommercial Traveller then goes on to project the man's physical deformity onto his moral character. He thus indulges in the stereotyping of the French working-class male as brutal and perhaps criminal that had been fostered by press reports about the revolutionary violence in 1830 and 1848, as well as by the historically more distant revolution of 1789, whose excesses were kept alive in the public consciousness by Carlyle's *French Revolution* and Madame Tussaud's "Chamber of Horrors" among others. Victorian readers would also have found memorable examples of this type in contemporary French fiction, such as Eugène Sue's highly popular *Les Mystères de Paris* (1842–43), which was also a bestseller in Britain. Although both of our illustrations of the morgue show middle-class visitors and a number of contemporary texts stress that the building was visited by the bourgeoisie ("The Morgue" 715, 717; Zola 132), the visitors in Dickens's episode seem to be exclusively working-class. This may be a coincidence or selective amnesia on the part of the middle-class tourist in order to distance himself from the crowd's sensationalism.

The confrontation of the Uncommercial Traveller with the potentially more sensitive members of society, women and children, in "Travelling Abroad" suggests that the distance between him and the crowd is not just one of class but also one of national culture:

> It was very hot weather, and he [the corpse] was none the better for that, and I was much the worse. Indeed, a very neat and pleasant little woman, with the key of her lodging on her forefinger, who had been showing him to her little girl while she and the child ate sweetmeats, observed monsieur looking poorly

as we came out together, and asked monsieur, with her wondering little eye-
brows prettily raised, if there were anything the matter? Faintly replying in the
negative, monsieur crossed the road to a wineshop, got some brandy, and resolved to freshen himself with a dip in the great floating bath on the river.
                                                        (*Journalism* 4: 88–90)

There is an incongruity between, on the one hand, the callousness displayed
by this member of the softer sex as she enjoys her sweets in front of the
corpses and, on the other hand, her prettiness and concern for the pale tourist.
Although the self-portrayal of the Uncommercial Traveller as the faint "monsieur" shows some self-directed irony, the message is nevertheless that, being
British, he has a natural sensitivity that French women, and even children,
lack.[13]

   This sensitivity is further demonstrated in the following paragraphs which
recount how, while in the river bath, he is "seized with the unreasonable
idea that the large dark body was floating straight at [him]" (*Journalism* 4:
90). After swallowing some water which he imagines has been contaminated
by the corpse, he has a fit of nausea. It is only when he is lying on the sofa
back in his hotel that he can begin "to reason with [him]self" (*Journalism*
4: 90). Over the next few days, he is haunted by the dead man, seeing his
face everywhere: in theaters, shops, and even in his food. He also imagines
that he can smell the corpse in his hotel room. This irrational aftermath of
the visit to the morgue corresponds to what Mansel calls the "preaching to
the nerves instead of the judgment" of the sensation novel and the resulting
stimulation of the senses on which critics of sensation novels comment
(Mansel 482, 487; Wynne 6–7). A key factor which causes the characteristic
frisson in readers of sensation novels is the proximity of the sensational
(Mansel 488–89; Debenham 211). Here again, Dickens's text, which evokes
not metaphorical proximity in the sense of familiarity and contemporaneity
but literal, physical proximity, pushes the bounds of what the critics of sensation fiction find most objectionable. Still under the impact of viewing the
corpse, the imagination of the Uncommercial Traveller adds to this by fantasizing about other kinds of physical proximity (taste and smell) that he has
not actually experienced.

   Despite this traumatic experience, he does not discontinue his visits to the
morgue. His attraction to it is as irrational as his fantasies about the dead
man. The passage in "Travelling Abroad" opens with the insistence that he
goes to the morgue against his conscious will, even on the most unlikely days:

   Whenever I am in Paris, I am dragged by invisible force into the morgue. I
   never want to go there, but am always pulled there. One Christmas Day, when
   I would rather have been anywhere else, I was attracted in to see an old grey
   man . . . One New Year's Morning . . . I was pulled in again to look at a flaxen-
   haired boy of eighteen . . . This time, I was forced into the same dread place,
   to see a large dark man.   (*Journalism* 4: 88)

This confirms that the Uncommercial Traveller is not just visiting the morgue as a detached observer of the Parisians who identifies with them only temporarily and for dramatic effect; he is actually as addicted to its sensational exhibits and driven by the same voyeuristic desire as the people from whom he wants to distance himself.

The same unwilled attraction to the morgue lies at the heart of "Apparent Failure," but Browning's speaker is much better at disguising his interest in it. He humorously describes his effort to hide the expected effect of the corpses on his psyche before he enters the morgue in lines which show that he, too, defines the British national character in opposition to the French. Yet while the Uncommercial Traveller sees the opposition as one of British sensitivity versus French brutality, Browning's tourist contrasts British courage with French cowardice:

> I plucked up heart and entered,—stalked,
> Keeping a tolerable face
> Compared with some whose cheeks were chalked:
> Let them! No Britons to be baulked! (15–18)

In his conversation with a Frenchman that is represented in this dramatic monologue, he engages in a similar endeavor to keep up appearances and give the impression of not having been gripped by the sensational while he was inside the morgue.

While the Uncommercial Traveller is involuntarily drawn to the building, this tourist seems to happen upon it by chance—or so he wants his interlocutor to believe—after having attended the baptism of the French crown prince and son of Napoleon III, which allows us to date his visit as 14 June 1856:

> I passed through Paris, stopped a day
> To see the baptism of your Prince;
> Saw, made my bow, and went my way:
> Walking the heat and headache off,
> I took the Seine-side . .
> So sauntered till—what met my eye? (2–6, 9)

Having ticked off one big public spectacle, and plagued by a headache and the heat, he searches for fresh excitement to distract him. The only reason why he enters the morgue can be to get an entertaining *frisson*, yet most of the monologue tries to disavow this and to minimize the sensational aspect of the experience.

The fascination with the sensationalism of the morgue which Browning's tourist experiences is, as in "Some Recollections of Mortality," most visible when he invents the life stories of the corpses. On this day, three drowned men are on display who, the speaker assumes, have all committed suicide:

How did it happen, my poor boy?
You wanted to be Buonaparte
And have the Tuileries for toy,
And could not, so it broke your heart?
You, old one by his side, I judge,
Were, red as blood, a socialist,
A leveller! Does the empire grudge
You've gained what no Republic missed?
Be quiet, and unclench your fist!

And this—why, he was red in vain,
Or black,—poor fellow that is blue!
What fancy was it turned your brain?
Oh, women were the prize for you!
Money gets women, cards and dice
Get money, and ill-luck gets just
The copper couch and one clear nice
Cool squirt of water o'er your bust
The right thing to extinguish lust! (37–54)

The condescending, moralizing tone betrays the speaker's feeling of superiority over these characters who have left life not by dying a respectable death surrounded by their families but in a disgraceful manner, which entails the loss of their identity and gives the speaker the power to create fictional identities for them.

The morgue's registers for the 1860s show that at this time roughly half of all corpses were found in the Seine and that men outnumbered women by about 6:1. The statistics for 1867, for instance, are: 89 newborn babies, 58 fetuses, 21 body parts, 513 men, 65 women. Of these 578 adults, 312 were fished out of the Seine and 163 were recorded as suicides. Drowning was far more frequent than other methods of suicide like hanging (30), shots in the head (6), suffocation (7) and poisoning (7). Moreover, there seems to have been a considerable number of "unofficial" suicides which were passed off as accidents, so that the dead could have a Christian funeral (Du Camp 431–33; Gozlan 327). The situation in "Apparent Failure," where three out of three corpses are those of males whose deaths are attributed to suicide by drowning, is therefore credible. However, the coincidence of three characters with the biographies that the speaker ascribes to them clearly is not. The would-be Napoleon, the socialist revolutionary, and the gambling womanizer are spectacular French stereotypes. The speaker's choice of these types suggests that he wants to see suicide as the result of a disorderly and specifically French life. Like other Victorians, he implicitly rejects the predominantly French stereotyping of suicide as the "English malady" (Gates 23–26). Judging from the morgue's statistics, the most frequent causes of suicide—insanity, domestic trouble, drunkenness, misery, or disappointed love—had nothing

specifically French about them, and the occupations that furnished most suicide victims—needlewomen, day laborers, and soldiers—also seem quite far
removed from Browning's flamboyant types (Maillard 75; Costello 115; "The
Morgue" 717).[14] By not including more "ordinary" and representative causes
of suicide that could be found in any urban context, the speaker seems implicitly to distance suicide from British urban culture. Such a move would not
be surprising, as the insistence that London does not suffer from the same
high rate of suicides as Paris is a recurring feature in British texts about the
morgue ("The Morgue" 717). Although it seems that suicide (especially by
drowning) was more widespread in Paris, the problem was also well known
in London. Suicide by jumping into the river was not uncommon, attracted
the attention of the press—as in Dickenss Down With the Tide of 1853
(*Journalism* 3: 113–26)—and inspired novelists, painters and poets, most
famously Thomas Hood in "The Bridge of Sighs" (1844).[15]

The three character stereotypes are not only what the middle-class Briton
would consider to embody French culture at its worst; they also hint at the
common fear of the impact of French autocratic rule, revolution, or debauch-
ery on British culture. The spectacular life stories seem to be inspired less
by real people than by literary types in nineteenth-century French novels,
which played a key role in shaping the image of France among British readers
and the middle-class prejudices about French depravity. The gambling womanizer probably alludes to aristocrats of the *ancien régime*; the would-be
Napoleon clearly recalls the ambitious young heroes of the post-Napoleonic
generation who have no opportunity for military heroism, like Julien Sorel
in Stendhal's *Le Rouge et le noir* (1830) or Balzac's Rastignac in the *Comédie
humaine* (1834–50); and the socialist evokes the depiction of revolutionary
uprisings in works like Hugo's recent *Les Misérables* (1862). Unlike the
Uncommercial Traveller, who attributes to his corpse the generic crime plots
to be found in newspapers, Browning's speaker appears to be driven by an
appetite for the kind of spectacular plots that are narrated by the French realist
novels that helped to prepare the British readership for the sensation novel.

Despite the predominance of a distanced, moralizing tone, these two stanzas
also betray that the speaker takes pleasure in this opportunity to invent sensational plots. In the first stanza, this is only expressed through the neat rhymes
which summarize the first two men ("boy—toy," "socialist—fist"), but the
next stanza abounds with playful devices through which the speaker displays
his ingenuity and wit. He repeats the verb "get[s]" three times in increasingly
complex and surprising parallel phrases, and in the second half of the stanza,
he builds up tension through enjambments which are combined with a striking
accumulation of stressed syllables ("cléar níce/Cóol squírt"). He also shows
sardonic humor in the puns, first, on the red and black of the roulette table
that lead to a blue corpse, and then, on the desire for money which is rewarded

with a place on a couch made from copper, the metal used for the cheapest coins.

However, these brief flashes that hint at a certain enjoyment of the situation are framed by much more subdued passages that eclipse the sensational aspect of the morgue. In contrast to Dickens's articles and most other texts on the morgue, there is no reference to the voyeurism of the other visitors, who are only mentioned in one line: "First came the silent gazers; next,/A screen of glass, we're thankful for" (19–20). The reference to the glass screen shows the speaker's eagerness to mark a sanitizing boundary between himself and the corpses rather than his enjoyment of the proximity to the dead, which adds to the effect of the sensational. While in "Some Recollections of Mortality" the first-person plural is used when the crowd is struggling to get closer to the corpse, the morgue's visitors are here united in their desire to distance themselves from the dead. In the description of the corpses that follows, he chooses strangely incongruous religious imagery that evokes church effigies rather than the spectacle imagery which pervades other accounts of the morgue:

> Last, the sight's self, the sermon's text,
> The three men who did most abhor
> Their life in Paris yesterday,
> So killed themselves: and now, enthroned
> Each on his copper couch, they lay
> Fronting me, waiting to be owned.
> I thought, and think, their sin's atoned.
>
> Poor men, God made, and all for that!
> The reverence struck me; o'er each head
> Religiously was hung its hat,
> Each coat dripped by the owner's bed,
> Sacred from touch: (21–32)

The religious terms not only express the speaker's compassion for the three supposed suicide victims; they also constitute a provocative attack on the Church doctrine that suicide is punished with eternal damnation, a stance the tourist here defies by likening these sinners to saints and bishops who are honored by sumptuous tombs. This parallel is ambiguous, though. On the one hand, the reader familiar with Browning's "The Bishop Orders His Tomb at St. Praxed's Church" (1845) will know that the (anticipated) elaborate tomb of this bishop is not evidence of an exemplary life and faith. Through the intertexual allusion to his sinful and unrepentant bishop, the author may thus be undermining the speaker's assertion that the suicide victims have attained salvation; on the other hand, the suggestion of a belief in divine forgiveness would be in line with Browning's optimistic creed. However, the moral lesson the speaker claims to have gained at the end of the poem is simply too trite and unselfconscious to be Browning's serious authorial statement:

> It's wiser being good than bad;
> It's safer being meek than fierce:
> It's fitter being sane than mad. (55–57)

The trivial moral and the criticism of Church doctrine are indications that the speaker is trying hard to pass off his visit to the morgue as a moment of moral and religious insight, distracting from the desire for excitement that took him there and the fascination with sensational narratives which is evident when he invents the life stories of the three corpses. The abrupt transition from sympathy with the three men and "reverence" (lines 21–36) to distanced condescension and attempted wit (lines 37–54) and then to moral common-places (lines 55–63) exposes the speaker's difficulty in coming up with a coherent response to the sights of the morgue and in playing his role as the composed, philosophizing Briton whose nerves are, in contrast to those of the French with their "chalked" cheeks, not excited by the sensational corpse.[16] The meaning of the poem is already signaled through the ambiguity of its title, "Apparent Failure." On the one hand, the speaker comes to the conclusion that the three men's failure in life is not actual but only apparent, as they have been saved. On the other hand, it also becomes apparent—that is, obvious—to the reader that the speaker fails in his attempt to contrive an adequate reaction to these sensational corpses.[17]

To conclude, while Brownings speaker is more successful than Dickenss Uncommercial Traveller at dissimulating his attraction to the sensational spectacle of the morgue, the texts by both authors portray essentially the same problem: the visit to the morgue allows the British tourist to indulge in his taste for the sensational narratives that he is used to consuming in the form of journalism and fiction. But the direct, visual confrontation with real corpses, to which he, unlike the Parisians, is not accustomed, the physical proximity to the real object of sensation, leads to a shocking realization of the morbidity that lies at the heart of the taste for the sensational. Conveniently, the middle-class Briton can distance himself from sensationalism by projecting it onto the foreign, working-class crowd and claiming the moral high ground. Through their focus on the psychology of their protagonists, Dickens's and Browning's texts display the moral dilemma which the sensational poses for the Victorian middle class, while at the same time exploiting the reader's fascination with spectacular death.

NOTES

1. Numbers of visitors are usually newspaper estimates. When a woman who had been cut into two was exhibited, Schwartz cites an official source—arguably less plausible—that estimates a number of 5,000 to 6,000 visitors per hour (72–73).
2. For a discussion of novels featuring the morgue, see Vita (246, 253–54). For a brief example of a fictional sensational story about the morgue, see Pilgrimages in Paris.''
3. In Wilkie Collins's *The Woman in White*, the corpse of the villain Count Fosco is also discovered in the morgue (580–82). For Dickens's references to visits to the morgue, see, e.g., Forster (444, 449). The morgue features in the following articles: "A Monument to French Folly," *Household Words* (8 March 1851); "Lying Awake," *Household Words* (30 October 1852); "Railway Dreaming," *Household Words* (10 May 1856); "Travelling Abroad," *All the Year Round* (7 April 1860); "Some Recollections of Mortality," *All the Year Round* (16 May 1863).
4. The new morgue was certainly efficient: some two-thirds of all corpses were identified by viewers (Maillard 86).
5. All translations are my own. Cf. Zola (132); also "La Vitrine" in the collection of songs by Clovis Pierre, a former clerk of the morgue (33–37).
6. See also Zola (132). For other examples of these comparisons, see Schwartz (59–62).
7. See also the "mountebank with a feather on his nose, within a yard of the gate" of the morgue in "Travelling Abroad" (*Journalism* 4: 88).
8. See also Trollope (259).
9. For a sociological case study of guidebooks to Paris at the turn of the century, see MacCannell (53–76).
10. The sensation novelist Charles Reade defended himself against an attack in the *Times* by stating that this very newspaper had been the main source for his plots (322–24).
11. See also Mansel (485, 501). For further examples of the food metaphor in criticism on the sensation novel, see Wynne (4–5).
12. Cf. Guillot (196–203). The primary aim of Guillot's book is the abolition of public displays of corpses.
13. Vita argues that this passage expresses Dickens's view that the Parisians' lack of sympathy is a result of their constant exposure to deaths in the morgue (249–50). However, the eating child and "two little girls (one showing [the corpses] to a doll)" (*Journalism* 4: 222) suggests rather that the text presents their indifference not as acquired but as innate.
14. The cited sources draw on research and statistics by the first medical inspector of the morgue, Alphonse Devergie.
15. On real and literary cases of death in the Thames, see Gates (135–42). Although Morselli cites statistics for suicides in England (15–35), a reliable comparison of the numbers and causes of suicide in the two capitals in the nineteenth century is not possible. Whereas the French kept very detailed registers of the circumstances

surrounding each case of death, the British authorities did not routinely record such information.

16. Cf. Lucas, who takes the poem for Browning's own utterance but reads it as an honest expression of his insecurity and inability to cope with the shocking confrontation with death, an experience from which he tries to retreat into ''cleverness'' (20).

17. In Vita's view, the apparent failure in the sense of ''obvious failure'' is that of the morgue ''not as a functioning institution, but as a symbol for social ills, individual despair, grief and misery'' (253). This interpretation assumes that the key purpose of the poem is Browning's critique of the morgue. However, the paramount purpose of his dramatic monologues is always to expose how the speaker (mis)conceives the world around him. The title of this poem would hence be the author's comment on the speaker and not on the subject of the speaker's monologue.

WORKS CITED

Brantlinger, Patrick. *The Reading Lesson: The Threat of Mass Literacy in Nineteenth-Century British Fiction*. Bloomington: Indiana UP, 1998.

Browning, Robert. *Robert Browning: The Poems*. Ed. John Pettigrew and Thomas J. Collins. Vol. 1. Harmondsworth: Penguin, 1996.

Carey, John. *The Violent Effigy: A Study of Dickens' Imagination*. London: Faber & Faber, 1973.

Carlyle, Thomas. *Early Letters of Thomas Carlyle*. Ed. Charles Eliot Norton. Vol. 2. London: Macmillan, 1886.

Collins, Wilkie. *The Woman in White*. 1859–60. Oxford: Oxford UP, 1973.

Costello, Dudley. ''Dead Reckoning at the Morgue.'' *Household Words* (1 October 1853): 112–16.

Debenham, Helen. ''The Victorian Sensation Novel.'' *A Companion to the Victorian Novel*. Ed. William Baker and Kenneth Womack. Westport: Greenwood, 2002. 209–21.

Devergie, Alphonse. *Notions générales sur la morgue de Paris, sa description, son service, son système hygiénique; de l'autopsie judiciaire comparée à l'autopsie pathologique*. Paris: Félix Malteste, 1877.

―――. *Statistique décennale de la morgue (1836–1846)*. Paris: J.-B. Baillère, 1851.

Dickens, Charles. *The Dent Uniform Edition of Dickens' Journalism*. Ed. Michael Slater and John M. L. Drew. 4 vols. London: Dent, 1994–2000.

———. *The Letters of Charles Dickens*. Ed. Kathleen Tillotson. Vol. 4. Oxford: Clarendon, 1977.

———. *The Old Curiosity Shop*. 1841. London: Oxford UP, 1951.

Drew, John M. L. "Voyages Extraordinaires: Dickens' 'Travelling Essays' and *The Uncommercial Traveller* (Part Two)." *Dickens Quarterly* 13. 3 (1996): 127–50.

Du Camp, Maxime. *Paris. Ses organes, ses fonctions et sa vie dans la seconde moitié du XIXe siècle*. Vol. 1. Paris: Hachette, 1869.

Du Maurier, George. *Trilby*. 1894. Oxford: Oxford UP, 1999.

Elliott, Philip L. "Browning's 'Apparent Failure.' " *Victorian Poetry* 27. 2 (1989): 209–13.

Forster, John. *The Life of Charles Dickens*. Vol. 2. London: Dent, 1966.

Galignani's New Paris Guide for 1851. Paris: Galignani, n.d.

Gates, Barbara. *Victorian Suicide: Mad Crimes and Sad Histories*. Princeton: Princeton UP, 1989.

Gatrell, V. A. C. *The Hanging Tree: Execution and the English People 1770–1868*. Oxford: Oxford UP, 1994.

Gittings, Robert. *Young Thomas Hardy*. London: Heinemann, 1975.

Gozlan, Léon. "La Morgue." *Paris ou le livre des cent-et-un*. Vol. 1. Paris: Ladvocat, 1831. 301–32.

Guillot, Adolphe. *Paris qui souffre. La basse Geôle du Grand Châtelet et les Morgues modernes*. Paris: Chez Rouquette, 1887.

Jewsbury, Geraldine. Review of *The Moonstone*. *Athenaeum* 2126 (25 July 1868): 106.

Korg, Jacob. *George Gissing: A Critical Biography*. London: Methuen, 1965.

Lucas, John. "Apparent Failure." *Browning Society Notes* 5. 1 (1976): 17–23.

MacCannell, Dean. *The Tourist: A New Theory of the Leisure Class*. 2nd ed. New York: Schocken Books, 1989.

Maillard, Firmin. *Recherches historiques et critiques sur la morgue*. Paris: Adolphe Delahays, 1860.

Mansel, Henry L. "Sensation Novels." *Quarterly Review* 113 (April 1863): 481–514.

Moore, George. *Flowers of Passion*. London: Provost & Co., 1878.

"The Morgue." *Once A Week* 11 (17 December 1864): 714–19.

Morselli, Henry. *Suicide: An Essay in Comparative Moral Statistics.* London: Kegan Paul, 1881.

Pater, Walter. "The Child in the House." *Miscellaneous Studies: A Series of Essays.* London: Macmillan, 1910.

"Pilgrimages in Paris: No. I: La Morgue." *Fraser's Magazine* 27 (March 1843): 260–71.

Pierre, Clovis. *Les Gaietés de la Morgue.* Paris: Gallimard, 1895.

Pilbeam, Pamela. *Madame Tussaud and the History of Waxworks.* London: Hambledon & London, 2002.

Pykett, Lyn. *The Sensation Novel from The Woman in White to The Moonstone.* Plymouth: Northcote House, 1994.

Rae, W. Fraser. "Sensation Novelists: Miss Braddon." *North British Review* 43 (September 1865): 180–204.

Reade, Charles. *Readiana: Comments on Current Events.* London: Chatto & Windus, 1883.

Rossetti, Dante Gabriel. *Letters of Dante Gabriel Rossetti.* Eds. Oswald Doughty and John R. Wahl. Vol. 1. Oxford: Clarendon, 1965.

Ruskin, John. *The Stones of Venice.* Ed. J. G. Links. Harmondsworth: Penguin, 2001.

———. *The Works of John Ruskin.* Ed. E. T. Cook and Alexander Wedderburn. Vols. 19 and 34. London: George Allen, 1905 and 1908.

Sanders, Andrew. *Charles Dickens, Resurrectionist.* London: Macmillan, 1982.

———. *Dickens and the Spirit of the Age.* Oxford: Clarendon, 1999.

Schwartz, Vanessa R. *Spectacular Realities: Early Mass Culture in Fin-de-Siècle Paris.* Berkeley: U of California P, 1998.

Stone, Harry. *The Night Side of Dickens: Cannibalism, Passion, Necessity.* Columbus: Ohio State UP, 1994.

Symons, Arthur. *The Collected Works of Arthur Symons.* Vol. 3. London: Martin Secker, 1924.

Trollope, Frances. *Paris and the Parisians in 1835.* Vol. 1. Paris: Galignani, 1836.

Twain, Mark. *The Innocents Abroad or the New Pilgrim's Progress.* New York: Oxford UP, 1996.

Veyriras, Paul. "Visiteurs britanniques à la morgue de Paris au dix-neuvième siècle." *Cahiers victoriens et édouardiens* 15 (1982): 51–61.

Vita, Paul. "Returning the Look: Victorian Writers at the Paris Morgue." *Nineteenth-Century Contexts* 25. 3 (2003): 241–56.

Wilde, Oscar. *More Letters of Oscar Wilde*. Ed. Rupert Hart-Davis. London: John Murray, 1985.

Wynne, Deborah. *The Sensational Novel and the Victorian Family Magazine*. Houndmills: Palgrave, 2001.

Zola, Emile. *Thérèse Raquin*. 1867. Paris: Garnier-Flammarion, 1970.

Mortimer Lightwood

Bert Hornback

Dickens regularly asks us to put things together, to make sense. How things fit together—or don't—is always part of his theme. The first part of this essay analyzes several examples of how Dickens weaves Our Mutual Friend *into a meaningful whole. The novel is full of little societies, each of the first six chapters introducing one of them. The second part of the essay looks at some of the various characters in the novel who put things together or try to do so, ranging from Mr. Inspector, who fails miserably, to the Analytical Chemist who knows what things are made of and Mr. Venus who "articulates" skeletons, from Mr. Inspector who tries "putting things together" but fails miserably, to Mr. Dolls who once makes "a dignified attempt to gather himself together." As readers, we put things together to make sense of them. The best example Dickens gives us of a good reader is Mortimer Lightwood. Were it not for his story of "the Man from Somewhere"—which becomes the story of "our mutual friend," this novel might not exist. Certainly Mortimer would not be an important character in it.*

Our Mutual Friend is a wonderful title. Chesterton complained that it was vulgar; that Dickens should have known to say "Our Common Friend" (21). But Dickens was fond of the locution, and used it commonly enough so that it appears in a number of the novels after *Nicholas Nickleby*, where it first occurs (454; ch. 29; 423; ch. 48).[1] In *Martin Chuzzlewit*, "our mutual friend" is even a momentary character named "Mr. Pip" (522, ch. 28). Anyway, Noddy Boffin—who no doubt speaks what Chesterton thought of as "vulgar"

English—is the one who calls John Harmon Handford Rokesmith "Our Mutual Friend" (157; bk. 1, ch. 9; 226; bk. 1, ch. 15).

The novel isn't only about John Harmon, however, or about old Harmon's will, or about John and Bella falling in love and marrying and having a baby daughter delivered by ship from the sea. The novel is about society: about how we live together. And *Our Mutual Friend* is its triply social title.

The novel is full of separate little societies, some of them more social than others. First we meet Gaffer Hexam and his self-proclaimed "Pardner," Rogue Riderhood (47; bk. 1, ch. 1). Then we meet all the best friends of the Veneerings (48 ff., bk. 1, ch. 2). Then we visit the home Lizzie has made for Charley and their father (63–73, bk. 1, ch. 3). Next we meet the Wilfers (74 ff.; bk. 1, ch. 4), and then visit the estate called Boffin's Bower (98–104; bk. 1, ch. 5). Then we are introduced to the society which Miss Abbey Potterson governs at the Six Jolly Fellowship-Porters (104–10; bk.1, ch. 6). "It has been hard work to establish order here," she says, "and make the Fellowships what it is, and it is daily and nightly hard work to keep it so." We are six chapters into the novel, and we have seen six little societies of sorts. A remarkably multiple tale is unfolding. Of course, Dickens's plot will eventually tie them all together—but we don't read for plot. And a richer, more meaningful kind of tying together will happen by the time we get to the end.

The novel will mean differently, to be sure, depending on how it is tied together and by whom. In this essay I want to explore what seem to me the ways in which Dickens asks us to put *Our Mutual Friend* together. In doing so, I will look at how Dickens presents characters and events in relation to each other, and try to figure out what those relations might signify. And I will look at who *within* the novel best puts things together, and to what end, on the assumption that his understanding could be a guide for ours. Such analysis will help us to see how—and why—a seemingly minor character, Mortimer Lightwood, is in this respect the novel's central character.

There are many things to understand in *Our Mutual Friend*. In the second paragraph the narrator challenges us to guess what Gaffer Hexam does for a living: "He had no net, hook, or line, and he could not be a fisherman; his boat had no cushion for a sitter, no paint, no inscription . . . and he could not be a waterman; his boat was too crazy and too small to take on cargo . . . and he could not be a lighterman or river-carrier."[2] Then comes the mystery of the Man from Somewhere, who seems to have been murdered.

Charley Hexam can understand writing, but Lizzie cannot. Nor can Noddy Boffin, who—thanks to Silas Wegg, his "literary man"—has the whole of the Rooshan empire to comprehend. To comprehend is to hold together—and etymologically, "together" is the *gathering* that is presumed to be *good*. Mr. Inspector, we are told, tries hard to solve the supposed Harmon murder by "putting things together." But he can't do it very well: "according to the success with which you put this and that together, you get a woman and a fish apart, or a Mermaid in combination. And Mr. Inspector could turn out nothing better than a Mermaid, which no Judge and Jury would believe in'' (74; bk. 1, ch. 3)[3]

What we do as readers is put things together. At least, that's what great writers ask us to do. They provide us with numerous ways to put things together, and expect us to make sense of what they have written that way. When Hamlet, dying, asks that his story be told, he isn't asking for the plot-outline of who killed whom, revenge tragedy style, that Horatio promises to tell. It's a far greater and more meaningful story than that. If we have read well—in our books or in the theater—we will understand Hamlet's story, and know its significance.

Simple ''reading'' isn't enough. Silas Wegg is a ''literary man,'' and however much he mangles things, he can read print. But when he reads character, he mangles things even worse. Charley Hexam can read—and count; and his values are accumulative ones, not understanding. Blinded by greed, Sophronia and Alfred misread each other. Carelessly, everybody who is anybody in Society misreads the Veneerings. Eugene can read, of course, and he is capable of reading seriously, but he won't read himself: ''Riddle-me, riddle-me-ree,'' he says, tapping his head and his heart, ''perhaps you can't tell me what this may be?—No, upon my life I can't. I give it up!'' (349; bk. 2, ch. 6).

Eugene comments later on Mortimer's insightful ''reading'' of his character. Then he says:

> ''(By-the-by, that very word, Reading, in its critical use, always charms me. An actress's Reading of a chambermaid, a dancer's Reading of a hornpipe, a singer's Reading of a song, a marine painter's Reading of the sea, the kettle-drum's Reading of an instrumental passage, are phrases ever youthful and delightful.)''
> (605; bk. 3, ch. 10)

A good *reader*—of songs or tea leaves or X-rays, entrails or novels—looks at details and puts them together. And Dickens, reading life, is fond of putting things together—and fond of characters who put things together—particularly in the novels from *David Copperfield* on. But even Mr. Pickwick honored the principle, however inadequate his practice usually was: he already knew, for Dickens, that the end is to comprehend the world you live in. In *Our Mutual Friend* the Analytical Chemist takes things apart, to see what they're made of, and Mr. Venus puts them together: ''articulating'' them (126; bk. 1, ch. 7). Loading the context for Mr. Venus's occupation, Silas Wegg compliments his ''skill in piecing little things together'' as well as his being ''a fellow-man, holily pledged in a friendly move to his brother man'' (357; bk. 2, ch. 7).[4] Old Betty Higden wants ''to be of a piece'' (441; bk. 2, ch. 14), and even Mr. Dolls makes ''a dignified attempt to gather himself together''

(603; bk. 3, ch. 10). Jenny Wren puts together all the fashionable people in London—and she's very, very clever about knowing people's "tricks and manners." The Veneerings put people together, too—after a fashion—without even knowing who they are; they also put together a remarkable semblance of wealth. There are many marriage plots in the novel, and little Georgiana Podsnap thinks that she might kill her "partner," if ever she has one.

Dickens puts characters together—pairs them, throughout the novel. Gaffer and Rogue are "pardners"; Mortimer is "founded on" Eugene. Sophronia Akershem and Alfred Lammle are paired by their names as well as by their descriptions: she is the "mature young lady," he the "mature young gentle-man" (52; bk. 1, ch. 2). Veneering, too, is paired with Lammle by name; they are indeed both dealers, confidence men. For our unbiased edification, Fascination Fledgeby, the Christian, is paired with Mr. Riah, the Jew. When we see Mr. Twemlow in Pubsey & Co., we start to think of others of our acquaintance who are in debt. When little Johnny makes his will, giving away everything he has even before he dies (386; bk. 2, ch. 9), we are reminded that this, like so many of Dickens's novels, is a novel of wills.

Putting things together is what Shelley called metaphor-making. The heart of what we call poetry, he said, is finding "the before unapprehended relations of things" (4)—and that may be true not just of poetry but of all art. Dickens sets up metaphors where we least expect and most need them. And his metaphors tell us truths.

I have explained elsewhere in detail how the metaphor in chapter 6 of book 2 develops.[5] Eugene is sitting in the window of his and Mortimer's new lodgings in the Temple when Charley and Bradley Headstone approach. As they stand in the doorway below, Eugene drops a pellet on Charley's hat. Then he prepares two more pellets to drop on them as they leave. Eugene torments Bradley throughout the scene. At its climax Bradley cries, "You reproach me with my origin . . . you cast insinuations at my bringing-up." Eugene answers that he cannot "cast stones that were never in [his] hand" (346; bk. 2, ch. 6). We know, however, that he has two pellets at hand if not in his hand, "prepared" for use on Bradley and Charley. If we are reading carefully we know now at another level—on the narrator's authority, as it were—that Eugene is false. And when, later in the scene, Eugene denies having any sort of "design" or intention or purpose in anything he does, we know otherwise. The narrator has shown him to us, preparing those pellets. We have the evidence.

Rogue Riderhood complains of "Poll Parrots" regularly. There's nothing really meaningful about the words, until Mr. Venus explains to Wegg how he happened to meet Riderhood's daughter Pleasant: he was "looking for parrots" down by the waterside, among the sailors, "and looking for a nice pair of rattlesnakes" (563; bk. 3, ch. 7). Maybe the *image* registers for us, with the introduction of the rattlesnakes, and maybe it says that Riderhood is a rattlesnake as well as a rogue. Maybe.

A better and more reliable example of Dickens creating metaphors and making them say things to us is Silas Wegg's demonstrative wooden leg. As Wegg reads to Noddy Boffin about misers, his wooden leg "slowly elevate[s] itself" in front of him. At the "crisis" of the story of Daniel Dancer's hiding his money, "Mr. Wegg's wooden leg had gradually elevated itself more and more," and then he fell over "in a kind of pecuniary swoon" (544–45; bk. 3, ch. 6). The image shows us Wegg's wooden-legged orgasm; the narrative representation of that elaborating image tells us that Wegg lusts—literally—for money.

Dickens invites us to pay attention to Bradley Headstone's hands almost as soon as he is introduced. But his gesture, then, is—twice—nothing more than his biting the side of his forefinger at Charley (265; bk. 2, ch. 1). More impressive is the sense we get of Bradley from the description of him in his "decent" everything, with all his "mechanically" acquired bits of knowledge—and his "suppression" of himself (266–67; bk. 2, ch. 1). The next time we see him the narrator concentrates his attention and ours on Bradley's "suppressed" and "restrained" manner, his "smouldering" nature, the "passion" that always threatens to "burst into flames" (396; bk. 2, ch. 11).

As he talks to Lizzie, then, our notice is redirected to his hands: to the "curious tight-screwing movement of his right hand in the clenching palm of his left" (400; bk. 2, ch. 11). This scene prepares us for the scene in St. Peter's churchyard, which begins with her "still holding Charley's hand," and proceeds as she and Charley "walked hand in hand" (451; bk. 2, ch. 15). When Charley tries to leave Lizzie alone with Bradley she resists, "detaining his hand as he withdrew it" (452; bk. 2, ch. 15). "There; let go," Charley says—and she is left with Bradley.

As Bradley speaks, Lizzie watches "the passionate action of his hands," and then the "action of his hands which was like flinging his heart's blood down before her." Five more times in three pages, we are told of Bradley's hands. Then, as he stands beside a low stone wall, facing Lizzie, he "bring[s] his clenched hand down upon the stone with a force that laid the knuckles raw and bleeding," and he stands "holding out his smeared hand." He catches Lizzie's arm with his hand, releases her, then stands, "folding his hands in front of him." And he has recovered: is the suppressed, restrained man again.

After this we see Bradley with Rogue at Plashwater, and then at the railway station. But Dickens's focus has changed again. Now Bradley has fits. Earlier, in an interview with Lizzie, he complains that "there is a spell" upon him. Then, having seen Lizzie walking with Eugene, he has sudden violent nosebleeds—"three times—four times—I don't know how many times" (704;

bk. 4, ch. 1). When Frank Milvey sees Bradley at the station he is having a "fit" (821; bk. 4, ch. 11), and he has another "fit" thinking about the futility of his attack on Eugene. When he first sees Rogue at his school, he feels a "fit" coming on him; as Rogue leaves, "the fit which had been long impending," overwhelms him.

In his last scene, with Rogue, Bradley sits "grasp[ing] his left wrist with his right hand." Throughout the night, not once does he "loosen his hold upon his wrist" (872; bk. 4, ch. 15). The next morning early, when he kills Rogue—throws them both into Plashwater Weir Mill Lock—he maintains that grip. When the bodies are found, Rogue is "girdled still with Bradley's iron ring."

"Evil will out," Dickens's favorite author wrote. And the point, I suspect, of Bradley's presentation to us is that evil—suppressed and restrained—will out in various ways. We see Bradley's evil in his active, dangerous hands, as well as in the fits of passion, rage, and frustration that erupt from within him.

Bella confides to her Pa, early on, that she is avaricious. The language she uses to express this sad confidence is important. "Talk to me of love!" she says; "Talk to me of fiery dragons! But talk to me of poverty and wealth, and there indeed we touch upon realities" (376; bk. 2, ch. 8). Bella subsequently uses those same terms—fulfils and redeems the image by getting the *values* involved untwisted—as she tells John, whom she loves, "your wishes are as real to me as the wishes in the Fairy story, that were fulfilled as soon as spoken" (748; bk. 4, ch. 5).

Charley Hexam complains about Lizzie being "such a dreamer" in her fancies, which was "all very well when we sat before the fire—when we looked into the hollow down by the flare—but we are looking into the real world, now." His sister answers, "Ah, we were looking into the real world then, Charley" (278; bk. 2, ch. 1). Lizzie's understanding is an imaginative and consequently informed understanding, and thus very different from her brother's.

When Eugene first meets Jenny Wren he dismisses her "fancies" of smelling flowers and hearing birds sing (289; bk. 2, ch. 2). But when he seems to be dying, he sends for her. He asks about her "pretty fancy" of flowers and birds, and says, "I should like you to have the fancy here, before I die" (807; bk. 4, ch. 10). Jenny Wren does have the fancy for him. She makes the birds' music real as she sings her low song softly for him.

Bella and Lizzie meet midway through the novel, and become fast friends. Immediately, Bella becomes "serious." Lizzie's adversity and her response to it change Bella: "I feel," she tells John, "as if much had happened—to myself, you know" (593; bk. 2, ch. 9). John is elated, and so is the narrator. As John's and Bella's train prepares to leave for London, the railway signal is described as "shutting up its green eye and opening its red one"—which has caused a great deal of Dickensian consternation.

It has seemed to many people that Dickens got the image wrong: the signal for the train to set out is a green light, not a red one. But if we read well the chapter which brings us to this phenomenon—and the narration describes it as a fantastic occurrence—we should be able to understand the image as Dickens gives it to us. If we understand both Bella's change and John's ecstatic delight in it, we should be able to read the whimsical, fantastic image without worrying about proper railway signalling. The train hurtles on through the night toward London, the stations through which it passes "all knowingly shutting up their green eyes and opening their red ones when they prepared to let the boofer lady pass" (594; bk. 2, ch. 9). At station after station, all the way to London, the same image: the green eye closed, the red one below it opened. Eyes closed, mouth puckered, each station offers "a kiss for the boofer lady" as she passes, sweetly confirming John's—and little Johnny's—judgment of Bella.

As usual, when trying to understand a Dickens novel, it's always best to stay *within* the novel. When old Gruff and Glum appears the first time and follows John and Bella to the little church in Greenwich to see them married, I only see an image. When he reappears out on Blackheath a few hours later (734; bk. 4, ch. 4), I have to stop to think about it. It's the David Copperfield principle: writing his life for himself, trying to understand his life, David scans through innumerable small details. When he repeats a seemingly insignificant one—jumping headfirst into the Roman Baths, for example (567; ch. 35; 582; ch. 36)—I suspect that at some level this is of some significance to David, so I try to figure it out. When Gruff and Glum reappears—with his two wooden legs—I wonder if Dickens isn't making up for Silas Wegg. This old pensioner with "timber toes" is a charming man despite his situation, and when Bella asks what she might do to make him happy, he asks only leave to kiss her hand. A small thing, but worth seeing. A good thing.

Pa is happiest when he is with Bella. When he comes to her house for an evening, in the last book of the novel, she pretends he is a schoolboy: "And how have they used you at school to-day, my dear?" He replies,

> "Why . . . [it has] taken a little out of me to-day, my dear, but that was to be expected. There's no royal road to learning; and what is life but learning!"
>
> "And what do you do with yourself when you have got your learning by heart, you silly child?"
>
> "Why then, my dear," said the cherub, after a little consideration, "I suppose I die."
>
> "You are a very bad boy," retorted Bella, "to talk about dismal things and be out of spirits."
>
> "My Bella," rejoined her father, I am not out of spirits. I am as gay as a lark."
> (751–52; bk. 4, ch. 5)

This little conversation is central to the novel. It gives us a context for so much that the novel is about. If only Lizzie could teach Gaffer to value learning, she would herself "be a'most content to die" (70; bk. 1, ch. 3), and Pa's wisdom would relieve Twemlow of "the unvanquishable difficulty of his existence" (52; bk. 1, ch. 2). But it is a fanstastic wisdom, as the wisdom of tragedy always is.[6] And what Pa has proposed to Bella is precisely that wisdom. It is also akin to the wisdom the narrative voice professed in his toast to Bella and John on their wedding day at the end of the previous chapter: "And O there are days in this life worth life and worth death. And O what a bright old song it is, that O 'tis love, 'tis love, 'tis love, that makes the world go round!'' (738; bk. 4; ch.4).

At the beginning of this scene, Bella is being "more than usually fantastic" with her father (751; bk. 4, ch. 5). At its conclusion the narrator repeats that note: "Fantastic as it all was . . . '' (753; bk. 4, ch. 5). And at the end of the chapter, the prospective birth of the new little Harmon is announced. Framing Pa's wisdom this wayin fantasyis not to diminish it, however: in *Our Mutual Friend* the fantastic is often realized.[7] And the beginning of a new generation is itself fantastic,when you stop to think about it.

Not all fantasies are good fantasies, however, nor are all ways of understanding things equally valid. Wegg's fantasies about Aunt Jane and Uncle Parker are innocent—and ignorant—enough, but his fantasies about money aren't, and get him thrown into a scavenger's cart at last (862; bk. 4, ch. 14). Mr. Podsnap's firm belief that the world does, thinks, and lives exactly as he does is a ridiculous autobiographical fancy that serves only Mr. Podsnap. Jenny's fantasies about the flowers and birds and the blessed children who take her up are escapist, but understandably so; when she realizes her fancy for Eugene, it is a generous, good, and healing gift.

Mortimer is a fantasist, at least in part. He is a reader, too: his being "founded on" Eugene doesn't mean that he is in all things like Eugene. He isn't a clone, a second-hand character, or what Dickens calls a "Buffer." In addition to being a reader, he is a storyteller, the novel's designated storyteller. There are various other characters—Lizzie Hexam, Silas Wegg, Jenny Wren—who tell stories. But Mortimer is the best and most important storyteller: he puts things together reliably, both paying attention to details and imagining beyond them. And his story is the story of "the Man from Somewhere," otherwise known as "Our Mutual Friend." Or *Our Mutual Friend*.

Dickens wrote two novels—*David Copperfield* and *Great* Expectations—with first person narrators. *The Old Curiosity Shop* starts out as such as well, and Esther Summerson's "portion" of *Bleak House* is a first-person narrative. Miss Wade's chapter presenting "The History of a Self-Tormentor" in *Little Dorrit* is much smaller, but it too is a first-person narrative. To give John Harmon a voice in *Our Mutual Friend*, Dickens uses soliloquies. And in *The Mystery of Edwin Drood* he gives us Dick Datchery, not so much a narrator as a chief observer—and Dickens's own last stand-in.

I want to suggest now, not that Mortimer is the narrator of *Our Mutual Friend*, but that his role in the novel hints teasingly to us that he could be such, and that his understanding of the world is what Dickens proposes to us in the end. Mortimer enters the novel as the intended but reluctant talker in Society, "inveigled by Lady Tippins . . . to come to these people's and talk, and who won't talk" (53; bk. 1, ch. 2). At the inquest he is described as being both "one of the witnesses" and "the eminent solicitor who watched the proceedings on behalf of the representatives of the deceased" (73; bk. 1, ch. 3). This latter is the only direct reference to Mortimer's role as observer, though we see him mostly in that way. His role as storyteller, however, is pointed up on several occasions. His story is that of "Our Mutual Friend"—as Noddy calls Harmon—to start with; but it ends focusing on Eugene and Lizzie and the idea of society.

Once forced to talk, Mortimer turns out to be an apologetically self-conscious narrator with a sharply critical imagination. His sermon upon the mounds is as remarkable as were the mounds themselves. Old Harmon, he relates, "grew rich as a Dust Contractor, and lived in a hollow in a hilly country entirely composed of Dust. On his own small estate the growling old vagabond threw up his own mountain range, like an old volcano, and its geological formation was Dust. Coal-dust, vegetable-dust, bone-dust, crockery dust, rough dust and sifted dust,—all manner of Dust" (55–56; bk. 1, ch. 2). Then Mortimer starts reminding his audience, not that *he* is the storyteller, but that he is a *storyteller*. He is imitating "the novelists" whom Society reads. He refers to "that popular character whom the novelists and versifiers call Another," and remarks that he "must now return, as the novelists say, and as we all wish they wouldn't, to the man from Somewhere" (56–57; bk. 1, ch. 2). Mortimer is called upon again at the Lammle anniversary party—another Society gathering—to play narrator. Lady Tippins reminding everyone of his earlier success with the man from Somewhere, Mortimer replies, "Yes . . . as they say on the stage, 'Even so' " (470; bk. 2, ch. 16). Though "on the stage" doesn't refer to Mortimer as narrator, it does focus on his role—and his role as storyteller is perhaps more important than the tale. Mortimer insists that he has "nothing to tell" or "nothing worth mentioning" (470; bk. 2, ch. 16); significantly, however, he relates the story of the man from Somewhere to the story of Lizzie and Eugene, and can tell Society that Lizzie has disappeared: that is all. "And so ends the story" (472; bk. 2, ch. 16), he says.

We have just been told that Mortimer has "a reputation for his manner of relating a story," and has "made this story quite his own"—which would be true, except that he hasn't yet met John Rokesmith. The story he is making "quite his own" is elaborating, bringing together more and more people—just as the novel is. It may well be that the significance of Mortimer's self-consciousness about "novelists" is Dickens's way of inviting us to see Mortimer as *something like* the first-person narrator of *Our Mutual Friend*, whose job is to bring the various threads of the novel together, to hold all its pieces together. To make sense of it for himself.

When James Joyce wrote *A Portrait of the Artist as a Young Man*, he wrote about a young man—Stephen Dedalus—who would prefer to be writing about himself. But if Joyce let Stephen write an autobiography, it would be *only* about himself. The great success of *David Copperfield* is that David manages to write about his understanding of this world, and calls it his life. Mortimer, of course, is neither Stephen nor David. Mortimer isn't concerned with his own life, except as he is concerned about Eugene, upon whom he has "founded himself." His primary role is that of observer and narrator, though his observations are such that he would prefer not to have anything to do with what he sees, and thus he sees at this point in the novel no reason to tell anything at all, let alone stories, when he goes into Society.

At the third Social assemblage, Mortimer's role is minor. This time the story for the evening is of the Lammles' crash. Mortimer acknowledges having been "consulted," and knows what there is to know: that the Lammles were "living beyond their means" (691; bk. 3, ch. 17). We add the Lammles to Mortimer's list of people understood. It grows like Lady Tippins's "Cupidon"—except that this list of her lovers is a "grisly little fiction" (54; bk. 1, ch. 2), and Mortimer's understandings of people are reliable and useful, and end up making him happy.

When I was speaking of pairs and pairings, I should have suggested a quick look at marriages in *Our Mutual Friend*. On the bad side we have old Harmon and his abused family, the Wilfers, Rogue and Gaffer as fathers, Jenny's father, the marriage M.R.F. (Eugene's abbreviation for "My Respected Father") has planned for Eugene, the the Lammles, the false Veneerings. On the good side, the Boffins, John and Bella. Eugene and Lizzie, to be sure, though Society doesn't think so. Jenny's "Him" turns out to be Mr. Sloppy, which is good.

Mortimer isn't scheduled to marry at all, perhaps because he sees too many bad marriages around. But no: he knows two young couples his age whose marriages are happy, and promise even more happiness. When Mortimer goes alone back into Society for the last time he has the central part, as "the eyes of Europe" again focus on the story of the man from Somewhere. And again he is uncooperative—but in an aggressive way now. As a storyteller Mortimer has become—like David, Dickens's "favorite" novelist—a social critic.

By the end of the novel, Mortimer's criticism is much more biting and direct and open than it was when, whimsically, he told the story about old Harmon and his mountain range of dust. And after his skirmish with Lady

Tippins she protests to Veneering: Mortimer "means to tell us, that a horrid female waterman is graceful." Mortimer replies, "I mean to tell you nothing" (888; bk. 4, ch. 17). He is required to answer questions about Lizzie's background, and does so: offensively. Lizzie "sometimes rowed in a boat" with her father, but is not "a female waterman"; she "had some employment in a paper mill," but is not "a factory girl" (889; bk. 4, ch. 17). Society is outraged, of course, by his manner, by his ideas, by his betrayal of his class. But then Twemlow—of all people—stands beside him. Lizzie is a "lady," just as Eugene is a "gentleman." And not only that: he declares—on this "point of great delicacy," at any rate—his independence from Lord Snigsworth of Snigsworthy Park.

In the aftermath of all this, "a canopy of wet blanket seems to descend upon the company." But Mortimer brightens: there is an alternative to Society—and *as* that alternative, Mortimer "sees Twemlow home, shakes hands heartily with him at parting, and fares to the Temple gaily" (892; bk. 4, ch. 17).

Mortimer has put things together, at the end, and understood them. He is a busy, efficient solicitor, and a man of principle and understanding. The novel we have just read—*Our Mutual Friend*—is in a sense his response to this world. He is Dickens's character, oddly so in the beginning with his references to "the novelists" and quite seriously so in the end. He is the main observer in the novel as well as its designated storyteller. And despite the Podsnaps and Veneerings and Lammles, despite Lady Tippins, despite poor, pathetic, murderous Bradley and selfish little Charley, despite Rogue, despite the Fledgebys of this world, Mortimer is happy at the end. He "fares to the Temple gaily" because of people like the Boffins and Pa Wilfer, people like John and Bella, Lizzie and Eugene, people like Mr. Riah, people like the watchful, good, and loving Mr. Sloppy, and the ever-vigilant (I know your tricks and manners) Jenny Wren. And Twemlow—who knows what a gentleman is, and what a lady is. He isn't Veneering's oldest friend, but he is Mortimer's friend, and Mortimer "shakes hands with him cordially at parting" (892; bk. 4, ch. 17).

There are various partings toward the end of the novel, but the main force of its resolution is not so much what has happened as what has been understood. The character to whom nothing happens—he doesn't get murdered or married (though Bella, sensing how he watches her, thinks once that he might propose to her), is neither blessed with fortune nor bankrupt and headed for Francefinally becomes the focus of our attention. He understands this world he lives in,and is satisfied that he needn't retreat or retire or despair. In the end, Mortimer's understanding—his putting everything together and making sense of it—lets the novel have its wonderful, social title, *Our Mutual Friend.* His shaking hands with Twemlow—they have a great deal in common—says that yes, we can have a society, in spite of almost everything. And thus Mortimer "fares to the Temple gaily."

NOTES

1. "Our mutual friend" appears in *Martin Chuzzlewit, David Copperfield, Bleak House* (four times), and *Little Dorrit* (twice). References to a "mutual friend" appear in *Pickwick Papers, Nicholas Nickleby, Barnaby Rudge,* and *American Notes.*
2. The same trick is repeated, briefly, in the introduction of Mr. Venus (122; bk. 1, ch. 7).
3. At the beginning of chapter 4, Pa Wilfer's "modest ambition ... to wear a complete new suit of clothes, hat and boots included, at one time" (75; bk. 1) is introduced; and this, I suppose, is also an image—a modest one—of an ambition to put things together.
4. In *David Copperfield,* Mr. Chillup "can't find authority for Mr. and Miss Murdstone in the New Testament." Similarly, Mr. Venus has bones—a whole box of "bones warious" that he can't find a place for, can't "articulate." Wegg says that Venus can "fit together on wires the whole framework of society" (540; bk. 3, ch. 6)—but he can't.
5. See "Talk to me of love!" in *The Hero of My Life,* 91–94.
6. W. B. Yeats called tragedy "heaven blazing into the head." See "Lapis Lazuli" in Yeats, 565.
7. As Norman Nelson, an old colleague of mine, was dying he waved one big fist in the air and said, "Fantastic!" Thinking he referred to the care he was receiving in the hospice, his companion agreed: yes, Norman was being well cared for. But Norman waved that off, and said again, "Fantastic! The trees, the people, the books, the talk, the love—fantastic!"

WORKS CITED

Chesterton, Gilbert Keith. *Appreciations and Criticisms of the Works of Charles Dickens.* London: Dent, 1911.

Dickens, Charles. *David Copperfield* (1849–59). Ed. Trever Blount. New York: Penguin, 1976.

———. *Martin Chuzzlewit* (1843–44). Ed. P.N. Furbank. New York: Penguin, 1968.

———. *Nicholas Nickleby* (1838–39). Ed. Michael Slater. New York: Penguin, 1978.

———. *Our Mutual Friend* (1864–65). Ed. Stephen Gill. New York: Penguin, 1972.

Hornback, Bert G. *"The Hero of My Life": Essays on Dickens.* Athens: Ohio University Press, 1981.

Shelley, Percy B. *A Defense of Poetry.* Ed. Albert S. Cook. Boston: Ginn, 1903.

Yeats, William Butler. *The Variorum Edition of the Poems of W. B. Yeats.* Ed. Peter Allt and Russell K. Alspach. New York: Macmillan, 1957.

Reading and Repeating
Our Mutual Friend

Daniel Pollack-Pelzner

For many readers, the pleasures and frustrations of Dickens's last com-
pleted novel come into focus when they are deluded into believing that
the kindly Mr. Boffin has become a miser and are then informed that
he has only been acting the part—a deception that has spurred critical
controversy for well over one hundred years. Rather than engage in
another sally for or against this "pious fraud," I explore how the
historical drama of the Boffin plot's critical reception repeats the repre-
sentations of its development and interpretation within the novel. Link-
ing the treatment of reading in the novel to its scholarly responses, I
show how Dickens inscribes the conceptions that his critics enact, for
readings of Dickens's plot fit into plots themselves—the very plots, in
fact, that they seek to analyze. This critical reenactment arises from the
narrative texture of Our Mutual Friend, *which forces us into belatedness*
by reading itself before we can, leading us on to repeat its scripted
turns, and casting reading itself as an act of imitation.

I. Reading the Script: Boffin and the Critics

Dickens's last completed novel, *Our Mutual Friend*, has it in for readers. In addition to presenting the reader with a bewildering array of characters assuming alternate identities in a sequence of intersecting plots recounted from multiple perspectives, the novel explicitly and repeatedly challenges the act of reading itself. Characters who claim to be literate misidentify books, misquote

Dickens Studies Annual, Volume 39, Copyright © 2008 by AMS Press, Inc. All rights reserved.

261

poetry, and misread faces; they alienate their families with their literacy, threaten to dismember unruly readers, and nearly kill one another over the right to teach the illiterate to read; they force enemies to read as punishment, claim to have been debased by books, and even challenge the use of the word "reading." The wooden-legged Silas Wegg, hired as a "literary man" to read aloud to the illiterate Noddy Boffin, complains that his employer has treated him "like a set of skittles, to be set up and knocked over, set up and knocked over, by whatever balls—or books—he chose to bring against me" (570; bk. 3, ch. 14), and many of Dickens's readers have felt similarly buffeted and baffled by the novel's dizzying turns.

The perils of reading *Our Mutual Friend* have become particularly acute for many critics in the plot of Mr. Boffin's feigned descent into miserliness. In contrast to most of the novel's frauds and disguises—the Lammles' as people of means, Mr. Riah's as a loan shark, John Harmon's as John Rokesmith—the fact that Mr. Boffin is only, in his words, "playing a part" (756; bk. 4, ch. 13), is concealed from the reader as well as from other characters. As a result, many readers have felt surprised, indignant, or even violated when, towards the novel's end, Boffin reverts to his benevolent self and reveals that his ostensible greed was only a ruse to cure the beautiful Bella of her avarice and prove her a fit wife for Harmon. "It is a mistake," wrote G. K. Chesterton of the Boffin plot in his introduction to the Everyman's Library edition of *Our Mutual Friend* in 1907 (xii); "It is a shock," wrote Stephen Gill in his introduction to the 1971 Penguin edition (24). In his proposal to adapt the novel for the stage in 1999, the playwright and critic John Glavin declared that the "Boffin about-face is notoriously unacceptable" (49), and in his influential 1968 study, Grahame Smith called it "one of the biggest disappointments in literature" (182). Wegg's feeling of being "set up and knocked over" emerges frequently in these critiques, most strongly, perhaps, in H. M. Daleski's 1970 protest that Dickens "has cheated us" (329).

Nevertheless, Mr. Boffin's "pious fraud," as the narrator dubs it (751; bk. 4, ch. 13), has received many powerful defenses from prominent Dickensians, for the outraged responses I quoted above are only snippets of a debate over the merits of *Our Mutual Friend* that has raged since the novel's publication in 1865, when the noted critic E. S. Dallas championed the novel's "ingenious" plot in *The Times* (6) and a young Henry James savaged Mr. Boffin as "lifeless, forced, mechanical" in *The Nation* (786–87). Despite defenders' frequent pronouncements of closure (meaning a happy ending for them), the controversy has persisted to the present. In 1999, for example, a prominent article by John Farrell on *Our Mutual Friend* noted approvingly that the novel's "tricks" on the reader, previously misconstrued as a sign of "inauthenticity," had been "by now effectively redefined" as "a deepening of the novel's performative design'' (n. 64), but one of the most recent studies of the novel I have encountered—a theoretically astute analysis by Tore Rem—kept up the attack on Dickens's tricks and his manners, charging him with ''an arrogant display of power'' in the Boffin plot and lamenting, ''the contract with the reader has been broken'' (143, 148), and a 2006 article by Seth Rudy claimed that the revelation of Boffin's fraud ''strains the credibility of the narrative to the breaking point'' (72). Of course, this debate is not merely a long-running poll tabulating votes for and against Dickens's success in the novel; supporters and detractors alike construct their positions from an evolving set of criteria for evaluating literary merit, as terms such as ''performative'' and ''contract'' indicate. Indeed, we will see that criteria initially used to defend Dickens—authorial control, for instance—became grounds for attacking him as critical paradigms shifted. The range of excerpts I have provided thus far, however, should indicate that the furor around the Boffin plot is not merely an artifact of dated theoretical positions, but an enduring feature of Dickens criticism.

What interests me is the extent to which this debate over *Our Mutual Friend* appears to reenact the novel's own terms. To take one example: just after Mr. Boffin has begun to act as a miser and just before he asks Wegg to read aloud the books about misers he has purchased—at the point, that, is between acting and reading—Dickens raises the problem of interpretation that has plagued many of his critics. ''What to believe, in the course of his reading,'' the narrator tells us, ''was Mr. Boffin's chief literary difficulty indeed; for some time he was divided in his mind between half, all, or none; at length, when he decided, as a moderate man, to compound with half, the question still remained, which half? And that stumbling-block he never got over'' (470; bk. 3, ch. 6). Mr. Boffin himself is, of course, the stumbling-block that critics have never gotten over, and their chief literary difficulty has been what part of him to believe: half, all, or none. Some have deemed his entire character implausible—''Boffins are all bosh,'' Glavin decided (61)—while others have bought the whole package, judging it impossible to separate the ''performing'' Boffin from an ''authentic'' Boffin. Some critics have believed in the benevolent half of Boffin alone, treating the miser as a sham; others have found the miser the most persuasive part, overwhelming the benevolent ending; and others still have professed their inability to decide which half of Boffin to believe.[1] However the critics come down, they take a part in a script Dickens has already written.

Rather than trip over the stumbling-block once again by offering yet another attack on or defense of the Boffin plot, I would like to explore how the historical drama of the Boffin plot's critical reception repeats the representations of its development and interpretation within the novel. Plenty of ink has been spilled over themes of reading in *Our Mutual Friend*, and there have been several surveys of critical responses to the novel as well, but to my knowledge there has yet been no attempt to bridge thematic analysis and reception history—to link the treatment of reading in the novel to its scholarly responses and show how Dickens inscribes the conceptions that the critics enact.[2] Even those critics who regard characters in the novel as figures for ''the reader'' do not historicize the concept of ''the reader'' or note how the characters that figure ''the reader'' shift as readers' demands of *Our Mutual Friend* change over time. For readings of Dickens's plot fit into plots themselves—the very plots, in fact, that they seek to analyze—in addition to repeating many motifs from the novel that have hitherto gone unnoticed. Writing about the reception of another nineteenth-century novel driven by the will of a departed master, Shoshana Felman argues that ''The scene of the critical debate is . . . a *repetition* of the scene dramatized in the text'' (101). Freud's uncanny compulsion to repeat is very much at play in the debate over Boffin's ''pious fraud,'' and it, too, as we will see, is anticipated within the novel itself.

II. Reading the Plot: No Change of Will

The first hundred-odd years of critical debate on the Boffin plot centered on the question of authorial intent: had Dickens always planned to reverse Mr. Boffin's degeneration into miserliness at the novel's end and declare his avarice an act? Or had Dickens originally intended to have Boffin actually degenerate, in keeping with the novel's treatment of the corrupting effects of wealth, and only changed his mind at the last minute? G. K. Chesterton was the chief apostle of the change-of-mind school, to which such leading early Dickens critics as George Gissing, Humphry House, and Peter Quennell also subscribed, until F. X. Shea investigated Dickens's holograph manuscript to ''settle once and for all,'' as he put it, the question of authorial intent. Shea used Dickens's working notes to show that the Boffin plot was in keeping with Dickens's original design, and the Chesterton charge was largely dropped.[3] Whether or not any legitimate question could be settled ''by consulting the oracle,'' as Shea tried to do, my interest lies less in evaluating the merits of the question or its answer than in plotting its trajectory through Dickens criticism. For the debate over Dickens's intention with regards to the Boffin plot had a plot of its own, with a beginning, middle, and end, and it uncannily repeated one of the central plots of the novel: the course of a will.

Both the intention debate and *Our Mutual Friend* trace what Dickens dubs in his postscript ''Will Cases'': they are concerned with investigating the master's will, in its legal and volitional senses. Just as the intention debate attempted successive responses to the question ''What was Dickens's will for Mr. Boffin?'', so one plot of the novel consists in providing a series of surprising answers to the question: ''What was Old Harmon's will for Mr. Boffin?'' In his postscript, Dickens associated his will—his plan for the Boffin plot—with Old Harmon's will. After describing the challenge of keeping Mr. Boffin's play-acting ''for a long time unsuspected, yet always working itself out'' as ''the most interesting and the most difficult part of [his] design,'' and acknowledging that readers of the monthly installments in which the novel was first published might not appreciate the integrity of his ''whole pattern,'' Dickens immediately proceeded to justify his representation of Harmon's wills, using the terms ''fiction,'' ''fact,'' and ''fancied'' to explain ''Will Cases'' like Harmon's (798). Structurally and stylistically, then, the postscript implies a parallel between Dickens's authorial will and Harmon's legal will. And the two, of course, have a parallel function. Within the novel, Harmon's will determines his progeny's course of action: since he ''had written [the Boffins'] names down in his will'' (106; bk. 1, ch. 9), they must enact his intention, just as Dickens's intention, manifested in writing, generated his creations' deeds. The will drives the plot. [4]

The key development in the intention debate plot, as in *Our Mutual Friend*, came when that initial motivating will was challenged. Just as the Boffins were surprised by the terms of Old Harmon's will, so early reviewers of the novel wondered at Dickens's design and raised the possibility that Dickens had originally intended to make Mr. Boffin's corruption genuine. They deferred, however, to the authority Dickens claimed in his postscript, obeying his suggestion that ''an artist (of whatever denomination) may perhaps be trusted to know what he is about in his vocation'' (798).[5] The real action arose in Chesterton's 1907 introduction to the novel. Chesterton found the Boffin plot unconvincing, and he came up with an explanation for it:

> The truth of the whole matter I think, almost certainly, is that Dickens did not originally mean Boffin's lapse to be fictitious. He originally meant Boffin really to be corrupted by wealth, slowly to degenerate and as slowly to repent. But the story went too quickly for this long, double, and difficult process; therefore Dickens at the last moment made a sudden recovery possible by representing that the whole business had been a trick. Consequently, this episode is not an error merely in the sense that we may find many errors in a great writer like Dickens; it is a mistake patched up with another mistake. It is a case of that ossification which occurs round the healing of an actual fracture; the story had broken down and been mended.   (xii)

This is, of course, highly speculative, but it is nonetheless interesting for its echoes of the novel's motifs. Although Chesterton hardly mentions Mr. Venus in his introduction, he seems unwittingly to cast Dickens as an inferior version of the ''Articulator of Human Bones'' when he portrays the resolution of the

Boffin plot as a poorly articulated bone, fractured and ossified. If only Dickens were as adept an articulator as Venus, he could "name your smallest bones blindfold equally with your largest, as fast as I could pick 'em out, and I'd sort 'em all, and sort your wertebræ, in a manner that would equally surprise and charm you" (89; bk. 1, ch. 7). And if Dickens is an inept Venus, Chesterton is an aspiring Wegg, contending that Dickens changed his will "at the last moment" to reverse Boffin's miserly status, just as Wegg brandishes the latest Harmon will he dug up from the dust mounds to prove that Boffin can play the Golden Dustman no longer. The departed master changed his will, Chesterton and Wegg insist; Boffin is in jeopardy; the plot thickens.

But fortunately for the forces of narratological equilibrium, the digging is not yet done. When Mr. Boffin hires Wegg to read for him, he declares himself too old to learn to read, "to begin shoveling and sifting at alphabeds and grammar-books" (58; bk. 1, ch. 5), yet he does shovel and sift through Harmon's dust mounds to find still another Harmon will, which John brandishes in the novel's "checkmate" scene to render Wegg's will worthless. And in the resolution to the intention debate, Shea reenacted the novel's plot, shoveling and sifting through Dickens's manuscript dust mound to find a document that would authenticate the master's will. Like Mr. Boffin, he emerged with the salvaged paper to trump the challenger's charge: the manuscript notes for the chapter where Boffin begins to act like a miser, which he quoted triumphantly: "Mr. Boffin and Rokesmith and Mrs. Boffin, having, unknown to reader, arranged their plan, now strike in with it" (38).[6] Dickens, it seems, had intended Mr. Boffin merely to feign his degradation all along, and Chesterton's assertion could be tossed, like the worthless Wegg, into the scavenger's cart.

Shea titled his article, which has been cited by nearly every subsequent discussion of the Boffin plot, "No Change of Intention in *Our Mutual Friend*"—a title that could apply equally well to Dickens's will or Harmon's. Ironically, the latter's "latest will" turns out effectively to restore the terms of his first will, since Mr. Boffin hands over everything to John except the small mound he was to have in the first place (767; bk. 4, ch. 14). So there is, after all, no lasting change of intention: John gets the girl and the fortune, and good servant Mr. Boffin gets the little mound, just as Old Harmon had originally willed.[7] "It looks as if the old man's spirit had found rest at last" (757; bk. 4, ch. 13), Mrs. Boffin observes as Harmon's will generates harmony, and with Dickens's original intention vindicated, it looks as if it had. The Boffin plot succeeded through the triumph of the will. Case closed.

III. Reading the Characters: Playing a Part

But if there's one thing everyone knows about plot, it's that closure is artificial; "Fictions of Resolution" is the title of one study by Deirdre David that includes an analysis of *Our Mutual Friend*. D. A. Miller writes that "closure needs to be a moment of suppression, where something is 'a little disguised, or a little mistaken' " (xii); certainly, later critics, at least, need to argue for such a fictional closure in order to open up their own inquiry, to continue the plot of reading. And so, just over one hundred years after the novel's publication, the debate over the Boffin plot started to heat up again. "No Change of Intention in *Our Mutual Friend*" appeared in 1967, just as the concept of "the author" was receiving death threats. Shea was a Jesuit priest with a doctorate in English, and his respect for the author may have sounded too reverential at a time when Roland Barthes was writing that "We know now that a text is not a line of words releasing a single 'theological' meaning (the 'message' of the Author-God) but a multi-dimensional space in which a variety of writings, none of them original, blend and clash" (1468). Defending the centrality of an Author-God's unalterable will no longer looked quite so desirable.

The challenge to Shea's closure came in 1968 when a Dickens study by Grahame Smith provided the fiercest attack on the Boffin plot to date. In the checkmate scene, John tells Wegg that he persuaded Mr. Boffin "to let us lead you on, deluded, to the last possible moment, in order that your disappointment might be the heaviest possible disappointment" (768; bk. 4, ch. 14). If Wegg's disappointment failed to live up to that standard, John would have been satisfied by Smith, who lamented that the scene was "one of the greatest disappointments in literature." He objected particularly to what Wegg might call being "set up and knocked over": by duping the reader into thinking Mr. Boffin's corruption was genuine, Dickens had exhibited an "almost contemptuous dealing in deception at the expense of human feeling" that Smith found morally untenable. "Such manipulation of people, in life or in art, is at once arrogant and frivolous," he declared (182–83).[8] This view may seem an overstatement, but Smith became the Chesterton of the post-Shea generation: almost every subsequent critic who attempted to justify the Boffin plot responded to him. The terms of the first debate were being reversed, as the fear became not too little authorial control, but too much. The problem with the Boffin plot was no longer an unsteady authorial will; the problem was an authoritarian will that diminished the reader's humanity.

A different way to justify the Boffin plot also began to take shape around this time—a playful, rather than willful, defense, taking its cue from Mr. Boffin's suggestion that he was "playing a part" (756; bk. 4, ch. 13). In 1966, Jacques Derrida delivered his famous deconstruction of the center in "Structure, Sign, and Play in the Human Sciences" to a conference at Johns Hopkins, where the chairman of the English Department and the Humanities Group was J. Hillis Miller. Eight years earlier, Miller had published his seminal study of Dickens, in which he argued that characters in *Our Mutual*

Friend can "change their real identities into roles, and live their lives as if they were a play or a game." He cited "the play-acting" of Mr. Boffin and John as "a way of assuming their real situations, and yet of transforming them from something merely imposed to something in a sense free and chosen" (308). Miller's concept of a situation free and chosen, not merely imposed, echoed the resolution of the Harmon plot, which, of course, is not a triumph of the will, but a triumph of goodwill. Explaining his final situation to Wegg, John praises the power of benevolence to overcome cruel legality: "You supposed me just now, to be the possessor of my father's property.—So I am. But through any act of my father's, or by any right I have? No. Through the munificence of Mr. Boffin" (768; bk. 4, ch. 14). True, the terms of Old Harmon's original will come to pass, but because of Boffin's free choice, his mutuality, not because of established inheritance structures or patriarchal intentions.

After Miller, free play became the thing: pantomime, theater, fancy, and performance have been the buzzwords for defenses of the Boffin ruse in the last three decades, with critics chuckling along with Mr. Boffin at the inspired dramatic skill of his "grandest demonstration" (756; bk. 4, ch. 13).[9] Several post-structuralist critics have shown how Dickens surrounds the Boffin plot with challenges to concepts of fixed or "real" identity, developing a representation of fluid, "performative" identity that reaches its most creative, unstable form in Mr. Boffin. This is the context in which, in the passage I quoted earlier, John Farrell contended that recent scholarship had "effectively redefined the 'tricks' [such as the Boffin ruse] as a deepening of the novel's performative design," leaving Grahame Smith's objection to sink like a stone.

But by the logic of drowning and rebirth that governs *Our Mutual Friend*, anything that sinks is bound to bob up again, and Smith's protest against the manipulation of the reader has proved as enduring as Miller's defense of free play. At issue in this post-1968 round of debate over the Boffin plot has been the question of who gets to play. Boffin and Harmon do, certainly, but does anyone else—particularly the reader? Whereas the pre-Shea debate worried about the author's control over the novel, the question of the reader's power has seized the spotlight in recent scholarship. But just as the writerly debate reenacted the novel's plot, with Dickens's will repeating Harmon's, so the readerly debate has evinced the compulsion to repeat, with the reader figured alternately as Bella Wilfer or Silas Wegg, the dupes of Boffin's plot.

The analogy between the reader and Bella was originally presented by a critic defending Dickens's authorial sovereignty. In a sort of coda to Shea's article, Rosemary Mundhenk tried to explain the consistent intention that Shea had shown by arguing that "Dickens does for the reader what Boffin does for Bella" (42); that is, benevolently deceive us to change our ways and reveal to us the limits of our capacity for judging character. It was a compelling argument, but it provoked many subsequent critics to object that they did not approve of what Boffin does for Bella, nor did they want Dickens to do them in a similar manner. Feminist critics in the 1980s led this charge. Kate Flint detected harm, not harmony, in the unveiling of the Boffin plot: "It is this unmasking of purpose shared by the Boffins and Rokesmith which in fact reveals the very worst aspect of Bella's subordinate role, manipulated, kept in the dark, deprived of making choices freely, by those who presume to know better than she" (119–20). Flint here sounded Smith's protest against manipulation and implied the limits of Miller's perception of "free and cho- sen" identity—available to Bella's male deceivers, but not Bella herself. A contemporary study of gender relations in the Victorian novel explicitly linked Bella's torment to the reader's: "Though Bella survives the test, the strain on her seems simply cruel. At the moment of revelation she beseeches Harmon, 'I don't know what it means, but it is too much for me.' We suspect it is also too much for most readers" (Barickman, MacDonald, and Stark 30). To the extent that critics are representative of most readers, this suspicion has some merit, for quite a few manipulated critics have echoed Bella's Ibsen- inspiring cry: "I want to be something so much worthier than the doll in the doll's house" (663; bk. 4, ch. 5).

In the last decade, reader-response critics have taken up the feminist protest against an authoritarian author, adopting the voice of the frustrated partner and reader Silas Wegg. Critics like Garrett Stewart, John Glavin, and Tore Rem view Wegg as their maligned martyr, the limping Caliban to Boffin's despotic Prospero, unfairly victimized for his creative interpretations.[10] Wegg is the postmodern performative reader par excellence, playfully adapting his ballads to the present context "to beguile the monotony of a literary life" (486; bk. 3, ch. 7), and when he is dumped in a scavenger's cart, his interpret- ers (generally valuing his dramatic flair over his avaricious scheming) feel as though they have been dumped, too. Just as John Harmon, seeking a position with Mr. Boffin, finds himself "in some sort anticipated" by Boffin's literary man (103; bk. 1, ch. 8), so Wegg has anticipated the later secretaries who would sort out Boffin's affairs. Like Wegg, the reader-response critics' sense of injury arises from their presumption of mutuality—though theirs stems from the history of Dickens's much-vaunted relationship to his readers, rather than the fantasy that a house whose inhabitants they have never met is their own. Wegg tells Venus that Boffin has appropriated "Our House" (303; bk. 2, ch. 7) and tampered with "our property" (568; bk. 3, ch. 14); so, too, the critics who side with him resent in the Boffin ruse an author who "noxiously insists [he] won't go halves" (Glavin 61), for whom "the contract with the reader has been broken" (Rem 148) and who "*subjects* a reader" instead of extending the mutuality promised in the novel's title (Stewart 232). Harmony may be restored at the novel's end, but it's the harmony of Harmony Jail, with the novel as "correctional institution," in Stewart's phrase (234). "Our

House'' has become our cell, with readers behind bars and Dickens outside, holding the key. Forcing the reader to endure tales of misers under false pretenses is a sadistic act: Boffin tells Bella that he decided to have Wegg read aloud the lives of misers he had purchased ''for the punishment of . . . - Wegg'' (755; bk. 4, ch. 13). Had Voltaire been a reader-response critic, he might have contended that *Our Mutual Friend* is neither ours, nor mutual, nor a friend.

As befits a reader whose authorial club does not want him for a member, Wegg finds that his attempts to gain control of Old Harmon's will are repeatedly threatened with dismemberment. When Wegg tries to hold onto the copy of the will he found in the dust mound, Venus threatens to cut off his arms, pointing to a skeleton that lacks a pair, and reminding Wegg: ''I like my art, and I know how to exercise my art, and I mean to have the keeping of this document'' (489; bk. 3, ch. 7). When Wegg proposes to his ''partner'' that they ''cut it in half, and each keep a half,'' Venus, exercising more legal acumen, rejects the offer—in the novel that, Glavin claims, ''noxiously insists it won't go halves'' (61)—saying ''It wouldn't do to mutilate it, partner'' (489; bk. 3, ch. 7), with the tacit threat that if Wegg mutilated it, he would mutilate Wegg. This sequence highlights the ominous side of Dickens's reminder to the reader in his postscript that ''an artist (of whatever denomination) may perhaps be trusted to know what he is about in his vocation.'' Trust the artist—Venus or Dickens—to know what he is about, hand over your readerly text to the master articulator, or else you may lose your limbs. In addition to Venus's threat of amputation, John tells Wegg that after Wegg tried to appropriate Old Harmon's will he had to restrain himself from trying ''to twist your head off, and fling *that* out of window!'' (768; bk. 4, ch. 14). A capital penalty awaits the reader who would tamper with an author's will.[11]

The intention debate over the Boffin plot, as we have seen, reenacted the temporal thrust of the Harmon will plot and reached a similar point of closure, affirming the power of a directing authorial will. The post-1968 readerly debate challenged that will, with one side emulating characters who could define themselves freely and the other side playing characters who were dominated by the free players. Repeating the role of characters, rather than reenacting a plot, the readerly debate has yet to reach closure. Despite repeated assertions that the Boffin plot is not problematic, criticisms continue from reputable sources. All the major objections to Dickens's overweening power play come from critics included in the 2001 *Cambridge Companion to Charles Dickens* (Smith, Flint, Stewart, Glavin), which also gave space to the critics who celebrate the novel's free play (J. Hillis Miller, Newsom, Baumgarten). None of these critics, however, wrote the essay in the *Cambridge Companion* on *Our Mutual Friend*. That distinction went to a South African critic, Brian Cheadle, who came down strongly on the side of the subjugated reader, arguing that Dickens achieves "his elaborate deception at the expense of temporarily destroying, in a most disconcerting way, the gratifying complicity between author and reader which had hitherto been crucial to Dickensian narrative" (85). The reader has not won entirely, however, for the *Cambridge Companion* was edited by John O. Jordan, who founded the Dickens Project—the preeminent academic Dickens conference—with Edwin M. Eigner, a champion of the "pious fraud," and runs it along with Baumgarten, a leader of the Boffinesque performative school. The Weggian detractors Stewart and Glavin have been invited to speak at the conference, but the Boffin contingent presides.

IV. Reading in its Critical Use: The Compulsion to Repeat

Why have the critics been compelled to repeat Dickens's plot and characters in their debate over the Boffin plot? We are always "after Dickens," in Glavin's useful phrase, not only because we follow him chronologically, seek him out, and work in his style, but because the narrative of *Our Mutual Friend* forces us into belatedness by reading itself before we can. Just as *Our Mutual Friend* abounds with fiction(al) authors,[12] so it bursts with readers—and not just of the daily papers, like Sloppy, but of its own story. The story of the Harmon will is presented to us as, indeed, a story, narrated by Mortimer Lightwood to an amused audience of "society." His self-conscious narration links his story to the novel we are reading; he explicitly invokes the convention of "novelists" in his account of "the Man from Somewhere" and "Another"—both the triteness of a romance muddied by disinheritance, and the tedious switching between plot lines heralded by phrases like "We must now return" (24–25; bk. 1, ch. 2). This is a bit of self-mockery on Dickens's part, since his own novel treads the love-despite-poverty ground while juggling a remarkable number of stories at once, and indeed Mortimer Lightwood (whose very name, compounded of mortality and buoyancy, echoes the novel's central trope of drowning and rebirth) doubles as an authorial figure, providing the exposition of the plot in the second chapter and revealing plot turns to heighten suspense ("Man's drowned!"; "She's vanished"). But the direction of the doubling grows complicated as Dickens lifts Mortimer's phrases for his own chapter titles: "The Man from Somewhere" and "Another Man." Whose story are we reading? The novel becomes Mortimer's story, just as Mortimer's story becomes the novel, appropriating its narrative technique from what "the novelists say," just as Dickens borrows his titles from what Mortimer says (25; bk. 1, ch. 2). Dickens quoting Mortimer becomes Mortimer quoting Dickens; the novel reads itself before we can begin turning its pages.

In the Boffin plot, the novel also turns its pages before we can begin reading it: the narrator tells us that the Golden Dustman begins his miserly act "as Bella turned the leaves of her book" (456; bk. 3, ch. 5). The plot is furthered by Wegg's reading the books about misers that Boffin has purchased, and is resolved when Mrs. Boffin assures Bella that she "shall be told all the story" (751; bk. 4, ch. 13). Bella even provides a preemptive conclusion: having read the start of the plot and been told the middle, she cries that she does not need anyone "to tell me the rest of the story" for "I can tell it to *you*" (754; bk. 4, ch. 13).[13] We are woefully belated: the plot has been composed, narrated, sold, purchased, and read before we can start. It has even been reread by Mr. Boffin, who repeatedly asks his audience to return to the scene of his "grandest demonstration" when he dismissed his Secretary with "Mew says the cat, Quack quack says the duck, and Bow-wow-wow says the dog" (756; bk. 4, ch. 13).[14]

The reader's response to the story has also been read and responded to by Dickens in his "Postscript." There he writes that he has anticipated what "a class of readers and commentators" would suppose, and is not alarmed, because that "supposition might in part arise out of some ingenuity in the story" (798). The "artist (of whatever denomination) may perhaps be trusted to know what he is about in his vocation," so readers should relax in the knowledge that however they respond, Dickens saw it coming. What is there left for us to do but reenact what has come before? The novel begins with a tease of mutuality, "In these times of ours," but then refuses the information that would allow the bond to be shared: "though concerning the exact year there is no need to be precise" (13; bk. 1, ch. 1). We may float in the novel's restorative waters, as the Hexam boat "floated on the Thames," but we are constrained by inflexible boundaries, "between Southwark Bridge which is of iron, and London Bridge which is of stone" (13; bk. 1, ch. 1). We are conscripted, in Stewart's apt term, by a text that has read us before we can read it.

Amid all the novel's preemptive explorations of reading, the most distressing are those that suggest the impossibility of doing so. In the scene when Mr. Boffin begins to act the miser, Bella pretends to read in order to keep Mrs. Boffin from reading her face, letting her eyes droop over her book so that Mrs. Boffin's eyes can't discover her reactions to Mr. Boffin's cruelty (458; bk. 3, ch. 5). Similarly, Mr. Boffin's reading of misers prevents others from reading him. As he descends into miserliness, "a kind of illegibility . . . stole over Mr. Boffin's face . . . His very smile was cunning, as if he had been studying smiles among the portraits of his misers" (467; bk. 3, ch. 5). Reading in *Our Mutual Friend* generates self-protective illegibility: while characters are reading, no one can read them. Can we, then, read a novel that so obsessively reads itself?

Or one that grows increasingly reluctant to continue its narrative? Mortimer, the chief storyteller within the novel, appears to become increasingly uncomfortable with his role as narrator to such a shallow audience as the Veneerings' circle, refusing to yield details to the inquisitive Lady Tippins or even to grant her status as a responsive reader. "I mean to tell you nothing, Lady Tippins" (794; bk. 4, ch. 17), Mortimer announces in the novel's final chapter. Overly solicitous readers nearly get killed in this novel: Eugene Wrayburn tells Mortimer that if he were to commit a crime, Lady Tippins should "look to it. Her life's in danger" (167; bk. 1, ch. 13); and John Harmon tells Wegg that he'd "give a thousand pounds for leave to knock your brains out" (767; bk. 4, ch. 14).

But what good is reading in the novel's world? When Fledgeby hears that Lizzie Hexam and Jenny Wren spend their free time at "book-learning," he replies that there's "not much good to be got out of that" (278; bk. 2, ch. 5), and Mr. Boffin tells his secretary that he may only "take up a book for a minute or two when you've nothing better to do, though I think you'll a'most always find something useful to do" (457; bk. 3, ch. 5), suggesting that reading, by contrast, is useless. Even though the comments of a scheming bigot and an ostensibly cruel miser may not serve as the novel's authoritative word on reading, especially in contrast to Lizzie's benevolent literacy, the arrogance that reading brings Charlie Hexam and the impotence of Wegg, the man to whom "all Print is open" (57; bk. 1, ch. 5), suggest that Fledgeby's assessment of reading is not entirely undermined.

The fear of any trusting reader is that he will simply be led on a path that goes nowhere, as Eugene leads Bradley Headstone on his uncannily doubling walks through the London streets in a pattern lacking any design except to sustain Bradley's desire. Eugene presents his tormenting of Bradley as a process of transference: Bradley has put him in a "ludicrous situation of being followed and observed," rather like a critic coming after (in Glavin's sense) an author, and in response, he "transfer[s] the position to the scouts" (532–32; bk. 3, ch. 10). This explanation comes immediately after Eugene's ostensibly digressive gloss on the word "reading":

> "By the by, that very word, Reading, in its critical use, always charms me. An actress's Reading of a chambermaid, a dancer's Reading of a hornpipe, a singer's Reading of a song, a marine painter's Reading of the sea, the kettle-drum's Reading of an instrumental passage, are phrases ever youthful and delightful."
> (532; bk. 3, ch. 10)

As every critic who treats this passage points out, it is not irrelevant at all, but deeply implicated in the novel's motifs of reading and interpretation.[15] But it is also deeply embedded in a narrative context that most critics neglect: immediately after Eugene casts reading as imitative performance ("an actress's Reading of a chambermaid"), he describes how he torments Bradley by inducing the schoolmaster to imitate his performance; in short, to read him. This is speaking "soberly and plainly," as opposed to his riddling riff on reading, and implies an explication of the previous disquisition. Mortimer's "reading of [Eugene's] weakness" engenders Eugene's exposition of reading, which in turn leads to a situation of sadistic reading, ending in Bradley's "grinding torments" (532–33; bk. 3, ch. 10). Just as Bradley is later compelled by Rogue Riderhood into putting his own name under erasure (literally wiping his signature off the blackboard), so here Eugene tortures him into self-annihilation, twisting him to the point that "the force of his expression cancel[led] his figure" (534; bk. 3, ch. 10). "Whichever way the reader turns," writes Shoshana Felman, "he can but be turned by the text, he can but *perform* it by *repeating* it" (101). Bradley is thus condemned by the compulsion to repeat: as Eugene decides to "rapidly turn the corner, and . . . as rapidly turn back," he is turned into oblivion (533; bk. 3, ch. 10).

This grim figure of reading's peril—erasing oneself being perhaps even worse than being dismembered, like Wegg, by one's author—is linked to Dickens's design on the reader not only by Eugene's gloss on "reading" but by his earlier riff on "design." In his postscript, Dickens writes that keeping the Boffin plot "unsuspected" and "turning it" to a good purpose in the end "was at once the most interesting and the most difficult part of my design" (798). That "design" provides the basis for the conviction Dickens wants us to hold that the artist should "be trusted," that even if inattentive readers cannot "perceive the relations of [the story's] finer threads to the whole pattern," such a pattern "is always before the eyes of the story-weaver at his loom" (798). If the text—in its etymological sense of a woven texture—is to be trusted, it is because the weaver has a design. But when Mortimer questions Eugene about his designs on Lizzie, which have infuriated Bradley, Eugene denies each of the designs Mortimer guesses, concluding: "My dear fellow, I don't design anything. I have no design whatever. I am incapable of designs. If I conceived a design, I should speedily abandon it, exhausted by the operation" (292; bk. 2, ch. 6). We have seen already at this point in the novel that Eugene is perfectly capable of designing schemes to amuse himself: his "reading" of a shipper in the lime-trade dupes the barman at the Six Jolly Fellowship Porters and gives him a "fiction of an occupation" to rival Young Blight's (92, bk. 1, ch. 8). Similarly, he can "study" to lead Bradley down the most circuitous route in London, and finds himself not exhausted, but delighted by "the healthful exercise" (533; bk. 3, ch. 10). Such designs, however, serve no clear purpose; Eugene can contrive to "loiter artfully" (534; bk. 3, ch. 10) but his art is squandered in a pursuit that annihilates its subjects, such as the self-effacing Headstone. Eugene as loitering artist functions then as a disturbing double to Dickens, raising the specter of doubt that if we follow the artist down his turning, twisting paths, we may end up like Bradley, finding nothing but our deceiver's impassive face passing us by. Like Mr. Boffin's face, as he practices his artful acting, the text can descend into illegibility.

One hundred and forty years of criticism on *Our Mutual Friend* may belie the suggestion that the novel cannot be read. But, as Eugene glosses "reading," it is an imitative act, an impersonation, a performance of another character. So the critical controversy over the Boffin plot, the most provoking challenge for the reader in the novel, has compelled the critics to read repetitively: to do a "reading" of Bella or Wegg as an actress does a "Reading of a chambermaid," or to perform the plot of the novel as they read its plotting. I, of course, am no more exempt from this reading cycle than they, and as a belated critic double-reading the novel and its reception, I may be doubly doomed to repeat.

NOTES

1. For critics who believe none of Boffin, see Glavin and James. For critics who believe all, see Eigner, *The Dickens Pantomime*, and Kincaid. For critics who believe in the miserly half, see Chesterton, Gill, and Hobsbaum. For critics who believe in the benevolent half, see Mundhenk and Baumgarten. For critics who can't decide which half to believe, see Lindsay and Ginsburg.
2. For studies of reading in *Our Mutual Friend*, see Mundhenk, Friedman, Newsom, Kiely, Hecimovich, and Farrell. For surveys of *Our Mutual Friend* criticism, see Brattin and Hornback's annotated bibliography and Heaman. For critical surveys that focus on the Boffin plot, see Hobsbaum and Newsom. In *Dear Reader*, Stewart has ably shown how Dickens conscripts one particular reader, but he does not link his findings to the historical receptions of the novel (231–34).
3. For a summary of the intention debate, see Hobsbaum, Shea, and Brattin, "Constancy, Change, and the Dust Mounds."
4. In *Fictions of Resolution*, David also notes that a will resembles a novel in laying down a plot for its beneficiaries (74), and Brooks links "the problem of transmission" in wills and authorship—how to pass on property to its inheritors or a story to its readers—in the nineteenth-century novel (27–28).
5. See, for example, *The London Review* 28 Oct. 1865 (qtd. in Shea 37).
6. The number plans for *Our Mutual Friend* are reprinted in Stone's edition of *Dickens' Working Notes*.
7. Ginsburg also points out that the plot of *Our Mutual Friend* consists in restoring the characters' status at the beginning of the novel.
8. Smith also worried that the late Dickens showed a "lack of control" (191), but the particular problem for Smith seemed to be that Dickens responded to his weakness as a faltering authoritarian leader might: by exercising too much control in response.

9. See Kincaid 12, Eigner, "Shakespeare, Milton, Dickens," 19, Newsom 53, Hecimovich 972, Farrell n. 64, 784, Baumgarten 18, and Rudy 71–72.
10. See Farrell n. 71, 787 for a less malignant association of Boffin with Prospero.
11. All the novel's villains, in fact, are threatened with dismemberment: besides
Venus eyeing Wegg's arms, Bradley is reduced by Eugene's labyrinthine night
walks to the state of "a haggard head suspended in the air" (534; bk. 3, ch. 10);
Lammle commands Fledgeby to "Give me your nose" (271; bk. 2, ch. 5); and
the steamer that nearly drowns Riderhood "cut him in two," and though the
witness's account "is so far figurative, touching the dismemberment, as that he
means the boat, and not the man," the threat remains (439; bk. 3, ch. 3). Hutter
discusses dismemberment on the narrative level.
12. For example, Wegg's refers to his leg as a "timber fiction" (300; bk. 2, ch. 7);
Lady Tippins maintains her "grisly little fiction" of a lover (23; bk. 1, ch. 2);
Young Blight sustains his "fiction of an occupation" (92, bk. 1, ch. 8); Miss
Peecher keeps up her "transparent fiction" of examining Mary Anne (335; bk.
2, ch. 11); and Eugene plays an actor, director, and writer in his useless and
ridiculous "lime fiction" (163; bk. 1, ch. 13). The Lammles fictionalize their
social status, as does Fledgeby, with his "convenient fiction" that Riah is a
greedy Jew and he an honest businessman (276; bk. 2, ch. 5), as do the Veneerings, whose guests, Twemlow notes, "become infected with the Veneering fiction" (119; bk. 1, ch. 10)—not to mention John's disclosure that the novel's
"plot was made" by him and Radfoot (361; bk. 2, ch. 13). Kiely also notes that
"Nearly everyone in the novel . . . is an author" (271).
13. Stewart sees Bella's narration as a model for conscripting the reader into accepting
the Boffin plot and reads Wegg as a satire of the resentful reader (234).
14. In response to Smith's contention that the passages where Boffin impersonates a
miser "can never be read again with patience" after his deception is revealed
(182), Newsom argues that "Mr. Boffin himself asks the reader to reread his
story and to take pleasure in it—as he himself does in looking back upon his
performance and remembering, among other things, what he calls his 'grandest
demonstration' " (53).
15. See, for example, Friedman 38 and Stewart 232.

WORKS CITED

Barickman, Richard, Susan MacDonald, and Myra Stark. *Corrupt Relations: Dickens, Thackeray, Trollope, Collins, and the Victorian Sexual System.* New York: Columbia UP, 1982.

Barthes, Roland. "The Death of the Author." Trans. Stephen Heath. *The Norton Anthology of Theory and Criticism.* Ed. Vincent Leitch, William Caine, Louise Finke, Barbara Johnson, John McGowan, and Jeffrey Williams. New York: Norton, 2001. 1466–70.

Baumgarten, Murray. "Boffin, *Our Mutual Friend*, and the Theatre of Fiction." *Dickens Quarterly* 19.1 (2002): 17–22.

Brattin, Joel J. "Constancy, Change, and the Dust Mounds of *Our Mutual Friend*." *Dickens Quarterly* 19.1 (March 2002): 23–30.

———, and Bert G. Hornback. *Our Mutual Friend: An Annotated Bibliography*. New York: Garland, 1984.

Brooks, Peter. *Reading for the Plot*. Oxford: Oxford UP, 1984.

Cheadle, Brian. "The Late Novels." *The Cambridge Companion to Charles Dickens*. Ed. John O. Jordan. Cambridge: Cambridge UP, 2001. 78–91.

Chesterton, G. K. "Introduction." *Our Mutual Friend*. By Charles Dickens. London: Dent, 1907.

Daleski, H. M. *Dickens and the Art of Analogy*. New York: Schocken, 1970.

Dallas, E. S. "Our Mutual Friend." *The Times* 29 Nov. 1865: 6.

David, Deirdre. *Fictions of Resolution in Three Victorian Novels*. New York: Columbia UP, 1981.

Dickens, Charles. *Dickens' Working Notes for His Novels*. Ed. Harry Stone. Chicago: U of Chicago P, 1987.

———. *Our Mutual Friend*. Ed. Adrian Poole. London: Penguin, 1997.

Eigner, Edwin M. "Shakespeare, Milton, Dickens and the Morality of the Pious Fraud." *Dickens Studies Annual* 21 (1992), 1–26.

———. *The Dickens Pantomime*. Berkeley: U of California P, 1989.

Farrell, John P. "The Partners' Tale: Dickens and *Our Mutual Friend*." *ELH* 66.3 (1999): 759–99.

Felman, Shoshana. "Turning the Screw of Interpretation." *Yale French Studies* 55/56 (1977): 94–207.

Flint, Kate. *Dickens*. Atlantic Highlands, NJ: Humanities, 1986.

Friedman, Stanley. "The Motif of Reading in *Our Mutual Friend*." *Nineteenth-Century Fiction* 28.1 (1973): 38–61.

Gill, Stephen. "Introduction." *Our Mutual Friend*. By Charles Dickens. London: Penguin, 1971. 11–32.

Ginsburg, Michal Peled. "The Case against Plot in *Bleak House* and *Our Mutual Friend*." *Economies of Change: Form and Transformation in the Nineteenth-Century Novel*. Stanford: Stanford UP, 1996. 138–56.

Glavin, John. *After Dickens: Reading, Adaptation and Performance*. Cambridge: Cambridge UP, 1999.

Heaman, Robert J. "Our Mutual Friend: An Annotated Bibliography, Supplement I-1984–2000." *Dickens Studies Annual* 33 (2003): 425–514.

Hecimovich, Gregg A. "The Cup and the Lip and the Riddle of *Our Mutual Friend*." *ELH* 62.4 (1995): 955–77.

Hobsbaum, Philip. "The Critics and *Our Mutual Friend*." *Essays in Criticism* 13 (1963): 231–40.

Hutter, Albert D. "Dismemberment and Articulation in *Our Mutual Friend*." *Dickens Studies Annual* 11 (1983): 135–75.

James, Henry. "Our Mutual Friend." *The Nation* 21 Dec. 1865: 786–87.

Kiely, Robert. "Plotting and Scheming: The Design of Design in *Our Mutual Friend*." *Dickens Studies Annual* 12 (1983): 267–83.

Kincaid, James R. "Performance, Roles, and the Nature of the Self in Dickens." *Dramatic Dickens*. Ed. Carol Hanbery MacKay. London: Macmillan, 1989. 11–26.

Lindsay, Jack. *Charles Dickens: A Biographical and Critical Study*. London: Dakers, 1950.

Miller, D. A. *Narrative and Its Discontents: Problems of Closure in the Traditional Novel*. Princeton: Princeton UP, 1981. ix–xv.

Miller, J. Hillis. *Charles Dickens: The World of His Novels*. Cambridge: Harvard UP, 1958.

Mundhenk, Rosemary. "The Education of the Reader in *Our Mutual Friend*." *Nineteenth-Century Fiction* 34.1 (1979): 41–58.

Newsom, Robert. " 'To Scatter Dust': Fancy and Authenticity in *Our Mutual Friend*." *Dickens Studies Annual* 8 (1980): 39–60.

Rem, Tore. *Dickens, Melodrama, and the Parodic Imagination*. New York: AMS, 2002.

Rudy, Seth. "Stage Presence: Performance and Theatricality in Dickens's *Our Mutual Friend*." *Dickens Studies Annual* 37 (2006): 65–80.

Sedgwick, Eve Kosofsky. *Between Men: English Literature and Male Homosocial Desire*. New York: Columbia UP, 1985.

Shea, F. X. "No Change of Intention in *Our Mutual Friend*." *Dickensian* 63 (1967): 37–40.

Smith, Grahame. *Dickens, Money, and Society.* Berkeley: U of California P, 1968.

Stewart, Garrett. "That very word, Reading, in its critical use." *Dear Reader: The Conscripted Audience in Nineteenth-Century British Fiction.* Baltimore: Johns Hopkins UP, 1996. 231–34.

War of the Roses: Hybridity in *The Moonstone*

John Glendening

Wilkie Collins's The Moonstone *examines and enacts hybridity—an idea influentially theorized by a number of critics—through the many references to roses and their cultivation that appear throughout the novel. This preoccupation is focused by the disagreement between Inspector Cuff, the famed London detective, and the head gardener of Lady Verinder, who has called in Cuff to investigate the disappearance of the great Indian diamond, the Moonstone, a spoil of imperialism. Cuff claims that the non-native moss rose can be bred on its own, while the gardener contends that it requires being budded onto the indigenous dog rose for its cultivation. This controversy begins the novel's investigation of various forms of hybridity—the potentially propagative mingling of distinct human groups or their attributes, and especially of combinations in which conventional equations of power and value are destabilized. Through its many direct references to roses and through the subtextual presence of historical events current to the time in which it is set, the novel imagines hybridity in regard not only to imperialist subjection but also to more specific cultural arenas—constructions of race, ethnicity, gender, and class—where imbalances of power create confusion about the combination of things generally believed fundamentally distinct and naturally incompatible. Particularly important are two of the novel's main characters, the multiculturalist Franklin Blake and his eventual friend, the racial hybrid Ezra Jennings. Associated with roses, these two characters hint at the notion, radical for its time, that various forms of mixing might ultimately prove more a boon to Britain than a threat. This is the chief implication of what the novel characterizes as "the battle of the roses."*

Dickens Studies Annual, Volume 39, Copyright © 2008 by AMS Press, Inc. All rights reserved.

I

One of the most memorable characters in Wilkie Collins's novel *The Moonstone: A Romance* (1868) is Sergeant Cuff, the famed London detective summoned to Lady Verinder's Yorkshire estate to look into the disappearance the Moonstone, the great diamond inherited by her daughter Rachel. Eccentric in manner and method, Cuff is notable for his love of roses, his keen comments about which punctuate his investigations. In particular, he engages in an ongoing dispute with the Verinders' head gardener about whether the moss rose can be bred on its own or requires being budded onto the dog rose for its cultivation; Cuff contends it can be grown independently. Surfacing a number of times, this recondite, seemingly incidental issue proves relevant to the major concerns of *The Moonstone*—although the novel fails to note that the moss rose, unlike the common dog rose, is not indigenous to Britain.[1] Knowledge of this background, however, along with that of the disputed horticultural relationship, focuses the novel's interest in cultural, ethnic, and racial hybridity. Although budding moss roses upon dog roses does not constitute actual interbreeding, it strongly suggests hybridity in this broader sense while connecting it to the theme of imperialism and its effects.

Through the mystery of the Moonstone, an illicit spoil of war removed from India to England years before, Cuff and his investigation reflect the influence of colonialism on Britain. Although he fails to solve the mystery on his own and retires from the action throughout much of the second half of the novel, Cuff and the subject of roses—a topic about which Collins likely possessed considerable firsthand knowledge—become significant elements in working out the novel's stance on imperialism.[2] Like *Heart of Darkness*, *The Moonstone* recognizes imperialist depredations. Unlike Conrad's novella, however, it hints that the influence of imperialism on the home country, properly channeled, might mitigate the combination of jingoism, racism, and greed that enables its abuses. This hopeful possibility fits with the happy ending enjoyed by the protagonists, but Collins's novel tempers this optimism and challenges its self-asserted status as a romance by also suggesting that Britain's career as an imperial power, beset by real-world political and economic contingencies, might be short-lived. *The Moonstone* expresses the potential of dangerous factors connected with colonies to infiltrate, intermix with, and subvert the imperial center, developing this anxiety in regard to other types of problematic mixing involving nation, class, gender, and race—permutations hinted at by roses and hybridity. The novel, however, is concerned not only with foreign threats, but with internal vices such as greed and intolerance that contribute to imperialist excesses in the first place. Overall, reciprocities between metropolis and empire encourage various

forms of mixing, and whether they will prove good or bad the novel leaves
to futurity. Still, going against popular sentiment, it radically imagines comprehensive hybridity as a form of progress.

Similarly, in recent years postcolonial theory has celebrated "hybridity"
as a vital form of cultural amalgamation produced by mingled diversities and
notably evidenced in authors from former colonies who invigorate colonial
languages and literatures with the traditional cultural and linguistic resources
of their homelands. In regard to colonial discourse, however, the term has
also been theorized as an unstable form of doubleness that occurs when
the dominance of one group is asserted but also undermined, indirectly but
necessarily, as the conceived otherness of the subjugated subverts the dominant discourse. Such is the influential position of Homi Bhabha, although it
derives ultimately from Mikhail Bakhtin, whose theory of dialogic imagination identifies the mutual interaction of centripetal and centrifugal linguistic
forces as a process of hybridity defined as "an *encounter*, within the arena
of an utterance, between two different linguistic consciousnesses" (358).
Expanding on Bakhtin's idea, Bhabha asserts that in such an encounter colonialist epistemology betrays implicit knowledge of and susceptibility to
counter-counsciousness, thus revealing a hybridity that "reverses the effects
of colonialist disavowal, so that other 'denied' knowledges enter upon the
dominant discourse and estrange the basis of its authority—its rules of recognition." But Bhabha also understands hybridity as part of a circular dynamic
in which it not only reverses the process of disavowal but is the product
of such:

> Produced through the strategy of disavowal, the *reference* of discrimination is
> always to a process of splitting as the condition of subjection: a discrimination
> between the mother culture and its bastards, the self and its doubles, where the
> trace of what is disavowed is not repressed but repeated as something *differ-
> ent*—a mutation, a hybrid. It is such a partial and double force that . . . disturbs
> the visibility of the colonial presence and makes the recognition of its author-
> ity problematic.

The "colonial hybrid," Bhabha contends, "is the articulation of the ambivalent space where the rite of power is enacted on the site of desire" (162,
159, 160).

Also positing forms of ambivalence and desire, Robert J. C. Young has returned hybridity to its nineteenth-century context in which its original biological focus was extended to anxieties about the sexual combining of races—a
subject that greatly interested Collins.[3] According to Young, these anxieties
were complicated by ambivalent desire for the very objects of racist denigration: "theories of race in the nineteenth century, by settling on the possibility
or impossibility of hybridity, focused explicitly on the issue of sexuality and

the issue of sexual unions between whites and blacks. Theories of race were thus also covert theories of desire.'' According to Young, ''anxiety about hybridity reflected the desire to keep races separate, which meant that attention was immediately focused on the mixed race offspring that resulted from interracial sexual intercourse, the proliferating . . . legacies that abrupt, casual, often coerced, unions had left behind'' (9, 25).

For the purposes of this essay, *hybridity* means a potentially propagative mingling of distinct human groups or their attributes, and especially of combinations in which conventional equations of power and value are destabilized. This occurs when the foreign and devalued interfuses the domestic and privileged, threatening to dilute its perceived virtues or, just possibly, increase its actual worth. The elements stressed by contemporary theorizations of hybridity—ambivalence, dialogism, and desire—are, in various ways, part of the response of *The Moonstone* to imperialism and to other cultural arenas in which imbalances of power create confusion about the combination of things generally believed fundamentally distinct and naturally incompatible.[4] Particularly in the later stages of the novel these elements build upon the subject, introduced early on, of Inspector Cuff's passion for roses, an enthusiasm he expresses even when he hums his favorite tune, ''The Last Rose of Autumn.'' Although the novel itself seems ambivalent about important issues that it only obliquely engages, obscuring its ideological underpinnings, its polemical inclinations emerge nonetheless. *The Moonstone* not only critiques imperialism and acknowledges its perils, but recognizes widespread cultural, ethnic, and even racial mixing as disturbing but not inevitably destructive for Britain; potentially, and in the long run, it may prove quite the reverse. This is the chief implication of the novel's interest in roses and their cultivation, a concern that offers both a key for understanding the text's various enactments of hybridity and a corrective to some recent critical trends.[5]

II

The subject of roses first unobtrusively arises when Franklin Blake—Rachel Verinder's cousin, childhood playmate, and soon-to-be suitor—after long absence returns to England from the Continent where he had been educated in several different countries. Blake brings with him the Moonstone, a bequest to Rachel from his and her recently deceased uncle, Colonel John Herncastle; as a young man Herncastle had stolen it from Tipoo Sultan's palace during the 1799 British victory at Seringapatam in India. Upon arriving at the Verinder estate Blake seeks out the elderly steward, his old friend Gabriel Betteredge, whose narration comprises the first half of the novel. He finds Betteredge consoling a depressed, guilt-afflicted housemaid whom the widowed Lady Verinder had employed in an act of philanthropy, trying to redeem the young woman from her former life of poverty and crime in London. The maid's name is Rosanna Spearman, and Blake is wearing a rose in his buttonhole.

The maid's first name and Blake's rose indicate a connection that begins by her falling in love with him on first sight. Later, another servant discovers Rosanna at Blake's "dressing-table, secretly removing a rose which Miss Rachel had given him to wear in his button-hole, and putting another rose like it, of her own picking, in its place" (69–70); both roses no doubt come from the Verinders' elaborate rose garden. The dressing table incident is hushed up, but this exercise in symbolic wish fulfillment expresses the tragedy of the maid's infatuation with Blake, who is nearly oblivious to her existence. Her unrequited love across class barriers ends in suicide—committed in the horrible, all-engulfing quicksand of a place known as the Shivering Sand. Before this self-destruction, however, she protects Blake from suspicion, again without his awareness, after he unknowingly takes the Moonstone in a drugged stupor and inadvertently transmits it to Rachel's other cousin and fellow suitor, the hypocritical do-gooder Godfrey Ablewhite. This linkage between Blake, Rosanna, and the rose will take on further significance in light of Sergeant Cuff's love for that flower.

Almost immediately upon his arrival at the Verinder estate, Cuff veers off to admire the rose garden but chafes the head gardener about its paths: "Grass, Mr. Gardener—grass walks between your roses; gravel's too hard for them. That's a pretty bed of white roses and blush roses." Roses in his view are feminine; they are delicate, genteel, and innocent (white and blushing) and thus in need of protection. He continues in that vein: " 'Here's a white musk rose, Mr. Betteredge—our old English rose holding up its head along with the best and the newest of them. Pretty dear!' says the Sergeant, fondling the Musk Rose with his lanky fingers, and speaking to it as if he was speaking to a child" (107). The detective's solicitude toward the domestic rose and his interest in different sorts of roses feed into a complex of associations concerning, among other things, the relationship of Britain to various far-off areas of the world where imports originate. Of central concern is his position, expressed later, about whether white moss roses can be bred successfully on their own or require dog roses. Betteredge reports Cuff's disagreement with the gardener on this subject: "As far as I could understand it, the question between them was, whether the white moss rose did, or did not, require to be budded on the dog rose to make it grow well" (145).

The ongoing controversy about the relationship between the indigenous dog rose and the moss rose concerns the novel's interest in the problematic mixing of the domestic and foreign. Victorian authorities agreed that the origin of the moss rose was mysterious but could perhaps be traced to Provence and, furthermore, that the flower occasionally arose in Britain as bud mutations—what Victorians called "sports"—on the Provence rose. In and of themselves, the dog and moss roses bear little relevance to the action of the novel; Victorian gardeners simply prized the moss rose for qualities that made it generally more desirable than the commonplace dog rose. Within the symbolic economy of the novel, however, the implications are different. Here the moss rose is the outsider, mysteriously appearing and threatening to intermix with and perhaps displace domestic varieties. Cuff's desire to grow it independently, whatever his actual motivation, relates to cultural concerns about the mingling of human physical and cultural differences. Like the "old English rose" that Cuff personifies as a pretty girl, the dog rose, required by the Verinders' gardener, assumes overtones of domestic virtue, an integrity associated with the common touch that the family retains despite its wealth and status. That the moss rose in question is white, a development from earlier colored varieties, carries several implications: variability and entanglement within and between races, ameliorationist desire—the white man's burden—to improve foreign races, and the potential worth of the alien once it is assimilated enough that familiarity obscures foreignness. These understandings become particularly important once Ezra Jennings, the biracial assistant to the Verinders' physician Dr. Candy, appears as a central character.

The novel develops the foregoing points into several themes, including the reactionary protection of national and class self-identity and the confusions that arise from cultural and racial mixing in a society that, by acquiring an empire, had opened itself up to nontraditional and sometimes unwelcome external influences. Class hybridity and that of gender—women abandoning traditional feminine traits and activities in favor of supposedly masculine ones—are related matters likewise concerning the displacements of a rapidly changing society. The subject of roses will hint at another theme as well: the possible virtue, for the nation and its people, of racial or ethnic hybridism.

Hybridity on the national level perhaps relates to the special significance of the dog rose for England. When, through war and marriage, Henry Tudor ended the War of the Roses between the houses of York and Lancaster, becoming Henry VII, he emblematized the new union by merging the White Rose of York and the Red Rose of Lancaster into the Tudor Rose, a heraldic hybrid based upon the dog rose, a common wildflower of varied colors. The dog rose therefore might intimate a traditional England, whole and unified, with de-emphasis of the actual conflictive forces and factors, including diverse ethnic, religious, and economic groups, that through the centuries had to be brought together to create that ideal but as yet were only imperfectly joined. Cuff reinforces the idea of national solidarity through his praise of the old English musk rose and his desire not to mingle the dog rose with an alien variety that, he feels, an English gardener should be able to foster or master without resorting to such mixing—a process that later in the novel he claims to have accomplished. Betteredge calls Cuff's debate with the gardener ''the battle of the roses'' (186), with Cuff fighting for one side rather than seeking a merger indicative of a potentially new, more comprehensive Britain, a nation embracing rather than dominating other lands and cultures while healing internal divisions as well.

Cuff's professional life fits with his symbolic support of conservative England implied by his attitudes toward roses. He tries to help an aristocratic family escape from the difficulties of a foreign invasion of sorts; Betteredge perceives ''our quiet English home suddenly invaded by a devilish Indian Diamond'' (46) and early on fears the potential for further violation posed by the three disguised Brahmins who had come to England to recover the diamond. Futhermore, Cuff respects the need to keep the matter private, saving his high-born clients from scandal. ''Don't be alarmed! I have put the muzzle on worse family difficulties than this,'' he reassures Betteredge (141). Part of his career had involved representing the interests of the well-to-do, as he explains in stating his belief that Rachel engineered the disappearance of the stone to pay off debts; he says he had dealt with many other young, upper-class girls who had overspent on credit and then secretly sold or pawned valuables to meet their obligations (172, 173). Cuff's vocational connection with the traditional upper class fits with his avocational preoccupation with rose cultivation. He fondly anticipates retiring from detective work and dedicating himself to this pastime once pursued primarily by his social betters.

III

Despite all that is impressive about Cuff—and he gets much right before his services are temporarily suspended, such as predicting unlikely events that subsequently occur—his passion for roses represents a retreat from the outside world and, consistent with the realm of a self-styled romance, from overt reference to the dominant and often harsh social, economic, and political realities of 1848–49 when the novel is set. These relate the subject of roses and their cultivation to matters of political and cultural history. One of the harsh underlying realities troubling the text's veneer of romance is the Irish Potato Famine. Toward the end of *The Moonstone* Cuff's expertise again is required, but at first he is unavailable because he is in Ireland where ''[s]ome great man's gardener . . . has found out something new in the growing of roses—and Mr. Cuff's away to inquire into it'' (360). But this inquiry seems trivial in comparison to what was actually happening in Ireland at precisely the time of Cuff's fictional visit. Between 1846 and 1850 over a million people died from starvation and related conditions, and a like number were forced to immigrate under horrid circumstances. Some of the great estates, the vast bulk of them owned by the Anglo-Irish whose English ancestors had taken over most of the country, forced impoverished tenants from their lands. The famine occasionally provoked revolts by desperate peasants, and these insurrections sometimes were brutally put down by local governments. In general, the British government's attempts to allay the famine were delayed and poorly managed.

Although the "great man" is not identified, he is almost certainly an Anglo-Irish owner of a great estate, quite possibly an absentee landlord living in England. And whether he deals well or ill with his Irish tenants during the famine, the allusion to him is necessarily tainted by the widespread perception, particularly among liberals like Wilkie Collins, that the British government and the Anglo-Irish were culpable, not only in either ignoring or responding inadequately to the devastation, but in contributing to the causes of the famine in the first place. For Cuff to be visiting Ireland at such a time, attending to the parochial and, in context, frivolous matter of roses, makes him indirectly representative of the values of an entrenched English upper class and indirectly of imperialism such as that the English long had practiced upon the Irish. The year 1848 also witnessed revolution in Europe as republican and radical forces threatened to bring down old regimes, in part as a response to poor harvests and widespread hunger on the Continent. The remainder of this essay will further discuss the relevant historical context of the novel, relate that to varieties of cultural hybridity represented in the persons and actions of various characters, and then return specifically to the subject of roses, especially in regard to the racial hybrid, Ezra Jennings.

The shadows of history that mark the text—various traces of suffering and disorder—take on greater substance in connection to the prologue about the Siege of Seringapatam, the novel's one overt reference to an historical event. In their lust for booty, the troops of the East India Company run amok in sacking Tipoo's palace, while John Herncastle murders, steals, and lies to secure the Moonstone. These piratical actions form an inverted reflection of rioting Irish peasants, oppressed and desperate, while the British troops, driven by greed instead of injustice and hunger, play a role analogous to that of rack-renting landlords or to the moral chaos of an imperial power reaping profits through the subjugation of foreign lands. The fabled curse attached to the Moonstone in fact prophesies an empire cursed by the internal consequences of its external excesses, much as the characters of the novel are afflicted by the arrival of the gem, which leaves the Verinder family in shambles, haunted by suspicions and doubts.

These consequences are further presaged by the failed Indian Mutiny of 1853 and its aftermath, memory of which was fresh and still alarming in the minds of Collins and his readers when the novel was written and published.

Indeed, several critics have explored the connection between revolt and novel.[6] The native insurrection, prompted by the misrule of the East India Company and by Christian missionaries' denigration of native religions, appalled the British and caused many to support harsh reprisals against the mutineers. Some citizens, however, were equally appalled by the viciousness of their soldiers' responses, while recognizing the mistreatment of Indians that had contributed to the revolt. Both the depicted Siege of Seringapatam and the background presence of the Mutiny resonate with social and political disruptions contemporary to the action of the novel. The Irish famine, along with Continental hunger and attempted revolts, goes unmentioned, but the subtextual presence of such important events, viewed in relation to the overt transgressions recounted in the prologue, inflects the novel with anxiety about the integrity, in both senses of the word, of the British homeland. This latent fear is not only of forces associated with colonies that might corrupt or spill back into the metropolis, but of dangers arising from those internal foreigners, the impoverished and crime-prone masses of the lower classes. Here again, actual history impinges on the novel.

Social disruptions were occurring not only in Ireland and on the Continent but in England as well, particularly in relation to Chartism, the movement representing lower-class workers that over the course of a decade unsuccessfully pressed Parliament for democratic reforms, including universal manhood suffrage and the secret ballot. Although the government rejected its requests and a series of uprisings and strikes in the late 1830s and early 1840s were unproductive, Chartism and the dissatisfactions it crystallized continued to exert an unsettling influence up until the time the *Moonstone* is set. General agitation for reform and relatively minor but alarming disturbances of the peace contextualize the outburst, a snatch of overheard conversation, of a local MP at Lady Verinder's dinner on the night of the Moonstone's theft: ''our county member, growing hot . . . about the spread of democracy in England, burst out as follows: 'If we once lose our ancient safeguards . . . what have we got?' '' (80–81). One safeguard had just disappeared with the repeal of the Corn Laws in 1847; no longer would protective tariffs discourage the importation of foreign grain, keeping prices artificially high in Britain, enriching the land-owning aristocracy and gentry and harming the poor who had to pay the price of protectionism. Universal male suffrage, were it allowed, would destroy another safeguard, threatening the affluent and the few by allowing—in another version of dangerous mixing—the infiltration of government, and perhaps much else, by the poor and the many.

To this group belongs the maid Rosanna. She is not directly connected to foreign or domestic political upheavals, but she nevertheless, looked at from a conservative mid-nineteenth-century perspective, points to insidious forms of social hybridism. Although supposedly reformed, she remains representative of the urban criminal class, and after the disappearance of the Moonstone she is suspected of committing the theft or, in Cuff's view, of being an accomplice in Rachel's removal of the jewel. It would seem she has no right to mix with the upper class, and especially so since her behavior, after falling in love with Blake, violates the deference expected of her. Betteredge and his daughter Penelope feel compassion for her, but they also note, in pushing herself onto Blake's attention, behavior inappropriate in a servant: "It's quite monstrous that she should forget herself and her station in that way," Penelope allows (153). Her effrontery in not only loving a gentleman but actually pursuing him constitutes a violation of both gender and class conventions. And that she is homely and has a deformed shoulder emphasizes the impropriety of her behavior. Although named Rosanna, her qualities contradict those of Cuff's personified rose as a compilation of idealized feminine qualities—beauty, delicateness, modesty, weakness. Her last name, Spearman, with its suggestion of masculine aggression, or perhaps of a rose with thorns, captures her transgression of both sexual and class boundaries, an attempt by an inferior to force herself where she does not belong.

The most notable and, seen in a negative light, unwarranted of Rosanna's qualities is the right she proudly and desperately claims, despite guilt over her former life of crime, to love whom she pleases regardless of class obstacles and the unlikelihood of being reciprocated. Her assertion of self-worth in this regard appears everywhere in the long letter (17 pages in the 1998 Penguin edition) to Franklin Blake, recovered after her death. The letter mixes overt dignity and implicit pathos in expressing, not so much her love, but the circumstances surrounding her love so that Blake perhaps will afford her respectful acknowledgment once she is dead; her explanations include her central action of hiding his nightdress, marked on the night of the theft with the wet paint he and Rachel had used to decorate the inside of her door. Furthermore, Rosanna challenges the ideology of inherent class difference—specifically, the notion of aristocratic breeding stemming from both heredity and environment—by suggesting that the differences between herself and Rachel are relative and contingent: "Suppose you put Miss Rachel in a servant's dress, and took her ornaments off—?" she speculates (318). Finally, support for Rosanna's unsettling of classist assumptions appears in Betteredge's comment that "there was just a dash of something that wasn't like a housemaid, and that *was* like a lady, about her" (35)—this idea is supported by the quality of her letter and Lucy's notice of Rosanna's good education, apparently received before circumstances made her mother into a streetwalker and her daughter became (with shades of *Oliver Twist*) "apprenticed" to a life of crime (191, 317, 330). Acknowledging that chance shapes status, the novel offers Rosanna sympathy and respect.

It does the same for her friend, callously nicknamed "Limping Lucy" because of her crippled leg. As with Rosanna, the novel extenuates the rebellious resentment of one victimized by socially mandated class and gender identities, but it does so in even stronger terms. Anguished by the fate of Rosanna, whom she loved, Lucy prophesies to Betteredge that ''the day is not far off when the poor will rise against the rich,'' adding that ''I pray to Heaven they may begin with *him,* '' a reference to Blake, whom she blames for Rosanna's destruction (192). Her revolutionary sentiments seem all the more subversive because, by appealing to divine justice, she implies an apocalyptic social revolution sanctioned by the Christian God. Lucy strongly protests against social injustice in the name all of its victims, and her attitude no doubt would appall those who, like the outraged MP at Lady Verinder's dinner party, fear even the spread of democracy. Betteredge, however, is willing to listen. Lucy denounces a social order responsible for Rosanna's ''miserable life,'' and Betteredge refrains from reproving her; his habitual compassion for the poor and suffering appears all the more evident because, as usual, it first has to break through the conservative veneer he maintains as friend and servant of a great family. Tacitly acknowledging that the poor have good reason for dissatisfaction, Betterege observes of Lucy, ''I noticed her wretchedness . . . and wretchedness is not uncommonly insolent, you will find, in humble life.'' She has been ''pushed too far,'' he says (191, 190).

Lucy concentrates her anger over social injustice upon Franklin Blake, whom she holds accountable for Rosanna's suicide and for ruining her and her friend's dream of living together in London with economic independence and without men. The confrontation between Lucy and Blake—he comes for Rosanna's note to him that will lead to the discovery of the incriminating letter and the stained nightdress—dramatizes Lucy's disdain for class distinctions. When Betteredge informs Blake of who has the note, Blake responds, ''The fisherman's daughter?'' The steward tells him that ''Limping Lucy has a will of her own, sir. She wouldn't give it into any hands but yours'' (306). She expresses this willfulness, along with her strength and independence, by treating him, a gentleman, with contempt. In introducing Blake, Betteredge tries to impress proper class attitudes: '' 'This gentleman's name . . . ' (with strong emphasis on *gentleman*), 'is Mr. Franklin Blake' '' (308). But she makes Blake stand still while she scrutinizes his face ''with abhorrence and disgust.'' Blake admits that ''no woman [ever before] had let me perceive'' such an opinion. Then, after he asks about the letter, she forces him to repeat his inquiry verbatim, making him feel ''like a good child learning its lessons'' while she continues to glower (308, 309). Lucy's behavior mixes up—hybridizes—normal class and gender valuations; like Rosanna, she ''forgets her place,'' and Blake is cowed by a fisherman's daughter.

Physically deformed and homely, Rosanna and Lucy represent the social handicaps of being poor and female. Yet they claim the right, however tenuously, to confront their superiors on the basis of equality while adumbrating aspects of the racial and cultural hybridism that later in the novel become associated with Ezra Jennings. In their different ways these characters are harbingers of a better England, albeit a sketchily imagined one, as are the members of the Verinder family: Lady Verinder; her daughter, Rachel; her nephew, Franklin Blake, attached to them by mutual affection; Gabriel Betteredge and his daughter Penelope, who live with the family as friends as well as servants; and their admiring lawyer, Mr. Bruff, who long has watched over their interests. Many critics have followed the lead of John R. Reed in arguing that *The Moonstone* indicts British society for vices such as greed, hypocrisy, racism, and exploitation; however, when pushed too far that position readily distorts the character of a novel rife with ambivalence and, in particular, ignores a great deal of countervailing evidence concerning the Verinders. Although necessarily implicated in the social order from which it benefits, the Verinder circle nevertheless adduces the possibility for Britain of keener moral insight and a more comprehensive outlook concerning outcasts within and without. Ironically, it is the Moonstone, the evil fruit of empire, that heralds this revision. But the rose, a less apparent source of symbolic resonance, also conveys this vision of change and does so more meaningfully.

IV

Providing roses for Rachel, Rosanna, and Blake and mixing domestic with foreign varieties, the Verinders' elaborate garden, aristocratic perk though it be, underscores the inclusiveness of the family and the mere possibility of a like quality for all of Britain—and the garden's connection with virtue is only enhanced by the fact that it is the place where Rachel rejects Ablewhite's marriage proposal (75). Lady Verinder knowingly takes on a former professional thief as a housemaid, and old-time servants are close and trusted friends of the family. Furthermore, the strength of Lady Verinder and her daughter entails a mingling of gender ideals. Capably running an estate without a husband, Lady Verinder is respected by everyone, including Sergeant Cuff, who finds her his match in resourcefulness and force of personality. Meanwhile Rachel—whom both Betteredge and Bruff, despite their conservative leanings, celebrate for her independent mind—resolutely refuses to divulge what she knows about the disappearance of the Moonstone, as well as her reasons for rejecting Blake. Mother and daughter mirror aspects of Rosanna and Lucy, who, despite low social status, likewise are females who combine strong and purposeful natures with a great capacity for love. Lady Verinder displays both heart and discernment in dismissing Cuff's belief that Rachel and Rosanna are responsible for the theft, and Rachel continues to love Blake even after rejecting him for his apparent thievery. The Verinder women combine the love traditionally associated with roses with, more specifically, the strength of the common, wild-growing dog rose ennobled by Henry Tudor.

The inclusiveness, as well as the humanity of the Verinders, appears in other ways, but especially in regard to Franklin Blake, the dominant character of the novel.[7] Considered in terms of the romance structure of *The Moonstone*, the Verinders' fondness for Blake, their affinity for roses, and Rachel's gifts of roses to him (69–70, 318) hint at his eventual worthiness to marry her, a worthiness highlighted by his reformation from his earlier youthful career of womanizing and improvidence. And, like the Verinders, the rose-wearing Blake also is notable for open-mindedness. His close terms with Betteredge and his daughter and his admiration for the independent Rachel and Lady Verinder establish his own relative independence in thinking about class and gender, and he is similarly unconstrained in his attitudes toward foreign lands and peoples. He had been educated in several different European countries, which, according to Betteredge, explains the changeability he detects in Blake's attitudes and actions. Recognizing this cultural fluidity in his friend's character, Betteredge predicts that Blake, following his rejection by Rachel, will set off on journeys around the world, and indeed the next we hear of his whereabouts he is ''wandering in the East'' (194, 296). Like others of the Verinder circle, he is presented as the opposite of provincial and hidebound.

The worst that can be said about Blake's behavior is that he is largely indifferent to Rosanna when she tries to get his attention, although at the time he is preoccupied with his love for Rachel, her inexplicable rejection of him, and the disappearance of the Moonstone. A number of critics, however, have cast Blake in a negative or at least morally equivocal role by interpreting his taking of the jewel as commentary—generally feminist, postcolonial, psychoanalytic, or some combination thereof—about sexual and imperialist transgressions committed by males and Europeans. Indeed, various factors imply a symbolic deflowering, consensual or not: Blake's secret visit to Rachel's rooms late at night, Rosanna's initial suspicion of a sexual motive (321), the stealing of a jewel associated with the moon and its cycles (11) and hence with female sexuality, the stained nightgown, Rachel's unwillingness to tell what has occurred, and her unexplained unhappiness with Blake. A related group of connections suggests the openness of colonies to despoliation and the absorption of their resources into British or European economies: the unlocked Indian cabinet, a valuable taken from it by an Englishman related to its original English despoiler, and Ablewhite's intention to have it taken to the Continent, cut into smaller stones, and sold piecemeal. Rachel fits as victim into this imperialist pattern because she bears a name suggestive of India (Verinder—''true Indian'') and because her complexion is dark, part of a complex of symbolic references to skin color (158, 64).[8]

But the multiculturalist Blake does not readily fit the role of either sexual or colonial predator. An overall estimation of his character does not associate him with imperialist offenses any more than these seem directly attributable to the rest of the Verinder group. His motivation in unconsciously taking the jewel concerns his desire to keep it safe for Rachel's sake (423, 424)—not an unreasonable impulse since he is responsible for bringing it, knows of Herncastle's possibly nefarious motives in leaving it to her, has heard the explorer Murthwaite speak of the dangers associated with it, and is aware that the three Indians are nearby and not what they seem (53, 78, 83). It is true that Blake and the Verinders, like the other English characters, show little concern about the injustice involved in possessing a spoil of British imperialism (though already a spoil of the imperialistic Moguls); the onus falls entirely upon Herncastle, not upon those who received the jewel from him. Here the novel's pervasive ambivalence implicates even its open-minded protagonists, along with the rest of Victorian society, in the evil of imperialism; morally they are something like people today who buy wooden furniture without considering its possible origin in the clear-cutting of tropical forests. But Blake, whose "wandering in the East" makes him appear as receptive to Oriental as to European cultures, should not be singled out as bearer of transgressive guilt. His association with the East, in fact, links him to his dark-skinned and suggestively named love interest, counteracting the notion that his actions place him, more than any other unreflective consumer of colonial products, in a negative light. And if one wishes to interpret his unconscious actions in regard to sexuality, then they need not mean any more than what a man in his position naturally would feel about a highly desirable young woman. The symbolic overtones of his taking the diamond, while compelling, should not obscure the novel's endorsement of Blake's character.

It also should be noted that Blake solicited and compiled the individual accounts that make up the novel, urging each participant to tell truthfully what he or she had seen and heard, even though part of that collective narrative undoubtedly would reflect poorly on him. He shows himself committed to truth and, again, receptive to varied understandings. But perhaps what speaks most highly of Blake is his friendship with Jennings. Often neglected in *Moonstone* criticism, their relationship points back to the subject of roses and then to the novel's attitude toward the various forms of hybridism it represents.

V

Late in the novel the now retired Cuff sends word that he has proved his point, triumphing over the Verinders' gardener by propagating the moss rose without first budding it onto the dog rose (304). Accomplished within a garden surrounded by a wall and hedge (360), this feat indicates that the domestic and the foreign have not been allowed to merge in a way that dilutes Englishness; the domestic space of the enclosed garden has, in effect, kept out foreign threats to the solid English virtues often associated with cottages, at least the tidy cottages of successful bourgeois types like Cuff. Similarly, the wall sets a boundary to incorporated foreign influences, constraining them to acceptable British usages. By the time we learn of Cuff's horticultural triumph, however, we already have met Ezra Jennings, the novel's most important experiment in hybridity and a response to the significations that the relationship between dog and moss rose introduces.

The novel's first reference to the doctor's assistant is brief; he is mentioned, and Betteredge then remarks that "nobody knew much about him in our parts. . . . and, right or wrong, we none of us liked him or trusted him" (155). The "right or wrong" concedes that the dislike is not well founded, being based upon his status as an outsider with a mysterious past and, most of all, on his extraordinary looks. Of Jennings's sudden and dramatic first appearance in the novel, Blake says, "The door opened, and there entered to us, quietly, the most remarkable-looking man that I had ever seen." His remarkableness includes "a complexion . . . of gypsy darkness," a multitude of "marks and wrinkles" despite his relatively young age, and his astonishing hair:

> Over the top of his head it was still of the deep black which was its natural colour. Round the sides of his head—without the slightest graduation of grey to break the force of the extraordinary contrast—it had turned completely white. The line between the two colors preserved no sort of regularity. At one place, the white hair ran up into the black; at another, the black hair ran down into the white.   (326)

Betteredge relates that the locals are so adverse to Jennings, whose "appearance is against him" and who supposedly was hired "with a very doubtful character," that only the poor will avail themselves of his services; however, Jennings serves these patients with dedication (327). Later Jennings tells Blake something of his background, including his mixed parentage: "I was born, and partly brought up, in one of our colonies. My father was an Englishman; but my mother—." He leaves the statement unfinished, but Blake remarks that "there was the mixture of some foreign race in his English blood" (371). He also tells Blake of a "horrible accusation" that had separated him from the woman he loved, pursued him everywhere he went, and blighted his life (379).

Because its nature is left unspecified, this unjust accusation readily attaches itself to the matter of his appearance and origins, which quite possibly motivated the "vile slander that struck [him] down at once and forever" and that, occurring at "the outset of [his] career" in England, caused his "own family" to subject him "to merciless treatment" (379). The family was likely that of his English relatives, their antipathy generated by an appearance disfigured by signs of extreme foreignness and by knowledge that their blood had been mixed with that of a dark-skinned colonial subject. In fact, he is described in such a way as not only to suggest but to signify miscegenation. His appearance might have seemed foreign enough had it simply merged black and white, but Jennings's hair holds the two aspects apart, thereby emphasizing a separateness so great that their conjoining appears unnatural in the extreme. Furthermore, the lack of "regularity" in the line separating white hair from black identifies Jennings's combination of racial components as chaotic—as, again, a threatening violation of the natural order. He appears so monstrous that—as with Frankenstein's creation, who by nature is as innocent and virtuous as Jennings and likewise suffers because of his appearance—a woman screams when she first sees him (416). Unlike the Frankenstein monster, however, persecution does not make him vicious, although it does etch his face with marks of suffering that make him more fearful as a racial abomination. Jennings's appearance is calculated to be especially distasteful to anybody fearful that "pure" English blood might become polluted by foreign racial elements.

The three factors that emerge from various postcolonial understandings of hybridity—ambivalence, dialogism, and desire—roughly describe the significance of Jennings revealed through his relationship with Blake. Cuff's concern about dog and moss roses had introduced these factors early on. The novel establishes ambivalence about the worth and relationship of the two varieties, especially as they relate to the Brahmins who arrive at Lady Verinder's estate to recover the Moonstone; Cuff's running argument with the head gardener, once it is recast in the connection between Blake and Jennings, produces meaning through dialogism; and the rose-lovers' wish to grow moss roses in the first place, a prizing of the nonindigenous, expresses desire. Ambivalence informs the relationship between, on the one hand, a commonplace English rose that nevertheless represents Englishness, and, on the other, a more highly valued outsider nevertheless lacking the hardiness of the native variety; it also describes the novel's attitude toward Indians, who are "murdering thieves" to Betteredge but "wonderful people" to Murthwaite, the famed explorer present at the dinner party on the night of the theft. Blake's initial ambivalence toward Jennings results from his bad reputation and the imputation of scandal and misbehavior; his being an alien; and, most of all, his appearance. Although initially he is anything but a prized outsider, he becomes such as his character gradually is revealed. And once Blake cultivates his friendship, their interactions become dialogic, not just because they reciprocate by sharing personal matters with one another, but because each grows stronger and happier through a friendship that begins because of Blake's desire directed toward this "other."

Indeed, Blake develops an immediate interest in Jennings that even in retrospect he cannot fully explain. He says that Jennings "had produced too

strong an impression on me to be immediately dismissed from my thoughts''
and refers to ''the impression produced on me by Ezra Jennings—it seemed
perfectly unaccountable, in such a situation [Betteredge has been reading
Rosanna's shocking letter to him] that any human being should have produced
an impression on me at all!'' (326, 328). He is unable to articulate what that
impression is. Later, he finds that almost unconsciously he has sketched from
memory ''a dozen portraits, at least, of the man with the piebald hair'' (361).
Perhaps Blake's sympathy is first enlisted because he senses that the other
man suffers from a severe illness and struggles with pain; his condition, we
learn, has caused him to become addicted to opium. What Blake sees most
clearly in Jennings, however, is an extremely unorthodox appearance coupled
with civility, sensitivity, and intelligence; in particular he refers to Jennings's
''unsought self-possession, which is a sure sign of good breeding, not in
England only, but everywhere else in the civilised world'' (370). Despite the
class consciousness and hint of condescension that underlie such an observation, he must recognize something not only out of the ordinary but potentially
helpful in Jennings—a wise and sympathetic professional who represents new
possibilities. Blake is in need of emotional as well as practical help: he has
been spurned by the woman he loves, has just lost his father, has learned that
Rosanna died through love for him after protecting him from the law, and
has received her posthumous testimony that, inexplicably, it was he who took
the diamond. But Jennings also might somehow help him discover the truth
about Rachel's aversion and the mystery of his own purported involvement
in the disappearance of the Moonstone. And Blake, himself something of a
cultural hybrid and a man uncommonly receptive to that which is foreign,
also appears attracted to the otherness of this man superficially so unlike
himself and yet giving hints of like-mindedness and reciprocated sympathy.
Therefore he says, ''it is not to be denied that Ezra Jennings made some
inscrutable appeal to my sympathies, which I found it impossible to resist''
(369).

   Attracted to this man marked as other, Blake's desire connects him to the
desire of Jennings's father for a dark-skinned woman—the ambivalent white
desire that, as Robert J. C. Young explains in a passage previously quoted,
informed ''theories of race in the nineteenth century [that], by settling on the
possibility or impossibility of hybridity, focused explicitly on the issue of
sexuality and the issue of sexual unions between whites and blacks.'' It is
even possible there is a sexual component in Blake's desire: while necessarily
aware that by race and social position he is dominant, he may also find
attractive that his new friend is one of those men ''born with female constitu-
tions,'' as Jennings says about his reticence and delicacy of temperament
(373). In any event, Blake needs what Jennings represents, and Jennings
needs Blake's sympathy and, as he later explains, vicarious involvement in

the belonging and happiness that seem Blake's by birthright (381); Rosanna, another outcast, possibly was attracted to Blake in part for much the same reason.

It is the learned, intelligent, and imaginative Jennings, bearing the stigmata of alien origins, who transcribes and reconstructs the meanings of Doctor Candy's delirious ramblings, uttered during his sickness and providing valuable clues, about the dinner party on the night of the theft. And it is Jennings who, by using this information, by applying various kinds of theoretical knowledge, and by staging the reenactment of that night, solves the main part of the mystery. In effect, he becomes the hero-detective, supplanting Cuff in that role even though Cuff becomes instrumental in uncovering Ablewhite's part in the affair. Jennings fully justifies Blake's mysterious interest in him, confirming the greatness of soul of a man whom, after Jennings's death, the partially recovered Dr. Candy describes as a virtual saint: "This was, as I think, a great man. . . . He bore a hard life bravely. He had the sweetest temper I have ever met with" (461). By solving the mystery of the Moonstone's disappearance from Rachel's room, by allowing Blake to recover her approval and eventually marry her, and by being embraced by the Verinder circle, Jennings, the thematic lynchpin of the novel, finds happiness, enables it in others, and makes a strong argument against prejudice. As Timothy L. Carens states, this "colonial hybrid kindles sympathy and compassion" and "counteracts the projection of criminal instincts and savage impulses onto racial others by guiding Blake toward a degree of self-knowledge" (257).

His admirable nature, however, has been apparent early in his relationship with Blake, revealing itself when the latter accompanies Jennings on a country walk while the doctor's assistant is on his way to treat the poor. At this time, they unfold their lives and concerns to one another. In particular, Jennings, with great delicacy, reveals that he knows something of the other's problems involving the Moonstone and offers to help—it would entail revealing the content of Candy's delirious utterances—if Blake can confide enough in him to justify the sharing of confidential information. Indirectly reintroducing the subject of roses, this excursion establishes that Jennings's hybridity has produced a mentally and morally superior individual, a potential boon to England rather than a threat of foreign corruption. But his virtue has gone unrewarded because of his alien appearance, the real issue behind an incident that Blake relates: "Jennings stopped for a moment, and picked some wild flowers from the hedge by the roadside. 'How beautiful they are!' he said simply, showing the nosegay to me. 'And how few people in England seem to admire them as they deserve!' " (371). The kinds of flowers are not identified, but because the novel has referred to roses scores of times already (the noun "rose" occurs around eighty times), and because the novel mentions no other variety of flower, a reader is justified in thinking of roses, and a rural English reader of dog roses especially. These are common hedge flowers, and their relatively short growing season occurs in late spring and early summer, when this scene is set. As already established, dog roses speak of Englishness, as do hedgerows. A perpetual outsider, Jennings wistfully calls attention to a commonplace sort of domestic beauty encompassing all that England had withheld from him. Later during the walk the two men sit down, and "Jennings laid aside his hat, and passed his hand wearily over his forehead, wearily through his startling white and black hair. He tossed his little nosegay of wild flowers away from him, as if the remembrances which it recalled were remembrances which hurt him now" (378). He has been reminded of the love he lost, probably because of his mixed racial heritage that the reference to his hair implies. Roses mean love—the erasure of barriers between people—or, in this case, the sadness when that cannot be accomplished, as entries in Jennings's journal seem to suggest.

At the beginning of the posthumous narrative "Extracted from the Journal of Ezra Jennings," the word "rose" appears twice as a verb but in a way that might indicate the flower as well if we take into account Jennings's associative thinking and the effects of opium: "June 16th.—Rose late, after a dreadful night; the vengeance of yesterday's opium, pursuing me through a series of frightful dreams. At one time, I was whirling through empty space with the phantoms of the dead. . . . At another, the one beloved face which I shall never see again, rose at my bedside" (397). Because the first "rose" lacks an explicit subject and the second is separated from its subject by a comma, both instances call attention to the word itself, making it possible to imagine it as a thing as well as an action in this novel full of roses. The association of that flower with love, both in general understanding and in *The Moonstone*, and with Jennings's lost love as suggested in the episode of the hedge flowers, makes this speculation plausible. And if that much is allowed, then the idea of a "rose [that is] late" can be seen to fit with the flowers thrown away by Jennings because they convey discarded hopes of belonging and of experiencing romantic fulfillment—a rose-like presence by his bedside—because it is too late for him. These interpretations recall Jenning's somewhat similar exercise in interpreting Candy's fragmented utterances.

In any event, roses suffuse the text as they do Cuff's garden. The subject appears one last time when, as narrated in his journal, Jennings and Rachel meet before the reenactment of the jewel's disappearance. Rachel greets him warmly because of the help he is giving, and she also expresses to him her love for Blake, a love she confesses she had never abandoned despite his apparent dishonesty and violation of her trust. Jennings brightens in the glow of her happiness, and when he tells her she need not worry about Blake's reciprocating her love, "[h]er face brightened." He reveals that Rachel, seeking further reassurance, "came a step nearer to me. Her fingers trifled nervously with a flower which I had picked in the [Verinders'] garden, and which

I had put into the button-hole of my coat'' (415). This flower recalls the
roses that Blake habitually wears in his buttonhole, as he does upon his first
appearance in the novel, and which both Rachel and the suggestively named
Rosanna provide him from the same garden. It is safe to assume that Jennings's flower is another rose, an emblem of love embracing Blake, the two
women, the whole Verinder group, and now Jennings as well. Ultimately, it
represents a potential for inclusiveness, the embracing of differences between
individuals, genders, classes, and races. It conveys a form of hybridity from
which all of Britain, and the entire world, could benefit. As for the most
disturbing aspect of hybridity for Victorians, that of racial mixing, the novel
shows that such merging, like that of many actual hybrids among plant and
animal varieties, might produce increased vigor rather than debility and degeneration if not stifled through fear and hatred: the much thwarted virtues
and ambitions of Jennings indicate as much. The novel's epilogue, however,
implies something else, not contrary but additional.

VI

In the epilogue, the explorer Murthwaite, having returned to the Orient and
disguised himself as a native, reports seeing the Moonstone, in an awe-
inspiring ceremony attended by multitudes, returned to the forehead of the
idol from which it had been stolen centuries before by the Moguls. The three
Indians have completed their mission after killing and taking the diamond
from Ablewhite, and although the novel often racially stereotypes them, they
nevertheless have demonstrated, along with murderousness, the virtues of
faithfulness, selflessness, intelligence, resourcefulness, courage, and determination. But such qualities in colonial subjects could make them a threat to
the Britain and its empire. Perhaps the Brahmans' visit to England presages
a much deadlier invasion, a dark consequence of imperialism something like
the secret importation of the Moonstone or the opium that had addicted both
Ezra Jennings and John Herncastle. At the time of the novel's publication
the British had recently experienced a serious threat to their world and self-
satisfaction in the form of revolt by native Indian troops, who had harbored
a deadly potential like that of the three Brahmins. Knowledgeable and open-
minded people like Wilkie Collins were aware that both the Mutiny and the
prevalence of opium had been enabled by British oppression. Hindu civilization had been conquered by the Mogul Empire, and its political descendants
in turn by Britain, a conquest figured in the novel's prologue by Herncastle's
theft of the Moonstone: perhaps aggrieved colonial subjects would become
the next conquerors.

   Although the epilogue, with its exotic setting and actions, supports the
subtitle, *A Romance*, that dimension of *The Moonstone* is undercut not only

by the representation of imperialism, but by oblique references elsewhere to problems closer to home such as the Irish Famine and political strife in England itself. Thus, its final sentences, provided by Murthwaite and referring to the circular travels of the Moonstone, convey not only romance but an ominous warning to the British about the real world: "So the years pass, and repeat each other, so the same events revolve in the cycles of time. What will be the next adventures of the Moonstone? Who can tell!" The future may not be fixed, but it is possible that native peoples will take from Britain more than just the Moonstone, or that domestic instability might be equally destructive. The reference to cycles of time offers a reminder that any nation's day in the sun, like an individual life, is fleeting relative to the vastness of time; nineteenth-century archeology and geology made this realization unavoidable for many people. Therefore the gloom of harsh reality figures in the end of the novel along with the gleam of romance, identifying *The Moonstone* as a generic hybrid, even if its elements sometimes clash, like the two aspects of Jennings's hair. Although Blake, Rachel, and their friends enjoy a happy ending, the epilogue alludes to the impersonal, all-engulfing supremacy of time, which is like the Shivering Sand where Rosanna takes her life or the effect of Cuff's continual humming of "The Last Rose of Autumn."

A diamond symbolizes the outlasting of time, but civilizations soon are undone, not just by external foes, but by the effects of internal corrosion through vices such as greed and hostility toward those perceived as different. Such corruption is like the flaw said to exist "in the very heart" of the Moonstone (50), a jewel that has spawned murder and strife. If a diamond is forever, then much better is the fleeting softness of a rose. Its organic beauty speaks of the human fragility that makes love and fidelity imperative. Seen this way—seen as representing, not separation between individuals and groups or a "battle of the roses" signifying ideological strife, but rather hybridity in the broadest sense—a rose is the better emblem for a people and for what might prolong their existence. Cuff is right in saying, "I think a rose much better worth looking at than a diamond" (179).

NOTES

1. English readers would have recognized the moss rose as one of their own.
2. Wilkie Collins's father, the well-known painter William Collins, kept a garden when his son was growing up and employed a gardener to tend it (Collins, *Memoirs* 1:29; 2:9).
3. In fiction and plays Collins treats these unions sympathetically and, in general, as potentially beneficial for those directly involved and for others. For relevant discussions, see articles by Nayder (" 'Blue' ") and by Audrey Fisch.

4. For discussion of the postmodern application of hybridity to *The Moonstone*, especially regarding gender and Collins's own life, see Heller, Afterword 363–65.
5. In the 1970s John Reed initiated the trend of focusing on the novel's moral relationship to the social structures underlying imperialism. For Reed, the novel reveals "England imperial depredations" and offers "a broad indictment of an entire way of life" (286, 288). While some critics followed his lead—for example, Lillian Nayder states that the novel carries out "ideology critique" ("Robinson" 216)—by the 1990s others were viewing *The Moonstone* as an endorsement of British imperialism, albeit a complex and indirect one. In this vein, Robert Crooks maintains that Collins's novel engages in "recoding western imperialism (or, more generally, legitimized oppression and exploitation) as a criminal assault upon western civilization" (226). Likewise, Jaya Mehta asserts that the novel "both re-inscribes and subverts imperialist constructs" but ultimately supports "a colonial strategy that displaces violence and theft onto the geographic and narrative periphery in order to preserve a central space for the pleasure of domestic romance" (645, 647). Ashish Roy makes a similar assessment (see n. 8 below). I would say that the novel impressively negotiates between, on the one hand, its veneer of romance and domestic reassurance and, on the other, its persistent, underlying criticism, available to attentive critics and readers, of imperialism and of racism. This is a necessarily conflicted and unstable doubleness stemming from Collins's own ambivalences but also from his need, as Nayder points out (" 'Blue' " 278), not to alienate a conventional readership. While Tamar Heller states that for Collins "the price of . . . popularity is self-suppression," a voluntary censorship of "radical Romanticism" ("Dead" 162, 159), it would be almost as correct to say that he suppresses his pursuit of conventional romance in favor of the revolutionary impulses he continually reveals. I believe Nayder is more accurate in her perception that the novel engages in a dialogic interrelationship between contrary tendencies ("Robinson" 213).
6. Ian Duncan argues that in *The Moonstone* the implicit presence of the Mutiny expresses a seemingly "demonic counter-imperialism" that unsettles "a conventional English domestic order" by intimating "the history-making vastness of a world economy"; thus, "the British themselves turn out to be the colonized subjects of empire at its global zenith" and victims of an historical process they cannot control (300, 319). For Duncan this disclosure of the real nature of "imperialist panic" neither expresses "an anti-imperialist sympathy for oppressed colonial peoples" nor "does it enthrone the imperialist subject-position" (300). Albert D. Pionke believes the novel "issues a challenge to earlier racist and imperialist responses to the rebellion" by disclosing the moral culpability of the English and by dignifying Indians (131–32). Ashish Roy, however, contends that the novel legitimizes British rule, in part through its "oblique appeal to the public memory of the Indian Sepoy Revolt," an appeal expressive of "a strong recuperative concern" (658). The novel does this by promoting a self-justifying myth of "internal resistance connoting a potential malevolence of the other" while co-opting "a desired otherness [that], while disabling the other whose possession it is, makes *The Moonstone* a prototypical imperialist text" (675, 676). For Jaya Mehta, the Siege of Seringapatam serves as stand-in for the Mutiny and

"shadow[s] the Mutiny's resistance to British rule while deflecting the hysteria surrounding it" (620), thereby allowing "displacement of violence and knowledge of violence" (620, 621).

7. Not only is Blake on the scene for most of the major actions in the novel, but he is the fictional editor of the narrative, it being his idea to combine reports from various sources so as to give the complete story.

8. For example, the villainous Geoffrey Ablewhite, with his allegorically ironic surname, dies while wearing blackface disguise, thus subverting the conventional equation between whiteness and rightness. His whiteness disguises moral darkness that releases his assumed blackness from its negative associations by emphasizing their superficiality.

WORKS CITED

Bakhtin, M. M. *The Dialogic Imagination.* Trans. Michael Holquist and Caryl Emerson. Ed. Michael Holquist. Austin: U of Texas P, 1981.

Bhabha, Homi K. *The Location of Culture.* London: Routledge, 2004.

Carens, Timothy L. "Outlandish English Subjects in *The Moonstone.*" *Reality's Dark Light: The Sensational Wilkie Collins.* Ed. Maria K. Bachman and Don Richard Cox. Tennessee Studies in Literature 41. Knoxville: U of Tennessee P, 2003. 239–65.

Collins, W. Wilkie. *Memoirs of the Life of William Collins, Esq., R.A.: With Selections from His Correspondence.* 2 vols. London: Longman, 1848.

———. *The Moonstone.* Ed. Sandra Kemp. London: Penguin, 1998.

Crooks, Robert. "Reopening the Mysteries: Colonialist Logic and Cultural Difference in *The Moonstone* and *The Horse Latitudes.*" *Literature Interpretation Theory* 4 (1993): 215–28.

Duncan, Ian. "*The Moonstone*, the Victorian Novel, and Imperialist Panic." *Modern Language Quarterly* 55 (1994): 297–319.

Fisch, Audrey. "Collins, Race, and Slavery." *Reality's Dark Light: The Sensational Wilkie Collins.* Ed. Maria K. Bachman and Don Richard Cox. Tennessee Studies in Literature 41. Knoxville: U of Tennessee P, 2003. 313–28.

Heller, Tamar. Afterword: "*Masterpiece Theatre* and Ezra Jennings's Hair: Some Reflections on Where We've Been and Where We're Going in Collins Studies." *Reality's Dark Light: The Sensational Wilkie Collins.* Ed. Maria K. Bachman and Don Richard Cox. Tennessee Studies in Literature 41. Knoxville: U of Tennessee P, 2003. 361–70.

————. *Dead Secrets: Wilkie Collins and the Female Gothic.* New Haven: Yale UP, 1992.

Mehta, Jaya. "English Romance; Indian Violence." *The Centennial Review* 39 (1995): 611–57.

Nayder, Lillian. " 'Blue Like Me': Collins, *Poor Miss Finch*, and the Construction of Racial Identity." *Reality's Dark Light: The Sensational Wilkie Collins.* Ed. Maria K. Bachman and Don Richard Cox. Tennessee Studies in Literature 41. Knoxville: U of Tennessee P, 2003. 266–82.

————. "Robinson Crusoe and Friday in Victorian Britain: 'Discipline,' 'Dialogue,' and Collins's Critique of Empire in *The Moonstone*." *Dickens Studies Annual* 21 (1992): 213–31.

Pionke, Albert D. "Secreting Rebellion: From the Mutiny to the Moonstone." *Victorians Institute Journal* 28 (2000): 109–40.

Reed, John R. "English Imperialism and the Unacknowledged Crime of *The Moonstone*." *Clio* 2 (1973): 281–90.

Roy, Ashish. "The Fabulous Imperialist Semiotic of Wilkie Collins's *The Moonstone*." *New Literary History* 24 (1993): 657–81.

Young, Robert J. C. *Colonial Desire: Hybridity in Theory, Culture and Race.* London: Routledge, 1995.

Dickens and Gender:
Recent Studies, 1992–2007

Natalie B. Cole

This review essay of gender in Dickens studies, 1992–2007, surveys ten books and over 100 book chapters and journal essays, aiming to give the reader a sense of the range, richness, and complexity of work done by scholars on this subject. Defining gender *as "the social process of dividing people and social practices along* sexed *identities. . . . creating hierarchies between the divisions it enacts" (Beasley 11), the essay is divided into eight sections: Review Essays; Monographs; Biography; Sexualities; Masculinities; Femininities; Cultural Studies; and Gender and Narrative. The essay begins with a brief consideration of how Dickens began to imagine classes and genders different from his own early in his career in* Sketches by Boz *and links this to recent historical novelists' reconstructions of gender and how such reconstructions may play a part in shaping the literary criticism of contemporary scholars.*

I.

> "We saw the prison, and saw the prisoners; and what we did see, and what we thought, we will tell at once in our way."
>
> ("A Visit to Newgate," *Sketches by Boz*)

II.

"There ain't nuffink *in* this world but men and women, is there? So you *got* to care about 'em, else what you got to care about?"

(Michel Faber, *The Crimson Petal and the White*)

Introduction

The prison may seem an unpropitious place with which to begin a review essay on fifteen years of gender criticism in Dickens studies, yet in his *Boz* sketch of Newgate prison Dickens pairs the condition of female fallenness with a childhood deprived of imagination, exhorting others to care for such "girls." Thus begins Dickens's exploration of a gender and class identity different from his own, the sensitive Dickens being already well acquainted with the instability of Victorian class identity, and extending this flexible sense of identity to gender as well. From the women he sees in Newgate, he constructs the prototype of the Nancy that he was to perform in public readings almost up until his death:

> the girl belonged to a class—unhappily but too extensive—the very existence
> of which should make men's hearts bleed. Barely past her childhood . . . she
> was one of those children born and bred in poverty and vice who have never
> known what childhood is.   (*Sketches*, 238)

Dickens's own blacking warehouse shadow appears in "one of those children" who missed a full childhood; seeing her, he sees himself, and the bleeding heart blurs the boundaries between self and lost girl.

The girl bound to the streets through "poverty and vice" retains her hold on our contemporary imagination, as today's historical fiction readily testifies. In *The Crimson Petal and the White* (2002), Michel Faber's less lucky prostitute Caroline says to her friend, the upscale prostitute Sugar, "There ain't nuffink *in* this world but men and women, is there? So you *got* to care about 'em, else what you go to care about?" (517). Although the categories of "men and women" seem simple enough, Sugar, Faber's market-savvy and quick-study protagonist, makes the transition from prostitute to governess with wonderful ease, vexing the separate male and female Victorian gender identities as her head for business proves superior to any male's in the novel. She is the poster girl for Judith Butler's definition of *gender trouble*, gender as "an identity tenuously constituted in time, instituted in interior space through a stylized repetition of acts," which can be turned around, through "the unanticipated agency, of a female 'object' who inexplicably reverses

the gaze, and contests the place and authority of the masculine position''
(140; ch. ix). The creation of characters like Sugar coincides with the increased critical attention paid to a wide variety of gender trouble in Dickens.
The scholars whose work is reviewed here redefine how gender is constructed
and explore various constructions of gender throughout the Dickens canon.

Other historical fiction by Louis Bayard, Peter Carey, Sheri Holman, John
Irving, and Sarah Waters also has a place in our discussion, for they each
construct metaphorical Newgates, only to plot their way ingeniously out of
them, inspired by the gendered characters and social conscience of that master
plotter, Charles Dickens. A brief look at these fictions serves as a prelude to
this review of gender criticism in Dickens studies.

Irving's *Cider House Rules* (1985, filmed and also reissued in paperback
in 1999), Carey's *Jack Maggs* (1999), Holman's *The Dress Lodger* (2000),
Waters's *Affinity* (1999) and *Fingersmith* (2002), and Bayard's *Mr. Timothy*
(2003) owe a large measure of their power to the ways in which their authors
imagine gender. In Irving's novel, the male orphans are read aloud to each
night from *Great Expectations*. Irving also writes of an intense male bond,
following the male friendships so important in novels from *Martin Chuzzlewit*
to *The Mystery of Edwin Drood*, between Homer and Dr. Larch, ending with
Larch's posthumously delivering Homer into a new identity. However, no
Dickens text is deemed suitable for the female orphans, and so *Jane Eyre*,
its female heroine considered to have more agency and self-determination
than Dickens's female characters, is read to them instead. Melony, the rene-
gade female double to Homer, Irving's updated Pip, literally tears down a
house, and in telling Melony's unconventional story, Irving, like so many of
the critics doing work on Dickens and gender in the last fifteen years, recovers
women's stories. If the good nurses at St. Clouds could not find in Dickens's
novels a suitable ''woman's story,'' Dickens scholars have made up for this
in their recent work.

Bayard, in his creation of an adult Tim Crachit, empowers the formerly
diminutive and crippled child, who becomes a bachelor protagonist, protector
of at-risk children, reviser of history, and storyteller. Bayard's technique of
recognizing the structural macrocosm in the microcosm, of holding a magni-
fying glass to the miniature, is a prominent feature of criticism on Dickens
and gender; his recovery of Crachit's story parallels the critical activities of
the Dickens scholar in recovering the narratives of Dickensian bachelor masculinities.

Sheri Holman's *The Dress Lodger* (2000) tells a story darkly derived from
Dickens's concerns about Victorian sanitation, medicine, body-stealing,
fallen sexuality, and narrative practice. Holman articulates another central
issue of gender studies in Dickens's work, the question of narrative authority
and its relation to gender and identity:

> To every story there is a narration and a greater narration. Perhaps it never occurred to you to ask who it is that tells this story, whether or not the narrators are truthful and kind or wish their characters well. Maybe one or two of you have paused and wondered at the voices behind the voice—who is this "us" who knows so much and yet claims not to know at all—but most, we would wager, have given us no second thought. Perhaps by now you have guessed that this is not the inspiring story of medical heroism and scientific breakthrough.
> (255–56)

Cultural authority does not belong to the middle class in Holman's text, and we see in Dickensian gender studies also a major shift towards the examination of the working—class woman and man and their bodies and sexualities—the Uriah Heeps, Marchionesses, Susan Nippers, Mrs. Joes, and Mollys.

The increasing recognition of multiple narrations in gender studies and of competing voices in texts creates new complexities and opens new areas for study. Scholars discover overlooked female and male characters; women's stories emerge in the first-person narratives of *David Copperfield* and *Great Expectations*; stories within stories receive new attention; the gendered dual narratives of *Bleak House* come under scrutiny; and Dickens's writing and its reception as a gendered discourse becomes the subject of examination.

Two particularly rich areas of study have come from sexuality and queer studies, and here again, fiction reflects these scholarly foci. Sarah Waters with her fictions *Affinity*, set in Millbank women's prison, and *Fingersmith*, set in part in a prison-like library of recondite pornography, locates a world of female desire in a historicized Victorian setting, reminiscent of Dickens's intense female relationships (Esther Summerson and Ada Clare, Miss Wade and Tattycoram, Rosa Budd and Helena Landless). Not only female erotic relationships, but also male eroticism, inform much of the gender criticism of Dickens that follows here. On the fictional front, Peter Carey's *Jack Maggs* constructs in Tobias Oates a mesmeric, adulterous, scribbling resemblance of Dickens, in Henry Phipps a profligate, homosexual "gentleman," and in Maggs, the returned convict and surrogate father, who rescues housemaid Mercy Larkin, another "child born and bred in poverty and vice who [has] never known what childhood is" (*Sketches* 238), all reflecting the complex male sexualities of the Victorian era and of Dickens's work. Further, the act of mesmerism or hypnotism, and how it constructs both Dickens's masculinity and the Dickens marriage, become the critical/biographical subject for several Dickens scholars.

Although we draw necessary and important distinctions between authentic fiction from a literary period and historical fiction that attempts to re-create that period, this outpouring of high-quality historical fiction nourishes the consciousness and imagination of many Victorianists who write about Dickens's fiction, and forms part of the matrix in which gender criticism of Dickens is written.

This survey examines the published scholarship on Dickens and gender, including gender and sexuality, from 1992 to 2007. A working definition of gender may be useful at the start: "*Gender* typically refers to the social process of dividing people and social practices along the lines of *sexed identities*. The gendering process frequently involves creating hierarchies between the divisions it enacts" (Beasley 11). Since "most writers in Feminist and Masculinity Studies (that is, in Gender Studies) view gender as intertwined with sexuality," this review essay follows that lead and considers work published on gender and sexuality (Cranny-Francis et al., 2003:7, quoted in Beasley 14). This essay is divided into eight sections: Reviews of Gender Criticism, Monographs, Biography, Sexualities, Masculinities, Femininities, Cultural Studies, and Gender and Narrative. The survey concludes with two bibliographies, a "Dickens and Gender" bibliography of the studies reviewed within the essay, and an "Other Sources Cited" bibliography. I express here my apologies to anyone whose work I inadvertently overlooked, and my appreciation to all the scholars who contributed to this rich and varied gumbo called "Dickens and gender."

Reviews of Gender Criticism

Flavia Alaya's "Feminists on the Victorians: The Pardoning Frame of Mind," although a few years before the parameters of this essay, deserves mention here. Alaya begins with this epigraph from *Middlemarch*: "But why always Dorothea?" The essay discusses "Mrs. Dickens" as the elephant in the (scholars') room (*She wasn't there again today. Damn, I wish she'd go away!*)," marking the beginning of radical change in Victorian studies from 1969 when Kate Millett's *Sexual Politics* came out, to the 1979 milestone of Sandra Gilbert and Susan Gubar's *Madwoman in the Attic*, and the rediscovery of a host of nineteenth—and twentieth-century women writers (Alaya, 337). See Alaya's essay to review Victorian gender studies at midpoint in the 1980s.

Natalie McKnight's "Dickens and Gender" provides a useful introduction to the subject, reviewing some of the works included in this essay (Ingham, Holbrook, Waters [1997]). To these, McKnight adds Michael Slater's *Dickens and Women* (1983), characterizing it as "one of the earliest and most comprehensive defenses of Dickens's characterizations of women," and Diane Sadoff's *Monsters of Affection* (1982), which theorizes Dickens's characters through Freud's primal scene fantasies. McKnight identifies important cultural histories for the study of Dickens, in work by Elizabeth Langland, on the notion of separate spheres; Elaine Showalter, on madness and gender expectations; Mary Poovey, on the "gendered organization of social relations at mid-century''; Linda Shires, on gender as socially constructed; and Leonore Davidoff and Catherine Hall, as well as Langland, on "the intersection of expectations of gender and family roles." Turning to masculinities, McKnight points to work by Eve Kosofsky Sedgwick (1985, 1991), on homophobic behaviors and changes in expectations for masculine behavior; the collection edited by Michael Roper and John Tosh, on changing forms of masculinity in the Victorian era; John Tosh, on the changing role of the Victorian father; and Herbert Sussman, on the Victorians' managing of sexual energy through constructive labor. McKnight also provides social/historical context, describing conduct books for women such as Sarah Stickney Ellis's *The Women of England*; the angel in the house ideal and its origin in Coventry Patmore's poem (1856); Victorian laws concerning marriage, children, and property; and the role Queen Victoria played in establishing the feminine cultural ideal. The essay concludes with an overview of "gender trends in Dickens's life and work," emphasizing Dickens's relationships with his mother and wife, and some of the female characters he created in his fiction.

Ella Westland, in "Dickens and Critical Change," emphasizes that the rise of feminist criticism in the 1970s and 1980s was particularly influenced by the work of Kate Millett's *Sexual Politics* and Nina Auerbach's *Communities of Women* and *Woman and the Demon* (1978, 1982), as well as by Nancy Armstrong's *Desire and Domestic Fiction* (1987) and Mary Poovey's *Uneven Developments* (1988), the latter two studies showing the connections between capitalism and gender. Three other landmark studies in Dickens gender studies to which Westland points are Laurie Langbauer's blending of "gender and genre, sexuality and male psychology" in *Women and Romance*, Claire Tomalin's biography of Ellen Ternan *The Invisible Woman*, and Patricia Ingham's linguistic analysis of Dickens's constructions of gender in *Dickens, Women and Language* (Westland 192). Westland concludes by reminding her readers, "Feminists always remember that there are women unread" (195), a reference to both Ellen Ternan and Lizzie Hexam, who are being read in new ways after the publication of Tomalin's book. Today, such a statement would be modified to reflect the surging interest in Victorian masculinities and cross-gendered characters, and to remember that there are other men, gender-bending, and gender-blending, yet unread.

Monographs

Biographical

Katey, a biography by Dickens's great-great-great granddaughter Lucinda Hawksley, recounts the long and interesting life of one the two Dickens daughters who survived to adulthood, Katey (1839–1929). The balancing act for this biographer is in terms of the interest of Katey's life in itself and for historians and readers interested in recovering the stories of nineteenth-century women, and in Katey's relationship to Dickens, without which the biography would perhaps seem less significant for some readers. Yet it is hard to separate the two, for being Dickens's daughter did define Katey's experience in ways she couldn't always control, and Hawksley has to rely on information provided, to some extent, by sources that paid attention to Katey only because of her famous father.

Hawksley describes Dickens's devotion to Katey in her childhood, as for example, when, during difficult illnesses, she allowed only Dickens to nurse her, and he would willingly "[push] aside his work schedule" to do so (39). Some interesting highlights include the Dickens family's first trip to Italy and what Hawksley characterizes as an idyllic stay in the Palace Peschiere, a time when "the children felt secure in their parents' contentment" (40); Katey's unrequited infatuation with Edmund Yates, who traded on his association with Dickens; the amateur theatricals in which the Dickens daughters joined their father and which led to Katey's consultation with Dickens at Gads Hill about a theatrical career; Katey's marriage to Charles Collins; her long-standing friendship with the Thackeray family; Katey's secret, then public, marriage to Carlo Perugini; her work as a painter and painter's model; and her ambiguous friendship with Gladys Storey.

Marring the biography for some more scholarly-minded readers, however, is anecdotal evidence about the Dickens's family life with neither source nor date provided, as when Hawksley generalizes about the Dickens daughters' education, or about what occurred at dinner in the 1850s between Charles and Catherine Dickens. It would indeed be interesting to know what visitors recalled about the Dickens girls as teens, or to have some evidence about the mental health diagnoses Hawksley makes about Katey's suffering from SAD (seasonal affective disorder) or Dickens's suffering from depression, but more specific evidence is needed. Hawksley is at her best in writing about the artists and their circles, and in describing the paintings (some of them reproduced in her biography) that Katey made and those for which she modeled. Katey comes most alive in this part of the biography. Hovering at the edge of the text is Catherine Dickens, tantalizing, but making Dickensians eager to see Lillian Nayder's upcoming biography of her. Hawksley's book reveals how very right Charles Dickens was when he instructed his children about the value of his name, but she also shows how Kate Perugini tried to find an art of her own.

Critical

In *Gender and Madness*, Marianne Camus claims that Dickens's "madwomen are original, somehow more human, than his normal women" (2), and that

Dickens "felt no need for a coherent definition or representation of the condition of the mentally ill," accepting instead "the fluidity of these shifting approaches": that a mad person was both responsible for her madness and that madness was an illness that could be cured with proper treatment (7). Unlike Natalie McKnight's *Idiots, Madmen and Other Prisoners in Dickens*, Camus's study fails to differentiate between the types of madness or mental illness suffered by the various characters she classifies under the heading of "madness": she lumps together brain damage, alcoholism, retardation, narcissism, delusion, homicidal tendencies, paranoia, and senility. Further, McKnight also makes a useful distinction between Dickens's attitudes to madness in his nonfiction and fiction, while Camus does not. Camus's generalizations, such as "violent madness tends to be reserved for men," clearly do not hold true throughout the Dickens canon, and her analysis of gender differences in relation to madness seems oversimplified: men go mad as a result of "freedom of movement of action" whereas women go mad as result of "too much constriction" (23). Most worthwhile are Camus's reading of madness and gender in the case of William Dorrit; her analysis of the "dead spaces" in which Miss Wade, Mrs. Clennam, and Miss Havisham reside; and her argument about the ambiguity in Dickens's punishment of his madwomen: they are humiliated and excluded from the return to order at the novel's ending. They are, however, accorded a kind of tragic stature.

Elizabeth Campbell in *Fortune's Wheel* describes two icons of fortune Dickens inherits from his literary predecessors: the goddess Fortune that comes from Hogarth and Fielding, associated with wealth, upper-class status, and beauty, and a fortune-teller figure from chapbooks and street literature, associated with grim fortune and death. While Campbell's discussions of emblem books, chapbooks, and the iconography of cover wrappers are carefully elucidated, they do not always focus squarely on constructions of gender. This is really a study of archetypes and temporality, and Campbell does not refer to recent gender criticism on Dickens's novels. Campbell's claim that Dickens enters "women's time" in 1840 when "Kate's labors seem to have synchronized with his own" (73) and that he writes *The Old Curiosity Shop* with a "focus on female temporality" (74) does not require the whole apparatus of Fortune's wheel and archetypes of Fortune. Moreover, the reading of Nell would benefit from acquaintance with Robert Polhemus's "Comic and Erotic Faith Meet Faith in the Child" which discusses all the symbolic burdens Nell is made to bear. Unhelpfully, Campbell interprets Nell as a Janus-Fortune, both avatar of fortune and goddess of death.

Campbell seems most specifically focused on gender in her study of *Dombey and Son*, in which she considers the religious iconography of the monthly wrappers, since these depict Fanny Dombey as *Maria Regina*, the Queen of Heaven, and represent Polly Toodle as *Maria Lactans*, the nursing Madonna

(96, 100). Campbell also notes that illustrations for the first two numbers drew attention to "Polly's bond with children" (101). Campbell stresses the importance of Polly's bosom as "the signifying bosom," "the bodily part most suggestive of womanly value," able to nourish, provide tea and sympathy, create calm in the household, and satisfy the husband (102–03). In contrast to the comfortable Polly, Mrs. Skewton is a "cruel divinity" and "dea ex machina" (107).

Campbell's attention to the visual can be striking and creative, as when she explicates Hogarth's *South Sea Scheme* and compares its mutilation of the statue-goddess to the social scapegoating of Lady Dedlock (45–47, 134–35). *Bleak House* is the first novel in which the goddess Fortune is repeatedly mentioned, and in which the wheel is used as a controlling metaphor, Campbell remarks, and yet this observation does not lead to a particularly rich reading. Confusingly, after associating Esther with the Mother Shipton of fortune-telling tradition, Campbell concludes that Esther embodies both good Fortune and Providence, apparently rendering the excursion into the chapbook association irrelevant. Frustratingly, the essay dips into issues that other scholars have written about concerning Esther—identity, illegitimacy, her association with the dead child, her scarring—but Campbell's research in Dickens criticism since 1990 is lacking. For Campbell, *Little Dorrit* offers "the most repellent—and dangerous—of Dickens's decrepit death goddesses," Mrs. Clennam (167). Following Metz and Warner, Campbell examines the significance of Little Dorrit's "poor tiny woman" who spins: she is a figure who works out time and fate, and spinning can assuage grief and soothe emotions (186–87). The miniaturizing of Little Dorrit "reasserts her identity as Fairy Fortune: a tiny goddess whose very ephemerality is a sign of her monumental powers" (190). The final chapter on *Great Expectations* uses a chapbook, *The World Turned Upside Down*, and its woodcuts, to examine gender role reversals. One woodcut shows "the old soldier turned nurse," in which a male soldier nurses a baby, while a woman wears a helmet and totes a rifle (195). This "motif of a reversible world" is enacted by the convict who turns Pip upside down in *Great Expectations*, and in Dickens's feminizing of Joe and masculinizing of Mrs. Joe. Overall, Campbell's project remains ambitious and thought—provoking in reading across literary periods and across a range of cultural texts. One can learn much from this cross-disciplinary work, although its focus is not always squarely on gender.

Hilary Schor, in her *Dickens and the Daughter of the House*, shines striking new critical light on the daughters of Dickens's fictional houses in this recovery of the novels' women's stories. The least cohesive chapter is the first, on *Oliver Twist* and *The Old Curiosity Shop*, in which Schor finds "uncertainty" about the narration of Nancy's character but argues convincingly about Nell as a *freak* or *emblem of legend* in the context of Victorian spectatorship.

After this, *Daughter of the House* reads *Dombey and Son* in terms of the daughter's responsibility to "embody and recompose the past" (60). Schor relocates the novel's climax as Florence's last encounter with Edith, rather than her reunion with her father. The refocus on Edith as a master plotter rather than the "instrument of male plots," as well as the close reading of the imagery surrounding both Florence and Edith, make for compelling reading.

Schor asks "what use is the daughter?" in *Hard Times* and *A Tale of Two Cities*, in *Hard Times* connecting Louisa with Stephen in Dickens's adultery plot, and in *A Tale of Two Cities* connecting the daughters Lucy Mannette and Madame Defarge through their simultaneous entry into "the adultery plot and the plot of historical change" (78, 84). In *Bleak House*, the question posed is "what can the dispossessed, illegitimate daughter inherit?"; answers include "narrative secrets, contagion, resemblance, a bastard line of property" (101,110). *Bleak House* is seen as the culmination of Dickensian fictions in which daughters try to bring their mothers back to life, a story that gives "the quiet daughter and the angry mother both their due" (123).

Schor devotes individual chapters to *Little Dorrit*, *Great Expectations*, and *Our Mutual Friend*. The explanations of Amy Dorrit's "renunciatory fervor" and the novel's "prizing of constraint" are splendid, as are her counter-readings of Miss Wade's resistance and readings of female characters with independent property such as Miss Rugg, Flora Finching, and Mrs. Clennam. This ability to see the women's stories from multiple ideological sides enhances the value of Schor's work on gender in Dickens.

Schor complements Estella's story with a recognition of Pip's identification with the feminine, what Schor characterizes as the "victimized, battered, self-emasculated male," and by discussions of the motherless Miss Havisham and Mrs. Joe (159). Schor uses Freud (1914), Mary Jacobus, and Sarah Kofman, to theorize male and female narcissism, positing narcissism as part of Pip's difficulty in actually *seeing* Estella or recognizing her needs as separate from his. Schor argues effectively about Pip's misreading of Estella through the distorting lens of metaphor, a point that may remind us that he is not so different from the rest of "us, grave or light [who] get our thoughts entangled in metaphors, and act fatally on the strength of them" (*Middlemarch*, ch. 10).

In *Our Mutual Friend*, the dispossession of the daughter is traced in the cases of Bella Wilfer and Lizzie Hexam, but the daughter's ability to possess is carefully elucidated in Pleasant Riderhood's life and "leaving" shop. The daughters of *Our Mutual Friend* "redeem" the dirt of the streets and of the Victorian commodity culture, "through productive self-alienation" (191). Schor rebuts Henry James's famous attack on Jenny Wren as a female eccentric and the sign of Dickens's lack of literary realism, following in some respects Helena Michie's argument (1989) about Jenny's eroticization and empowerment; for Schor, Jenny is Dickens's "uncanny partner" (204).

Schor's rich recoveries of these daughters' stories make a major contribution to recent gender criticism in Dickens studies.

Brenda Ayres's thesis in *Dissenting Women in Dickens' Novels* is "to identify where and when the Dickens novel fails to promote" the domestic ideology that had the angel in the house at its center, the woman who exhibited the virtues of "piety, purity, submissiveness and domesticity" described by Barbara Welter (1966; Ayres 5, 4). Ayres finds many "dissenting" women in Dickens's canon, but her thesis limits her analysis of them. She starts with the women of *David Copperfield*, finding Dora Spenlow not necessarily a wrong fit for David as a Victorian child-bride, since the Strong marriage shows such a marriage can succeed. Given time, Dora "would have represented a revolutionary new image of desirable woman and preferred wife" (31). Ayres follows with a thoughtful discussion of the "plump and buxom" Martha Varden and her servant Miggs in *Barnaby Rudge*. Martha's religious zealotry must be redirected into more submissive wifehood and domesticity, while Miggs, guilty of unfeminine behaviors such as conspiring against her own sex and initiating sexual relationships, gains a position as turnkey at Bridewell, an institution that incarcerates prostitutes (45, 58–59). Although Ayres's discussion of Miggs's ambiguous position as jailer/jailed and punished/punisher is interesting, she does not connect how Miggs might function as a social shadow or alter ego for her mistress, Mrs. Varden, or even how Miggs might perhaps be perceived as masculinized through her appropriation of power. In short, Ayres could theorize gender more fully and currently, here and throughout her book.

Chapters 5 and 6 are snapshots of Dickensian woman: "Little Women" in *Martin Chuzzlewit, The Old Curiosity Shop, Little Dorrit, Our Mutual Friend*, and *The Mystery of Edwin Drood*, and "She-Dragons," in *The Old Curiosity Shop, Hard Times, Little Dorrit, A Tale of Two Cities*, and *Great Expectations*. Chapter 7 classifies women under an indiscriminate umbrella of "misfits": religious zealots, women thinkers, widows, spinsters, dwarves, and gypsies, while chapter 8 belatedly focuses on Agnes, Rose, and Nancy in *Oliver Twist*. Ayres's final chapter, on *Bleak House*, views this novel as a "meta-narrative" but does not rigorously engage this idea, nor does it offer an original reading of the text. Ayres's project has some good features but it is too diffuse, lacking strongly argued and theorized individual readings of Dickens's works.

Catherine Waters, in *Dickens and the Politics of the Family*, notes that the concept of *family* is a construct in Dickens's writing and, as such, "inescapably political" (12). Although Waters is interested in the theoretical model of the family as a disciplinary mechanism, as propounded by Donzelot and Foucault (1990, 1995), she finds they do not sufficiently account for gender and political resistance (27). She wants to "[situate] Dickens's representation of the family within nineteenth-century ideological constructions of class and gender," and to trace a shift away from a definition of *family* that emphasizes "the importance of lineage and blood towards a new ideal of domesticity assumed to be the natural form of the family" (27). *Oliver Twist* is the first Dickens novel to reveal this shift, since "the family reconstituted at the end . . . contains only one relationship based on blood" (32). Instead, it underscores "surrogate familial relationships and the cozy harmony of this *little society* . . . according to the middle-class ideal of domesticity" (32). *Dombey and Son* also highlights surrogate familial relationships in its resolution, where Florence's home "transcends the divisions of class and gender" (57).

Waters's chapter on the Christmas stories does not at first seem to advance her thesis, but later in the book she returns to the theme of the Christmas dinner/family dinner as a normative domestic scene for the middle-class family in many of Dickens's novels. The chapter on *Little Dorrit* takes up again the issue of how the family is defined and how class, gender, and economic status affect and are affected by concepts of *family*. Here *family* is defined as a "small kin-group sharing the same household," but also *family* can be "a tribe" (90). Particularly useful are Waters's discussions of Miss Wade and Tattycoram, examining how each is stratified and excluded in new domestic units or *families*, and showing how Tattycoram's return to the Meagles' home is only an "ambiguous reaffirmation of the middle-class family" (100). Normative domesticity appears in the Plornish family home, while the Meagles' parental spoiling of Pet, and their inability to prevent threatening intrusions, of Henry Gowan and Miss Wade, cause them to forfeit normative status. The false paternalism of Mr. Casby and William Dorrit are contrasted to the "true" paternalism of Arthur Clennam, who feels compassion for others. Little Dorrit's domestic labor is the "normative vision of the family" in the novel (120).

Discussing *A Tale of Two Cities*, Waters challenges Lukacs's criticism of Dickens's treatment of the French revolution as a romantic background, arguing instead that Dickens's representation of the middle-class family is a "historically significant strategy" (Lukacs, 1962, Waters 124), in which Charles Darnay embodies the self-made male at a time when the concept of occupation was becoming "an integral part of masculine identity" (Davidoff and Hall 199). Waters, following Nancy Armstrong (1987), argues that Carton's alienation reaffirms "the unifying power of the domestic woman," while his self-sacrifice suggests that family is a matter of the "ideology of domesticity, rather than blood-relatedness . . . [,]an endorsement of *surrogate* familial relationships" (147–48).

Waters begins her discussion of *Great Expectations* by focusing on how Pip's identity is determined by familial context, beginning with the gendering of language on the family tombstones through which Pip imagines his deceased parents. Middle-class ideals of family and femininity are satirized through Mrs. Joe, Mrs. Pocket, and Miss Havisham—all "deviant" maternal types (152–59). Waters posits the Finches of the Grove as a male enclave, a sign of Pip's new class, and finds its opposite term in Biddy and the forge as signs of home, domesticity, and the working class (162–64). *Great Expectations* "rewrites" *Oliver Twist* and *David Copperfield*, both of which feature male protagonists who find "exemplary homemakers"; Pip, although he makes a home with Herbert and Clara Pocket, does not find his own domestically grounded partner, losing Biddy to Joe (166). Further, Estella is "a profoundly unstable foundation for male identity," failing to provide the female nature that is the normative, domestic "other" to the male, and this failure, Waters believes, reveals the ideological significance of gender in this novel (170).

Finally, Waters argues that *Our Mutual Friend* indicates Dickens's investment in the ideology of middle-class domesticity even though his narrative form remains deeply ambivalent. The lodger's proximity and access to the family with whom he lodges as well as the narrator's access to female identity, link "novelistic form" and "domestic ideology," so that the text depends on a "phallocentrism of the visual" (185). Harmon's benevolent watching takes on a more ambiguous meaning with Wrayburn's surveillance or "erotic theft" of Lizzie Hexam (186). The normative ideal of domesticity is reinscribed outside the home to places like the Greenwich wedding party and the "Feast of the Three Hobgoblins" in Mr. Wilfer's office, and later, inside Bella and John's marital home. The narrator's satire of the Wilfers' dourly observed wedding anniversary is similar to the satirical tone of Wrayburn's rhapsodizing about the "domestic virtues" of flour barrels and spice boxes when he shares a flat with Mortimer Lightwood, both points of view making more ambiguous the aforementioned celebrations of domesticity in other parts of the novel. Waters concludes that Dickens's fictions "resist the closure of the middle-class family" (206). *Dickens and the Politics of the Family* repays the reader who wants to see how concepts so vital to the study of Dickens such as *family* and *gender identity* have been theorized, historicized, and thoughtfully analyzed in their different constructions in parts of Dickens's canon. Waters's ability to see variant ideologies of domesticity and gender within a single text is a strength, although the terms "normative" and "deviant" now seem to have been preparing the way for future gender criticism to ask still more questions about what "normative," "deviant," and "family" mean. This book remains a valuable touchstone for Dickens critics.

In Rita Lubitz's *Marital Power in Dickens's Fiction*, a phrase like *marital power* begs for definition: to whom does such power properly belong, according to social practice and according to the law? Did its meaning change over the course of Dickens's career, from the 1830s to 1870? Did Dickens vary in his representation of marital relationships? If so, how, and why?

Lubitz, however, does not historicize or theorize this study in the most basic
way by defining what she means by *power*. The only attempt to do so is a
quotation from Barickman, Macdonald, and Stark in her discussion of *Martin
Chuzzlewit*: ''the husband is master, the wife totally dutiful, suffering his
brutal treatment and being still'' (8). Lubitz's chapter-headings themselves
suggest a lack of subtlety in the analyses that will follow: ''Dominant Husbands and Submissive Wives: The Brutal, the Dissolute, the Malicious and
the Meek'' and ''Dominant Wives and Submissive Husbands: The Shrewish,
the Proud, the Obsessive and the Henpecked'' are two examples. While concentrating largely on the novels, Lubitz deals with some short fiction and
interpolated tales, but without considering the latter's relationship to the
larger texts in which they appear, with a disorienting effect. Typical of the
weaknesses of this book are excessive reliance on citations from other scholars and individual chapters that read like laundry lists, with little primary
textual analysis. Overall, the author needs to dig deeper, as when she asks
about Mrs. Gradgrind's headaches and Mrs. Blackpool's alcoholism as possible symptoms of inner conflict in the power relations of their marriages but
does not pursue this idea. The ''whys'' of ''marital power'' require further
exploration. Fortunately, scholars can look to the work of Marlene Tromp
and Lisa Surridge reviewed here.

In *Consuming Fictions: Gender, Class and Hunger in Dickens's Novels*,
Gail Turley Houston brings to the forefront a topic that runs throughout
Dickens's work and with which the bodies of his characters are so often
concerned, the consumption of food and how this food expresses desire
and social relationships. Using Rita Felski's *Beyond Feminist Aesthetics* and
Mikhail Bakhtin's *Rabelais and His World* to theorize her discussion, Houston
argues consistently that the ''appetitive desires'' of middle-class and upper-
class characters are displaced onto carnivalesque, ''lower'' social bodies,
who express those desires. Houston begins with *Pickwick Papers* and *Oliver
Twist*, concluding that Dickens in the former novel allows finally for Pickwickian desires to be ''sacralized,'' but uses ''starvation as a punishment for
sexual folly'' in *Oliver Twist* (30, 31).

Houston's focus on the diagnostic birth of anorexia nervosa makes an
interesting historical case for Dickens's fictional use of the ''small body''
and also reveals the way in which men's illnesses signified different cultural
and political meanings than women's ailments in the Victorian period: ''*Old
Curiosity Shop, Martin Chuzzlewit, Dombey and Son*, and *David Copperfield*
represent the height of the miraculously anorectic heroine and Dickens's most
unquestioning acceptance of the need for female bodily economies to support
male economies'' (60). Continuums of eating, less and more, appear in *The
Old Curiosity Shop* and *Martin Chuzzlewit*, with Houston arguing that ascetic
heroines ''binge'' psychologically when off-page (in private) or when practicing a kind of ''luxurious self-denial,'' like Little Nell's (66–67). In *Martin*

Chuzzlewit, characters such as Mrs. Gamp, Mrs. Todgers, and Mrs. Lupin "know their food" and "act out the other side of Mary's asceticism" (81). *Dombey and Son* and *David Copperfield* redeem a conflict between the "nurturing female-ordered home" and the "voraciousness" of the male consumer economy outside the home. Houston follows Mary Poovey's argument about Agnes as David's "hidden—spiritualized—business partner," but goes further to argue that Agnes performs an act of ventriloquy or possession, becoming "more David than David himself" (122).

The discussion of *Bleak House* adds little to Houston's argument and might have been omitted, but *Little Dorrit* is seen as a turning point in Dickens's novels. Here Dickens at last looks at "the consequences of the repressed female bodily economies of his earlier heroines" in the "little" self of Amy Dorrit (134). Houston offers a nuanced reading of Little Dorrit's appetite through her relationship to Maggy, her fairy tale, her encounter with the prostitute, and her nursing of Clennam. Finally, Houston maintains, "*Great Expectations* suggests that consumer society is the ultimate Gothic horror. . . . endlessly [producing] images of ingestion for the reader's consumption" (168). Pip's appetite is displaced onto other characters, all of whom are punished for it. Houston's book provides many fine readings of the tropes of appetite, consumption, nurturing, and other issues related to the most basic human needs and desires. Her conclusion, "that the maternal feminine must underwrite Victorian economy" for a healthier society, continues to inform other scholarly writing about Dickens and gender (170).

David Holbrook announces in his introduction to *Charles Dickens and the Image of Woman*, that his methodology is psychoanalytic—more specifically, the object relations theory of D. W. Winnicott and Melanie Klein, but with Jungian inflections as well. He follows with chapters on *Bleak House*, *Our Mutual Friend*, *Little Dorrit*, and *Great Expectations*, concluding with a chapter on Dickens's relationships with women. Ignoring the wave of French feminist psychoanalytic criticism available when his work was done (Cixous, Kristeva), Holbrook also does not refer to the feminist psychoanalytic work of Jane Gallup. Holbrook at times seems careless, as when he admits surprise that *Great Expectations* comes late in Dickens's canon, and forgets about Mrs. Joe in stating, "There is not in this novel the punitive woman who seeks to promote guilt and to inflict expiation on an infant who thereby inherits disgrace" (132). He notes that "fantasies" "of women being abused, threatened or attacked by man" were important to Dickens, and examines such fantasies by referring to Melanie Klein's theory of the *paranoid-schizoid stage*, which allows Holbrook to explore "the problem of whether love is dangerous and is liable to consume the other and annihilate her" (133). Holbrook, using the expression *homosexual element*, anticipates Eve Sedgwick's discussion of homosociality in Victorian fiction in his comments on

Pip's relationships with Joe and Magwitch, which he sees as playful and tender, respectively, and "positive and enriching" (144). In contrast, Holbrook finds "the false manliness" of Orlick and Bentley Drummle has led them to "sadistic cruelty" (144). The discussion of *Bleak House*, in which Holbrook moves through a discussion of themes such as death, illegitimacy, emotional deprivation, and the household, before concluding that the novel is a "fantasy of reparation" based on Klein's concept of the child's reparation of love to the mother after fantasies of destruction and hate (Klein 50–51), is paradigmatic of the problems of the book as a whole. Inconsistent application of psychoanalytic theory, which some chapters lack or which comes too late in others, and inconsistent attention to "the image of the woman" mar this study.

Patricia Ingham begins *Dickens, Women & Language* by noting Dickens's familiarity with the Victorian code of physiognomy drawn on by his contemporaries, a code Dickens employs in his representation of women. Ingham divides Dickens's female characters into five linguistic signs: *nubile girls, fallen girls, excessive females, passionate women,* and *true mothers* (16). The nubile girl is written through what Ingham calls a "ghost pornography," a verbal exploitation that under the guise of idealizing her, objectified her solely as a sexual object (37). Nubile girls exhibit a "lack of physicality," a "slight" figure, and a "fragmentation" or "morselisation," as, for example, when Dora becomes an inventory of straw hat, curls, and slender arms (18, 21, 23). Ingham argues that Dickens displaces desire for the nubile girls onto the food near them, "giving them that lusciousness denied to them in descriptions of their physical appearance" (31). Nubile girls include Rose Maylie, Little Nell, Ruth Pinch, Ada Clare, Amy Dorrit, Dolly Varden, Dora Spenlow, and Rosa Budd, among others.

Fallen girls are understood as "antithetical" to the nubile girls (40). Ingham asserts that Dickens participated in the "recoding" and shifting of the language describing prostitution and fallen women in early and midcentury Victorian England, beginning with conventional treatment of the subject in *Sketches by Boz* and progressing to more "economic" and "skillful" troping of them in *Oliver Twist* (42, 45). Ingham discusses how Dickens depicts in the figure of Nancy, "womanly compassion," and in that of Martha Endell, a "female Samaritan," conflicts of meaning in the Virgin/whore and nubile girl/fallen girl dichotomies (46–47). Ingham also notes how Nancy's speech is rehabilitated, "so that the lower-class markers become fewer" (51). In addition, Ingham makes an important argument concerning the agency of the fallen girl. Martha, she contends, serves as a surrogate for Emily, "acting out a more extreme version of Emily's fall and so preserving her from carrying the full significance of the fallen woman" (55); and Alice Marwood performs a similar function in *Dombey and Son* (55). Ingham sees Nancy's death as a way she can exercise agency, and rather than her death performing a cleansing, Nancy "remains unambiguously a victim," and thus she is "Dickens's Tess" (59). Ingham concludes that Dickens grants his fallen girls agency that is denied to the nubile girls; this agency comes with the sexual identity of the fallen girl (61).

Excessive females consist of middle-class married women "left to nature without nurture"; these include Mrs. Nickleby, Mrs. Varden, Mrs. Gamp, Mrs. Skewton, Mrs. Joe Gargery, Mrs. Jellyby, Mrs. Pardiggle, Flora Finching, and Mrs. Wilfer (69). This group is defined by their voices, in keeping with "Dickens's obsession with every aspect of how individuals speak, from voice quality to syntax. It also follows naturally from narrative sequences in which, typically, agency is denied to women since it is virtually the only form of self-expression left" (71). Ingham sets her discussion of gendered speech in the context of nineteenth-century discourse on gender and intellect, which assumes a split between men as rational and women as intuitive and emotional (71). Dickens's excessive females, though, not only lack intellectual power and rationality, but show "garrulous inconsequentiality," "incoherence," solipsistic fantasies, loquacity, and posings as romantic heroines (72–78). This "rampant femaleness" escapes class boundaries and results in "unnatural domesticity," epitomized in the Gargery household (78, 81). In some cases, this unruly female excess is punished into silence (83). Ingham notes that this "silencing" is part of the "enjoyable" restoration of order in a Dickens novel, and that what is punished as tyranny in the *excessive female* is also "the very essence of femaleness" and "theoretically privileged in the depiction of nubile girls" (86).

Passionate women are already married and non-virgins, but unfallen; however, they are connected to the fallen girl through "near-miss adultery" (87). Ingham reminds readers that Lady Dedlock, Edith Dombey, and Louisa Bounderby are characters created in the years approaching the Matrimonial Causes Act of 1857 and that Dickens uses the "language of negation" to "maximize" the effect of his characters' near-adultery (89).

Their "deliberate refusal to communicate . . . encodes the essential self"; "Not speaking is at once a means of resistance and a form of self-definition, an ironic reversal of the stereotypical garrulousness that renders excessive females uniformly undesirable, knowable and despicable," thereby making these women "unknowable and desirable" (103). Ingham notes that Dickens counters the tradition of associating passion with low social rank, since these three passionate women possess high social rank (103). In the "near-miss adultery" texts by Dickens's contemporaries Craik and Jewsbury, the passionate women are punished and a "mild degree of culpability" is assigned to their husbands (104), whereas in Dickens's novels, "it is the men whose place in society is lost" and the husbands seem more directly linked to the wives' flights into adultery (105, 104). Ingham concludes that the "chaos" brought by passionate women is "exciting and desirable, like the women themselves," and that they are more highly valued than the nubile girls (110).

True mothers, Ingham's fifth sign of Dickens's women, are understood best through Sarah Stickney Ellis's concept of *disinterested kindness*. Ingham explains that *true mothers* must have disinterested kindness along with "the capacity to 'mother' or nurture," and that many of Dickens's biological mothers are "monsters of selfishness" (115). Many biological parents are mothered in role reversals by their daughters, who are womanly true mothers: Edith Dombey, Alice Marwood, Harriet Carker, Esther Summerson, Fanny Cleaver, and Little Nell (a grandchild mothering a grandparent), among others. There are also unexpected true mothers, such as Miss Tox who shows solicitude to Rob the Grinder and Miss Flite who gives domestic training to Caddy Jellyby. Thus, "the overall grouping of womanly figures into a sign, *true mothers*, creates a method of evaluation and at the same time displaces biological mothers from their central place in the family" (118). Dickens's propensity for "unmothering" families "cannot be directly related to referents in the real world," and must be considered in relation to Dickens's interest in "creating a new relationship between father and child" argues Ingham (118–19). Amy Dorrit is the "apotheosis of all those girls who reach 'wifehood' via surrogate motherhood"; the true mother who is "simultaneously perfect and corrupt" (120, 123). Unlike Sadoff, who finds Little Dorrit's mothering of her father redemptive, Ingham sees Amy as morally compromised, a "grotesque image of a person half-woman and half-child, suckling her own father and becoming simultaneously his mother and his wife" (Ingham 122). Ingham calls attention to the intense same-sex relationships of Esther and Ada in *Bleak House*, Helena and Rosa in *Edwin Drood*, and Miss Wade and Tattycoram/Harriet in *Little Dorrit*, attributing this to "the dissolution of rigid familial categories and of gender difference . . . [resulting in] the individual's loss of a clear sense of self" (127–128, 129). *Dickens, Women & Language* informs much subsequent scholarship on Dickens and gender. Ingham's explanations of the five "signs" of *nubile girl, fallen girl, passionate woman, excessive female*, and *true mother* and her carefully elucidated readings of Dickens's characters make her study essential for Dickens scholars interested in gender.

Sexualities

Collection of Essays in a Book

Dickens Refigured: Bodies, Desires and Other Histories, a collection edited by John Schad, features four essays focused on sexuality and gender in Dickens's work, beginning with Nicholas Royle's essay "Our Mutual Friend," which discusses the many figures of reading and readability in *Our Mutual Friend*, as Royle attempts to extend Sedgwick's reading of homoeroticism, anality, desire, and murderous rage in *Our Mutual Friend* to what he calls "the relation between anality and writing" (52). Royle locates evidence of the "faecal" subtext of the novel in the conversation between Podsnap, whom he re-christens "Bowelbreak," and the Frenchman about the soiled English pavement. For Royle *Our Mutual Friend* is "at once a kind of textual coprolith and a discourse *on* the coprolith" (53). However, the coprolith as waste material that is readable needs to be linked to other legible urban waste in the novel.

Richard Dellamora, in " 'Pure Oliver: or, Representation without Agency,' " provocatively reads as diptypchs Cruikshank's pair of illustrations, "Oliver asking for More" and "Oliver introduced to the Respectable Old Gentleman," in which he sees Oliver's phallicism and his at-risk purity as signified through the objects he holds at an angle, a giant spoon at the workhouse in the first illustration, and a walking stick in the second. In the first, the gaze of the workhouse boys and the Workhouse master in his apron (read by Dellamora as the beadle) are directed at Oliver's "spoon," and in the second, the gaze of Fagin and his "boys" are all directed at Oliver's "stick," suggesting in the first case that the bodies of the working poor both consume (the large bowl of the spoon) and spend, and in the second case, that Oliver brings his "stick" into the secret, shared, and illicit bond between Fagin and his "boys." Dellamora's homoerotic interpretation explicates Oliver's body, as well as other working-class bodies in the novel, as objects of the Malthusian gaze. Such bodies are vulnerable to or cause what Foucault calls "social and psychic *zones of disorder*" (68). Identifying the perverse possibilities of Fagin's relationship with his den of boys, and following Steven Marcus and William Cohen, Dellamora analyzes the concept of *queerness* in relation to Dickens's representation of Oliver's character and his "adoption by a ring of bachelors," which both fascinated and repulsed Henry James (75).

Helena Michie, in "The Avuncular and Beyond: Family Melo(drama) in *Nicholas Nickleby*," defines the *family idiom* as "the system of terms which transforms what might at first seem non-familial relations into familial ones" and examines this idiom at work in two kinds of discourses about the family: the legal and the theatrical or performative (80). She explains, "If the conflict between nature and culture in the realm of the legal leads to questions of inheritance and the rights of children, tensions in the realms of the theatrical lead directly to questions of affect or feeling" (82). She continues, "We can then set in motion a chain of anxieties at once spectacularly displayed and repressed in this novel: all paternity is legal; all paternity a legal fiction; all paternity fiction; all fiction writing about the recovery of paternity" (84).

Michie springboards from Eve Sedgwick's idea of the *avuncular*, "a possible place for the reproduction of adult non-reproductive sexuality" (85), to consider Ralph Nickleby, and coins the term *tantular* to describe an "aunt-like role" of sexual but non-reproductive women in the novel (85). Michie argues that Dickens's critique of the avuncular Ralph Nickleby and his home in Golden Square is a displacement of a critique of the absent, deceased father and of patriarchy itself (87). Michie skillfully elucidates the nexus of Ralph's financial "interests" and incestuous interests in Kate, his usury associating him with pawnbrokers, another Victorian type that is "avuncular," and his role as procurer of money and possibly other goods, for other men. Incest breaks down familial boundaries, affecting fathers, uncles, and even brothers. "Even the most sacred familial relations are not free of the erotic and the violent" (88). Also noted is the "gynophobic humor directed against the female body" (91). Ultimately, Dickens does imagine, briefly, an alternative to the marriage plot, in the brother-sister relationship of Kate and Nicholas, an "idyll [in which they] share a cottage and grow old together" (96).

Patricia Ingham's " 'Nobody's Fault': The Scope of the Negative in *Little Dorrit*" demonstrates that novel's emphatic and gendered language of negation, from the "nobody" of Arthur Clennam to the "nothing"-ness of Little Dorrit. Little Dorrit's femininity follows the cultural requirements of Sarah Stickney Ellis's "disinterested kindnesss" and provides surrogate mothering. Little Dorrit is distinct from other Dickensian women, such as Mrs. Nickleby, whose "femaleness [is] a biologically determined set of characteristics of non-intellectual, intuitive, reactive kind" that can lead to "unreasonable, demanding, emotional" behavior (107). Ingham defines Little Dorrit as one of Dickens's "nubile girls" who becomes a virginal wife, and this leads to the second part of Ingham's reading of her character, the alternative persona, Amy. The "Amy" self can be read as incestuously possessive of her father's love, giving her father "endless mother's milk" (111), like the "classical daughter" from Italian painting to which Dickens alludes and which Ingham provides pictorially in her text (Andrea Sirani's "Roman Charity," dated 1632–34). Further, the relationship between Clennam and Amy is seen as "desexualized" on both sides, with Clennam having the harder struggle, as Amy makes an easier transition from mothering her father to mothering Clennam, while Clennam must struggle against sexual love for her [that] would be paedophiliac" (110).

Special Journal Issue

Critical Survey 17:2 (2005), *Dickens and Sex*

In their introduction to this 2005 special issue of *Critical Survey* titled *Dickens and Sex*, guest editors Holly Furneaux and Anne Schwan note the dominance

of the Foucauldian "disciplinary thesis," a thesis so widespread in Dickensian and Victorian criticism that it may have perhaps constrained readings
of Dickens's work. This special issue aims, therefore, to move beyond the
Foucauldian paradigm "to open up new critical avenues into Dickens and
sex" (2).

William A. Cohen opens with "Interiors: Sex and the Body in Dickens,"
seeking to examine "the embodied relation between interior and exterior"
in *The Old Curiosity Shop* and *David Copperfield* (8). Beginning with the
image of the keyhole, Cohen reads this psychoanalytically as an opening in
the body, and sees keys and keyholes in *The Old Curiosity Shop* as central
to the plot of the Marchioness. Although Cohen does not mention Gaston
Bachelard's discussion of the keyhole, he convincingly argues that "the keyhole suggests a continuity between perception and other forms of bodily
ingestion" and the keyhole signifies "connection between two bodies" (13).
In *David Copperfield*, the keyhole's "language of absorption and ingestion
sets the pattern for Copperfield's future expression of intense feeling" as
Clara Peggotty's kind words enter David's mouth and then his heart, through
the keyhole (15). Later, David is similarly "saturated" with love for Dora,
and frightened by the sticky contamination of Uriah Heep's hand and the
"pervious membrane" of Heep as he watches him sleep (15–17). Intriguingly,
Cohen argues, "In Dickens, the interior of the person is reached and reshaped
through the bodily openings through which the material world enters it" (17).

Vybaar Cregan-Reid's "Bodies, Boundaries and Queer Waters: Drowning
and Prosopopoeia in Later Dickens," reexamines water as an "embodied,
raging and stampeding agent," as well as sexualized and "queer," and the
body in water as vulnerable to sexual penetration and violation. Disappoint-
ingly, the essay does not acknowledge as a part of its critical conversation
key works on the image of the river in Dickens by Avrom Fleishman and
Leon Litvack, or a recent cultural studies text by Elaine Freedgood, *Victorian
Writing About Risk*. Dickens's personification of water is contextualized by
the legal case of *Rylands and Horrocks v. Fletcher*, involving a burst reservoir
that had catastrophic potential but did not result in loss of life, and other true
waterworks disasters, which Cregan-Reid argues led to the "pervasive cultural concept of water as an embodied agent of destruction" (24). Thus, one
may interpret Quilp's drowning in *The Old Curiosity Shop* as a male rape,
and Steerforth's drowning as an effeminizing, sexualized penetration in *David
Copperfield* (24, 28–29). The essay concludes with a look at *The Uncommercial Traveller*'s "Travelling Abroad," in which, after a visit to the Paris
morgue, the narrator swims in the river and feels he has ingested one of the
corpses he has viewed. Cregan-Reid understands this as Dickens's fears of
drowning becoming "commingled with a disgust of same-sex desire," and
concludes by noting the mutability of water's meanings and its ability to act

as a "catalyst of degeneration"; without placing this discussion within the context of other critical discussions of Dickens, the Thames, and the city, this essay fails to persuade (31, 32).

Holly Furneaux, taking her title quotation from the scene in which Herbert Pocket carefully dresses Pip's burned arm in *Great Expectations*, " 'It is impossible to be gentler': The Homoerotics of Male Nursing in Dickens's Fiction," wants to counter Eve Sedgwick's reading of male sexualities emerging exclusively through violence in Dickens's work, offering instead Dickens's "affirmative, tender strategies for articulating desire between men" (34). Furneaux argues that Pip's "sensitive place[s]" react erotically to Herbert's touches and words during his telling of Estella's "back-story," and again to Herbert's rescue when Orlick is about to kill him, since Pip shows "excessive eagerness at Herbert's physical support" (38). Nursing made male touching legitimate. Furneaux, however, notes that although Miriam Bailin, in her landmark study of the Victorian sickroom, recognized the heterosexual erotics of Dickensian nursing, she did not write about its potential homoerotics. Following Bailin, Furneax theorizes that "Nursing, then, provided a major metaphor for erotic contact in nineteenth-century fiction, and Dickens's own novels operate as an explicit index to the growing, pre-coital intimacy of premarital couples such as Arthur Clennam and Little Dorrit, and Dick Swiveller and the Marchioness" (39–40). In class-crossed homoerotic relationships, nursing can bring about breakdowns of class boundaries, as when Pip's delirium expresses an "erotic transgression of social boundaries" between himself and Joe (40). Eden becomes the cultural site for this male romance in *Martin Chuzzlewit*, following Robert Lougy, but Furneax goes further to explain how, through the experience of nursing, Martin and Mark become emotionally intimate, developing a relationship so intense that upon their return to England, it threatens to overtake the "boundaries of the domestic plot" between Martin and Mary (45).

Tara Macdonald's " 'red-headed animal': Race, Sexuality and Dickens's Uriah Heep" identifies Heep's "unruly," associatively Semitic, and sexually deviant body as diverging from "the English masculine ideal" (49). Following Edgar Rosenberg's idea of the economic parasite (1960), Macdonald identifies the link between David and Uriah, and places Uriah's deviance in the context of Victorian race theories such as Robert Knox's *Races of Men* (1850) and Thomas Carlyle's "Occasional Discourse on the Negro Question" (1849). Uriah's skin, hair, unstable class position, and parasitism combine to underscore his difference/deviance. David, however, both carnally fixates on Uriah and paranoically disavows him; this "suggests an intense homoerotic relation between the two men" (56). Macdonald reads David's rage at Uriah after the latter admits to loving Agnes, as suggestively homoerotic and characterized by heterosexual jealousy, at the same time: [David wishes to run] the phallic image of a red-hot poker . . . through Uriah's body, and [Uriah's confession of love goes through David like] a ball fired from a rifle, which implies a kind of orgasmic discharge. As a red-headed animal, Uriah is himself represented as a threatening phallus'' (58). Macdonald's reading combines race and sexuality in her reading of David's response to Uriah; a major influence is Oliver Buckton's interpretation, discussed below, also under **Sexualities**.

Jenny Hartley provides one of the most enjoyable essays in this collection, ''Undertexts and Intertexts: The Women of Urania Cottage, Secrets and *Little Dorrit*.'' The essay carefully reads from Dickens's letters about the Urania Cottage project, as do Amanda Anderson (1993) and Margaret Darby (2000), but also considers the manuscript of *Little Dorrit* in the Forster Collection in the National Art Library (Victoria and Albert) in London, as well as the concurrent writing project of *Dombey and Son* when the Urania Cottage project was begun. By studying the confluence of Dickens's fictional projects and his access to women's sexual histories through Urania Cottage, what Hartley calls ''this casebook of back-stories,'' she unfolds an essay that feels not like an academic presentation but, instead like the very best kind of literary discussion written for a broader audience, an essay that is itself a locked box that gradually opens to reveals its contents to the reader. Hartley describes Dickens's involvement in Urania Cottage engagingly as ''part theatre, part Big Brother social experiment, part reform penal colony, and part data bank'' (64), noting how Dickens himself wrote down the histories of the Urania Cottage women, in a casebook now lost and therefore forever secret.

This literal text of women's secrets becomes the fictional text of *Little Dorrit*, a novel full of women's secrets, and also men's (66). Arthur's birth-mother's story remains largely secret, as does Little Dorrit's desire. Studying Dickens's manuscript, Hartley notes that twice in the last of eight volumes of the manuscript, in ''Mrs. Clennam's long speeches of revelation,'' there is a pasting of a fresh version over an original undertext and ''strokes which dig into the paper as in acts of suppression'' (68), as Dickens self-edits like his heroine Little Dorrit (68). Miss Wade's intertext, ''The History of a Self-Tormentor,'' remains one of the most-discussed structural and narrative elements of the novel, and Hartley takes this up in her essay, calling Miss Wade ''an ex-Urania girl,'' the awkwardness of whose story ''alerts us to the contradictory processes at work in Dickens about women and their stories, and how to pass them on or not'' (71). Although acknowledging Wilkie Collins, through his own ''bohemian'' experience and his fictional assumption of women's voices, was an ally of Dickens, Hartley notes Dickens's worry about the prosecution of Flaubert in France for *Madame Bovary*. Dickens at this time was halfway through *Little Dorrit*, and the prosecution of Flaubert contributed to Dickens's decision to desexualize the character of

Little Dorrit (72–73). Thus *Little Dorrit*'s women are silenced or unheeded, whether the exiled Miss Wade, the paralyzed Mrs. Clennam, the silenced Affery, or the self-policed Tattycoram (73). Only Flora Finching, the "woman with the sexual secret gone comic," gets to express female desire (74).

Anne Schwan's "The Limitations of a Somatics of Resistance: Sexual Performativity and Gender Dissonance in Dickens's *Dombey and Son*" critiques individualized corporeal practices at the expense of "social relationships on a structural level" through the coding of "Paul and Edith's resistance to Dombey's regime of gender-discipline as . . . deviance" (93). Schwan notes the importance of "relational criticism," studying masculinities next to femininities, and cites Robert Newsom on Dombey's "radical questioning of the psychology of gender" (94, 95). Following James Kincaid's *Child-Loving*, Schwan finds that Little Paul's refusal to take on middle-class masculinity embodies "somatic resistance" that is coded as sexually deviant (96). Further, Paul's weakness in his "legs" may be seen as a euphemism for "contemporaneous discourses around the masturbating child," figuratively marking Paul's resistance to Dombey's "mode of bourgeois masculinity" (97). Like Major Bagstock, whose association with Victorian flowers codes him as homosexual, Paul, a "pretty flower," is also coded as queer (100–01). Continuing the "gender dissonance" begun by Paul, Dickens codes Edith Dombey an hysteric, a "performative resistance [which] fails as a social strategy of opposition" (101). Schwan argues that Paul's and Edith's resistance has limited value as an agent of social change "on the structural level," because Dickens has "individualis[ed] the problem of gender dissonance" (102–03). Schwan's essay concludes the collection of six essays on Dickensian sexualities in this issue of *Critical Survey* by urging critics not only to "subject canonical figures like Dickens to a continuous reassessment of his representational strategies, and their broader political implications, but also [to examine] those of our own contemporary critical practice and its own political dimension" (103).

Journal Essays and Single Book Chapters

The fallen woman's sexual taint as constructed by Dickens is the subject of Amanda Anderson's " 'The Taint the Very Tale Conveyed': Self-Reading, Suspicion, and Fallenness in Dickens." She foregrounds her study of *Dombey and Son* and *David Copperfield* with Dickens's work on the Urania Cottage project and his essay "A Nightly Scene in London" (1856). "For Dickens, the fallen woman displaces three primary threats: the threat of environment over character, the power of 'stories' over their tellers, and the alienating effects of self-consciousness" (67). Dickens challenged Victorian "religious and moral discourses of the fall," blaming "a degraded environment, [and] diminished options'' (68). Consequently, he denied agency to the fallen woman. ''A Nightly Scene in London,'' in which the narrator gives money to fallen women who dissolve into the night, shows that fallen women ''cannot sustain the status of a subject in that society'' (71). Seeking control over the Urania Cottage girls, ''Dickens fetishized and insisted on personally conducting the initial interviews of all candidates for admission to Urania Cottage'' (73). His adoption of gaol commander Captain Maconochie's system of marks enabled girls to earn marks for good behavior and lose marks for poor behavior, but Anderson shows that ''reading'' the Urania Cottage women as ''marks'' rather than ''stories'' objectifies them much as prostitution does, thus expressing ''the forms of falseness and attenuated autonomy that define these women'' (78). Also a ''public woman'' textually marked by her bad behavior, Alice Marwood of *Dombey and Son*, the double for Edith Dombey, ''the prostituted wife,'' combines various elements of fallenness. She is a product of her environment (her mother and home), she has a ''compulsion to 'communicate her history,' '' like all ''public'' women, and her subjectivity is precarious. Thus, we see with her ''an eventual erasure or forced fading'' (83). The subject of critical comment by Tillotson and the Leavises, Edith's theatricality ''transcend[s] ''crude melodrama'' because it functions in two important ways: to ''display . . . her commodity status,'' and ''to establish a troubling inverse relation between . . . reading the self and having a self'' (85).

In discussing *David Copperfield*, Anderson finds that David ''achieves consolidation and recovery of self largely by defining himself against . . . versions of fallenness''; these include Emily, Martha Endell, and Annie Strong. Emily is often figured in postures of falling (97, 98), while Martha Endell ''as a fallen woman represents Emily's telos'' (97–98). Martha's London habitat shows the ''interpenetration of feminine vice and polluted environment'' (99). Annie Strong's suspected fall ''[embodies] the force of the narrative,'' analogous to how the fallen woman embodies ''the force of the environment'' (105). Annie's ''stain'' or suspicion of guilt is ''anticipation, suspicion, narrative exigency itself'' (104). Finally, Dickens's own anxieties about autonomy are displaced onto the fallen woman (106–07).

Showing how an identification between female prostitutes and male thieves in *Oliver Twist* genders prostitution, and ''allowed for the possibility of child prostitution among the boys'' (230), Larry Wolff in '' 'The Boys are Pickpockets, and the Girl is a Prostitute,' '' makes the historical and sociological case for sexual abuse in Fagin's den. Wolff notes Dr. Michael Ryan's founding of the London Society for the Protection of Young Females and the Prevention of Juvenile Prostitution in 1835 and also observes that the society's manifesto contains language which resembles the story of Oliver's recapture and confinement (236). Wolff uses William Acton's *Prostitution* (1857) and Henry

Mayhew's *London Labour and the London Poor* (vol. 1, 1861–62) to explore further Victorian attitudes to juvenile female and male prostitution, and concludes with a discussion of Oliver's "looks" as an "asset" both in the criminal world and in the respectable world (239).

Lesbian erotics swirl around *Dombey and Son*'s construction of its nineteenth-century sentimental heroine, Florence Dombey, claims Mary Armstrong in "Pursuing Perfection." After first connecting "female sentimental suffering" with "female homoerotic possibilities" in the early example of Florence's kidnapping by Mrs. Brown, Armstrong shows how Susan Nipper reconstructs her identity through Florence's sentimental suffering, "displac[-ing] her language of critique onto her body/self," and leading to class rebellion (285–86, 291). Susan's "dangerous" erotic attachment to Florence, narrated through the "low melodrama" of Susan and the sentimental suffering of Florence, is eventually made safe through Susan's marriage to Mr. Toots (291). Further, Armstrong demonstrates how stepmother Edith fetishizes Florence's innocence and beauty, but lacks the redemptive comedy of Susan. While Dickens may attempt to regulate Edith's desires through the villain Carker, Edith cannot be "defused," and *Dombey and Son* "introduces unquenchable erotic possibilities between and among women" (296, 298).

Dickens's displacement of "problematic desire" onto "expressions of maudlin sentimentality" or "scenes of violent antipathy" reveals the homoerotics of *David Copperfield* as read by Oliver S. Buckton, in " 'The Reader Whom I Love': Homoerotic Secrets in *David Copperfield*." Buckton theorizes the novel through Dickens's autobiographical confessions to his friend John Forster, with whom he discussed many of the narrative techniques he used; through narrative theorist Philippe Lejeune's concept of autobiographical space; and through Judith Butler's idea of melancholia stemming from the loss of an object of same-sex desire (Lejeune; Butler 189–90). Further, Buckton shows that Dickens, having disclosed his past to Forster, in his novel seeks to forbid intimacies between his protagonists and other characters in his novel in order to recuperate his lost privacy and, in doing so, employs a language that strikingly resembles "the vocabulary of homoerotic desire" (191). The role of *Copperfield*'s narrator, Buckton points out, has been the fodder of much critical discourse, as scholars debate the degree of relationship between life and fictional construction, and between constructed autobiography and the author's life. Buckton calls "*Copperfield*'s narrator "an insecure interpreter," who invites the reader to "hunt" for the "reader whom I love" (preface to 1850 edition), to search for private disclosures, in reading the novel (191, 193–94). This invitation by Dickens opens up the autobiographical space Lejeune theorizes as a way authors invite readers to explore the self-referentiality of their work. Buckton demonstrates David's attraction first to Murdstone, called by David "a very handsome man," then to Steerforth, and shows how these attractions construct David as a masculine subject who lacks the masculine power of Murdstone and Steerforth (202–03). David's remarks about the shame he feels following the night of men-only dissipation is "coded as a *class* transgression in Dickens's novel" and is also "only too legible as an instance of the systematic homophobic policing that attempts to keep male intimacy 'pure' " in the novel (205). Despite Steerforth's death, David never recovers from his infatuation with his friend Steerforth (209). Buckton concludes with a discussion of Uriah Heep's visit to David's London lodgings, and the "queer complementarity" of the two characters (211). Buckton reads Uriah's "posture of sexual receptivity" and his working class proximity to David as conflating "class and sexual anxieties," making him a representative body for the "narrative's shameful past" (212, 211). Thus, argues Buckton, David's repulsion towards Uriah must be strong, and also, his fantasies of assaulting Uriah strongly envisioned, in order to belie David's erotic attraction to Uriah.

Investigating the relationship between sexual prudishness and Victorian novels through references to sex scandals in fiction and newsprint, William A. Cohen, in "Manual Conduct in *Great Expectations*," argues that these reveal conflicts about the generation and prohibition of discourse about sexuality. Cohen notes the historical correspondences between novel-reading and masturbatory practice in the mid-nineteenth century: the novel had to "learn" to manage its discourse about sexuality, to "encrypt" its representations of sexuality, just as Victorians had to learn to manage appropriately or repress their autoerotic impulses. Cohen quotes the "prig" conversation between Oliver, Charley, and Dodger in *Oliver Twist* as a scene of "initiation into the secret community of male adolescence" (28), before pointing to two implicitly masturbatory scenes in *Great Expectations*, the first in which the child Pip hides bread and butter in his pants, and the second in which the adult Pip finds boiled fowl, parsley, and congealed butter in his bed at Barnard's Inn. Cohen's project will be to find "at the very heart of the Victorian literary canon a deeply saturated perversity. . . . a literary language that expresses eroticism even as it designates sexuality the supremely unmentionable subject" (31).

Foregrounding his study of Dickens with the medical history of masturbation, and Victorian texts on palmistry and the hand, Cohen shows "the kind of attention the hand received in the period" (35). Hands in the novel function metonymically both to suggest and warn against masturbation. Cohen reads Pip's shame at Estella's scoffing at his "coarse" hands as embarrassment about forbidden "manual conduct" or masturbation: "Humiliation over the laboring (productive) hand converges on shame over the autoerotic (wasteful) one" (37). Cohen also reads Jaggers as an autoerotically coded character, a man with a massive hand who refuses to offer it or offers it only sparingly.

Cohen also contends that Herbert's and Pip's early sparring is tactile eroticism preceded by visual "cruising" and that Pip's conflict with Orlick is both violent and erotic. Therefore, Cohen surmises, the novel's homophobia "proposes several alternate routes": heterosexual "spectacles of impropriety" such as Mr. Wemmick's embrace of Miss Skiffins (56), domesticity "canceling" eros in marriage (57), "male homosocial desire expressed as brutality" (57), and eros sublimated as "comfortably homosocialized relation," as in Pip and Herbert's friendship at the end (59). Cohen creatively pairs the dinner scene at which Herbert instructs Pip about his "manual conduct" at table, teaching him manners, with the later scene during which Herbert dresses Pip's burned hands, stating that their intimacy "can be more frankly noted" in the latter scene (59).

Magwitch is the other character whose handling of Pip's hands has a troubling eroticism, writes Cohen. This meaning is recuperated by Pip into "straight desire" through Magwitch's death and kinship to Estella. Cohen also discusses the manual conduct of Biddy, Molly, and Estella before stating that "the novel's concluding ambivalence may reinscribe the mode of sexual deferral by which it has operated from the first: in the manner of an imaginary object held perpetually at bay by autoerotic reverie, its eroticism can persist precisely by being suspended as undecidable" (71). Finally, *Great Expectations* holds scandal at bay in its very mode, but depends on the threat of the revelation of scandal for its effect (72).

"Relentlessly scrutinized" female sexuality masks anxiety about the novel's deviant male sexuality, argues Colette Colligan, in "Raising the House Tops: Sexual Surveillance in Charles Dickens's *Dombey and Son* (1846–48)." Theorizing her argument through film specialist Laura Mulvey and cultural historians Lynda Nead and Anne McClintock, Colligan posits that not only the text, but also Hablot K. Browne's illustrations, emphasize a panoptic gaze, often directed at potentially transgressive female sexuality. However, at the novel's midpoint, the focus shifts to the male subject, Mr. Dombey, to uncover his impotence and "homosexual proclivities," expressed in Dombey's relationships with Bagstock and Carker, and through Dickens's characterizations of them (101, 116–17).

Anna Wilson's "On History, Case History, and Deviance: Miss Wade's Symptoms and Their Interpretation" reads Miss Wade as a lesbian and considers her roles as governess and madwoman. Although Wilson notes that previous critics have denied eroticism or lesbianism in Miss Wade's character (Lucas, Heatley, Splitter), she suggests that readings of this character have suppressed her lesbianism in favor of exclusively psychological interpretations, diagnosing her as revealing psychotic rage, neurosis, or paranoia (189). Instead, Wilson approaches Miss Wade first through her role as a governess, positioned precariously between social advance and decline, and second through her lesbian identity. Observing that the social instability of the governess was linked in the public mind with insanity, Wilson argues that in Miss Wade's case, Dickens does not assign social injustice experienced by the governess as the cause of madness, and, further, it is Miss Wade herself who "becomes not the victim of insanity but its propagator" (193). However, while Tattycoram's madness can be rehabilitated through Victorian moral treatment, Miss Wade's pathology is untreatable, beyond history, and "self-inscribed" (193). Wilson's reading of Miss Wade as a lesbian refers to Victorian sources that warn against "overpowering feeling . . . in opposition to the definite laws of God," particularly "special friendships" between adult women that might detract from domestic duties and responsibilities (194–95). Wilson concludes that Miss Wade's history is "[linked] to other threats to class and gender stability" (197). Thus, lesbian identity acts as a "metaphor" for disruptions of class.

Rebutting readings of Miss Wade as a lesbian, Janet Retseck, in "Sexing Miss Wade," reexamines Dickens's Number Plans for *Little Dorrit* and Victorian current affairs to show how this character "embodies the threat of political rebellion" (217). With attention to Dickens's concern in the mid-fifties about how the British government treated its subjects, Retseck reads Miss Wade's body in the novel's initial quarantine scene as defiant and angry and believes she is introduced into the novel to inflame Tattycoram's rebelliousness and emphasize what "Dickens feared the subjects of the British crown might do in the absence of reform" (221). In conclusion, Retseck argues that the purpose of "The History of a Self-Tormentor" is not to establish Miss Wade's sexual identity, but to show "readers that all her anger and defiance is founded in delusion" (223).

Sharon Marcus, in "The Female Accessory in *Great Expectations*," fascinatingly describes how Miss Havisham and Estella form a female "dyad" that resembles lesbian pulp fiction of the 1950s, except that Pip does not get the girl in the end and must watch his exclusion throughout the novel (169). Reading Miss Havisham's relationship with Estella as fetishistic, Marcus foregrounds this with Dickens's familiarity with Mark Lemon's children's book *The Enchanted Doll*, showing how Dickens transforms the image of the doll into a weapon in his female character's hands. Marcus characterizes this weapon, which is the foster-daughter Estella, variously: as "a dildo, a surrogate appendage . . . endowed with the power of the woman who wields her but has no sensation of her own"; "attached to and detachable from Miss Havisham"; and, "Miss Havisham's fashion plate and doll" (175). While Miss Havisham exercises her fetishistic authority, Pip is experiencing the death of masculinity, since masculinity becomes associated in myriad ways with a lack of gentility. He moves from the contemptible "boy" Estella calls him, to his coming of age, in an apprenticeship that he associates with criminality and being socially low, to a view of "Trabb's boy [who] impersonates a bestial, uncontrollable priaprism inseparable from low social status" (179). Marcus's explications of the novel's "sartorial imagination" and Pip's feminized identification with Estella and Miss Havisham are compelling. Pip, the spendthrift of Barnard's Inn, is reconstructed through close attention to Dickens's text and Pip's material world and his responses to it, in an unforgettable critical ride for the Victorian scholar ready for something completely different.

Gender and Biography

David Parker, in "Dickens and the Death of Mary Hogarth," traces the influence of Dickens's sister-in-law Mary Hogarth on his life and work, carefully reevaluating evidence from letters and Forster's biography. Pointing to the practical role played by her both before and after the marriage, first as chaperone, later as companion, nurse, and general helper, Parker shows how Mary from the age of fourteen took on a role in the household that was mutually beneficial for Mary herself and the young couple (68). While reminding readers of Victorian customs, values, and "Dickens's own rectitude," Parker states that "it seems unlikely that a man of Dickens's experience, instincts and imagination would never have fantasized about a sexual relationship between them [Mary and himself]" (69). However, Parker notes that the intensity of Dickens's feelings for Mary emerges only after her death and is permissible only as an expression of grief, reminding readers of the Deceased Wife's Sister Bill that remained in effect until 1908, prohibiting marriage to a sister-in-law, and further, that sexual congress with a sister-in-law was condemned as incest by the *Book of Common Prayer* (69–70). Parker demonstrates how after Mary's death, Catherine and Charles at first record their grief as being shared and felt equally, but then this shifts, until "he became heedlessly eager to proclaim his grief and loss greater than anyone's" (71). This event led to "a myth-making habit of mind" for Dickens, argues Parker, because Dickens belonged to a "literary generation fascinated by dangerous ambiguities of love" (72). Thus, Nell stands for the lost Mary. Nell "becomes an "object of religious veneration, angelic, no less," a precursor of Dickens's Genovese dream, three years later, of Mary Hogarth, "his own complexly revered" virgin, talking to him of Catholicism (73–74).

In part 1 of "Dickens, *Household Words*, and The Paris Boulevards" Michael Hollington examines Dickens's role as a "quintessentially male" flâneur in the city of Paris, a city figured as "regularly female" (155). Describing the routine that Dickens and Wilkie Collins followed in the Carnival season of 1855, Hollington writes that the two men, after dining at five, would enjoy the multiple privileges of *flânerie* (155–56). When Dickens found lodgings on the Champs-Elysées, "the family had a front row seat for the spectacle of Parisian life," a spectacle toward which Dickens had "an ambivalent, or even contradictory" attitude (158–59). Nevertheless, Dickens was fascinated by Paris's sexual spectacle on this boulevard where "*lorettes* display the latest fashion" (Jerrold, *Household Words*, 2 Dec. 1854, quoted in Hollington 161).

Hollington begins part 2 of this study with Haussmann's and Louis Napoleon's efforts "to drive prostitution indoors," efforts favored by Dickens (199). "The question of public display" concerning prostitution was most vexing to Dickens, seen in a letter of 22 April 1856 from Dickens to Collins, demonstrating Dickens's fascination with a "handsome, regardless, brooding" prostitute about whom he wishes to know more (199–200). Hollington sees Dickens here as a man who refuses to engage in the Second Empire's authorized erotic contact, hoping instead to encounter this woman a second time, out of doors: "Dickens approves of it [the Second Empire's policy of removing prostitutes to indoors in salons and ballrooms] yet he seems to want to meet this exceptional person alone, outdoors, in the 'masculine' world of the street where after dark men might hunt, master and 'penetrate' the female night" (201). A privileged male in the city, enjoying *flânerie* (and probably the sexual freedoms available to males without their wives), Dickens also participated in the modernist loss inherent in city-building, sharing with Baudelaire a regret for the loss of "paving stones and their replacement by smooth macadamized tar and pitch" (205). Hollington's essay shows how Dickens's urban pedestrianism was gendered as a male activity and enriched his art during his time in France. See Deborah Epstein Nord (1995), under **Feminitities,** for another view on his flânerie.

In "Nell and Sophronia—Catherine, Mary and Georgina," Rosemary Coleman provides a well-argued essay that exemplifies the difficulty of classifying some of the studies on Dickens and gender. She uses the metaphor of the puzzle to argue that Dickens segmented women into separate pieces, according each woman/piece a dominant quality that fit together in his literary text and in his life. These pieces/qualities are spiritual (deceased Nell and Mary Hogarth), domestic (the Marchioness and Georgina Hogarth), and sexual (living Nell and Catherine Dickens) (33). Coleman begins by theorizing male "energy" through Herbert Sussman's important work on Victorian masculinities, noting it is "potent and dangerous," requiring regulation (35). Thus, *The Old Curiosity Shop* performs what Coleman terms as "surgeries" on its female characters, in order to control these male energies, starting with Nell, whose overexposed, innocent yet eroticized body must be killed in order for the narrator to "take his pleasure with the never-lovelier body" (40). The next patient for "surgery" is the Marchioness, who is silenced and whose reproductive capacity is eliminated, as she emerges "the perfect sister-wife," not unlike Georgina Hogarth (44–45). The dangerously erotic Sally Brass, however, is not controlled, but only "temporarily marginalized" (49). Coleman notes that Georgina joined the Dickens household in 1842, the same year in which some legislators attempted to overturn the "Deceased Wife's Sister Bill"; looking ahead, Coleman implies that Dickens may have acted Quilpishly in the case of Ellen Ternan, " 'a young and lovely girl' growing into a woman expressly on Dickens's account" (51).

Examining the intersection between Dickens's life and three women's stories, Margaret Flanders Darby in part 1 of "Dickens and Women's Stories: 1845–1848" looks at the narratives of Augusta de la Rue, the women of Urania Cottage, and that of his former sweetheart, Maria Beadnell Winter. Darby argues that during these years, 1845–48, Dickens's mesmerism of de la Rue, work on Urania Cottage, and attempt to write an autobiography, fed his "storyteller's appetite to extract feminine secrets through willpower and compassion" (68). Darby explains how Dickens's mesmeric powers gave him the opportunity to tell Madame de la Rue's story in his own words in letters and a journal he kept, since he had total access to the "recesses of her identity . . . beyond her conscious control," and also how this must have been therapeutic for him as well, a way "to heal the wounded child through memory" from the blacking factory days (69). Dickens creates the persona "The Phantom" to embody her disease and "the anxious Physician" to represent himself battling the "Phantom." Dickens's metaphoric language reveals the "sexual overtones" of the melodrama in which he participated with the de la Rues, despite some objections from Mr. de la Rue and Catherine Dickens (72–73). The second set of "women's stories" Darby investigates are the ones at Urania Cottage, in the planning of which Dickens shows "a remarkably humane and imaginative flexibility," according to Darby (73).

In part 2 of this essay, Darby emphasizes Dickens's principles of not referring to the past and of not treating the inmates of Urania House "as children," as well as his own keen curiosity about their stories: "His letters make clear his ready indulgence in this power of his position, as well as his fascination, again protected by the highest motives" (127–28). The only surviving record of the girls' histories are in Dickens's letters about them; here, "the girls come vividly to life," as Darby shows, quoting Dickens's description of Sestina, "I never saw such a draggled piece of fringe upon the skirts of all that is bad," and recalling Sarah Hyam, who seduced a policeman hired to guard Urania Cottage (128–29). Darby argues that Dickens's fascination with these women's stories was due in part to their resistance to him: "they had real lives beyond the reach of his language" (130). Further, Darby compellingly suggests that Dickens may have felt an "affinity" with them, writing "a displaced and subterranean autobiography [which was] much easier and safer to write than the acknowledged one he worked on during these years"

(132). She links Dickens's mesmerism of Augusta de la Rue in Italy and his recording of the case histories of the Cottage girls as instances in which Dickens exercised his "dominating will in which in his view they had to submit in order to be cured" and in which he "[displaces] his autobiographical impulse onto others' lives" (134). Darby also sees Dickens doing this in his short-lived attempt to reconnect with Mrs. Winter in 1855, an attempt that fails because of his "self-indulgent version of the past" (136).

John Bowen, in " 'Bebelle and 'His Boots': Dickens, Ellen Ternan and the *Christmas Stories*," examines the possible birth of an illegitimate child born to Ellen Ternan and Charles Dickens, and its subsequent influence upon Dickens's *Christmas Stories*. Dickens wrote "His Boots" during the fall of 1862 as part of a group of stories called "Somebody's Luggage," a period of "miserable anxieties" for him (201). The tale has a redemptive theme like *A Christmas Carol*, but features an illegitimate French child, *Bebelle*, who loses her soldier-surrogate parent and is adopted by a crusty Englishman who takes her back to England determined to reconcile with his own disinherited daughter (198–99). By introducing into this fictional text the real-life Monsieur Mutuel (a landlord from Boulogne), Dickens, Bowen posits "is using autobiographical material and invoking his life in France in 1862" (202). Further, Bowen advances "the hypothesis that Dickens feared Ellen Ternan to be pregnant in the autumn of 1862, cast[ing] light on this story about an illegitimate child, adoption, fatherhood and forgiveness" (202). Noting that "Mrs. Lirriper's Lodgings" and "Mrs. Lirriper's Legacy," the Christmas stories that followed "His Boots," focus on "questions of illegitimacy, fatherhood and adoption," Bowen concludes his essay by drawing attention to Dickens's 1865 Christmas story *Dr. Marigold's Prescriptions* (206–07). This story, he reminds us, shows Marigold continuing "his public patter while his own child dies in his arms, unbeknownst to his amused and laughing audience." Thus, suggests Bowen, Dickens may have lost his own infant child and out of that loss created a public reading in the character of Marigold, simultaneously performing, exposing, and concealing his loss (207).

Robert R. Garnett, in "The Crisis of 1863," offers further evidence for a pregnancy by closely examining Dickens's letters from 1862–63, arguing that they point to the birth of a child of Dickens and Ellen Ternan, an idea supported by statements made after Dickens's death by his children Kate Perugini and Henry Dickens. Dickens told friends that his sister-in-law Georgina had a heart ailment, but his erratic and frequent travels for eight months between England and France in 1862–63 appear to belie this. Dickens's letters show he is unable to reveal the cause of his anxiety to others, even the liberal-minded Wilkie Collins, and imply some discomfort about the position in which he may have placed his beloved Ellen, a young, unmarried woman. Garnett asks why this information should matter and answers that Dickens's relationship with Ellen, and the possibility that their child was born and perhaps died in infancy, can help us understand the genesis of his next novel, *Our Mutual Friend*.

Chris Louttit, in "Lowell Revisited: Dickens and the Working Girl," reinvestigates the significance of Dickens's account of his visit to the textile town of Lowell, Massachusetts, on 3 February 1842. Louttit disagrees with the readings of Natalie McKnight and Jerome Meckier. Neither of these, he argues, has noticed that "the factory workers are working *women*," and that "the mill girls maintain markers of femininity in Dickens's account" (28). Noting the contemporary controversy surrounding the labor of women and children and citing the work of Patricia E. Johnson and Catherine Robson (reviewed below), Louttit first traces Dickens's involvement with the Children's Employment Commission in 1842–43, before noting the contradiction between Dickens's public objections to women's mine work and his apparent approval of the Lowell textile workers (28–30). While Dickens does have "reservations . . . about the issue of women working outside the home," he also responds to the Lowell workers as "ladylike" and even sexually attractive (30–31). He asks his secretary on his American tour, George Putnam, an aspiring artist, to make a painting of them, and urges him to "make them very handsome" (31–32), but, no painting was ever made. Louttit concludes that Dickens is "more like a factory inspector on holiday intent on coolly detailing the workers' garb and general health" than a tourist "with a roving eye" (32). Rather than being based on any long-lasting reflections of sexual attraction or beauty Dickens had of the workers, information about the Lowell women probably came from a pamphlet given him by Elisha Bartlett, "onetime Mayor of Lowell," which Louttit suggests was probably "beside [Dickens] as a source of ready information when he was writing up the impressions of the day he spent there" (32). Further, Dickens also would have been impressed by the "morals and manners of the Lowell women" and would have regarded their employment as authorized in part by its temporariness, as well as by their femininity, which rendered the factory "a feminized space of domesticity and security" very much at odds with the workplaces being decried as unfit places for women and children back home in England (33–34).

Also examining Dickens's American experience, Lillian Nayder's "The Other Dickens and America: Catherine in 1842" maintains that Dickens's narrative reconstructions of his trip to America in speeches, letters, and later writings attempt to "write Catherine out of his life story" (141). Nayder reminds readers of popular, literary, and scholarly attempts to tell Catherine's story, beginning with Michael Slater's touchstone work *Dickens and Women*, followed by Jean Elliott's one-woman play *My Dearest Kate*, and Daniel Panger's *Hard Times: The Lost Diary of Mrs. Charles Dickens*. While Nayder notes that Panger attempts to offer Catherine's side of the story, she finds that he reinforces the stereotype of Kate as "the marital incubus" Dickens accused her of being (143). Nayder reconsiders Catherine's American tour in light of the six-month separation from her children and the difficulty and pleasures of this separation; the travel experience as a proving ground for Kate as a "game" traveler, amateur actress, and devoted wife (146–47). In America, Kate's willingness to undergo mesmerism was the ultimate sign of her submission and of Dickens's "manly powers" (149).

Nayder's "Catherine Dickens and Her Colonial Sons" unpacks the multiple meanings of Dickens's plans for his sons as he sent them out across the empire: "The making of manhood; mark of ambition, promise and self-reliance; a chance for superfluous and less-than-brilliant boys; the consequence of inadequacy or failure; exile, banishment" (82). She argues further that these five sons' imperial service abroad constituted an exile that meaningfully coincided with the exile of Catherine Dickens from the Dickens household: "The sons' stories point to the needs and dynamics of the British empire during a time of expansion and peril. Yet they also reveal the needs and dynamics of a family in which imperial authority and the authority of the father coincided" (82). Although Dickens may have fantasized "stories of struggle and triumph that would demonstrate [his sons'] manly strength and their resemblance to their father," a different narrative emerges in his letters: "they are in the colonies because of their weaknesses, not their strengths, and are the sons of their mother rather than his own" (86). Building carefully upon Dickens's letters concerning his sons' futures from 1854 to his last letter to Plorn three weeks before Dickens's death in 1870, with special attention to the letters to Frederick Lehmann, and Catherine Dickens's letters and "Last Will and Testament," Nayder reveals how these latter two sources especially show Catherine Dickens "bringing margins to center" through her ability to use "the souvenirs of empire and relics of partings with her sons to draw connections among family members" (90).

Masculinities

The masculinities of Dickensian "bacheldores" or odd men out such as Tom Pinch, George Rouncewell, Reverend Crisparkle, and the Pickwickians are the subject of essays by Karen Chase and Michael Levenson, Natalie Cole, David Faulkner, and Brian McCuskey.

Karen Chase and Michael Levenson, in "Tom's Pinch: The Sexual Serpent Beside the Dickensian Fireside," look at Dickens's fiction of the 1840s and contemplate the suppression of individual pleasure for the achievement of a certain ideal of domestic pleasure that the character of Tom Pinch embodies: "what does generosity have to do with sexuality?" (92). Tom sacrifices a sexual life of his own, and gets instead popularity, what Chase and Levenson eloquently call "the sensuous solidarity of the group as the alternative to the troubling energies of the pair" (94). The essay claims that unfulfilled sexual energies present in Dickens's domestic circles find release in "the chaste buzz of public regard" bestowed upon and received by unpaired characters like Tom.

Examining Trooper George Rouncewell's ability to offer physical and emotional comfort, Natalie B. Cole in " 'Attached to Life Again': The 'Queer Beauty' of Convalescence in *Bleak House*," reads George as a paragon of Victorian male health, building on Miriam Bailin's touchstone work on the Victorian sickroom and Bruce Haley's seminal study on Victorian health. Cole shifts the critical focus from female health to consider Rouncewell's role as an embodiment of masculine vitality and healing who is able to recognize the "queer beauty" of characters like the singed and battered Phil Squod, to meet the needs of outcasts like Gridley and Jo, and also to care for the stricken Sir Leceister Dedlock. Dickens, Cole argues, not only shows a more complex and feminized Victorian masculinity in the class-crossed male bonding of George and Phil, and of George and Sir Leceister, but he also demonstrates the importance of medical realism in his narrative practices.

David Faulkner's "The Confidence Man: Empire and The Deconstruction of Muscular Christianity in *The Mystery of Edwin Drood*" takes issue with Eve Sedgwick's interpretation of the novel's "homophobia of empire" to argue that "Crisparkle presides over this novel," claiming that he as a "global policeman," is the foil and double for Jasper, and that his "wholehearted innocence [is for Dickens] a cultural still-point in a turning world" (175–76). Faulkner, however, may overstate the case for making Crisparkle the narrative center of moral authority, for the Dickensian masculinities at play seem more complex than this essay acknowledges.

Offering to read the Pickwickian bachelor and his sexuality anew is Brian W. McCuskey, in " 'Your Love-Sick Pickwick': The Erotics of Service." Responding to readings by Houston, Kincaid ("Fattening Up"), and Glavin that interpret Pickwickian sexuality as regressive or displaced, McCuskey argues that the novel looks instead for "alternative spaces and relations where excessive erotic energy might be contained, explored, and exploited," most specifically, outside heterosexual marriage, and most often with the help of the novel's many servants (246). McCuskey maintains that Pickwickian characters that seek satisfaction beyond conventional spaces of courtship and marriage may achieve it without the loss of bourgeois male authority. The observation that Dickens's "parody of male anxieties is less an act of subversion than it is an offer of catharsis" is the essay's unresolved crux, an issue of narrative point of view that requires further examination. The essay would benefit from further research on the Victorian servant. For example, reference to Pamela Horn's *Rise and Fall of the Victorian Servant* (1991) would have updated and added additional perspective to Bruce Robbins's *The Servant's Hand* (1986). The discussion of masters ogling buxom servants (252–53) doesn't seem that different from Kincaid's view of sexuality in *Pickwick Papers* as the "voracious oral drive of infancy," a stance that McCuskey earlier dismissed. That servants are connected or involved in some way with the erotic lives of their masters, and that servants have "certain kinds of license and authority" in some sexual matters but are restricted in others, do not seem like large enough claims (257). Discussion of the homosociality of Pickwick and Sam's master-servant relationship should come earlier in the essay and deserves added development (263–64).

Masculinities and work have received much critical attention, especially in *David Copperfield*, but in some of the other novels as well. A variety of Victorian male workers are considered: in *David Copperfield* the writer as narrator and author by Mary Poovey, Laura Fasick, and Lyn Pykett; the artist in the *Kunstlerroman* by Gail Houston, and the writer as Romantic artist by Andrew Dowling; the factory worker in *Hard Times* by Peter Scheckner and Martin Danahay; the physician in *Bleak House* by Laura Fasick; the intellectual worker and teacher in *Our Mutual Friend* by Cathy Shuman and Laura Fasick.

Mary Poovey's study of David Copperfield's concealed authorial labor and of Dickens's socially unstable labor, "The Man-of-Letters Hero," remains one of the most cited essays on this novel and on Dickensian masculinities. She begins her discussion of David's gendering with his mother, Clara Copperfield, a contradictory woman who offers a seemingly "perfect love," but then "[undermines] David's vision of union and perfect love" (83–84). David re-creates his relationship with his mother in marrying Dora, as well as in his association with figures like Annie Strong which exposes his own "undisciplined heart." Before this, these problems are anticipated by David's childhood infatuation with Emily, who, for Poovey, "is intimately connected to David's fantasies of a childish 'marriage' and to his fears about his own and his mother's infidelity" (89). Poovey shows how, even though David desires Emily, Dickens doesn't assign responsibility for such desire to him in the narrative; instead, the novel assigns "the 'stain' of sexual provocation to the woman" (90). Moreover, Steerforth seduces Emily in David's stead, so that the problem of forbidden sexuality and class is transferred "onto the figure of *woman* where it can be symbolically addressed" (91). Poovey likens the male novelist's transfer of power to a woman he has created, but claims merely to describe, to "the process by which contaminating sexuality is rhetorically controlled by being projected onto the woman" (92).

Poovey also observes that Dickens's treatment of the work of writing differs from his representation of other work in *David Copperfield* in that it remains "almost invisible," "euphemistic or nonchalant"(93). Similarly, Agnes's housekeeping is performed as "effortlessly as love is given" (93). Poovey contextualizes her discussion with the uncertain social, gender, and professional roles of midcentury British novelists and underscores the normative values of the Victorian patriarchy, within which the woman's role is a supporting one. Examining Uriah Heep's proximity to David and Agnes, Poovey observes that the physical contact with Heep metonymically functions for other "more degrading contamination": moral corruption wherein Heep conflates sexual and economic motives, pointing to a similarity of behavior between him and David (96). But Poovey maintains that Dickens struggles to make clear the difference between Heep and David, and that such a difference depends on distinguishing between the narrator-David and the character-David, so that the former knows of Heep's evil, while the latter remains innocent of it (98). Such distinctions seem inconsistent, however, since the character-David does understand Emily's fall and Annie Strong's possible corruption. Therefore, Poovey contends, Dickens does not fully individuate David's character, because it is "split and distributed among so many other characters and parts," possibly a "function of sexual knowledge and of female sexuality in particular" (99). In conclusion, Dickens's own labor, as a "literary man," was enhanced by his representation of work that derived from the ideologies of "separate spheres" and "women's domestic labour as non-alienated labour" (104–05).

Laura Fasick's *Professional Men and Domesticity in the Mid-Victorian Novel* is sparked by the central idea expressed by Claudia Nelson in her preface to Fasick's book, "we lose something when we overlook Victorian's men's roles within the home" (i), and she coins the term "Dickensian critique" to describe Dickens's recognition of an ideal of hyperaggressive and brutally energetic masculinity that needed a cultural critique in fiction. Fasick's discussion of *David Copperfield* examines this novel in the context of Carlyle's work on hero-worship, with its inclusion of the hero as a man of letters (see Poovey 1988, above).

David's passivity, feminization, and victimhood are emphasized by Fasick in her first chapter, "Portrait of the Writer as a Young Waif: Authorship in Dickens, Thackeray and Kingsley," as she argues that the character David Copperfield deviates from Carlyle's masculine hero. Despite David's immersion in the "overbearingly masculine novels" of Fielding, Smollett and Defoe, the child David remains, Fasick indicates, surprisingly uncorrupted and innocent after reading them (38). Further, David's "horror" over his demeaning work at Murdstone and Grinby's "unbalances" the narrative when considered in relation to the largely omitted description of the labor of writing (39). Fasick cites Mary Poovey's comparison of the invisibility of housekeeping to the labor of writing (Poovey, 1988). It is in Fasick's placement of

Dickens's construction of a feminized masculine hero next to Kingsley's Alton Locke and Elsley Vavasour, theorized in Kaja Silverman's terms as participating in "marginal male subjectivities" (61), that Fasick's argument is most interesting. She concludes that Dickens and Thackeray were unwilling to unleash in the sight of readers the more overt masculine energies in their fictional authors that they themselves employed to succeed as writers, and that "they refuse to represent any pleasure in the exercise of artistic powers for their own sake" (65). Instead, all three writers choose to over-represent male pain, a strategy that Fasick characterizes as: "nothing succeeds like failure—succeeds, that is, in establishing an easy sympathy and even a heroic status for the protagonist" (11).

Lyn Pykett in "The Gendered Subject of Writing: *David Copperfield*," also notes the detailed account of the young David's suffering, compared to Dickens's reticence concerning David's labor as a writer (114–15). Following Poovey (1988), Pykett skillfully reexamines the linkage of David's writing and domestic labor, and David's feminization as a Scheherazade figure (119–20). In addition, Pykett places the novel as a narrative of David's gendering in the context of Dickens's narrative of the "hero's quest for a family," reviewing the various models of family to which David is witness before he forms his own (120–21). Further, Pykett explains lucidly and carefully how this novel became a central text in Victorian fiction, particularly for "feminist representations of women and the construction of gendered and classed identities, and psychoanalytic explorations of Oedipal dramas and narratives of maternal lack" (112). Such representations include not only the figure of the writer, but also "the representation of the home, the family, the neglected, bereaved, or abandoned child, the Angel in the House and the fallen woman" (112).

Gail Houston's "Gender Construction and the *Kunstlerroman*: *David Copperfield* and *Aurora Leigh*," compares the male and female artists in novel and poem, showing how both Dickens and Barrett Browning propose androgynous models for their artist protagonists. The *Kunstlerroman*, or *artist-novel*, "displays a stabilized and authorized reading of the writer" (213), who is typically male, thereby making this form and the different ways Dickens and Browning appropriate it good sites for investigating Victorian gender construction. Houston argues that the artist is associated both with engendering and whoring in the cheap nineteenth-century marketplace (214). She contends that both David Copperfield and Aurora Leigh find that the binaries of rigid male-female sex divisions "continually collapse into each other" (215). "Dickens imagines his alter ego as a female-manqué" (216), "a boy who must assume the pen to assume the penis," (216), but the feminized writers Mr. Dick and Dr. Strong also signal what David might have become, had he not attained "masterful writing" (217–20). Ultimately, for Houston, "Dickens' self-serving figuration of androgyny equates the feminine with copying and submission and masculinity with creating and author-ity" (223).

Andrew Dowling, in "Dickens, Manliness, and the Myth of the Romantic Artist," attempts to show how "the male novelist defines himself against the multiple images of unmanliness" and tries "to open up the meanings of the male 'other' beyond the homosocial" (3). The masculinity of the literary man can be enhanced by the figure of the Romantic artist, since such a role includes suffering and the endurance of pain (8, 40). Dowling examines reviews of Dickens's works that either find Dickens too "feminine" in mind or else see him as writing or "thrusting the novel into a masculine world of contentious debate" (32).

Peter Scheckner's "Gender and Class in Dickens: Making Connections" argues that in *The Chimes*, *Hard Times*, and *Great Expectations* women function as metaphors for the worker. A corollary argument that Stephen Blackpool is a prototype of the Dickensian worker and also in some ways of "a certain type of female character" (243) deserves further exploration. Gender could be more explicitly historicized and theorized, since the essay seems to be focused more on class issues than on constructions of gender proper.

Martin Danahay, in "Dickens, Work and Sexuality," sees the male workers' fate in Coketown as symbolized by Louisa's Evelike status and consequent sin and fall from grace. Danahay, however, does not sufficiently explain why male workers are displaced onto the character of a leisured, upper middle-class female character (as Fasick does). Statements like "Esther's character is separated from sexuality by her illness" would benefit from studies like Helena Michie's on illness and scarring. Danahay argues: "Rather than represent male labor directly, Dickens uses female figures as representatives of excluded or repressed desires that cannot find expression directly within the world of masculine work" (84). Contending that "Dickens indirectly represents his own position [as a writer] through Esther, but cannot directly represent the labor of writing," for "his own subject position within the Victorian gendered hierarchy of labor . . . [is] as problematic as that of a woman performing domestic labor as a feminized form of work," (73–74), Danahay never makes clear why Dickens's position as a writer would have been especially problematic in the 1840s and 1850s, when Dickens was well established as a popular novelist. Danahay writes that Dickens's work at this time was "informed" by the "spectre of indolence," (68), but this charge requires more support. Mining Dickens's letters at this time could help, and more attention to Esther's labor in the context of male labor and to Louisa's sexuality in the context of other sexualities in *Hard Times*, would be welcome. Danahay extensively cites *Mrs. Beeton's Book of Household Management* (1861) to foreground Esther's housekeeping, but does not remind readers, as

Chris Louttit has observed, that Beeton's book was published eight years after *Bleak House* began serialization.

In "The Hero as Healer," Fasick briefly notes that those with a less medically trained approach to the sickbed (such as Esther and Charley) perform the most effective healing (108). Fasick also argues that *Bleak House* celebrates the gentlemanly status of Alan Woodcourt as physician, indicating that gentlemen physicians in Victorian fiction seem to make better healers. Woodcourt, however, though empathetic, loses many patients, his largely unsuccessful practice of medicine reaching its apex with the ambiguous disappearance (through the blindness of his love?) of Esther's scars at the end of *Bleak House* (125–26). Timothy Carens's essay takes up the issue of Woodcourt as a type of masculine social reformer in his essay (see Carens in the **Femininities** section).

Cathy Shuman, in "Invigilating *Our Mutual Friend*: Gender and the Legitimation of Professional Authority," argues that Dickens employs the paradigm of the examination for relationships between test-takers and test-givers in *Our Mutual Friend* (169). First, Wegg and Boffin "classify intellectual work . . . by invoking the doctrine of separate spheres" (156). Second, Bella's wifehood is set up as a test or examination, so that domesticity itself is examined by a "male invigilator," who is also the husband conducting surveillance (159). Third, Shuman argues that in this novel, homes may fail to allow female domesticity to prosper, while professional power thrives in state institutions, which mimic the coziness of the family home (161–62). Reading the scene between Rogue Riderhood and Bradley Headstone in the latter's classroom, Shuman shows how Riderhood's invigilation of Headstone "enacts a profound uneasiness about institutionalized free-trade education and the ease with which it can be perverted to private—indeed to criminal—ends" (166). Shuman extends this argument in her chapter " 'In the Way of School': Dickens's *Our Mutual Friend*," where she further demonstrates how market and "extraeconomic boundaries are blurred," paralleled by the blurring of class and gender boundaries, for example, in the scavenging of Lizzie's and Jenny's occupations (131). Job classification, the novel suggests, now belongs with the intellectual worker such as Headstone, emphasizing "the difficulty of categorizing and controlling work performed at the borders of the marketplace" (133). Offering a more extended reading of the novel's model of invigilation, she calls it the "replacement of the domestic angel with the schoolgirl," a turning from the "domestic haven" to the "classroom" (143). Theorizing the transmission of knowledge through Bourdieu and Passeron (1977) and Bourdieu (1996), Shuman shows how female development in the novel paradoxically depends on resistance to the invigilators of male knowledge. She sums up: "it is the incoherent formation of a female *subjectivity* that empowers a specifically nineteenth-century construction of masculinity through identification rather than differentiation" (169).

Focusing on the denigration of intellectual acquisition, Fasick, in "Love and Work in *Great Expectations* and *Our Mutual Friend*," shows how Dickens insists on the value of work as "an act of self-abnegation" (146). Here Dickens "actually distorts most severely and abandons most thoroughly the values of energy, effort, and endeavor that Carlyle preached" (12). The striving after self-improvement that characterizes Bradley Headstone is interpreted as egotism and condemned, while Eugene Wrayburn's behavior is seen as less self-conscious and therefore more authentic. Showing Dickens's denigration of intellectual acquisition, especially in Charley Hexam, Bradley Headstone, and Pip, for all of whom it coincides with an overly aggressive pursuit of class mobility, Fasick also shows that, for Biddy, proper learning is motivated by the desire "to be a more effective domestic angel," and for Lizzie Hexam, "reading or not reading is . . . always a sign of love" (155, 154).

Men work at being men at home in essays by Natalie McKnight and Donald Hall on fathers and patriarchs, which are not quite the same thing. McKnight, in "Dickens's Philosophy of Fathering," notes that Dickens's career is bookended by "bumbling but affectionate" surrogate fathers in Pickwick and Boffin, with Captain Cuttle a similar exemplar from Dickens's mid-career. Biological fathers do not parent so well as surrogates in Dickens's fiction. McKnight foregrounds her discussion with John Tosh's *A Man's Place: Victorian Masculinity and Male Domesticity*, an important study that explores Victorian masculinity in relation to home and family life. McKnight uses the conceit of the "male conduct book" to develop a "how to do it" list of fathering in Dickens, beginning with the traits "affectionate, solicitous, and available," and continuing with the rhetorical playfulness of *David Copperfield*'s Micawber, colorful language of *Dombey*'s Captain Cuttle, and childlike flights of fancy of *Copperfield*'s Mr. Dick. The simple but affectionate tag-phrases of Joe Gargery in *Great Expectations*, "Ever the best of friends" and "wot larks," enable him to "serve as a healing father figure to a needy child," Pip (133). Even Scrooge participates in linguistic play, argues McKnight, thus preparing the reader "for his dramatic change" later in the story (134).

Nonverbal play is a sign of the good father, and McKnight cites S. J. Newman's *Dickens at Play* to draw a connection between Dickens's playful fathers and Dickens the author playfully fathering his characters and imbuing them with the spirit of play (135). She claims that "No other English author, with the possible exception of Shakespeare, *plays* so relentlessly and productively in his writing" (135). She notes too, that Dickens's depiction of playful fathers changes as his career progresses, so that as his own children grew up and he felt the need to exert more control over them, his father-figures, such as John Jarndyce in *Bleak House* and Noddy Boffin in *Our Mutual Friend*, became less playful and more controlling. Finally, McKnight calls God "the ultimate father'' in the Dickens world and notes that in *The Life of Our Lord*, a text written exclusively for his children, "Dickens stresses the aspects of Jesus and God that most match his fictional depictions of good fathers'' (136). In doing so, he overlooks the punitive messages, and concentrates on love and forgiveness. In the end, McKnight proposes that Dickens and his ideal fathers, heavenly and fictional, combine qualities of lovingness, accessibility, play, creativity with language, and control.

Discussing the patriarch in " 'None of Your Eyes at Me': The Patriarchal Gaze in *Little Dorrit*,'' also from *Fixing Patriarchy*, Donald Hall argues that Arthur Clennam's quest "excludes women and the feminine.'' Hall summarizes Luce Irigaray's theory from *The Speculum of the Other Woman* by stating that "individuals within Western discourse remain fixed in discourses that are inherently patriarchal . . . [and] pre-empt the feminine,'' and finds the novel's "love/hate relationship with the father is a central tension'' (116). Patriarchs include William Dorrit, Mr. Casby, Clennam's father-in-law, and Clennam, while those who challenge the patriarchy include characters like Mr. F.'s Aunt, Mrs. Clennam, and Miss Wade. Yet Hall seems to contradict his own thesis as he argues that "Amy Dorrit's soul is gradually 'specularized' (to use Irigaray's terminology), opened up and revealed to us'' (118), after stating that the feminine is "pre-empted'' (116). While Hall says this is the "patriarchal gaze'' on Amy, he does not deal with narration that *is* Amy's, such as her fairy tale or her letters to Clennam, and his thesis is weakened. Hall is more effective on the power of Flora Finching's gaze (120), and indeed, on the trope of the gaze itself. Hall convincingly argues that Mrs. Clennam and Miss Wade, appropriators of the phallic gaze and therefore unnaturally powerful women, allow Dickens to displace "some of the grossest dynamics of patriarchal oppression [onto] the 'women's space' '' (127). In sum, *Little Dorrit*'s final image of the gaze is benevolent, compared to the oppressive image with which the novel began, and Dickens ends on a note of "revivified patriarchy'' (129).

Interrogating David Copperfield's gendered identity and relationships are Margaret Myers, Carolyn Oulton, and Andrew Dowling, and peering into the complicated constructs of Pip's gender are Robert Garnett and Kathleen Sell.

Margaret Myers's "The Lost Self: Gender in *David Copperfield*,'' argues that *David Copperfield* "indicts the cultural extremes of masculinity and femininity,'' eventually offering a reconciliation in the form of Agnes Wickfield and Tommy Traddles, who represent, respectively, the best of feminine and masculine worlds. Following work by Welsh and Friedman, Myers considers the importance of Agnes in a series of juxtaposed losses and achievements important to David's gender identity. David engages in gender role-playing at Salem House, but his loss of Steerforth coincides with two other masculine rites of passage: his falling in love with Dora, and his assumption of financial responsibility when Aunt Betsy claims to have lost her money. Despite David's adoption of what seem to be "rigorous" masculine roles, Myers argues that novel's audience "is warned from the outset of the inherent moral ambivalence of David's masculine role-playing" (114). David's "rediscovery of selfhood" occurs in the Alps, with Agnes's help, after the loss of Dora, Steerforth, and his "feminised male" self Daisy and "corrupted male" self Doady (118). Back in England, David must first visit Traddles, who embodies "the reconciliation between the masculine and the feminine," demonstrating both the work ethic and the intellectual effort men need for the public sphere, but balancing this with "the moral and the emotional" values of the private sphere (119). At the end, the protagonist and writer David retreats into "a safe domestic harbour, a Victorian middle-class home," his writing "feminised" and his wife Agnes just "an idea in the mind of the narrator" (122, 121).

Exploring the David-Steerforth friendship as a Victorian "romantic friendship," Carolyn Oulton in " 'My Undisciplined Heart': Romantic Friendship in *David Copperfield*," sees it in the context of other such friendships in the Victorian era. Dickens admired such friendship. In a letter to Forster, regarding a friend of the explorer John Franklin, he called it "one of the noblest things I ever knew in my life" (159). Oulton notes "the power and the contradictoriness of an ideal that was prevalent in a society supposedly based around the sanctity of marriage," and observes that the discourse of male romantic friendship employed the "rhetoric of love and marriage" (160). Romantic friendship set "boundaries for the containment of emotion," including youth and obliviousness to the inherent erotic possibilities of the friendships (161–62). She finds that in romantic friendship, eroticism may be managed through "the splitting of characteristics between protagonists"—in this case the "innocent enthusiast" David and the "predatory agent of forbidden passion" Steerforth (162, 168). Oulton contends that after an initial intense romantic friendship with Steerforth, David recovers his masculine identity through professional writing and heterosexual marriage (167).

Finding David surrounded by "deviant" men in Murdstone, Heep, and Steerforth, Andrew Dowling in "Masculinity and Its Discontents in *David Copperfield*" sees these characters "establish[ing] an intense relationship with David through the codes of manly discipline they violate" (50). Murdstone's violence is ascribed to his "hegemonic masculinity" that breaks and hardens the hero (52). Heep's desire for Agnes provides the text with "a titillating image of the 'pure woman' corrupted," while Heep himself is the "deviant double who oozes and leaks [while he] also incorporates a displaced anxiety over female sexuality" (55). Steerforth displays a "Byronic temperament that disdains decorum, a heterosexual desire that refuses marriage" (56). Dowling's "queering" of Heep is the most interesting reading offered here.

Pip's unruly desire is paired with that of Miss Havisham in Robert R. Garnett's "The Good and the Unruly in *Great Expectations*—and Estella." For Garnett, both characters stand in marked contrast to the "mild-mannered, cheerful and patient" behavior of the novel's "moderates"—Joe, Wemmick, and Herbert—who serve as exemplars of male nursing (25–26). Miss Havisham's unruly passion as a Dido-figure stretches out her funeral pyre "over years of smoldering decay," while Jaggers is a "crypto-passionate figure" who may hold his servant Molly in concubinage to him (31). Because of his unruly passion, Pip "reveals an essentially sacramental imagination," despite his isolation and homelessness (32–33). Garnett directs attention to Estella's defending against her desirability and susceptibility to desire, and to Pip's recognition of her "passionate blood" (36). He carries this argument forward to the novel's end, where he notes that Estella's penitence still does not clarify for Pip or the reader Estella's heart concerning the issue of *her desires*.

In "The Narrator's Shame: Masculine Identity in *Great Expectations*," an essay that influenced Sharon Marcus's recent reading of Pip as a victim of the novel's female dyad, Kathleen Sell notes that Pip's failure to find a "heterosexual dyad," along with the intensity of Pip's male friendships, leads to his inability "to consolidate securely a masculine identity" (212). Sell distinguishes between guilt (uneasiness over one's actions) and shame (uneasiness over one's self), arguing that Pip simultaneously desires to turn the shaming gaze away from himself and also to expose himself totally to the reader's gaze (203). Sell explores how the dual narration calls attention to but then diverts shame, so that the reader sympathizes with the young Pip and approves of the narrating self (209). The shame of Pip's failure to form a heterosexual dyad results in a narrative shift, whereby the shaming gaze is turned onto the women of the novel (212). Those women fail Pip because their domestic spaces are hells rather than havens: Mrs. Joe fails to be maternal and fails to "ameliorate class conflict and the violent competition potentially provoked by this conflict" (213). Miss Havisham also fails to model maternal behavior, and instead perverts it, "damaging Estella . . . [and] by extension . . . Pip" (214). Finally, Estella is the novel's "ultimate scapegoat," the female who fails to turn Pip's transgressive desires into a safe channel through a marriage that *she* does not desire. Sell astutely reasons that "through marriage, he [Pip] would rule out the potentially shameful quality of his close relationships with men and ameliorate his need to compete and labor" (220). Pip's bachelorhood at the end signals his exclusion from the narratives of heterosexual desire and heroism, condemning him to a hinterland of ambiguous identity and "wretched hankering" (222).

Femininities

Communities of women, organized by kinship or common traits, form an important part of the Dickensian critical discourse on femininities. First among this group are the Dickensian mother and surrogate mother.

Natalie McKnight, in "Making Mother Suffer, and Other Fun in Dickens," reminds the reader of Dickens's propensity to tame, beat, burn, scar, and paralyze a host of mother figures in his fiction. McKnight situates Dickens's "delight in making mothers suffer" between a "desire to wreak vengeance on his own mother" and a need for autonomy from the mother who could threaten his identity and creative abilities (37). Theorizing identity-formation and mothering through work by Nancy Chodorow, Adrienne Rich, and Isaac Balbus, McKnight judiciously weighs the biographical effect of Elizabeth Dickens on Dickens's fictional mothers, stating that while Dickens felt betrayed by his mother for her wish to send him back to the blacking factory, his "fictional creations are much more complex than" simply "reactions against his mother" (38). That said, Elizabeth Dickens's love of juvenile dress and finery persisted into old age, and may influence depictions of Mrs. Skewton of *Dombey and Son* and Miss Havisham of *Great Expectations*. Further, "Mrs. Skewton basically sells her daughter in marriage to the highest bidder," a betrayal like that Dickens attributed to his mother (43). Mrs. Joe, a surrogate mother who also "seems willing to sell a young boy to the highest bidder," is stricken down like Mrs. Skewton, Miss Havisham, and Miss Barbary (44).

"Cold, inadequate mothers stand guard at either end of *Bleak House*," while the garrulous Mrs. Nickleby fails to maintain the family's respectability, comically receiving a mild taming, while the ineffective Clara Copperfield fails to protect her son from the vicious Murdstone and is disciplined through death (46–47). However, Betsy Trotwood is "one of Dickens's most complete portraits of an ideal mother"—a non-biological mother, sexless, loving, intelligent, redeemed from tyranny because she can defer to a man's judgment (albeit Mr. Dick's), and never failing the child once she has accepted charge of him or her (48). Other good mothers are also non-biological, such as Mrs. Lirriper ("Mrs. Lirriper's Lodgings" in *Christmas Stories*) and Mrs. Boffin in *Our Mutual Friend* (49).

McKnight concludes her examination of Dickens's mothers by turning to Dickens's treatment of his wife, Catherine Dickens, whose story he rewrote as that of a bad mother, beginning with the "violated letter" that was published in *The New York Tribune*, casting Catherine as an uncaring parent whose own children were unattached to her: "But Catherine's own letters and the reports of her children and other family members contradict these accounts of her mothering'' (50–51). Moreover, McKnight shows how Dickens fled the scene or wrote to friends arranging to be absent from the house on many occasions after Kate had given birth. While recognizing that ''Victorian fathers did not hang around the birth scene as dotingly as some fathers do today,'' McKnight still questions the rapidity and vehemence with which Dickens needed to escape. Noting Dickens's great need for physical order in relation to the chaos of childbirth with its ''messy vitality'' (53), McKnight concludes that making ''mother suffer'' may have even deeper psychological origins in Dickens than we yet recognize.

Associating the wet-nurse with the working-class laborer and the railroad worker, Laura C. Berry, ''In the Bosom of the Family,'' considers the role of the wet-nurse Polly Toodle. By thus ''conjoining two of the more troubling modes through which the classes intermix,'' argues Berry, the wet-nurse's ''class-effacing sign of feminine *influence*'' works to correct or eliminate working-class contamination from the breach of class boundaries (3). A medical debate in the 1850s about the ways in which wet-nursing ''reinscribes the social differences between classes'' forms the backdrop for Berry's ensuing discussion of the ''traffic'' between the Toodle and Dombey families (7, 11). Working-class appetites are transferred to Carker, who ''becomes the repository for the appetitive picture of the poor that operates outside the novel,'' while Polly Toodle's maternal attributes gradually become Florence's (19, 20–21). Ultimately, Berry argues, *Dombey and Son* supports William Acton's medical argument (1859) that the working class wet-nurse need not be feared as a ''devouring'' force, because Florence, through the example of the maternal and nurturing Polly Toodle, has supplied a ''new little Paul,'' and thus the wet-nurse is ''edible'' rather than ''devouring,'' used to sustain and reform the Victorian family (22).

Melisa Klimaszewski's ''Examining the Wet Nurse: Breasts, Power, and Penetration in Victorian England'' compares the cultural attitudes to wet-nurses in Dickens's *Dombey and Son* to those in *Mrs. Beeton's Book of Household Management*, both involving ''invasive approaches to their bodies'' (324). Beeton's shift into a ''medical tone'' regarding the examination of the physical attributes of the wet-nurse's breast is compared to Mrs. Chick's interview of Polly Toodle, with Polly ''coming out unscathed by this ordeal'' (328–31, 336). Klimaszewski suggests that Polly may have undergone the rigorous physical examination prescribed by Mrs. Beeton and that, further, Mr. Dombey panoptically watches her breastfeed (337). This surveillance attempts to ''impose class difference'' even as breastfeeding links disparate classes through its intimacy, evoking class anxiety for the higher social class the wet-nurse serves.

Examining the nursemaid's role as both crucial and disruptive to the middle-class home and British empire, Klimaszewski, in another study, ''The

Contested Site of Maternity in Charles Dickens's *Dombey and Son*,'' offers a more extended discussion of *Dombey and Son* that follows Berry in considering the role of the nursemaid, but goes further to expose "the interdependence of domestic and imperial relationships" (139). Building on work on Victorian servants by John O. Jordan, Klimaszewski explores the ambiguity of Polly Toodle's role in the Dombey household as a "replacement" for the dead mother, a source of sustenance for the infant Paul, a depersonalized servant and commodity, and a challenge to Mr. Dombey's patriarchal control. Recovering Polly's point of view in her reading of the nursemaid, linking Polly's perspective to the reader's and, ultimately, to a critique of Dombey's domestic authority, Klimaszewski argues that Susan Nipper "[extends] the nursemaids' contestation of Mr. Dombey's authority within the domestic sphere to a critique of him as an imperial leader" (147). However, Susan is more transgressive, yelling at Mr. Dombey and dramatizing her rebellion with comments about "being a black slave and a mulotter" (148). Klimaszewski notes, too, how Dickens racializes Susan with "jet-black eyes, black hair, and nickname—'the black-eyed' " (148). Susan's moral authority is derived from her maternal role in the household. Skillfully explicating Susan's invocation of sati (also known as suttee), an Indian ritual involving the sacrificial immolation of a widow on her husband's funeral pyre, Klimaszewkski shows how allusion to sati complicates Susan's maternal authority (150–51). The paired discussion of Polly Toodle and Susan Nipper enriches the reader's understanding of surrogate or replacement mothering and its implications for patriarchal identity at home and abroad in *Dombey and Son*.

Female friendships are discussed in Wendy Jacobson's "Freedom and Friendship: Women in *The Mystery of Edwin Drood*." Beginning with the observation that "in literature friendship between women is usually thrust aside" (70), Jacobson defines friendship through references to Nietszche, Cicero, and Emerson, and she locates in Rosa and Helena's friendship in *Drood* "the Aristotelian ideal that friends love each other for the virtues they discern in each other" (73). Rosa has emotional integrity and the will to act in removing herself to London, Jacobson notes, and it is a mistake to see her in stereotypical terms as a "fairy bride," as Crisparkle does (74–75). Except for Rosa, only Helena Landless perceives Jasper's menace and has the fortitude to speak of it; this is the "foundation of Helena's intimacy with Rosa" (76).

Investigations of the subversive femininities of working women are found in essays by Elsie Michie on Dickens, Gaskell and the "inappropriately public woman," Juliet John on the sincere theatricality of Edith Dombey, Joellen Masters on Little Dorrit as a needlewoman, Linda Raphael on Miss Havisham's cultural constraints, and Lucy Frost on the "taming" of women in *Great Expectations*. Susan Walsh uncovers Miss Havisham's "climacteric" economic body, while Timothy Carens performs a case study on Esther's work as social reform. Essays by Christine van-Boheeman-Saaf and Deborah Vlock also consider the work of the woman's body, since they focus on Flora Finching in order to study the body and the voice of the "odd woman."

Elsie Michie's " 'My story as My Own Property': Gaskell, Dickens, and the Rhetoric of Prostitution" reads Dickens's editorial interaction with Gaskell in the 1850s in the context of the "inappropriately public woman" (79), noting that both Dickens and Gaskell were engaged in public work with fallen women and writing about them in fiction during this decade. Gaskell's concern about a lack of control over her work, how she was paid, and Dickens's naming of her as "Scheherazade" coincides with the masculine authority he exercised over inmates at Urania Cottage. Women there were forbidden to tell their stories to each other or to the female matrons, but could reveal them to the male directors, including Dickens (92). Following Langbauer, Michie reads David as Steerforth's Scheherazade, replaced later by Emily, who is "voiceless," but his "nighttime entertainer" nonetheless (94). Gaskell resisted Dickens's editorial attempts to "appropriate" her work and play literary "husband" to her, and in the serialization of *North and South*, Gaskell regarded *Household Words* as a "prison" (95, 98). Policing trumps rescue work in *Bleak House* and they are revealed to be similar in the pursuit and death of Lady Dedlock. Comparing Dickens's treatment in *Bleak House* of the public and private woman in terms of a split between toxic/healthy and dirty/clean to Gaskell's representation of the title character of *Ruth*, Michie emphasizes the wholeness of Ruth, who is "simultaneously pure and impure . . . [allowing] Victorian women to recognize the split inherent in contemporaneous definitions of femininity" (107). Michie concludes that both Dickens's letters to Gaskell and his representations of rescue workers in *Bleak House* show that apparent benevolence and patience can also be understood as constraints on Gaskell's writing and on female identity in *Bleak House*.

How the sexual and economic spheres intersect is the subject of Michie's following chapter, " 'Those That Will Not Work': Prostitutes, Property, Gaskell, and Dickens," as she reads marriage through a Marxist understanding of private property. Michie sees an authorial uneasiness in both *Mary Barton* and *Hard Times* about the worker's claiming power, so that both authors switch to an erotic plot concerning a fallen woman or woman at risk of falling. Emotional conversion replaces the need for economic change in *Hard Times*, and theatrical spectacle diverts the audience from economic issues in *Mary Barton* (129–30).

Juliet John in "Seriously Deviant Women" argues that the nineteenth-century theater importantly contextualizes Dickens's female characters: first, through revealing the Victorian cultural attitude to actresses, who subverted the feminine cultural ideals of authenticity, sincerity, and domesticity; and second, through the portrayal of melodrama's female characters' "passional interiority," complicating the good/evil binaries of melodrama (200, 205–06). John presents fascinating historical background material on the Victorian actress, and "deviant" female characters in English melodrama, before commencing her discussion proper of Dickens's work. Characterizing Dickens's deviant women as "gender offenders" who have violated the "*unwritten* Victorian code or ideal of femininity," John includes among these women Madame Defarge, Edith Dombey, Lady Dedlock, and Miss Havisham (213). Following the example of Ingham (1992), John wants to further "[muddy] the essentialist view of Dickens's women" (213). Excepting prostitution, John finds "criminality for most women in Dickens perversely . . . [offers] a carnivalesque freedom from the restrictions of the patriarchal order," and recognizes Dickens's dual interest in "openly fiery women" and women who "repress their passion and don a social mask"—the latter commit the gender crimes of being both passionate and duplicitous (213, 214). John argues, then, that Dickens uses melodrama in his representation of Edith in gendering and managing her emotions (215). Alice Marwood is Edith's double, significant because of the "synonymity . . . between actresses and prostitutes in Victorian Britain" and because of "Alice's wild nature" (216, 217). While Edith is described as a statue or sculpture, Alice is active in destroying her own good looks, which "the narrator finds it difficult to forgive" (217). Invoking Erving Goffman's concept of the "true self," John argues that Edith is in fact more sincere than Dickensian heroines Kate Nickleby and Lizzie Hexam, understanding in Judith Butler's words, "gender as a performance with clearly punitive consequences" (Goffman 1959: 28–29; Butler 1990: 139, qtd. in John 218). Edith's melodramatic behavior is reevaluated, then, as her self-conscious role-playing of public and private selves. Her outcast status at the end reaffirms her integrity and "true self," while Alice Marwood's conversion is "artistically and psychologically inappropriate" (221).

John urges a reconsideration of Edith, one that is heroic, feminist, and subversive in rejecting the authority of Dombey and Carker and thus the Victorian patriarchy (222). She also emphasizes Edith's love for Florence, and her complex interiority, moving her out of the critical "prison of essentialism" (223). John resumes her discussion with Simone de Beauvoir's statement in *The Second Sex* (1949) that identifies the dressed woman as an art object, what de Beauvoir calls "this identification with something unreal, fixed" (qtd. in John 223). Relating this to both Edith Dombey and Lady Dedlock, whom John calls "prisoners of their own beauty," John argues that both women are represented as subjects and objects in their respective narratives (224–25). While both women "are complicit in turning themselves into art objects," they are not motivated by vanity (226–27). Dickens uses the objectification of women to explore "female repression of passion, the social enforcement of female interiority, fashionable society's admiration of the statuesque, and commercial society's valuing of the female as commodity'' (228). Concluding her essay, John quotes Kate Millet's assessment of Dickens's heroines as ''insipid goodies carved from the same soap as Ruskin's *Queens*'' (Millet 89–90, qtd. in John 232–33); John, however, shows that Dickens's deviant women are not only ''objects of sexual attraction,'' but often express the desire to dominate others and to exercise sexual power (230, 232). John's reading of Dickens's ''sincerely deviant women'' brings the valuable genre perspective of Victorian theater to the study of Dickens and gender.

Placing Little Dorrit in the social and historical context of the seamstress figure, Joellen Masters in '' 'Let herself out to do needlework': Female Agency and the Workhouse of Gender in Charles Dickens's *Little Dorrit*,'' finds that Little Dorrit combines ''the powerful savior woman with the passive and nurturing woman but in the process of bringing her to life, Dickens simultaneously erases and empties her out'' (54–55). A figure with whom women sympathize, whom men find nonthreatening, who is linked to the quiet safety of the home, Little Dorrit, Masters notes, provides connections ''between characters and episodes, between the text and the reader'' (56). Dickens's ''uneasy conception of the working woman'' also appears in the figure of the seamstress Little Dorrit in three ways: women's labor is hidden, shown by Little Dorrit's sewing being unacknowledged by her father; Dickens never gives Little Dorrit a stronger voice or ''the extended inward reverie of indirect discourse'' (59, 61); and Little Dorrit is not given much female agency, Dickens only allowing her ''to stitch up the weaknesses in those patriarchal traditions he so bitingly critiques'' (62).

Linda Raphael's ''A Re-vision of Miss Havisham: Her Expectations and Our Responses'' urges readers to reconsider Miss Havisham both in her Victorian cultural context and in more recent cultural, literary, and social contexts. She begins by noting how this character ''enact[s] a gap between opportunity and desire which frequently occurred in the lives of Victorian women'' (218). She was motherless, isolated by her wealth, and perhaps served as an emotional focus for her widowed father, as Davidoff and Hall have described the daughter's role (220). Although she was privileged, her father's status as a brewer was only marginally upper class and may have compromised her status in the marriage market (219). Miss Havisham's choice appeared to be authorized by her brother's introduction of Compeyson, guaranteeing him as respectable; hence her rage when Compeyson jilted her. Raphael further reasons, though, that Miss Havisham made this choice herself, taking ''advantage of the new potential independence of a woman making a choice based on emotional intuition'' (223). Dickens not only carefully draws the social shades here, but studies reclusive women, writing about them in letters to John Forster, in *Household Words*, and in his *Christmas Stories*. Raphael follows Kristeva's explanation of narcissism in her understanding of Miss Havisham as having "installed the loved one in herself, while all aspects of her behavior belie a violent self-hatred directed at the lost one who is now part of the self" (Kristeva 1982: 226). This explains her tattered wedding garb and her living amidst the mouldering remnants of her wedding feast. Yet, following Kucich, Raphael considers how "repressed material forms identity," and therefore Miss Havisham enacts a male role as the owner of property, the owner of a female (Estella), and the wielder of power over a male, Pip (226). Raphael concludes with Pip's refusal to tell Mrs. Joe about the "real" Miss Havisham, and the link between "female repression and class immobility" (228). As the best essays do, Raphael's offers not only a "re-vision" of Miss Havisham, but a wider understanding of what she calls "the full workings of the novel" (228).

"Psychologically aberrant" women in *Great Expectations* engage Dickens's imaginative energies more powerfully than the novel's conventional women, argues Lucy Frost in "Taming to Improve: Dickens and the Women in *Great Expectations*." Nevertheless, these women are "tamed" into submission through violence. Diagnosing Mrs. Joe as "the neurotic who clings to her neurosis," imprisoned by housework and lashing out at those around her, Frost questions Dickens's conversion of Mrs. Joe into the docile figure so strangely attached to Orlick, and concludes that "Mrs. Joe is revelling in Orlick's mastery of her," including a possible sexual mastery (64). Frost discusses a nuanced characterization of Estella, in which Dickens has carefully analyzed her as a woman with "awareness of her own peculiarities . . . [able] to distinguish among versions of reality, [who has an] understanding of people whose feelings are not her own" (66), but finds again that Dickens artificially "tames" her through violence. Frost hypothesizes that Dickens was threatened by "women with strong personalities," and thus driven to humble or tame them in his narrative (70). In the case of Miss Havisham's conversion, and her gift of money to complete the purchase of Herbert's partnership, Frost questions whether this atonement is as "straightforward" as Pip thinks it is, given the moral ambiguities surrounding Magwitch's patronage of Pip (74). In Pip's fiery "struggles" with the burning Miss Havisham, Frost also detects Dickens's "impulse to destroy fictional women in the guise of improving them" (75).

Reading Miss Havisham's body as a menopausal narrative of Victorian economic practices of inheritance, investment, and bankruptcy, Susan Walsh in "Bodies of Capital: *Great Expectations* and the Climacteric Economy" offers a closely argued and original interpretation of character and novel. She maintains that although Dickens sets *Great Expectations* in the 1820s, he uses Miss Havisham's "sterile wealth" and "aging female body" to respond to the "shifting socio-economic grounds of the 1840s and 1850s," exploring how that body functions analogously to "a dysfunctional market economy" (78, 73). Following Catherine Gallagher, Walsh notes the "homologous relationship between the social body and the human body," which leads her to a curious historical association: "*Punch* artists [were led] to an even more specific analogy: the change-of-life woman is an economy of men in acute financial distress" (75, 79). Walsh examines *Punch* cartoons of the Old Lady of Threadneedle Street, which use a female figure to represent both the "climacteric crisis" of menopause and an economically precarious state of banking or business, as the context for understanding the climacteric condition of Miss Havisham and her "worrisome . . . financial powers" (79–84, 85). Miss Havisham's unwillingness to carry on her father's business and "to sponsor her male relatives" is obstructive, paralleling the medical diagnosis of obstruction of the blood flow in the climacteric woman (90). Miss Havisham analogously "blocks her financial capital from circulating within the proper channels of investment and trade, thus rendering it economically barren," just as she "condemns her sexual body to infertile disuse and enters her forties as a textbook case of the tragically embittered climacteric woman" (90–91). Having lost her role as "silent partner" in a premature economic exchange prior to the beginning of her matrimonial experience, Miss Havisham lays waste to everything (92). However, Walsh concludes by seeing the glass as half full and half empty: Miss Havisham does invest in Matthew and Herbert Pocket, and Biddy gives some "historical and economic equilibrium" to the Gargery home, but Miss Havisham's economic practices, her ruthless "Beggar My Neighbor" economics, have a lasting, detrimental effect on Pip and Estella (93–96).

Women's philanthropy must be restricted to the domestic sphere, while male reformers must link their imperial adventures and military service to urban reform, in Timothy L. Carens's reading of Dickens's gendering of national reform in *Bleak House*: "The Civilizing Mission at Home: Empire, Gender, and National Reform in *Bleak House*." Carens follows Deirdre David (1995) in claiming that "writing about empire both appropriates and elaborates Victorian gender politics" (David 1995:5, qtd. in Carens 123). After first demonstrating how Mrs. Jellyby has inverted "normative sexual power relations" (125) and produced "savages" in her "wilderness" of a home (125), Carens shows how Esther embodies Dickens's "approved model of female reform, a 'civilizing mission' in which domestic order expands incrementally from a well-managed domestic sphere" (125–27). Even Esther's powers, though, are "curtailed" beyond the middle-class home, as Dickens suggests by the trip to the brickmakers' (129). Dickens satirizes "Telescopic Philanthropy" in Mrs. Jellyby and Mrs. Pardiggle, but praises empire when linked to female duty as in the character of Mrs. Bagnet (130).

Through Woodcourt's and Rouncewell's experiences in the service of empire, Dickens "simultaneously justifies the possession of distant 'dominions' and defines a masculine type of compassionate philanthropy" (136). But Carens concludes that the gendered missions represented by Esther and Alan through Esther's rescue/hiring of Charley's sister and Alan's doctoring of a poor Yorkshire village are a "variety of utopian evasion" (140).

A far cry from Esther are Flora Finching and Molly Bloom. Christine Van Boheemen-Saaf's "Joyce's Answer to Philosophy: Writing the Dematerializing Object" understands Joyce's Molly Bloom and Dickens's Flora Finching as iconic female "flowers" and exposes "the fear of dematerialization and the loss of natural relationship to the body" in both texts (33). Molly's menstruation reveals a mythically fertile female, a Penelope, whose flow can be displaced into "flowers of rhetoric" that reveal the modernism of Joyce's text. Dickens also figures his Flora as a Penelope-figure to Clennam's returning Odysseus. As a flower, she is already blown, her "flush, added girth, and shortness of breath point to menopause, the end of menstruation, the mother of all unmentionables," and her verbal flow is not a sign of fertility, but of "the pathology of the continuation of flirtation after the end of youth and fertility" (38). Therefore, Clennam's masculine subjectivity must be restored by Little Dorrit, who mirrors back to him "young, flowing femininity."

Redundant women and their patter-based dialogue are Deborah Vlock's subject in "Patter and the Problem of Redundancy: Odd Women and *Little Dorrit*." Both "frivolous and true, patter is a literal embodiment of redundancy, and a motivated sign of certain kinds of social marginality" (161). Vlock points out that Dickens worked from sketches by Charles Matthews, but also used a much broader cultural text on single women in the Victorian age (162). Dickens, Vlock notes, shared his culture's feelings about "odd" or "redundant" women: he felt aversion and anxiety, "sweetened, perhaps, with a touch of pity" (165). Vlock claims that the madness and spectacle of industrial culture had its counterpart in bourgeois women and came out in patter, a kind of "verbal deformity" (171). Patter may be both funny and threatening, belonging to both the comic and tragic modes (177). Flora Finching's patter underscores her redundant woman status, and demonstrates open-endedness, diffuseness, and imbalance (188–89). Vlock, although observing that Flora is memorable, could do more to show why the tradition of theatrical patter is such an important cultural backdrop to Dickens's work and, in particular, to *Little Dorrit*'s Flora (189).

Defining the family and its significance in the Dickens canon is Catherine Waters, while Britta Zangen focuses on Dickens's "marriageable women." Marlene Tromp, Lisa Surridge, and Susan Zlotnick examine women, gender, and the law, on issues of spousal abuse and bastardy. Taking up genre and gender are Anne Humpherys on marriage and sensation fiction in *Hard Times*, and Caroline Levine on narrative suspense, realism, and Biddy as the ethical ideal in *Great Expectations*.

Catherine Waters's "Gender, Family, and Domestic Ideology," concisely introduces this complex subject by explaining how Dickens's stories became woven into the Victorian cultural fabric through his portrayal of the family and domesticity: "He used family relations—often represented in distorted forms—to explore the social, political and economic tensions of his age" (120). Waters argues that Dickens studies have moved in the last two decades from traditional examinations of families toward "the ways class and gender differences are implicated in the affirmation of the values of the middle-class family" (122). Waters notices that Dickensian "scenes of family harmony tend to be set in small spaces": the Peerybingles' hearth, the Peggottys' boathouse, Wemmick's castle, Boffin's bower, and even the bachelor quarters of Lightwood and Wrayburn. Designating *Dombey and Son* as a turning point in Dickens's canon in which he engages with the family as "a complex cultural construct," and one which values domestic affection over pride of lineage, Waters further notes the importance of surrogacy and homemaking in this novel (128). Waters's analysis of *Bleak House* focuses on the instability of private, familial space and the family's failure to regulate itself or be regulated by society. Class may displace gender as a basis for identity. Throughout Dickens's fiction, while the deviant woman helps establish the normative ideal, these deviant women also challenge the domestic ideology of many novels. Orphanhood and illegitimacy reveal "middle-class self-making" that "harbor[s] an anxiety about familial origins that Dickens will explore more fully in *Great Expectations*" (132).

In *Our Daughters Must be Wives*, Britta Zangen's decision to split the book's discussion of "Socio-Historical Context" and "Fiction" into separate sections is infelicitous. While the "socio-historical context" is generally well-researched and provides important foregrounding for understanding nineteenth-century cultural expectations concerning eligibility for marriage, the individual discussions of Dickens's work are thin and list-like, not allowing for full consideration of questions of what comprises *marriageability* in specific gender, class, or moral terms. Nor does Zangen show whether or not this concept changes over the course of Dickens's canon. Similarly, her decision to treat Dickens, Eliot, and Hardy in separate sections does not allow for comparison of these writers' representations of this idea, which also might have enriched her discussion. Zangen calls her methodology "close-reading," but she would benefit from attention to previous feminist studies of Dickens. The treatment of female characters is uneven, with no mention of the Marchioness in *The Old Curiosity Shop* or of Martha Endell in *David Copperfield*, and only cursory discussions of Agnes in *David Copperfield*, Estella in *Great*

Expectations, and Bella and Lizzie in *Our Mutual Friend*. Zangen's best analysis is that of *Martin Chuzzlewit*, in which she notes that Dickens for the first time critiques ''the sacrificial endurance and self-denying patience'' as ''feminine qualities of his heroine Mary Graham'' (111). The study is limited by Zangen's decision not to examine ''unmarriageability'' in Dickens's fiction.

Bill Sikes's abuse of Nancy constitutes the starting point of Marlene Tromp's ''A'Pound' of Flesh: Morality and the Economy of Sexual Violence in *Oliver Twist*.'' Tromp looks back at *The Newgate Calendar*'s objectification of the battered woman to show how Dickens provides a more sympathetic representation. Tromp begins by noting the physical purity of Agnes and Oliver, and the moral goodness of their tears compared to crocodile tears of ''failed women'' such as Mrs. Sowerberry and Mrs. Bumble (30–32). Nancy's physicality becomes a ''narrative obsession'' for Dickens, and Dickens's sympathetic portrayal of Nancy changes the trajectory of the spousal abuse narrative, making Nancy ''the pound of flesh'' by which both Oliver and Dickens ''purchase their status'' (35, 60). In the 1830s, working-class women's bodies were naturalized as targets for abuse, as seen in Dickens's representation of Nancy, although they gained new attention, while middle-class and upper-class women were disembodied, making violence against them invisible (65).

Spousal assault had two highly visible turning points, writes Lisa Surridge in her book, *Bleak Houses*, three chapters of which show how spousal abuse and legislative and social attitudes surrounding it importantly inform Dickens's work. First, the 1828 Offenses Against the Person Act was ''legislation that opened magistrates' courts to abused working class wives'' (6) and second, the 1857 Divorce Act ensured that ''middle-class assaults received the same level of publicity'' as working-class assaults (8). She notes that spousal assault debates were linked to tropes of animal cruelty, anti-vivisection debates, and child abuse debates (9). The ''Introduction'' provides a useful overview of legal and social historians' work on marital violence and marriage laws. Of particular note are studies by Shani D'Cruze and Mary Lyndon Shanley.

Surridge's context for spousal violence in Dickens's ''Early Writings'' in her second chapter is the 1828 Offenses Against the Person Act and the subsequent newspaper coverage of marital assault trials. Surridge explains that battered women appear in five early sketches, indicating that ''even as Dickens's texts participate in the newfound visibility of marital violence, they reveal a deep ambivalence concerning public intrusion into domestic privacy'' (18). In *The Old Curiosity Shop*, Mrs. Jiniwin's aggressive resistance in countering Quilp's abuse is frowned upon by Dickens, while Nell's passivity is exalted by Dickens and his readers (29–30). In a skillful reading of ''The

Hospital Patient,'' Surridge demonstrates how the privacy of the domestic sphere remains protected even as the battered woman's body is displayed and thereby shown to deserve the protection of the law and courts (35). Extending her discussion to *Oliver Twist*, Surridge notes how both the death of the hospital patient and the death of Nancy receive ''an almost excessive degree of public scrutiny'' (41). She reads Nancy's loyalty to Bill as a type of ''the emergent middle-class ideal of selfless femininity'' (37). Although she is associated with the animal, unlike the dog Bull's-eye, Nancy is passively loyal, rather than combative (37–39). Both cling suicidally to Bill, Nancy hanging onto him as he strikes her down, and Bull's-eye leaping after his dead master.

With Dombey as a ''full anatomy of failed manliness,'' *Dombey and Son* causes its title character to become ''unmanly and unclassed,'' argues Surridge, in ''Domestic Violence and Middle-Class Manliness: *Dombey and Son*,'' the third chapter of *Bleak Houses* (45). Surridge notes the shifting definitions of masculinity at play in this era, in which middle-class ''manliness [was] inextricably linked to domesticity'' and ''self-control over both sexual and violent urges'' (46). The novel struggles with closure, in that it ''[re-creates] protective manliness rather than critiquing the unequal gender relations underlying spousal assault'' (47). To remake the home, it also ''excludes and vilifies Edith, its most powerful female figure'' (47). The 1853 Bill for the Better Protection and Punishment of Aggravated Assaults Upon Women and Children, known popularly as the ''Good Wives' Rod,'' was based on the idea that ''genuine British manliness'' was incompatible with marital violence (48). Instances like the 1840 Cochrane case, however, had in the meantime, reinforced the husband's absolute authority over the wife (52–53). Police reports in the *Times* provided accounts of spousal assaults and attempted murder as part 1 of *Dombey and Son* was serialized (56). Nevertheless, the novel, Surridge contends, still maintains that ''at some level, Florence, by leaving, is responsible for the shattering of the middle-class home'' (63). In response to Patricia Ingham's reading of Edith as an ''excessive female,'' who garners ''narrative admiration,'' Surridge finds Edith only gets such admiration within marriage, not after she leaves the Dombey house (65): ''Dombey's reeducation in manliness depends on the woman's. . . . 'self-denial and devotion' '' (66). Dombey is temporarily feminized when he assumes Florence's role and mourns Paul in humility. But this is simply preparation for restored manliness later on, manliness that may be problematic, given Edith's uneasy exile (67). Ultimately, Surridge concludes, Edith's ''unfeminine recalcitrance'' belies the restoration of masculine authority and feminine self-denial in the home.

Contending that *Oliver Twist* offers a critique of the New Poor Law's bastardy clause, Susan Zlotnick, in '' '*The Law's a Bachelor*,' '' shows how the law placed the responsibility for illegitimate offspring onto the mother. As the novel genders its competing subjectivities differently in the cases of Oliver and Rose, Nancy and Agnes, it aligns Oliver most closely with the melodramatic mode and the women with literary realism and the New Poor Law. Zlotnick notes that the debate over the bastardy clause became "a referendum on the moral nature and true character of women," with some members of Parliament emphasizing women's moral agency and others "highlight[ing] women's vulnerability and victimhood" (137, 138). Dickens conflates Agnes and Nancy just as critics of the New Poor Law said the law conflated all women who bore illegitimate children, closing the gap between prostitute and single mother. Zlotnick notes that both Agnes and Nancy "rehearse their own punishments," Agnes by leaving home only to end incarcerated in a workhouse, and Nancy in imagining a lonely emigration without Sikes (141–42). Zlotnick offers a reinvigorated interpretation of Rose Maylie as well, explaining the significance of her self-discipline in rehabilitating Harry Maylie from an aristocrat into the "moralized, domesticated gentleman of the middle-ranks" and in "revis[ing] both women's stories" through her own exercise of self-control, which Zlotnick claims "grants her a degree of psychological realism and tortured subjectivity" (142).

Studying genre and gender through marriage in *Hard Times*, Anne Humpherys, in "Louisa Gradgrind's Secret: Marriage and Divorce in *Hard Times*," considers Louisa Gradgrind's story through the sensation novel as a version of the Gothic. Humpherys notes that one crucial gap in the text is the "sexual nature" of the Bounderby marriage, expressed prior to the wedding through Louisa's obvious disgust for Bounderby, and his clear desire for her (179). Humpherys also recovers the stories of Mrs. Sparsit and Mrs. Gradgrind, arguing that both women are victims of abusive marriages, and brilliantly elucidates the structural and thematic links between Louisa and Stephen, many of them adumbrating the issue of marriage. Discussing the separation of Bounderby and Louisa, Humpherys notes that Bounderby's refusal to separate would appear justified at the time of the aborted 1854 Matrimonial Causes Act. Louisa's confrontation of her father culminates in a "narrative death" for her, absorbing her into her father's story, rather than allowing her a story of her own. Ultimately, *Hard Times* anticipates the sensation heroine's "story of repression and lack of fulfillment in marriage," and thus Louisa's story goes underground alongside the live burial of Stephen.

Gendering the suspense genre as feminine, Caroline Levine's "Realism as Self-Forgetfulness: Gender, Ethics, and *Great Expectations*" posits that "*Great Expectations* belongs to the tradition of detective fiction" and that "Biddy emerges as the epistemological ideal" of the novel (85). Defining the plot's "ethical imperative" as "the arresting of arbitrary desires and prejudices in the face of tested knowledge," Levine first explains how Pip's "bringing up by hand" and cross-examinations by Jaggers have not prepared him to be this kind of ethical reader of realism (89). Nor does Jaggers have these traits, because "the realist text teaches us skepticism *in the face of* desire and prejudice," and Jaggers has only skepticism (91). Biddy is the novel's fair-minded reader, who labors to read Mrs. Joe's signs (92–93). "[U]nlike the abstractly fair Jaggers, Biddy's ethical-epistemological model is supple, *flexible*: she is not bound by written principles—the conventionalized letter of the law—but moves easily among paradigms of interpretation when confronted with the enigmas of the other" (93). Biddy's self-forgetfulness" allows her to attend to the radical otherness of a mind unlike her own" (93). Levine's reading is persuasive, and a welcome respite from jaded criticism in its celebration of Biddy's humane and skilled interpretive art.

Other nineteenth-century contexts within which narrative femininities are constructed have received much critical attention in the last fifteen years. Catherine Robson places *The Old Curiosity Shop* in the legislative and visual context of the nineteenth century, while Diana Archibald and Donald Hall set *Martin Chuzzlewit* in its American and British social and historical contexts. Deirdre David and Caroline Rooney consider *The Old Curiosity Shop* and *Bleak House* as narratives of empire. Richard Currie examines Esther Summerson's femininity in the context of female conduct books. Deborah Epstein Nord and Karl Smith analyze the interplay between the Victorian city and characters in *Sketches by Boz* and *Bleak House*. David L. Cowles explains *Hard Times*'s double-bind of Utilitarianism and gender double-standards, and Susan Zlotnick breaks down Dickens's contemporaries' representations of industrialization and working class women. Donald Hall writes about the transgressive women of *Great Expectations* in relation to the Contagious Diseases Act legislation.

Catherine Robson, in "The Ideal Girl in Industrial England," contextualizes her discussion of Nell Trent in *The Old Curiosity Shop* with William Frith's painting *Many Happy Returns of the Day (*1856) and writing by Ruskin and Ellis. Noting that "The symbolic burden placed on Nell Trent's famously frail shoulders is perhaps the heaviest carried by any girl in literature," Robson finds that Little Nell "must act as the ideal representative of the three precious havens of safe home, a happy childhood, and an idyllic past," at a time when Royal Commission reports on child labor in the early 1840s told of widespread exploitation of the working-class child (75). Robson contrasts Nell and the Marchioness, noting the extreme focus on Nell's body, and how "the working-class girl's body is shrouded from our view" (85). She comments on the incestuous eroticization of Nell's body, finding that it goes unresolved in the text.

American wives have been attractive to British husbands, both historically and fictionally, notes Diana Archibald in "American Women and English

Angels in Dickens, Reade, Trollope, and Thackeray.'' Dickens portrays the masculine individualism of Americans in *Martin Chuzzlewit* in a way that resembles the ''frontier thesis'' of Turner, and shows too, that ''America masculinized its women, corrupting the 'natural' sweetness of their true feminine nature and producing something 'monstrous' instead'' (145–46). Thus, the American women of *Chuzzlewit* make a pretense of gentility but don't devote time to domestic management. They have grotesque intellectual pretensions, spending their time attending lectures and improving their minds, and thus are seen to be, according to the feminine ideal in *Martin Chuzzlewit*, ''deformed and unnatural'' (147). Martin returns home to his English ''angel'' to find a woman who is a ''true lady,'' a ''loving wife and mother.'' Archibald notes the ''fatal consequences'' for emigrating to the masculinizing New World for a poor woman that Martin and Mark rescue—the loss of all three of her children (148).

Donald E. Hall in '' 'Betsy Prig . . . Try the Cowcumbers, God Bless You!': Hierarchies, Transgression and Trouble in *Martin Chuzzlewit*,'' establishes that novel's context through Dickens's trip to America and his experience of American slavery and bluestockings, which led to his ''harsh characterizations of anti-patriarchal women there and in Britain'' and revealed his concerns about the future of England (24). Theorizing his reading of *Chuzzlewit* through Judith Butler's *Gender Trouble* and Catherine Hall's *White, Male and Middle Class*, Donald Hall emphasizes the binarism of the Victorian patriarchy, which easily accommodates Tom Pinch's androgyny/male passivity (28–29). Even though male-dominated systems inevitably become corrupted, ''patriarchy manages to self-correct''; in the cases of the two Martins, both learn to be less selfish, and thus Dickens reaffirms ''benevolent male hegemony'' (31). Inverted hierarchies receive much narrative attention, such as Cherry Pecksniff's domination of her suitor Moddle or Jonas Chuzzlewit's abuse of his aged father. The novel's most powerful insistence of *gender trouble* is Sairey Gamp, labeled by Hall ''a woman of amazing transgressive power who violates numerous rules of proper behavior and domain'' (35). Hall links British transgressive women first to the ''brash Americans'' encountered by Martin and Mark who have ''pretensions of superiority over the British,'' and second, to the American feminists Martin would like to ''knock on the head'' (40). These rebel groups cause anxiety about the breakdown of hierarchy, and threaten the patriarchy with being supplanted by a form of 'gender war' '' (39).

Explaining *The Old Curiosity Shop* as a story of empire, Deirdre David in ''Children of Empire: Victorian Imperialism and Sexual Politics in Dickens and Kipling,'' compares Nell's adventuring through England's Middlesex to the wanderings of Kipling's Kim's through Lahore and the surrounding Indian landscape—but notes there are ''differences in terms of gender and race politics'' (125). David argues that "gender politics inflect imperialist politics and imperialist politics inflect gender politics,'' and demonstrates how Quilp is figured as a savage and a heathen, compared to Nell's being figured as civilized and Christian. These differences are also coded for Victorian readers within "the context of Dickens's writings about Africa and the 'Noble Savage' '' and within the context of "early nineteenth-century writings about woman's civilizing mission" (125, 127). Further, Quilp is associated with cannibals as a barbaric male savage, while Nell epitomizes the suffering Englishwoman sacrificed for empire, "a common figure in early Victorian writing about imperialism" (131). Quilp invades Nell's domestic space, emulating the '' 'devilish Indian diamond' (symbol of the colonized)'' in *The Moonstone* (182). Nell's death "signifies Dickens's view that the changes wrought in Victorian culture by mercantile empire-building are inescapable, cannot be eradicated, must be problematically symbolized, and are thereby occluded" (132–33).

The "gender imperialism" of *Bleak House* is paired with Ama Ata Aidoo's *Our Sister Killjoy* in Caroline Rooney's "The Gender Differential, Again and Not Yet." Rooney finds that Mrs. Jellyby's household is depicted as "having 'gone native' '' within a text that reflects contemporary debates over slavery (141). Still, "class upstages race," and even class is "put to one side" so that Dickens can focus on the domestic household where "gender . . . makes all the difference" (142). Rooney sees in Esther's illness, caught from do-gooding beyond the home, a Dickensian critique of any female activity outside the "keep" of the house; instead, Esther must focus on the exemplary home—"hygienic, well-run, well-regulated—an example to all classes" (143). Rooney concludes that Esther is her own colonial subject: "Esther's freedom from poverty and homelessness is a debt to be interminably repaid by her agreeing to police, enslave, colonise herself as a housewife" (143).

Dickens draws on and subverts nineteenth-century conduct books in his portrayal of Esther Summerson, argues Richard Currie in "Against the Feminine Stereotype: Dickens's Esther Summerson and Conduct-Book Heroines." He notes previous work on conduct books by Nancy Armstrong, Mary Poovey, Elizabeth Wallace-Kowalski, Ruth Yeazell, Peter Gay, and Elizabeth Langland. Currie shows that conduct books condemned the expression of anger and counseled self-discipline, while exalting affection, cheerfulness, and gratitude (14–15). They forbade selfishness, while extolling discretion and modesty. Esther exhibits many of these traits, but, Currie argues, she struggles to contain her anger and does not practice self-denial in her sickroom (19). Arguing against Bailin and Peltason, Currie finds Esther's concern about her new face and how Ada may respond, to be "a love of self," that is out of keeping with prescribed conduct-book behavior (19). Further, Currie claims, Esther contravenes conduct-book guidelines when she expresses desire for

Woodcourt when reading of his rescue exploits, and when she shows her scarred face to him, thereby lacking modesty and discretion.

Deborah Epstein Nord's "*Sketches by Boz*: The Middle-Class City and the Quarantine of Urban Suffering," shows how Dickens's "interest in process" makes his *Sketches* different from other urban descriptions by Pierce Egan, Lamb, and Leigh Hunt (57). Dickens "quarantines" the poor and working class from his middle-class readers, and represents "the sexually tainted and victimized woman" (50). In "The Pawnbroker's Shop" and other sketches, Dickens "uses the barrier of gender to introduce yet quarantine urban misery" (68). "The world of Boz's London emerges largely, although not exclusively, as a masculine preserve," which Nord compares to the Pickwickian London (69–70). However, Nord notes that victimized women appear in both *Pickwick Papers* and *Sketches by Boz*, most notably in "The Hospital Patient," a battered woman's story in which Nord sees a prefiguring of Nancy; the patient's death comes as a relief to the reader (73–74). "The Prisoner's Van," in which two young prostitutes are arrested, appears to unfold like "The Hospital Patient" to expose "femaleness" and "otherness," while also containing "extremes of urban life" for the middle-class reader (75). However, Nord argues that this apparent containment is undermined by Dickens's sentence: "The progress of these girls in crime will be as rapid as the flight of a pestilence, resembling it too in its baneful influence and wide-spreading infection" (Nord 75). By invoking *infection*, Dickens "alludes to the potential literal and metaphoric contamination that the prostitute represents," bringing his middle-class audience "down into the dark shadows of London" and potentially, into contact with disease (75, 80). In her following chapter, " 'Vitiated Air': The Polluted City and Female Sexuality in *Dombey and Son* and *Bleak House*," Nord argues that the "prostitute has now become a wife," bringing along with her "urban pollution [that] has invaded the preserves of middle-class life" (81). Wives who do this are Edith Dombey and Honoria Dedlock. Reading Dickens's use of Edith's masochistic scarring of her own arm and hand not as melodramatic but as "Dickens's careful portrayal of a sexual pathology that is specifically the result of buying and selling what he believes ought to be naturally given," Nord interprets Edith as a sexually debased female who must be removed from Florence's proximity and who is linked implicitly with the urban contagion of syphilis and the "barrenness of middle-class marriage" (94). Carker, though a villain, "merely exploits the weaknesses [Edith and Alice] inherited from their mothers" (95). Nord explains that the threats of debased female sexual inheritance, contamination and rebellion are made safe in the next generation through Florence's marriage to Walter, a "brotherly figure," who rather than being "proto-Lawrencian," evokes the "ancient mythic power of a Dick Whittington" (95). One other rebellious woman, Susan Nipper, is only "a bit player whose class position and comic presence make her particular kind of rebelliousness instructive yet benign'' (96). Nord's discussion of *Bleak House* aims to show "that the various threats to social health represented by the slums of Tom-All-Alone's are ultimately resolved in the novel in the realm of female sexuality" (98). She locates this resolution primarily in Esther's marriage to the physician Alan Woodcourt at the novel's end, an "unsettling middle-class romance of maternal sexuality" that allows Esther to bear daughters out of a healthy sexuality that "expunges" any inherited "taint" from Lady Dedlock (109, 107). Nord remarks, though, that the replication of Bleak House elsewhere links it to "the legacies of the past," as well as to the slum "that breeds fevers still" (109). What is missing to provide a parallel to the analysis of *Dombey and Son* is discussion of the ways that Lady Dedlock has brought urban contamination into the Dedlock marriage and consideration of whether and how Dickens figures her as a prostitute-wife in the way he does Edith Dombey. Nord's focus is instead shifted to Esther and her rehabilitation of social health via her own sexual health.

Karl Smith, in "Little Dorrit's 'speck' and Florence's 'daily blight': Urban Contamination and the Dickensian Heroine," theorizes gender through Mary Douglas's *Purity and Danger*, linking London's polluted state, which required sanitary reform, and the purity of Dickensian heroines like Florence Dombey, Esther Summerson, and Amy Dorrit, who are able to "reassert" the "proper categories of matter" in an increasingly "dirty, disordered" London (117, 116). London's dirty state produced physical, social, and mental harm (118–20). Smith also describes how Victorian sanitary reformers' ideas of hygiene and appropriate sexual conduct were influenced by "symbolic systems of purity" (Douglas 36, qtd. in Smith, 120). The "daily blight" of emotional neglect by Dombey to which Florence is subjected and which parallels the contamination of the city, causes Florence to suffer, "[depriving her] of something priceless," yet Dickens does not allow her essential goodness to be marred (124–25). Florence, Esther, and Little Dorrit "assert humanity's place in a scheme of things eroded in the potentially degenerative environment of the filthy city" (150).

Tracking the cultural Catch-22s for women in *Hard Times*, David L. Cowles, in "Having It Both Ways: Gender and Paradox in *Hard Times*," finds that Louisa is the character most caught up in this difficulty, since her Utilitarian education is "particularly hostile to the traditional female virtues so essential to her 'real' nature," virtues and nature that she *does* have, however suppressed they may be. She must perform a constant balancing act, showing these virtues as an act of loyalty to Tom (sisterly duty), but not showing disloyalty to her father (by revealing to him how his education has failed both herself and Tom), and often these two are in opposition. Cowles shows how Dickens the author is in a Tom-like position, exploiting Louisa's sisterly devotion for his own artistic purposes (441). Further, Dickens, rather than carrying his critique to the Victorian patriarchy, punishes *Louisa* for her "unfeminine actions and attributes" of desiring "a man who is not her husband" and marrying a man "old enough to be her father" (442). Cowles sees Dickens attempting to mitigate her punishment through the love of Sissy's children (442). In conclusion, Cowles finds a parallel between Dickens's contradictory attitudes towards "disempowered workers like Stephen and Rachael" and the novel's "disempowered women"(443). Dickens wants workers and wives to "put faith in their oppressors," making *Hard Times* full of "cover-ups" needed by mid-Victorians struggling with industrialization and "the woman question" (444).

Susan Zlotnick's "A 'World Turned Upside Downwards,' " discusses *Hard Times* in the context of responses to industrialism by Disraeli, Ruskin, Arnold, and, most important, Carlyle and Dickens, arguing that their responses were "rooted in an endangered sense of male privilege that arose out of the sexual anarchy associated with early industrialism" (8). Zlotnick places Mrs. Blackpool in the context of "modernity as a female destroyer" along with Carlyle's Irish widow, Arnold's infanticidal mother, and the "masculine" mill women in Lord Ashley's and Engel's texts (18). Dickens's "allegiances to Carlyle force him to depreciate the value of the material realm he wishes to critique and to dismiss as inconsequential the perilous industrial world he labors to create"; consequently, "the industrial milieu, first invoked as an inhumane, life-threatening environment, is reduced to the status of local color" (33). Zlotnick bleakly but astutely concludes, "Joining a long line of middle-class Victorians who blamed the degraded state of the working man on the domestic inadequacies of his wife, Dickens scripts the working man's redemption as the transformation of the notorious factory girl into a model of femininity" (42).

Donald Hall, in "Great Expectations and Harsh Realities," discusses *Great Expectations* in the context of the first Contagious Diseases Act (CDA) and other reactionary responses to feminism in the 1860s, although Hall does not date the passage of the CDA for the reader as 1864, occurring in fact after the publication of the novel, 1860–61. Hall notes the appearance of "transgressive women" in the novel, beginning with Mrs. Joe, "a gynecocrat" who tyrannizes over her husband and younger brother (185). Hall contends, however, that Mrs. Joe's power is authorized, her "basket like the Great Seal of England," herself a " 'sovereign' in the tradition of Cleopatra and indeed, Victoria," so that even though she misuses her power, that power is validated (186). On the point of her beating and conversion by Orlick, Hall argues that she begs forgiveness not for her assumption of power, but for her abuse of it (187). Hall says that both Mrs. Joe's abuse of power and renunciation of power are excessive, and in showing this, Dickens prepares for the moderate ideal (187). Biddy is credited as "a substantial evolution in the Dickens heroine" because she instructs Joe and counsels Pip (188). Hall sees elements in the novel anticipating the debate around the Contagious Diseases Act through "certain gender-inflected notions of culpability and punishability" (189). Foremost are Estella's prostitute-like toying with men's affections and Miss Havisham as the Kristevian *abject*, also madam of a "house of corruption," displaying her own erotic delight in Estella's beauty, anticipating Sharon Marcus's interpretation (Kristeva 1982, 190; see Marcus 2007). Hall argues that Dickens pathologizes Miss Havisham's same-sex desire; he observes that inherent in the notion of its pathology is the challenge to the patriarchy and its need to reproduce and colonize the nation (191). Further, Hall posits, Miss Havisham's "sickness" is like that of prostitutes and nineteenth-century feminism, a "blight" that spreads unhappiness as a contagion and that is therefore punishable. Hall, like Frost, emphasizes the violence brought to bear on Estella and Miss Havisham by Bentley Drummle and Pip, especially the fire "as a symbolic act of rape perpetrated by Pip" (192). Hall unconvincingly concludes that despite the violence against empowered women in *Great Expectations*, the novel's ending indicates "the slow process of social change," leading to the new property rights acts in 1870 and 1882, and to the repeal of the Contagious Diseases Acts in 1886 (195).

Cultural Studies

This is an unsatisfactory categorization of this rich group of essays, many of which have visual, iconographic, or archetypal elements. Shuli Barzilai, Galia Ofek, Piya Pal-Lapinski, Linda Lewis, and Rob Garnett examine folkloric and iconographic figures of very different origins: Bluebeard, Rapunzel, the female vampire, French icons of La Liberté, and the Virgin Mary. Barbara Black examines a "sisterhood of rage" in Rosa Dartle, Miss Wade, and Madame Defarge. Christine Huguet finds Dickens provocatively changing the rules as he dresses different characters, and Susan Nygaard, studying *Dombey and Son*, finds an analogy between the Crystal Palace and the gendered reupholstering job, narratively and in the novel's gendered mise-en-scènes.

"Unable to keep women and meat discrete," Captain Murderer never lost hold of Charles Dickens's imagination, as Shuli Barzilai reminds us in "The Bluebeard Barometer: Charles Dickens and Captain Murderer" (508). Barzilai examines Dickens's "Captain Murderer" tale and its sources, including Perrault's classic fairy tale "The Blue Beard," the English folktale "Mr. Fox" and the Grimm brothers' "The Robber Bridegroom" (507). Seeing Dickens's retelling of previous versions in "Captain Murderer" as a combining of genres—fairy tale, comic, Gothic and social performance—that implicates the wife in the husband's criminality and implies the "institutional

constraints of marriage,'' Barzilai finds the ''Captain Murderer'' figure not
only in Dickens's oral performances and its source in ''Nurse's Stories,'' but
also in *Pickwick Papers, Barnaby Rudge, Bleak House,* and *Hard Times*
(510–11). In the latter two novels, Bluebeard is invoked in association with
John Jarndyce and Thomas Gradgrind, Sr., only to be repudiated, in what
Freud characterized as a ''tendentious joke,'' serving ''satiric, hostile, aggressive or self-defensive purposes'' under the mask of a joke (Freud 8: 514–18,
qtd. in Barzilai 506). Concluding her essay with a final invocation of the
Bluebeard tale in *Our Mutual Friend,* Barzilai shows how Dickens sentimen-
talizes rather than satirizes the idea of Bluebeard in John Rokesmith (519).

Hair fetishism typifies the materialism of the Victorian commodity culture,
in Galia Ofek's '' 'Tie Her Up By The Hair': Dickens's Retelling of the
Medusa and Rapunzel Myths.'' Ofek argues that ''association between hair
despoliation and sexual despoliation was likely to be clear and immediate
for many readers'' in the case of Mrs. Brown's exploitation of her daughter
Alice and her ecstasy over Florence's locks (186). Positing that Dickens uses
hair as a synechdoche, to encode ''his heroine's character, and [as] a means
to conceptualize and circulate images of femininity as a whole,'' Ofek reads
Lucy Manette as another Rapunzel figure with her golden thread of domestic-
ity/hair, while Madame Defarge is the Medusa whose ''snaky hair evoked a
castration anxiety not necessarily localized as the loss of a specific organ''
but rather ''associated with female empowerment'' and ''the loss of virile
power and patriarchal order'' (189, 190). Ofek further sees Catherine Dickens
the wife and Elizabeth Dickens the mother as other Medusa-figures in Charles
Dickens's life—bad-mother figures who threatened him or had done so in the
past. Medusas in *Little Dorrit* are Flora Finching's aunt by marriage and the
''emasculating'' Mrs. Clennam, who makes Arthur feel ''completely power-
less'' (192). Ofek concludes with Margaret Atwood's idea of ''Rapunzel's
Syndrome'' in literature and its biographical significance to Dickens: ''These
heroines have internalized the values of their culture to such an extent that
they have become their own prisons'' (Atwood 209). This paradigm fits Jenny
Wren and Bella Wilfer in *Our Mutual Friend.* Bella, in allowing Rokesmith
to possess her hair in the form of a keepsake, reiterates Dickens's ''shaping
and fixing'' of Mary Hogarth's image (195–96).

The vampiric powers of Miss Wade in comparison to and as a possible
source for Lefanu's Carmilla are the subject of Piya Pal-Lapinski's ''Dickens's Miss Wade and J. S. Lefanu's Carmilla: The Female Vampire in *Little
Dorrit.*'' Pal-Lapinski argues that the resistance afforded by Miss Wade's
narrative to integration in the larger story engages the reader through the
lesbian and social ''otherness'' of Miss Wade. Further, Pal-Lapinski sees
Miss Wade in Jungian terms, as a ''shadow figure'' for other characters such
as Pet Meagles, Harriet/Tattycoram, and Amy Dorrit, ''carrying a collective

burden of repression, denial and guilt'' (85). The vampire motif also expresses a type of devouring mother that links maternal sympathy with secrets and death (86).

Tapping into French icons of activist, even monstrous women is Linda M. Lewis's ''Madame Defarge as Political Icon in Dickens's *A Tale of Two Cities.*'' Claiming that Madame Defarge is Dickens's ''most memorable allegory for radical feminism,'' Lewis enumerates how she is a double for Lucie Manette: a Frenchwoman to her ''true Englishwoman,'' a destroyer to Lucie's creator, and death-knitter, recording the names of those to go to the guillotine, to Lucie's ''golden thread'' of domesticity (32–33). Madame Defarge dies privately and comically, denied the tragic glory of a national death, so that Dickens, like Carlyle, can interpret ''woman's rule as misrule'' (33). Lewis traces the allegory of the female body as a political icon in French art, to Delacroix's anachronistic ''Liberty Guiding the People,'' iconography with which Dickens was familiar and which he borrowed in his novel (36–37). Lewis observes: ''As French women became more volatile as activists, protesters, and warriors, the icon of woman evolved from beauty to horror, and the female body came to represent Discord, License, Disobedience, Malignancy, Wickedness, Calumny, and Vengeance'' (37). Dickens uses this icon for his ''Vengeance,'' Madame Defarge. Lewis's essay reproduces images of women in scenes of revolution—wearing weapons, attending meetings, allegorized as monsters—and juxtaposes these to Hablot K. Browne's ''The Sea Still Rises,'' an illustration in book II, chapter 22, providing a rich visual context with which to understand her discussion of female iconography during the French Revolution. This allegorical Madame Defarge, ''who becomes a stepmother to the children of violence,'' and ''iconoclast, feminist and king-killer,'' is, in the end, Lewis contends, a reprise of Dickens's belief in ''women's unfitness for political life'' (43, 44, 46).

Beginning, but not ending, with the virginal Mary Hogarth and her associations with Catholicism and the Virgin Mary, Robert R. Garnett's ''Dickens, the Virgin, and the Dredger's Daughter'' urges readers to break away from facile dichotomies to consider how Dickens himself moved toward blending the spiritual and erotic influences of Mary Hogarth and Ellen Ternan in his creation of Lizzie Hexam in *Our Mutual Friend*. Garnett notes that Dickens's ''concept of the highest Good took the form of a sublime feminine benevolence'' (48). In explicating the 1844 Italian dream in which Dickens envisions his deceased sister-in-law Mary Hogarth advising him that Catholicism is ''the best'' religion for him, Garnett shows how Dickens conflates Mary Hogarth and the Virgin Mary, noting the irony that Dickens's ''demythologized Christianity . . . lacked the passionate yearning with which he reached out to embrace the Spirit of Mary'' (50–51, 52). Garnett's discussion of Dickens's ''worship'' of the virgin begins with Rose Maylie, followed by

Little Nell, Ruth Pinch, Florence Dombey, Agnes Wickfield, Esther Summerson, and Amy Dorrit (54). Pointing to Agnes's symbolic gesture at Dora's death, Garnett emphasizes the iconographic uses to which Dickens puts his virgins. Dickens's saintly heroines provide a refuge and "wishful sanctuary even from erotic energies," and, Garnett stresses, from the "novels' centrifugal energies" as well (54–55). However, Garnet believes Dickens in his last decade moves beyond "his Mary Hogarth religion," influenced by his relationship with Ellen Ternan, which challenged his previous ideal of the ethereal heroine (56). Garnett shows how Lizzie Hexam's morally ambiguous association with the Thames shadows her with desire and death, corruption, lust, and violence (58–59). In Lizzie, the river-dredger's daughter, the opposite extremes of river "ooze and slime," out of which she came, and her noble nature, as well as her sexual allure, unite, and Garnett sees this union as a way for Dickens to combine his earthly desire for Ellen with his idealization of the spiritualized Mary Hogarth. Finally, Garnett locates in *Our Mutual Friend* a "sacramental awareness" that "transcendental love begins in the passionate, corruptible flesh" (63).

Barbara Black, in "A Sisterhood of Rage and Beauty: Dickens' Rosa Dartle, Miss Wade, and Madame Defarge," discusses women who don't fit into the "domestic sublime" in Dickens's fiction, who, in fact, rage against it. She theorizes her discussion of these characters through Peter Brooks's reading of the psyche through what is inscribed on the body. Madame Defarge's clothing signs her uncanny quality and "primal fleshiness," while Rosa Dartle and Miss Wade are sexualized by a male gaze that also sees "the presence of pain" (94–95). All three women destabilize their texts because they want to be agents, not just objects of the gaze (96). All three women "share origins in dependency and rejection and/or violence at the hands of privileged males," and all "fall at the hands of a female tribunal" (100, 103).

The class-crossed dressing up and down of Nancy in *Oliver Twist* and Lady Dedlock is Christine Huguet's starting point in " 'There's not a doubt of the dress': Changing Clothes in Dickens's Fiction." In choosing these disguises, Dickens inverts "their symbolic power." Nancy, after pretending and dressing as if Oliver is her "young defenceless brother," does act to defend and save him: "In *Oliver Twist* Dickens thus perverts the conventional, straightforward reading of disguise: instead of creating abnormality through misrepresentation, it indirectly manifests the disguised person's true identity" (26). In *Bleak House*, Dickens "neatly inverts the dialectics functioning in *Oliver Twist*, that is by denying Lady Dedlock's humble attire any enduring moral significance" (26). Although Lady Dedlock changes clothes with Jenny to take on the disguise of the "lowest of the low," the novel asserts the idea of "true legitimacy" and Sir Leicester refuses her lowly disguise, according her the honor of burial in the family vault and continuing to pay his respects to her there (26). Dickens's interest in women's dress as a displacement for prostituted sexuality is evident also in *Nicholas Nickleby* and *Dombey and Son*. Kate Nickleby's mourning dress is embellished to attract the attention of her uncle's disrespectful guests; here and at Madame Mantalini's, the "disguised woman becomes a desirable object of exchange and possession" (28). Huguet also refers to Arthur Gride as a "cross-dressed bride" in *Nickleby* (28). Madeleine Bray also dresses in "ghastly bridal garb" that "ironically prefigures . . . mourning weeds and her second wedding dress" (28). An "episode of social/moral transvestitism" also occurs in *Dombey and Son*, Huguet argues, when Florence Dombey is redressed by good Mrs. Brown after her abduction, and Florence is devalued further by her father when she returns home, seen by him now as belonging "*on* the street" (29). Huguet concludes that "altered clothing authorizes bold ambiguities," and that "Dickens's 'philosophy of clothes' often entertainingly situates him halfway between physiognomy and detective work, between social realism and sensationalism or gothicism" (30).

In "Redecorating Dombey," Susan Nygaard compares the "cluttered Palace interior" of the Great Exhibition of 1851 with the interior of the Dombey home, and argues that Dickens "uses 'upholstery' as a metaphor for all the domestic comforts and ameliorative feminine qualities absent from the Dombey household" (43). Dombey's redecoration of his home does not follow the traditional Victorian use of upholstery in which furnishings help produce "the illusion of a world separated into public and private spheres" (44); instead, "it marks the denial of femininity" (47). Dombey's house reflects his masculine authority through its scale and its being a "wilderness of a home": its staircase, hall, and imposing rooms create what Nygaard terms "the same effect as being lost in the wilderness of London" (50). Further, the Dombey home is punctuated throughout with marble busts and portraits, depicted in the illustrations by Hablot K. Browne, making this home, like the Crystal Palace, a showcase for commodities that include art objects, plate and furniture, and women (52). Nygaard sees Edith's Amazonian anger and ability to control domestic space underscored in Browne's illustration, "Mr. Carker in his hour of triumph," which features an Amazon statuette behind the figure of Edith. The reupholstery battle between Dombey and Edith "restages the establishment of domestic authority" (56–57). However, Edith won't play, opting out by seeking out Florence's spaces (57). Finding that the most "intense moments of emotional connection are between members of the same sex, and most developed and complicated relations are between women," Nygaard determines that ultimately, Dickens is so uncomfortable with Edith's anger against Dombey that he "must banish her" (62). Moving to the illustration "Florence and Edith on the staircase" that accompanies Edith's flight from the Dombey home, the essay analyzes the stairway's sculptures, whose stories are resonant with paternal violence, sexual submission, risk-taking, and authorities both male and female. In concluding her argument, Nygaard questions Julian Moynahan's male-centered reading of the novel's ending and claims that Dombey's "male privileges (violence and misogyny) are not eradicated, only forgotten, upholstered" (67). Nygaard makes an important distinction between true reform and "redecoration" in this character's masculine identity, arguing that Dombey learns to display emotion, but "still does not like women" (68–69). Nygaard also draws an analogy between the disorienting "evanescent" space of the Crystal Palace that attempted to "roof over the outer world and the domestic sphere," and the brightly lit scene at "Gills and Cuttle," a male household where Dombey can pursue "the pleasures of male friendship," in a space in which "feminine" feeling circulates among men, and women are forgotten (74).

Gender and Narrative

Helen Moglen establishes important theoretical parameters for gendered discourse in Dickensian narrative in her discussion of *Dombey and Son*, while Jean Ferguson Carr discusses the gendering of narrative in *Hard Times*, and Anny Sadrin, Virginia Blain, and LuAnn McCracken Fletcher examine the gendering of voices in *Bleak House*. Ellen Burton Harrington shows how Wilkie Collins's female narrator in *The Law and the Lady* appropriates Esther's and Inspector Bucket's voices to narrate her story. Mary Lenard and Kathleen Sell-Sandoval analyze Victorian literary and political discourses and their possible effects upon Dickens's writing and the reception of his work.

By examining the apparent binary oppositions of male and female culture/ nature in *Dombey and Son*, Helen Moglen shows the limitations of such binary feminist critical approaches in her essay "Theorizing Fiction/Fictionalizing Theory." Moglen sees "two distinct but interdependent narratives":

> Dombey's is a narrative of social realism, an anxious critique of the economic and ethical forces transforming Britain from a country of merchants and landowners to one ruled increasingly by industrial entrepreneurs. . . . [And in] Florence's narrative, social realism is rewritten as romance, a pastoral romance of Woman and of nature which anticipates, in striking ways, the romance of women's culture which some contemporary feminists have told.   (160)

Moglen adds that "melodramatic and sentimental interrogations" are also brought to bear on this narrative (160). Importantly, "the social relations of a culture are not simply oppositional after all, but are multiple and complexly interactive," and thus binary oppositions are too limited a way of approaching this text (160–61). Paul Dombey is seen as an "undecidable" hero who faces a discord between "the demands of a masculine society and the needs of a hidden feminine self" (162). Dombey senior has repressed and negated the female "other," and considers little Paul's childhood "wasted woman-time," since it "forestalls" Paul's absolute identification as a male (163). Dombey allows others, like Carker and Bagstock, to mediate between him and the business and social worlds. Carker resembles other criminals and class rebels in Dickens such as Rigaud, Heep, and Headstone and uses his feminized qualities for erotic domination (166). Moglen also, however, sees Carker and Dombey as possessing "unrelenting 'masculinity,' victims of the genderic struggle that defines and fragments their private and public worlds" (166).

Turning to Edith, Moglen interprets her character as a "supporting player" pimped by her mother, Bagstock, and Carker, who reclaims both her body and control of her story, although she turns it from romance into melodrama (167–68). Moglen makes this important distinction: "In melodrama it is the characters themselves who are the locus of expression," while "sentimentality tends to obscure the significance of class and gender that melodrama underscores" (169). Like other Dickensian women, Edith, despite her complexity and ability to rebel against her marginalization, is displaced at the novel's end, so that melodrama can be replaced with sentimentality, and Florence can "[link] the potentially tragic world of Dombey to the regenerative world of Captain Cuttle and Sol Gills," ending in a "sentimental romance" (173, 175).

In the last section of her essay, Moglen usefully reminds us of major feminist gender theorists who offer accounts of identity formation in girls and whose theories are rooted in feminist ideology "grounded in the same inverted hierarchy of binary terms that Dickens ultimately affirms" (176; see, in "Other Works Cited": Benjamin, Chodorov, Gilligan, Keller 1983 and 1985, and Ruddick). But, argues Moglen, doing so leaves no room for "marginal or undecidable concepts that will deconstruct the absolutism of binary terms," and it "disguises crucial differences among women" (176). Moglen attempts to correct this by reading *Dombey* against the grain, finding an incest fantasy in Dombey's treatment of Florence, connected to Dickens's own idealization of the dead-at-seventeen Mary Hogarth (177–78). This rich, often-cited essay has influenced many subsequent readings of *Dombey and Son*.

Jean Ferguson Carr, in "Writing as a Woman: Dickens, *Hard Times*, and Feminine Discourses," considers both the ways in which Dickens explored feminine discourse and the manner in which like George Henry Lewes sought to identify Dickens's writing as aligned with feminized discourse. Calling Dickens's rhetorical stance in *Household Words* "a gesture of cultural cross-dressing," Carr emphasizes Dickens's preoccupation with women's wrongs in midcentury as the context for her discussion of *Hard Times* (199). Carr brilliantly elucidates the "faint transparency," Mrs. Gradgrind, as material and metaphoric transparency, as stunned object, as disregarded mother left out of the father's discourse of knowledge, and as "a no-meaning that can be neither heard nor reformed" (205). Carr points out the wife-killer Blue Beard's appearance in the government blue books, to suggest Gradgrind's responsibility, due to his enforcement of the Gradgrind system, for his wife's social death and his daughter's lack of "female resources" (206). Carr sees Dickens "writing as a woman" by creating an "oppositional discourse of fancy," which is voiced by Sleary and Sissy (208–09). Sissy's confrontation with Harthouse only works because Sissy acts as a modest go-between, forgetting herself, and gathering her power from her status as a working-class child (209). Carr contends that Dickens exploits the oppression of women and the poor "when they serve as analogies for his own more temperate marginality as a lower-middle class writer of fiction in a literary culture that preferred educated reason over experienced fancy" (210–11).

Anny Sadrin's "Charlotte Dickens: The Female Narrator of *Bleak House*," echoes Ellen Moers in maintaining that Dickens "certainly knew *Jane Eyre*" (Moers 1973: 13–24, qtd. in Sadrin 47), and provocatively urges readers to reconsider Dickens as a writer who is "Charlotte Dickens." Esther is viewed as a character who is "conceived in a spirit of experimentation and sympathy" and a narrator who is "almost an inverted parody of Dickens's style," exhibiting "negation, understatement and equivocation" (51). Noting the many female authors with whom Dickens held regular correspondence, and particularly Mrs. Gaskell, whose meticulousness, mildness, truthfulness, and "tact and feeling" were much admired by him, Sadrin explains how Dickens uses this knowledge to render Esther's repressed desires, improper for a Victorian woman, and especially one with Esther's history, through "a rhetoric of omission and negation" (50, 52). While Sadrin does not argue that Dickens's creation of Esther as a narrator is feminist, she does show that he turns Esther into "an autonomous, desiring subject" through writing, and that Esther's unveiling to show Alan Woodcourt her scarred face is an act of sexual disclosure and desire, "an almost indecent scene" (54, 56).

Virginia Blain, in "Double Vision and the Double Standard in *Bleak House*: A Feminist Perspective," importantly brings to the forefront the "submerged dialectic between male and female viewpoints" in the narration of *Bleak House* (65), arguing that such an examination enhances the reader's understanding of the novel's structure, of Esther's character, and of Lady Dedlock's relationship to the legal patriarchy and to Esther (65). Blain differentiates between the two points of view: "Esther's is the 'inner' voice, his the 'outer' voice; hers is the subjective voice, his the objective; hers is personal, his is impersonal" (67). Blain points out that Dickens can subversively appoint each of his narrators to be a "purveyor of criticism of the other's domain,'' such as having Esther narrate Richard Carstone's struggles with Chancery or having the male narrative voice tell Lady Dedlock's guilty domestic secret (68). Finding a secret community among women in the novel for whom Lady Dedlock is the subversive representative, Blain argues that the latter serves as representative scapegoat among a host of outsiders—Hortense, the foreigner; Jenny, the social outcast; and Esther, the illegitimate child (74, 77). Blain reasserts the significance of Esther's ''sexual stigma'' by explicating Esther Hawdon as ''whore/hoyden,'' as well as interpreting her scarring, her humiliation by Guppy and Mrs. Woodcourt, and her final testing by Jarndyce as evidence of a sexual stain deriving not from Lady Dedlock's premarital sex but from ''the hostility to women endemic in a patriarchal society'' (79). Blain contests Taylor Stoehr's view that the finding of Lady Dedlock's corpse brings together the two narrative points of view (Stoehr 149, qtd. in Blain 80). Rather, ''the dialectic of the dual narrative paradoxically offers both an enactment and a critique of the sexual division into separate spheres,'' because, while Esther gets a happy ending, this ending fails to contain violence against female sexuality (82). As Blain startlingly concludes, Esther ''connive[s] at what amounts to her own clitoridectomy'' (82).

LuAnn McCracken Fletcher's ''A Recipe for Perversion'' also explores the connection between gender and narrative, but questions previous assumptions about the designation of the third-person omniscient voice as masculine or wholly authoritative. Noting that Judith Wilt has called the two voices ''two sides of the same narrator'' (Wilt 285, qtd. in Fletcher 69), Fletcher argues the voices do not differ much in actual technique, but that Esther's is marked by a self-reflexivity concerning the act of storytelling (70). Fletcher, theorizing omniscience through Audrey Jaffe (1987, 1991), wants to show the fiction of narrative ''transparency'' in *Bleak House*'s omniscient narration. Esther's narrative points frankly to the limits of narrative objectivity and to probable narrative deception of the reader (77). In doing so, her narrative makes the reader aware of the narrative conventions used by both of the novel's narrative voices. Fletcher quotes Mrs. Ellis's tenet about woman as a ''relative creature'' who should ''[blend] her own existence with'' others (78) to contextualize Esther's dilemma in telling a narrative without making herself too conspicuous in it (78). In response to critics who want Esther's final sentence to be more definitive, Fletcher writes that Dickens uses Esther as a feminine narrator to ''suggest the fictitiousness of social definition, of essential identity, of authoritative interpretation'' (83).

Ellen Burton Harrington, in ''From the Lady and the Law to the Lady Detective: Gender and Voice in Dickens and Collins,'' claims that Dickens's *Bleak House* strongly influenced Collins's *The Law and the Lady* (1875), and that Collins modeled his lady detective upon Esther Summerson. Harrington emphasizes the gendering of detective narration in *Bleak House* by juxtaposing Esther's narrative to Bucket's male detective authority and highlighting Esther's irrational female mind in comparison to the male detective's "scientific" mind. Collins's *The Law and the Lady* gives the abandoned wife some of the male detective's agency, while she retains a feminized discourse that includes reasoning and intellectual powers. Since her goal is to restore order in the domestic sphere, she is allied with Esther Summerson, and "her voice is the most potent connection to her predecessor" (22).

Dickens employed the feminized "sentimentalist social reform" discourse of female social reformers like Charlotte Elizabeth Tonna, argues Mary Lenard, in " 'Mr. Popular Sentiment': Dickens and the Gender Politics of Sentimentalism and Social Reform Literature" (46). This discourse includes Christian preaching and scenes of physical and emotional suffering, and is demonstrated in "exaggerated" figures such as Jo and Betty Higden (46). Lenard places the young boy's sentimentalized deathbed scene in the context of the feminized social reform discourse that Dickens opposes to a " 'masculine,' self-serving Utilitarianism which attempts to crush sympathy and sentiment in the name of a 'philosophical' self-interest" (48). Lenard notes, however, that excessive feeling makes characters vulnerable, and thereby shows the "instability of the gender binaries" in Victorian domestic ideology. Therefore, male sentimentalists were at risk, just like the frequently weeping Oliver.

Kathleen Sell-Sandoval's "In the Market-Place: Dickens, the Critics and the Gendering of Authorship" discusses the ways in which Dickens was affected by a gendered cultural discourse that arose by midcentury, characterizing writers and their work according to gender traits, and also classifying work as popular versus "serious" (225). According to Victorian critics like George Henry Lewes, female novelists were thought to lack intellectual range while having "power of emotion," while male novelists could both feel powerfully and think deeply (227). Sell-Sandoval carefully shows how critics like Lewes characterize Dickens's writing and Dickens himself in feminized language and terms, repeatedly emphasizing his "appeal to feeling and lack of intellect" (232). In part this may be due to the fact that "Dickens's immense popularity and commercial success posed a dilemma for critics" (232). Sell-Sandoval concludes that this "mobility of gendered attributes became essential in the burgeoning attempt of critics to define the genre of the novel, undermining at the same time the ideological underpinnings of such attempts" (224).

Acknowledgments

Many thanks to Professor Lillian Nayder, Bates College, for reading the introduction and making helpful recommendations, and to Dr. Chris Louttit,

University of Leicester, for reading the Masculinities section and providing useful suggestions. For help and encouragement, I also thank Professors Goldie Morgentaler, University of Lethbridge, Joel Brattin, Worcester Polytechnic Institute, and John Jordan, University of California, Santa Cruz.

Dickens and Gender: Recent Studies, 1992–2007

Aikens, Kristina. "The Daughter's Desire in *Dombey and Son*." *Critical Survey* (special issue: *Dickens and Sex*) 17:2 (2005): 77–91.

Alaya, Flavia. "Feminists on the Victorians: The Pardoning Frame of Mind." *Dickens Studies Annual* 14 (1985): 337–80.

Anderson, Amanda. " 'The Taint the Very Tale Conveyed': Self-Reading, Suspicion, and Fallenness in Dickens." *Tainted Souls and Painted Faces: The Rhetoric of Fallenness in Victorian Culture*. Ithaca: Cornell UP, 1993. 66–07.

Archibald, Diana. "American Women and English Angels in Dickens, Reade, Trollope and Thackeray." *Domesticity, Imperialism, and Emigration in the Victorian Novel*. Columbia: University of Missouri Press, 2002. 135–82.

Armstrong, Mary. "Pursuing Perfection: *Dombey and Son*, Female Homoerotic Desire, and the Sentimental Heroine." *Studies in the Novel* 28:3 (Fall 1996): 281–303.

Ayres, Brenda. *Dissenting Women in Dickens' Novels: The Subversion of Domestic Ideology*. Westport, CT: Greenwood, 1998.

Barzilai, Shuli. "The Bluebeard Barometer: Charles Dickens and Captain Murderer," *Victorian Literature and Culture* 32:2 (2004): 505–24.

Berry, Laura C. "In the Bosom of the Family: The Wet-Nurse, the Railroad, and *Dombey and Son*." *Dickens Studies Annual* 25 (1996): 1–28.

Black, Barbara. "A Sisterhood of Rage and Beauty: Dickens' Rosa Dartle, Miss Wade, and Madame Defarge." *Dickens Studies Annual* 26 (1998): 91–106.

Blain, Virginia. "Double Vision and the Double Standard in *Bleak House*: A Feminist Perspective." *New Casebooks: Bleak House*. Ed. Jeremy Tambling. New York: St. Martin's, 1998. 65–86. [Published originally as "Double Vision and the Double Standard," *Literature and History* 2:1 (1985): 31–46.]

Bowen, John. '' 'Bebelle and 'His Boots': Dickens, Ellen Ternan and the *Christmas Stories*.'' *The Dickensian* 96:3 (Winter 2000): 197–208.

Buckton, Oliver. '' 'The Reader Whom I Love': Homoerotic Secrets in *David Copperfield*.'' *ELH* 64 (1997): 189–201.

Campbell, Elizabeth. *Fortune's Wheel: Dickens and the Iconography of Time*. Athens: Ohio UP, 2003.

Camus, Marianne. *Gender and Madness in the Novels of Charles Dickens*. Lewiston, ME: Edwin Mellen, 2004.

Carens, Timothy L. "The Civilizing Mission at Home: Empire, Gender and National Reform in *Bleak House*." *Dickens Studies Annual* 26 (1998): 121–45.

Carr, Jean Ferguson. "Writing as a Woman: Dickens, *Hard Times*, and Feminine Discourse." *David Copperfield and Hard Times*. Ed. John Peck. New York: St. Martin's, 1995. 197–218. [Published originally as "Dickens, *Hard Times*, and Feminine Discourses." *Dickens Studies Annual* 18 (1989): 161–78.]

Chase, Karen, and Michael Levenson. "Tom's Pinch: The Sexual Serpent Beside the Dickensian Fireside." *The Spectacle of Intimacy: A Public Life for the Victorian Family*. Princeton: Princeton UP, 2000. 86–101.

Cohen, William A. "Interiors: Sex and the Body in Dickens." *Critical Survey* (special issue: *Dickens and Sex*) 17:2 (2005): 5–19.

——— "Manual Conduct in *Great Expectations*." *Sex Scandals: The Private Parts of Victorian Fiction*. Durham: Duke UP, 1996. 26–72.

Cole, Natalie B. '' 'Attached to life again': The 'Queer Beauty' of Convalescence in *Bleak House*." *Victorian Newsletter* No. 103 (Spring 2003): 16–19.

Coleman, Rosemary, "Nell and Sophronia—Catherine, Mary, and Georgina: Solving the Female Puzzle and the Gender Conundrum in *The Old Curiosity Shop*." *Dickens Studies Annual* 36 (2005): 33–55.

Colligan, Colette. "Raising the House Tops: Sexual Surveillance in Charles Dickens's *Dombey and Son*." *Dickens Studies Annual* 29 (2000): 99–144.

Cowles, David L. "Having It Both Ways: Gender and Paradox in *Hard Times*." *Hard Times*. Ed. Fred Kaplan and Sylvere Monod. New York: Norton, 2001. 439–44. [Originally published in *Dickens Quarterly* 8:2 (June 1991): 79–84.]

Cregan-Reid, Vybarr. "Bodies, Boundaries and Queer Waters: Drowning and Prosopopeia in Later Dickens." *Critical Survey* (special issue: *Dickens and Sex*) 17:2 (2005): 20–33.

Currie, Richard. A. "Against the Stereotype: Dickens's Esther Summerson and Conduct Book Heroines." *Dickens Quarterly* 16:1 (March 1999): 3–12

Danahay, Martin, "Dickens, Work and Sexuality." *Gender at Work in Victorian Culture: Literature, Art and Masculinity*. Aldershot: Ashgate, 2005. 67–86.

Darby, Margaret Flanders. "Dickens and Women's Stories: 1845–1848" (Part 1) *Dickens Quarterly* 17:2 (June 2000): 67–76; "Dickens and Women's Stories: 1845–1848." (Part 2). *Dickens Quarterly* 17:3 (Sept. 2000): 127–38.

David, Deirdre. "Children of Empire: Victorian Imperialism and Sexual Politics in Dickens and Kipling." *Gender and Discourse in Victorian Literature and Art*. Ed. Antony H. Harrison and Beverly Taylor. Dekalb: Northern Illinois UP, 1992. 125–42.

Dellamora, Richard. "Pure Oliver: or, Representation without Agency." *Dickens Refigured: Bodies, Desires and Other Histories*. Ed. John Schad. Manchester: Manchester UP, 1996. 55–79.

Dowling, Andrew. "Dickens, Manliness, and the Myth of the Romantic Artist," "Masculinity and Its Discontents." *Manliness and the Male Novelist in Victorian Literature*. Aldershot: Ashgate, 2001. 26–45, 46–61.

Fasick, Laura. "Portrait of the Writer as a Young Waif: Authorship in Dickens, Thackeray, and Kingsley," "Love and Work in *Great Expectations* and *Our Mutual Friend*," "The Hero as Healer." *Professional Men and Domesticity in the Mid-Victorian Novel*. Lewiston, ME: Edwin Mellen, 2003. 17–72, 101–39, 141–72.

Faulkner, David. "The Confidence Man: Empire and the Deconstruction of Muscular Christianity in *The Mystery of Edwin Drood*." Ed. Donald E. Hall. *Muscular Christianity: Embodying the Victorian Age*. Cambridge UP, 1994. 175–93.

Fletcher, LuAnn McCracken. "A Recipe for Perversion: The Feminine Narrative Challenge in *Bleak House*." *Dickens Studies Annual* 25 (1996): 67–89.

Frost, Lucy. " 'Taming to Improve': Dickens and the Women of *Great Expectations*. *Great Expectations*. Ed. Roger Sell. New York: St. Martin's, 1994. 60–78. [Originally published in *Meridian* 1 (1982): 11–20.]

Furneaux, Holly. " 'It is impossible to be gentler': The Homoerotics of Male Nursing in Dickens's Fiction." *Critical Survey* (special issue: *Dickens and Sex*) 17:2 (2005): 34–47.

———, and Anne Schwan. "Introduction: Dickens and Sex." *Critical Survey* (special issue: *Dickens and Sex*) 17:2 (2005): 1–3.

Garnett, Robert R. "The Crisis of 1863." *Dickens Quarterly* 23:3 (Sept. 2006): 181–91.

———. "Dickens, the Virgin, and the Dredger's Daughter." *Dickens Studies Annual* 28 (1999): 45–64.

———. "The Good and the Unruly in *Great Expectations*—and Estella." *Dickens Quarterly* 16:1 (March 1999): 24–41.

Hall, Donald E. " 'Betsy Prig . . . Try the Cowcumbers, God Bless You!': Hierarchies, Transgression and Trouble in *Martin Chuzzlewit*," "Great Expectations and Harsh Realities," " 'None of Your Eyes at Me': The Patriarchal Gaze in *Little Dorrit*." *Fixing Patriarchy: Feminism and Mid-Victorian Male Novelists*. New York: New York UP, 1996. 21–43, 107–30, 175–95.

Harrington, Ellen Burton. "From *The Lady and the Law* to the Lady Detective: Gender and Voice in Collins and Dickens." *Storytelling* 6:1 (2006): 19–31.

Hartley, Jenny. "Undertexts and Intertexts: The Women of Urania Cottage, Secrets and *Little Dorrit*." *Critical Survey* (special issue: *Dickens and Sex*) 17:2 (2005): 63–76.

Hawksley, Lucinda. *Katey: The Life and Loves of Dickens's Daughter*. London: Doubleday, 2006.

Holbrook, David. *Dickens and the Image of Woman*. New York: New York UP, 1993.

Hollington, Michael. "Dickens, *Household Words*, and the Paris Boulevards" (Part 1). *Dickens Quarterly* 14:3 (Sept. 1997): 154–64; "Dickens, *Household Words*, and the Paris Boulevards" (Part 2). *Dickens Quarterly* 14:4 (Dec. 1997): 199–212.

Houston, Gail Turley. *Consuming Fictions: Gender, Class and Hunger in Dickens's Novels*. Carbondale: Southern Illinois UP, 1992.

———. "Gender Construction and the *Kunstlerroman*: *David Copperfield* and *Aurora Leigh*." *Philological Quarterly* 72:2 (Spring 1993): 213–36.

Huguet, Christine. " 'There's not a doubt of the dress': Changing Clothes in Dickens's Fiction." *The Dickensian* 102:1 (Spring 2006): 24–31.

Humpherys, Anne. "Louisa Gradgrind's Secret Marriage and Divorce in *Hard Times*." *Dickens Studies Annual* 25 (1996): 177–95.

Ingham, Patricia. *Dickens, Women & Language*. Toronto: UP of Toronto, 1992.

———. " 'Nobody's Fault': The Scope of the Negative in *Little Dorrit*." *Dickens Refigured: Bodies, Desires and Other Histories*. Ed. John Schad. Manchester: Manchester UP, 1996. 98–111.

Jackson, Lisa Hartsell. "Little Nell's Nightmare: Sexual Awakening and Insomnia in Dickens's *The Old Curiosity Shop*." *Dickens Studies Annual* 39 (2008): 43–58. Not reviewed.

Jacobson, Wendy. "Freedom and Friendship: Women in *The Mystery of Edwin Drood*." *Dickens Quarterly* 18:2 (June 2001): 70–82.

John, Juliet. "Sincerely Deviant Women." *Dickens's Villains: Melodrama, Character, Popular Culture*. Oxford: Oxford UP, 2001. 199–234.

Joshi, Priti. "Mutiny Echoes: India, Britons, and *A Tale of Two Cities*." *Nineteenth-Century Literature*. Forthcoming. Not reviewed.

Klimaszewski, Melisa. "The Contested Sites of Maternity in Charles Dickens's *Dombey and Son*." *The Literary Mother: Essays on Representations of Maternity and Child Care*. Ed. Susan C. Staub. Jefferson, NC: McFarland, 2007. 138–58.

———. "Examining the Wet Nurse: Breasts, Power, and Penetration in Victorian England." *Women's Studies: An Interdisciplinary Journal* 35:4 (2006): 323–46.

Lenard, Mary. " 'Mr. Popular Sentiment': Dickens and the Gender Politics of Sentimentalism and Social Reform Literature." *Dickens Studies Annual* 27 (1998): 45–68.

Levine, Caroline, "Realism as Self-Forgetfulness: Gender, Ethics, and *Great Expectations*." *The Serious Pleasures of Suspense: Victorian Realism and Narrative Doubt*. Charlottesville: UP of Virginia, 2003. 84–98

Lewis, Linda. "Madame Defarge as Political Icon in Dickens's *A Tale of Two Cities*." *Dickens Studies Annual* 37 (2006): 31–49.

Louttit, Chris. "Lowell Revisited: Dickens and the Working Girl." *Dickens Quarterly* 24:1 (March 2007): 27–36.

Lubitz, Rita. *Marital Power in Dickens's Fiction.* New York: Peter Lang, 1996.

MacDonald, Tara. " 'red-headed animal': Race, Sexuality and Dickens's Uriah Heep." *Critical Survey* (special issue: *Dickens and Sex*) 17:2 (2005): 48–62.

Marcus, Sharon. "The Female Accessory in *Great Expectations*." *Between Women: Friendship, Desire, and Marriage in Victorian England.* Princeton: Princeton UP, 2007. 167–90.

Masters, Joellen. " 'Let herself out to do needlework': Female Agency and the Workhouse of Gender in Charles Dickens's *Little Dorrit*." *Famine and Fashion: Needlewomen in the Nineteenth Century.* Ed. Beth Harris. Aldershot: Ashgate, 2005. 53–66.

McCuskey, Brian. W. " 'Your Love-Sick Pickwick': The Erotics of Service." *Dickens Studies Annual* 25 (1996): 245–66.

McKnight, Natalie. "Dickens and Gender." *A Companion to Charles Dickens.* Ed. David Paroissien. Oxford: Blackwell, 2007: 186–98.

———. "Dickens's Philosophy of Fathering." *Dickens Quarterly* 18:3 (Sept. 2001): 129–38.

———. "Making Mother Suffer and Other Fun in Dickens." *Suffering Mothers in Mid-Victorian Novels.* New York: St. Martin's, 1997. 37–56. [Originally published in *Dickens Quarterly* 11:4 (Dec. 1996): 177–86. Not reviewed.]

Michie, Elsie B. " 'My Story as My Own Property': Gaskell, Dickens, and the Rhetoric of Prostitution," " 'Those That Will Not Work': Prostitutes, Property, Gaskell and Dickens." *Outside the Pale: Cultural Exclusion, Gender Difference, and the Victorian Woman Writer.* Ithaca: Cornell UP, 1993. 79–112, 113–41.

Michie, Helena. "The Avuncular and Beyond: Family (Melo)drama in *Nicholas Nickleby*." *Dickens Refigured: Bodies, Desires and Other Histories.* Ed. John Schad. Manchester: Manchester UP, 1996. 80–97.

Moglen, Helene. "Theorizing Fiction/Fictionalizing Theory: The Case of *Dombey and Son*." *Victorian Studies* 35 (Winter 1992): 159–84.

Myers, Margaret, "The Lost Self: Gender in *David Copperfield*." *David Copperfield and Hard Times.* Ed. John Peck. New York: St. Martin's, 1995. 108–24. [Published originally in *Gender Studies: New Directions in Feminist Criticism.* Ed. Judith Spector. Bowling Green: Creative Writing Program, 1986. 120–36.

Nayder, Lillian. "Catherine Dickens and Her Colonial Sons." *Dickens Studies Annual* 37 (2006): 81–93.

———. "The Other Dickens and America: Catherine in 1842." *Dickens Quarterly* 19:3 (Sept. 2002): 141–50.

Nord, Deborah Epstein. "*Sketches by Boz*: The Middle-Class City and the Quarantine of Urban Suffering," " 'Vitiated Air': The Polluted City and Female Sexuality in *Dombey and Son* and *Bleak House*." *Walking the Victorian Streets: Women, Representation, and the City*. Ithaca: Cornell UP, 1995. 49–80, 81–111.

Nygaard, Susan. "Redecorating Dombey: The Power of 'a Woman's Anger' versus Upholstery in *Dombey and Son*." *Critical Matrix* 81 (1994): 40–80.

Ofek, Galia. " 'Tie Her Up by the Hair': Dickens's Retelling of the Medusa and Rapunzel Myths." *Dickens Quarterly* 20:3 (Sept. 2003): 184–99.

Oulton, Carolyn. " 'My Undisciplined Heart':Romantic Friendship in *David Copperfield*." *Dickens Quarterly* 21:3 (Sept. 2004): 157–69.

Pal-Lapinski, Piya. "Dickens's Miss Wade and J. S. Lefanu's Carmilla: The Female Vampire in *Little Dorrit*." *Dickens Quarterly* 11:2 (Aug. 1994): 81–87.

Parker, David. "Dickens and the Death of Mary Hogarth." *Dickens Quarterly* 13:2 (June 1996): 67–75.

Poovey, Mary. "The Man-as-Letters Hero: *David Copperfield* and the Professional Writer." *David Copperfield and Hard Times*. Ed. John Peck. New York: St. Martin's, 1995: 81–107. [Published originally in Poovey's *Uneven Developments: The Ideological Work of Gender in Mid-Victorian England*. Chicago: U of Chicago P, 1988. 89–101, 116–25.]

Pykett, Lynn. "The Gendered Subject of Writing: *David Copperfield*." *Charles Dickens*. Houndmills, Basingstoke: Palgrave, 2002. 109–20.

Raphael, Linda. "A Re-vision of Miss Havisham: Her Expectations and Our Responses." *Great Expectations*. Ed. Roger D. Sell. New York: St. Martin's, 1994: 216–32. [Originally published in *Studies in the Novel* 21 (1989): 400–12.]

Retseck, Janet. "Sexing Miss Wade." *Dickens Quarterly* 15:4 (Dec. 1998): 217–25.

Robson, Catherine. "The Ideal Girl in Industrial England." *Men in Wonderland: The Lost Girlhood of the Victorian Gentleman*. Princeton: Princeton UP, 2001. 46–93.

Rooney, Caroline. "The Gender Differential, Again and Not Yet." *Literature and the Contemporary: Fictions and Theories of the Present.* Ed. Roger Luckhurst and Peter Marks. New York: Longman, 1999. 139–55.

Royle, Nicholas. "Our Mutual Friend." *Dickens Refigured: Bodies, Desires and Other Histories.* Ed. John Schad. Manchester: Manchester UP, 1996. 39–54.

Sadrin, Anny. "Charlotte Dickens: The Female Narrator of *Bleak House.*" *Dickens Quarterly* 9:2 (June 1992): 47–57.

Schad, John, Ed. *Dickens Refigured: Bodies, Desires and Other Histories.* Manchester: Manchester UP, 1996.

Scheckner, Peter. "Gender and Class in Dickens: Making Connections." *Midwest Quarterly* 41:3 (Spring 2000): 236–50.

Schor, Hilary. *Dickens and the Daughter of the House.* Cambridge: Cambridge UP, 1999.

———. " 'If He Should Turn to and Beat Her': Violence, Desire, and the Woman's Story in *Great Expectations.*" *Great Expectations.* Ed. Janice Carlisle. Boston: Bedford Books, 1996. 541–57. [Earlier version of ch. 6 in Schor's *Dickens and the Daughter of the House*]. Not reviewed.

Schwan, Anne. "The Limitations of a Somatics of Resistance: Sexual Performativity and Gender Dissonance in Dickens's *Dombey and Son.*" *Critical Survey* (special issue: *Dickens and Sex*) 17:2 (2005): 92–106.

Sell, Kathleen. "The Narrator's Shame: Masculine Identity in *Great Expectations. Dickens Studies Annual* 26 (1998): 203–26.

Sell-Sandoval, Kathleen. "In the Market Place: Dickens, the Critics and the Gendering of Authorship." *Dickens Quarterly* 17:4 (Dec. 2000): 224–35.

Shuman, Cathy. " 'In the Way of School': Dickens's *Our Mutual Friend.*" *Pedagogical Economies: The Examination and the Victorian Literary Man.* Stanford: Stanford UP, 2000. 123–69.

———. "Invigilating *Our Mutual Friend*: Gender and the Legitimating of Professional Authority." *Novel: A Forum on Fiction* 28:2 (Winter 1995): 154–72.

Simmons, James, Jr. "No Expectations at All: Women in Charles Dickens's *Great Expectations.*" *Women in Literature; Reading Through the Lens of Gender.* Ed. Jerilyn Fisher and Ellen S. Silber. Westport, CT: Greenwood, 2003. Not reviewed. [For use in middle-schools and secondary schools.]

Skabarnicki, Anne M. " 'Dear Little Women': Down-Sizing the Feminine in Carlyle and Dickens." *Carlyle Studies Annual* 14 (1994): 32–42. Not reviewed.

Smith, Karl. "Little Dorrit's 'speck' and Florence's 'daily blight': Urban Contamination and the Dickensian Heroine." *Dickens Studies Annual* 34 (2004): 117–54.

Surridge, Lisa. "Introduction," "Private Violence in the Public Eye: The Early Writings of Charles Dickens," "Domestic Violence and Middle-Class Manliness: *Dombey and Son.*" *Bleak Houses: Marital Violence in Victorian Fiction*. Athens: Ohio UP, 2005. 1–14, 14–43, 44–71.

———. "Domestic Violence, Female Self-Mutilation, and the Healing of the Male in *Dombey and Son.*" *Victorians Institute* 25 (1997): 77–103. [Earlier version of ch. 2 on *Dombey and Son* in *Bleak Houses* above.] Not reviewed.

Tromp, Marlene. "A 'Pound' of Flesh: Morality and the Economy of Sexual Violence in *Oliver Twist.*" *The Private Rod: Marital Violence, Sensation, and the Law in Victorian Britain*. Charlottesville: UP of Virginia, 2000. 23–68.

Van Boheemen-Saaf, Christine. "Joyce's Answer to Philosophy: Writing the Dematerializing Object." *Joyce, 'Penelope' and the Body*. Ed. Richard Brown. Amsterdam: Rodopi, 2006. 31–46.

Vlock, Deborah. "Patter and the Problem of Redundancy: Odd Women and *Little Dorrit.*" *Dickens, Novel Reading, and the Victorian Popular Theatre*. Cambridge: Cambridge UP, 1998. 159–89.

Waters, Catherine. *Dickens and the Politics of the Family*. Cambridge: Cambridge UP, 1997.

———. "Gender, Family, and Domestic Ideology." *Cambridge Companion to Charles Dickens*. Cambridge: Cambridge UP, 2000. 120–35.

Westland, Ella. "Dickens and Critical Change: Dickens and Women." *Dickens Quarterly* 11:4 (Dec. 1994): 187–96.

Walsh, Susan. "Bodies of Capital: *Great Expectations* and the Climacteric Economy." *Victorian Studies* 37:1 (1993): 73–98.

Wilson, Anna. "On History, Case History, and Deviance: Miss Wade's Symptoms and Their Interpretation." *Dickens Studies Annual* 26 (1998): 187–201

Wolff, Larry. " 'The Boys are Pickpockets, and the Girl is a Prostitute': Gender and Juvenile Criminality in Early Victorian England from *Oliver Twist* to *London Labour.*" *New Literary History* 27:2 (1996): 227–49.

Zangen, Britta. *Our Daughters Must Be Wives: Marriageable Young women in the Novels of Dickens, Eliot and Hardy.* Frankfurt: Peter Lang, 2004.

Zlotnick, Susan. "A 'World Turned Upside Downwards': Men, Dematerialization, and the Disposition-of-England Question." *Women, Writing, and the Industrial Revolution.* Baltimore: Johns Hopkins UP, 1998. 13–61.

———. " 'The Law's a Bachelor': *Oliver Twist*, Bastardy, and the New Poor Law." *Victorian Literature and Culture* 34 (2006): 131–46.

Other Works Cited

Acton, William. *Prostitution.* (1857). New York: Praeger, 1969.

———. "Unmarried Wet-nurses." *Lancet* 1 (1859): 175–76.

Aidoo, Ama Ata. *Our Sister Killjoy: Reflections of a Black-Eyed Squint.* London: Longman, 1977.

Armstrong, Nancy. *Desire and Domestic Fiction: A Political History of the Novel.* New York: Oxford UP, 1987.

Atwood, Margaret. *Survival: A Thematic Guide to Canadian Literature.* Toronto: Anansi, 1972.

Auerbach, Nina. *Communities of Women: An Idea in Fiction.* Cambridge: Harvard UP, 1978.

———. *Woman and the Demon: The Life of a Victorian Myth.* Cambridge: Harvard UP, 1982.

Bachelard, Gaston. *The Poetics of Space.* Trans. Maria Jolas. 1964; Boston: Beacon, 1994.

Bailin, Miriam. *The Sickroom in Victorian Fiction: The Art of Being Ill.* Cambridge: Cambridge UP, 1994.

Bakhtin, Mikhail. *Rabelais and His World.* Trans. H. Iswolsky. Cambridge: MIT P, 1968.

Balbus, Isaac D. "Disciplining Women: Michel Foucault and the Power of Feminist Discourse." *After Foucault: Humanistic Knowledge, Postmodern Challenges.* New Brunswick, NJ: Rutgers UP, 1988. 138–60.

Barickman, Richard, Susan MacDonald, and Myra Stark. *Corrupt Relations: Dickens, Thackeray, Trollope, Collins, and the Victorian Sexual System.* New York: Columbia UP, 1982.

Bayard, Louis. *Mr. Timothy.* New York: HarperCollins, 2003.

Beasley, Chris. *Gender and Sexuality: Critical Theories, Critical Thinkers.* London: Sage, 2005.

de Beauvoir, Simone. *The Second Sex.* New York: Knopf, 1952.

Beer, Gillian. *Darwin's Plots: Evolutionary Narrative in Darwin, Great Expectations, and Nineteenth-Century Fiction.* London: Routledge and Kegan Paul, 1983.

Beeton, Isabella. *Mrs. Beeton's Book of Household Management.* 1859–61. Oxford: Oxford UP, 2000.

Benjamin, Jessica. *The Bonds of Love: Psychoanalysis, Feminism, and the Problem of Domination.* New York: Pantheon, 1988.

Bourdieu, Pierre. *The State Nobility: Elite Schools in the Field of Power.* Trans. L. C. Clough. Cambridge: Polity, 1996.

———, and Jean-Claude Passeron. *Reproduction in Education, Society, and Culture.* Trans. Richard Nice. London: Sage, 1977.

Brooks, Peter. *Body Work: Objects of Desire in Modern Narrative.* Cambridge: Harvard UP, 1993.

Butler, Judith. *Gender Trouble: Feminism and the Subversion of Identity.* New York: Routledge, 1990.

Carey, Peter. *Jack Maggs.* New York: Vintage, 1997.

Carlyle, Thomas. ''Occasional Discourse on the Negro Question.'' *Fraser's* 40 (Dec. 1849): 670–79.

Chodorov, Nancy. *The Reproduction of Mothering: Psychoanalysis and the Sociology of Gender.* Berkeley: U of California P, 1978.

Cixous, Hélène. ''The Laugh of the Medusa.'' Trans. Keith Cohen and Paula Cohen. *Signs* 1 (1976): 875–93.

———, and Catherine Clement. *The Newly Born Woman.* Trans. Betsy Wing. Minneapolis: U of Minnesota P, 1986.

Collins, Wilkie. *The Law and the Lady.* Oxford: Oxford UP, 1999.

Cranny-Francis, Anne, Wendy Waring, Pam Stavropoulos, and Joan Kirby. *Gender Studies: Terms and Debates.* Houndmills, Basingstoke: Palgrave: 2003.

David, Deirdre. *Rule Britannia: Women, Empire and Victorian Writing.* Ithaca: Cornell UP, 1995.

Davidoff, Leonore and Catherine Hall. *Family Fortunes: Men and Women of the English Middle Class, 1780–1850.* Chicago: U of Chicago P, 1987.

D'Cruze, Shani. *Crimes of Outrage: Sex, Violence and Victorian Working Women.* DeKalb: Northern Illinois UP, 1998.

Dickens, Charles. "Dr. Marigold." *The Christmas Stories.* 1956. Oxford: Oxford UP, 1989. 433–72.

———. "The Hospital Patient." *Sketches by Boz.* London: Penguin, 1995. 277–82.

———. *The Letters of Charles Dickens.* Pilgrim Edition. Ed. Madeline House, Graham Storey, Kathleen Tillotson, et al. 12 vols. Oxford: Clarendon, 1965–2002.

———. "Mrs. Lirriper's Legacy." *The Christmas Stories.* 1956. Oxford: Oxford UP, 1989. 403–32.

———. "Mrs. Lirriper's Lodgings." *The Christmas Stories.* 1956. Oxford: Oxford UP, 1989. 369–401.

———. "A Nightly Scene in London." *'Gone Astray' and Other Papers from Household Words, 1851–1859.* Ed. Michael Slater. Vol. 3 of *The Dent Uniform Edition of Dickens' Journalism.* Columbus: Ohio State UP, 1999. 346–51.

———. "Nurse's Stories." *The Uncommercial Traveller and Other Papers, 1859–1870.* Vol. 4 of *The Dent Uniform Edition of Dickens' Journalism.* Ed. Michael Slater and John Drew. Columbus: Ohio State UP, 2000. 169–80.

———. "The Pawnbroker's Shop." *Sketches by Boz.* Ed. Dennis Walder. London: Penguin, 1995. 220–29.

———. "Somebody's Luggage." *The Christmas Stories.* 1956. Oxford: Oxford UP, 1989. 315–65.

———. "Travelling Abroad." *The Uncommercial Traveller and Other Papers, 1859–1870.* Vol. 4 of *The Dent Uniform Edition of Dickens' Journalism.* Ed. Michael Slater and John Drew. Columbus: Ohio State UP, 2000. 83–95.

————. "A Visit to Newgate." *Sketches by Boz*. Ed. Dennis Walder. London: Penguin, 1995. 234–48.

Donzelot, Jacques. *The Policing of Families*. Trans. Robert Hurley. London: Hutchinson, 1979. Trans. of *La Police des Familles*. Paris: Les Editions de Minuit, 1977.

Douglas, Mary. *Purity and Danger*. London: Routledge, 1966, 1984.

Eliot, George. *Middlemarch*. Ed. Gordon S. Haight. Boston: Houghton Mifflin, 1956.

Elliott, Jean. *My Dearest Kate: The Marriage of Mrs. Charles Dickens*. Unpublished typescript. [1983.]

Ellis, Sarah Stickney. *The Women of England, Their Social Duties and Domestic Habits*. London: Fisher, 1839.

Faber, Michel. *The Crimson Petal and the White*. New York: Harcourt, 2002.

Felski, Rita. *Beyond Feminist Aesthetics: Feminist Literature and Social Change*. Cambridge: Harvard UP, 1989.

Fleishman, Avrom. "The City and the River: Dickens's Symbolic Landscape." *Studies in the Later Dickens*. Montpelier: Université Paul Valéry, Centre d'Etudes et de Recherches Victoriennes et Edouardiennes, 1974. 111–26.

Forster, John. *Life of Charles Dickens*. 2 vols. London: Dent, 1966.

Foucault, Michel, *Discipline and Punish: The Birth of the Prison*. Trans. Alan Sheridan. New York: Random House, 1995.

————. *The History of Sexuality: An Introduction*. Trans. Robert Hurley. New York: Random House, 1990.

Freedgood, Elaine. *Victorian Writing About Risk: Imagining a Safe England in a Dangerous World*. Cambridge: Cambridge UP, 2000.

Freud, Sigmund. *Jokes and Their Relation to the Unconscious*. Vol. 8. *The Standard Edition of the Complete Psychological Works of Sigmund Freud*. Ed. and trans. James Strachey. London: Hogarth, 1953–74. 24 vols.

————. "On Narcissism: An Introduction." Vol. 14. *The Standard Edition*. 73–102.

Friedman, Stanley. "Dickens's Mid-Victorian Theodicy." *Dickens Studies Annual* 7 (1978): 128–50.

Gallagher, Catherine. "The Body versus the Social Body in Malthus and Henry Mayhew." *The Making of the Modern Body: Sexuality and Society in the Nineteenth Century.* Berkeley: U of California P, 1987. 83–106.

Gallup, Jane. *The Daughter's Seduction: Feminism and Psychoanalysis.* Ithaca: Cornell UP, 1982.

Gay, Peter. *The Cultivation of Hatred.* New York: Norton, 1993.

Gilligan, Carol. *In a Different Voice: Psychological Theory and Women's Development.* Cambridge: Harvard UP, 1982.

Glavin, John. "Pickwick on the Wrong Side of the Door." *Dickens Studies Annual* 22 (1993): 1–19.

Goffman, Erving. *The Presentation of Self in Everyday Life.* Harmondsworth: Penguin, 1959.

Haley, Bruce. *The Healthy Body and Victorian Culture.* Cambridge: Harvard UP, 1978.

Hall, Catherine. *White, Male and Middle-Class: Explorations in Feminism and History.* Cambridge: Polity, 1992.

Heatley, Edward. "The Redeemed Feminine of *Little Dorrit.*" *Dickens Studies Annual* 4 (1975): 153–64.

Holman, Sheri. *The Dress Lodger.* New York: Ballantine: 2000.

Horn, Pamela. *The Rise and Fall of the Victorian Servant.* Wolfeboro Falls, NH: A. Sutton, 1991.

Houston, Gail Turley. "Broadsides at the Board: Collations of *Pickwick Papers* and *Oliver Twist.*" *SEL* 31 (1991): 735–55.

Irigaray, Luce. *An Ethics of Sexual Difference.* Trans. Carolyn Burke and Gillian C. Gill. Ithaca: Cornell UP, 1993.

———. *The Speculum of the Other Woman.* Trans. Gillian C. Gill. Ithaca: Cornell UP, 1985.

———. *This Sex Which Is Not One.* Trans. Catherine Porter. Ithaca: Cornell UP, 1985.

Irving, John. *The Cider House Rules.* New York: Ballantine, 1993.

Jacobus, Mary. "Is there a Woman in This Text?" *Reading Woman: Essays in Feminist Criticism.* New York: Columbia UP, 1986.

Jaffe, Audrey. "Omniscience in *Our Mutual Friend*: On Taking the Reader by Surprise." *Journal of Narrative Technique* 17 (1987): 91–101.

————. *Vanishing Points: Dickens, Narrative, and the Subject of Omniscience.* Berkeley: U of California P, 1991.

Johnson, Patricia E. *Hidden Hands: Working-Class Women and Victorian Social-Problem Fiction.* Athens: Ohio UP, 2001

Jordan, John O. "Domestic Servants and the Victorian Home." *Homes and Homelessness in the Victorian Imagination.* Ed. Murray Baumgarten and H. M. Daleski. New York: AMS Press, 1998. 79–90.

Keller, Evelyn. *A Feeling for the Organism.* San Francisco: Freeman, 1983.

————. *Reflections on Gender and Science.* New Haven: Yale UP, 1985.

Kincaid, James. *Child-Loving: The Erotic Child and Victorian Culture.* New York: Routledge, 1992.

————. "Fattening Up on Pickwick." *Novel* 25 (1992): 235–44.

————. "The Education of Mr. Pickwick." *Nineteenth Century Fiction* 24 (1969): 127–41.

Kipling, Rudyard. *Kim.* Harmondsworth: Penguin, 1987.

Klein, Melanie. *New Directions in Psychoanalysis.* 1955. London: Routledge, 2003.

Knox, Robert. *Races of Men, a Fragment.* London: Renshaw, 1850.

Kofman, Sarah. *The Enigma of Woman: Woman in Freud's Writings.* Trans. Catherine Porter. Ithaca: Cornell UP, 1985.

Kristeva, Julia. *The Powers of Horror: An Essay on Abjection.* New York: Columbia UP, 1982.

————. *The Kristeva Reader.* Ed. Toril Moi. New York: Columbia UP, 1986.

Kucich, John. *Repression in Victorian Fiction: Charlotte Bronte, George Eliot and Charles Dickens.* Berkeley: University of CA Press, 1987.

Langbauer, Laurie. "Dickens's Streetwalkers: Women and the Form of Romance." *ELH* 53 (1986): 411–31.

————. *Women and Romance: The Consolations of Gender in the English Novel.* Ithaca: Cornell UP, 1990.

Langland, Elizabeth. *Nobody's Angels: Domestic Ideology and Middle-Class Women in the Victorian Novel.* New York: Cornell UP, 1995.

Leavis, F. R. and Q. D. Leavis. *Dickens the Novelist.* London: Chatto and Windus, 1970.

LeFanu, Sheridan. *Carmilla*. *The Penguin Book of Vampire Stories*. Ed. Alan Ryan. New York: Penguin, 1988. 71–137.

Lejeune, Phillipe. *On Autobiography*. Trans. Katherine Leary. Minneapolis: U of Minneapolis P, 1989.

Litvack, Leon. "Images of the River in *Our Mutual Friend*." *Dickens Quarterly* 20 (March 2003): 134–55.

Lougy, Robert "Nationalism and Violence: America in Dickens's *Martin Chuzzlewit*." *Dickens and the Children of the Empire*. Ed. Wendy Jacobson. Houndmills, Basingstoke: Palgrave, 2000. 105–15.

Louttit, Chris. Reviews of Andrew Dowling's *Manliness and the Male Novelist in Victorian Literature* and Martin A. Danahay's *Gender at Work in Victorian Culture: Literature, Art and Masculinity*. *Dickens Quarterly* 23:2 (Sept. 2006): 199–202.

Lucas, John. *The Melancholy Man: A Study of Dickens's Novels*. Brighton: Harvester, 1980.

Lukacs, Georg. *The Historical Novel*. Trans. Hannah and Stanley Mitchell. London: Merlin, 1962.

Marcus, Steven. *Dickens: From Pickwick to Dombey*. New York: Basic Books, 1965.

Mayhew, Henry. *London Labour and the London Poor*. Vol. 1. London, 1860–1861.

McClintock, Anne. *Imperial Leather: Race, Gender and Sexuality in the Colonial Contest*. London: Routledge, 1995.

McKnight, Natalie. "Dickens and Industry." *Dickens Quarterly* 19 (2002): 133–40.

———. *Idiots, Madmen and Other Prisoners in Dickens*. New York: St. Martin's, 1993.

Meckier, Jerome. "Chapter Four of *American Notes*: Self Discovery in Lowell; Or Why Little Nell Would Have Been Happy There But Dickens Was Not." *Dickens Quarterly* 19 (2002): 123–32.

Metz, Nancy. " 'The Blighted Tree' and the Book of Fate: Female Models of Storytelling in *Little Dorrit*." *Dickens Studies Annual* 18 (1989): 221–41.

Michie, Helena. " 'Who Is This in Pain?': Scarring, Disfigurement, and Female Identity in *Bleak House* and *Our Mutual Friend*." *Novel: A Forum on Fiction* 22:2 (Winter 1989): 199–212.

Millet, Kate. *Sexual Politics*. New York: Doubleday, 1970.

Moers, Ellen. "*Bleak House*: The Agitating Woman." *Dickensian* (1973): 13–24.

Moynahan, Julian. "Dealing with the Firm of Dombey and Son: Firmness *versus* Wetness." *Dickens and the Twentieth Century*. Ed. John Gross and Gabriel Pearson. London: Routledge and Kegan Paul, 1963. 121–31.

Mulvey, Laura. *Visual and Other Pleasures*. London: Macmillan, 1989.

Nead, Lynda. *Myths of Sexuality: Representations of Women in Victorian Britain*. Oxford: Blackwell, 1988.

Newman, S. J. *Dickens at Play*. New York: St. Martin's, 1981.

Newsom, Robert. "Embodying Dombey: Whole and in Part." *Dickens Studies Annual* 18 (1989): 197–219.

Panger, Daniel. *Hard Times: The Lost Diary of Mrs. Charles Dickens*. Berkeley: Creative Arts, 2000.

Patmore, Coventry. *The Angel in the House*. Boston: Ticknor and Fields, 1856.

Peltason, Timothy. "Esther's Will." *ELH* 59 (Fall 1992): 671–91.

Polhemus, Robert. "Comic and Erotic Faith Meet Faith in the Child: Charles Dickens's *The Old Curiosity Shop* ('The Old Cupiosity Shape')." *Critical Reconstructions: The Relationship of Fiction and Life*. Stanford: Stanford UP, 1994. 71–89.

Rich, Adrienne. *Of Woman Born: Motherhood as Experience and Institution*. New York: Norton, 1986.

Robbins, Bruce. *The Servant's Hand: English Fiction from Below*. New York: Columbia UP, 1986.

Roper, Michael and John Tosh. *Manful Assertions: Masculinities in Britain since 1800*. New York: Routledge, 1991.

Rosenberg, Edgar. *From Shylock to Svengali: Jewish Stereotypes in English Fiction*. Stanford: Stanford UP, 1960.

Ruddick, Sara. "Maternal Thinking." *Feminist Studies* 16 (1980): 342–67.

Sadoff, Diane. *Monsters of Affection: Dickens, Eliot and Brontë on Fatherhood*. Baltimore: Johns Hopkins UP, 1982.

Sedgwick, Eve Kosofsky. *Between Men: English Literature and Male Homosocial Desire*. Berkeley: U of California P, 1985.

———. *The Epistemology of the Closet*. Berkeley: U of California P, 1991.

Shanley, Mary Lyndon. *Feminism, Marriage, and the Law in Victorian England, 1850–1895*. Princeton: Princeton UP, 1989.

Shires, Linda M., ed. *Rewriting the Victorians: Theory, History, and the Politics of Gender*. New York: Routledge, 1992.

Showalter, Elaine. *The Female Malady: Women, Madness, and English Culture, 1830–1980*. New York: Pantheon, 1985.

Silverman, Kaja. *Male Subjectivity at the Margins*. New York: Routledge, 1992.

Slater, Michael. *Dickens and Women*. London: Dent, 1983.

Splitter, Randolph. "Guilt and the Trappings of Melodrama in *Little Dorrit*." *Dickens Studies Annual* 6 (1977): 119–33.

Stoehr, Taylor. *Dickens: The Dreamer's Stance*. Ithaca: Cornell UP, 1965.

Sussman, Herbert. *Victorian Masculinities: Manhood and Masculine Poetics in Early Victorian Literature and Art*. Cambridge: Cambridge UP, 1995.

Tillotson, Kathleen. *Novelists of the Eighteen-Forties*. Oxford: Clarendon, 1954.

Tomalin, Claire. *The Invisible Woman: The Story of Nelly Ternan and Charles Dickens*. New York: Knopf, 1991.

Tosh, John. *A Man's Place: Masculinity and the Middle-Class Home in Victorian England*. New Haven: Yale UP, 1999.

Wallace-Kowalski, Elizabeth. *Their Father's Daughters: Hannah More, Maria Edgeworth and Patriarchal Complicity*. Oxford: Oxford UP, 1991.

Warner, Marina. *Alone of All Her Sex*. New York: Knopf, 1976.

Waters, Sarah. *Affinity*. New York: Riverhead, 1999.

———. *Fingersmith*. New York: Riverhead, 2002.

Welsh, Alexander. *The City of Dickens*. Cambridge: Harvard UP, 1971.

Welter, Barbara. "The Cult of True Womanhood: 1820–1860." *American Quarterly* 19 (Spring 1966): 151–74.

Wilt, Judith. "Confusion and Consciousness in Dickens's Esther." *Nineteenth-Century Fiction* 32 (1977): 285–309.

Winnicott, D. W. *Playing and Reality*. 1971. New York: Routledge, 1989.

Yeazell, Ruth. *Fictions of Modesty: Women and Courtship in the English Novel*. Chicago: U of Chicago P, 1991.

Recent Dickens Studies, 2006

Timothy Spurgin

This essay reviews books, articles, and essays published on Dickens in 2006. The year was a good one, featuring publications from established scholars along with the work of many rising stars. Sharply different images of Dickens emerged from these publications, with some essays describing him as a confident and capable writer and others painting him in less flattering tones. In future years, Dickensians might more directly address the question of why their author continues to provoke such widely varying responses. For now, it may be enough to note that 2006 seemed to mark a renewed engagement with Dickensian strangeness and a growing frustration with the new historicist approaches of the 1980s and 1990s. This essay groups its materials thematically or topically, ranging from "America and Britain" to "Theory" and "Vision." The largest single category was "Politics," which takes in everything from class conflict to mob violence. Most of the works in that category begin with questions about Dickens's reputation as a reformer, and many share an interest in his representation of social forces and social bodies.

Introduction

I have no complaints. Mine was a year in which several eminent Dickensians issued new publications, with a few established scholars (John Bowen, Rosemarie Bodenheimer, and Malcolm Andrews) appearing in print more than once. It was also a year in which striking new voices were heard. So, in addition to helping me catch up with old favorites like James Kincaid, 2006

Dickens Studies Annual, Volume 39, Copyright © 2008 by AMS Press, Inc. All rights reserved.

introduced me to rising stars like Jennifer Ruth and Jason Jones. Their work, issued in the new Victorian Critical Interventions series from Ohio State University Press, was thoroughly impressive, suggesting new possibilities for the study of Victorian fiction. So, whatever the reason for my good fortune, I'm happy to echo earlier reviewers in announcing that the task of assembling this review, though sometimes daunting, was always fun.

One question was somewhat perplexing: how to organize all this material? Would it be better to go book by book, starting with the *Sketches* and ending with *Drood*? Or would it make more sense to begin with monographs, go on to essay collections, and wrap up with articles and encyclopedia entries? Both approaches had clear advantages, as well as obvious drawbacks. In the end, it seemed best to group materials thematically. This approach is not without its own defects—should essays on class issues be included with other work on political and social themes, or spun off into a separate category?—but it also has the great advantage of allowing most readers to find what they need quickly.

Having reached that conclusion, I sorted the almost sixty publications from 2006 into the following categories:

1. America and Britain
2. Biography
3. China
4. Christmas
5. Drood mysteries
6. Film and TV
7. Gender
8. Literary form
9. Literary life
10. Other writers
11. Performance
12. Politics and social reform
13. Race
14. Theory
15. Vision

Some of these terms require further explanation. ''America and Britain'' takes in discussions of *American Notes* as well as considerations of national identity. ''Literary form'' brings together studies of technical issues like characterization and plotting. ''Literary life'' is concerned with publication practices, reception histories, and the impact of plagiarism on Dickens's career. With ''Other writers,'' we turn to questions of influence and intertextuality, comparing Dickens with literary figures from Darwin and Dostoevsky to

Joyce and Somerset Maugham. "Performance" includes Dickens's public readings, as well as his treatment of theatricality and acting. "Vision," the final category on my list, takes in our visualization of Dickens's stories along with Dickensian attitudes toward looking and seeing.

The largest categories, as you'll see, were "Biography," "Gender," "Other writers," and "Politics." "Gender" includes work on masculinity and domesticity, in addition to studies of Dickens's attitude toward women. "Politics" is an elastic term, capturing everything from class conflict to mob violence. Much of the scholarship treated under this heading took off from a question about Dickens's reputation as a social reformer, and almost all of it displayed an interest in his representation of social forces and social bodies. Because political issues loom large in books like *Oliver Twist, Barnaby Rudge*, and *A Tale of Two Cities*, they received a good deal of attention in 2006. The books discussed most frequently, for the record, were *Bleak House* and *Our Mutual Friend*. By contrast, relatively little work was done on *The Pickwick Papers, Dombey and Son*, or *Great Expectations*.

I was surprised by some of these developments—only two publications on *Great Expectations?*—and intrigued by many others. The Dickens who emerged from one essay often bore little resemblance to the man described elsewhere. At times he was portrayed as supremely confident, a keen observer of human behavior, and an endlessly ambitious writer. At other times, he seemed insecure and stupid, worrying about the possibility of being misread, scrambling to stifle criticism, and falling back on clichés. Nowhere was the contrast more obvious than in two compelling readings of *Little Dorrit*, both the work of insightful and accomplished scholars. For Hilary Schor, the Dickens of *Little Dorrit* was an old pro, an absolute master, conducting "brilliant experiments" (101), challenging his critics, and outdoing his rivals. For Kincaid, as you'll discover, he was a fraud and a bore, covering his mistakes with "beatific mush" (18). "*Little Dorrit*," says Kincaid,

> is a novel so smug, so unforgiving and spiteful, so self-satisfied and static, stewing in its own resentments, rehearsing its own wrongs, that few readers would ever bother with it, except Dickens enthusiasts who, like the insufferable Amy Dorrit, are locked into the most tedious of all Vices, a devotion to duty.
>
> (19)

So who's right? Are we really "locked into" some weird devotion to Dickens? Is it a "tedious" sense of duty that keeps us going back to some of these books? Or are we, as Schor suggests, only just beginning to value Dickens's "experiments"?

It's my hope that instead of attempting to resolve these undecidable questions, scholars will continue to explore and account for our difficulties with Dickens. It's worth asking why he gives us so much trouble—and why, compared with Eliot or James or even Hardy, he continues to prove so elusive. In much of the work treated here, I saw signs that my hopes might be realized. Many scholars noted the incoherence of Dickens's personality, his career, and his opinions, while others acknowledged the difficulty of fitting him into literary history or describing his contribution to the development of the novel. A memorable example came from the introduction to *Palgrave Advances in Charles Dickens Studies*, a fine collection of essays edited by John Bowen and Robert L. Patten: "For all the modern pleasures that they bring to their readers, [Dickens's books] do not pass readily into the category of the safely-consumed, but live on like an infection that cannot be shaken off, a ghost that cannot be exorcised, or a joke that returns and returns" (8). This wonderful passage was for me one of the highlights of the year. In it, Dickens is an infection, a ghost, and a joke. He makes his way into our bodies, then he messes with our minds, and then he leaves us laughing.

The editors' emphasis on strangeness, incoherence, and contradiction is carried through the rest of the *Palgrave Advances* collection. Reviewing a long tradition of biographical criticism on Dickens, Rosemarie Bodenheimer credits Edmund Wilson with "open[ing] the way to appreciate the sheer strangeness of Dickens" and also applauds Peter Ackroyd for his attention to the "essential strangeness of Dickens" (65). In Hilary Schor's essay on Dickens's plotting, from which I've already quoted, she announces her desire to "restore some of the strangeness and difficulty" to books like *Bleak House* and *Little Dorrit* (90). And in his own contribution to the volume, appearing at the very end of the collection, editor Bowen describes "Dickens's writing" as "one of the strangest force-fields a critic can enter" (258). The essays in the Palgrave volume aren't alone, either. In many other books and articles—Julian Wolfreys's study of vision and visuality in *Pickwick*, say, or Elaine Freedgood's work on race, commodification, and realism in *Great Expectations*—I found evidence of a growing willingness to talk about our troubles with Dickens. Who was he? What did he think he was doing? Why do we still care? These are the questions we're now beginning to confront, and they're the ones we'll want to explore more carefully in future years.

Given my investment in 2006, I don't suppose I can be blamed for hoping that it will be remembered not only as a banner year but also as a turning point, a time when we found new ways of reckoning with Dickens. One way or another, it has been a great pleasure to work on this review. In closing, I must thank Joanne Johnson, administrative assistant to the humanities departments at Lawrence University, for her help with proofreading. Any remaining mistakes are, of course, my own. I also want to follow recent reviewers in apologizing to anyone whose work I've overlooked or misunderstood. I did my best to find everything, and to write on whatever I found, but I suspect that at least a few items have eluded my grasp, and for that I am sorry.

America and Britain

Dickens's view of America was the subject of two fine articles. The first, Christopher Keirstead's "In Search of the 'Great Human Family,' " explores the "temporary companionship" experienced by Dickens and other travelers (123). Keirstead's essay is most impressive in its discussion of Dickens's experiences aboard railway carriages and canal boats, places where he was "confined, immobilized, and presented for observation" (124). As Dickens fought to preserve some sense of privacy, he also found himself bonded to other passengers. Though silent and unwanted, these bonds could prove to be quite powerful, creating what Keirstead calls a "reluctant community of victimization" (126).

The best evidence for Keirstead's argument comes in a scene from *American Notes*, where Dickens describes the ambivalent feelings stirred up by a dissatisfied passenger on a Pennsylvania boat trip. When this passenger shouts out his complaints about overcrowding, Dickens is both appalled and enthused. As Keirstead explains, the man has begun to speak on behalf of the other passengers, "express[ing] the feelings they all share but are reluctant to voice" (126). For anyone who flies coach, the situation will seem familiar, but to Dickens and his readers it was new, and it's this sense of novelty that prompts Keirstead's identification of *American Notes* as a "seminal text of modern tourism" (118). That idea is worth developing further—it would be interesting to see how Dickens differs from other travel writers in the period—but for now it seems enough to say that Keirstead has deepened our understanding of Dickens's travels and sharpened our view of *American Notes*.

Other important contexts for *American Notes* are suggested by Amanda Claybaugh, whose "Toward a New Transatlanticism" places Dickens within a "shared Anglo-American culture of social reform" (439). This shared reform culture was focused on the "campaigns against slavery and for suffrage reform" (444), and it allowed for the possibility of lively, mutually beneficial transatlantic exchanges. "At times, one nation served as an example for reformers in the other nation," Claybaugh says, while "at other times, reformers in both nations worked in tandem" (444). Claybaugh leaves little doubt that Dickens was "fully alive to the reform possibilities" of his tour and travel book (447), citing a reporter's observation of Dickens "surrounded" by reforming travel books on the eve of his departure for the U.S. (445–46).

With these ideas in the background, Claybaugh turns to a detailed analysis of "Slavery," one of the most controversial chapters in *American Notes*. In this chapter, Dickens borrows from the writings of abolitionist Theodore

Weld, which is to say that he engages in the "same acts of reprinting against which he was campaigning elsewhere" (440). Like Weld, Dickens reprints advertisements placed by whites seeking the return of their runaway slaves, thereby forcing his Southern readers to "see what their own newspapers looked like through unfamiliar eyes" (453). This strategy, sharply described by Claybaugh as one of "defamiliarization" (see 448, 452–53), helped Dickens to explode the notion that public opinion might be rallied against slavery or used to mitigate its worst excesses. "Public opinion!" Dickens cries at one point, "Why, public opinion in the slave States *is* slavery, is it not?" (*American Notes* 271).

Among the many impressive features of Claybaugh's article is its attention to the crucial place of *American Notes* in Dickens's career. Through her readings of *Martin Chuzzlewit* and *Bleak House*, Claybaugh shows that Dickens's disillusionment with the United States led him to "withdraw from the very Anglo-American networks that his tour and travel book had exemplified" (454). This withdrawl had serious consequences, as Claybaugh also demonstrates: Dickens refused to negotiate with American publishers, abandoned his earlier commitment to suffrage, strengthened his opposition to Chartism, and became more deeply skeptical of the transnational antislavery campaign (see 454). In *Chuzzlewit*, Claybaugh argues, Dickens "posits an absolute separation" between the U.S. and Britain, one that he "knew did not exist" (454), and in *Bleak House*, he goes even further, "ridicul[ing] any attention to the world beyond the nation" (457). Thus, instead of simply telling us that Dickens's trip was a turning point in his life or saying that his disappointments reinforced a general sense of pessimism, she traces the impact of his unhappy experiences on particular works of fiction. For future scholars of Dickens's engagements with America—and his evolution as a political and social thinker—her article will be an important reference point.

Though most scholars agree that Dickens's first trip to America sharpened his sense of what it meant to be British, few have taken up the question of English national identity in Dickens. Patrick Parrinder tries to fill that gap with a chapter on Dickens in *Nation and Novel*, his wide-ranging study of the "representation of Englishness" in works of fiction from 1485 to 2001. Parrinder claims that, for Dickens, England is "a nation centering on its metropolis" (213), and he has much to say about Dickens's "wrestling" with the myth of Dick Whittington, the legendary Lord Mayor (220). According to Parrinder, Dickens rejects some parts of the myth (including the hero's triumphs as merchant and politician) but actively embraces others (the hero's marriage to the master's daughter). Though he never quite manages to bring his argument back to the issue of "Englishness," Parrinder makes a useful contribution to our understanding of several other topics: Dickens and domesticity, for example, as well as Dickens and London. His work also offers much for the general reader, particularly in its discussion of crucial contradictions. Dickens may be drawn to the city, Parrinder explains, but he also feels a "profound distrust of urban society" (216).

Biography

Rosemarie Bodenheimer reflects on biographical approaches to Dickens in her contribution to the *Palgrave Advances* collection. Instead of trying to separate fact from fiction, Bodenheimer tries to "follow central strands in the biographical-critical legend of Dickens" (49). Along the way, she uncovers a long tradition of "moral judgment" (65), arguing that biographers from Forster to Hugh Kingsmill felt obliged to account for Dickens's later failings as both an artist and a man. In Forster's biography, for example, the dangerous "combination of early suffering with premature fame" not only exacerbates Dickens's feelings of class resentment but also denies him the opportunity to develop habits of "renunciation" and "self-sacrifice" (57).

In dealing with biographers like Forster, Bodenheimer is alert to the presence of larger narrative patterns. Taking her story up through the middle of the twentieth century, she illuminates biographical works by George Gissing and G. K. Chesterton, closing with a long, appreciative discussion of Edmund Wilson's "Dickens: The Two Scrooges." With the publication of Wilson's essay, she says, the tradition of moral judgment comes to an end. In Wilson's hands, later events like "the marital separation and the public readings are, like the novels, matters for interested interpretation," not signs of an "embarrassing collapse or a tragic decline" (65).

One example of biographical criticism, John Bowen's "A Garland for *The Old Curiosity Shop*," was so good that it made me feel like crying. In the first two sections of the essay, Bowen argues that *Curiosity Shop* is "a more significant and sophisticated text than is often recognized, and one that has a peculiar significance for Dickens's autobiographical self-understanding" (1). Here, Bowen shows that images of flowers and floral garlands are important to the story of Little Nell and suggests that her wanderings recreate Dickens's boyhood journeys through the streets of London. "We first see Nell wandering the streets at night, alone," he says, "just as young Dickens wandered back over Blackfriars Bridge, the route that made him cry, on errands for his imprisoned father, who could not do them himself" (10).

The most moving part of the essay comes later, as Bowen directs our attention to "a shadowy, nameless figure who is perhaps the most important link between the autobiographical fragment and *The Old Curiosity Shop*" (13). That figure, he explains, is the servant girl employed by the Dickens family when they lived on Bayham Street. This girl continued to wait on

Dickens's parents even after his father was imprisoned for debt, and she served as the inspiration for the Marchioness in *Curiosity Shop*. Bowen quotes Forster on the subject of the girl's chance meetings with Dickens on London Bridge:

> She too had a lodging in the neighborhood that she might be early on the scene of her duties; and when Charles met her, as he would do occasionally, in his lounging-place by London Bridge, he would occupy the time before the gates opened by telling her quite astonishing fictions about the wharves and the Tower. "But I hoped I believed them myself" he would say.
>
> (qtd. in Bowen 13)

In these pages, Bowen rewrites two of the most familiar stories in and about Dickens—the story of the blacking factory, and the death of Little Nell—forcing us to admit the carelessness with which we've always treated such things. He is here weaving his own garland, linking Dickens's boyhood trauma, his early creativity, and his impossible good luck. One of the children on that bridge would become world-famous, the subject of endless curiosity and commentary, while the other would be lost entirely. "Of the True history, ungarlanded, of the girl whom Dickens studied for the Marchioness's portrait, the maid-of-all-work from Bayham Street, the orphan girl of the Chatham workhouse, his companion to whom he told stories of the wharves and Tower," Bowen writes in a devastating final sentence, "there is here another blank" (14–15).

I had trouble with James Kincaid's "Blessings for the Worthy," and you know why: too many good lines, too many sharp questions—too much of everything, really. Kincaid's focus here is on *Little Dorrit*, a book he describes as "fenced-in and knowing, fearful and snarling" (18), "narrow and moralistic" (18), "frightened" (19), "misogynist" (19), "hostile to the imagination" (20), and "unforgiving" (21). I can't go on. I'll go on: the book is also "hysterical, forced, ungenerous, incurious" (28), "poisonous" (29), and "centered on casting blame" (29). Kincaid's own unforgiving hysteria seems to me perfectly reasonable. Amy Dorrit is indeed an enabler, and Arthur Clennam a crybaby. What's more, the politics in this one are—deep breath—"reactionary" (26), "resentful" (27), and "mindless" (27). Oh, and "hysterical" (27), too.

So he hates the book? Pretty much, though he does say some nice things about Flora Finching, "the novel's great artist and its major realist too" (28). And Dickens? Is he finally cutting the old boy loose after all these years? Not on your life. After two bruising biographical interludes, in which he reminds us of Dickens's "self-pitying rant against his mother" (20) and speculates on his "Lolita complex" (22), Kincaid goes on to rescue our hero from himself, identifying Dickens as "a titanic genius as well as a trivial thinker'' (28) and describing *Great Expectations* as ''the world's greatest novel of mercy and forgiveness'' (29). In his praise for *Great Expectations*, Kincaid does Shaw one better, describing the book not as an apology to Mealy Potatoes, but a compensation for *Little Dorrit*. ''The blessings conferred in *Little Dorrit* are false blessings, the blessings of a selfish preacher,'' Kincaid concludes. ''But in *Great Expectations* Dickens reaches Shakespearean heights, conferring blessings on the abusers themselves'' (29).

Biographical approaches were also featured in two short pieces for *The Dickensian*. In ''From Devonshire House to the Bull Ring, Birmingham,'' Allan Sutcliffe explains that the portable theater used by Dickens at Devonshire House was in 1853 auctioned off to the owner of a concert hall in Birmingham. Sutcliffe quotes from an advertisement in which the new owner was ''gratified to be able to announce that he has been fortunate to become the possessor of the memorable stage and scenery formerly in the possession of Charles Dickens, Esq.'' (21). A later advertisement identified the presence of Dickens's theater as a ''circumstance sufficient of itself to attach a prestige to this place of public resort, which cannot be claimed by any other similar establishment'' (23). In spite of that prestigious circumstance, the hall eventually closed its doors, and Dickens's theater was purchased by someone else. Its current whereabouts remain unknown.

In ''Dickens, Robert Lytton and a Newly Discovered Letter,'' Valerie Purton discusses a letter from Dickens to the son of his friend and fellow writer, Edward Bulwer-Lytton. The letter was written in the fall of 1861, when Dickens and Forster were acting as mentors for the young Lytton, and its immediate purpose was to announce that one of Lytton's poems had been accepted for publication in *All the Year Round*. The best part of Purton's essay is her discussion of the warm relationship between Dickens and Lytton, and the essay's conclusion, stressing ''the kindness with which Dickens could deal with his associates, particularly those less eminent than himself'' (115), seems entirely right.

The complete text of Dickens's letter to Robert Lytton appeared in the summer issue of *The Dickensian*, along with about a dozen other letters written in the period from 1861 to 1865. In some cases, the texts included by Angus Easson and Margaret Brown in *The Dickensian* are corrections to the versions printed in the Pilgrim edition; in place of a catalog extract, for instance, we now have the full text of a letter from Dickens to Lady Olliffe (see 118). In addition to these corrected texts, we also find notes and corrections for a number of other letters. Here, as always, the scrupulous scholarship of the Pilgrim editors cannot be praised too highly. In a brief headnote, the editors explain that ''[s]ome hundred letters are currently to hand for future supplements'' (117). We may have assumed that their work was finished—but as usual, they knew better.

Robert Garnett acknowledges his debts to the Pilgrim editors at the beginning of his essay on "The Crisis of 1863." Garnett finds in the later volumes of the Pilgrim edition "multiple streams of circumstantial evidence" that "Ellen Ternan became pregnant in the spring of 1862, and bore a child in France early in 1863" (181). "For years," Garnett says, "scholars have been justifiably cautious in speculating on the nature of Dickens's and Ellen Ternan's relationship, but volume 10 of the Pilgrim *Letters* reveals . . . that the evidence can scarcely be read in any other way" (181). At times, Garnett may overstate his case—he sometimes resorts to phrases like "virtually certain" (183) and "almost inescapable" (185)—but his reading of the evidence and the situation is convincing. Working with the new edition of the letters, he establishes several key facts: that Dickens "crossed to France as many as eight times in the summer of 1862" (182); that by early July he "had decided to settle in Paris for most of the autumn" (182); that he was confident his "French sojourn would be over by mid-February" (185); and that he made a number of other "brief, hasty excursions" in March and April (190). The letters do not tell us where those last few trips may have taken Dickens, but they do "hint at a second crisis connected with Ellen: perhaps the death of the son who, according to Kate Perugini and Henry Dickens, died in infancy" (190).

In addition to assembling the evidence and relating it to what he politely calls the "timetable of pregnancy" (186), Garnett provides insightful readings of the letters themselves. In dealing with a mysterious remark to Georgina Hogarth, for example, he shows that Dickens was playing with a "hackneyed phrase associated with pregnancy and childbirth" (189). Through all of this, Garnett performs a valuable service. His essay should be enough to persuade almost anyone that Dickens and Ellen were lovers and, however briefly, parents of a child together.

While Garnett focuses on Dickens's affair with Nelly Ternan, Lillian Nayder considers the other side of the story. In a preview of her biography of Catherine Dickens, Nayder explores the situation of the Dickenses' five "colonial sons." These children were "Walter, Frank, Alfred, Sydney, and Edward ('Plorn')," and all of them were "destined for India, Australia, and the high seas" (82). Nayder's main point here is that Dickens's "thinking about what the empire meant for his boys, their identities, and their manhood clearly intersected with his thinking about himself, his wife, and their differences" (84). She explains that his separation from Catherine "created a metaphoric metropole and colony within their family" (83) and argues that the separation created a further motive for exiling Charley, Walter, and the others: the need to remove "obstacles to [Dickens's] relationship with Ellen" (87).

As Nayder points out, the boys may have enjoyed a measure of revenge in the end. Their famous failures can be read as "types of resistance" to paternal authority (88), and their disposition of their father's estate offers even more convincing evidence of a rebellion against him. "In 1870, after Dickens's death," Nayder tells us, "Charley outbid the agent who represented his father's executors to become the new proprietor of Gad's Hill Place, and he often invited his mother to stay at the home from which she had been excluded by her husband" (89). In tracing all of these developments, Nayder's work is thoroughly impressive. Smart and sensitive, this essay shows why her biography of Catherine promises to be a landmark in Dickens studies.

China

The work of Kay Li adds much to our understanding of Dickens's reception in other parts of the world. Explaining that translations of writers like Dickens did not appear in China until the end of the nineteenth century, Li remarks on an explosion of new translations in the period from 1896 to 1917. Most versions of Dickens were the work of a single translator, Lin Shu, whose output included renderings of *Oliver Twist*, *Nicholas Nickleby*, *The Old Curiosity Shop*, *Dombey and Son*, *David Copperfield*, and *Hard Times*. Through his career, Lin translated over 160 foreign novels, ranging from Alexandre Dumas and Sir Walter Scott to H. Rider Haggard—this despite the fact that he "did not know any foreign language" (120–21)! As Li explains, Lin worked with a partner. While his collaborator "translated orally," he "wrote the words down in classical Chinese" (121). Not surprisingly, Lin was "famous for conveying the meaning and spirit of Western European novels rather than giving literal translations" (120), and though his versions of Dickens "deviated from the original, most notably in his use of the classical style as opposed to the original vernacular" (122), he "was able to grasp the spirit, mood, and humor instinctively" (121).

After tracing this history, Li turns to more recent events, examining the period following the Cultural Revolution. "Modern Chinese readings of Dickens have remained ideological rather than aesthetic" (123), she says, focusing on Dickens's "petit bourgeois background," his "humanism," and his "preference for mild social reform and abstract unrestrained universal love and tolerance" (128–29). As one might expect, his "bourgeois humanism and his support of the middle class" have often become "popular targets of attack for the socialist Chinese critics" (131). Li also notes another interesting fact, observing that "most of the articles written on Dickens are found in journals of teachers' colleges and journals of universities of science and technology, rather than in journals specializing in literature or foreign literature" (133). "The study of Dickens [in China] is utilitarian and pragmatic" (133), Li concludes, as Chinese critics and teachers "are looking for contextual inter-changes, ways of bringing the world to the country without compromising its national and social characteristics" (134).

Christmas

Also released in 2006, as part of the Oxford World's Classics series, was a new edition of the Christmas Books. This edition includes all five of Dickens's Christmas Books, along with an 1851 story from *Household Words*, "What Christmas Is, As We Grow Older." The texts are based on those in the 1868 Charles Dickens Edition, which "represents his final published intentions for the Christmas Books" (xxx). The edition also includes a chronology, two pages from the prompt-book that Dickens used in public readings from the *Carol*, reproductions of some of the original illustrations—I'm sorry to say that most of them look like fifth-generation photocopies—and several pages of helpful notes.

The introduction to the volume, by editor Robert Douglas-Fairhurst, is excellent. After remarking on the enduring popularity of the *Carol*, and referring to Martin Heidegger, Douglas-Fairhurst offers a subtle analysis of Dickens's "accretive style" (xi). "Repeatedly, the narrator lingers over examples of human activities that show companionability spreading from one person to another," he writes, "in a way that is as involuntary and catching as a cough" (ix). A bit later, he advances a very nice argument about the place of the *Carol* in Dickens's career. For Douglas-Fairhurst, the *Carol* is the "first narrative that [Dickens] had planned as 'a little *whole*,' " and it not only made up for the disappointing reception of *Martin Chuzzlewit* but also rebuilt Dickens's confidence in himself and his readers (xi). "[N]ever before had he set out so deliberately to bring together his style and his narrative subject," and never before had he been so "confident in his ability to keep his imagination from overspilling the boundaries of his plot" (xi).

Throughout this essay, Douglas-Fairhurst displays a poet's gift for metaphor—at one point he says that "Christmas is sunk into [Dickens's] imagination like a watermark" (xxi)—and his work is consistently intelligent and stylish. The essay closes with a brief discussion of the other Christmas Books, suggesting that Dickens outgrew the form he had created in the *Carol*. In 1843, it had been important to go back to something like *Pickwick*—and back even further, as Douglas-Fairhurst suggests, to the pantomime and *The Arabian Nights* (see xviii and xxiv). By 1848, the date of the last Christmas Book, things had changed. Dickens sensed that "for himself as much as for his readers, these stories were too orderly, too neat to be true to the complexity of the problems he was addressing" (xxvi). Similarly, he wondered "whether a set of short stories would help his development or turn out to be no more than a form of narrative stuttering'' (xxvi).

These problems were solved in 1853, according to Douglas-Fairhurst, when Dickens performed the first public reading of the *Carol*. With the readings, which he eventually repeated more than 120 times, Dickens freed himself from the burden of inventing a new Christmas story each year. What's more, he found a way to ''bring together a diverse readership into a single body of listeners, and then fire them with an affection for Dickens and for each other, creating a perfect Christmas on demand'' (xxviii). A new edition of the Christmas Books can't accomplish that much, but thanks to its illuminating introduction, this one comes close.

Drood Mysteries

Though the mystery of Edwin Drood remains unsolved—the authorities can't even agree on whether he's dead or alive—the case hasn't yet gone cold. In ''Jasper's Plot,'' Robert Tracy links Dickens's plans for *Drood* to his public readings from *Oliver Twist*. Describing John Jasper as ''a projection of Dickens himself'' (29), Tracy argues that ''Jasper's opium reveries are a metaphor for the novelist's brooding over a developing plot'' (31). Tracy supports this argument by noting a passage in which Forster describes Dickens's plans for the ending of *Drood*. Reading the passage as suggesting that Jasper would end by ''telling his own story as if it were someone else's'' (34), Tracy is reminded of Dickens's experience as the reader of *Sikes and Nancy*: ''To act Nancy's murder,'' Tracy says, ''Dickens had to become a brutal murderer and then a haunted murderer, and at the same time remain detached as observer/writer/performer'' (37). For Tracy, the nagging question is whether or not ''repeated readings'' from *Sikes and Nancy* inspired the idea of a ''murderer [who] would witness and describe the murder without realizing that he was himself the murderer'' (37).

Continuing work he began in the 1960s, Arthur J. Cox produced two articles on *Drood* for *Dickens Quarterly*. In the first, he traces Dickens's search for a title, offering a close reading of several possibilities. Noting that Dickens briefly considered titles such as ''The Two Kinsmen'' and ''The Mystery in the Drood Family,'' Cox asserts that the Drood family mystery ''cannot be . . . confined to the present generation,'' adding that ''Dickens must have had in mind other kinsmen, perhaps ones not presently on the scene or not presently identified as members of the Drood clan'' (21). Elsewhere in this article Cox suggests that the question of the title was settled not in late September of 1859, as most biographers have thought, but rather in mid-August (see 23).

Cox's second article also focuses on the origins of *Drood*, challenging Forster's account of Dickens's "first fancy" for the book. (On the issue of Forster's reliability, Cox and Tracy disagree sharply.) Though Forster says that Dickens began with the notion of a story involving two young people, Cox believes that his real plan was for one detailing a father's unrequited love for his daughter-in-law. Why would Forster suppress the real "first fancy" and substitute another idea in its place? Because he recognized the parallel between Dickens's story and his real-life affair with Ellen Ternan and felt "he would be putting a weapon into the hands of those detractors of Dickens who had sprung up after his separation from his wife" (114). An ingenious theory, to be sure, but not enough to justify a charge of obstruction against Forster. For now, his rap sheet stays clean.

Film and TV

In "We Ask for More," Toru Sasaki takes a critical look at Roman Polanski's adaptation of *Oliver Twist*. Though Sasaki admits that Polanski's film "is not without interesting elements" (241), he argues for the superiority of David Lean's 1948 version, explaining that "comparisons of the same scenes almost always show Lean to advantage" (241). In the scene of Nancy's murder, "Polanski is content to have the effect (mostly aural) of blood splashed towards the barking Bull's-eye, Lean conveys the horror by the frantic behaviour of the frightened dog" (241). The most striking part of Sasaki's article is its discovery of parallels between Polanski's version of *Oliver Twist* and *The Pianist*, the director's Oscar-winning film from 2002. In both cases, Sasaki shows, the hero survives "only because total strangers help him" (242). Thus, although Sasaki declares a firm preference for Lean, he proves to be an insightful and sensitive reader of Polanski.

If Dickens's presence was felt anywhere in 2006, it was on PBS, where a new adaptation of *Bleak House* became a surprise hit. Reviews ranged from ecstatic (John Leonard in *New York* magazine: "splendid television") to really ecstatic (Alessandra Stanley in the *Times*: "*Bleak House* is too good to be homework"). Praise was showered on the cast, especially Burn Gorman as Guppy, and on the screenplay by master adapter Andrew Davies. Close attention was also paid to the director's attempts to recreate the dislocating effects of Dickensian narration: instead of using jump-cuts or blackouts, this version suddenly swoops from London to Lincolnshire and back again. Critics also remarked on the parallels between the original serial publication of the book and weekly broadcasts of the film. The best and smartest discussion of the parallel came from Stephanie Zacharek, who reported that although the series would soon be available on DVD, "nearly everyone I know . . . prefers to see it the old-fashioned way, on successive Sunday nights."

Despite Zacharek's very sensible point about the delights of watching the story play out week by week, the DVD may in some ways be superior to the version aired on PBS. On Public TV, the film was shown in six installments, but on DVD it's presented in fifteen episodes, each about thirty minutes long. I don't have any way of proving it, but I felt that the shorter episodes on the DVD—which, by the way, preserves the format of the original broadcasts on British television—offered a better approximation of Dickens's monthly parts. Whether you buy that argument or not, I'm sure you'll enjoy this adaptation. It takes some liberties with the story, especially at the end, but it features lots of wonderful performers and captures the mood and energy of Dickens as well as any film I know. It gets four stars, two thumbs up, and A+ from me.

Gender

On the question of how Dickens thinks and talks about gender, critics were divided, with some describing him as progressive and others as reactionary. In sorting out their differences, we might begin with a fine essay on the subject of masculinity in Dickens. The essay is Rosemarie Bodenheimer's "Dickens, Fascinated," and as we might expect, it combines subtle biographical analysis with sharp readings of works from every phase of Dickens's career. Bodenheimer begins by explaining that in life, as in fiction, Dickens tended to "create triangular relationships of rivalry and desire" with other men (268). Her main example comes from 1844, when Dickens became infatuated with an eighteen-year-old piano prodigy named Christiana Weller. Resisting the usual temptation to treat this crush as a manifestation of "the Mary Hogarth syndrome" or the expression of an "arrested sexual instinct" (271), Bodenheimer shifts our attention to Dickens's "intense identification" with Thomas James Thompson, his friend and eventual rival for Christiana's affections (271). Before long, Bodenheimer says, Dickens had "patronized and identified with both Thompson and [Christiana's father]," playing "all possible roles except that of the legitimate lover" (271). Eve Sedgwick couldn't have wished for anything better than this fascinating story, and in Bodenheimer's retelling we see how the dynamics of Dickens's fiction writing and later public readings—his desire and his drive to play "all possible roles" (271)—were mirrored in his private life.

Turning to the fiction, Bodenheimer considers examples of "fascination," episodes "in which connections between male characters are eroticized by anxieties about class status, power, and masculinity" (268). Over the course of the nineteenth century, she explains, the meaning of the term "fascination" became associated with "enigma or mystery" (272). On this understanding of the term, "if one figure gazes fascinated at another, it is because the other seems to conceal some knowledge about the self that is not quite available to consciousness or language" (272). This is precisely what we see in face-to-face encounters between Barnaby's father and Gabriel Varden, David and Steerforth, or David and Uriah Heep: an image of some "suspected but secret knowledge" (273) and a confrontation with hidden or buried "aspects of the self" (274).

Not surprisingly, Bodenheimer finds her best examples in the "pairings and exchanges of male energy" in *Our Mutual Friend*, where Dickens seems to be "consciously and deliberately playing as many variations on the theme as he possibly could" (274). Exploring the initial meeting between Eugene Wrayburn and Bradley Headstone, Bodenheimer observes that "[t]here is little to choose between them," arguing that the "greatness of the dialogue lies in its fairness to the worst aspects of both participants" (275). The scene "reads as an intensely uncomfortable humiliation of a lower-middle-class man by an upper-class man," though it can also be viewed "as an offensive intrusion of paranoid and self-humiliating suspicion on Headstone's part" (275). Bodenheimer characterizes figures like Eugene and Bradley as "enthralled with—and by—the other men they might have been but for their pride, their shame, their class position, their age, or their need for respectability" (275). In that observation, and throughout this suggestive essay, she not only explores the issue of masculinity but also calls for a richer and more complex understanding of the erotic, concluding that the "erotic charge of fascination" should be viewed "less as an indicator of sexual attraction or repulsion than as a kind of internal shift in the fantasy of the self" (275). What really fascinates Dickens's men, and what they're most deeply in love with, she says, is "their own transformational possibilities, the potential, yearned-for multiplicity of themselves" (275).

Interesting arguments about gender roles and gender ideologies were also advanced in two essays about Dickensian domesticity. In "From Blood to Law: The Embarrassments of Family in Dickens," an essay for the *Palgrave Advances* volume, Helena Michie notes several striking features of the Dickensian household: it is often "made up of people unrelated by blood or marriage"; its members are frequently "bound together . . . by metonymy, contiguity, and chance"; and its relationships are highly unstable, with people "undergo[ing] shifts from the category of the sexually inappropriate to that of the sexually appropriate—[and] vice versa" (134–36). Working with examples from *Nickleby*, *Dombey*, and *Bleak House*, Michie quickly zeroes in on a "problem of definition" (135). How are we to describe the relationship between people like Esther Summerson and John Jarndyce? Is Jarndyce best understood as Esther's guardian, her lover, or her father? "Who are these people to each other," Michie asks, "and what names will make it safe for them to live together?" (135).

Michie is not the first to raise such questions, but she sets herself apart from earlier critics in several ways. First, she shows that Dickens shared our "discomfort about naming and placing relationships," relating his embarrassment to ongoing debates over the age of consent for girls (136). In addition, she studies the performative effects of terms like "guardian," "father," and "brother," focusing on the final chapters of *Bleak House*, where Jarndyce's language "triumphantly naturalizes" his relationship with Esther (151). In earlier novels, Dickens had shown how family members could turn into lovers—but here, he "reverses the process," raising the possibility that "sexuality can be undone, its work erased by self-sacrifice" (151).

Dickens's view of marriage is treated with considerable wit in Kelly Hager's "Jasper Packlemerton, Victorian Freak." Hager is happy to admit that her title is itself somewhat freakish, acknowledging that Jasper Packlemerton "occupies a very small moment" in *The Old Curiosity Shop*—just "one paragraph in a novel of seventy-three chapters" (226). So why does Hager stand by her man—and her title? Two reasons, it seems. First, because Packlemerton is not a real person, but a figure in Mrs. Jarley's waxworks, he helps us to think about Dickens's borrowings from popular culture. And, second, because he's a "serial killer and a serial husband," famous "for having tickled his fourteen wives to death" (211), Packlemerton also allows us to connect the themes of freakishness and marital dysfunction.

Working with these themes, Hager shows that the happy couples in *The Old Curiosity Shop* are treated like exhibits in a sideshow, "brought out for display, put on parade, marveled over and remarked upon as if they were each as miraculous and unusual a state of affairs as you could ever hope to come across" (215). Hager is thinking of characters like Kit Nubbles and Barbara, or Dick Swiveller and the Marchioness, and she goes on to render an almost definitive judgment on such characters, noting that "[t]hey are little and they make you smile and they are not meant to be taken seriously" (215).

Hager's discussion of the unhappy couples in Dickens's story is equally impressive. She zeroes in on the weird sexual chemistry between Mr. and Mrs. Quilp, suggesting that Betsy Quilp is right to suspect her friends of desiring her husband. She also has interesting things to say about the "wretched union" of Nell's parents (211), viewing it as crucial to the entire story. Hager may get off on the wrong foot when she claims, in her opening paragraph, that we still have a "vague sense that most marriages in Dickens are as happy as David and Agnes's" (209), but she moves with considerable authority at later stages in her argument, asking sharp, smart questions about Dickens's place in the history of the novel: are we right to think of the courtship plot as central to the tradition of English fiction? And, if so, what can we do with a writer like Dickens—clearly so important to the novel tradition, yet also so doubtful about the idea of wedded bliss? In raising these questions, Hager shows us that she's not kidding—or not *just* kidding—when she identifies the institution of marriage as "the real monster" and "the most chilling freak of nature" in *The Old Curiosity Shop* (211).

Two scholars, Diana Archibald and Christine Huguet, saw Dickens working to subvert conventional attitudes toward women. Archibald's essay on *Oliver Twist*, "Of All the Horrors . . . the Foulest and Most Cruel," appeared in a collection of articles on sensation fiction, and so her interest in gender issues is not obvious at first. Yet if Archibald has much to say about questions of form or genre, her chief concern is clearly Dickens's portrayal of Nancy. She credits Dickens with insight into the mindset of a " 'battered woman' . . . unable to extricate herself from an unhealthy codependency" (57). Eager to avoid charges of anachronism, she also states that "the concept [of code-pendency] was not foreign in the nineteenth century," noting that a "large burst of writing appeared about the 'Magdalen problem' in the 1830s and 1840s" (57).

Anticipating other possible objections to her argument, Archibald makes much of the encounters between Nancy and Rose Maylie. "Nancy's portrait might seem to uphold the notion that domestic violence is contained within the 'lower orders,' " she says. "But Nancy is linked so clearly to Rose Maylie that it is difficult to ignore the inference that all women are vulnerable to such abuse" (59). Rose's own sister Agnes has been "ruined by the treachery of a man she loved" (60), and although Rose is ignorant of her sister's fate, we might join Dickens in understanding that "Nancy is one of many" (61).

Dickens's "variance with mid-Victorian sexual ideology" (30) is also asserted by Christine Huguet. In " 'There's not a doubt of the dress,' " Huguet examines episodes in which women adopt disguises, concluding that they offer evidence of Dickens's interest in "freedom for women from the double standard" (27). In some cases, new clothes may help to reveal a woman's true identity; in other cases, like that of Lady Dedlock, the effect may be just the opposite. No matter what the result, Huguet says, the use of disguise allows Dickens to explore the complicating factors of sex and sexuality. When Kate Nickleby dresses up for her uncle's friends, or Madeline Bray prepares for her marriage to Arthur Gride, Dickens begins to "grapple with the issue of prostituted sexuality as openly as Victorian reticence in such matters would allow" (27).

In her suggestive reading of *Oliver Twist*, "The Law's a Bachelor," Susan Zlotnick considers Dickens's response to the most controversial provision of the New Poor Law: the bastardy clause, which "shifted the responsibility for [an] illegitimate child from both parents to the poor mother alone" (131). Supporters of the clause insisted on the distinction between women "who achieved respectable, dependent domesticity, and those who did not" (135), thereby transforming illegitimacy and illicit sexual experience into the "purely private matter of a woman's moral weakness" (137). Thus, in a reversal of what we might expect, it was supporters of the bastardy clause who "endowed women with free agency" and opponents who portrayed them as "fragile creatures, the easy prey of libertines and seducers" (138).

Zlotnick's account of these debates, drawn from the analysis of social historians Anna Clark and Lynn Lees, provides a solid foundation for her work on *Oliver Twist*. In Dickens's portrayal of Oliver, he sounds like a fierce opponent of the bastardy clause, "refus[ing] to allow good character to become the sole possession of the well-to-do" (133). But when he turns his attention to poor women, he often echoes the reformers he claimed to despise, praising a few women for their strength and blaming most for their moral weakness. In developing this argument, Zlotnick considers three examples, moving from Oliver's mother, Agnes, whom she identifies as the trickiest case, to Nancy and Rose. The argument ends with a revealing contrast between Rose and the other two characters: unlike her foils, Rose is able to resist sexual temptation, and her "power of refusal" is so great that it eventually "leads to the moral redemption of the seemingly innocuous Harry Maylie" (143). "Rose's denial accomplishes what Agnes's love could not," Zlotnick says; "she reforms the text's aristocrat into the moralized, domesticated gentleman of the middle ranks" (143).

Zlotnick's concern with the gendering of "competing subjectivities" allows her to reveal the larger "ideological confusions" of *Oliver Twist* (133). Her article stands as strong evidence, should anyone still need it, of how sustained attention to issues of gender can deepen our understanding of even the most familiar texts. There are times when the main lines of the argument begin to blur—Zlotnick overcomplicates her description of the differences between Dickens's "male plot" (which she labels "melodramatic") and his "female plot" (which she sees as somewhat more realistic)—but by the end, little confusion remains. Zlotnick's final paragraphs move briskly, gaining undeniable momentum as they go, and her closing remarks are enormously interesting. In Rose, she says, Dickens creates "the ideal domestic woman as defined by Nancy Armstrong," ascribing to such women "the self-control poor women lack" and effectively transforming the story of Oliver Twist into "an origin myth about the birth of the middle class" (143).

Dickens's fear of the female body and his "particular revulsion over woman activists" (38) receive close attention in Linda Lewis's "Madame Defarge as Political Icon." Lewis identifies Madame Defarge as Dickens's "most memorable allegory for radical feminism" (32), observing that "almost every major scene of violence against aristocrats, functionaries of the *ancien regime*, and enemies of the Revolution [in *A Tale of Two Cities*] features frenzied women and Madame Defarge at the center of the action" (38). Dickens views these characters as "unnatural and unwomanly" (38), yet he also presents their leader as almost ferociously sexy. Madame Defarge is "beautiful and graceful," so compelling that she "threatens to become the star of [the] novel" (33). Lewis is particularly good on the issue of Madame's sexuality and star power, noting its absence from the 1935 David O. Selznick adaptation of the book. As her article takes shape, Lewis turns to the iconography of the French Revolution, suggesting that it may have helped to inspire both Dickens and Phiz (see 36–38). She closes by comparing *A Tale of Two Cities* with *Bleak House*, concluding that in the shift from Mrs. Jellyby to Madame Defarge, Dickens "chose to raise the stakes" in his campaign against "the involvement of middle-class English women," including his own wife, "in feminist and political causes" (46). For Dickens, Lewis observes, Madame Defarge is not only a striking character but an "iconic warning against woman as leader, soldier, or politician" (47).

Literary Form

Essays on traditional literary topics—characterization, plotting, narrative structure—often turned on the question of realism. With "Performing Character," an essay for the *Palgrave Advances* collection, Malcolm Andrews considers the apparent "lack of interiority" in Dickens's characters (73). Andrews reviews a number of familiar objections to Dickens's methods—Why won't he behave like other novelists? Doesn't he know better?—arguing that for Dickens, interiority is often "visibly busy on the surface" (75). Extending this point, Andrews suggests that Dickens "is educating the reader in a kind of visual literacy" (74). Dickens sees a "general deficiency" in his readers, and by "presenting carefully wrought details of clothing, physique, mannerisms," he shows us how to "read character from outward style" (74).

Following Andrews's essay in the Palgrave volume is "Dickens and Plot," in which Hilary Schor takes up another apparent shortcoming in Dickens's fiction: the messiness and occasional clumsiness of his narrative constructions. Schor begins with contemporary responses to Dickens's plotting, suggesting that his reputation suffered with the emergence of new definitions of realism. According to these new definitions, she says, "the novelist must serve as a kind of filter, keeping his readers, through a carefully imposed artistic control, from being overwhelmed by the world around them" (93). By the 1850s, she adds, "[w]hat critics seem to want is less a plot than a map; less a 'coherent story' than a single strand to follow" (93).

At this point in his career, Dickens was hardly inclined to offer anything like a "single strand." As Schor points out, he had "started writing a new kind of novel" (93), "encouraging us to focus on parallel acts in widely separated scenes, among characters who may never have met'' (102). These innovations in Dickens's plotting help to account for the deepening ''discontent of [his] contemporaries'' (96), for as he ''work[ed] quite diligently to make *us* connect the various parts of the book'' (101–02), he also appeared to be shifting his responsibilities onto his readers, failing to follow through on his most serious artistic duties.

In the second part of her essay, Schor mounts a compelling defense of Dickens's plotting. Describing his later books as ''rejecting one form of coherence for another'' (96), Schor sees Dickens as creating a distinctive ''blend of temporal, psychological, and social experimentation'' (96). Whereas Charlotte Brontë and George Eliot tend to satisfy our wish for a tidy conclusion, the later Dickens confounds those wishes, presenting them as deceptive and potentially dangerous. At the beginning of *Little Dorrit*, we're invited to imagine an ending in which ''not only people but the past can be redeemed'' (103), but by the end we've come to question the ''fantasy of a redemptive plot'' (104). Here, quite clearly, Schor is offering a redemptive plot of her own, showing that apparent mistakes are actually strokes of genius. That's not a problem, though. She's not tidying up so much as clearing new ground, and her work in this essay will establish a solid foundation for future studies of Dickens's plotting.

Like Schor, John R. Reed defends Dickens from charges of shapelessness and disorder. Writing on the ''riches of redundancy'' in *Our Mutual Friend*, Reed argues that Dickens ''swamps his reader with information initially seeming to be redundant in the colloquial sense, but ultimately helping to deliver the novel's meaning more clearly'' (33n1). In developing these points, Reed draws on the language of information theory, suggesting that, like a geneticist working with ''junk DNA,'' Dickens saw how apparently excessive repetition actually ''facilitates the communication of messages'' (19). That may be true, but it has the effect of confusing a massive (and massively complicated) book like *Our Mutual Friend* with a simple, straightforward ''message'' or ''meaning.'' How, we might ask, is a multiplot novel like the information encoded in genes or transmitted over an Ethernet cable—and how is it different?

Literary Life

Dickens's literary life was the subject of two essays for the *Palgrave Advances* volume. In the first, ''Publishing in Parts,'' Robert Patten offers an exhaustive treatment of Dickens's career as a professional writer. Patten tells how Dickens was paid, how he managed his time, and how he got along with various illustrators. He also helps us to imagine the crushing demands of Dickens's monthly schedule, explaining that a twenty-number serial like *Copperfield* or *Bleak House* required the production of over 16,000 words a month—about sixty modern typescript pages—all of which had to be "imagined, written, revised, set in proof, revised again, proofed again, and published" (25).

Implicit in Patten's essay is a fresh account of Dickens's development as a serial writer. Patten points to several crucial breakthroughs from the time of *Pickwick*, including Dickens's proposal, following the death of illustrator Robert Seymour, for a change in the ration of illustrations to letterpress or text. In discussing this development, Patten contests one of the "hoariest of Dickens myths," arguing that the key event in the history of *Pickwick* was not the appearance of Sam Weller in the fourth installment but a prior "reformatting" that allowed Sam's "wonderful flow of words and observations" to "run on" (14–15).

As he takes us through the 1840s and 1850s, Patten calls attention to Dickens's growing frustrations with serial publication. "He wanted to move away from installments and deliver his fictions at one time, as a whole, in volumes" Patten argues, and "no longer wanted to share compositional labor with an illustrator" (38). Yet in the 1860s, after going through "a troubled period in his personal as well as professional life," Dickens halted his experiments with other formats and "reverted to type" with *Our Mutual Friend* (40). All of this is not only reported but analyzed by Patten, who quietly replaces our older sense of a movement from "early" to "late" (or "light" to "dark") phases with a far more satisfying image of growing ambition and gradual refinement.

Complementing Patten's essay on serial publication is another contribution to *Palgrave Advances*. In this piece, called "Dickens's Reading Public," David Vincent reminds us that Dickens's contemporaries saw him as having established a new kind of relationship with his audience. "Alongside the conventional judgments about plot and characterization," Vincent explains, "were extensive accounts of who the readers were and how they were interacting with the person of the author through and around the medium of the text" (177). Especially important to contemporaries, according to Vincent, was Dickens's ability to enter a new market—one that we might now describe as a mass market—without "sacrificing [his] moral or artistic standards" (187).

As he describes the particulars of Dickens's contemporary reception, Vincent advances a persuasive argument about the development of the British publishing industry. In opposition to scholars who align "developments in the production of literature . . . with a simple model of industrial[ization]" (183), he presents publishing as "a fundamentally undisciplined industry in which old and new forms of making money flourished because of and in spite of each other" (185). Though he never denies the growing unification and centralization of the market for books, Vincent points out the "profound unevenness of the process" (184), explaining that the transformation of the publishing industry "was essentially incomplete not only in the late 1830s but throughout Dickens's publishing lifetime" (183).

In *"Pickwick* and the Pirates," Irene Wiltshire considers one of the most unpleasant aspects of Dickens's literary career. After reviewing several early Dickens knock-offs, Wiltshire concludes that Dickens's desire to baffle "potential pirates" led to his later use of multiplot structures and symbolic forms (43). That argument was not, in the end, as exciting as Wiltshire's account of the original piracy of *Pickwick*. "Dickens had opened up new possibilities for the presentation of the fictional working-class hero," Wiltshire explains, but in their versions of the story "the pirates returned [Sam] to the conventional image in which he does not engage the reader's loyalty" (38). In *The Post-Humourous Notes of the Pickwickian Club*, Sam "practically grovels to Pickwick," proving to be "the cause of embarrassment" rather than "the agent of rescue" (35). In *Pickwick Abroad*, Sam is once again a "liability" (36); and in *Sam Weller: or, the Pickwickians*, he is "reduced to a knockabout character, a participator in events but not indispensable to his master" (35–36). Since cheap imitations of *Pickwick* would seem to have been designed for a less affluent and less sophisticated audience—Wiltshire says that one of the plagiarisms "was cheaply priced at a penny per number" (38)—all of this comes as a real surprise and makes a genuine contribution to our understanding of Dickens's early career.

Other Writers

Though many scholars were interested in issues of influence and intertextuality, only one considered Dickens's debts to Shakespeare. In "The Prince of the Marshes," Wendy Jacobson finds a number of parallels between *Hamlet* and *Great Expectations*: both begin with "an uncanny encounter with a creature from 'another world' " (200); both include " 'false' mother figures" who "seem afraid of the young men whose lives they have so profoundly disrupted" (206–07); and both feature protagonists possessed of an unmistakable nobility (see 208). To her credit, Jacobson also notices striking differences between the two works, contrasting Shakespeare's emphasis on revenge with Dickens's interest in forgiveness. She may overstate the extent to which *Hamlet* can be viewed as a revenge tragedy, but she is right to note the contrast between Shakespeare's aristocratic milieu and Dickens's "bourgeois age" (201). Pip must not only dispense forgiveness, as she notes, but also show himself to be worthy of it. If he is transformed into something like a prince, he pays for that achievement with what Jacobson describes as "grief, loss, and broken pride" (201).

Moving to studies of Dickens's relationships with his contemporaries, we discover unexpected connections. In "Dickens and Darwin," Natalie McKnight views Dickens's treatment of animals—and his blurring of "the boundaries between human and animal" (131)—as a foreshadowing of Darwin. McKnight never quite manages to link *Barnaby Rudge* or *The Old Curiosity Shop* to *The Origin of Species* and *The Descent of Man*, but she does make some interesting points about Dickens's view of animals. Especially persuasive is her analysis of a short scene from *Bleak House*, in which Jo is contrasted with a dog waiting for his master: "In this scene, perhaps more overtly than in any other," McKnight explains, we see "that very little fundamentally distinguishes humans from animals, and that care and education are essential to make either a functioning part of civilised society" (140–41).

In "Naked Truth is the Best Eloquence," Eleanor Courtemanche identifies Harriet Martineau's *Illustrations of Political Economy* as an "oblique influence" on midcentury industrial novels like *Hard Times* (403). Where Martineau uses stories to teach the lessons of political economy, helping her readers "resign themselves to the inevitability of the capitalist system" (393), Dickens mounts an assault on the "utilitarian-industrial complex" (399). Nevertheless, both writers believe in the political efficacy of fiction; both "base their claims to realism . . . on their fidelity to a truer vision of human behavior than mere observation can provide" (399); and both assume that "[their] characters' actions display the immutable laws of human interaction" (402). Thus, Courtemanche concludes, Martineau "creates the conditions for [later] novels' understanding of the political power of realist fiction" (384).

In "Parodic Prolongation in *North and South*," Jerome Meckier explores the relationship between Dickens and Elizabeth Gaskell, expanding on ideas sketched in his 1987 study, *Hidden Rivalries in Victorian Fiction*. According to Meckier, Gaskell used the first volume-edition of *North and South*, a novel originally serialized in *Household Words*, to "get even with Dickens for his editorial interference by ridiculing the popular novelist's stock in trade: allegedly unrealistic delays that artificially increase suspense" (220). Meckier knows that Gaskell "added two chapters and expanded three others" in preparing her story for publication in book form, and he suspects that she was eager to "obtain the elbow room that *Household Words* had denied her" (220). What he can't quite do is prove that she and Dickens were engaged in "mutual recrimination" (223). Gaskell may have been frustrated with her former editor, but that doesn't mean that she was trying to parody or ridicule him. Without additional biographical evidence revealing such motives, Meckier's argument, though suggestive, seems unconvincing.

In "Flight from the Snow Queen," Louis James examines another strained relationship, that between Dickens and Hans Christian Andersen. James begins where he must, discussing Andersen's uncomfortable visit to Gad's Hill in the summer of 1857. This visit not only stretched from two weeks to five, but also coincided with the "final stages" of Dickens's marriage (223). Turning to the works of the two writers, James argues that they "helped further a revolution in popular sensibility . . . , a change relating to attitudes to childhood and the childlike vision" (224): "where a poet like Wordsworth returned to the child in solitary harmony with primitive nature, Dickens and Andersen related childhood vision to the modern everyday life of their readers, both young and old" (224). Indeed, both "asserted that the adult, through the power of memory and the imagination, could recover the innocence, wonder and loving emotions of the child" (224). In this way, despite their famous falling-out, James concludes, the two writers can be seen as close collaborators, innovative figures who "wrote as two sides of the same coin" (230).

Turning to Dickens's influence on later writers, we find a wide range of references. In "Dostoevsky and the English Novel," a lively if somewhat diffuse essay, David Gervais begins on familiar ground, reviewing ideas first advanced by Edmund Wilson. For Gervais, however, the main point of contact between Dickens and Dostoevsky is not an interest in criminality but a shared sense of human character as "unfathomable" (53) and "beyond explanation" (58). Gervais reminds us of the ways in which Dostoevsky "goes beyond" Dickens (see 55, 70), suggesting that one of Dostoevsky's finest achievements was his unusually insightful reading of Dickens: "Dostoevsky saw a poetic spirituality beyond Dickens's morality and humour," Gervais writes, "at a time when most English readers regarded *The Pickwick Papers* as merely an entertainment" (52).

After linking Dickens to Dostoevsky, Gervais goes on to consider Dostoevsky's impact on two later writers, John Cowper Powys and D. H. Lawrence. More might be said about these connections, but for now it feels right to join Gervais in concluding that later English novelists were drawn to Dostoevsky because he seemed like a better version of Dickens. To writers like Powys and Lawrence, as Gervais says, Dostoevsky may have "represented a Dickensian intensity coupled with an unswerving honesty, like a Dickens without the Dickensian tendency to pull the strings" (71).

The influence of Dickens on popular fiction of the 1880s was traced by Peter Merchant. In "Tales Told Out of School," Merchant draws our attention to a novel called *Vice Versa*. This book was the work of Thomas Anstey Guthrie, known to the reading public as F. Anstey, and its plot recalls a number of Hollywood movies from the 1980s and 1990s. A middle-aged businessman wishes that he could change places with his teenage son, and then—because he happens to be holding an ancient Indian stone—he does, finding himself in the boy's place at boarding school. Eventually, through the agency of the stone, order is restored and father and son are reconciled.

Merchant never goes so far as to suggest that the storyline of *Vice Versa* can be traced back to Dickens—a more likely source, he admits, was the "Bab Ballads" of W. S. Gilbert—but he does do a lot to suggest the "prompting presence" of themes and characters from *Oliver Twist, Nicholas Nickleby,* and *David Copperfield* (235).

The appropriation of Dickensian motifs by W. H. Hudson is the subject of Michael Hollington's "The *Rebenque* and the Wax-tipped Cane." Hollington notes that Hudson was born and raised in Argentina, finding in Hudson's work a " 'proto-post-colonial' approach to Dickens—a method of reworking, inverting, parroting, and even mocking the great classic writer" (215). For Hollington, the best examples of Dickens's influence on Hudson come from Hudson's autobiography, *Far Away and Long Ago,* and "his finest novel," *The Purple Land* (214). Working with the autobiography, Hollington points out the resemblance between Hudson's schoolmaster and Wackford Squeers. As it happens, this "antipodean Squeers" (217) not only used a *rebenque* or horsewhip as an instrument of discipline; he was also an enthusiastic admirer of Dickens, reading aloud from *Pickwick* to the delight of some listeners (the adults) and the dismay of others (his pupils).

In "Joycean Dickens/Dickensian Joyce," Matthew Bolton argues that "[t]he great volubility of some of Dickens's dialogue . . . seems to provide Joyce with a model on which to construct his interior monologues" (243). Although Bolton explains that Joyce purchased four novels by Dickens between 1912 and 1920 (see 254n2), there may still be room for doubt about the extent of Dickens's influence on Joyce. We can easily trace Molly Bloom back to Flora Finching or Sairy Gamp, but can't we just as confidently link her to Mrs. Bennet or Miss Bates? Bolton realizes the limitations of his argument, and his final statements are appropriately modest. In the end, though he can assert that Dickens's "experiments . . . prefigure those of Joyce," suggesting that Dickens "may have provided some of the raw material" for *Ulysses* (254), he won't (and probably shouldn't) do more.

Another approach to the complex issue of intertextuality is offered by Ewa Kujawska-Lis. Kujawska-Lis examines a reference to Dickens in "The Round Dozen," a 1951 short story by Somerset Maugham. One of Maugham's characters is reading *Bleak House,* and according to Kujawska-Lis the reference is far from accidental, since both works share an interest in secrecy and feature "the motif of a ruined family life" (234). Accounting for differences as well as similarities, Kujawska-Lis says that "the situation of the short story's main heroine is in many ways the reversal of that of the *Bleak House* heroine" (235). She seems eager to sidestep the biographical issues raised by critics like Meckier and Bolton, speaking of "intertextual signals" rather than authorial intentions (240). Yet, because she's reluctant to ground her interpretations in biographical fact, her conclusions are rather limited: "ignoring the meaning of the borrowed elements [of 'The Round Dozen'] does not mean that the story will be misunderstood,'' she concedes, but ''decoding the semantic load of all allusions to English literature and culture, and to Dickens and *Bleak House* in particular, makes for a more informed reading'' (240).

Performance

Issues of performance and theatricality were crucial to Seth Rudy's ''Stage Presence.'' Rudy describes *Our Mutual Friend* as ''a novel dependent on multiple layers of performance'' (65), distinguishing the John Harmon plot, which he sees as indebted to Victorian melodrama, with the society plot centered on the Veneerings. Rudy does a fine job of contrasting these two plots, remarking on an interesting paradox: ''Dickens treats the theatrical characters [in the Harmon plot] as overtly real, and the real characters [of the Veneering plot] as overtly theatrical'' (75). John Harmon and Bella Wilfer are both given ''recognizable and sympathetic human qualities'' (75), while the Veneering set is shown to be incapable of development. For these characters, as for many of Dickens's readers, Rudy concludes, there is no alternative to performance—and thus no way out of the show. As Rudy puts it in a stylish final paragraph, ''*Our Mutual Friend* exposes the presence and power of theatrical conventions beyond the realm of fiction, but cannot tell its audience how safely to escape the theater'' (78).

Dickens's performances as a reader of his own work were treated in *Charles Dickens and His Performing Selves*, an impressive new book by Malcolm Andrews. Unlike most earlier studies of the readings, this book chooses not to dwell on the events of Dickens's private life. Andrews acknowledges that the readings were a byproduct of the separation from Kate (see 32), but his main interest is the relationship between Dickens and his audience. That relationship, though generally positive, was not without its difficulties, and Andrews shows how Dickens used the readings to expose and correct earlier misunderstandings of his work. In place of the broad caricatures he had been accused of producing, Dickens's readings featured strikingly naturalistic performances: ''without apparently any undue distortion,'' Andrews explains, familiar stories ''became broader, brighter, with higher resolution, and at the same time more *realistic*, than his readers had expected'' (231).

The originality of Andrews's approach is evident in the organization of his book. Instead of taking a chronological approach, Andrews asks us to consider the material facts of the readings. He describes the ''extraordinary (though typical) pains'' Dickens took in ''perfecting'' the set for his performances (126), concluding that the various elements of the set—the reading desk, the back-screen, and the lighting rig—"increased the isolation and distinctiveness of the Reader" (143). He also recognizes the physical challenges of the readings, observing that Dickens "did not have a particularly distinctive or full-bodied voice" and underscoring the "special pressures" of speaking in large halls (183). On such matters, his work should remain authoritative.

Throughout the book, Andrews is eager to answer charges first leveled by Forster—to show, in other words, that Dickens was not guilty of substituting "lower for higher aims" (see 33). Andrews defends Dickens in the best way possible: by revealing the artistry that went into the readings and by describing them as a natural extension of Dickens's earlier achievements as a writer of serial fiction. Andrews's brief for the defense is strengthened by his attention to issues of categorization or definition. He's alert to the ways in which Dickens's writing "break[s] down the . . . generic conventions associated with reading a novel" (17), and he argues that the same sort of confusion must have surrounded the readings. Were they "recitations, solo dramatics, or what?" (209). In the end, Andrews chooses not to pin Dickens down, encouraging us to see the readings as defamiliarizing and destabilizing forces, meant to confound distinctions between writers and readers, creators and consumers.

Only one aspect of the book seems misguided, and that is its use of "dramatic reconstructions" (viii) of readings from *A Christmas Carol* and *Oliver Twist*. In these passages, Andrews switches into a very different style and, working from "accumulated eyewitness accounts," invites us to "join the audience" (4). The results of this experiment are mixed, and the writing in these sections sometimes seems overdone. More effective, and more genuinely creative, are the many other passages in which Andrews develops his ideas about writing, reading, and reading aloud. As those ideas take shape, he points to a contrast between two competing visions of Dickens. On the one hand, the readings seem to present the audience with a powerful and supremely confident creator. This Dickens is the source and origin of his many famous characters; they all emerge from him, and they eventually return to him as well. On the other hand, the readings also feature a performer who shares his fans' amusement and amazement. This Dickens laughs along with the audience, enjoying its "surprised delight at the material being presented as if it were fresh to *him*" (212). The chance to consider this dual image of Dickens—a Dickens who manages both to produce and consume, to assert and erase himself—is one of the many things that makes this book worth reading.

Politics and Social Reform

Does Dickens deserve his reputation as a reformer? How far did his social criticism extend? When did he contest dominant social values, and when did he uphold them? Versions of these questions appeared frequently in 2006, and since this category is our biggest and busiest, it makes sense to begin our examination of the scholarship on Dickens's politics with general overviews of the subject.

In an entry for the new *Oxford Encyclopedia of British Literature*, John Kucich and Dianne Sadoff argue that Dickens's "phenomenal popularity derived largely from his ability to please multiple social constituencies" (154). Extending this point, Kucich and Sadoff analyze Dickens's appeal to different groups of readers, concluding that although he may have earned the title of "the people's novelist" (154), his deepest affinities were with the middle class. It's not just that he endorses the values of sincerity, honesty, and industriousness. He also "depict[s] oppositional political potentials as unthreatening" (156) and "participate[s] in the midcentury ideological project of separating the public from the private sphere" (158). What's more, he "depoliticizes the marketplace and class relations" (159) and helps to "promulgat[e] Coventry Patmore's celebrated Victorian ideal, the 'angel in the house' " (158).

It is somewhat dismaying, I must admit, to see the charges against Dickens presented in this way. It's not that the charges don't stick—many of them seem more than fair—but rather that they pile up so quickly. Kucich and Sadoff do acknowledge the complexity of Dickens's positions, especially in the section on "domestic angels," where he's said to provide "simultaneous confirmations and critiques of domestic ideology" (159). But even at the end of that section, they reassert Dickens's "deep—if vexed—reverence for the sanctities and sentimentalities of the middle-class home" (160).

In making these points, I don't mean to suggest that I envy these authors their assignment. It can't be easy to summarize a major career in a few short pages, and it must be even harder to imagine the audience for such a piece. At times, Kucich and Sadoff seem unsure of their purpose, mixing sophisticated commentary on Dickens's fiction with basic advice for beginning readers. They seem to hope that their praise for Dickens's "attention to the psyche's performativity" will redeem him in the eyes of some critics—clearly, they mean for us to admire his indifference to the "restrictive conventions of ego psychology" (160)—but those comments may come too late to make much difference. Bright students, especially undergraduates, will by that point have reason to wonder why they should bother with a "militantly antipapist and casually anti-Semitic" author, who may well have "represented the humble classes to themselves flatteringly, but . . . also domesticated them for the safe consumption of his middle-class readers" (155).

Two essays on Dickens's social vision, both focused on writings from *Household Words*, appear in the *Palgrave Advances* volume. In "Reforming Culture," Catherine Waters considers Dickens's responses to almost a dozen different issues, including poverty, prostitution, prisons, policing, sanitary reform, and marriage law. She argues—and this came as an interesting surprise to me—that "the fiercest campaign" ever waged in *Household Words* was arguably the one concerning factory accidents (166). Eight articles on factory safety appeared between March 1854 and January 1856, and their publication indicates Dickens's awareness of the "dehumanizing effects of the factory system and the political economy that supported it" (168).

Waters stops short of presenting Dickens as a thoroughly committed reformer, acknowledging his role in the creation of capitalist ideologies. Her Dickens is capable of allowing himself and his readers to retreat from social pressures into a "separate private sphere" (163), yet he is also, at least on occasion, ready to subvert "overlapping race and gender ideologies" (165) and expose the "abstraction and objectification involved in the development of modern industrial capitalism" (170). Through all of this, the key word for Waters seems to be "ambivalent." Though she uses the word to describe Dickens's "narrative perspective" (156), his "concern with issues of discipline and punishment" (160), and his "response to modernity" (170), Waters is not herself ambivalent. She's just trying to avoid the twin temptations of valorizing or demonizing Dickens. Her work in this essay offers a splendid example of how to envision and characterize his various engagements with the world around him. If we want to see him as "construct[ing]" the "culture attendant upon nineteenth-century capitalism," she argues, we must also see him as "contest[ing] it" (158).

Joseph Childers returns to the image of "Dickens the reformer" (198) in his contribution to the *Palgrave Advances* volume. Like Waters, Childers takes his evidence from Dickens's journalism. But where she surveyed Dickens's views of many different topics, he hones in on a handful of articles from the 1850s. His first major example is "On Strike," published in 1854, which he sees as offering a "somewhat romantic" solution to the conflict between labor and capital (205). Childers soon moves beyond familiar conclusions, noting that Dickens's emphasis on mutual understanding and shared sympathy requires the extension of his fictional methods to the entire population: "in essence," he says, "Dickens is asking that everyone involved think like the novelist, imaginatively inhabit the space of the other and articulate those imaginings" (205).

In dealing with his other major example, "To Working Men," an essay on the cholera epidemic of 1854, Childers examines Dickens's call for an alliance of the working and middle classes. Though he admires the essay's willingness to accept "responsibility for the welfare of the nation—and its national character—by the middle classes" (208), he ultimately views the piece as an early example of "liberal guilt" (208). "Dickens's version of a confession of middle-class failure and isolation in 'To Working Men' masterfully reclaims identity for the middle classes," he argues, "while maintaining the sanitized distance from the workers that the bourgeoisie originally established" (209). Because Dickens's essay also "legitimizes the subjectivity of the worker as liberal" (209), it encourages workers not only to imagine themselves as free but also to reproduce the values of a system that actually works to exploit them. Childers's treatment of these materials is compelling and provocative, and his essay offers a splendid model of a more thoroughly Foucauldian approach to Dickens's politics. Though his essay serves as an excellent foil to Waters's piece, it also stands on its own as a valuable contribution to the Palgrave collection.

In "From Caricature to Character," published in three parts by *Dickens Quarterly*, Paul Marchbanks offers his estimate of Dickens as "author-cum-social activist" (179). Marchbanks is interested in Dickens's "representations of the intellectually deficient" (4), and his examples range from Smike and Barnaby Rudge to Mr. Dick, Maggy, and Sloppy. Though he begins by considering the origins of the characters' disabilities, noting that whereas Smike and Maggy are victims of physical abuse, Barnaby seems to bear the curse of a murderous father, his real concern is ideology, not etiology. Describing himself as working from "a cultural studies perspective concerned with how fictional mimesis both reflects and shapes societal forms" (10), Marchbanks often finds fault with Dickens, characterizing the portrait of Smike as condescending and the image of Barnaby as unstable, imperfect, and inconsistent. In both cases, he's concerned with the novelist's power to shape his readers' views of the intellectually disadvantaged: If Dickens treats Smike as a "pitiable dependent" (67), and if he presents Barnaby's partial recovery as a precondition for his reassimilation into society, then isn't this presumably liberal, humanitarian author in some way responsible for the spread of harmful stereotypes?

Crediting Dickens with a gradual movement toward "increasingly empowering portraits of the intellectually disabled" (5), Marchbanks praises the greater "self-reliance and social competence" of characters like Maggy and Sloppy (177). In accounting for this development, he points to Dickens's 1853 tour of the Hall Asylum for Idiots and to a later essay for *Household Words*. Aside from this, however, he offers little in the way of historical background, making it difficult to see how Dickens's books might be related to larger social trends. If Marchbanks continues to work on this intriguing topic—and I do hope he will—he should find broader cultural contexts for Dickens's representation of "intellectual otherness" (178).

Dickens's social vision is the subject of Olga Stuchebrukhov's "*Bleak House* as an Allegory of a Middle-Class Nation." This essay begins by examining Dickens's view of the relationship between feudal aristocracy and emergent industrial capitalism. If the old system embodied by Sir Leicester is outmoded and irrational, the new one embodied by the ironmaster Mr. Rouncewell is "overly rational" and lacking in "humanitarian concerns" (154). As an alternative to these unfeeling extremes, Dickens offers the middle-class virtues of Esther Summerson: self-control; a sense of duty to others; "common sense, domesticity, and modesty" (159). Through the practice of such virtues, Esther "pattern[s] the way for the entire nation" (163), inspiring hopes for a new society predicated on "authentically human relations" (165).

So far, so good. The problem, for Stuchebrukhov at least, is that Dickens can't quite believe in his own happy ending. He wants to present Esther's marriage to Allan Woodcourt as "a perfect balance" between masculine and feminine spheres (160), but his allegory of "national salvation" (148) is beset by nostalgia and melancholy. (In this, she says, following Benjamin, it's like all modern allegories.) Thus, "Esther's pastoral idyll at the end of the novel refers nostalgically to the absence rather than embod[ying] the presence of the ideal nation" (165). The only remaining question is whether or not Dickens intends such effects. Stuchebrukhov often seems to think so, but she never makes the point directly. Sometimes the unsatisfying quality of the ending is presented as Dickens's own creation, part of a larger attempt to "expose the melancholy of modern capitalist reality" (165); at other times it's treated as a built-in function of allegory itself, an inevitable result of writing in that mode. One way or another, this essay is at its best when hinting at Dickens's dissatisfaction with all of the political and social options available to him. He wanted more than his world could give him, and Stuchebrukhov helps us to see why.

Dickens's responses to contemporary political movements were central to the work of other critics. In "Fictions of the Crowd," Mark Willis links Dickens's largely negative view of Chartism to his portrayal of rioting crowds in works like *Barnaby Rudge* and *A Tale of Two Cities*. Willis's interpretations of Dickens's crowd scenes often seem predictable, and he veers off course when aligning Dickens with Plato. (I can't tell why Willis thinks that Plato's "idealized *polis* stands behind Dickens's London of the 1840s" [94].) Later, Willis soon gets back on track, making useful connections between Dickens and other writers on mass psychology. He also makes good use of Lukacs, drawing on *The Theory of the Novel* for suggestive remarks about the tradition of bourgeois realism and the emergence of a new worldview, "one more conscious of class dynamics" (104), in the middle of the nineteenth century.

Like Willis, Deborah Wynne is fascinated by scenes of political unrest. For Wynne, the most immediate context for *A Tale of Two Cities* is not the Chartist movement of the 1840s but the Irish religious revivals of 1858 and 1859. Wynne explains that Irish revival meetings "involved outbreaks of hysteria, convulsions, and temporary loss of hearing and sight" (53), noting that the meetings sometimes gave rise to a "form of social rebellion" (56), with revivalists claiming that their experiences had left them "weak and incapable of work" (53). Wynne has cogent points to make about the "strange carnival atmosphere" of these events, arguing that they offered a "sense of release from social restraints and industrial discipline" (56).

Wynne notes that the revivals coincided with Dickens's first reading tour of Ireland, and she also points out the frequency with which *All the Year Round* paired installments of *A Tale* with "features on religious extremism, revivals, and public violence" (55). She's careful not to promise more than she can deliver, acknowledging the other factors at work in Dickens's *Tale*, but in the end she makes a strong case for the influence of events in Ireland. As she puts it, "the vigor with which the link was made between revolutionary France and Irish revivalism would have made it difficult for readers of 1859 *not* to perceive *A Tale of Two Cities* as topical" (54).

Of the many studies of Dickens's politics, few are likely to have the impact of *The Body Economic*, Catherine Gallagher's study of the relationship between political economy and Victorian fiction. Gallagher admits that she is not alone in thinking that "political economists and their literary antagonists had a great deal in common" (2), but if she acknowledges her debts to earlier scholars, she also adds much to our understanding of the similarities between economics and literature. As usual, Gallagher's treatment of the issues is richly detailed. In her introduction, she traces two lines of development within the tradition of political economy, distinguishing what she calls "bioeconomics" from what she terms "somaeconomics." Whereas bioeconomics is generally Malthusian, focusing on "the interconnections among populations, the food supply, modes of production and exchange, and their impact on life forms generally" (3), somaeconomics descends from Bentham and focuses on the feelings and sensations "that are both causes and consequences of economic exertions" (3). On the one hand, as she points out, we have life and death; on the other, pleasure and pain. From the outset, then, Gallagher wants us to know that political economy was "not a static or monolithic entity" (3). She also wants to suggest that the influence of political economy on Victorian culture was neither simple nor straightforward. Economic theories "appear in numerous aspects" of novels like *Hard Times* or *Daniel Deronda*, Gallagher says, and these theories "have stylistic, structural, and thematic manifestations; they shape the plots and modes of characterization" (5).

Gallagher's distinctions are crucial to her later chapters on Dickens. In the first, she links *Hard Times* to the Benthamite tradition of somaeconomics, arguing that Dickens's work explores and extends the labor theory of value. Dickens may seem to offer a "transparent advertisement for the amusement business" (72), yet in his efforts to present the circus performers as productive workers, he shows that any kind of work for money—even work that might otherwise be classified as play—is deadening and demoralizing. The circus act may bring pleasure to others, but for the performers it's often quite painful: "what is comic but nevertheless poignant about players," Gallagher observes, "is that, unlike other workers, they must labor at seeming to play" (79).

In her second chapter on Dickens, Gallagher shifts her attention to *Our Mutual Friend*. Here the most pressing questions are bioeconomic: What's the worth of the human body? Does it matter if the body is dead or alive? Is value added or extracted when dead bodies are brought back to life? According to Gallagher, Dickens follows other Victorian thinkers in taking the dead body as a "starting place" for his exploration of the relationship between "economic value" and "vital power" (87). Yet he departs from them in offering a "celebration of the transformative potential in drying out and storing up life's remains" (92). "Despite the death versus life metaphors in the passages that introduce us to the dustmen," Gallagher argues, "the transmission of life into inorganic matter and thence into money is not consistently presented as life destroying in the novel. On the contrary, it is portrayed as a sanitizing process and one in which a pure potential called 'Life' is released" (93).

Examples? John Harmon, most obviously, but also Rogue Riderhood, Eugene Wrayburn, the dustheaps, and even the form of the book itself. Both of Dickens's love-plots "work through . . . images of suspended animation and discardable bodies," Gallagher argues, and "for both, the period of suspended animation, or apparent death, is the moment when life takes on value" (109). What's more, the words on the page may themselves exist in a similar state of suspended animation, their "stored life force" (112) available to any "properly subordinate" reader (114).

In both of these chapters, Gallagher reflects on the situation of the artist. In the case of *Hard Times*, she sees a Dickens capable of extraordinary self-knowledge, a writer who confronts "the endemic, hidden and therefore deep, sadness of those who work to make people laugh" (80). In *Our Mutual Friend*, she finds a distrustful and suspicious Dickens, one who fears that "readers, especially new readers, will be incapable of bringing the text back to life" (111). Through her various constructions of "that elusive creature known variously as the implied author, the authorial persona, or the author effect," Gallagher is careful to imagine a "creative subject who is emphatically also a productive economic subject . . . one whose life and feelings have been transmitted to the textual product" (5).

Gallagher makes another impressive move in her conclusion, linking Victorian ideologies to our own disciplinary self-understandings. Her first step is to show how late-nineteenth—and early-twentieth-century economists shed their connections to moral philosophy and psychology, effectively renouncing "both their old and their new interdisciplinary commitments" (190). Partly in response to these developments, Gallagher explains, literary criticism "professionalized in the opposite direction," with midcentury critics like John Crowe Ransom "insisting on the difference between literature and all analytic modes of thought" (191). There is a further twist on both sides of the story; for as literature departments took in those "who challenged the binary structures of thought that gave literature its putative uniqueness" (191), adventuresome economists confidently announced their break with rational choice theory and their rediscovery of emotion and sensation—apparently leaving us poor humanists in the dust. When working through these narratives, Gallagher seems capable of explaining almost everything, including our own intellectual predicaments. Though she never offers an explicit defense of the humanities, she may—in her treatment of materials ranging across three centuries and her insistence on the values of historicizing and of close reading—give us something even better: an image of humanistic learning at its best.

If Gallagher's latest book reminds us of her preeminent place in our field, then the work of Jennifer Ruth marks the arrival of a new generation of Victorianists. In *Novel Professions*, Ruth confidently positions her work in relation to that of Gallagher's generation, taking a seemingly moribund topic—professionalism and its legacies—and giving it new life. Unlike earlier scholars, who often appeared eager to demystify the ideals of professionalism, Ruth takes a "dialectical" approach to the subject (see 19, 22). She agrees that professionalism can be used to mask self-interest, but also insists that the options for professionals are not "purity versus complicity" (21). Professionals are both "inside and outside the market—at once complicit and transcendent" (22), and their "paradoxical position . . . works both ways, enabling but also destabilizing the system within which it functions" (22).

In making these points, Ruth challenges Mary Poovey, whose influence on our understanding of Victorian professionalism she rightly describes as enormous. Both Ruth and Poovey recognize the position of the professional writer as anomalous, with Poovey arguing for literary work as "the work par excellence that denied *and* exemplified the alienation written into capitalist work" (106). Yet, whereas Poovey insists that such crises had to be "covered over" or covered up (123)—usually through the alignment of male writers with middle-class women—Ruth argues that they more often remained unresolved. Her guide in such matters is Pierre Bourdieu, and in particular the Bourdieu of *Rules of Art*. According to Ruth, this later Bourdieu "moves beyond a hermeneutics of suspicion, yielding a dialectical advance: he argues that the principle of aesthetic and intellectual autonomy is an element of class mystification and, *at the same time*, is among the 'most precious collective achievements of intellectuals' (19). Bourdieu's argument about the "principle of aesthetic and intellectual autonomy'' is more or less Ruth's argument about professionalism: these things are dangerous and precious; if their costs must be tallied, then so must their benefits.

With such ideas in mind, Ruth offers a ''post-Foucauldian reading'' of books like *David Copperfield* (56). Identifying David as ''the ur-object of a hermeneutics of suspicion'' (27)—she's thinking here of both Poovey and D. A. Miller—she makes a number of striking observations: David hates the factory, but the ''internalization'' of its ''time-discipline'' is crucial to his later success as a writer (56); writers like David must develop a peculiar relationship to time, rejecting both the ''piecework time'' of an earlier economy (76) and the ''greedily accelerated temporality'' of emergent finance capitalism (81); the literary professional ''must undergo the labor'' of learning what he already seems to know, bridging the gap between effort and ability, doing and being (79). Unlike Miller and Poovey, then, Ruth finds something complimentary to say about David. She even sees David's courtship of Agnes as admirable, or at least interesting, arguing that with his marriage to Agnes, David not only ''*earns* what he already possesses,'' but also becomes the epitome of the ''modern professional,'' realizing his goals and achieving his heart's desire in the ''trustworthy time of industrial labor'' (81).

At such moments, Ruth challenges her readers to see themselves in David, prodding us to think through the reasons for our intense dislike of ''Victorian studies' most unbecoming professional'' (53). Might our reactions be a product of resentment and self-abnegation, or a delayed response to the demands of a ''shrinking academic market'' (10)? As she explores such questions, Ruth notes the differences between the situation of academics writing in, say, 1987, and critics struggling to make it today. If the 1980s and 1990s ''put critics under unprecedented pressure to professionalize'' (10), she says, then the current decade has confronted us with the realities of ''deprofessionalization,'' as more and more departments ''replace retiring tenured faculty . . . with adjunct labor'' (13). In light of that dramatic shift in our own circumstances, Ruth argues, we need to reconsider our habitual ambivalence toward the figure of the Victorian professional:

> such a figure might encourage us to recognize that the ''crisis of the profession'' is not a crisis of too much professionalization, as it is often portrayed, but of too little—an erosion of professional control over the autonomous work practices that are simultaneously the guarantee of and the reward for our interested disinterestedness.   (21–2)

As this quotation shows, the rewards of Ruth's book are many: a smart and generous reading of *Copperfield*, a fresh approach to an important topic, and an insightful take on how we live (and write) now. I can hardly imagine a more welcome contribution to our professional discourse.

Race

Issues of race and racial difference received a good deal of attention in 2006. In "Honeythunder, Exeter Hall and the Jamaican Uprising," Karl Smith explores Dickens's response to the Jamaican uprising of 1865. Like many modern critics, Smith is disturbed by Dickens's support for colonial governor E. J. Eyre. How could someone as "humane and liberal" as Dickens "condone the racist bloodshed unleashed by Eyre's orders" (16)? Smith suspects that Dickens "was aware of criticisms that his racial attitudes were a betrayal of his otherwise liberal values" (18), and he sees Dickens working to answer his critics in a crucial scene from *The Mystery of Edwin Drood*. In this scene, according to Smith, Mr. Honeythunder's insinuations against Neville Landless are meant to recall the charges against Eyre, while Rev. Crisparkle's heroic refusal to endorse those accusations has the effect of aligning Dickens and the other members of the Eyre Defence Committee with the larger "Radical principle of standing up for the misrepresented" (16). Thus, the scene refigures support for Eyre as the "genuinely liberal position" and clears away any lingering image of Dickens as a hypocrite (18).

Similar issues are addressed by Sean Purchase in "The less said about it the better," an essay on Dickens's views of slavery. Purchase explores Dickens's relationship with Harriet Beecher Stowe as well as his support for Governor Eyre, concluding that although Dickens felt compelled to take up the question of slavery, he was unsure of what could be said about it. According to Purchase, slavery is "at once repressed and irrepressible, visible and invisible in [Dickens's] work" (146), and the meanings of his writings on the subject must be seen to emerge from the relation between "that which the text says and that which it cannot say" (147). Extending his argument with examples from *Martin Chuzzlewit*, *Bleak House*, and *Our Mutual Friend*—not to mention a letter on the Jamaica uprising—Purchase reveals "moment[s] of hesitancy in language" (154), times when characters are clearly thinking but not talking about slavery, "chary of saying the word 'slave', so that it stays on the tips of their tongues forever" (154).

The most challenging treatment of racial issues in Dickens was advanced by Elaine Freedgood, whose new book, *The Ideas in Things*, might be described as a study of Victorian material culture, with examples ranging from "mahogany furniture in *Jane Eyre*" to "calico curtains in *Mary Barton*" (2). Since Freedgood's chapter on Dickens focuses on "Negro head tobacco" in *Great Expectations*, she wastes little time in turning to themes of race and ethnicity. References to Negro head tobacco appear in the chapters describing Magwitch's return to London, and they raise several questions for Freedgood. Why, for example, doesn't the presence of Negro head prompt Magwitch to associate his virtual enslavement by Compeyson with the extermination of "the other 'black slaves' of colonial Australia" (98)? At one point, Freedgood observes, Magwitch seems to be on the verge of noting this connection—only to pull back in the end.

The most obvious explanation for Magwitch's behavior is advanced by Pip, who senses that the convict is reluctant to "perplex the thread of his narrative" (see *Great Expectations* 345). Freedgood insists on pushing further, and she makes it clear that Dickens was well aware of recent events in Australia. Indeed, she shows that there was a "massive chronicling of Australia in general and of Aboriginal everyday life—and death—in particular, beginning in the 1830s and persisting through the 1860s, the decade of the novel's publication" (85); and she notes that a volume of writings by the secretary of the Society for the Protection of Aborigines eventually made its way to Dickens.

So what is Dickens doing with that tobacco, and what does he expect his readers to make of it? Does he want us to confront the "crime of Aboriginal genocide" (84)? Or would he prefer that we look past such crimes, focusing instead on the story of Magwitch and Pip? On such questions, Freedgood's argument is admirably complex. She suggests that Dickens seeks to limit readerly waywardness by "the practice of a nearly crazed supplementation," which is to say that he fills his books with so many references to so many things that none of them is likely to provoke much thought (103). As a result, Freedgood says, objects in Dickens usually serve as "partial" or "fractional" symbols: neither entirely meaningless nor obviously meaningful, these partial symbols allow "the bad news of history [to] risk representation, since it will probably be left undecoded" (107). In the case of *Great Expectations*, "Negro head tobacco symbolizes the crime of Aboriginal genocide without requiring conscious acknowledgement of it" (83–84).

Freedgood extends her arguments about Dickens by contrasting him with other writers. In a chapter on *Middlemarch*, she says that although George Eliot shares Dickens's worries about misreading and misunderstanding, she responds to those anxieties in completely different ways. Instead of overwhelming us with long lists of objects, Eliot restricts our attention and works to stabilize her meanings. She tells us exactly how to interpret the Puritan dress of her heroine Dorothea Brooke, transforming Dodo's costume into something much more like a conventional symbol. By drawing this sharp contrast between Dickens and Eliot, Freedgood helps us to appreciate the force of her claim that Dickens's writing "marks the end of a chapter in the history of the novel" (105). "[T]he apex of the random accumulation of objects in the novel must also mark the moment of its decline," she says. After Dickens, "the representation of fictional objects begins to change," and the novel form "begins to organize its object relations with more symbolic care" (105).

In addition to its treatment of the differences between Dickens and Eliot, the book offers an original approach to the rise of commodity culture, which Freedgood sees as emerging slowly and unevenly. In a splendid conclusion, touching again on Eliot and moving on to Hardy, Freedgood shows that "commodification was less secure, less consistently triumphant than we have imagined" (157). There are times, over the course of the book, when Freedgood may overlook some key pieces of evidence. It would be interesting to see what she'd say about the rest of Magwitch's portable property—his pistol and knife, his "great thick pocket-book" (*Great Expectations* 332) and "greasy little clasped black Testament," stolen, Pip assumes, from "some court of justice" (*Great Expectations* 334). But that's just a quibble. *The Ideas in Things* is a very good book with a genuinely interesting thesis. Its theoretical sophistication is evident on every page—you may want to brush up on Jakobson and Barthes before diving in—and its arguments will prove useful to anyone interested in Dickens's realism, his differences from other authors, and his perpetually uncertain place in the history of British fiction.

Theory

Only a few scholars made theory or theorizing their main business. Three such essays appeared at the end of the *Palgrave Advances* volume, giving the collection a satisfying sense of closure. Psychoanalytic approaches are covered by Carolyn Dever, who begins by noting that for both Dickens and Freud, "present-day consciousness is composed of the endless repetition of unresolved psychic conflicts" (221). In *A Tale of Two Cities*, characters first remember, then repeat, and finally work through "the trauma of shame and violence" (231). Thus, the story traces a "process of exorcism," eventually pointing toward "a redemptive future located squarely in the heart of Victorian London" (222) and embodied in the figure of "the boy child Sydney Darnay" (231). As she develops this argument, Dever credits Dickens with understanding the importance of "social circumstances" in constituting "the agency of any particular [character]," adding that "[i]n this effort Dickens might have had something to teach Freud" (225).

Next in line is historicism, both old and new, with Catherine Robson focusing less on Dickens's understanding of history than on what she calls "[t]he history of historical approaches to Dickens" (240). In describing these developments, Robson expresses great affection for the work and the worldview of scholars like Humphry House and Kathleen Tillotson. Because midcentury historicists tended to be of a "populist cast of mind," Robson explains, they "generally ended up with a rather problematic Dickens on their hands," unsure of "whether his 'good' tendencies (i.e., his championship of

the people) outweighed his 'bad' ones (i.e., his betrayal of the people)''
(241). Shifting her attention to more recent scholarship, Robson praises the
contributions of Catherine Gallagher and D. A. Miller. Through these pages,
however, as in some other publications from 2006, there's a sense of impatience with new historicism and a wish to move beyond its now-familiar
characterization of Dickens as ''unwitting mouthpiece of his culture's controlling beliefs'' (247). Robson observes that ''it is incredibly easy to parody the
worst examples of this kind of scholarship,'' tossing off a spoof of a ''flat-
footed new historicist'' reading of *Dombey and Son* (245). Her parody imagines a ''less able'' scholar fixing on the detail of ''Carker's mouth,'' producing
a ''concise summary of the history of false teeth,'' and ending with an ''anecdote about a Victorian and his dentures'' (245–46).

As her argument unfolds, however, Robson gets serious, arguing that new
historicist assumptions about the nature of capitalism can have ''the effect of
quashing attention to real and felt inequities'' (246). On many new historicist
readings, she contends, ''differences within a society are flattened out, for all
its various parts tell one and the same story'' (246). What's striking here is
not so much Robson's general critique of new historicism, which should seem
familiar to anyone who's worked on Foucault, but rather her forceful account
of the disconnect between Foucault and Dickens. Offering an unapologetically
admiring characterization of Dickens, Robson insists on his ''persistent preoccupation with who actually gets hurt within a society,'' which she refuses to
see ''only as a cynical, tear-jerking ploy'' (246). With that ''only,'' Robson
makes an important strategic concession, yet as she moves forward she continues to stress the special quality of Dickens's response to suffering. ''Dickens is both more outraged about particular injustices and more hopeful about
their possible amelioration than [most new historicist critics] will allow,''
Robson states (246), suggesting that both his outrage and his hope deserve
more careful attention from historicist critics.

Finally, there's poststructuralism. This time, the situation is tricky, at least
at first, since John Bowen's title is not ''Deconstructing Dickens'' but rather
''Dickens and the Force of Writing.'' ''Dickens's writing has been a trouble
as well as a pleasure ever since it began,'' Bowen says, explaining that his
goal is to ''ask what are the distinctive qualities of Dickens's writing and
how it might be best to describe them'' (255). In the next paragraph, however,
Bowen has already established his poststructuralist credentials, not only introducing ''[t]he idea of force'' but also following his description of force as
something that ''both enables and decomposes literary form'' with a citation
of Derrida (255, 269n1). Before long, he is describing Dickens as a kind of
literary historical pharmakon, ''both inside and out[side the history of the
novel], of supreme importance and placed in a note'' (256). Though he later
says that ''Dickens's fiction . . . has never been a particularly privileged example for contemporary poststructuralist literary theory,'' adding that ''[t]his is

an overwhelmingly good thing'' (257), there's no doubt that this essay has been informed and enriched by his reading of Nietzsche, Wittgenstein, Bakhtin, and Lyotard.

In the later sections of his essay, Bowen considers "the complexity of Dickens's relationship to the philosophical" (261), offering an especially thoughtful assessment of Richard Rorty's comments on Dickens in *Contingency, Irony, and Solidarity*. Why has it taken us so long to engage with Rorty, I wonder? As Bowen points out, his is "one of the most fertile discussions of Dickens's work by a major philosopher," and one "which values Dickens's work at the very highest level" (263). In any case, though Bowen is grateful to Rorty for treating Dickens as a "figure of world historical importance," he also sees the larger argument of *Contingency* as "in many ways run[ning] explicitly counter to the central strengths of the novels themselves" (263). Put briefly, Bowen's position is that where Rorty recommends a division between "self-creation and solidarity with other people," Dickens usually moves to "break down such a division" (264): "What we encounter in Dickens is not a search for private perfection on the one hand and a sense of human or social solidarity on the other," Bowen says, "but a constant mutual implication of the two" (264).

Interestingly, Bowen's prose style is in many ways inspired by G. K. Chesterton, whom he identifies as "Dickens's most acute critic" (272), and his witty mashup of Chesterton and Derrida is somehow in keeping with his larger emphasis on strangeness, weirdness, and resistance. Bowen is convinced that Dickens's work "outplays and indeed, at some level, destroys some of our more cherished cultural and aesthetic assumptions" (257), and by the end of his essay, we can't help but agree. Indeed, we must join this gifted critic in throwing in the towel, conceding defeat, and acknowledging the "extraordinary force, the extraordinary forces, at play in the work" of this great writer (269).

Theoretical issues were also important to the very impressive debut of Jason B. Jones. In *Lost Causes*, a book with a downbeat title and a refreshingly affirmative argument, Jones examines Dickens's theory of history, beginning with the issue of historical causation—and the notion, widely attributed to Victorian writers and thinkers, that the present is "only a product of the past" (38). Jones argues that, far from endorsing such views, Dickens attributes them to characters like Madame Defarge; and, in a fine reading of *A Tale of Two Cities*—one of the best I encountered all year—he explains that such characters are sure of two things: first, that they know the meaning of the past; and second, that they can see "what its implications are for the present" (45). Dickens recommends a different approach to history, Jones says, one that acknowledges its own uncertainty and thereby allows for the "possibility of change" (48).

In exposing the limits of historical overconfidence, Dickens never suggests that we can safely ignore the past. The dangers of such ignorance are made clear in *Barnaby Rudge*, Jones explains, where the murderous acts of Barnaby's father are hushed up or hidden for years. Although these crimes are denied by both of Barnaby's parents, such efforts prove futile. Barnaby is eventually brought to a reckoning with both his father and the past, and the experience transforms him into the sort of person "who understands, however rudimentarily, that one's past actions bear upon the present—although always enigmatically" (52).

Because Jones's Dickens "reminds us of the ambiguity and conflicting interpretations at the core of what we take to be certain" (49), he can be said to anticipate the insights of psychoanalysis, "which similarly tries to battle against certainty in the name of a more supple, but also more responsible, relationship with the past" (59). This last move has the desirable effect of aligning Dickens with Jones's intellectual heroes—namely, Freud and Lacan—and, perhaps more surprisingly, of redescribing Dickensian perspectives on history as generally hopeful and liberating ones. "The work of history and the work of analysis is not only to uncover new facts about past events," Jones concludes, "but also thereby to disrupt the familiar, equally self-serving and self-harming stories we tell ourselves—all in the name of a new story that is perhaps more capacious, more able to tolerate the demands of the present" (60).

On this reading, Dickens is associated not with closure and certainty but openness: he's willing to imagine and reimagine both personal and national histories. Like Jones and many other psychoanalytic thinkers, this Dickens can accept the loss of all causes, and perhaps of causation itself, recognizing that the "meaning of the past is never settled or finite" (6) and that "the demand for coherence is fraudulent" (17). This vision is an appealing and encouraging one, and though it may resemble a kind of wish fulfillment—Jones's image of Dickens is almost too good to be true—it strikes me as a valuable supplement to other, less generous readings. *Lost Causes* shows that Dickensian "meditations on history" are "interesting and nuanced" (3), suggesting that we neglect their complexity at our peril.

Vision

John Sutherland begins "Visualizing Dickens," his contribution to the *Palgrave Advances* volume, by noting a stark contrast. Whereas the Victorians "sentimentally conceived [Dickens's] great brain as an inexhaustible generator of visual imagery," we tend to be "rigorously unvisual" (111). "Blindfolded in a worthy cause," Sutherland says, "[w]e do not *see* Dickens's creations, we *read* his texts—and feel the more virtuous for it'' (111–12). Sutherland can't resist the temptation to blame the devisualization of Dickens on ''modern schools of critical doctrine'' (112), and his case here is not unpersuasive. As Sutherland's examples reveal, theorists from I. A. Richards to J. Hillis Miller have often encouraged a prejudice against seeing and a sense of visualization as ''bad, primitive, childish, or irrelevant'' (112).

The result of all this, according to Sutherland, is often a ''gross misreading'' of Dickens (113). In *Dombey and Son*, we must visualize Dombey's railway trip to Leamington as it ''would have been 'seen' by Dickens's contemporary readers'' (114), understanding that Dombey is seated not in a speeding carriage, but rather ''in his *own* coach,'' which has been ''rolled on to a flat-bed truck and then secured by tie-ropes'' (118). Sutherland sees the ''strange hybridity'' of the railway journey—old-fashioned coach atop new-fangled train—as ''congruent with larger patterns in the story'' (119), including Dombey's devastating ''failure . . . to appreciate that he is on the cusp of drastic technological change'' (123). Similarly, in the opening from *Bleak House*, we must recognize Holborn Hill ''as metonymic of pervasive English inefficiency,'' since it presented a ''scandalous obstruction'' for urban pedestrians, ''dipping down . . . to the level of the Fleet sewer, before forcing the traveler to fight his way back up'' (124). ''The hill made the principal eastern thoroughfare into the metropolis horribly difficult and dangerous in bad or—worse still—icy weather,'' creating a ''barrier, actual and symbolic, between the City of London (the commercial center) on one side and the Inns of Court on the other'' (124).

Sutherland closes by speculating on the impact of photography on Dickens's view of the world. His argument here, though sketchy, is nevertheless interesting, contrasting passages from *Oliver Twist* and *Our Mutual Friend* and concluding with the suggestion that Dickens's later compositions are ''infinitely fuller, more anatomically detailed'' and ''fluidly mobile''—more ''photographic''—than his earlier efforts (129). Through all of this, Sutherland links visualizing to historicizing. It's not enough that we see; we must also see what the Victorians saw: ''the more we penetrate the ideological and historical fabric of Dickens's fiction,'' Sutherland says, ''the better we shall understand him'' (125). No one would dispute that point, but a few may feel discouraged by it, since there's no way to know if you know enough to see what you're supposed to be seeing. Besides, if distinguished scholars like Richard Altick can misread the image of Dombey's railway journey—and Sutherland offers proof that they can—then what chance do the rest of us have?

In *The Old Story, With a Difference: Pickwick's Vision*, Julian Wolfreys takes a very different approach to looking, seeing, and visualizing. Wolfreys has little patience for any sort of historicism, announcing that his book ''is not about text and context, at least not in any direct or straightforward fashion'' (2). Why not? Because processes of historicizing and contextualizing often have the effect of ''making the strangeness of literature safe, of domesticating, corralling, and policing its play'' (2). Wolfreys means to show the continuing relevance and value of poststructuralist readings of Dickens—and if you have not longed for a return to the days when *Pickwick* could be described as a ''rhizomic excess'' (10) or a ''*novel* and a *novelty*, a *novel novel* as it were'' (20), then this is not the book for you. I will admit to losing patience with Wolfreys from time to time—he often seems terribly pleased with himself, boasting of his own '' 'brash' spirit'' (105n3) and suggesting that he alone remains committed to a vision of ''the literary text as *literary*'' (3)—but more often, I found him engaging and rewarding, a pleasure to read and to argue with.

As his subtitle indicates, Wolfreys sees himself as exploring ''*Pickwick*'s vision''—or, more precisely, its vision of vision. He begins his second chapter, which offers his longest and most detailed discussion of the subject, in a fairly predictable way, noting the ''recurrence of motifs, figures, and terms having to do with visuality, vision, observation, . . . the visible, and visible effects'' (45). After exploring a few examples of what he calls ''reciprocal relay''—moments when characters stare or gaze at each other—Wolfreys makes some suggestive connections between seeing and reading, explaining that both operations take us from the visible to the invisible. His later arguments, in which he identifies the ''frequency of so many figures of vision and sight . . . as a symptom of broader epistemological and ontological changes in the nineteenth century'' (54), are less satisfying. What's more, many of the conclusions advanced in this section seem rather obvious. We are reminded, for example, that ''[w]e should always be wary of *how* we see'' (61) and that we should remain ''suspicious of any claims to clarity or supposedly unmediated vision'' (59). Since it's hard to imagine a literary work that wouldn't teach similar lessons, this section of the book often seems to undermine Wolfreys's earlier insistence on the ''strangeness'' and ''singularity'' of Dickens's text (2, 4). Instead of making *Pickwick* seem distinctive, these pages sometimes have the effect of flattening or standardizing it.

For students of Dickens, and lovers of *Pickwick* in particular, Wolfreys's best moments may come when he turns his attention to the novel's setting—he makes much of the fact that the story takes place about ten years before the publication of Dickens's first installment—and its use of the same proper name, ''Sam/uel,'' for both Mr. Pickwick and his Cockney servant (83). In dealing with these points, Wolfreys describes *Pickwick* as a work that both widens and bridges the gap between past and future: ''The name passes from one [character] to the other,'' he explains, yet because ''its attenuated form,

Sam, . . . is used only for, and by Sam Weller,'' we must conclude that the
''name is the same and yet not the same'' (83). Since ''Pickwick is somewhat
out of date,'' while ''Sam, on the other hand, is modern, a man of the future,''
the repetition (with a difference) of the name may be seen to dramatize ''the
play of, and between, two distinct historicized moments of Englishness'' (84).
Here, by offering a fresh look at one of the most important pairings in
Dickens, Wolfreys makes good on his earlier boasts. His version of the ''old
story,'' of how Dickens thinks about time, thinks about identity, and thinks
about community, is indeed ''different,'' effectively reminding us that ''despite our best efforts to decode it the text remains other, and thus remains to
be read, to come'' (103).

Coda

Since I've often returned to the issue of Dickensian strangeness, I'd like to
close by remarking on one of the strangest things I saw—or didn't see—in
2006. I'm thinking of the virtual absence of Dickens from the massive two-
volume anthology of writings on the novel assembled by Franco Moretti. To
be sure, there were a few passing references to Dickens, along with two brief
discussions of his work: Frederic Jameson gives a couple of pages to the
''providential endings'' of *Bleak House* and *Our Mutual Friend*, and Alex
Woloch devotes about five pages to the treatment of minor characters like
Mr. Guppy.

That's it, though. I realize that Moretti's aim is to expand our sense of the
novel, to treat it as the ''first truly planetary form'' (''On *The Novel*'' ix),
and I know that I should put these things in perspective. Jane Austen and
George Eliot don't fare any better than Dickens, and Henry James comes out
worse. Still, only a handful of pages in those two fat books? For Dickens?
The Inimitable? The Sparkler? Somehow that doesn't seem right.

I almost hate to ask those questions. It seems grudging, given the many
great things in Moretti's anthology, to ask for more. Yet Dickens, as we
know, believes in asking for more. One of the biggest clichés in all of literary
criticism—and thus one of the biggest clichés anywhere—is that there's always more to say about great books and great writers. In the case of these
books and this writer it appears to be true. The rich and varied work produced
in 2006 shows that Dickens belongs in the pantheon, that he not only demands
more attention—and more and more attention—but also repays it hand-
somely.

Works Cited

Andrews, Malcolm. *Charles Dickens and His Performing Selves: Dickens and the Public Readings*. Oxford: Oxford UP, 2006.

———. "Performing Character." *Palgrave Advances in Charles Dickens Studies*. Ed. John Bowen and Robert L. Patten. New York: Palgrave, 2006. 69–89.

Archibald, Diana C. " 'Of All the Horrors . . . the Foulest and Most Cruel': Sensation and Dickens's *Oliver Twist.*" *Victorian Sensations: Essays on a Scandalous Genre*. Ed. Kimberly Harrison and Richard Fantina. Columbus: Ohio State UP, 2006. 53–63.

Bleak House. Dirs. Justin Chadwick and Susanna White. Perf. Gillian Anderson, Charles Dance, Denis Lawson, and Anna Maxwell Martin. 2005. DVD. BBC Warner. 2006.

Bodenheimer, Rosemarie. "Dickens and the Writing of a Life." *Palgrave Advances in Charles Dickens Studies*. Ed. John Bowen and Robert L. Patten. New York: Palgrave, 2006. 48–68.

———. "Dickens, Fascinated." *Victorian Studies* 48:2 (Winter 2006): 268–76.

Bolton, Matthew. "Joycean Dickens/Dickensian Joyce." *Dickens Quarterly* 23:4 (Dec. 2006): 243–55.

Bowen, John. "Dickens and the Force of Writing." *Palgrave Advances in Charles Dickens Studies*. Ed. John Bowen and Robert L. Patten. New York: Palgrave, 2006. 255–72.

———. "A Garland for *The Old Curiosity Shop.*" *Dickens Studies Annual* 37 (2006): 1–16.

———, and Robert L. Patten. Introduction. *Palgrave Advances in Charles Dickens Studies*. Ed. John Bowen and Robert L. Patten. New York: Palgrave, 2006. 1–10.

Childers, Joseph. "Politicized Dickens: The Journalism of the 1850s." *Palgrave Advances in Charles Dickens Studies*. Ed. John Bowen and Robert L. Patten. New York: Palgrave, 2006. 198–215.

Claybaugh, Amanda. "Toward a New Transatlanticism: Dickens in the United States." *Victorian Studies* 48:3 (Spring 2006): 439–60.

Courtemanche, Eleanor. " 'Naked Truth Is the Best Eloquence': Martineau, Dickens, and the Moral Science of Realism." *ELH* 73:2 (Summer 2006): 383–407.

Cox, Arthur J. "The *Drood* Remains Revisited: 'First Fancy.' " *Dickens Quarterly* 23:2 (June 2006): 108–20.

————. "The *Drood* Remains Revisited: The Title Page." *Dickens Quarterly* 23:1 (Mar. 2006): 14–28.

Dever, Carolyn. "Psychoanalyzing Dickens." *Palgrave Advances in Charles Dickens Studies*. Ed. John Bowen and Robert L. Patten. New York: Palgrave, 2006. 216–33.

Dickens, Charles. *American Notes for General Circulation*. Ed. Arnold Goldman and John Whitley. London: Penguin, 1985.

————. *A Christmas Carol and Other Christmas Books*. Ed. Robert Douglas-Fairhurst. Oxford: Oxford UP, 2006.

————. *Great Expectations*. Intro. David Trotter. Ed. Charlotte Mitchell. London: Penguin, 1996.

Douglas-Fairhurst, Robert. Introduction. *A Christmas Carol and Other Christmas Books*. By Charles Dickens. Oxford: Oxford UP, 2006.

Easson, Angus and Margaret Brown. "The Letters of Charles Dickens: Supplement VI." *The Dickensian* 102 (2006): 117–30.

Freedgood, Elaine. *The Ideas in Things: Fugitive Meaning in the Victorian Novel*. Chicago: U of Chicago P, 2006.

Gallagher, Catherine. *The Body Economic: Life, Death, and Sensation in Political Economy and the Victorian Novel*. Princeton, NJ: Princeton UP, 2006.

Garnett, Robert. "The Crisis of 1863." *Dickens Quarterly* 23:3 (Sep. 2006): 181–91.

Gervais, David. "Dostoevsky and the English Novel: Dickens, John Cowper Powys and D. H. Lawrence." *Cambridge Quarterly* 35:1 (2006): 49–71.

Hager, Kelly. "Jasper Packlemerton, Victorian Freak." *Victorian Literature and Culture* 34:1 (2006): 209–32.

Hollington, Michael. "The *Rebenque* and the Wax-tipped Cane: W. H. Hudson and Dickens." *The Dickensian* 102 (2006): 212–20.

Huguet, Christine. " 'There's not a doubt of the dress': Changing Clothes in Dickens's Fiction." *The Dickensian* 102 (2006): 24–31.

Jacobson, Wendy. "The Prince of the Marshes: *Hamlet* and *Great Expectations*." *The Dickensian* 102 (2006): 197–211.

James, Louis. "Flight from the Snow Queen: Childhood and the Imaginative Worlds of Dickens and Hans Christian Andersen." *The Dickensian* 102 (2006): 222–31.

Jameson, Frederic. "The Experiments of Time: Providence and Realism." *The Novel*. Ed. Franco Moretti. Vol. 2. Princeton: Princeton UP, 2006. 95–127.

Jones, Jason B. *Lost Causes: Historical Consciousness in Victorian Literature*. Columbus: Ohio State UP, 2006.

Keirstead, Christopher M. "In Search of the 'Great Human Family': Tourism, Mass Culture, and the Knowable Community of Dickens' *American Notes.*" *Nineteenth-Century Prose* 33:1 (Spring 2006): 117–32

Kincaid, James R. "Blessings for the Worthy: Dickens's *Little Dorrit* and the Nature of Rants." *Dickens Studies Annual* 37 (2006): 17–30.

Kucich, John, and Dianne Sadoff. "Charles Dickens." *The Oxford Encyclopedia of British Literature.* Ed. David Scott Kasten. Oxford: Oxford UP, 2006.

Kujawska-Lis, Ewa. "*Bleak House* as the Source of Intertextuality in Somerset Maugham's 'The Round Dozen.' " *Dickens Quarterly* 23:4 (Dec. 2006): 229–42.

Leonard, John. "Charles in Charge." *New York* 23 Jan. 2006. 17 Nov. 2007. <http://nymag.com/nymetro/arts/tv/reviews/15525/>

Lewis, Linda M. "Madame Defarge as Political Icon in Dickens's *A Tale of Two Cities.*" *Dickens Studies Annual* 37 (2006): 31–49.

Li, Kay. "Dickens and China: Contextual Interchanges in Cultural Globalization." *Dickens Studies Annual* 37 (2006): 117–36.

Marchbanks, Paul. "From Caricature to Character: The Intellectually Disabled in Dickens's Novels." *Dickens Quarterly* 23 (2006): 3–13, 67–84, 169–80.

McKnight, Natalie. "Dickens and Darwin: A Rhetoric of Pets." *The Dickensian* 102 (2006): 131–43.

Meckier, Jerome. "Parodic Prolongation in *North and South*: Elizabeth Gaskell Reevaluates Dickens's Suspenseful Delays." *Dickens Quarterly* 23:4 (Dec. 2006): 217–28.

Merchant, Peter. "Tales Told out of School: Anstey's Relation to Dickens and *Vice Versa.*" *The Dickensian* 102 (2006): 232–39.

Michie, Helena. "From Blood to Law: The Embarrassments of Family in Dickens." *Palgrave Advances in Charles Dickens Studies.* Ed. John Bowen and Robert L. Patten. New York: Palgrave, 2006. 131–54.

Moretti, Franco. "On *The Novel.*" *The Novel.* Ed. Franco Moretti. Vol. 1. Princeton: Princeton UP, 2006. ix–x.

———, ed. *The Novel.* 2 vols. Princeton: Princeton UP, 2006.

Nayder, Lillian. "Catherine Dickens and Her Colonial Sons." *Dickens Studies Annual* 3 (2006): 81–93.

Parrinder, Patrick. *Nation & Novel: The English Novel from its Origins to the Present Day.* Oxford: Oxford UP, 2006.

Patten, Robert L. "Publishing in Parts." *Palgrave Advances in Charles Dickens Studies.* Ed. John Bowen and Robert L. Patten. New York: Palgrave, 2006. 11–47.

Poovey, Mary. *Uneven Developments: The Ideological Work of Gender in Mid-Victorian England.* Chicago: U of Chicago P, 1988.

Purchase, Sean. " 'The less said about it the better': Slavery and Silence in Dickens." *The Dickensian* 102 (2006): 144–58.

Purton, Valerie. "Dickens, Robert Lytton and a Newly Discovered Letter." *The Dickensian* 102 (2006): 101–16.

Reed, John R. "The Riches of Redundancy: *Our Mutual Friend.*" *Studies in the Novel* 38:1 (Spring 2006): 15–35.

Robson, Catherine. "Historicizing Dickens." *Palgrave Advances in Charles Dickens Studies.* Ed. John Bowen and Robert L. Patten. New York: Palgrave, 2006. 234–54.

Rudy, Seth. "Stage Presence: Performance and Theatricality in Dickens's *Our Mutual Friend.*" *Dickens Studies Annual* 37 (2006): 65–80.

Ruth, Jennifer. *Novel Professions: Interested Disinterest and the Making of the Professional in the Victorian Novel.* Columbus: Ohio State UP, 2006.

Sasaki, Toru. "We Ask for More: A Note on Polanski's *Oliver Twist.*" *The Dickensian* 102 (2006): 240–42.

Schor, Hilary M. "Dickens and Plot." *Palgrave Advances in Charles Dickens Studies.* Ed. John Bowen and Robert L. Patten. New York: Palgrave, 2006. 90–110.

Smith, Karl. "Honeythunder, Exeter Hall, and the Jamaica Uprising." *The Dickensian* 102 (2006): 5–20.

Stanley, Alessandra. "A Very Modern Dickens, Still Haunting but Lively." *The New York Times* 20 Jan. 2006. 17 Nov. 2007. <http://www.nytimes.com/2006/01/20/arts/television/20blea.html>

Stuchebrukhov, Olga. "*Bleak House* as an Allegory of a Middle-Class Nation." *Dickens Quarterly* 23:3 (Sept. 2006): 147–68.

Sutcliffe, Allan. "From Devonshire House to the Bull Ring, Birmingham: A Dickensian Contribution to the Music Hall." *The Dickensian* 102 (2006): 21–23.

Sutherland, John. "Visualizing Dickens." *Palgrave Advances in Charles Dickens Studies.* Ed. John Bowen and Robert L. Patten. New York: Palgrave, 2006. 111–30.

Tracy, Robert. "Jasper's Plot: Inventing *The Mystery of Edwin Drood.*" *Dickens Quarterly* 23:1 (Mar. 2006): 29–38.

Vincent, David. "Dickens's Reading Public." *Palgrave Advances in Charles Dickens Studies.* Ed. John Bowen and Robert L. Patten. New York: Palgrave, 2006. 176–97.

Waters, Catherine. "Reforming Culture." *Palgrave Advances in Charles Dickens Studies.* Ed. John Bowen and Robert L. Patten. New York: Palgrave, 2006. 155–75.

Willis, Mark. "Charles Dickens and Fictions of the Crowd." *Dickens Quarterly* 23:2 (June 2006): 85–107.

Wiltshire, Irene. "Pickwick and the Pirates." *The Dickensian* 102 (2006): 32–44.

Wolfreys, Julian. *The Old Story, with a Difference: Pickwick's Vision.* Columbus: Ohio State UP, 2006.

Woloch, Alex. "Minor Characters." *The Novel.* Ed. Franco Moretti. Vol. 2. Princeton: Princeton UP, 2006. 295–323.

Wynne, Deborah. "Scenes of 'Incredible Outrage': Dickens, Ireland, and *A Tale of Two Cities.*" *Dickens Studies Annual* 37 (2006): 51–64.

Zacharek, Stephanie. "Refuge in 'Bleak House.' " *Salon* 4 February 2006. 17 Nov. 2007. <http://www.salon.com/ent/tv/review/2006/02/04/bleak_house/>.

Zlotnick, Susan. " 'The Law's a Bachelor': *Oliver Twist*, Bastardy, and the New Poor Law." *Victorian Literature and Culture* 34:1 (2006): 131–46.

INDEX

(Page numbers in italics represent illustrations)

447